THE ANNALS
OF
AMERICA

THE ANNALS OF AMERICA

Volume 18

1961 - 1968

The Burdens of World Power

ENCYCLOPÆDIA BRITANNICA, INC.

Chicago London Toronto Geneva Sydney Tokyo Manila Johannesburg Seoul

The editors wish to express their gratitude for permission to reprint material from the following sources:

The Academy of Political Science for Selection 17, from the *Political Science Quarterly,* June 1962 (Vol. LXXII, no. 2).

Aldine Publishing Company and Orlando W. Wilson for Selection 8, from *Police Power and Individual Freedom,* ed. by Claude R. Sowle, © 1960, 1961, 1962 by Northwestern University School of Law.

The American Academy of Political and Social Science and Gerald Stern for Selection 78, from *The Annals* of the American Academy of Political and Social Science, © 1967 by The American Academy of Political and Social Science.

The American Forestry Association for Selection 95, from *American Forests,* Copyright 1967 by The American Forestry Association.

Americas for Selection 14, from *Americas,* monthly magazine published by the Pan American Union in English, Spanish, and Portuguese.

Army Magazine for Selection 107, from *Army,* Copyright © 1968 by Association of the United States Army.

Atheneum Publishers for Selection 4, from *Equal Time,* by Newton N. Minow, Copyright © 1964 by Newton N. Minow.

The Baltimore Sun and Clinton I. Winslow for Selection 99 (Clinton I. Winslow, "Description of the Proposed Constitution"), from *The Baltimore Sun,* January 10, 1968.

Bulletin of the Atomic Scientists for Selection 96, "New Years Thoughts 1968," by Eugene Rabinowitch; Selection 97, "The Use and Abuse of Psychedelic Drugs," by Daniel X. Freedman; and Selection 98, "The Kennedy Effect," by Richard S. Lewis, reprinted from the January, April, March, 1968 issues, respectively, of the *Bulletin of the Atomic Scientists,* Copyright 1968 by the Educational Foundation for Nuclear Science.

Center for the Study of Democratic Institutions for Selection 11, from *A World Without War,* by Walter Millis, Copyright © 1961 by The Fund for the Republic, Inc. Also for Selection 15, from *Bulletin* of the Center for the Study of Democratic Institutions. Also for Selection 64, from *Center Diary: 15,* Copyright © 1966 by The Fund for the Republic, Inc. Also for Selection 70, from *Center Diary: 14,* Copyright © 1966 by The Fund for the Republic, Inc. Also for Selection 84, from *The Center Magazine,* © 1967 by The Fund for the Republic, Inc. Also for Selection 114, from *The Center Magazine,* © 1968 by The Fund for the Republic, Inc.

The Christian Century for Selection 27, from *The Christian Century,* Copyright © 1963 by the Christian Century Foundation.

Consumers Union of U.S., Inc. for Selection 56, from *Consumer Reports,* Copyright © 1965 by Consumers Union of U.S., Inc. Also for Selection 80, from *Consumer Reports,* Copyright © 1967 by Consumers Union of U.S., Inc.

Daedalus, Journal of the American Academy of Arts

(continued on p. 689)

CODED SOURCES IN THIS VOLUME

Bulletin

Department of State Bulletin. Published weekly by the Office of Public Services, Bureau of Public Affairs. Supersedes two previous publications: *Press Releases* and *Treaty Information Bulletin.* Washington, July 1, 1939 *et seq.*

Record

Congressional Record. A record of the proceedings of Congress from March 3, 1873, to date, arranged by number of Congress and by session. Washington, 1874 *et seq.*

Record, App.

Congressional Record Appendix. A supplement to the *Congressional Record* (see above), paged separately and also arranged by Congress and session.

United States Reports [Supreme Court]

369 U.S. 186
383 U.S. 463
384 U.S. 333
384 U.S. 436

Vol. 369, pp. 186ff.;
Vol. 383, pp. 463ff.;
Vol. 384, pp. 333ff.;
Vol. 384, pp. 436ff.

VSD

Vital Speeches of the Day. Published twice a month. New York, 1934 *et seq.*

Contents

1963

THE BURDENS OF WORLD POWER
In Pictures

In the decade of the 1960s the new society that had been in the
making since World War II came to maturity, sufficiently so, at
least, to become introspective and concerned with its own validity.
The problems and anomalies imbedded in the social system, at first
only grudgingly acknowledged, came to be actively sought out
and considered. The nation came face to face with a complex of
issues, and there followed a period of public debate, division, and
even strife such as had seldom been seen in any time.

The achievement of equality in weapons systems and destructive
capability by the U.S. and the U.S.S.R. in the early 1960s
led to a deadlock situation in the race for world power.
The growing political and economic independence of European
nations, both Eastern and Western, removed from the area the
danger of active Cold War confrontation and hinted at a possible
future third power center. The competition for influence moved to
the less developed areas in Africa, Asia, and Latin America.

As the gap between rich and poor nations continued to widen
despite foreign aid programs carried on by Western and
Communist countries alike, the growing possibility of concert
among the undeveloped nations of the world, some long-established
as in Latin America, and some newly emerged from colonialism
as in Africa and Asia, gave rise to the concept of the Third
World. The generally high degree of nationalism among the
people of these poor nations led them to resist the political
implications of foreign aid from superpowers; when, as in Vietnam,
it did not, armed conflict was often the result.

During the 1960s the civil rights movement, hitherto concentrated
in the South and concerned with specific instances of discrimination,
spread to include the entire country and the vastly more difficult
problems of de facto segregation and the urban ghetto. The
emphasis on the realization of already-guaranteed rights was absorbed
into the larger aim of developing an active black consciousness and
combating the effects of a centuries-old conviction of inferiority.

America's booming economy left a number of unresolved
problems in its wake. One of the most difficult was the problem
of pollution; industrial waste and by-products progressively
poisoned the air and water, rendering them unsuitable for
human or animal life and earning for the nation the sardonic
title of the "effluent society." Wildlife and the little remaining
wilderness were constantly endangered by the thoughtless
handling of natural resources. It was in the city, however,
that such problems were most acute.

The decade was a time of protest. Largely a phenomenon of the
young, vocal and physical protests were directed at a number
of issues such as war, racism, and various facets of what was
conceived of as a society devoted to merely technological and profit
values. The problem of responsiveness to people's needs was central,
and dissent was aimed at pointing up and, perhaps, remedying the
attenuation of human values in business and government activity.

1961

1.

Dwight D. Eisenhower: Farewell Address

A "new" Eisenhower seemed to emerge during 1959 and 1960, when the President, at last in health, and acting without the advisers — Secretary of the Treasury George M. Humphrey, Secretary of State John Foster Dulles, and Presidential Assistant Sherman Adams — who had dominated the early years of his administration, began to use the powers of his office to implement his policies and to check the rise of certain influential factions in the government. One group that particularly worried Eisenhower was the alliance that he dubbed the "military-industrial complex." He warned on several occasions, most notably in his Farewell Address of January 17, 1961, that advances in technology combined with the growing defense needs of the country had created an opportunity for the military establishment and the armaments industry to exert undue and improper influence on the formation and conduct of national policy. The warning was especially striking coming from Eisenhower, product as he was of the military and good friend, as it had been assumed, of "Big Business." Eisenhower's Farewell Address is reprinted here.

Source: *Bulletin*, February 6, 1961.

My Fellow Americans:

Three days from now, after half a century in the service of our country, I shall lay down the responsibilities of office as, in traditional and solemn ceremony, the authority of the presidency is vested in my successor.

This evening I come to you with a message of leavetaking and farewell, and to share a few final thoughts with you, my countrymen.

Like every other citizen, I wish the new President and all who will labor with him Godspeed. I pray that the coming years will be blessed with peace and prosperity for all.

Our people expect their President and the Congress to find essential agreement on issues of great moment, the wise resolution of which will better shape the future of the nation.

My own relations with the Congress, which began on a remote and tenuous basis, when long ago a member of the Senate appointed me to West Point, have since ranged to the intimate during the war and immediate postwar period and, finally, to the mutually interdependent during these past eight years.

In this final relationship, the Congress and the administration have, on most vital issues, cooperated well to serve the national good rather than mere partisanship, and so have assured that the business of the nation should go forward. So my official relationship with the Congress ends in a feeling on my part of gratitude that we have been able to do so much together.

We now stand ten years past the midpoint of a century that has witnessed four major wars among great nations. Three of these involved our own country. Despite these holocausts, America is today the strongest, the most influential, and most productive nation in the world. Understandably proud of this preeminence, we yet realize that America's leadership and prestige depend not merely upon our unmatched material progress, riches, and military strength but on how we use our power in the interests of world peace and human betterment.

Throughout America's adventure in free government our basic purposes have been to keep the peace, to foster progress in human achievement, and to enhance liberty, dignity, and integrity among people and among nations. To strive for less would be unworthy of a free and religious people. Any failure traceable to arrogance or our lack of comprehension or readiness to sacrifice would inflict upon us grievous hurt both at home and abroad.

Progress toward these noble goals is persistently threatened by the conflict now engulfing the world. It commands our whole attention, absorbs our very beings. We face a hostile ideology — global in scope, atheistic in character, ruthless in purpose, and insidious in method. Unhappily, the danger it poses promises to be of indefinite duration. To meet it successfully there is called

for not so much the emotional and transitory sacrifices of crisis but rather those which enable us to carry forward steadily, surely, and without complaint the burdens of a prolonged and complex struggle — with liberty the stake. Only thus shall we remain, despite every provocation, on our charted course toward permanent peace and human betterment.

Crises there will continue to be. In meeting them, whether foreign or domestic, great or small, there is a recurring temptation to feel that some spectacular and costly action could become the miraculous solution to all current difficulties. A huge increase in newer elements of our defense, development of unrealistic programs to cure every ill in agriculture, a dramatic expansion in basic and applied research — these and many other possibilities, each possibly promising in itself, may be suggested as the only way to the road we wish to travel.

But each proposal must be weighed in the light of a broader consideration: the need to maintain balance in and among national programs — balance between the private and the public economy, balance between cost and hoped-for advantage, balance between the clearly necessary and the comfortably desirable, balance between our essential requirements as a nation and the duties imposed by the nation upon the individual, balance between actions of the moment and the national welfare of the future. Good judgment seeks balance and progress; lack of it eventually finds imbalance and frustration.

The record of many decades stands as proof that our people and their government have, in the main, understood these truths and have responded to them well in the face of stress and threat. But threats, new in kind or degree, constantly arise. I mention two only.

A vital element in keeping the peace is our military establishment. Our arms must

President Eisenhower speaking before the United Nations in October 1960

be mighty, ready for instant action, so that no potential aggressor may be tempted to risk his own destruction.

Our military organization today bears little relation to that known by any of my predecessors in peacetime, or indeed by the fighting men of World War II or Korea.

Until the latest of our world conflicts, the United States had no armaments industry. American makers of plowshares could, with time and as required, make swords as well. But now we can no longer risk emergency improvisation of national defense; we have been compelled to create a permanent armaments industry of vast proportions. Added to this, 3.5 million men and women are directly engaged in the defense establishment. We annually spend on military security more than the net income of all United States corporations.

This conjunction of an immense military establishment and a large arms industry is new in the American experience. The total influence — economic, political, even spiri-

tual — is felt in every city, every statehouse, every office of the federal government. We recognize the imperative need for this development. Yet we must not fail to comprehend its grave implications. Our toil, resources, and livelihood are all involved; so is the very structure of our society.

In the councils of government we must guard against the acquisition of unwarranted influence, whether sought or unsought, by the military-industrial complex. The potential for the disastrous rise of misplaced power exists and will persist.

We must never let the weight of this combination endanger our liberties or democratic processes. We should take nothing for granted. Only an alert and knowledgeable citizenry can compel the proper meshing of the huge industrial and military machinery of defense with our peaceful methods and goals so that security and liberty may prosper together.

Akin to, and largely responsible for, the sweeping changes in our industrial-military posture has been the technological revolution during recent decades. In this revolution, research has become central; it also becomes more formalized, complex, and costly. A steadily increasing share is conducted for, by, or at the direction of the federal government.

Today, the solitary inventor, tinkering in his shop, has been overshadowed by task forces of scientists in laboratories and testing fields. In the same fashion, the free university, historically the fountainhead of free ideas and scientific discovery, has experienced a revolution in the conduct of research. Partly because of the huge costs involved, a government contract becomes virtually a substitute for intellectual curiosity. For every old blackboard there are now hundreds of new electronic computers.

The prospect of domination of the nation's scholars by federal employment, project allocations, and the power of money is ever present and is gravely to be regarded. Yet, in holding scientific research and discovery in respect, as we should, we must also be alert to the equal and opposite danger that public policy could itself become the captive of a scientific-technological elite. It is the task of statesmanship to mold, to balance, and to integrate these and other forces, new and old, within the principles of our democratic system — ever aiming toward the supreme goals of our free society.

Another factor in maintaining balance involves the element of time. As we peer into society's future, we — you and I, and our government — must avoid the impulse to live only for today, plundering for our own ease and convenience the precious resources of tomorrow. We cannot mortgage the material assets of our grandchildren without risking the loss also of their political and spiritual heritage. We want democracy to survive for all generations to come, not to become the insolvent phantom of tomorrow.

Down the long lane of the history yet to be written, America knows that this world of ours, ever growing smaller, must avoid becoming a community of dreadful fear and hate, and be, instead, a proud confederation of mutual trust and respect. Such a confederation must be one of equals. The weakest must come to the conference table with the same confidence as do we, protected as we are by our moral, economic, and military strength. That table, though scarred by many past frustrations, cannot be abandoned for the certain agony of the battlefield.

Disarmament, with mutual honor and confidence, is a continuing imperative. Together we must learn how to compose differences, not with arms but with intellect and decent purpose. Because this need is so sharp and apparent, I confess that I lay down my official responsibilities in this field with a definite sense of disappointment. As one who has witnessed the horror and the lingering sadness of war, as one who knows that another war could utterly destroy this civilization which has been so slowly and painfully built over thousands of years, I wish I could say tonight that a lasting peace is in sight.

Happily, I can say that war has been avoided. Steady progress toward our ultimate goal has been made. But so much remains to be done. As a private citizen I shall never cease to do what little I can to help the world advance along that road.

So, in this, my last good night to you as your President, I thank you for the many opportunities you have given me for public service in war and peace. I trust that in that service you find some things worthy; as for the rest of it, I know you will find ways to improve performance in the future.

You and I, my fellow citizens, need to be strong in our faith that all nations, under God, will reach the goal of peace with justice. May we be ever unswerving in devotion to principle, confident but humble with power, diligent in pursuit of the nation's great goals.

To all the peoples of the world, I once more give expression to America's prayerful and continuing aspiration:

We pray that peoples of all faiths, all races, all nations, may have their great human needs satisfied; that those now denied opportunity shall come to enjoy it to the full; that all who yearn for freedom may experience its spiritual blessings; that those who have freedom will understand, also, its heavy responsibilities; that all who are insensitive to the needs of others will learn charity; that the scourges of poverty, disease, and ignorance will be made to disappear from the earth; and that, in the goodness of time, all peoples will come to live together in a peace guaranteed by the binding force of mutual respect and love.

2.

John F. Kennedy: Inaugural Address

January 20, 1961, in Washington was a cold, windy day. A brilliant sun shone on snow that had fallen the night before. A rabbi, a Protestant minister, a Catholic cardinal, and a Greek Orthodox archbishop prayed for guidance; all four emphasized freedom of religion. Robert Frost, a friend of the Kennedy family, read a poem. The man who stepped to the rostrum to take the oath as chief executive was the youngest man ever to be elected President. Many noted his youthfulness, and as they spoke of the hopes for his administration they did so in terms of a new kind of politics that would be appropriate to the needs of a new generation of citizens, and of a new world. "The inauguration of JFK as 35th President of the U.S. will stand," asserted Commonweal, *"as one of the most dramatic political events of this century." The even more dramatic event that was to occur on November 22, 1963, would cause people to remember the Inaugural Address of that January day with a special regard. The address is reprinted here.*

Source: *Bulletin*, February 6, 1961.

WE OBSERVE TODAY not a victory of party but a celebration of freedom — symbolizing an end as well as a beginning — signifying renewal as well as change. For I have sworn before you and Almighty God the same solemn oath our forebears prescribed nearly a century and three-quarters ago.

The world is very different now. For man holds in his mortal hands the power to abolish all forms of human poverty and all forms of human life. And yet the same revolutionary beliefs for which our forebears fought are still at issue around the globe — the belief that the rights of man come not from the generosity of the state but from the hand of God.

We dare not forget today that we are the heirs of that first revolution. Let the word go forth from this time and place, to friend and foe alike, that the torch has been passed to a new generation of Americans — born in this century, tempered by war, disciplined by a hard and bitter peace, proud of our ancient heritage — and unwilling to witness or permit the slow undoing of those human rights to which this nation has always been committed, and to which we are committed today at home and around the world.

Let every nation know, whether it wishes us well or ill, that we shall pay any price, bear any burden, meet any hardship, support any friend, oppose any foe to assure the survival and the success of liberty.

This much we pledge — and more.

To those old allies whose cultural and spiritual origins we share, we pledge the loyalty of faithful friends. United, there is little we cannot do in a host of cooperative ventures. Divided, there is little we can do — for we dare not meet a powerful challenge at odds and split asunder.

To those new states whom we welcome to the ranks of the free, we pledge our word that one form of colonial control shall not have passed away merely to be replaced by a far more iron tyranny. We shall not always expect to find them supporting our view. But we shall always hope to find them strongly supporting their own freedom — and to remember that, in the past, those who foolishly sought power by riding the back of the tiger ended up inside.

To those people in the huts and villages of half the globe struggling to break the bonds of mass misery, we pledge our best efforts to help them help themselves, for whatever period is required — not because the Communists may be doing it, not because we seek their votes, but because it is right. If a free society cannot help the many who are poor, it cannot save the few who are rich.

To our sister republics south of our border, we offer a special pledge — to convert our good words into good deeds — in a new alliance for progress — to assist free men and free governments in casting off the chains of poverty. But this peaceful revolution of hope cannot become the prey of hostile powers. Let all our neighbors know

Ted Spiegel from Rapho Guillumette

John F. Kennedy, photographed in Seattle, Sept. 1960

that we shall join with them to oppose aggression or subversion anywhere in the Americas. And let every other power know that this hemisphere intends to remain the master of its own house.

To that world assembly of sovereign states, the United Nations, our last best hope in an age where the instruments of war have far outpaced the instruments of peace, we renew our pledge of support — to prevent it from becoming merely a forum for invective — to strengthen its shield of the new and the weak — and to enlarge the area in which its writ may run.

Finally, to those nations who would make themselves our adversary, we offer not a pledge but a request — that both sides begin anew the quest for peace before the dark powers of destruction unleashed by science engulf all humanity in planned or accidental self-destruction. We dare not tempt them with weakness. For only when our arms are sufficient beyond doubt can we be certain beyond doubt that they will never be employed.

But neither can two great and powerful groups of nations take comfort from our present course — both sides overburdened by the cost of modern weapons, both rightly alarmed by the steady spread of the deadly atom, yet both racing to alter that uncertain balance of terror that stays the hand of mankind's final war.

So let us begin anew — remembering on both sides that civility is not a sign of weakness, and sincerity is always subject to proof. Let us never negotiate out of fear. But let us never fear to negotiate.

Let both sides explore what problems unite us instead of belaboring those problems which divide us.

Let both sides, for the first time, formulate serious and precise proposals for the inspection and control of arms — and bring the absolute power to destroy other nations under the absolute control of all nations.

Let both sides seek to invoke the wonders of science instead of its terrors. Together let us explore the stars, conquer the deserts, eradicate disease, tap the ocean depths, and encourage the arts and commerce.

Let both sides unite to heed in all corners of the earth the command of Isaiah — to "undo the heavy burdens . . . [and] let the oppressed go free."

And if a beachhead of cooperation may push back the jungle of suspicion, let both sides join in creating a new endeavor, not a new balance of power but a new world of law, where the strong are just and the weak secure and the peace preserved.

All this will not be finished in the first 100 days. Nor will it be finished in the first 1,000 days, nor in the life of this administration, nor even perhaps in our lifetime on this planet. But let us begin.

In your hands, my fellow citizens, more than mine, will rest the final success or failure of our course. Since this country was founded, each generation of Americans has been summoned to give testimony to its national loyalty. The graves of young Americans who answered the call to service surround the globe.

Now the trumpet summons us again — not as a call to bear arms, though arms we need — not as a call to battle, though embattled we are — but a call to bear the burden of a long twilight struggle, year in and year out, "rejoicing in hope, patient in tribulation" — a struggle against the common enemies of man: tyranny, poverty, disease, and war itself.

Can we forge against these enemies a grand and global alliance, North and South, East and West, that can assure a more fruitful life for all mankind? Will you join in that historic effort?

In the long history of the world, only a few generations have been granted the role of defending freedom in its hour of maximum danger. I do not shrink from this responsibility — I welcome it. I do not believe that any of us would exchange places with any other people or any other generation. The energy, the faith, the devotion which we bring to this endeavor will light our country and all who serve it — and the glow from that fire can truly light the world.

And so, my fellow Americans — ask not what your country can do for you — ask what you can do for your country.

My fellow citizens of the world — ask not what America will do for you but what together we can do for the freedom of man.

Finally, whether you are citizens of America or citizens of the world, ask of us here the same high standards of strength and sacrifice which we ask of you. With a good conscience our only sure reward, with history the final judge of our deeds, let us go forth to lead the land we love, asking His blessing and His help, but knowing that here on earth God's work must truly be our own.

3.

John F. Kennedy: Federal Aid to Education

*Between 1920 and 1960 the U.S. population increased by 55 percent. Such growth
would probably have caused trouble for the country's educational establishment in
any event, but in fact the high school population increased by 500 percent during the
period, and college and university enrollment increased sixfold. John F. Kennedy,
the first President to be born in the twentieth century and in an important sense the
representative of the generation that had grown up during World War II,
came to office committed to a program of federal aid to education at all levels — a
program that he outlined in his message to Congress of February 20, 1961, part of
which is reprinted here. The President's proposals encountered strong opposition
from states' rightists and from those who feared for the traditional policy of
separation of church and state.*

Source: *Record*, 87 Cong., 1 Sess., pp. 2389-2391.

OUR PROGRESS AS A NATION can be no swift-
er than our progress in education. Our requirements for world leadership, our hopes
for economic growth, and the demands of
citizenship itself in an era such as this all
require the maximum development of every
young American's capacity.

The human mind is our fundamental resource. A balanced federal program must go
well beyond incentives for investment in
plant and equipment. It must include equally determined measures to invest in human
beings — both in their basic education and
training and in their more advanced preparation for professional work. Without such
measures, the federal government will not
be carrying out its responsibilities for expanding the base of our economic and military strength.

Our progress in education over the last
generation has been substantial. We are educating a greater proportion of our youth to
a higher degree of competency than any
other country on earth. One-fourth of our
total population is enrolled in our schools
and colleges. This year $26 billion will be
spent on education alone.

But the needs of the next generation —
the needs of the next decade and the next
school year — will not be met at this level
of effort. More effort will be required —
on the part of students, teachers, schools,
colleges, and all fifty states — and on the
part of the federal government.

Education must remain a matter of state
and local control and higher education a
matter of individual choice. But education is
increasingly expensive. Too many state and
local governments lack the resources to assure an adequate education for every child.
Too many classrooms are overcrowded.
Too many teachers are underpaid. Too
many talented individuals cannot afford the
benefits of higher education. Too many aca-

Courtesy, Herbert Block, "Washington Post"

"We Can't Burden Our Children with Deficit Spending"; cartoon by Herblock for the "Washington Post" in 1963

demic institutions cannot afford the cost of, or find room for, the growing numbers of students seeking admission in the Sixties.

Our twin goals must be: A new standard of excellence in education and the availability of such excellence to all who are willing and able to pursue it. . . .

I recommend to the Congress a three-year program of general federal assistance for public elementary and secondary classroom construction and teachers' salaries.

Based essentially on the bill which passed the Senate last year (S. 8), although beginning at a more modest level of expenditures, this program would assure every state of no less than $15 for every public school student in average daily attendance, with the total amount appropriated ($666 million being authorized in the first year, rising to $866 million over a three-year period) distributed according to the equalization formula contained in the last year's Senate bill, and already familiar to the Congress by

virtue of its similarity to the formulas contained in the Hill-Burton Hospital Construction and other acts. Ten percent of the funds allocated to each state in the first year, and an equal amount thereafter, is to be used to help meet the unique problems of each state's areas of special educational need — depressed areas, slum neighborhoods, and others.

This is a modest program with ambitious goals. The sums involved are relatively small when we think in terms of more than 36 million public school children, and the billions of dollars necessary to educate them properly. Nevertheless, a limited beginning now — consistent with our obligations in other areas of responsibility — will encourage all states to expand their facilities to meet the increasing demand and enrich the quality of education offered, and gradually assist our relatively low-income states in the elevation of their educational standards to a national level.

The bill which will follow this message has been carefully drawn to eliminate disproportionately large or small inequities, and to make the maximum use of a limited number of dollars. In accordance with the clear prohibition of the Constitution, no elementary or secondary school funds are allocated for constructing church schools or paying church school teachers' salaries; and thus nonpublic school children are rightfully not counted in determining the funds each state will receive for its public schools. Each state will be expected to maintain its own effort or contribution; and every state whose effort is below the national average will be expected to increase that proportion of its income which is devoted to public elementary and secondary education.

This investment will pay rich dividends in the years ahead — in increased economic growth, in enlightened citizens, in national excellence. For some forty years, the Congress has wrestled with this problem and searched for a workable solution. I believe that we now have such a solution; and that this Congress in this year will make a landmark contribution to American education.

Our colleges and universities represent our ultimate educational resource. In these institutions are produced the leaders and other trained persons whom we need to carry forward our highly developed civilization. If the colleges and universities fail to do their job, there is no substitute to fulfill their responsibility. The threat of opposing military and ideological forces in the world lends urgency to their task. But that task would exist in any case.

The burden of increased enrollments — imposed upon our elementary and secondary schools already in the fifties — will fall heavily upon our colleges and universities during the sixties. By the autumn of 1966, an estimated 1 million more students will be in attendance at institutions of higher learning than enrolled last fall — for a total more than twice as high as the total college enrollment of 1950. Our colleges, already hard pressed to meet rising enrollments since 1950 during a period of rising costs, will be in critical straits merely to provide the necessary facilities, much less the cost of quality education.

The country as a whole is already spending nearly $1 billion a year on academic and residential facilities for higher education — some 20 percent of the total spent for higher education. Even with increased contributions from state, local, and private sources, a gap of $2.9 billion between aggregate needs and expenditures is anticipated by 1965, and a gap of $5.2 billion by 1970.

The national interest requires an educational system on the college level sufficiently financed and equipped to provide every student with adequate physical facilities to meet his instructional, research, and residential needs.

I, therefore, recommend legislation which will:

1. Extend the current college housing loan program with a five-year, $250-million-a-year program designed to meet the federal government's appropriate share of residential housing for students and faculty. As a start, additional lending authority is necessary to speed action during fiscal 1961 on approvable loan applications already at hand.

2. Establish a new, though similar, long-term, low-interest-rate loan program for academic facilities, authorizing $300 million in loans each year for five years to assist in the construction of classrooms, laboratories, libraries, and related structures sufficient to enable public and private higher institutions to accommodate the expanding enrollments they anticipate over the next five years; and also to assist in the renovation, rehabilitation, and modernization of such facilities.

This nation, a century or so ago, established as a basic objective the provision of a good elementary and secondary school education to every child, regardless of means. In 1961, patterns of occupation, citizenship, and world affairs have so changed that we must set a higher goal. We must assure ourselves that every talented young person who has the ability to pursue a program of higher education will be able to do so if he chooses, regardless of his financial means.

Today private and public scholarship and loan programs established by numerous states, private sources, and the student loan program under the National Defense Education Act are making substantial contributions to the financial needs of many who attend our colleges. But they still fall short of doing the job that must be done. An estimated one-third of our brightest high school graduates are unable to go on to college principally for financial reasons.

While I shall subsequently ask the Congress to amend and extend the student loan and other provisions of the National Defense Education Act, it is clear that even with this program many talented but needy students are unable to assume further indebtedness in order to continue their education.

I therefore recommend the establishment of a five-year program with an initial authorization of $26,250,000 of state-administered scholarships for talented and needy young people which will supplement but not supplant those programs of financial assistance to students which are now in operation.

Funds would be allocated to the states during the first year for a total of 25,000 scholarships averaging $700 each, 37,500 scholarships the second year, and 50,000 for each succeeding year thereafter. These scholarships, which would range according to need up to a maximum stipend of $1,000, would be open to all young persons, without regard to sex, race, creed, or color, solely on the basis of their ability — as determined on a competitive basis — and their financial need. They would be permitted to attend the college of their choice, and free to select their own program of study. Inasmuch as tuition and fees do not normally cover the institution's actual expenses in educating the student, additional allowances to the college or university attended should accompany each scholarship to enable these institutions to accept the additional students without charging an undue increase in fees or suffering an undue financial loss.

The National Vocational Education Acts, first enacted by the Congress in 1917 and subsequently amended, have provided a program of training for industry, agriculture, and other occupational areas. The basic purpose of our vocational education effort is sound and sufficiently broad to provide a basis for meeting future needs. However, the technological changes which have occurred in all occupations call for a review and reevaluation of these acts, with a view toward their modernization.

To that end, I am requesting the secretary of health, education, and welfare to convene an advisory body drawn from the educational profession, labor-industry, and agriculture as well as the lay public, together with representation from the Departments of Agriculture and Labor, to be charged with the responsibility of reviewing and evaluating the current National Vocational Education Acts, and making recommendations for improving and redirecting the program.

These stimulatory measures represent an essential though modest contribution which the federal government must make to American education at every level. One-sided aid is not enough. We must give attention to both teachers' salaries and classrooms, both college academic facilities and dormitories, both scholarships and loans, both vocational and general education.

We do not undertake to meet our growing educational problems merely to compare our achievements with those of our adversaries. These measures are justified on their own merits — in times of peace as well as peril, to educate better citizens as well as better scientists and soldiers. The federal government's responsibility in this area has been established since the earliest days of the republic — it is time now to act decisively to fulfill that responsibility for the Sixties.

Soap and education are not as sudden as a massacre, but they are more deadly in the long run.

MARK TWAIN, *The Facts Concerning My Recent Resignation*

4.

NEWTON N. MINOW: The Vast Wasteland

President Kennedy caught the imagination of the country not only by his own youth and by that of his wife and children, but also by the appointment to federal offices of a number of energetic young men who had more talent and intelligence than reputation to recommend them. One of the youngest of such appointees was Newton Minow, whom Kennedy named chairman of the Federal Communications Commission. Minow shocked the broadcasting industry — and gained front page headlines across the nation — in May 1961, when, in his first major speech in his new position, he described television as a "vast wasteland." The speech, which in fact seemed to have little effect on the quality of television fare, is reprinted here.

Source: *Equal Time*, Lawrence Laurent, ed., New York, 1964, pp. 48-64.

THANK YOU for this opportunity to meet with you today. This is my first public address since I took over my new job. When the New Frontiersmen rode into town, I locked myself in my office to do my homework and get my feet wet. But apparently I haven't managed to stay out of hot water. I seem to have detected a certain nervous apprehension about what I might say or do when I emerged from that locked office for this, my maiden station break.

First, let me begin by dispelling a rumor. I was not picked for this job because I regard myself as the fastest draw on the New Frontier.

Second, let me start a rumor. Like you, I have carefully read President Kennedy's messages about the regulatory agencies, conflict of interest, and the dangers of *ex parte* contacts. And, of course, we at the Federal Communications Commission will do our part. Indeed, I may even suggest that we change the name of the FCC to The Seven Untouchables!

It may also come as a surprise to some of you but I want you to know that you have my admiration and respect. Yours is a most honorable profession. Anyone who is in the broadcasting business has a tough row to hoe. You earn your bread by using public property. When you work in broadcasting, you volunteer for public service, public pressure, and public regulation. You must compete with other attractions and other investments, and the only way you can do it is to prove to us every three years that you should have been in business in the first place.

I can think of easier ways to make a living. But I cannot think of more satisfying ways.

I admire your courage — but that doesn't mean I would make life any easier for you. Your license lets you use the public's airwaves as trustees for 180 million Americans. The public is your beneficiary. If you want to stay on as trustees, you must deliver a decent return to the public — not only to your stockholders. So, as a representative of the public, your health and your product are among my chief concerns.

As to your health: let's talk only of television today. In 1960 gross broadcast revenues of the television industry were over $1,268,000,000; profit before taxes was $243,900,000 — an average return on revenue of 19.2 percent. Compare this with 1959, when gross broadcast revenues were $1,163,900,000 and profit before taxes was $222,300,000, an average return on revenue of 19.1 percent. So, the percentage increase of total revenues from 1959 to 1960 was 9 percent and the percentage increase of profit was 9.7 percent. This, despite a recession. For your investors, the price has indeed been right.

I have confidence in your health. But not in your product.

It is with this and much more in mind that I come before you today.

One editorialist in the trade press wrote that "the FCC of the New Frontier is going to be one of the toughest FCC's in the history of broadcast regulation." If he meant that we intend to enforce the law in the public interest, let me make it perfectly clear that he is right — we do. If he meant that we intend to muzzle or censor broadcasting, he is dead wrong.

It would not surprise me if some of you had expected me to come here today and say in effect, "Clean up your own house or the government will do it for you." Well, in a limited sense, you would be right — I've just said it. But I want to say to you earnestly that it is not in that spirit that I come before you today, nor is it in that spirit that I intend to serve the FCC.

I am in Washington to help broadcasting, not to harm it; to strengthen it, not weaken it; to reward it, not punish it; to encourage it, not threaten it; to stimulate it, not censor it. Above all, I am here to uphold and protect the public interest.

What do we mean by "the public interest"? Some say the public interest is merely what interests the public. I disagree. So

does your distinguished president, Governor Collins. In a recent speech he said:

> Broadcasting, to serve the public interest, must have a soul and a conscience, a burning desire to excel, as well as to sell; the urge to build the character, citizenship, and intellectual stature of people, as well as to expand the gross national product. . . . By no means do I imply that broadcasters disregard the public interest. . . . But a much better job can be done, and should be done.

I could not agree more.

And I would add that in today's world, with chaos in Laos and the Congo aflame, with Communist tyranny on our Caribbean doorstep and relentless pressure on our Atlantic alliance, with social and economic problems at home of the gravest nature, yes, and with technological knowledge that makes it possible, as our President has said, not only to destroy our world but to destroy poverty around the world — in a time of peril and opportunity, the old complacent, unbalanced fare of action-adventure and situation comedies is simply not good enough.

Your industry possesses the most powerful voice in America. It has an inescapable duty to make that voice ring with intelligence and with leadership. In a few years this exciting industry has grown from a novelty to an instrument of overwhelming impact on the American people. It should be making ready for the kind of leadership that newspapers and magazines assumed years ago, to make our people aware of their world.

Ours has been called the jet age, the atomic age, the space age. It is also, I submit, the television age. And just as history will decide whether the leaders of today's world employed the atom to destroy the world or rebuild it for mankind's benefit, so will history decide whether today's broadcasters employed their powerful voice to enrich the people or debase them.

If I seem today to address myself chiefly to the problems of television, I don't want any of you radio broadcasters to think we've gone to sleep at your switch — we haven't. We still listen. But in recent years most of the controversies and crosscurrents in broadcast programming have swirled around television. And so my subject today is the television industry and the public interest.

Like everybody, I wear more than one hat. I am the chairman of the FCC. I am also a television viewer and the husband and father of other television viewers. I have seen a great many television programs that seemed to me eminently worthwhile, and I am not talking about the much-bemoaned good old days of "Playhouse 90" and "Studio One."

I am talking about this past season. Some were wonderfully entertaining, such as "The Fabulous Fifties," the "Fred Astaire Show" and the "Bing Crosby Special"; some were dramatic and moving, such as Conrad's "Victory" and "Twilight Zone"; some were marvelously informative, such as "The Nation's Future," "CBS Reports," and "The Valiant Years." I could list many more — programs that I am sure everyone here felt enriched his own life and that of his family. When television is good, nothing — not the theater, not the magazines or newspapers — nothing is better.

But when television is bad, nothing is worse. I invite you to sit down in front of your television set when your station goes on the air and stay there without a book, magazine, newspaper, profit-and-loss sheet, or rating book to distract you — and keep your eyes glued to that set until the station signs off. I can assure you that you will observe a vast wasteland.

You will see a procession of game shows, violence, audience participation shows, formula comedies about totally unbelievable families, blood and thunder, mayhem, violence, sadism, murder, Western badmen,

Western good men, private eyes, gangsters, more violence and cartoons. And, endlessly, commercials — many screaming, cajoling, and offending. And, most of all, boredom. True, you will see a few things you will enjoy. But they will be very, very few. And if you think I exaggerate, try it.

Is there one person in this room who claims that broadcasting can't do better?

Well, a glance at next season's proposed programming can give us little heart. Of seventy-three and a half hours of prime evening time, the networks have tentatively scheduled fifty-nine hours to categories of "action-adventure," situation comedy, variety, quiz, and movies.

Is there one network president in this room who claims he can't do better? Well, is there at least one network president who believes that the other networks can't do better?

Gentlemen, your trust accounting with your beneficiaries is overdue. Never have so few owed so much to so many.

Why is so much of television so bad? I have heard many answers: demands of your advertisers; competition for ever higher ratings; the need always to attract a mass audience; the high cost of television programs; the insatiable appetite for programming material — these are some of them. Unquestionably these are tough problems not susceptible to easy answers.

But I am not convinced that you have tried hard enough to solve them. I do not accept the idea that the present overall programming is aimed accurately at the public taste. The ratings tell us only that some people have their television sets turned on, and, of that number, so many are tuned to one channel and so many to another. They don't tell us what the public might watch if they were offered half a dozen additional choices. A rating, at best, is an indication of how many people saw what you gave them. Unfortunately it does not reveal the depth of the penetration or the intensity of reaction, and it never reveals what the acceptance would have been if what you gave them had been better — if all the forces of art and creativity and daring and imagination had been unleashed. I believe in the people's good sense and good taste, and I am not convinced that the people's taste is as low as some of you assume.

My concern with the rating services is not with their accuracy. Perhaps they are accurate. I really don't know. What, then, is wrong with the ratings? It's not been their accuracy — it's been their use.

Certainly I hope you will agree that ratings should have little influence where children are concerned. The best estimates indicate that during the hours of 5 to 6 P.M., 60 percent of your audience is composed of children under twelve. And most young children today, believe it or not, spend as much time watching television as they do in the schoolroom. I repeat — let that sink in — most young children today spend as much time watching television as they do in the schoolroom. It used to be said that there were three great influences on a child: home, school, and church. Today there is a fourth great influence, and you ladies and gentlemen control it.

If parents, teachers, and ministers conducted their responsibilities by following the ratings, children would have a steady diet of ice cream, school holidays, and no Sunday school. What about your responsibilities? Is there no room on television to teach, to inform, to uplift, to stretch, to enlarge the capacities of our children? Is there no room for programs deepening their understanding of children in other lands? Is there no room for a children's news show explaining something about the world to them at their level of understanding? Is there no room for reading the great literature of the past, teaching them the great traditions of freedom? There are some fine children's shows, but they are drowned out in the massive doses of cartoons, violence,

and more violence. Must these be your trademarks? Search your consciences and see if you cannot offer more to your young beneficiaries whose future you guide so many hours each and every day.

What about adult programming and ratings? You know, newspaper publishers take popularity ratings too. The answers are pretty clear; it is almost always the comics, followed by the advice-to-the-lovelorn columns. But, ladies and gentlemen, the news is still on the front page of all newspapers, the editorials are not replaced by more comics, the newspapers have not become one long collection of advice to the lovelorn. Yet newspapers do not need a license from the government to be in business — they do not use public property. But in television — where your responsibilities as public trustees are so plain — the moment that the ratings indicate that Westerns are popular, there are new imitations of Westerns on the air faster than the old coaxial cable could take us from Hollywood to New York. Broadcasting cannot continue to live by the numbers. Ratings ought to be the slave of the broadcaster, not his master. And you and I both know that the rating services themselves would agree.

Let me make clear that what I am talking about is balance. I believe that the public interest is made up of many interests. There are many people in this great country, and you must serve all of us. You will get no argument from me if you say that, given a choice between a Western and a symphony, more people will watch the Western. I like Westerns and private eyes too — but a steady diet for the whole country is obviously not in the public interest. We all know that people would more often prefer to be entertained than stimulated or informed. But your obligations are not satisfied if you look only to popularity as a test of what to broadcast. You are not only in show business; you are free to communicate ideas as well as relaxation. You must pro-

Newton N. Minow, appointed chairman of the Federal Communications Commission by Kennedy in 1961

vide a wider range of choices, more diversity, more alternatives. It is not enough to cater to the nation's whims — you must also serve the nation's needs.

And I would add this — that if some of you persist in a relentless search for the highest rating and the lowest common denominator, you may very well lose your audience. Because, to paraphrase a great American who was recently my law partner, the people are wise, wiser than some of the broadcasters — and politicians — think.

As you may have gathered, I would like to see television improved. But how is this to be brought about? By voluntary action by the broadcasters themselves? By direct government intervention? Or how?

Let me address myself now to my role, not as a viewer but as chairman of the FCC. I could not if I would chart for you this afternoon in detail all of the actions I contemplate. Instead, I want to make clear some of the fundamental principles which guide me.

First, the people own the air. They own it as much in prime evening time as they do at 6 o'clock Sunday morning. For every hour that the people give you, you owe them something. I intend to see that your debt is paid with service.

Second, I think it would be foolish and wasteful for us to continue any worn-out wrangle over the problems of payola, rigged quiz shows, and other mistakes of the past. There are laws on the books which we will enforce. But there is no chip on my shoulder. We live together in perilous, uncertain times; we face together staggering problems; and we must not waste much time now by rehashing the clichés of past controversy. To quarrel over the past is to lose the future.

Third, I believe in the free enterprise system. I want to see broadcasting improved and I want you to do the job. I am proud to champion your cause. It is not rare for American businessmen to serve a public trust. Yours is a special trust because it is imposed by law.

Fourth, I will do all I can to help educational television. There are still not enough educational stations, and major centers of the country still lack usable educational channels. If there were a limited number of printing presses in this country, you may be sure that a fair proportion of them would be put to educational use. Educational television has an enormous contribution to make to the future, and I intend to give it a hand along the way. If there is not a nationwide educational television system in this country, it will not be the fault of the FCC.

Fifth, I am unalterably opposed to governmental censorship. There will be no suppression of programming which does not meet with bureaucratic tastes. Censorship strikes at the taproot of our free society.

Sixth, I did not come to Washington to idly observe the squandering of the public's airwaves. The squandering of our airwaves is no less important than the lavish waste of any precious natural resource. I intend to take the job of chairman of the FCC very seriously. I believe in the gravity of my own particular sector of the New Frontier. There will be times perhaps when you will consider that I take myself or my job *too* seriously. Frankly, I don't care if you do. For I am convinced that either one takes his job seriously — or one can be seriously taken.

Now, how will these principles be applied? Clearly, at the heart of the FCC's authority lies its power to license, to renew or fail to renew, or to revoke a license. As you know, when your license comes up for renewal, your performance is compared with your promises. I understand that many people feel that in the past licenses were often renewed *pro forma*. I say to you now: renewal will not be *pro forma* in the future. There is nothing permanent or sacred about a broadcast license.

But simply matching promises and performance is not enough. I intend to do more. I intend to find out whether the people care. I intend to find out whether the community which each broadcaster serves believes he has been serving the public interest. When a renewal is set down for hearing, I intend — wherever possible — to hold a well-advertised public hearing, right in the community you have promised to serve. I want the people who own the air and the homes that television enters to tell you and the FCC what's been going on. I want the people — if they are truly interested in the service you give them — to make notes, document cases, tell us the facts. For those few of you who really believe that the public interest is merely what interests the public — I hope that these hearings will arouse no little interest.

The FCC has a fine reserve of monitors — almost 180 million Americans gathered around 56 million sets. If you want those monitors to be your friends at court — it's up to you.

Some of you may say, "Yes, but I still do not know where the line is between a grant of a renewal and the hearing you just spoke of." My answer is: Why should you want to know how close you can come to the edge of the cliff? What the Commission asks of you is to make a conscientious good-faith effort to serve the public interest. Every one of you serves a community in which the people would benefit by educational, religious, instructive, or other public service programming. Every one of you serves an area which has local needs — as to local elections, controversial issues, local news, local talent. Make a serious, genuine effort to put on that programming. When you do, you will not be playing brinkmanship with the public interest.

What I've been saying applies to broadcast stations. Now a station break for the networks:

You know your importance in this great industry. Today, more than one-half of all hours of television station programming comes from the networks; in prime time, this rises to more than three-fourths of the available hours. You know that the FCC has been studying network operations for some time. I intend to press this to a speedy conclusion with useful results. I can tell you right now, however, that I am deeply concerned with concentration of power in the hands of the networks. As a result, too many local stations have forgone any efforts at local programming, with little use of live talent and local service. Too many local stations operate with one hand on the network switch and the other on a projector loaded with old movies. We want the individual stations to be free to meet their legal responsibilities to serve their communities.

I join Governor Collins in his views so

well expressed to the advertisers who use the public air. I urge the networks to join him and undertake a very special mission on behalf of this industry: you can tell your advertisers, "This is the high quality we are going to serve — take it or other people will. If you think you can find a better place to move automobiles, cigarettes, and soap — go ahead and try." Tell your sponsors to be less concerned with costs per thousand and more concerned with understanding per millions. And remind your stockholders that an investment in broadcasting is buying a share in public responsibility.

The networks can start this industry on the road to freedom from the dictatorship of numbers.

But there is more to the problem than network influences on stations or advertiser influences on networks. I know the problems networks face in trying to clear some of their best programs — the informational programs that exemplify public service. They are your finest hours, whether sustaining or commercial, whether regularly scheduled or special; these are the signs that broadcasting knows the way to leadership. They make the public's trust in you a wise choice.

They should be seen. As you know, we are readying for use new forms by which broadcast stations will report their programming to the Commission. You probably also know that special attention will be paid in these reports to public-service programming. I believe that stations taking network service should also be required to report the extent of the local clearance of network public service programming, and when they fail to clear them, they should explain why. If it is to put on some outstanding local program, this is one reason. But if it is simply to carry some old movie, that is an entirely different matter. The Commission should consider such clearance reports carefully when making up its mind about the licensee's overall programming.

We intend to move — and as you know, indeed the FCC was rapidly moving in other new areas before the new administration arrived in Washington. And I want to pay my public respects to my very able predecessor, Fred Ford, and my colleagues on the Commission who have welcomed me to the FCC with warmth and cooperation.

We have approved an experiment with pay TV, and in New York we are testing the potential of UHF broadcasting. Either or both of these may revolutionize television. Only a foolish prophet would venture to guess the direction they will take, and their effect. But we intend that they shall be explored fully — for they are part of broadcasting's new frontier.

The questions surrounding pay TV are largely economic. The questions surrounding UHF are largely technological. We are going to give the infant pay TV a chance to prove whether it can offer a useful service; we are going to protect it from those who would strangle it in its crib.

As for UHF, I'm sure you know about our test in the canyons of New York City. We will take every possible positive step to break through the allocations barrier into UHF. We will put this sleeping giant to use, and in the years ahead we may have twice as many channels operating in cities where now there are only two or three. We may have a half-dozen networks instead of three.

I have told you that I believe in the free enterprise system. I believe that most of television's problems stem from lack of competition. This is the importance of UHF to me: with more channels on the air, we will be able to provide every community with enough stations to offer service to all parts of the public. Programs with a mass-market appeal required by mass-product advertisers certainly will still be available. But other stations will recognize the need to appeal to more limited markets and to special tastes. In this way we can all have a much wider range of programs.

Television should thrive on this competition — and the country should benefit from alternative sources of service to the public. And, Governor Collins, I hope the NAB will benefit from many new members.

Another, and perhaps the most important, frontier: television will rapidly join the parade into space. International television will be with us soon. No one knows how long it will be until a broadcast from a studio in New York will be viewed in India as well as in Indiana, will be seen in the Congo as it is seen in Chicago. But as surely as we are meeting here today, that day will come — and once again our world will shrink.

What will the people of other countries think of us when they see our Western badmen and good men punching each other in the jaw in between the shooting? What will the Latin-American or African child learn of America from our great communications industry? We cannot permit television in its present form to be our voice overseas.

There is your challenge to leadership. You must reexamine some fundamentals of your industry. You must open your minds and open your hearts to the limitless horizons of tomorrow.

I can suggest some words that should serve to guide you:

> Television and all who participate in it are jointly accountable to the American public for respect for the special needs of children, for community responsibility, for the advancement of education and culture, for the acceptability of the program materials chosen, for decency and decorum in production, and for propriety in advertising. This responsibility cannot be discharged by any given group of programs, but can be discharged only through the highest standards of respect for the American home, applied to every moment of every program presented by television.

> Program materials should enlarge the horizons of the viewer, provide him with wholesome entertainment, afford helpful stimulation, and remind him of the responsibilities which the citizen has toward his society.

These words are not mine. They are yours. They are taken literally from your own Television Code. They reflect the leadership and aspirations of your own great industry. I urge you to respect them as I do. And I urge you to respect the intelligent and farsighted leadership of Governor LeRoy Collins and to make this meeting a creative act. I urge you at this meeting and, after you leave, back home, at your stations and your networks, to strive ceaselessly to improve your product and to better serve your viewers, the American people.

I hope that we at the FCC will not allow ourselves to become so bogged down in the mountain of papers, hearings, memoranda, orders, and the daily routine that we close our eyes to the wider view of the public interest. And I hope that you broadcasters will not permit yourselves to become so absorbed in the chase for ratings, sales, and profits that you lose this wider view. Now more than ever before in broadcasting's history the times demand the best of all of us.

We need imagination in programming, not sterility; creativity, not imitation; experimentation, not conformity; excellence, not mediocrity. Television is filled with creative, imaginative people. You must strive to set them free.

Television in its young life has had many hours of greatness — its "Victory at Sea," its Army-McCarthy hearings, its "Peter Pan," its "Kraft Theater," its "See It Now," its "Project 20," the World Series, its political conventions and campaigns, the Great Debates — and it has had its endless hours of mediocrity and its moments of public disgrace. There are estimates that today the average viewer spends about 200 minutes daily with television, while the average reader spends 38 minutes with magazines and 40 minutes with newspapers. Television has grown faster than a teenager, and now it is time to grow up.

What you gentlemen broadcast through the people's air affects the people's taste, their knowledge, their opinions, their understanding of themselves and of their world. And their future. The power of instantaneous sight and sound is without precedent in mankind's history. This is an awesome power. It has limitless capabilities for good — and for evil. And it carries with it awesome responsibilities — responsibilities which you and I cannot escape.

In his stirring Inaugural Address, our President said, "And so, my fellow Americans: ask not what your country can do for you — ask what you can do for your country."

Ladies and Gentlemen: Ask not what broadcasting can do for you — ask what you can do for broadcasting.

I urge you to put the people's airwaves to the service of the people and the cause of freedom. You must help prepare a generation for great decisions. You must help a great nation fulfill its future. Do this, and I pledge you our help.

5.

Dean Rusk: Formulating Foreign Policy

President Kennedy and his secretary of state, Dean Rusk, were confronted with urgent international problems from the moment they took office. Turmoil in Laos, civil war in the Congo, the diplomatic break with Cuba, and strained relations with the Soviet Union all made it difficult to formulate policies consonant with the goals of the new administration and at the same time adequate to deal with problems inherited from the old. Rusk emphasized the difficulty of creating both a just and a workable policy in some informal remarks to his aides in the State Department on February 20, 1961. His words echoed a warning that he had enunciated ten years before, when he had declared that "there are few fields of human endeavor where wishful thinking and self-delusion are as common, or as dangerous, as in foreign policy. . . . We should like an easy way to carry a heavy burden, an agreeable way to perform disagreeable tasks, a cheap way to bring about an expensive result."

Source: *Bulletin*, March 20, 1961: "A Fresh Look at the Formulation of Foreign Policy."

I suppose you are wondering what the significance of a new administration is. You haven't experienced a change of party administration since 1952, and before that not since 1932.

I think the principal point is that a change in administration gives us a chance to take a fresh look at a good many of our policies, to make fresh approaches, and to see whether we are going in the direction in which we as a nation really want to go. . . .

It is quite true that the central themes of American foreign policy are more or less constant. They derive from the kind of people we are in this country and from the shape of the world situation. It has been interesting over the years to see how, in our democratic society based on the consent of the governed, movements off the main path of the ideas and aspirations of the American people have tended to swing back to the main path as a result of the steady pressures of public opinion.

Nevertheless, we are today in a highly revolutionary world situation. Change is its dominant theme. I suppose that the central question before us is how we can properly relate ourselves to these fundamental and far-reaching changes. . . .

Older political forms have disintegrated. New international forms are coming into being. We are experiencing enormous pressures to achieve economic and social improvements in all parts of the world as masses of people who have largely been isolated from currents of world opinion, knowledge, and information are coming to realize that their miseries are not a part of an ordained environment about which nothing can be done.

We could be passive in relation to these changes and take our chances. I think the view of the new administration is that, were we to be passive, we could not expect the institutions of freedom to survive. We could undertake an active defense of the status quo. My own guess is that, were we to do that, we would be fighting a losing battle. We can, on the other hand, attempt to take a certain leadership in change itself; certainly the world is not as we should like to see it, and the world is not as peoples elsewhere find tolerable. . . .

I think another important factor for us to consider as we move into a new period turns on the President and his attitude toward the conduct of foreign relations. We have a President with great interest in foreign affairs. We have a President who will rely heavily upon the Department of State for the conduct of our foreign relations. This will not be a passive reliance but an active expectation on his part that this department will in fact take charge of foreign policy. The recent executive order which abolished the Operations Coordinating

Board bore witness to the fact that the Department of State is expected to assume the leadership of foreign policy. . . .

With this enlarged role in mind, I should like to make a few suggestions: What we in the United States do or do not do will make a very large difference in what happens in the rest of the world. We in this department must think about foreign policy in its total context. We cannot regard foreign policy as something left over after defense policy or trade policy or fiscal policy has been extracted. Foreign policy is the total involvement of the American people with peoples and governments abroad. . . . It is also the concern of the Department of State that our trading relationships with the rest of the world are vigorous, profitable, and active — this is not just a passing interest or a matter of concern only to the Department of Commerce. We can no longer rely on interdepartmental machinery "somewhere upstairs" to resolve differences between this and other departments. Assistant secretaries of state will now carry an increased burden of active formulation and coordination of policies. Means must be found to enable us to keep in touch as regularly and as efficiently as possible with our colleagues in other departments concerned with foreign policy.

I think we need to concern ourselves also with the timeliness of action. Every policy officer cannot help but be a planning officer. Unless we keep our eyes on the horizon ahead, we shall fail to bring ourselves on target with the present. The movement of events is so fast, the pace so severe that an attempt to peer into the future is essential if we are to think accurately about the present. . . .

I also hope that we can do something about reducing the infant mortality rate of ideas — an affliction of all bureaucracies. We want to stimulate ideas from the bottom to the top of the department. We want to make sure that our junior colleagues realize that ideas are welcome, that initiative goes right down to the bottom and goes all the way to the top. I hope no one expects that only presidential appointees are looked upon as sources of ideas. The responsibility for taking the initiative in generating ideas is that of every officer in the department who has a policy function, regardless of rank.

Further, I would hope that we could pay attention to little things. While observing the operations of our government in various parts of the world, I have felt that in many situations where our policies were good we have tended to ignore minor problems which spoiled our main effort. To cite only a few examples: The wrong man in the wrong position, perhaps even in a junior position abroad, can be a source of great harm to our policy; the attitudes of a UN delegate who experiences difficulty in finding adequate housing in New York City, or of a foreign diplomat in similar circumstances in our Capital, can easily be directed against the United States and all that it stands for. Dozens of seemingly small matters go wrong all over the world. Sometimes those who know about them are too far down the line to be able to do anything about them. I would hope that we could create the recognition in the department and overseas that those who come across little things going wrong have the responsibility for bringing these to the attention of those who can do something about them.

If the Department of State is to take primary responsibility for foreign policy in Washington, it follows that the ambassador is expected to take charge overseas. This does not mean in a purely bureaucratic sense but in an active, operational, interested, responsible fashion. He is expected to know about what is going on among the representatives of other agencies who are stationed in his country. . . .

It occurred to me that you might be in-terested in some thoughts which I expressed privately in recent years, in the hope of clearing up a certain confusion in the public mind about what foreign policy is all about and what it means, and of developing a certain compassion for those who are carrying such responsibilities inside government. I tried to do so by calling to their attention some of the problems that a senior departmental policy officer faces. This means practically everybody in this room. Whether it will strike home for you or not will be for you to determine.

The senior policy officer may be moved to think hard about a problem by any of an infinite variety of stimuli: an idea in his own head, the suggestions of a colleague, a question from the secretary or the President, a proposal by another department, a communication from a foreign government or an American ambassador abroad, the filing of an item for the agenda of the United Nations or of any other of dozens of international bodies, a news item read at the breakfast table, a question to the President or the secretary at a news conference, a speech by a senator or congressman, an article in a periodical, a resolution from a national organization, a request for assistance from some private American interests abroad, et cetera, ad infinitum. The policy officer lives with his antennae alerted for the questions which fall within his range of responsibility.

His first thought is about the question itself: Is there a question here for American foreign policy, and, if so, what is it? For he knows that the first and sometimes most difficult job is to know what the question is — that when it is accurately identified it sometimes answers itself, and that the way in which it is posed frequently shapes the answer. Chewing it over with his colleagues and in his own mind, he reaches a tentative identification of the question — tentative because it may change as he explores it further and because, if no tolerable answer can be found, it may have to be changed into one which can be answered.

Meanwhile he has been thinking about the facts surrounding the problem, facts which he knows can never be complete, and the general background, much of which has already been lost to history. He is appreciative of the expert help available to him and draws these resources into play, taking care to examine at least some of the raw material which underlies their frequently policy-oriented conclusions. He knows that he must give the expert his place, but he knows that he must also keep him in it.

He is already beginning to box the compass of alternative lines of action, including doing nothing. He knows that he is thinking about action in relation to a future which can be perceived but dimly through a merciful fog. But he takes his bearings from the great guidelines of policy, well-established precedents, the commitments of the United States under international charters and treaties, basic statutes, and well-understood notions of the American people about how we are to conduct ourselves, in policy literature such as country papers and National Security Council papers accumulated in the department.

He will not be surprised to find that general principles produce conflicting results in the factual situation with which he is confronted. He must think about which of these principles must take precedence. He will know that general policy papers written months before may not fit his problem because of crucial changes in circumstance. He is aware that every moderately important problem merges imperceptibly into every other problem. He must deal with the question of how to manage a part when it cannot be handled without relation to the whole — when the whole is too large to grasp.

He must think of others who have a

Lagos — Pix from Publix

Dean Rusk, appointed secretary of state by Kennedy

stake in the question and in its answer. . . . If action is indicated, what kind of action is relevant to the problem? The selection of the wrong tools can mean waste, at best, and, at worst, an unwanted inflammation of the problem itself. . . .

What type of action can hope to win public support, first in this country and then abroad? For the policy officer will know that action can almost never be secret and that in general the effectiveness of policy will be conditioned by the readiness of the country to sustain it. He is interested in public opinion for two reasons: first, because it is important in itself; and, second, because he knows that the American public cares about a decent respect for the opinions of mankind. And, given probable public attitudes — about which reasonably good estimates can be made — what action is called for to insure necessary support?

May I add a caution on this particular

point? We do not want policy officers below the level of presidential appointees to concern themselves too much with problems of domestic politics in recommending foreign policy action. In the first place, our business is foreign policy, and it is the business of the presidential leadership and his appointees in the department to consider the domestic political aspects of a problem. Mr. Truman emphasized this point by saying, "You fellows in the Department of State don't know much about domestic politics."

This is an important consideration. If we sit here reading editorials and looking at public-opinion polls and other reports that cross our desks, we should realize that this is raw, undigested opinion expressed in the absence of leadership. What the American people will do turns in large degree on their leadership. We cannot test public opinion until the President and the leaders of the country have gone to the public to explain what is required and have asked them for support for the necessary action. I doubt, for example, that, three months before the leadership began to talk about what came to be the Marshall Plan, any public-opinion expert would have said that the country would have accepted such proposals.

The problem in the policy officer's mind thus begins to take shape as a galaxy of utterly complicated factors — political, military, economic, financial, legal, legislative, procedural, administrative — to be sorted out and handled within a political system which moves by consent in relation to an external environment which cannot be under control.

And the policy officer has the hounds of time snapping at his heels. He knows that there is a time to act and a time to wait. . . . If he waits, he has already made a decision, sometimes the right one, but the white heat of responsibility is upon him and

he cannot escape it, however strenuously he tries.

There is one type of study which I have not seen, which I hope we can do something about in the months ahead. The pilot of a jet aircraft has a checklist of many dozen questions which he must answer satisfactorily before he takes off his plane on a flight. Would it not be interesting and revealing if we had a checklist of questions which we should answer systematically before we take off on a policy?

Perhaps this is a point at which to inject another passing comment. The processes of government have sometimes been described as a struggle for power among those holding public office. I am convinced that this is true only in a certain formal and bureaucratic sense, having to do with appropriations, job descriptions, trappings of prestige, water bottles, and things of that sort. There is another struggle of far more consequence, the effort to diffuse or avoid responsibility. Power gravitates to those who are willing to make decisions and live with the results, simply because there are so many who readily yield to the intrepid few who take their duties seriously.

On this particular point the Department of State is entering, I think, something of a new phase in its existence. We are expected to take charge. We shall be supported in taking charge, but it throws upon us an enormous responsibility to think broadly and deeply and in a timely fashion about how the United States shall conduct itself in this tumultuous world in which we live.

I want to transmit to you not only my own complete confidence but the confidence of the President in our determination to back you in one of the most onerous responsibilities in the country, and indeed in the world today, and ask you for your maximum help as we try to get on with this job in the months ahead.

6.

Adlai E. Stevenson: The Bay of Pigs

One of the most pressing problems inherited from the Eisenhower administration by President Kennedy was Cuba. There was in Central America a force of anti-Castro Cuban refugees that had been trained and equipped for an invasion of their homeland since 1960. Kennedy had the choice of disbanding this group or letting it go ahead, and he chose the latter course. On April 17, 1961, about 1,400 Cubans landed at the Bahia de Cochinos (Bay of Pigs) on the southern coast of Cuba. The beachhead was maintained for only three days, after which the invasion collapsed. News of the event spurred heated charges in the United Nations that the United States was pursuing an imperialist policy toward Cuba and was the secret force behind the invasion. Adlai E. Stevenson, U.S. ambassador to the UN, answered the charges in three statements on April 17, 18, and 20, portions of which are reprinted here.

Source: *Bulletin*, May 8, 1961, pp. 668-685.

April 17. What Dr. Roa seeks from us today is the protection of the Castro regime from the natural wrath of the Cuban people. We have all read the recent newspaper stories about these activities which he has described with such lurid oratory — of men who hope to return to Cuba for the purpose of establishing a free government in their homeland. At least some members of such groups have been captured or imprisoned or executed by Cuban firing squads. We have given asylum to tens of thousands of Cuban citizens who have been forced to flee from their homeland to these shores. These exiles nurse a natural, burning desire to bring freedom to Cuba, and toward that end they work with the dedicated concentration which José Martí and other Cuban exiles in the United States have shown in the tradition which is now nearly 100 years old.

But what does the present Cuban regime have to fear from these groups? What ac-

counts for Dr. Roa's agitation? Is Dr. Roa demanding that the Cuban exiles throughout the Americas be suppressed and controlled in the same ruthless manner as the people within Cuba today?

It cannot be that he fears the armed might of small armed bands of resistance fighters. His prime minister has often boasted of the armed strength of Cuba. Cuba has by far the largest ground forces of any country in Latin America, possessed, by Dr. Castro's own admission, with ample supplies of automatic rifles, machine guns, artillery, grenades, tanks, and other modern armament obtained from his new friends. Well over 30,000 tons of Soviet equipment has arrived in the last few months. This includes at least 15 Soviet 50-ton tanks, 19 Soviet assault guns, 15 Soviet 35-ton tanks, 78 Soviet 76-millimeter field guns, 4 Soviet 122-millimeter field guns, and over 100 Soviet heavy machine guns. Over 200 Soviet and Czechoslovak military advisers are in

Cuba, and over 150 Cuban military personnel have been sent to the bloc for training.

In view of all of this, we must look for the answer to Castro's fears somewhere else: in the internal situation in Cuba and in Prime Minister Castro's own experience with the difficulties which small dissident groups can cause for a dictator who has betrayed his own revolution, as in the case of Batista.

If the Cuban government is so deeply concerned about a few isolated groups, it must be because Dr. Castro has lost confidence in his own people. He evidently really believes that small armed groups are likely to find support enough to become dangerous. If this is the case, it seems a remarkable confession of doubt as to whether his own people approve his regime and its practices, and Dr. Castro is surely right to be afraid. Even with full government control of the press, the radio, television, all forms of communication, every evidence, including the daily defections of his close associates and supporters, suggests that the people of Cuba are rejecting this regime.

Let me make it clear that we do not regard the Cuban problem as a problem between Cuba and the United States. The challenge is not to the United States but to the hemisphere and its duly constituted body, the Organization of American States. The Castro regime has betrayed the Cuban revolution. It is now collaborating in organized attempts by means of propaganda, agitation, and subversion to bring about the overthrow of existing governments by force and replace them with regimes subservient to an extracontinental power. These events help to explain why the Cuban government continues to bypass the Organization of American States, even if they do not explain why Cuba, which is thus in open violation of its obligations under inter-American treaties and agreements, continues to charge the United States with violations of these same obligations.

Soon after the Castro government assumed power, it launched a program looking to the export of its system to other countries of the hemisphere, particularly in the Caribbean area. The intervention of Cuban diplomatic personnel in the internal affairs of other nations of the hemisphere has become flagrant. Cuban diplomatic and consular establishments are used as distribution points for propaganda material calling on the peoples of Latin America to follow Cuba's example. Even Cuban diplomatic pouches destined for various Latin-American countries have been found to contain inflammatory and subversive propaganda directed against friendly governments.

In public support of these activities Prime Minister Castro, President Dorticós, Dr. Roa himself, and many other high-ranking members of the revolutionary government have openly stated that "the peoples of Latin America should follow Cuba's example." They have frankly declared that the Cuban system is for export. On August 30, 1960, Prime Minister Castro said: "What happened in Cuba will someday happen in America, and if for saying this we are accused of being continental revolutionaries, let them accuse us." But in case that was not clear enough, it was followed two days later by Mr. Roa's statement that the Cuban revolution "will act as a springboard for all the popular forces in Latin America following a destiny identical to Cuba."

And as late as March 4 of this year, last month, President Dorticós did not hesitate to urge a group of Latin-American agricultural workers meeting in Habana to "initiate similar movements in their own countries" when they returned home. He promised them the "solidarity of a people who have already won their victory and are ready to help other people achieve theirs."

In spite of all of this, Dr. Roa now tells us that the revolutionary government wants only to live in peace, that it does not threaten its neighbors, that it has not attempted nor intends to export its revolution.

Statements of Soviet Russian and Chinese Communist leaders indicate that, by Dr. Castro's own actions, the Cuban revolution has become an instrument of the foreign policies of these extracontinental powers. The increasingly intimate relationship between Cuba and the Soviet Union, the People's Republic of China, and other countries associated with them, in conjunction with the huge shipments of arms, munitions, and other equipment from the Sino-Soviet bloc, must therefore be matters of deep concern to independent governments everywhere.

The Castro regime has mercilessly destroyed the hope of freedom the Cuban people had briefly glimpsed at the beginning of 1959. Cuba has never witnessed such political persecution as exists today. The arrests, the prisons bulging with political prisoners, and the firing squads testify to this. Since the Castro regime came to power, more than 600 persons have been executed, with a shocking disregard of the standards of due process of law and fair trial generally accepted and practised in the civilized community of nations. The government has even threatened to replace its slogan for this year — "the year of education" — with a new slogan — "the year of the execution wall."

There is no democratic participation of the Cuban people in the determination of their destiny. Staged rallies, at which small percentages of the population are harangued and asked to express approval of policies by shouts or show of hands, represent the procedure of a totalitarian demagog and not free and democratic expression of opinion through the secret ballot.

The Cuban farm worker, who was promised his own plot of land, finds that he is an employee of the state, working on collective or state-run farms. The independent labor movement, once one of the strongest in the hemisphere, is today in chains. Freely elected Cuban labor leaders, who as late as the end of 1960 protested the destruction of

workers' rights, were imprisoned for their pains, or took asylum in foreign embassies, or fled the country to escape imprisonment. When, in addition, the people are confronted, despite aid from the Sino-Soviet bloc, with a drastic reduction in their standard of living, it is not surprising opposition to their present master grows. . . .

The roster of disillusioned, persecuted, imprisoned, exiled, and executed men and women who originally supported Dr. Castro — and who are now labeled as "traitors and mercenaries" by Dr. Roa because they tried to make the Castro regime live up to its own promises — is long and getting longer. These are the men who are now leading the struggle to restore the Cuban revolution to its original premises.

In his letter of February 23, circulated in document A/4701, Dr. Roa claims that it is the policy of the United States "to punish the Cuban people on account of their legitimate aspirations for the political freedom, economic development, and social advancement of the underdeveloped or dependent peoples of Latin America, Africa, Asia, and Oceania." Such a ludicrous charge deserves no serious reply. But I should remind Dr. Castro that he had many friends in the United States at the time he took power in Cuba. The ideals which he then expressed of establishing honest and efficient government, perfecting democratic processes, and creating higher standards of living, full employment, and land reform were welcomed warmly both in the United States and in other parts of the Western Hemisphere. I sincerely wish that was still the case.

The problem created in the Western Hemisphere by the Cuban revolution is not one of revolution. As President Kennedy said on March 13:

> . . . political freedom must be accompanied by social change. For unless necessary social reforms, including land and tax reform, are freely made, unless we broaden the opportunity of all of our people, unless the great mass of Ameri-

cans share in increasing prosperity, then our alliance, our revolution, our dream, and our freedom will fail. But we call for social change by freemen — change in the spirit of Washington and Jefferson, of Bolívar and San Martín and Martí — not change which seeks to impose on men tyrannies which we cast out a century and a half ago. Our motto is what it has always been — progress yes, tyranny no. . . .

No, the problem is not social change, which is both inevitable and just. The problem is that every effort is being made to use Cuba as a base to force totalitarian ideology into other parts of the Americas.

The Cuban government has disparaged the plans of the American states to pool their resources to accelerate social and economic development in the Americas. At the Bogotá meeting of the Committee of 21 in September 1960, the Cuban delegation missed few opportunities to insult the representatives of other American states and to play an obstructionist role. They refused to sign the Act of Bogotá and thereby to take part in the hemisphere-wide cooperative effort of social reform to accompany programs of economic development. The Cuban official reaction to President Kennedy's Alliance for Progress program for the Americas was in a similar vein. In a speech on March 12, 1961, Dr. Castro denounced the program, portraying it as a program of "alms" using "usurious dollars" to buy the economic independence and national dignity of the countries which participate in the program.

This is insulting to the countries which participate in the program. But equally important, he chose to ignore the underlying premise of the program: a vast cooperative effort to satisfy the basic needs of the American peoples and thereby to demonstrate to the entire world that man's unsatisfied aspiration for economic progress and social justice can best be achieved by freemen working within a framework of democratic institutions. The hostility of the Castro regime to these constructive efforts for social and economic progress in the Americas — and even the language — recalls the similar hostility of the U.S.S.R. to the Marshall Plan in Europe.

Dr. Castro has carefully and purposefully destroyed the great hope the hemisphere invested in him when he came to power two years ago. No one in his senses could have expected to embark on such a course as this with impunity. No sane man would suppose that he could speak Dr. Castro's words, proclaim his aggressive intentions, carry out his policies of intervention and subversion — and at the same time retain the friendship, the respect, and the confidence of Cuba's sister republics in the Americas. He sowed the wind and reaps the whirlwind.

It is not the United States which is the cause of Dr. Castro's trouble; it is Dr. Castro himself. It is not Washington which has turned so many thousands of his fellow countrymen against his regime — men who fought beside him in the Cuban hills, men who risked their lives for him in the underground movements in Cuban cities, men who lined Cuban streets to hail him as the liberator from tyranny, men who occupied the most prominent places in the first government of the Cuban revolution. It is these men who constitute the threat — if threat there is — to Dr. Castro's hope of consolidating his power and intensifying his tyranny. . . .

The problem which the United States confronts today is our attitude toward such men as these. Three years ago many American citizens looked with sympathy on the cause espoused by Castro and offered hospitality to his followers in their battle against the tyranny of Batista. We cannot expect Americans today to look with less sympathy on those Cubans who, out of love for their country and for liberty, now struggle against the tyranny of Castro.

Ambassador Adlai E. Stevenson, photographed at the United Nations during the Bay of Pigs incident, 1961

If the Castro regime has hostility to fear, it is the hostility of Cubans, not of Americans. If today Castro's militia are hunting down guerrillas in the hills where Castro himself once fought, they are hunting down Cubans, not Americans. If the Castro regime is overthrown, it will be overthrown by Cubans, not by Americans.

April 18. I have listened here to every kind of epithet and abuse of my country. All of the familiar Communist words have been poured in a torrent on a nation that has fought in two world wars to defeat the designs of tyrants and protect your freedom as well as ours; a nation that bore the greatest burden of the first great battle for collective security in Korea and the protection of a small country from cynical and unprovoked attack by its neighbor; a nation that has poured out its treasure to aid the reconstruction and rehabilitation, the defense and prosperity, of friends and foes alike, with a magnanimity without historical precedents. And for our pains the words that reverberate in this chamber are too often "greedy monopolists," "mercenaries,"

"economic imperialists," "exploiters," "pirates," "aggressors," and all the familiar Communist jargon, including the worst of all — "counterrevolutionary" — which of course means anti-Communist. And I must say that after listening to this I welcome the healthy and wholesome suggestion of the representative of Ecuador that we declare a moratorium on epithets and poison in our discussion.

Not content with calling us all the names in the glossary of epithets and abuse, not content with confiscating all of our properties, with closing our Embassy, with persecuting our citizens, I have heard the United States denounced over and over for not buying our assailant's sugar — and at a price above the world market. I am reminded of the little boy who killed his mother and his father and then pleaded for clemency on the ground that he was an orphan.

But I assure you that Cuba is no orphan. Cuba has a new and powerful friend, just like Little Red Riding Hood in the fable. And now that their imperialist invasion of Cuba has succeeded and the Cuban revolution has been conformed to their pattern, we hear them deny the right of revolution to another people — the Cubans. I heard no such bitter protests when Mr. Castro was establishing his foothold in the Cuban mountains after returning from abroad with his followers. . . .

The current uprising in Cuba is the product of the progressively more violent opposition of the Cuban people to the policies and practices of this regime. Let us not forget that there have been hundreds of freedom fighters in the mountains of central Cuba for almost a year; that during the last six months skirmishes with the Castro police, attacks upon individual members of his armed forces, nightly acts of sabotage by the revolutionaries, have been increasing in number and intensity. Protest demonstrations have taken place by workers whose trade-union rights have been betrayed, by Catholics whose freedom of expression and worship has been circumscribed, by professional men whose right to free association has been violated. The response of the Castro regime has been repression, arrests without warrant, trial without constitutional guarantees, imprisonment without term and without mercy, and, finally, the execution wall.

Let me be absolutely clear: that the present events are the uprising of the Cuban people against an oppressive regime which has never given them the opportunity in peace and by democratic process to approve or to reject the domestic and foreign policies which it has followed. . . . It is hostility of Cubans, not Americans, that Dr. Castro has to fear. It is not our obligation to protect him from the consequences of his treason to the revolution, to the hopes of the Cuban people, and to the democratic aspirations of the hemisphere.

April 20. Although I am loath to speak as often or as long as the representative of the Soviet Union, this is, after all, an item that involves the United States and not the U.S.S.R. So I have some final words that I should like to say in this debate. I am grateful to those of my colleagues who have expressed respect for my country and for the honesty of its spokesmen here and in Washington.

First let me say that we don't deny that the exiles from Cuba have received the sympathy of many people inside and outside the United States — even as Dr. Castro had the sympathy of many in the United States, Mexico, and elsewhere. But the extent to which so many speakers have deliberately confused this with intervention and aggression by the United States government has exceeded all bounds of fact or fancy. Obviously the incessant repetition of such charges as though they had been proved reveals a greater anxiety to mislead and to corrupt world opinion than to keep the discussion on the tracks.

Let me commence where I started a couple of days ago. I said at the outset of this debate about Cuba:

> The United States sincerely hopes that any difficulties which we or other American countries may have with Cuba will be settled peacefully. We have committed no aggression against Cuba. We have no aggressive purposes against Cuba. We intend no military intervention in Cuba. I repeat, no military intervention in Cuba. We seek to see a restoration of the friendly relations which once prevailed between Cuba and the United States. We hope that the Cuban people will settle their own problems in their own interests and in a manner which will assure social justice, true independence, and political liberty to the Cuban people.

Since I said those words, I have heard a torrent — a deluge — of ugly words from Communist speakers here accusing the United States of aggression and invasion against Cuba. I will resist the temptation to invite attention to the record of aggression of the countries represented by some of those speakers — or to inquire as to which country has *really* intervened in Cuba, which country has perverted the Cuban revolution, and why these same speakers are so emotional about the revolt of the Cuban refugees against the new tyranny in Cuba and the new imperialism in the world.

Let me just ask — if this was a United States military operation, do you think it would succeed or fail? How long do you think Cuba could resist the military power of the United States? Perhaps the best evidence of the falsity of the shrill charges of American aggression in Cuba is the melancholy fact that this blow for freedom has not yet succeeded. And if the United States had been in charge I submit that fighting would hardly have broken out on the day debate was to start in this committee.

Aside from these loud charges of aggression, I have also heard the Communists echo over and over like parrots the old theme that the United States is trying to impose economic slavery — this time on Cuba.

Some of these speakers are evidently unaware — or perhaps they don't care — about the fact that I have written and talked about the need for economic and social reform and political democracy throughout Latin America for years. I would also remind these cold warriors that President Kennedy has recently proposed a large and thoughtful program of social reforms and economic assistance to Latin America. But I confess I have no hope that the Communist speakers will be any more interested in the truth tomorrow than they were yesterday or today.

There are those who will say that in the last forty-eight hours the Cuban people have spoken. Who can doubt the outcome if the events of the last few days had given the Cuban people the opportunity to choose between tyranny and freedom? The Cuban people have not spoken. Their yearning to be free of Castro's executions, of his betrayal of the revolution, of his controlled press, and of his yoke and rule by mailed fist has not been extinguished. The more than 100,000 refugees from his tyranny are undeniable proof of the historic aspirations of the Cuban people for freedom. The Cubans will continue to look forward to the day when they can determine their own future by democratic processes and through free institutions.

And what are the lessons to be learned? For those Cuban patriots who gave their lives, the lesson is one of tragic finality. But what of those who live on and will shape the future? The events of the last few days are indelible reminders to all of us in the Western Hemisphere. The penetration of force from outside our hemisphere, dominating a puppet government and providing it with arms, tanks, and fighter aircraft, is already dangerously strong and deep. It is now demonstrably stronger, deeper, and more dangerous to all of us who value freedom than most Americans — and most of our neighbors in the Western Hemisphere — have been willing to think.

If there is hope in the events of the last few days it is that it will awaken all of us in the Americas to a renewed determination to mobilize every resource and energy to advance the cause of economic growth and social progress throughout the hemisphere — to foster conditions of freedom and political democracy. They summon all of us to expand freedom and abundance with education of all peoples. If we dedicate ourselves with renewed resolve to bringing greater social reform, greater economic opportunity, greater human dignity, the sacrifices of the last few days will not have been in vain.

7.

LOUIS EISENSTEIN: Tax Ideologies

*Wars are always expensive, and taxes tend to rise as a consequence; they usually fall
again after the war is over. This was not true after World War II. Although taxes
fell somewhat, they remained at a generally high level, with the result that for most
U.S. citizens taxes came to be, and remained, the single largest item of expenditure.
(Anyone who doubted this was not counting in his budget the concealed taxes of one sort
or another that are thought by economists and politicians to be the least painful to pay.)
In this situation it was natural that a new profession should arise, composed of men
and women who were experts in the art of paying no more taxes than were due. Such a
tax accountant and lawyer was Louis Eisenstein, who in 1961 published a book on taxes
and on who paid them (and who didn't) from which the following selection is taken.*

Source: *The Ideologies of Taxation,* Copyright © 1961, The Ronald
Press Company, New York, pp. 3-15.

AT TIMES there is much to be said for stating the obvious. And so I start with what seems beyond dispute. Our taxes reflect a continuing struggle among contending interests for the privilege of paying the least. I am not unaware that others have a loftier view of the matter. They prefer to believe that our tax laws are usually inspired by more generous motives, which are then insidiously subverted for some unworthy purpose. The triumph of a special interest is considered an unfortunate deviation from the general rule. However, if we are to discuss taxes intelligently, we should gracefully abandon such pleasing illusions. In the words of an admirable conservative, we must clear our minds of cant. Tax legislation commonly derives from private pressures exerted for selfish ends. . . .

Mr. Justice Holmes tried to make taxes less disagreeable by means of a definition. Taxes, he wrote, "are what we pay for civilized society." He even said, "I like to pay taxes. With them I buy civilization." Yet a skillful definition can only accomplish so much and no more. We may cheerfully concede that taxes are an inevitable overhead of civilization, and that civilization is well worth having and saving. But it hardly follows that everyone should be happy to bear his allotted share of the overhead. For the question always remains whether the cost is properly allocated among the many beneficiaries. A taxpayer may readily wonder whether he is paying too much of that cost. If he regards his burden as excessive, he may even infer that civilization is in a very sorry state. Holmes also overlooked another difficulty in his effort to be helpful. Various groups are firmly persuaded that their functions are peculiarly vital to the progress of civilization. And so they easily reason that since their contributions are exceptional, their taxes should be small. Holmes' aphorism on civilization is more quotable than meaningful. . . .

Whether taxes are high or low, they are a constitutional means of appropriating private property without just compensation. The power to¹ tax is the power to confiscate. In short, taxes are distinctly disagreeable burdens, and so there is a constant striving to place them on the backs of others. The tax laws record the terms of the uneasy peace which happens to prevail at a particular moment. The terms periodically change as the contentions continue. I am not suggesting that taxes raise only questions of how they are to be distributed among those disinclined to pay them. The elected statesmen and the appointed experts who labor over taxes are troubled by other questions as well. They have to decide how much money is to be collected and how much money is to be spent. They have to say whether it is better to try for a surplus or to acquiesce in a deficit. They have to consider economic effects and political consequences. But so far as taxpayers are concerned, all such questions are subsidiary to the critical issue of distribution. As our tax hearings repeatedly reveal, it is usually assumed that other problems may be best resolved by shifting the burdens elsewhere. And there is no lack of ingenuity in providing the necessary rationalizations for the desired results.

I have been pursuing the thought that our tax laws reflect the fiscal aspirations of classes or groups. The time has come to be more precise. What do I mean when I speak of a "class" or "group"? Here, as on other occasions, we may return with profit to the Founding Fathers.

In the days of the Fathers a class or group was called a "faction" — which Madison defined as "a number of citizens, whether amounting to a majority or a minority of the whole, who are united and actuated by some common impulse of passion" emanating from self-interest. "From the protection of different and unequal faculties of acquiring property," he wrote, "the possession of different degrees and kinds of property immediately results; and from the

influence of these on the sentiments and views of the respective proprietors, ensues a division of the society into different interests and parties." Madison recognized that there are other sources of factions, but he concluded that "the most common and durable source" is "the various and unequal distribution of property."

"Those who hold and those who are without property have ever formed distinct interests in society. Those who are creditors, and those who are debtors, fall under a like discrimination. A landed interest, a manufacturing interest, a mercantile interest, a moneyed interest, with many lesser interests, grow up of necessity in civilized nations, and divide them into different classes, actuated by different sentiments and views." Madison, unlike Karl Marx, had no desire to remove "the *causes* of faction." He sought the more modest relief "of controlling its *effects*."

I am content to follow in the footsteps of the formidable Fathers. For present purposes I generally define a class or group as a number of persons who are animated by a common economic concern in their own behalf. I would be glad to speak of "factions," for the distinct interests in society still have their special sentiments and views. But, unfortunately, we have lost the capacity to be as frank as the Fathers, and we no longer speak of factions. Apparently the word is considered too indecorous. It has connotations of immoderate combativeness which should be more politely expressed. Perhaps the word "class" will soon disappear as well, because it is too closely associated with Marx. Already we rarely speak of "the poor." Instead we refer with due detachment to "the low income groups." While the word "class" does not make me shudder, many others prefer to do without it. Hence the accepted terminology now consists largely of "groups" and "interests"; and usually these approved nouns are preceded by the adjective "special."

Not every change is a change for the worse. A good deal can be said for the present vocabulary, apart from its respectability. The words "groups" and "interests" are much more flexible and adaptable than the word "class." A class is rather rigidly conceived in terms of some basic economic function or attribute. The customary categories are relatively few. They consist of such ultimate divisions as wage earners, farmers, businessmen, and capitalists. These categories are very useful when properly applied. But they are not useful enough for tax purposes because they do not adequately illuminate the variety of pressures from which the tax laws derive. "Groups" and "interests" more aptly describe the many voices that are heard and the many influences that are felt. The pressures that normally count are effectively exerted by smaller clusters of those who would pay less. As Madison pointed out, there are different interests, "with many lesser interests."

The words "groups" and "interests" are admirably versatile. They enable us to understand all sorts of distinctions that Congress has made. As a matter of principle, for example, it is generally assumed that all who are engaged in a trade or business are entitled to be treated as kindred souls. Since they are companions in risk, their tax liabilities should not invidiously vary. Businessmen, no less than others, may rightfully expect the equal protection of the laws. However, there are businessmen and businessmen, and some are considered more deserving than others. If a businessman grows and sells grain, his profit is ordinary income. But if he grows and sells timber, his profit may be capital gain. If he raises and sells poultry, his profit is ordinary income. But if he raises and sells livestock, his profit may be capital gain. If he buys and sells real estate, his profit is ordinary income. But if he buys and sells stock, his profit may be capital gain. If he produces steel, he can only deduct his actual costs. But if he produces

oil, he may also deduct imaginary costs known as percentage depletion.

The variations do not become less interesting as we continue our way through our Internal Revenue Code. If a royalty is received from an iron mine, it is ordinary income. But if a royalty is received from a coal mine, it may be capital gain. If an employee resides in this country, his earnings are taxable. But if he resides abroad, his earnings are not taxable. And if he resides here but works abroad, his earnings may be exempt up to $20,000. Needless to say, there are also scrupulous distinctions between one corporation and another. If a domestic corporation does business here, it pays 52 percent on income over $25,000. But if it does business elsewhere in the Western Hemisphere, it pays only 38 percent. The arts and sciences, too, are not ignored. Income from the sale of a book is ordinary income. But income from the sale of an invention may be capital gain. Composers and painters are regarded as no better than writers.

In listing these distinctions, I am not implying that they were necessarily conceived in error. Distinctions which are so delicately drawn may well reflect an estimable wisdom, though that wisdom may not be immediately apparent. The examples which I have given merely illustrate that "groups" and "interests" are more fitting nouns than "classes." They do a much better job of describing the beneficiaries of Congressional solicitude. Moreover, "groups" and "interests" serve another use which is not to be slighted. An increasing number of statutes are narrowly designed to relieve just a few select taxpayers. A good many, in fact, are carefully drawn to assure the salvation of only one or two. . . . While one taxpayer is too solitary to be a "group," he may still qualify as an "interest."

One other refinement is in order before we move further afield. Those who deplore the triumph of groups and interests repeatedly suggest that the Treasury is benevolently animated by different purposes. According to these unhappy observers, the Treasury is assiduously devoted to the public welfare as distinguished from private profit. This view of the Treasury is overly generous. It is an understandable effort to find comfort amid unpleasant circumstances.

The Treasury is not a neutral which is happily removed from the war of interests. On the contrary, it is intimately involved in their efforts to have their way. As Andrew Mellon disclosed, the precise sympathies of the Treasury will vary with those who are authorized to speak in its name. In the forties the Treasury was concerned with the burdens of small taxpayers. In the fifties it was comparably anxious on behalf of others.

The spokesmen for the Treasury, however, cannot always be as sympathetic as they would like to be. As custodians of the exchequer, they are troubled slaves to duty. Regardless of their compassion for certain groups and interests, they are obliged to gather the necessary revenues. Collections must correspond to expenditures. To a secretary of the Treasury a deficit may be the proverbial fate worse than death. The secretary who is especially worried over taxpayers in the upper brackets is also the secretary who is most disturbed by an unbalanced budget. Much as he may wish to alleviate their distress, he must weigh their suffering against the pain of diminished receipts. Even Mellon suggested higher estate taxes in the early thirties, when he was suddenly overtaken by the disaster of deficits. Finally, the Treasury must always evaluate the political effects of what it says and does. Whenever it lends its aid and comfort to a particular group or interest, it must do so with measured restraint. An undue display of enthusiasm may be condemned as a reckless failure of responsibility.

Taxes, then, are a changing product of earnest efforts to have others pay them. In a society where the few control the many, the efforts are rather simple. Levies are imposed in response to the preferences of the governing groups. Since their well-being is equated with the welfare of the community, they are inclined to burden themselves as lightly as possible. Those who have little to say are expected to pay. Rationalizations for this state of affairs are rarely necessary. It is assumed that the lower orders will be properly patriotic.

As political democracy comes upon the scene, complications soon emerge. Taxes can no longer be imposed without public consultation and debate. Those who have less property have more votes. Since heads are to be counted, they must first be persuaded. Reasons have to be given for the burdens that are variously proposed or approved. In time the contending reasons are skillfully elaborated into systems of belief or ideologies which are designed to induce the required acquiescence. Of course, if an ideology is to be effective, it must convey a vital sense of some immutable principle that rises majestically above partisan preferences. Except in dire circumstances, civilized men are not easily convinced by mere appeals to self-interest. What they are asked to believe must be identified with imposing concepts that transcend their pecuniary prejudices. . . .

I turn to what I regard as the three primary ideologies. For convenience I refer to them as the ideology of ability, the ideology of barriers and deterrents, and the ideology of equity. These three provide a framework of reason and rhetoric within which classes, groups, and interests assert themselves. . . .

The ideology of ability declares that taxes should be apportioned in accordance with the ability to pay them; and that ability to pay is properly measured by income or wealth. Therefore, the ideal levies are a progressive income tax and a progressive death tax. The ideology of barriers and deterrents takes a dim view of this conclusion. It embraces three related precepts that point to the inevitable disintegration of private enterprise if the precepts are disregarded. Progressive taxes dangerously diminish the desire to work; they fatally discourage the incentive to invest; and they irreparably impair the sources of new capital. Our economic system must come to an untimely end if private capital cannot accumulate and private initiative is destroyed. The three precepts merge into a more general perception of impending disaster. Progressive taxes are critically viewed as barriers and deterrents to the economic growth and stability of the nation. Even if the system is not on the verge of collapse, the barriers and deterrents must be rapidly removed. Otherwise the system must eventually decline and decay, since neither capital nor ambition will be available to sustain it. Finally, we have the ideology of equity. This ideology is closely concerned with the eloquent theme of equality among equals. It maintains that those who are similarly situated should be similarly treated, and those who are differently situated should be differently treated.

8.

Orlando W. Wilson: Police Arrest Privileges in a Free Society

The position of the police in a free society, Chicago Police Superintendent Orlando W. Wilson pointed out in the article reprinted here in part, is highly ambivalent. The policeman is the servant of the community and must heed the desire of its members for personal liberty; at the same time, however, it is his business to deprive certain members of the society of their liberty on occasions and in circumstances that the society defines. Before joining the Chicago police department Wilson had been for many years professor of police administration and dean of the school of criminology of the University of California at Berkeley. He took over Chicago's police department when it was riddled with dissension and had a reputation for corruption and inefficiency and in seven years converted it into one of the best in the country. He retired in 1967. The selection that follows is taken from an address delivered by Wilson in 1960 before the International Conference on Criminal Law Administration at Northwestern University. The speech was first published in 1961 and again in 1962.

Source: *Police Power and Individual Freedom*, Claude R. Sowle, ed., Chicago, 1962, pp. 21-28.

My TITLE, "Police Arrest Privileges in a Free Society," is merely one summation of the dilemma presented by the fact that you cannot have complete, absolute freedom in a free society when some people are confined or their freedom of movement and conduct is restricted. . . . It is my intention, in discussing police arrest privileges, to consider both the danger of unbounded liberty and the danger of bounding it, in the belief that a fair compromise is possible between the two — a compromise that will be to the advantage of a free society. The discussion will be within the framework of our Constitution; its amendment or violation is not proposed. This exclusion of the constitutional guarantees from the discussion cannot be absolute, however, for the reason that the reasonableness of search and seizure is often dependent upon the validity of the arrest.

Our free society has created a system designed to identify and apprehend the person who commits a crime and to give him a fair trial in which the truth of his guilt or innocence is to be established. This system is based on the principle that guilty persons should be adjudged guilty. The trial court is as ethically bound to ascertain the guilt of the guilty as it is to ascertain the innocence of the innocent. Rules that exclude material and relevant facts bearing on the guilt or innocence of the defendant are inconsistent with this principle and with the oath to tell the truth, the whole truth, and nothing but the truth. Since an invalid arrest may result in the exclusion of material and relevant facts, the liberalization of arrest privileges would lessen the likelihood of the exclusion of truth, and would also facilitate the apprehension of criminals and lessen the physical hazards of the police. . . .

Both unbounded liberty and its restriction place basic human rights in jeopardy. Unbounded liberty jeopardizes the security of life and property and, indeed, the security of our free society. Were this not so, there would be no need to place any restrictions on liberty. Restricting liberty, on the other hand, jeopardizes the basic human right to freedom in movement and conduct.

The problem, then, is to prescribe restrictions which will provide an acceptable degree of security without unduly infringing upon individual freedom. The restrictions on liberty now under discussion are adjusted by increasing or decreasing police arrest privileges. They must be so regulated that the price paid in inconvenience and restraint has an equal compensating value in the advantages of greater security. To keep the scales of justice in balance, the advantages to a free society resulting from a reasonable

degree of security in one pan must hold in precise equilibrium the other containing the disadvantages that result from restrictions.

This means compromise; some liberty must be sacrificed for the sake of security. A compromise is a modification of opposing views so that they may blend to the mutual satisfaction of the opponents. The opponents in the issue under discussion are not the assailant and his victim but instead law-abiding citizens who differ in their appraisals of the danger of unbounded liberty on the one hand and the danger of bounding it on the other. . . .

Compromise is a characteristic of a free society, the strength of which is derived from consolidating the most acceptable features of opposing views into a workable system. In compromise, each side appraises what it gains in advantage against what it loses in disadvantage; there is then a measure of give and take. The appraisal in a free society is participated in by the citizens with the legislature serving as the arbitrator to say, "This is the way it will be." This democratic process enables citizens to have their desires implemented by law.

In the absence of legislation bearing on some aspect of police arrest privileges, the appellate courts may make decisions that are as binding in their effect as legislative enactments. The process which results in an appellate decision is markedly different from the legislative process. The issue before the court relates to the rights of the appellant, who has been judged guilty by the most liberal system of criminal justice found anywhere in the world. The court considers whether the rights of the appellant have been violated, not by organized society but by a policeman whose actions are often viewed with distaste because all of the facts which may have justified the action are not on the record. The court ponders the alleged infringement of the rights of the convicted person as a legal abstraction and feels obliged to consider the question as it would apply were the individual innocent. Finally, the desires of the general public for some reasonable measure of security and for a redress of the wrong done to the innocent victim of the criminal are not made known nor are they readily available to the court. . . .

It is apparent that equilibrium in the scales of justice may necessitate adjustment of the weight in one pan to compensate for a change in weight in the other. Should reasonable security be jeopardized by an increase in criminality, further restrictions on liberty may be justified. On the other hand, a society that has minimum criminality may enjoy maximum liberty.

An accurate and valid comparison of the crime frequency of this country with that of other countries is not possible today, but analysis and fair interpretation of available statistics lead to the conclusion that our country is among those having the highest crime rates. This fact in itself is apparently not alarming to a people accustomed to excel in industrial production, in standard of living — and in liberty.

Some cause for concern is found, however, in that the extent of criminality in our country is not remaining constant at this excessively high level. Instead, it is increasing at an alarming rate year by year. For example, the frequency of those crimes categorized by the FBI as "Part I crimes" increased four times more rapidly than the population of this country during the first seven years of this decade.

In 1958, the FBI adopted a new crime index which differed from the previously used Part I crimes by the exclusion of negligent manslaughter, statutory rape, and larceny under $50. This new and more accurate index revealed that crime increased five times more rapidly than population from 1957 to 1958.

Reports for the first nine months of 1959 from cities with a total population of 69 million showed an overall decrease of 1 percent in the number of crimes from the comparable 1958 statistics. It seems unwise to conclude from these incomplete figures, however, that the upward crime trend has been halted.

During the past decade, the police of this country have been strengthened in number, in training, and in equipment. They are better organized and are using more progressive procedures to prevent crime and to apprehend criminals than ever before in their history. Crime increases during the past decade have not resulted from a decrease in police effectiveness; they must be accounted for by other factors.

The effectiveness of a free society in controlling criminals may be measured in part by its success in convicting defendants. Comparison of 1957 and 1958 conviction rates with the average for the previous five-year periods in offenses included in the new crime index (excluding forcible rape, for which statistics are not available prior to 1958) and in four other classes of crimes (stolen property offenses, weapons offenses, narcotic law violations, and gambling) reveal a startling trend. . . .

In each of these crime categories (except homicides and narcotic offenses in 1957), the 1957 and 1958 conviction rates are lower than the average for the preceding five years. In 1957 the conviction rate for robbery, compared to the previous five-year average, decreased 19 percent; for aggravated assault, 18 percent; for burglary, 11 percent; for stolen property offenses, 12 percent; for weapons offenses, 16 percent; for gambling, 30 percent. In 1958, the conviction rate for robbery, compared to the previous five-year average, decreased 18 percent; for aggravated assault, 14 percent; for burglary, 7 percent; for stolen property offenses, 14 percent; for gambling, 29 percent; for homicide, 4 percent; for narcotic offenses, 6 percent.

Decreases of such magnitude in conviction rates may be taken, with the persistent increase in crime, as a warning that the scales of justice are getting out of balance.

Where lies the fault? There is no indication that police procedures used in marshaling evidence against the defendant are becoming less effective; indeed, the reverse seems more likely. Nor does it seem that prosecutors have grown less vigorous or that defense attorneys have suddenly discovered new and more successful techniques. May the explanation be found in the restrictions that have been imposed on the police by appellate decisions?

People on the whole want protection from criminal attack; they want to feel secure in their homes and on the streets from disturbances and molestations. To meet this need, local communities in our free society have created uniformed bodies of police to prevent crimes and to bring to court those who commit them. Responsibility for the prevention of crime rests principally on city police forces, sheriffs' departments, and local detachments of state police.

A crime occurs when a person who desires to commit it discovers the opportunity to do so. Such unwholesome desires spring from and are a measure of criminality. The police cannot prevent the development of criminality, except as their contacts with potential and actual offenders may have this wholesome effect; nor are the police charged with this responsibility. Their basic purpose is to remove or lessen by both physical and psychological means the opportunity to commit crimes.

To prevent crime, the police must either stand guard at every point of possible attack, which is a physical and economic impossibility, or intercept the person with criminal intent before he robs, rapes, or kills. It is better to have an alert police force that prevents the crime than one that devotes its time to seeking to identify the assailant after the life has been taken, the daughter ravished, or the pedestrian slugged and robbed.

The task of the police in preventing crime is quite different from that of identifying the perpetrator and marshaling evidence to

prove his guilt. To prevent crime by intercepting the criminal while he seeks his prey is not unlike hunting a predatory animal; prompt and decisive action is called for at a critical moment not of the huntsman's choosing. The policeman who fails to act at the critical moment may nonetheless prevent an impending crime, but the criminal, who more times than not is wanted for previous unsolved crimes, remains at large to continue his depredations. Restrictions on arrest privileges hamper the police, not only in preventing crime but also in clearing cases by the arrest of the perpetrator and in marshaling evidence to support prosecution.

The local police feel the restrictions imposed on arrest privileges more keenly than do the specialized police agencies whose principal responsibility is the gathering of evidence to identify and convict persons after they have committed a crime rather than to prevent the act in the first instance. Frequently the criminal, whose act is within the jurisdiction of a specialized police agency, has already been arrested by local police, who often apprehend him in the act or in flight from the crime scene. These are critical moments for police action. In cases where the culprit has not been arrested, the critical moment for arrest can often be set by the specialized police; it is planned after sufficient evidence is marshaled to justify the arrest, which is often authorized by warrant. In contrast, most arrests by local police are made without warrant at a critical moment not of their choosing before they have had an opportunity to marshal evidence beyond what they personally observed at the time.

The typical citizen would feel that the police were remiss in their duty should they fail on their own initiative, or refuse on legal grounds, to investigate by questioning a person who was lurking in the neighborhood for no apparent reason. The disturbed citizen would expect the police to discover whether the suspect was armed and, if so, to disarm him and prosecute him should it be discovered that he was carrying the weapon illegally. Should the suspect refuse to explain what he was doing in the neighborhood, and the policeman apologized for questioning him and then went about his duties leaving the suspect to continue his lurking, the citizen would consider that he was not receiving adequate protection.

The typical citizen is surprised when he discovers that in many jurisdictions police arrest privileges are so carefully circumscribed by statutory and case law as to render the policeman virtually powerless to deal effectively and safely with situations that confront him almost hourly during his duty tour. The police action demanded by the citizen from his protector is illegal in many jurisdictions.

The police, under local control as in our form of government, are inclined to provide the protection their citizen-employers demand; otherwise the police fail to prevent crime and are subject to sharp criticism for their failure to protect the public. Also, since they usually act with courtesy, discretion, and good judgment, only infrequently is the legality of their acts questioned, and then by a citizen who fails to understand and appreciate the police motive or by a lawyer who uses the incident in the defense of his guilty client.

The discrepancy between what the people expect the police to do and what the police are privileged to do in protecting public peace and security results principally from a lack of understanding of the police purpose and of what the police must do to accomplish it. . . .

Lack of public understanding of the police purpose and what the police must do to accomplish it is accentuated by two circumstances that tend to cast the police in the role of agents bent on unnecessarily oppressing freedom. The first grows out of police responsibility in the enforcement of traffic and other regulatory laws sometimes violated by the most conscientious citizen, an enforcement that aligns good citizens

against the police. The other is ignorance of the facts involved in the war against crime in a free society. People are apt to fear and hate what they do not understand — and the hate is often stimulated by traffic violation experiences.

These misunderstandings continue unabated because the police are not a vocal, scholarly group that devotes much time to presenting in a favorable light the facts that bear on the problem. The literature, in consequence, is principally devoted to the case against the police; little has been written in their defense. The press, the literature, and even case law are all directed at incidents that discredit the police. Small wonder that those who read the papers or research the literature and case law conclude that the police are evil. Information on which a fairer judgment might be based is not generally circulated. . . .

Law enforcement may be strengthened by legalizing common police practices, already legal in some jurisdictions, which would have the effect of facilitating the discovery of criminals and evidence of their guilt and of lessening the exclusion of relevant evidence from their trials. The police should be authorized to question persons whose actions under the circumstances then existing are such as to arouse reasonable suspicion that the suspect may be seeking an opportunity to commit a crime. A police officer should be privileged to search such a suspect for weapons when the officer has reasonable grounds to believe that he is in danger if the person possesses a dangerous weapon, and, should the suspect be illegally armed, to arrest him for this offense. Should the suspect be unable or unwilling to explain satisfactorily the reasons for his presence and actions, the officer should be authorized to take him to a police station and hold him while the investigation is continued, for a period of two hours, without placing him under arrest.

The police should be privileged to release an arrested person without bringing him before a magistrate when their investigation reveals his innocence or when a drunk has become sober. The police should be authorized to hold an arrested person before bringing him before a magistrate for at least twenty-four hours, excluding days when courts are not in session. Magistrates should be authorized to order the defendant to be held for an additional period when good cause for such detention is shown.

A police officer should be authorized to arrest under a warrant when the warrant is not in his possession, to arrest without a warrant for any misdemeanor committed in his presence, and to arrest without a warrant for petty thefts and other misdemeanors not committed in his presence when he has reasonable grounds to believe that the defendant could not be found after the warrant was issued.

Suspects should be denied the right to resist illegal arrest by a person the suspect has reasonable grounds to believe to be a police officer. The police should be authorized and urged to use notices to appear in court in lieu of physical arrest in suitable misdemeanor cases when they believe the defendant will appear as agreed. Persons the police have reasonable grounds to believe to be witnesses to crimes should be legally required to identify themselves to the police.

These are essentially the provisions of the Uniform Arrest Act. To them should be added authority for the police to search any convicted narcotic offender for contraband, without a warrant, when his actions, under the circumstances then existing, are such as to arouse reasonable suspicion that the suspect may have contraband in his possession.

The reasonable arrest privileges mentioned above would facilitate the achievement of objectives in law enforcement desired by all persons except the criminals themselves. The privileges would enable the police to exercise such control over persons in public places as to enhance the peace and security of all citizens.

These privileges do not threaten the lives or health of the innocent; the inconvenience of two hours of detention, short of arrest, is experienced only by the innocent person who inadvertently or by poor judgment is found in a situation that arouses police suspicion and which the suspect is unable or unwilling to explain on the spot. In view of the present jeopardy to public security, such inconvenience seems a small price to pay for the privilege of living securely and peacefully.

Police abuse of authority with criminal intent resulting in serious offenses must always be dealt with by criminal prosecution and disciplinary action. Establishing safeguards against abuse of authority by the overzealous policeman in the day-to-day performance of his duty presents quite a different problem. Safeguards that weaken law enforcement or free the guilty are socially undesirable; if possible the problem should be solved in some other way.

Civil suits for damages filed against the individual officer have not proved adequately effective in preventing police abuse of authority. Were this procedure effective, however, it would emasculate vigorous police action and law enforcement would be weakened at a time when it needs to be strengthened.

Negating police overzealousness by freeing guilty defendants violates the principle that the guilty should be adjudged guilty, punishes society rather than the policeman, rewards the guilty, and is a miscarriage of justice. Its effectiveness as a control of police abuse of authority has not been demonstrated.

The Committee on Criminal Law and Procedure of the California State Bar proposed that:

> . . . the answer might lie in a new kind of civil action, or better, a summary type of proceeding, for a substantial money judgment in favor of the wronged individual, whether innocent or guilty, and against the political subdivision whose enforcement officers violated that person's rights. After not many outlays of

public funds the taxpayers and administrative heads would insist upon curbing unlawful police action.

Professor Edward L. Barrett, Jr., of the University of California Law School, in commenting on this proposal, stated:

> Legislative action along these general lines gives promise of providing a more adequate solution than the exclusionary rule at a smaller social cost. . . . The remedy would be available to the innocent as well as the guilty, for the illegal arrest as well as the illegal search. The courts would have frequent opportunities for ruling on the legality of police action, for enunciating and developing the governing law. If in any community a substantial number of such actions become successful, the financial pressure on the police to conform more closely to judicial standards would doubtless follow. Finally, if a careful line is drawn between those situations where increased personal liability should be placed upon the individual policeman (basically those involving serious and intentional violations of law) and those where he should be immunized and sole liability placed upon the governmental agency, interference with the efficient functioning of law enforcement would be minimized.

9.

Barry Goldwater: Total Victory in the Cold War

The problem of creating a viable American foreign policy during the Cold War was complicated by the opposition of certain factions within the U.S. to any accommodation with the U.S.S.R. These factions, regarding the concept of "peaceful coexistence" as a screen behind which the proponents of Communism were working to dominate the world, saw the Cold War as necessarily continuing until either freedom or Communism was destroyed. One of the leading supporters of this view was Senator Barry Goldwater of Arizona, the Republican candidate for President in 1964. In a speech in the Senate on July 14, 1961, a portion of which appears below, Goldwater urged that the U.S. seek total victory over Communism in all of its dealings with the Soviet bloc of nations. In the course of his speech he made several references to Senator J. William Fulbright of Arkansas, a dissenter from the Goldwater philosophy. Fulbright rejected the goal of total victory as one that exceeded the capabilities of the U.S. and the requirements of the world situation, and warned that even a total military victory would burden the U.S. with the problem of rehabilitating millions of Russians and Chinese.

Source: *Record*, 87 Cong., 1 Sess., pp. 12582-12584.

Mr. President:

As I study the address delivered by the distinguished chairman of the Committee on Foreign Relations, I find myself becoming first surprised, then amazed, and finally, alarmed. In essence, it strikes me as an argument for continued drifting in the wrong direction; for inaction on all major cold war fronts; for further costly implementation of an outmoded, weak-kneed foreign policy which accomplishes nothing but more and greater losses of freedom's territory to the forces of international communism. It is a plea for more useless expenditures in the

name of more hopeless objectives. It is part
and parcel with the prevalent belief in administration circles that all we have to do is
increase the foreign aid budget and Khrushchev will back off, Castro will be rendered ineffective, and a tremendous host of
nations will quickly effect social and economic reforms and clasp the United States
to their bosom as the savior of underdeveloped areas.

If our largesse is increased, we are led to
believe neutrality among the uncommitted
nations of the world will be merely a disguise for free world partisanship, and countries struggling with centuries-old social and
economic institutions and habits will suddenly develop a form of dynamic anti-
Communist progress similar to that which
has taken place in Western Europe.

Mr. President, I say also that the reflections of the chairman of the Foreign Relations Committee would seem to rest our
entire case against the powerful Soviet-Sino
axis on economic, social, and political arguments to the exclusion of military considerations. For example, the senator from Arkansas seems to view with alarm the voices,
as he puts it, that "are saying the United
States is the strongest country in the world,
and should not hesitate to commit its
strength to the active defense of its policies
anywhere outside the Communist empire." . . .

It might be well for the administration to
give more consideration to why the American people are skeptical. Some day, Mr.
President — and the way things are going I
am beginning to wonder whether it will
ever come — those in official capacity in
this country will have to stand up and tell
the American people why it is that this approach to the realities of the cold war has
cost us billions and billions of dollars while
communism continues to gain, both in prestige and territory. The plain fact is that this
is not a way to meet effectively the challenge of the cold war. It is the way to

Barry Goldwater, photographed in 1964

weaken freedom by draining our strength
and undermining our economy. . . .

I believe there is something that would
please the Communists more than the costly commitments of military strength, and
that is the action we are taking right now. I
assure you, Mr. President, that a show of
American strength, even in peripheral areas,
would not please the Communists. What
pleases them is our present policy of making costly commitments throughout the
world, commitments which carry with them
no elements of real strength, but which rest
on theoretical dreaming that the way to
fight Communist bullets is with relief pack-
ages, Communist tanks with plows, Communist bombs with elaborate charts for
monetary reform.

I disagree also with the inference of the
senator from Arkansas that peripheral areas
are negligible in a military sense. The areas
he talks about are the periphery of freedom
— a periphery, I might add, that is growing
steadily smaller in direct ratio to our failure

to act from strength. I cannot say I find any concern for this development in the scholarly words of the chairman of the Committee on Foreign Relations. This is particularly true when he speaks about the closest point of freedom's encirclement — Cuba — which the senator concedes has been transformed into "a Communist-oriented totalitarian state," but which he does not want us to regard as a threat requiring action. . . .

The remarks of my esteemed colleague from Arkansas on these important matters do not provide us with a new insight into how the nation's foreign affairs should be conducted. At the most, they add up to an apologia for inaction, to an excuse for a continuation of stumbling and groping in the cold war.

Mr. President, I should like to see us get on the right track, once and for all, in our approach to foreign policy matters. And I believe the first step is for the President of the United States to declare officially that it is our purpose to win the cold war, not merely wage it in the hope of attaining a standoff. Further, I would like to see the chairman of the Senate Foreign Relations Committee urge this action on the President, and back him to the hilt if he agrees.

Mr. President, it is really astounding that our government has never stated its purpose to be that of complete victory over the tyrannical forces of international communism. I am sure that the American people cannot understand why we spend billions upon billions of dollars to engage in a struggle of worldwide proportions unless we have a clearly defined purpose to achieve victory. Anything less than victory, over the long run, can only be defeat, degradation, and slavery. Are these stakes not high enough for us? Is not this reason enough for us to fight to win?

I suggest that our failure to declare total victory as our fundamental purpose is a measure of an official timidity that refuses to recognize the all-embracing determination of communism to capture the world and destroy the United States. This timidity has sold us short, time and time again. It denied us victory in the Korean War, when victory was there for the taking. It refused General MacArthur the right to prosecute a war for the purpose of winning, and caused him to utter these prophetic words:

The best that might be said for the policy makers responsible for these monumental blunders is that they did not comprehend the truism, as old as history itself, that a great nation which voluntarily enters upon war and does not fight it through to victory must ultimately accept all of the consequences of defeat — that in war, there is no substitute for victory.

Mr. President, we would do well to heed those words of General MacArthur, and apply them to the present — apply them to our position in the cold war, for if we engage in this cold war, and do not fight it through to victory, we must be prepared to accept the consequences of defeat. And the consequences of such a defeat, I can assure you, Mr. President, will be slavery for all the peoples of the world.

In addition to an overall objective of victory, we need a careful appraisal of what such an effort will cost, and a priority list of essentials to measure against the willy-nilly demands for spending on all sectors. This is a clarification which the American people are demanding. In this respect, I refer to the findings of Mr. Samuel Lubell, a public opinion expert who recently took samplings in nineteen states. He reached these conclusions:

If President Kennedy is to gain public support for a more intensive cold war effort, two basic reforms seem needed:
1. Existing programs must yield better results.
2. All of the government spending effort, domestic and foreign, must be unified into a thought through, first-things-first system of priorities.

Mr. President, I am not one who ordinarily takes the findings of public opinion pollsters as the last word in popular sentiment; but I must say that the findings of Mr. Lubell are in keeping with everything which my office mail, as well as conversations I have had with people across the face of this country, have been telling me. There is a great restiveness among our people, because they have the feeling that the administration's programs have been thrown together without sufficient regard for an overall objective or for final costs. They are disturbed at reports that the State Department is toying with a so-called two-China policy; at indications that we may negotiate with Khrushchev on Berlin instead of standing firm; at the possibility that a flimsy, "phony" pretext will be found for diplomatic recognition of Communist Outer Mongolia.

To date, Mr. President, the American people have nothing to which they can point as a positive indication that the New Frontier means to stand up to the forces of international communism, after the fashion of a great world power. They have waited patiently — and in vain — for this government to resume nuclear testing, against growing evidence that the Soviet Union is already secretly engaged in this vital activity. Let me say that I believe right here is where the New Frontier could act to show us that it does not intend to be hoodwinked forever by Soviet negotiators. I do not think there is any longer a reason for even fixing a deadline for the resumption of these tests. I believe the United States should just pull its representatives back from the test meetings and begin work — work that has been delayed too long, in the face of new and greater Communist threats around the world.

These are the things, I believe, that our nation needs right now, instead of more excuses for inaction and more justifications for an expanding foreign-aid program, which needs drastic alterations before it can yield results. We need a declaration that our intention is victory. We need a careful cost accounting of what will be required to meet this objective within the framework of our economic ability. And we need an official act, such as the resumption of nuclear testing, to show our own people and the other freedom-loving peoples of the world that we mean business.

These are minimum requirements, Mr. President, in the nature of first steps. But they are essential if we are to chart a positive course aimed at total victory in a struggle for the future of freedom.

There is no more dangerous misconception than this which misconstrues the arms race as the cause rather than a symptom of the tensions and divisions which threaten nuclear war. If the history of the past fifty years teaches us anything, it is that peace does not follow disarmament — disarmament follows peace.
BERNARD M. BARUCH, memorandum composed for U.S. government officials, 1961

10.

The Crisis of World Capitalism — A Soviet View

The Twenty-second Congress of the Communist Party of the Soviet Union met in Moscow in October 1961 (the eighth year of Khrushchev's reign) to approve a new long-term political and economic program. The new program replaced the one adopted by the Eighth Congress of 1919, written by or under the direction of Lenin, which had outlined the path to "Socialism." The Khrushchev program outlined the path to "Communism," which the document declared would be achieved by the generation then living (this was a radical departure from traditional Marxist ideas), and predicted that the Soviet people would enjoy the highest standard of living in the world by 1980. The program filled several hundred pages, two or three of which were taken up by the following description of the "crisis" of world capitalism. The selection is interesting not only in itself but also as an expression of the official Soviet view of the United States in the Cold War.

Source: *The Communist Blueprint for the Future*, compiled by Thomas P. Whitney, New York, 1962, pp. 124-133.

THE UNITED STATES monopoly bourgeoisie is the mainstay of international reaction. It has assumed the role of "savior" of capitalism. The United States financial tycoons are engineering a "holy alliance" of imperialists and founding aggressive military blocs. American troops and war bases are stationed at the most important points of the capitalist world.

But the facts reveal the utter incongruity of the United States imperialist claims to world domination. Imperialism has proved incapable of stemming the Socialist and national-liberation revolutions. The hopes which American imperialism pinned on its atomic-weapons monopoly fell through. The United States monopolies have not been able to retain their share in the economy of the capitalist world, although they are still its chief economic, financial, and military force. The United States, the strongest capitalist power, is past its zenith and has entered the stage of decline. Imperialist countries such as Great Britain, France, Germany, and Japan have also lost their former power.

The basic contradiction of the contemporary world, that between socialism and imperialism, does not eliminate the deep contradictions rending the capitalist world. The aggressive military blocs founded under the aegis of the United States of America are time and again faced with crises. The international state-monopoly organizations springing up under the motto of "integration," of mitigation of the market problem, are in reality new forms of the redivision of the world capitalist market and are becoming seats of acute strain and conflict.

The contradictions between the principal imperialist powers are growing deeper. The economic rehabilitation of the imperialist countries defeated in World War II leads to the revival of the old and the emergence of new knots of imperialist rivalry and conflict. The Anglo-American, Franco-American, Franco-German, American-German, Anglo-German, Japanese-American, and other contradictions will inevitably arise and grow in the imperialist camp.

The American monopolies and their British and French allies are openly assisting the resurgence of West German imperialism, which is cynically advocating aggressive aims of revenge and preparing a war against the Socialist countries and other European states. A dangerous center of aggression, imperiling the peace and security of all peoples, is being revived in the heart of Europe. In the Far East the American monopolies are reviving Japanese militarism, another dangerous hotbed of war threatening the countries of Asia and, above all, the Socialist countries.

The interests of the small group of imperialist powers are incompatible with the interests of the other countries, the interests of all peoples. Deep-rooted antagonism divides the imperialist countries from the countries that have won national independence and those that are fighting for liberation.

Contemporary capitalism is inimical to the vital interests and progressive aspirations of all mankind. Capitalism with its exploitation of man by man, with its chauvinist and racist ideology, with its moral degradation, its rampage of profiteering, corruption, and crime is defiling society, the family, and man.

The bourgeois system came into being with the alluring slogans of liberty, equality, fraternity. But the bourgeoisie made use of these slogans merely to elbow out the feudal gentry and to assume power. Instead of equality a new gaping abyss of social and economic inequality appeared. Not fraternity but ferocious class struggle reigns in bourgeois society. . . .

The ideologists of imperialism hide the dictatorship of monopoly capital behind specious slogans of freedom and democracy. They declare the imperialist powers to be countries of the "free world" and represent the ruling bourgeois circles as opponents of all dictatorship. In reality, however, freedom in the imperialist world signifies nothing but freedom to exploit the working class, the working people, not only at home, but in all the other countries that fall under the iron heel of the monopolies. . . .

Not even nuclear weapons can protect the monopoly bourgeoisie from the unalterable course of historical development. Mankind has learned the true face of capitalism. Hundreds of millions of people see that capitalism is a system of economic chaos and periodical crises, chronic unemployment, mass poverty, and indiscriminate waste of productive forces — a system constantly fraught with the danger of war. Mankind does not want to, and will not, tolerate the historically outdated capitalist system.

Whether you like it or not, history is on our side. We will bury you.
NIKITA S. KHRUSHCHEV, statement at Kremlin diplomatic reception, Nov. 18, 1956.

We face in Communist hostility and expansionism a formidable force, whether Mr. Khrushchev and Mr. Mao Tse-tung pull together or apart. They disagree so far only on whether capitalism should be peacefully or violently buried. They are both for the funeral.

ADLAI E. STEVENSON, July 1963

11.

Walter Millis: The Peace Game

*World War II ended in hope — at least on the Allied side: in the hope that the
United Nations would be a viable international organization, in the hope that the
world might at last look forward to a time when there would be a just and lasting
peace. But these hopes were soon dashed and as a matter of fact had never been
anything but illusory. As the recognition dawned of the depth and persistence of the
modern "total war system," various men and organizations published discussions
of what peace would be like if it were to come, and of what achieving it would entail.
A leading author in this genre was Walter Millis, who produced a pamphlet on the
subject — part of which is reprinted below — for the Center for the Study of
Democratic Institutions in 1961.*

Source: *A World Without War*, Santa Barbara, Calif., 1961, pp. 1-15.

THE PEACE GAME

The institution of organized international
war has become so deeply embedded in our
economy, our law, our politics, even in
many of our religious concepts, that it requires a really serious effort of the imagination to conceive of a world from which it
had been eliminated. The statesmen of our
own and of most other countries like to
speak of "a just and *lasting* peace." These
words can, rationally, convey the notion
only of a situation from which organized
war had been permanently excluded; yet
there is little to indicate that any of the officials who so frequently use the words have
ever tried to picture such a situation in any
detail, to consider what it would be like or
how they expect it to operate.

But however difficult it may be to imagine a world without war, this task is now
forced upon us. Two propositions are, I
think, irrefutable: that a continuation of the
present state of international affairs is bound

sooner or later to produce a catastrophe in
which most civilized values and all of the
present warring value systems must perish;
and that no strategic inventions, no new
"national security" policies, no jugglings
with weapons systems and armaments are
likely to alter this prognostication.

What this says is that the system of organized international war, as we have known
it through the ages, has reached a point of
no return. Such useful or necessary social
ends as it has served in the past it can serve
no longer, or can serve only at an ultimate
price which has become intolerably exorbi-
tant. It is like a religion so debased that it
can only degrade its adherents; a legal system so rigidified that it is incapable of determining justice; an economic system (and
one thinks of the various slave economies of
the past) so trapped in its own contradictions that it is no longer a viable method of
economic organization.

It can no longer serve its greatest social
function — that of *ultima ratio* in human

affairs — for it can no longer *decide*. It can render the first judgment of Solomon — to slaughter the disputed infant — but cannot render the second, which was to award it alive and whole to one or the other of the claimants. . . .

War is losing whatever social utility it ever had, at the same time that it is exaggerating out of all reason the social costs which it has always exacted. It is ever more insistently confronting us with the dilemma between the total abolition of the war institution and the total abolition of civilized society. There have, of course, been numerous attempts to escape the dilemma — to find some formula, whether through theories of "limited war," through the control and reduction of armaments, through building them to new heights of defensive terror and efficiency, through political assuagement or in other ways, whereby war can be retained as the convenient and comforting *ultima ratio* which it has always been, while at the same time divesting it of the cataclysmic consequences to which it now seems almost certainly to be leading. None of these attempts is persuasive. The problem is unsolved. This, it is here suggested, is probably because it is insoluble.

We are often told, for example, that "disarmament" is a subject of the greatest difficulty, calling for profound (and of course classified) technical knowledge and the most sensitive intellectual expertise. We are told that in order to avoid disastrous mistakes we must proceed very slowly — so slowly that progress must be reduced virtually to zero, while the possible disasters attendant upon making no progress at all accumulate to gigantic proportions.

But this notion of the "difficulty" of the subject is an illusion. Given a desire by all the great powers to disarm, there would be nothing very complicated about disarming; but given the desire (now firmly retained by all the great powers) merely to reduce the threats and burdens of arms while clinging tenaciously to the simplicities, the supposed securities, and the opportunities of the war system, the problem becomes one which all the technical and intellectual expertise in the world is unlikely to resolve. It is not just difficult, like "duplicating the cube," it is impossible.

Around the turn of the century the physicists' instruments began more insistently to report to them facts about the physical world that could not be met or explained by the classical concepts of space, time, matter, and energy which had theretofore ruled as absolutes in the world of science. It was necessary, through the work of Einstein and others, to modify or even reject the classical assumptions in favor of startlingly new conceptual systems before physics could advance to its modern triumphs. In the world of international relations there are no analogues to the instruments of the physicists, capable of reporting to us with similar authority and exactitude the facts about the system with which we are attempting to deal. We do, however, have a wealth of bloody experience to serve somewhat the same function; and it appears to be transmitting a report of much the same kind.

The problem of a "just and lasting peace" simply cannot be met or resolved by the classic concepts of the war system — the concepts of "defense," "aggression," "victory," "defeat," "freedom," "slavery," or "world domination" which we continue to bring to it. Is it possible to develop and apply to the field of international relations a new conceptual system under which the problem will become manageable? The remainder of this study is an attempt to answer this question.

Let us begin by assuming that war has actually been abolished and that the nations have by voluntary agreement disarmed themselves totally, down to police force level. Few will dissent from the notion that this is, under the existing concepts now universally applied to international relations (by "peace-loving" Americans no less than by "warmongering" Russians), an impossibility. But by adopting this assumption, an attempt will be made to establish institutional and conceptual systems which would be consistent with it. The institution of war, while obviously approaching the point of no return, is still deeply embedded in our structures of law, economics, and politics, in our whole system of ideas about ourselves and the world. Within these structures it serves many functions which to us seem indispensable. But by initially assuming a world that has abolished war, one can more clearly put the question of just what these functions are; how in such a world they would in fact be discharged, how such a world would operate; what systems of ideas and institutions would be consistent with a viable international life under the assumed state.

A somewhat simpler way of stating the underlying notion is to say that it proposes a kind of game — a "peace game," analogous to the war games played in all earnestness by military staffs and no less serious in intent. . . .

The war game starts by assuming an "aggressor," or at the least the possibility of "aggression," and then continues to consider what politico-military measures must be taken to render the nation secure against such eventualities. Is it in any way more irrational, or even more romantic, to start with the assumption of peace and then consider what politico-military measures would actually be required to insure the nation against the eventualities (by no means in all respects pleasant) that this situation would open?

It may be said that to start with the assumption of world peace — which does not now exist and seems for many reasons to be a virtual impossibility — is to start from a foundation of sand. But almost the same argument could be made against the war-gamers. To start from an assumption of military aggression — which is not now taking place and which may be, for reasons connected with the giant weapons, improbable if not impossible — is to start from a foundation not really much more solid. Peace has its perils and difficulties no less than war. In fact, they are, or have seemed to be, so great that most people fear the prospect of peace (except, of course, as it can be obtained on "our" terms) almost as much as they fear the modern prospect of war. But where the war game has led to no exit from the impasse of our times, it is possible that the peace game may at least suggest possibilities of escape. . . .

THE FUNCTIONS OF WAR

IN THE PEACE GAME the players are asked to assume that peace has broken out — that the nations have abolished war by international agreement and ratified their undertaking by reducing their armaments to police force level. They are then asked to say what could be expected to happen.

Two kinds of things could be expected to happen. The abolition of war would remove from international society many of the fears and pressures under which it has always operated. There can be no doubt that if every nuclear, biochemical, and other mass destruction weapon in the world, along with the heavy "conventional" weapons systems and the staffs and military and industrial organizations which now plan, support, and manage these things, were destroyed, the international problem itself would assume a totally new form. Much of what now concerns us about it would simply become pointless. It might even be argued that with this one change the already existing institutions of international order — institutions of diplomacy, international law, commerce, finance, and communications — could handle the remaining load well enough. Effects of this kind would follow and must be given proper weight in any theory of a warless world.

But a second kind of thing would also happen. While many of the problems involved in the operation of our existing institutions would be reduced, others would arise; and new institutional arrangements of some kind would presumably have to be developed to meet them or to discharge those vital functions for the performance of which we have been accustomed to rely upon the war system. This notion, of course, lies behind all proposals for attaining world peace through the establishment of some system of world government or world law.

If war is to be abolished, institutions must be created which will perform war's essential functions. But the weakness in such approaches is that they seldom analyze the functions for which a substitute institutional structure would really be required. Usually, they set up as a prerequisite to peace an institutional system which will be quite impossible of attainment until peace has occurred; they expect peace to flow out of the institutional system rather than asking what institutional system might be expected to flow out of peace. If the question is put in the latter way, the answers may not seem so very different. They will, perhaps, be rather more firmly grounded in international reality.

In peace-gaming the future, the initial attempt must be to identify these vital or useful functions, in both the internal and the international society, now apparently performed by war and the war system. If this can be done with reasonable plausibility, the next step must be to suggest how, practically, these functions could be or might be provided for in a world which had agreed to abolish international war. The peace game is not, as has been suggested before, an enterprise upon which one can enter with confidence of success. The accurate identification of the "functions" is not easy.

While the admitted purpose of the peace game (and of this paper) is to make the best possible case for systems of ideas or institutions which would successfully fulfill all these functions of war, the case may seem unconvincing. The suggestions may seem ineffective or at best inadequate to deal with the problems involved. If so, the game has been lost. But one cannot simply leave it there. Either the game can, with more thought and skill, be won or one must face the conclusion that peace is impossible. Somehow, one has to make a commitment. . . .

The functions of war are, in all societies, both internal and external. Its internal functions are more apparent to us when we examine foreign societies than when we look at our own. It is quite clear to us that most Latin-American military establishments are essentially internal power structures, with a great deal more relevance to internal problems of power and politics than to any external threats to the societies which they "defend" in hardly more than a mythical sense. It is quite clear to us that the internal cohesion of Soviet Russia depends in many ways upon the alleged existence of external threats and upon the military structures authorized by these supposed threats as well as the military attitudes and sanctions derived from them. We do not so readily perceive the same factors operating within our own society, but there can be no doubt that they are present.

The crude economic function is here the most obvious. About 10 percent of American production and employment is generated directly by the requirements of the war system. The generation of this substantial fraction of total goods and services is an internal function of war which, in a warless world, would have to be fulfilled in some way.

The social functions of war are many. It promotes scientific and especially technological advance. It promotes education and public subsidies to education. By vastly expanding the military services and the civilian bureaucracy, it offers careers of honor and profit to able people who would otherwise be lost in the shuffle of routine operations. The career opportunities which the war system opens within the domestic complex are a social fact perhaps quite as important as the economic opportunities which it provides.

It is usual to take a negative view of both sorts of opportunities — to argue that huge military expenditures result from industry's pressure for government contracts and that aggressive or at least militaristic policies are promoted by those whose status, prestige, and careers depend upon the war system. No doubt such pressures exist; but they are subtle, probably in large part unconscious, and too easily exaggerated. And it is clear that just as there are positive economic values in the war system, there are positive social values as well. Throughout the Western tradition the Law, the Church, and the Army have offered hierarchical structures of public service around which society has, as it were, congealed.

In many countries (Spain is a good example) the army lives, not because it is in any way necessary or even useful to the defense of the state against external aggression but because it is an instrument of social order and preferment which the country would have difficulty in doing without. If it should be rendered supernumerary tomorrow by the formal abolition of the war system, Spain would have difficulty not only in pensioning off her exaggerated officer corps but also in filling their place in the Spanish social organization. But we should not delude ourselves with the idea that we would not have many of the same difficulties if all the scientists, generals, admirals, bellicose congressmen, industrialists, State Department men, and journalists whose careers have been made out of the war problem also had to be pensioned off.

The political functions of the war system in the domestic organization of any society are prominent. War's cohesive force for any given society is tremendous, and it is no accident that the authors of the American Constitution phrased the Preamble as they did: "To provide for the common defense and the general welfare." Defense came before welfare; and it is at least doubtful whether the Constitution could have been written and adopted unless this had been the generally accepted idea of the functions of government in the late 18th century. The necessity for providing for a common defense has always been the most powerful bond of internal unity and domestic institutions of order.

Many of the anti-Communist measures taken in the name of "internal security" during the "McCarthy era" were really in the nature of tribal rites. If one can discern a purpose in them it was to cement the old social bonds, to organize the group, to reestablish common values in face of the anomie and atomization of the technological age. We do not readily recognize the functions which the "cold war" fulfills in our own political organization, but there can be no doubt that they are real and could not easily be discarded by any society.

It is, however, the external functions of the war system with which most are concerned. Once really faced with the problem we could, no doubt, convert both our military industry and our military bureaucracy to peaceful uses without too much difficulty; we could find other sanctions for the indispensable requirements of unity and social cohesion. But how would we meet the great problems of international order, peace, justice, economic organization, and "power," which have always been confided, in the final analysis, to the arbitrament of organized international war?

The external function of war that comes first to the minds of most is the protection of the territorial integrity of the state. All nations normally found their military policies on the maintenance of the inviolability of their frontiers; and no nation is likely to abandon its military defenses until it is insured in some way against the violent invasion or appropriation of its territory.

No completely static world order could, however, be expected to endure. It has also been a major function of war to provide for the revision of national boundaries, the reallocation of peoples or ethnic groups among the national sovereignties, the creation of new sovereign states, and the suppression of those that, for whatever reason, seemed no longer viable. A world without war would, if it were to survive, have to allow for such changes in some way.

In the past, at any rate, war has similarly provided the major instrument for the redistribution of natural resources and capital supplies, in accordance with what appeared to be the requirements of efficiency if not of justice. Again, we cannot accept the existing economic distribution as perpetual. Without the war system, a living international order would have to develop other means of effecting just and necessary changes.

International war has been a significant instrument of internal revolution and social change. The abolition of organized international war obviously cannot be expected to eliminate violence from the affairs of men, but the forms that such violence would take, its impacts on the international structure, the means for regulating its consequences all raise serious problems. If we do not need international war to foment or support necessary domestic revolution, we do need something to fulfill its function of controlling the effects of revolution.

The war system has provided the final sanction for the adjustment of many lesser international issues which would continue to arise. These are issues over such matters as the protection of foreign investments, both public and private, extractive and fish-ing rights, protection of nationals abroad, immigration rights, tariffs, and export-import quotas. While no doubt reflecting the greater international issues discussed above, these usually arise in less extreme and more justiciable form. The warless world would still have to provide its own means for adjudicating them.

War has also provided our *ultima ratio* in the greatest of the world's moral issues, turning on our convictions as to freedom, justice, and religious faith. To most Americans the rise of the Hitler dictatorship represented a positive evil, a flagrant denial of beliefs and principles without which, it seemed to us, no moral or even social order could be held together. To many, the Soviet dictatorship represents not simply a military threat but a moral evil of the same kind; with evils of this sort (which may arise again from other quarters) there can be no peace or enduring coexistence, but organized war has provided the only instrument whereby to decide the issues they present. Those who try to imagine a warless world cannot avoid this problem.

Finally, one may perhaps generalize these functions of war into one: War is the determinant of international power relations. How would the basic issues of power be resolved in a multinational world from which organized war had been excluded? The usual (if hasty) answer is that it would be impossible; to exclude war it would first be necessary to absorb the national sovereignties into some form of world government or superstate endowed with a monopoly of international force. But this is simplistic, and overlooks the difficulties inherent in the concept of "power" itself. "Power" is a shorthand word. Like the words "space" and "time" it reflects a common human experience. In all systems of human relationship, from the family to the superstate, there is an element of coercion, and this element, wherever it occurs and in

whatever degree it is significant or controlling, we conveniently designate as "power."
But in giving the element a name we do
not greatly elucidate its nature or operative
function.

No form of international organization is
likely to eliminate the coercive element
from the life of man. But it does not follow
that this element must be organized into
the form of multimegaton and biological
weapons, massive missile and military
forces, and all the rest of the apparatus of
modern military technology. The underlying problem of "power" on the world stage
is central for those interested in the possibility of a warless world, but it is not, *prima
facie,* insoluble.

These appear to be the chief functions
which the war system has served in the development of contemporary human society.
There may be others. But all these, at least,
must be taken into consideration by anyone
who would seriously set out to peace-game
the future.

12.

John F. Kennedy: A Long Twilight Struggle

*By the end of the 1950s it had become apparent to many observers that the power
struggle between East and West had developed into a stalemate, and in particular that
the lines of demarcation between Communism and the Western democracies had been
drawn in Europe and could not be changed without war. The United States had not
liberated Eastern Europe, nor was there any real hope that it could; the Soviet Union
had not extended its sphere either. The arms race had only increased the danger
of any conflict between them; there could be no victory for either side, at least in
traditional senses of the term. In many speeches, notably the following address
delivered at the University of Washington on November 16, 1961, President Kennedy
emphasized that America did not have unlimited power to control the world. He
warned that those people who sought easy answers, who demanded either peace at any
price or total victory, who saw the alternatives as being either "Red or dead," were
equally wrong and that their solutions would be equally disastrous. The only sane and
effective foreign policy in a nuclear age, he said over and over again, was one that
combined willingness to negotiate and to compromise with a determination to defend
basic values.*

Source: *Bulletin,* December 4, 1961: "Diplomacy and Defense: A Test of National Maturity."

In 1961 the world relations of this country have become tangled and complex. One
of our former allies has become our adversary — and he has his own adversaries who
are not our allies. Heroes are removed from
their tombs, history rewritten, the names of
cities changed overnight.

We increase our arms at a heavy cost,
primarily to make certain that we will not
have to use them. We must face up to the

chance of war if we are to maintain the peace. We must work with certain countries lacking in freedom in order to strengthen the cause of freedom. We find some who call themselves neutrals who are our friends and sympathetic to us, and others who call themselves neutral who are unremittingly hostile to us. And as the most powerful defender of freedom on earth, we find ourselves unable to escape the responsibilities of freedom and yet unable to exercise it without restraints imposed by the very freedoms we seek to protect. We cannot, as a free nation, compete with our adversaries in tactics of terror, assassination, false promises, counterfeit mobs, and crises.

We cannot, under the scrutiny of a free press and public, tell different stories to different audiences, foreign, domestic, friendly, and hostile.

We cannot abandon the slow processes of consulting with our allies to match the swift expediencies of those who merely dictate to their satellites. We can neither abandon nor control the international organization in which we now cast less than 1 percent of the vote in the General Assembly. We possess weapons of tremendous power, but they are least effective in combating the weapons most often used by freedom's foes: subversion, infiltration, guerrilla warfare, and civil disorder. We send arms to other peoples — just as we can send them the ideals of democracy in which we believe — but we cannot send them the will to use those arms or to abide by those ideals.

And while we believe not only in the force of arms but in the force of right and reason, we have learned that reason does not always appeal to unreasonable men, that it is not always true that "a soft answer turneth away wrath," and that right does not always make might.

In short we must face problems which do not lend themselves to easy or quick or permanent solutions. And we must face the fact that the United States is neither om-nipotent or omniscient, that we are only 6 percent of the world's population, that we cannot impose our will upon the other 94 percent of mankind, that we cannot right every wrong or reverse each adversity, and that therefore there cannot be an American solution to every world problem.

These burdens and frustrations are accepted by most Americans with maturity and understanding. They may long for the days when war meant charging up San Juan Hill, or when our isolation was guarded by two oceans, or when the atomic bomb was ours alone, or when much of the industrialized world depended upon our resources and our aid. But they now know that those days are gone and that gone with them are the old policies and the old complacencies. And they know, too, that we must make the best of our new problems and our new opportunities, whatever the risk and the cost.

But there are others who cannot bear the burden of a long twilight struggle. They lack confidence in our long-run capacity to survive and succeed. Hating communism, yet they see communism in the long run, perhaps, as the wave of the future. And they want some quick and easy and final and cheap solution — now.

There are two groups of these frustrated citizens, far apart in their views yet very much alike in their approach. On the one hand are those who urge upon us what I regard to be the pathway of surrender — appeasing our enemies, compromising our commitments, purchasing peace at any price, disavowing our arms, our friends, our obligations. If their view had prevailed the world of free choice would be smaller today.

On the other hand are those who urge upon us what I regard to be the pathway of war: equating negotiations with appeasement and substituting rigidity for firmness. If their view had prevailed, we would be at war today, and in more than one place.

It is a curious fact that each of these extreme opposites resembles the other. Each believes that we have only two choices: appeasement or war, suicide or surrender, humiliation or holocaust, to be either Red or dead. Each side sees only "hard" and "soft" nations, hard and soft policies, hard and soft men. Each believes that any departure from its own course inevitably leads to the other: one group believes that any peaceful solution means appeasement; the other believes that any arms buildup means war. One group regards everyone else as warmongers; the other regards everyone else as appeasers. Neither side admits its path will lead to disaster, but neither can tell us how or where to draw the line once we descend the slippery slopes of appeasement or constant intervention.

In short, while both extremes profess to be the true realists of our time, neither could be more unrealistic. While both claim to be doing the nation a service, they could do it no greater disservice. For this kind of talk and easy solution to difficult problems, if believed, could inspire a lack of confidence among our people when they must all — above all else — be united in recognizing the long and difficult days that lie ahead. It could inspire uncertainty among our allies when above all else they must be confident in us. And even more dangerously, it could, if believed, inspire doubt among our adversaries when they must above all be convinced that we will defend our vital interests.

The essential fact that both of these groups fail to grasp is that diplomacy and defense are not substitutes for one another. Either alone would fail. A willingness to resist force, unaccompanied by a willingness to talk, could provoke belligerence, while a willingness to talk, unaccompanied by a willingness to resist force, could invite disaster.

But as long as we know what comprises our vital interests and our long-range goals, we have nothing to fear from negotiations at the appropriate time and nothing to gain by refusing to play a part in them. At a time when a single clash could escalate overnight into a holocaust of mushroom clouds, a great power does not prove its firmness by leaving the task of exploring the other's intentions to sentries or those without full responsibility. Nor can ultimate weapons rightfully be employed, or the ultimate sacrifice rightfully demanded of our citizens, until every reasonable solution has been explored. "How many wars," Winston Churchill has written, "have been averted by patience and persisting goodwill! . . . How many wars have been precipitated by firebrands!"

If vital interests under duress can be preserved by peaceful means, negotiations will find that out. If our adversary will accept nothing less than a concession of our rights, negotiations will find that out. And if negotiations are to take place, this nation cannot abdicate to its adversaries the task of choosing the forum and the framework and the time.

For there are carefully defined limits within which any serious negotiations must take place. With respect to any future talks on Germany and Berlin, for example, we cannot, on the one hand, confine our proposals to a list of concessions we are willing to make, nor can we, on the other hand, advance any proposals which compromise the security of free Germans and West Berliners or endanger their ties with the West.

No one should be under the illusion that negotiations for the sake of negotiations always advance the cause of peace. If for lack of preparation they break up in bitterness, the prospects of peace have been endangered. If they are made a forum for propaganda or a cover for aggression, the processes of peace have been abused.

But it is a test of our national maturity to accept the fact that negotiations are not a contest spelling victory or defeat. They may succeed; they may fail. They are likely to be successful only if both sides reach an agreement which both regard as preferable to the status quo — an agreement in which each side can consider its own situation can be improved. And this is most difficult to obtain.

But, while we shall negotiate freely, we shall not negotiate freedom. Our answer to the classic question of Patrick Henry is still "No." Life is not so dear and peace is not so precious ". . . as to be purchased at the price of chains and slavery." And that is our answer even though, for the first time since the ancient battles between Greek city-states, war entails the threat of total annihilation, of everything we know, of society itself. For to save mankind's future freedom we must face up to any risk that is necessary. We will always seek peace — but we will never surrender.

In short, we are neither "warmongers" nor "appeasers," neither "hard" nor "soft." We are Americans, determined to defend the frontiers of freedom by an honorable peace if peace is possible, but by arms if arms are used against us. And if we are to move forward in that spirit, we shall need all the calm and thoughtful citizens that this great university can produce, all the light they can shed, all the wisdom they can bring to bear.

It is customary, both here and around the world, to regard life in the United States as easy. Our advantages are many. But more than any other people on earth, we bear burdens and accept risks unprecedented in their size and their duration, not for ourselves alone but for all who wish to be free. No other generation of free men in any country has ever faced so many and such difficult challenges — not even those who lived in the days when this university was founded in 1861.

This nation was then torn by war. This territory had only the simplest elements of civilization. And this city had barely begun to function. But a university was one of their earliest thoughts, and they summed it up in the motto that they adopted: "Let there be light." What more can be said today regarding all the dark and tangled problems we face than: Let there be light.

The world is not a big Red sea in which this country is being scuttled, but a vast arena of political upheaval, in which the quest for freedom, ever stronger, has overthrown the colonial empires of the past. It isn't a tidy world, nor is it a secure one. But it is one for which the United States set the revolutionary example.
FRANK CHURCH, speech in the U.S. Senate, January 12, 1965

1962

13.

MELVIN J. LASKY: America and Europe

*The perennial discussion, mostly on the part of Americans, of the New World's
relations to the Old out of which it had had its birth continued into the 1960s, as the
following selection, taken from an article published early in 1962, makes clear. Its
author, Melvin J. Lasky, was the American half of the Anglo-American team that
edited* Encounter *(Stephen Spender was the English half). In the article Lasky provided
a painstaking review of past "communication" between America and Europe, and
suggested the forms that such communication was likely to take in the near future.*

Source: *Encounter,* January 1962.

FOR THE GREATEST PART of the last three
centuries, few Europeans, with the exception of those single-minded souls who were
about to make their way across the Atlantic,
found it necessary to think about America.
But for Americans, Europe was from the
very beginning that other soul that dwelt
within their breasts. Europe was their past
and their heritage, their teacher and their
challenge as a new nation. No theme in
American history can really be divorced
from the background of Europe, whether it
be foreign policy, the pushing-back of the
frontier beyond the Mississippi and the
Rockies, or the creation of an individual
style in the national literature. Americans
have not always understood this, possibly
because they have been so preoccupied with
the thing itself: with nostalgia for the Old
Country, with bitter memories of the place
of their trial and shame, with admiration for
the richest civilization man had yet created,

with hope that the New World would
achieve something original and even fairer.

"The burden is necessarily greater for an
American," Henry James said some eighty
years ago, "for he must deal, more or less,
even if only by implication with Europe;
whereas no European is obliged to deal in
the least with America." Perhaps, he added,
in a hundred, or even fifty years
hence. . . ? Surely that time has come. In
every European land, "America" has become a main theme of parliament and press,
school, café, and household. We would
seem to be at the beginning of some new
epoch. Is it too melodramatic to think that
what we have called Western civilization is
now moving into a period of unprecedented
partnership between Europeans and Americans, a period of some kind of "transatlantic
community"?

In the United States of the fifteen postwar years, there has not only been a new

awareness of this problem but also the onset of a changing consciousness of "what it is to be an American" and of what attitudes a mature and "come-of-age" America is to take toward Europe and Europeans. American opinion has been in ferment. The country and its institutions are being regarded in a new way. In the past, America was, alas, culturally dependent on Europe; now Europe is militarily (and, not infrequently, economically) dependent upon America.

As the editors of *Partisan Review* announced some years ago:

> America is no longer the raw and unformed land of promise from which men of superior gifts like James, Santayana, and Eliot departed, seeking in Europe what they found lacking in America. Europe is no longer regarded as a sanctuary; it no longer assures that rich experience of culture which inspired and justified a criticism of American life. The wheel has come full circle, and now America has become the protector of Western civilization, at least in a military and economic sense.

The question which has fascinated me, in my own fifteen years in postwar Europe, is whether the wheel can ever break out of the traditional circle it has been making for centuries. *In Europe:* a utopian pro-Americanism in times of adventurous hope, and then the turn to a grumbling anti-Americanism in times of stress. *In America:* a naïve and nostalgic pro-Europeanism when life was raw and difficult, and then the turn to a strident anti-Europeanism when prosperity made for power and national confidence.

There have been the beginnings of a new and encouragingly self-conscious "transatlantic dialogue" on this theme. European writers have been prepared to concede that what separates America from the mind of Europe is an angry self-assertiveness on both sides of the Atlantic. Is it "the impatience of youth" on the American side and "the resentfulness of age" on the European? Surely, since the Declaration of Independence, the Americans had been looking across the ocean for inspiration, and when they were in Paris or in London to be "cultured" obviously meant to be un-American or even anti-American. How could this fail to be pleasing to the self-esteem of Europeans? They felt themselves to be the center of civilization, and even when in terms of power and economics there was a time of bankruptcy, a European intellectual could claim that "we had to borrow dollars from the U.S.A., but she still borrows our ideas. . . ."

The disturbance in this balance of payments caused a transatlantic discord. Americans no longer care to sit at the feet of Europeans and are delighted to exchange their old role with generous grants to visitors to come and see and learn. The American way of life is no longer shamefacedly contrasted with the European; on the contrary, certain U.S. patterns are vigorously recommended if in politics there was to be stability and in economics efficiency and affluence. An observer remarked at the time of Marshall Plan enthusiasm, "Today it is Europe's intellectuals who are fumbling with their psyche: the Americans have all the answers pat."

> This change is all the more distressing because neither side is fully conscious of it. Whether we are French or English or Scandinavian, we have forgotten how gloriously self-confident and how contemptuous of American ideas we Europeans still were even in 1938. We had the answers. Now we know that we haven't, and our new skepticism makes us rage against an American who thinks he has. He in his turn is quite oblivious of the intellectual somersault he has turned since the 1930s, and resents our skepticism as defeatism. If you can't pay your way and have no idea how to save the world, he says, the least you can do is to listen to my lecture before you grab my dollars. . . . (*R. H. S. Crossman*)

But the Americans, as I have been saying, are no longer as "oblivious" as all that. An American poetess wrote some years ago:

The American artist and intellectual must give over expecting the future to develop according to region or historic example. America is soaked with Europe, in any case; and there is no sign that Europe as it rebuilds itself may not provide vitality, variety, and perspective for American life, art, and thought. For although Carthage never recovered after its furrows were sown with salt, Rome, like Troy, rebuilt itself innumerable times; and what may Europe not produce out of its present ruins? . . . (*Louise Bogan*)

There has been not only this strand of American confidence in Europe but also an understanding that with the coming of world power it would be disastrous for the United States to retreat into a narrow and self-satisfied cultural nationalism. There were even suggestions that, as American foreign policy tried to make a reality out of the hypothetical unity of Western Europe, so should American intellectuals attempt to realize the Goethean concept of *Weltliteratur*. At any rate, for the first time in centuries there was in the search for a transatlantic identity no glee and no malice, no flight from self nor heaviness of heart.

> We cannot affirm America without reaffirming Europe and the West. Humans are beings with a history, a past; Europe is our past; and even God cannot will the past not to have been. . . .

But if this is the point that had to be reached, and from which there may be no turning back, it was not always this way, for the past is the history of a strange transatlantic tension within the American soul, of glee and malice, of withdrawal and return. . . .

THE WHOLE WORLD FOR STAGE

"THE WHEELS OF THE CLOCK have so completely stopped in Europe," wrote Randolph Bourne in August 1914, "and this civilization that I have been admiring so much seems so palpably to be torn to shreds that I do not even want to think about Europe until the war is over and life is running again. . . ."

Other Americans, in their shock at the outbreak and the horror of World War I, were even more bitter. The American ambassador in London noted:

> The idea that we were brought up on, that Europe is the home of civilization in general — nonsense! It's a periodical slaughter pen, with all the vices that this implies. I'd as lief live in the Chicago stockyards. (*Walter Hines Page*)

The President in Washington was soberer. In his inaugural address of 1917, Woodrow Wilson declared: "The greatest things that remain to be done must be done with the whole world for stage. . . . We are provincials no longer. . . . There can be no turning back."

After the War in Paris Gertrude Stein told young Hemingway, "You are all a lost generation . . ." and this became the inscription for his first novel and the name of a group of Americans who were to be transitional forces in the national culture. They were the adventurous young men in American history who went, not West but East. "They do things better in Europe, let's go there." And off they went from Greenwich Village to Montparnasse — Hemingway, Scott Fitzgerald, John Dos Passos, E. E. Cummings, Ezra Pound, Hart Crane, T. S. Eliot, and so many others. Their dream was of an "escape into European cities with crooked streets. . . ." Their idea was "salvation by exile." These were the *expatriates,* and they waved to each other from the windows of passing trains in Europe. Malcolm Cowley, the historian of this generation, writes in *Exile's Return:*

> . . . at heart they were not convinced that even the subject matter of a great novel could be supplied by this country.

American themes were lacking in dignity. Art and ideas were products manufactured under a European patent; all we could furnish toward them was raw talent destined usually to be wasted. Everywhere, in every department of culture, Europe offered the models to imitate — in painting, composing, philosophy, folk music, folk drinking, the drama, sex, politics, national consciousness — indeed, some doubted that this country was even a nation; it had no traditions except the fatal tradition of the pioneer. . . .

What would that pioneer of American culture, Jefferson, have thought who 150 years before had said to Monroe: "While we shall see multiplied instances of Europeans going to live in America, I will venture to say, no man now living will ever see an instance of an American removing to settle in Europe and continuing there. . . ." But perhaps he was wiser than he knew; for with the exception of Eliot who, like James before him, remained to become a British subject, almost none of them continued there.

Because whatever it was that these Americans had "lost," none of them could find it permanently in Europe. The pattern was an old one — we have already seen it innumerable times — the old pattern of alienation and reintegration, of departure and return. Cowley's poems about movies and skyscrapers and machines begin to have a nostalgic note about them, and he discovered that "I had learned from a distance to admire America's picturesque qualities. . . ." The expatriates began to quarrel amongst each other. Was America really vulgar, vicious, a failure? Cowley once burst out —

America is just as god-damned good as Europe — worse in some ways, better in others, just as appreciative, fresher material, inclined to stay at peace instead of marching into the Ruhr. As for its being the concentration point for all the vices and vulgarities — nuts. New York is refinement itself beside Berlin. French taste in most details is unbearable. London is a huge Gopher Prairie. I'm not ashamed to take off my coat anywhere and tell those degenerate Europeans that I'm an American citizen. Wave Old Glory! Peace! Normalcy!

America was, after all, their country and they began to feel a little homesick for it. The new generation of exiles came straggling back to New York.

The exiles were ready to find that their own nation had every attribute they had been taught to admire in those of Europe. It had developed its national types — who could fail to recognize an American in a crowd? — it possessed a folklore, and traditions, and the songs that embodied them; it had even produced new forms of art which the Europeans were glad to borrow. Some of the exiles had reached a turning point in their adventure and were preparing to embark on a voyage of rediscovery. Standing as it were on the Tour Eiffel, they looked southwestwards across the wheatfields of Beauce and the rain-drenched little hills of Brittany, until somewhere in the mist they saw the country of their childhood, which should henceforth be the country of their art. American themes, like other themes, had exactly the dignity that talent could lend them.

In 1930, when Sinclair Lewis was awarded the Nobel Prize, he stood up as the spokesman of his generation of American writers: "I salute them with a joy in being not yet too far removed from their determination to give to the America that has mountains and endless prairies, enormous cities and far-lost cabins, billions of money and tons of faith, to an America that is as strange as Russia and as complex as China, a literature worthy of her vastness. . . ." From Lewis himself to Faulkner, Thomas Wolfe, and Tennessee Williams, this can, I suppose, be considered as the achievement of the new generation; and this, in turn, made for confidence, for maturity, even for what Eliot called "the historical sense":

The historical sense involves a perception, not only of the pastness of the past but of its presence; the historical sense compels a man to write not merely with his own generation in his bones but with a feeling that the whole of the literature of Europe from Homer and within it the whole of the literature of his own country has a simultaneous existence. . . .

What this might mean for Americans is that an historical sense of their attitudes toward Europe could possibly provide the opportunity to escape from the dead hand of sentimental pieties.

One American scholar recently, troubled by the issues of "anti-Americanism," said:

Most people are not able to stand personal criticism of themselves, especially when it emanates from strangers. Criticism of one's country, particularly if one is an American, is even less tolerable than criticism of oneself. Americans, more than any other people, seem to feel that a criticism of any of their country's institutions or ways constitutes a criticism of and an insult to themselves. A psychologist cannot help wondering whether this sensitivity does not betray a rather deep-seated insecurity — individually and collectively — which causes most Americans to respond in this way to such criticisms. This insecurity explains a great many things about Americans which foreigners see but which many Americans are so frequently unwilling to face. What look to the foreigner like arrogance and conceit are simply the overcompensatory devices by means of which the American is trying to compensate for his feeling of inadequacy and show that he is a "success." . . . (Ashley Montagu)

In something of the same spirit an editor tried to face the "frightening misunderstandings" between Europe and America:

For in Europe there has grown up a kind of myth about America, and it might one day be written that the free world destroyed itself because of it. It would not be the Big Lie of the Russians; only the fools believed that. It would be something much more inexplicable: the myth that for all our bathtubs and our cars and our skyscrapers we are without moral purpose; that we are the New Carthago — all money, no spirit; that we are, in short, a country without a soul.

If America does not destroy this myth, it will destroy America. . . .

And, finally, a few years ago, this sensible (and already prophetic) thesis from Lewis Galantière:

The attempt to "spread Americanism" round the world is futile and offensive; to spread "understanding of America" is another thing.

I know of no revolutionary movement currently going on which, whatever its philosophic and ethical creed, does not have for its immediate pretext the material betterment of the life of the masses, East and West. In this art of material betterment, we of America are the leaders; and, because we are, we are accused of materialism by those very non-Americans whose first purpose is a better material life for their compatriots. Those who thus accuse us lose sight of the moral promptings behind our material system and assert that we have no culture, in the common sense of "refinement of taste," "acquaintance with the humanities," and so on. They do so because they judge us from the point of view of the culture of a bourgeois or aristocratic society, where nothing is easier than to run an avant-garde theater or magazine for a mere handful of "cultivated" spectators or readers, at the expense of underpaid printers, stagehands, and other workers.

Our critics are not aware that, as we tend materially toward a classless society, our cultural problem becomes a problem of culture for the mass, not for the few; that no European society has ever had to face the problem of, say, 100 million people who possess the purchasing power to satisfy their impulse to entertainment and instruction. In a closed society, those millions could be ordered to read, hear, and see what their masters thought "culture"; in a democratic society, cultural despotism cannot be imposed; every movie producer, comic-book publisher, TV manager is free to solicit the patronage of those millions — and he does.

This is our problem, and Europeans must learn to understand that it is a problem which will face them as soon as their masses have the purchasing power as well as the freedom which our people enjoy. In the cultural domain, as well as in the material domain, America is a proving ground which Europeans ought to regard with sympathy and study with interest — not disdain as inferior to the dark and shabby world in which a Flaubert or a Dickens was produced. . . .

Which leaves us, at the end of our documentary, with a number of questions. Was not the American notion of "exceptionalism," with all its unfriendly implications for Europe, the natural and understandable compensation for a strange transatlantic birth 3,000 miles away from the motherland? Was not the phenomenon of "expatriation" a unique tribute of a young society to an older culture? Is it sentimental piety on my own part to claim that the American tradition of "cosmopolitanism" is possibly the finest product of the national genius?

Perhaps the most significant fact of our time will be not, as Bismarck prophesied (with some characteristic continental envy and resentment), "the accident that in England and the United States the same language is spoken," but rather the fact that the Americans and all the Europeans, sharing as they do a libertarian ideal of a free and open society, were able in an epoch of historic challenge to communicate in a common tongue.

14.

EDWARD T. HALL: Why Are We "Ugly Americans"?

"Though the United States has spent billions of dollars on foreign aid programs," wrote anthropologist Edward T. Hall in The Silent Language *(1959), "it has captured neither the affection nor esteem of the rest of the world. In many countries today Americans are cordially disliked; in others merely tolerated." The reasons for this, Hall observed, are many and varied, but he added that "much of the foreigners' animosity has been generated by the way Americans behave." He mainly meant unconscious, rather than conscious, behavior, and* The Silent Language *was a first attempt — many by Hall and his fellow workers followed — to analyze it. A later article by Hall, published in* Science Digest *in 1962, is reprinted here.*

Source: *Science Digest,* August 1962: "Our Silent Language."

THERE ARE DEEP and subtle differences between the people of the United States and their South American neighbors. Surface differences can be seen and dealt with. What defeats all of us are the hidden elements in man's psychological makeup whose presence are all too often not even suspected.

I will use the Spanish word *ocultos* — "not seen" — in a new sense to stand for these hidden psychological patterns that stand between peoples. Like germs that can't be seen, there are many *ocultos* that cause psychological difficulty. All one sees are the symptoms, the outward manifestation of the *oculto*.

I will particularize about three specific topics to demonstrate a principle. These are time, space, and friendship. *Ocultos* between the U.S. citizen and his neighbors differ in all three.

I first became aware of space as a patterned aspect of human behavior when I noted that people raised in other cultures handled it differently. In the Middle East I felt crowded and was often made to feel anxious.

'NATURAL' DISTANCES

FELLOW U.S. CITIZENS, also, found it hard to adapt themselves to houses and offices arranged so differently, and often commented on how there was too little or too much space, and how much space was wasted. These spatial differences are not limited to offices and homes: towns, subway systems, and road networks usually follow patterns that appear curious to one not accustomed to the culture.

The "natural" way to describe space may be different in two cultures. For instance, I discovered in Japan that intersections of streets were named and the streets were not.

These differing ideas of space contain traps for the uninformed. A person raised in the United States is often likely to give an unintentional snub to a Latin American because of the way he handles space relationships, particularly the physical distance between individuals during conversations.

A conversation I once observed between a Latin and a North American began at one end of a 40-foot hall. I watched the two conversationalists until they had finally reached the other end of the hall. This maneuver had been effected by a continual series of small backward steps on the part of the North American as he unconsciously retreated, searching for a comfortable talking distance. Each time, there was an accompanying closing of the gap, as his Latin friend attempted to reestablish his own accustomed conversation distance.

In formal business conversations in North America, the "proper" distance to stand when talking to another adult male who is simply a business acquaintance is about two feet. This distance diminishes, of course, at social functions like the cocktail party, but anything under eight to ten inches is likely to irritate.

To the Latin, with his own *ocultos*, a distance of two feet seems remote and cold, sometimes even unfriendly. One of the things that gives the South or Central American the feeling that the North American is *simpatico* is when he is no longer made uncomfortable by closeness or being touched.

North Americans, working in offices in Latin America, may keep their local acquaintants at a distance — not the Latin-American distance — by remaining behind a desk or typewriter. Even North Americans who have lived in Latin America for years have been known to use the "barricade approach" to communication and to remain completely unaware of its cultural significance.

COLDLY COMFORTABLE

THEY ARE AWARE ONLY that they "feel comfortable" when not crowded, without realizing that the distance and the desk often create an *oculto* that distorts or gives a cold tone to virtually everything that takes place. The hold of the *oculto* is so strong, however, that the Latin is sometimes observed trying to "climb over" the intervening obstacles — leaning across the desk for instance — in order to achieve a distance at which he can communicate comfortably.

As with space, there are many time *ocultos* that characterize each people. The North American has developed a language of time that involves much more than being prompt. He can usually tell you when his own *ocultos* have been violated, but not how they work. His blood pressure rises, and he loses his temper when he is kept waiting; this is because time and the ego have been linked.

As a rule, the longer a North American is kept waiting in his own setting, the greater the discrepancy between the status of the two parties. Because of their high status, important people can keep less important people waiting. Also, very important business takes precedence over less important business. The North American has developed a pattern for seeing one person at a time, but individual appointments aren't usually scheduled by the Latin American to the exclusion of other appointments. The Latin often enjoys seeing several people at once even if he has to talk on different matters at the same time.

In this setting, the North American may feel he is not being properly treated, that his dignity is under attack, even though this simply is not true. The Latin-American clock on the wall may look the same, but it tells a different sort of time.

LATIN TIME LAG

BY THE U.S. CLOCK, a consistently tardy man is considered undependable. To judge a Latin American by the same time values is to risk a major error. This cultural error may be compounded by a further miscalculation. Suppose the *Norteamericano* has waited 45 minutes or an hour and finally gets to see the Latin American with whom he has an appointment, only to be told, with many apologies, that "there is only five minutes — maybe a meeting can be arranged for tomorrow or next week?"

At this point, the North American's schedule has been "shot." If it is important, he will have to make the time. What he may not understand is an *oculto* common in Mexico, for example, and that is that one is

very likely to take one's time before doing business, in order to provide time for "getting acquainted."

First meetings leave the North American with the feeling he isn't getting anywhere. If not forewarned he keeps trying to get down to business and stop "wasting time." This turns out to be a mistake.

In the United States, discussion is used as a means to an end; the deal. One tries to make his point with neatness and dispatch — quickly and efficiently. The North American begins by taking up major issues, leaving details for later, perhaps for technicians to work out.

Discussion, however, is to the Latin American an important part of life. It serves a different function and operates according to rules of form; it has to be done right. For the Latin American, the emphasis is on courtesy, not speed. Close friends who see each other frequently, shake hands when they meet and when they part.

For the Latin American it is the invisible social distance that is maintained, not the physical distance. Forming a new friendship or a business acquaintance must be done properly. The Latin first wants to know the human values of a new acquaintance — his cultural interests, his philosophy of life — not his efficiency. This is all accompanied by elaborate and graceful formal verbal expressions, which people in the United States have long felt too busy to take time for. They tend to assume familiarity very quickly, to invite new acquaintances to their homes after one or two meetings. But the Latin American entertains only friends of very long standing in his home — and never for business reasons.

BRIEF NORTHERN FRIENDSHIPS

OF COURSE, TIMES ARE CHANGING, because there are an increasing number of Latin businessmen who now demand punctuality even more strictly than in the North. However, there are still a great many times when the old patterns prevail and are not understood. The hidden differences seem to center around the fact that in the North, the ego of the man is more on the surface, whereas in the South preserving institutional forms is important.

It has been observed that in the United States, friendships may not be long lasting. People are apt to take up friends quickly and drop them just as quickly.

A feature influencing North American friendship patterns is that people move constantly (in the 12-year period from 1946-1958, according to U.S. census data, two-thirds of those owning homes had moved, while virtually all those renting property had moved). The North American, as a rule, looks for and finds his friends next door and among those with whom he works.

There are for him few well-defined, hard and fast rules governing the obligations of friendship. At just what point our friendships give way to business opportunism or pressure from above is difficult to say. In this, the United States seems to differ from many other countries in the world.

WEIGHT OF TRADITION

In Latin America, on the other hand, while friendships are not formed as quickly or as easily as in the United States, they often go much deeper and last longer. They almost always involve real obligations. It is important to stress that in Latin America your "friends" will not let you down. The fact that they, personally, are having difficulties is never an excuse for failing friends. You, in turn, are obligated to look out for their interests.

The weight of tradition presses the Latin American to do business within a circle of friends and relatives. If a product or service he needs is not available within his circle, he hesitates to go outside; if he does so, he looks for a new friend who can supply the want.

Apart from the cultural need to "feel right" about a new relationship, there is the logic of the business system. One of the realities of life is that it is dangerous to enter into business with someone over whom you have no "control." The difference between the two systems lies in the controls. One is formal, personal, and depends upon family and friends. The other is technical-legal, impersonal, and depends upon courts and contracts.

Europeans often comment on how candid the North American is. Being candid, he seeks this in others. What fools him is that the Latin American does not readily reciprocate. One has to be known and trusted — admitted into the circle of friendship — before this happens. Even then, what is not said may be just as important, and just as much noticed, as what is said.

Until we face up to the reality of the *ocultos,* and make them explicit, difficulties in communication are going to continue. *Ocultos* drain the great reservoir of goodwill that the people of the Americas feel in their hearts for each other.

Don't say things. What you are stands over you the while, and thunders so that I cannot hear what you say to the contrary.

EMERSON, *Letters and Social Aims*

Wayne Miller from Magnum

Housewife shopping in a richly stocked supermarket

A REEVALUATION

The general prosperity and well-being of the nation continued and expanded during the 1960s. Welfare capitalism and the consumer market remained the world's most successful operation. Occasional business recessions seemed only minor nuisances in a system that had apparently solved the dilemmas of economics. The quiet acquiescence in material wealth that had characterized the 1950s, however, passed away with surprising speed. Once affluence was accepted as normal, and especially once there arrived a generation that had known no otherwise, attention quickly turned elsewhere, to the anomalies, the injustices, the hypocrisies that became apparent in certain areas of American life. Some were truly anomalous and could be corrected relatively easily; others seemed to be inherent in the system and called for major revisions. Indeed, just such thought could now be given to reevaluating the whole of American society. The decade, then, seemed to take as its task a massive national self-analysis, led jointly by the dispossessed and the dedicated. Though such an undertaking naturally generates considerable friction, and though it was too early to make any clear assessment, it appeared to be a generally healthy exercise. It remained to be seen whether the schisms so created could be healed in a new progressive spirit.

Oil refinery in operation through the night at Shell Oil's Texas plant

(Above) Lush vegetable crop on an American farm. OPPOSITE PAGE: Wyoming sheep farmer and his family at supper

The most remarkable feature of the United States remained, in the 1960s, the incredible richness of life within its borders. Unprecedented productivity and affluence placed the average U.S. citizen among the world's wealthy. The nation's gross national product in 1967 was over $775 billion, and there was every expectation of a trillion-dollar year in the not-too-distant future. The economy shifted in emphasis as well; as more and more families reached a saturation point for material acquisition, the service industries accounted for a progressively larger share of the nation's output.

(Above) Tenement family watching television in Cleveland, Ohio; (below) television picture tubes in factory awaiting shipment

Televised debate between Richard Nixon and John Kennedy during 1960 campaign

The realization grew gradually that the ubiquitous television set — present in over 99 percent of American homes — performed, in addition to its obvious entertainment value, a strong cultural function. Spreading the scenes and values of the dominant urban middle class to every corner of the nation, TV was only beginning to explore its educative possibilities. Certainly it created a new relation between the viewer and the world; bringing political campaigns, world news, or the Vietnam War into everyone's home necessarily made the world smaller and ignorance less secure.

Television program showing U.S. soldier in Vietnam

America became known also as a highly mobile society. Once, of course, most Americans were born, grew up, and died in a small area, perhaps the same town; now, in a single year in the mid-1960s nearly one-fifth of the population moved, and of these over one-sixth moved to another state. The automobile had become a way of life; used for business, vacationing, going to the shopping center, or just passing the time, automobiles were so widely and constantly used that they perennially outperformed the highways provided for them and became a serious problem in the large cities. Automobiles and the hurried pace of life they both symbolized and made possible gave rise to new and peculiarly American institutions: drive-in restaurants, movies, banks, and even churches; motels; superhighways with billboards; traffic jams.

(Right) Family moving into a new home in a Connecticut suburb; (below) customer shouts his order into a microphone at a drive-in restaurant in Los Angeles, Calif. OPPOSITE PAGE: Annual gathering of Oklahomans living in California who meet to talk over old times "back home"

Elliott Erwitt from Magnum

Bruce Davidson from Magnum

OPPOSITE PAGE: Moon crater Copernicus as photographed by Lunar Orbiter II, Nov. 28, 1966; (Above) cake batter being readied for baking in a modern bakery; (right) computer supervisor at work, Cape Kennedy

The basis of American prosperity was an ever growing mastery of technology. Though the blind faith in America's natural technical superiority had been briefly shaken by the Russian's Sputnik coup, the national composure was soon regained and spectacular strides in astronautical science were made. Americans seemed both able and likely to produce machines to do almost anything; the arcane studies in electronics that bore subminiature components and huge computers were particularly suited to technological speculation that was no longer simply science fiction. With a determination to apply machinery wherever possible, America created whole new problems: what to do with the gained leisure time, and how to reequip displaced workers for productive occupations.

(Top left) The Beatles, British singing group; (top right) teen-ager tries out an electric guitar in a music store; (bottom) young surfers on a California beach

Burk Uzzle from Magnum

Steve Schapiro from Black Star

(Above) College students at commencement exercises in New York City; (right) youthful admirers surround Robert F. Kennedy as he campaigns for the Senate in New York City, 1964

The "Silent Generation" of the 1950s was succeeded by its exact opposite, an active, assertive, always vocal and often demonstrative generation whose prime characteristic was dissatisfaction with the status quo. The activist sentiment and strong political and moral consciousness that pervaded the era sent many into the early civil-rights campaigns, moved thousands to work and demonstrate against the Vietnam War, and made possible the Peace Corps, VISTA, and other service agencies set up as channels for constructive effort. Materially secure, the young were free to look beyond personal affluence toward the realization of universal justice and peace; they felt free to challenge institutions and ignore sacred cows, and were highly inventive in developing new methods of expression. The music that was the central element of their rich subculture grew more and more complex and in its originality, variety, and vitality epitomized the spirit of the time.

Elderly gentleman playing with his grandson

Citizens of a California retirement community enjoy a cycling outing

The heightened tempo of daily life, the increased mobility of the American family, and the small size of the average modern house had the side result of displacing the elderly from their traditional position of respect and authority in the home. Modern medicine and health care facilities have at the same time extended life expectancy. Retirement communities and expanded Social Security services, notably Medicare, have met part of the physical problem of old age, but little has been done toward maintaining the elderly in a real and mutual relation to society.

Nurse and elderly patient at a New York clinic which participates in Medicare

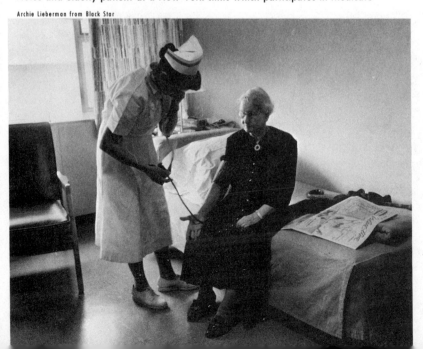

Children of an unemployed coal miner from Appalachia who came to Chicago to search for work

A notable achievement of the 1960s was the "discovery" of poverty in the United States. The poor had been largely held to rural areas or the slum sections of cities; this isolation, further masked by the general prosperity, had allowed most Americans to ignore the existence of poverty. Yet a Senate committee found in 1968 a shocking amount of actual starvation in some areas. A system of programs designed to go beyond simple welfare in meeting the problem made a fitful start against outmoded social ideas and national inertia, but it was barely a beginning.

Vocational training class in North Carolina

Eugene Anthony from Black Star

Unskilled worker looking for a job at a Harlem employment agency

(Above) Navajo mother and child on a reservation in Arizona; (below) migrant cotton pickers working a field in Mississippi

15.

W. H. FERRY: Problems of Abundance

During the 1960s the United States enjoyed a greater wealth and more widespread
affluence than had any country in the history of the world. However, although the fact
might have seemed surprising to men of an earlier age, the abundance that marked
the era appeared to bring almost as many problems with it as it solved. There was
no question that some problems were solved, but poverty continued to exist, in the
midst of great and widely dispersed riches, and, as many pointed out, this accented
rather than alleviated the plight of the poor. Poverty was a major factor in the civil
rights struggles, it was intimately involved with the decay of central cities, and it was
an element in the spread of Communism — for the richer the Americans became,
the poorer the rest of the world felt itself to be. W. H. Ferry, vice-president of the
Center for the Study of Democratic Institutions, discussed these and related matters in
a pamphlet published by the Center in January 1962. The work, appropriately titled
"Caught on the Horn of Plenty," is reprinted in part below.

Source: *Bulletin* of the Center for the Study of Democratic Institutions, January 1962.

STRANGELY ENOUGH, AMERICANS are having a hard time getting used to the idea of abundance. Abundance is not only a relatively recent state of affairs. There is also an idea current that it may not last very long. The barriers to general comprehension of the possibilities and demands of abundance are numerous. There is, for example, tradition, and a mythology that seeks to confine the growing abundance of this country inside the old political and social enclosures. Happily there is also the beginning of a less dusty literature on the topic.

As consumers, Americans are joyously sopping up affluence, quarter after quarter sending private debt for consumer goods to record levels, and inventing new categories of services. But the lesson of abundance is even here ambiguous; for while there is enough to go around for all, not all are sharing. There is enough in our ever-swollen granaries so that no American need to go to bed hungry. Yet millions do, while millions of others are vaguely uneasy and feel guilty about so absurd a situation. The American farm is technology's most notorious victory. That the disaster of abundance on our farms has so far resisted solution is a portent of greater dilemmas in other areas.

For the country may soon be in the same fix with regard to consumer goods and services — more than enough for all, but without the political wit to know how to bring about a just distribution. We may, in fact, be in that situation at present. There is evidence that something like 30 percent of our productive facilities are standing idle most of the time. Much of our machinery is obsolete. Everyone knows that the steel industry spent about a year in the doldrums of 50 percent of capacity production. Planned obsolescence, which is the design and sales strategy of many manufacturers, is latent abundance, just as the fields left unturned by wheat and barley and rice farmers are latent abundance. It is not only what is produced that counts up to a total of abundance but what is capable of being produced.

Not the least of our troubles occurs over definitions. Abundance of this self-evident variety, for example, is not the opposite of the classical idea of scarcity. And what are resources? How do you tell when a resource is scarce? Or not scarce? Are people resources? Are people without jobs or skills resources? What is prosperity? This is a particularly hard definition. The recession is said to be past. Newcomers by the millions are thronging into the stock market. The Gross National Product is at a 3.4 rate. And around 5 million people are out of jobs. Is this prosperity? What are today's definitions of work, leisure, play, affluence? Our vocabulary is tuned to yesterday's Industrial Revolution, not to today's scientific revolution. Abundance might, for instance, be defined as the capacity — here meaning resources, skill, capital, and potential and present production — the capacity to supply every citizen with a minimum decent life. We have the capacity, so this makes us an abundant society. Yet some 30 million Americans are living below the poverty line.

This paper focuses on a disagreeable abundance — the ironic and growing abundance of unemployment. Radical technological change is producing a surplus of labor, and radical measures will be required to deal with it. Since no such radical measures have been, or seem likely to be, proposed by the federal government, technological unemployment may soon grow to the proportions of a crisis. This is not a new phenomenon. Technological unemployment is what frightened the Luddites into riots and the destruction of machinery 150 years ago. John Maynard Keynes noticed it in 1930; his definition of the term is apt today:

"This means unemployment due to our discovery of means of economizing the use of labor outrunning the pace at which we can find new uses for labor."

If it is true that virtually all respectable economic theory is devoted to explaining and justifying the expansion of capitalism, then the oncoming of abundance is a crisis indeed. . . .

The immemorial view is that unemployment is a bad state of affairs. Although all the tendencies in recent generations have been toward leisure — shorter workdays and workweeks, more pay for less labor, education for constructive use of spare time — the country has assumed that the process would always come to a convenient halt close to the Full Employment sign. It seems not to have occurred to any statesman that leisure might as readily be a goal of society as employment. Now that such a possibility exists, no welcome mat is put out for it. On the contrary, dismay is the rule. Instead of embracing the hope that technology may be opening the way into a new style of civilization, one in which work and the economic machinery are not the preeminent concerns of society, the effort today is to show that nothing has been significantly altered by the onrush of technology, that we can lean back comfortably on ancient theories, and that old goals are best after all.

This attitude is particularly evident in the discussion of structural unemployment. For generations the dictum that Machines Make Jobs was demonstrably valid. Now the dictum is losing its force and generality. Machines are replacing workers. Some part of the 50,000 new jobs that have to be provided weekly to keep the American economy going are, to be sure, being supplied by new machines. But what the machine giveth at one place it taketh away at another: hence, structural unemployment. . . .

The question is whether jobs can be manufactured fast enough to approach full employment, using the present definition of jobs and the means of providing them that are presently regarded as acceptable. The essential contention of this paper is that the answer is no. An apparently unavoidable condition of the Age of Abundance is increasing structural unemployment and underemployment.

The novelty of this proposition is that the majority of victims of technological displacement will be *permanently* out of work. They will not just be "resting between engagements." They will not just be waiting for the next upturn, or for expansion of the industry or company in which they were working. They will no longer be the objects of unemployment insurance plans, for these plans are designed to fill the gap between jobs, not to provide a permanent dole. . . .

A spokesman for the Council of Economic Advisers declares that "no respectable intellectual case" has been made for the proposition that technology is inexorably displacing people. The Council says that what is labeled technological unemployment is actually nothing new and should be seen merely as a problem of inadequate demand. The Council's position is therefore the conventional Keynesian one of stimulating demand wherever feasible. Thus the official prescription for unemployment calls for restrained fiscal policy with judicious admixtures of public works, together with doses of therapeutic legislation — for example, extension of unemployment insurance, widening of coverage of minimum wage laws, and depressed-areas bills. A nice contemporary touch is added by the decision to shoot the moon, which from one point of view can be recognized as a long-range WPA for the electronic and missile industries.

Doubtless each of these measures will do something to mitigate unemployment and alleviate hardship. But none gets to the center of the difficulty, which is the rapidly emerging fact that every year from now on we shall be able, because of accelerating technology, to produce the goods and ser-vices needed by the nation with fewer and fewer of the available hands — say 90 percent or less. . . .

There will be no effort here to "prove" that technological unemployment is here to stay, that its progress is relentless, and that traditional means of producing jobs are inadequate. Professor William Gomberg warns against committing the "fallacy of extrapolating the future as an image of the past." The need for proof rests with those who assert, against most of the evident tendencies, that there is nothing novel about technological unemployment today, that it is just the same old sickness in slightly aggravated form and will yield to the same old nostrums. It may be true that "no intellectual case" can be made out of the statistics now available. But the Council of Economic Advisers appears to be relying exclusively on historical data and not on observations of what is going on around them. It is hard to read in the daily accounts of new substitutions of machines for men anything but the auguries of a far-reaching revolution in the offices and production centers of the nation. . . .

There is, to be sure, a way to defer indefinitely the need for coping with the problems of abundance in the United States. This is by deciding to return to a state of scarcity. Unabundance can be ours again by the simple act of deciding to share what we have with those who need it elsewhere in the world. This is not a proposal for more economic aid, though that is a small step in the right direction. It is for an enormously expanded foreign trade, based on radically different premises from the ones on which foreign trade now operates. The new premises would be those of need and justice. The need for what we have — for example, food and food-processing machinery — and our capacity to supply them are plain. The justice of the idea that the need of others and the capacity of the United States ought to be brought into some relation with one another is also obvious, though there might be a good deal of argument before some Americans could be persuaded that impoverished Africans or Asians have a "just" claim on American abundance. . . .

Forthright planning is required now if this country is to attune its trade policies to the swiftly shifting conditions of a new and restless world. The interests of the United States abroad have to be publicly planned and directed. They should not be left to the vagaries of private arrangements. Perhaps the dreamiest idea now current is that the emerging nations are waiting anxiously to adopt American-style free enterprise. Our policy should be that of promoting the general welfare through a mutually beneficial exchange of goods and services and talent, and not that of sustaining capitalism. The general welfare today is the general welfare of the world. This is a practical, not a utopian, assertion. A prospering and warless world is a more important aim than the survival of obsolete trade arrangements. Some planning, to be sure, is being done in this area; but the planning is usually disguised as something else, is always uncoordinated; and is often aimed at preserving private sinecures.

Federal intervention will also have to go far beyond defense contracting in depressed areas if structural unemployment is to be dealt with. This means planning too. Attempts thus far have amounted to little more than unimaginative patchwork. Legislation to move contingents of the jobless to places where they might find work bogged down in Congress, perhaps because that body sensed that the proposed statutes are makeshift and unplanned and may therefore result only in exporting hardship from one place to another. Planning would help to answer the questions, should jobs be moved to people, or people to jobs, and who's responsible anyway? . . . .

National planning is one step in a basic reorganization of our public and private institutions, but it is far from the only one. It must be emphasized that national planning and the radical alterations proposed with regard to such matters as foreign trade are put forth as minimum measures needed by this country if it is to cope successfully with technology and abundance, and get into step with a swiftly changing world. . . .

National planning will be recognition that the government bears the final responsibility for the quality and content and prosperity of the nation. This may perhaps be called modern mercantilism. Those who construe these proposals as some dark version of new and unholy economic doctrines are advised to refer to economic planning in 16th- and 17th-century England or, even better, to the economic history of the Eastern seaboard of this country in the 18th and early 19th centuries.

In an abundant society the problem is not an economic one of keeping the machine running regardless of what it puts out, but a political one of achieving the common good. And planning is one of its major means.

But whether or not we can figure out some such way of taking systematic advantage of the bewildering fact of abundance, we shall within a short while have to discard attitudes that grew up in the dog-eat-dog phase of capitalism and adopt others suitable to modern mercantilism. For example, we shall have to stop automatically regarding the unemployed as lazy, unlucky, indolent, and unworthy. We shall have to find means, public or private, of paying people to do no work.

This suggestion goes severely against the American grain, and it will have to be adopted slowly. The first steps have been taken. Unemployment insurance and supplementary unemployment benefit plans reached by company-union negotiations are examples. As these have come to be accepted as civic-industrial policy, so may plans for six-month work years, or retirement at fifty or fifty-five at full pay until pension schemes take hold. So may continuation of education well into adult years, at public expense. So may payment from the public treasury for nonproductive effort, such as writing novels, painting pictures, composing music, doing graduate work, and taking part in the expanding functions of government. Is a physicist more valuable to the community than a playwright? Why? The responsibility of the individual to the general welfare runs far beyond the purely economic. In his book *The Challenge of Abundance*, Robert Theobald observes:

> . . . In the last century and a half we have tried to solve two problems with a single mechanism. We have allowed the income received from the production of goods to determine the distribution of wealth. However, this system is no longer suitable for an economy moving toward abundance. The economy of abundance will have rules different from those applying in an economy of scarcity. *The fact that a proposed solution would be impossible in an economy of scarcity does not mean that it is not appropriate for an economy of abundance.* . . . In the past, society has claimed that its members were entitled to a living only if they carried out a task society defined as valuable and for which it was willing to pay. The creation of a society of abundance will make it possible to relax this requirement. We will be able to allow people to follow an interest they find vital, but that society would not support through the price mechanism.

The essential change in outlook will be to regard the new leisure — including the leisure of the liberated margin — as desirable, as a good, and to direct public policy to accepting it as a good in itself. This suggests some but far from all of the changes in conventional attitudes that will be compelled the moment that full employment is seen to be an obsolescent goal, and abandoned.

It will be hard to look on members of the liberated margin as useful participants in society, no matter how enlightened the arrangements may be, because "useful" has up to now strictly denoted people who work for economically productive enterprises and ends. Let me emphasize that I am not talking about idleness, only about what most people today regard as idleness, or near to it. The revolution in economic theory that is indicated by abundance is dramatically illustrated here. Whoever heard of economic theory with poets, painters, and philosophers among the premises?

Deliberation on the ways and the standards for getting purchasing power into the hands of the liberated margin may be the beginning of methodical social justice in the American political economy. Abundance may compel social justice as conscience never has. The liberated margin will have to get "what is its due." This means developing a basis of distribution of income which is not tied to work as a measure. For decisions about "due-ness" will have to be made without economic criteria; at least without the criterion of what members of the liberated margin are worth in the employment market, for there is no such market for them.

The criteria of capitalism, are, in fact, largely irrelevant to conditions of abundance. Efficiency, administration, progress, success, profit, competition, and private gain are words of high standing in the lexicon of capitalism. Presumably among these terms are some of the "pseudomoral principles" that Keynes saw on their way to the ashcan as society progressively solved its economic problems. In any event, a community of abundance will find less use for these ideas and will turn instead to ideas like justice, law, government, general welfare, virtue, cooperation, and public responsibility as the touchstones of policy.

Abundance will enable a reversal of the old order of things. Modern mercantilism will remove the economic machine from the middle of the landscape to one side, where, under planning by inducement, its ever more efficient automata will provide the goods and services required by the general welfare. Humanity, with its politics and pastimes and poetry and conversation, will then occupy the central place in the landscape. Management of machines for human ends, not management by them, is the true object of industrial civilization.

This is the promise of modern mercantilism, and if the time is not yet, it is yet a time worth striving for. Meanwhile the chief necessity is to revive respect for law and government as the proper instruments of the general welfare. Without this respect the economic future of this country and that of other nations linked to it will be determined, and stultified, by the accidents of private ambition and the hope of private gain. With this respect the Age of Abundance can be made into the Age of the General Welfare, and the United States can become in fact the moral commonwealth it has always claimed to be.

16.

Michael Harrington: Poverty in an Affluent Society

Discussions of the plight of the poor in affluent America seemed to become ever more common as the very affluence of the nation increased. Michael Harrington's The Other America *(1962) was one of the most widely read books on the subject during the 1960s. Harrington rejected with bitter eloquence the arguments of those who cited the encouraging economic statistics and pointed instead to that still large proportion of Americans who did not share in the unprecedented wealth that so many enjoyed. Parts of two chapters of the book appear here. The first dealt with what Harrington called the "economic underworld" of the large cities of the nation. The second dealt with the special problem of the Negro, who, Harrington said, is "black because he is poor," and not the other way around.*

Source: *The Other America*, New York, 1962, pp. 19-20, 71-81.

In New York City, some of my friends call 80 Warren Street "the slave market."

It is a big building in downtown Manhattan. Its corridors have the littered, trampled air of a courthouse. They are lined with employment-agency offices. Some of these places list good-paying and highly skilled jobs. But many of them provide the work force for the economic underworld in the big city: the dishwashers and day workers, the fly-by-night jobs.

Early every morning, there is a great press of human beings in 80 Warren Street. It is made up of Puerto Ricans and Negroes, alcoholics, drifters, and disturbed people. Some of them will pay a flat fee (usually around 10 percent) for a day's work. They pay $0.50 for a $5.00 job and they are given the address of a luncheonette. If all goes well, they will make their wage. If not, they have a legal right to come back and get their half-dollar. But many of them don't know that, for they are people that are not familiar with laws and rights.

But perhaps the most depressing time at 80 Warren Street is in the afternoon. The jobs have all been handed out, yet the people still mill around. Some of them sit on benches in the larger offices. There is no real point to their waiting, yet they have nothing else to do. For some, it is probably a point of pride to be here, a feeling that they are somehow still looking for a job even if they know that there is no chance to get one until early in the morning.

Most of the people at 80 Warren Street were born poor. (The alcoholics are an exception.) They are incompetent as far as American society is concerned, lacking the education and the skills to get decent work. If they find steady employment, it will be in a sweatshop or a kitchen.

In a Chicago factory, another group of people are working. A year or so ago, they were in a union shop making good wages, with sick leave, pension rights, and vacations. Now they are making artificial Christmas trees at less than half the pay they had been receiving. They have no contract rights, and the foreman is absolute monarch. Permission is required if a worker wants to go to the bathroom. A few are fired every day for insubordination.

These are people who have become poor. They possess skills, and they once moved upward with the rest of the society. But now their jobs have been destroyed, and their skills have been rendered useless. In the process, they have been pushed down toward the poverty from whence they came. This particular group is Negro, and the chances of ever breaking through, of returning to the old conditions, are very slim. Yet their plight is not exclusively racial, for it is shared by all the semiskilled and unskilled workers who are the victims of technological unemployment in the mass-production industries. They are involved in an interracial misery.

These people are the rejects of the affluent society. They never had the right skills in the first place, or they lost them when the rest of the economy advanced. They are the ones who make up a huge portion of the culture of poverty in the cities of America. They are to be counted in the millions. . . .

IF ALL THE DISCRIMINATORY LAWS in the United States were immediately repealed, race would still remain as one of the most pressing moral and political problems in the nation. Negroes and other minorities are not simply the victims of a series of iniquitous statutes. The American economy, the American society, the American unconscious, are all racist. If all the laws were framed to provide equal opportunity, a majority of the Negroes would not be able to take full advantage of the change. There would still be a vast, silent, and automatic system directed against men and women of color.

To belong to a racial minority is to be poor, but poor in a special way. The fear, the lack of self-confidence, the haunting, these have been described. But they, in turn, are the expressions of the most institutionalized poverty in the United States, the most vicious of the vicious circles. In a sense, the Negro is classically the "other" American, degraded and frustrated at every turn and not just because of laws.

There are sympathetic and concerned people who do not understand how deeply America has integrated racism into its structure. Given time, they argue, the Negroes will rise in the society like the Irish, the Jews, the Italians, and all the rest. But this notion misses two decisive facts: that the Negro is colored, and no other group in the United States has ever faced such a problem, and that the Negro of today is an internal migrant who will face racism wherever he goes, who cannot leave his oppression behind as if it were a czar or a potato famine. To be equal, the Negro requires something much more profound than a way "into" the society; he needs a transformation of some of the basic institutions of the society.

The Negro is poor because he is black; that is obvious enough. But, perhaps more importantly, the Negro is black because he

"Wall-to-Wall Under-the-Carpeting"; cartoon by Herblock, 1963

is poor. The laws against color can be removed, but that will leave the poverty that is the historic and institutionalized consequence of color. As long as this is the case, being born a Negro will continue to be the most profound disability that the United States imposes upon a citizen.

Perhaps the quickest way to point up the racism of the American economy is to recall a strange case of jubilation.

Late in 1960 the Department of Labor issued a study, "The Economic Situation of Negroes in the United States." It noted that in 1939, nonwhite workers earned, on the average, 41 percent as much as whites, and that by 1958 their wages had climbed to 58 percent of that of whites. Not a little elation greeted this announcement. Some of the editorialists cited these statistics as indicating that slow and steady progress was being made. (At this rate, the Negro would reach parity with the white some time well after the year 2000.)

To begin with, the figures were somewhat more optimistic than the reality. Part of the Negro gain reflected the shift of rural Negroes to cities and Southern Negroes to the North. In both cases, the people involved increased their incomes by going into a more prosperous section of the country. But within each area their relative position remained the same: at the bottom. Then, the statistics take a depression year (1939) as a base for comparison, and contrast it to a year of recession (1958). This tended to exaggerate the advance because Negroes in 1939 were particularly victimized.

Another important aspect of the problem was obscured by the sweeping comparisons most editorialists made between the 1939 and 1958 figures. Even the Department of Labor statistics themselves indicate that the major gain was made during World War II (the increase from 1939 to 1947 was from 41.4 percent to 54.3 of the white wage). In the postwar period the rate of advance slowed to a walk. Moreover, most of the optimism was based upon figures for Negro men. When the women are included, and when one takes a median family income from the Current Population Reports, Negroes rose from 51 percent of white family income in 1947 to 57 percent in 1952 — and then declined back to the 1947 level by 1959.

But even without these qualifications, the fact is stark enough: the United States found cause for celebration in the announcement that Negro workers had reached 58 percent of the wage level of their white co-workers. This situation is deeply imbedded in the very structure of American society.

Negroes in the United States are concentrated in the worst, dirtiest, lowest-paying jobs. A third continue to live in the rural South, most of them merely subsisting within a culture of poverty and a society of open terror. A third live in Southern cities and a third in Northern cities, and these have bettered their lot compared to the sharecroppers. But they are still the last hired and the first fired, and they are particularly vulnerable to recessions.

Thus, according to the Department of Labor in 1960, 4 percent of Negro employees were "professional, technical, and kindred workers" (compared to 11.3 percent for the whites); 2.7 percent were "managers, officials, and proprietors" (the white figure is 14.6 percent). In short, at the top of the economic structure there were 6.7 percent of the Negroes — and 25.9 percent of the whites. And this, in itself, represented considerable *gains* over the past two decades.

Going down the occupational scale, Negroes are primarily grouped in the bottom jobs. In 1960, 20 percent of the whites had high-skill industrial jobs, while the Negro share of this classification was 9 percent. Semiskilled mass production workers and laborers constituted around 48 percent of the Negro male population (and 25.3 percent of the white males). Negro women are the victims of a double discrimination. According to a New York State study, Negro female income as a percentage of white actually declined between 1949 and 1954 (and, in 1960, over a third of Negro women were still employed as domestics).

In part, this miserable structure of the Negro work force is an inheritance of the past. It reflects what happens to a people who have been systematically oppressed and denied access to skill and opportunity. If this completely defined the problem, there would be a basis for optimism. One could assume that the Negro would leave behind the mess of pottage bequeathed him by white America and move into a better future. But that is not the case. For the present position of the Negro in the economy has been institutionalized. Unless something basic is done, it will reproduce itself for years to come.

Take, as an example, the problem of automation. This has caused "structural" unemployment through the American work force, that is, the permanent destruction of jobs rather than cyclical layoffs. When this happens, the blow falls disproportionately upon the Negro. As the last significant group to enter the factory, the Negroes have low seniority (if they are lucky enough to be in union occupations), and they are laid off first. As one of the least skilled groups in the work force, they will have the hardest time getting another job. The "older" Negro (over forty) may well be condemned to job instability for the rest of his life.

All of this is immediate and automatic. It is done without the intervention of a single racist, yet it is a profound part of racism in the United States.

However, more is involved than the inevitable working of an impersonal system. The Negro lives in the other America of poverty for many reasons, and one of them is conscious racism reinforcing institutional patterns of the economy. In 1960, according to the report of Herbert Hill, Labor Secretary of the National Association for the Advancement of Colored People, Negroes made up only 1.69 percent of the total number of apprentices in the economy. The exact figure offered by Hill has been disputed; the shocking fact which he describes is agreed upon by everyone. This means that Negroes are denied access precisely to those jobs that are not low-paying and vulnerable to recession.

The main cause of this problem is the attitude of management, which fundamentally determines hiring policy. But in the case of apprenticeship programs, the labor movement and the Federal and state agencies involved also bear part of the responsibility. In the AFL-CIO, it is the politically conservative unions from the building trades who are the real stumbling block; the mass-production unions of the CIO have some bad areas, but on the whole they pioneered in bringing Negroes into the plants and integrating local organizations.

With the companies, one of the real difficulties in dealing with this structure of racism is that it is invisible. Here is a huge social fact, yet no one will accept responsibility for it. When questioned as to why there are no Negroes in sales, or in the office, the personnel man will say that he himself has nothing against Negroes. The problem, he will claim, is with subordinates who would revolt if Negroes were brought into their department, and with superiors who impose the policy. This response is standard up and down the line. The subordinates and the superiors make the same assertion.

Indeed, one of the difficulties in fighting against racist practices in the American economy is the popularity of a liberal rhetoric. Practically no one, outside of convinced white supremacists in the South, will admit to discriminatory policies. So it is that the Northern Negro has, in one sense, a more personally frustrating situation than his Southern brother. In Dixie, Jim Crow is personified, an actual living person who speaks in the accents of open racism. In the rest of the country, everybody is against discrimination for the record, and Jim Crow is a vast impersonal system that keeps the Negro down.

In the past few years, some Negro groups have been using the boycott to force companies to abandon racist hiring practices. This may well be an extraordinarily momentous development, for it is a step out of the other America, and equality will come only when the Negro is no longer poor.

But, as one goes up the occupational ladder, the resistance to hiring Negroes becomes more intense. The office, for example, is a bastion of racism in American society. To some of the people involved, white-collar work is regarded as more personal, and even social, than factory work. So the integration of work appears like the integration of the neighborhood or the home. And a wall of prejudice is erected to keep the Negroes out of advancement.

Perhaps the most shocking statistic in all this is the one that describes what happens when a Negro does acquire skill and training. North, East, South, and West the pattern is the same: the more education a Negro has, the more economic discrimination he faces. Herman Miller, one of the best-known authorities on income statistics, has computed that the white Southern college graduate receives 1.85 times the compensation of his Negro counterpart, and in the North the white edge is 1.59.

What is involved in these figures is a factor that sharply distinguishes racial minorities from the old immigrant groups. When the Irish, the Jews, or the Italians produced a doctor, it was possible for him to begin to develop a practice that would bring him into the great society. There was prejudice, but he was increasingly judged on his skill. As time went on, the professionals from the immigrant groups adapted themselves to the language and dress of the rest of America. They ceased to be visible, and there was a wide scope for their talents.

This is not true of the Negro. The doctor or the lawyer will find it extremely difficult to set up practice in a white neighborhood. By far and large, they will be confined to the ghetto, and since their fellow Negroes are poor they will not receive so much money as their white colleagues. The Negro academic often finds himself trapped in a segregated educational system in which Negro colleges are short on salaries, equipment, libraries, and so on. Their very professional advancement is truncated because of it.

For the mass in the racial ghetto the situation is even more extreme. As a result of the segregation of neighborhoods, it is possible for a city like New York to have a public policy in favor of integration, and yet to maintain a system of effective segregation. In the mid-fifties, for example, the New York public-school system took a look at itself, dividing schools into Group X, with a high concentration of Negroes or Puerto Ricans, and Group Y where Negroes and Puerto Ricans were less than 10 percent of the student body. They found that the X schools were older and less adequate, had more probationary and substitute teachers, more classes for retarded pupils, and fewer for bright children. This situation had developed with the framework of a public, legal commitment to integrated education. (Some steps have been taken to remedy the problem, but they are only a beginning.)

In the other America each group suffers from a psychological depression as well as from simple material want. And given the long history and the tremendous institutionalized power of racism, this is particularly and terribly true of the Negro.

Some commentators have argued that Negroes have a lower level of aspiration, of ambition, than whites. In this theory, the Jim Crow economy produces a mood of resignation and acceptance. But in a study of the New York State Commission Against Discrimination an even more serious situation was described: one in which Negro children had more aspiration than whites from the same income level, but less opportunity to fulfill their ambition.

In this study, Aaron Antonovsky and Melvin Lerner described the result as a "pathological condition . . . in our society." The Negro child, coming from a family in which the father has a miserable job, is forced to reject the life of his parents, and to put forth new goals for himself. In the case of the immigrant young some generations ago, this experience of breaking with the Old Country tradition and identifying with the great society of America was a decisive moment in moving upward. But the Negro does not find society as open as the

immigrant did. He has the hope and the desire, but not the possibility. The consequence is heartbreaking frustration.

Indeed, Antonovsky suggests that the image of Jackie Robinson or Ralph Bunche is a threat to the young Negro. These heroes are exceptional and talented men. Yet, in a time of ferment among Negroes, they tend to become norms and models for the young people. Once again, there is a tragic gap between the ideal and the possible. A sense of disillusion, of failure, is added to the indignity of poverty.

A more speculative description of the Negro psychology has been written by Norman Mailer. For Mailer, the concept of "coolness" is a defense reaction against a hostile world. Threatened by the Man, denied access to the society, the Negro, in Mailer's image, stays loose: he anticipates disillusion; he turns cynicism into a style.

But perhaps the final degradation the Negro must face is the image the white man has of him. White America keeps the Negro down. It forces him into a slum; it keeps him in the dirtiest and lowest-paying jobs. Having imposed this indignity, the white man theorizes about it. He does not see it as the tragic work of his own hands, as a social product. Rather, the racial ghetto reflects the "natural" character of the Negro: lazy, shiftless, irresponsible, and so on. So prejudice becomes self-justifying. It creates miserable conditions and then cites them as a rationale for inaction and complacency.

One could continue describing the psychological and spiritual consequences of discrimination almost endlessly. Yet, whatever the accurate theory may be, it is beyond dispute that one of the main components of poverty for the Negro is a maiming of personality. This is true generally for the poor; it is doubly and triply true for the race poor. . . .

If, as is quite possible, America refuses to deal with the social evils that persist in the sixties, it will at the same time have turned its back on the racial minorities. There will be speeches on equality; there will be gains as the nation moves toward a constitutional definition of itself as egalitarian. The Negro will watch all this from a world of double poverty. He will continue to know himself as a member of a race-class condemned by heredity to be poor. There will be occasional celebrations — perhaps the next one will be called in twenty years or so when it is announced that Negroes have reached 70 percent of the white wage level. But that other America which is the ghetto will still stand.

There is a bitter picket-line chant that one sometimes hears when a store is being boycotted in the North:

> If you're white, you're right,
> If you're black, stay back.

It is an accurate sociological statement of the plight of the Negro in American society.

17.

J. S. Dupré and W. E. Gustafson: Defense Contracting and the Public Interest

Not merely new weapons but new weapons systems were called for at shorter and shorter intervals in the arms race between the United States and the Soviet Union in the years after World War II, and particularly after the Korean War. The development of new weapons systems involved vast government expenditures, which obviously could have better or worse effects on the total economy depending on how and where they were spent. The question of the relation between defense contracting and the general public interest was discussed by Harvard faculty members J. Stefan Dupré and W. Eric Gustafson in an article published in 1962. The article, part of which is reprinted here, was based on an earlier paper read by Dupré and Gustafson at a meeting of the American Political Science Association, in New York in September 1960.

Source: *Political Science Quarterly,* June 1962: "Contracting for Defense: Private Firms and the Public Interest."

ONE OF THE MOST CHALLENGING and costly imperatives of the Cold War is the need for constant innovation in weapons systems. Given the advanced state of defense technology, such innovation requires systematic research and development, which in turn call for sophisticated technical capacity, refined managerial skills, and flexible financial arrangements. Accordingly, the government has had to devise new standards in its contractual relationships with business firms. Essentially, the government now assumes the financial risk involved in innovation. Free competition no longer characterizes the process of bidding for government contracts. While private firms have thus been freed from the restraints of the open market, they have acquired new public responsibilities. They are no longer merely suppliers to the government, but participants in the administration of public functions. The capacity of private firms to promote the public interest in the absence of market forces poses serious conceptual and administrative problems. . . .

New Contracting Methods: General Implications

THE POSITION OF THE CONTRACTOR under recently developed contractual methods can perhaps best be appreciated through a comparison of more traditional forms with the new. The advertised fixed-price contract lies at one extreme; the negotiated cost-plus-fixed-fee (CPFF) contract at the other.

The traditional firm fixed-price contract with open advertising is an attempt to bring full market forces into play. In order to use this system, the government must have a fairly exact idea of its requirements, and the items involved must be sufficiently standardized to enable a large number of firms to compete. In open advertising, the government lays down rigid specifications regarding the nature of the item it wishes to procure. With this information in hand, prospective suppliers submit bids which are publicly opened. The contract is automatically awarded to the qualified bidder who promises to meet the exact requirements for the lowest price.

Participating bidders are in open price competition. Their incentive is clear: to meet the government's requirements at the lowest possible cost. The lower their estimate of cost prior to bidding, the greater is

the possibility of securing the contract. Once the contract has been awarded, the contractor's profit is greatest if he holds actual costs as far below his previous estimate as possible. The risk lies squarely on the contractor. He will reap its full rewards or (if his actual costs are higher than his estimates) suffer its full penalties.

By comparison with this classic concept of contracting, the newer forms are all deviations from the market mechanism. Contracts involving research, development and prototype production must by their very nature be handled differently from the procurement of routine items. It is impossible to secure firm bids in advance from which the winner could be chosen. The contractor is expected to find the solution to a problem and clearly the costs of doing so can only be roughly estimated in advance. The government thus agrees to reimburse the contractor for the costs he incurs (subject to certain exclusions), and selects the contractor by negotiation on the basis of technical and managerial facilities and know-how, rather than price. In addition, the government has had to provide a great part of the capital equipment involved in these efforts, since otherwise (so the argument runs) companies could not be induced to commit themselves to large-scale contracts with highly specialized equipment.

As the pace of technological change has quickened in the military with the increasing dominance of advanced aircraft and missiles, a larger and larger share of procurement dollars has been spent on negotiated cost-reimbursement contracts. In fiscal 1952, 12.7 percent of defense procurement dollars were tied up in cost-reimbursement contracts; by fiscal 1960, the proportion had risen to 42.6 percent. In that year, the total value of military contracts was $22.9 billion, over 86 percent of which was negotiated. The disposition of a substantial fraction of our national income, therefore, is now the result of negotiation between the military departments and the contractor.

Weapons-System Contracting

THE MECHANICS OF NEGOTIATED cost-reimbursement contracting will become somewhat clearer if we look at concrete examples. Negotiated cost-reimbursement contracting offers largely the same problems whatever the nature of the task or the amount of money involved. These problems appear in sharpest relief in weapons-system contracting in its single-manager form. Under this mode of organization, conceived by the Air Force, a single prime contractor is charged with the responsibility of developing and producing a complete weapons system including all components or subsystems, with the help of a widespread network of subcontractors.

A weapons system has its beginnings in the formulation of general operating requirements by the Air Force, which then invites firms to submit designs and proposals. In the case of the B-70, currently in development, the Air Force invited six companies to submit designs in 1954. Late in 1957 North American Aviation won an intensive two-year competition after independent evaluations by the Air Research and Development Command, the Air Materiel Command, and the Strategic Air Command. As weapons-system prime contractor, North American was awarded a CPFF Phase I contract authorizing it to proceed with further design work and construction of mockups. Under normal circumstances this is followed by a Phase II contract (also usually CPFF) for completion of engineering and construction of prototypes and, finally, a Phase III contract for production. . . .

As prime contractor, North American essentially takes the place that would otherwise be occupied by Air Force procurement personnel. Seventy percent of the work on the B-70 is planned to be carried on by the subcontractors; 30 percent will remain with North American itself, and even this is the result of competition with other possible subcontractors.

Each subcontractor enters into contracts with a second tier of subcontractors. These may be on a CPFF or a fixed-price basis, depending on the end item to be obtained. It is normally at this level that small businesses will begin to get some portion of the work. North American, with due regard to government regulations, takes steps to insure that small firms will be considered. . . .

The entire subcontracting system, then, is based on continual administration and checking from top to bottom. Costs and economy are secondary considerations; technical efficiency and coordination hold prime importance. As each tier performs its managerial function, so do the fixed fees pyramid one on top of the other. Assuming a 6 percent fixed fee to the prime contractor, and a similar fee to two levels of subcontractors, a second tier subcontract for $100,000 will involve payment of over $18,000 in fixed fees. The government thus procures management as well as hardware at all levels.

The single-manager concept of weapons-system contracting gives a particularly good example of multi-tiered contracting with major administrative responsibilities borne by private business. But there are many others as well. The associate weapons-system manager concept is an important modification. Here a number of prime contracts are let, with one of the primes as an integrator, the government retaining somewhat more managerial control. In the case of the Atlas missile, for instance, two Air Force units together with a hired consultant, Space Technology Laboratories, are system managers. North American Aviation, General Electric, Burroughs, American Bosch Arma Corporation and Convair are all prime contractors, with Convair holding responsibilities as integrator. Somewhere between this system and the single-manager arrangement lies the Polaris Missile Program. Here the Special Projects Office of the Navy's Bureau of Naval Weapons is weapons-system manager. M.I.T. holds a prime contract for the development of the guidance system. The Lockheed Missiles and Space Division holds a prime contract as missile-system manager and has numerous subcontractors.

These cases all illustrate government contracting in its various modern weapons-system forms, tying hundreds of firms together through various tiers to produce a single end item. The use of such complex contracting methods has created a set of problems of the utmost importance for public policy.

Problems of the New Contracting Methods

THE NEW CONTRACTING METHODS create problems because they involve new concepts of the roles of government and business. Under our traditional contracting system, business firms are government suppliers whose responsibilities and performance are regulated by the competition and risk that characterize the market mechanism of the private economy. Government, for its part, plays a relatively passive role limited to assuring equitable competition for its business. Recently, however, there has emerged a mixture of the functions formerly considered "governmental" and "private" to the point where the old distinctions are inappropriate.

The result has been a number of problem areas in which old tools of control and old concepts prove ineffective in the modern context. Costs and performance are hard to regulate in the absence of the market discipline of competitive contracting; the requirements of the system have led to a concentration of business in a small number of hands, a situation which seems unavoidable under current practices; and the need for productive capacity has tied the hands of

the Defense Department in terms of the sources of supply available to it and in terms of its ability to terminate its relationship with a contractor.

1. Costs. Negotiated CPFF contracts offer a marked contrast to the advertised fixed-price variety. First, while competition is not precluded, the number of competing firms is limited to those that receive government invitations to bid. Second, competition concentrates on proffered designs, technical and managerial competence, and the like, rather than estimated costs. Third, the assumption of the contract by the successful firm involves no element of risk; the government undertakes to reimburse costs. The contractor as a result is left with no market incentive to hold costs down; such incentives as there are to hold down the level of costs are purely administrative.

By contrast to the market-imposed controls of advertised fixed-price contracting, negotiated CPFF contracts are the result of a bargaining process in which government and business are at opposite ends. Here business firms have decided advantages. They will have an incentive to negotiate for high target costs and will be in a favorable position to do so; their personnel is more knowledgeable and better acquainted with cost determinants. The government's position is bound to be weaker in a situation where experience with thousands of components is needed. The advantages of the business firms in negotiation have been confirmed by numerous cases in which audits have revealed that negotiated fixed-price contracts have been overpriced. For instance, in a recent case before the Tax Court, it emerged that Boeing had initially submitted a bid on a contract of $540 million. After negotiation with the Air Force, the price was reduced to $500 million. The FBI later turned up internal cost estimates made at the time by Boeing of only $460 million.

In an attempt to provide contractors with an inducement to hold costs down, the government has devised modified forms of contract. Cost-plus-incentive-fee and fixed-price incentive contracts permit the contractor to share in any cost reduction which takes place relative to negotiated target costs. (Contracts of this sort can normally be used only after research, development, and early prototype production.) In one frequent form, any savings on target costs go 80 percent to the contracting military department and 20 percent to the contractor. Incentive contracts, however, provide incentive for the contractor in two directions: to hold actual costs below target costs, but also to keep target costs as high as possible.

The effective operation of any of these contracting methods depends on the bargaining or "adversary" system which the contracting method assumes. The buyer must be an aloof and impartial decision-maker. Yet defense contracting officials must now work hand-in-glove with their opposite numbers in the contractors' establishments. To a large extent, the standing of government personnel within their departments (and the standing of the military department itself, for that matter) depends on cooperation from the contractor. The result, as one might predict, is frequently a live-and-let-live situation when crucial decisions arise. This attitude can be especially damaging to cost control when emphasis is placed on time of delivery, while little attention is paid to cost. If the contractor is permitted to buy shorter delivery time with increased costs, and the reasonableness of these costs is not too closely scrutinized, the opportunities for inefficiency are multiplied.

2. *Concentration.* The number of firms which can participate as prime contractors has tended to be rather limited. Some of the reasons are obvious: few firms have the management, technical personnel, and industrial capacity to build complex and costly hardware and to manage sizeable contracts involving many subcontractors. Large firms have frequently done essential background research and development using their own funds or under other government contracts, and already hold government financed facilities. As the contract comes closer to the all-inclusive weapons-system concept, without provision for associate contractors, the number of firms which can possibly compete for the contract becomes smaller.

But also important is the fact that there are pressures in the contracting situation which tend to limit the number of firms which can participate in the process. As one small businessman phrased it:

> All other things being equal, the average military procurement officer would rather give a contract to a big firm because he thinks it is safer and he takes less personal risk. If the contract doesn't work out, he always has the excuse that the big firm is well-known and well-established and should have performed better.

The result of these pressures has been to concentrate defense business in the hands of a relatively few large corporations. . . .

3. *Maintenance of Capacity.* The limited number of large firms qualified to bid for prime contracts in the field of weapons systems has placed the government in a peculiar position. The market incentives for cost and good performance are of course weak, due to the necessity of using negotiated contracts. Nonetheless, there is another incentive which might normally operate. In the words of a Boeing Airplane Company representative, "a reputation for high costs is damaging to any contractor seeking to remain in the defense contracting industry."

Given the special nature of defense contracting, however, the threat of loss of business has considerably less meaning than it would in the context of the purchase of common use items from normal commercial suppliers and manufacturers. Many observers feel that defense officials are almost compelled to keep the large contractors in business in order to maintain the country's defense research and production capabilities and the defense establishment's investment in these facilities. . . .

The necessity of maintaining research and production facilities conflicts with an important underlying assumption of contracting. The assumption is that if a contractor does not perform to standard, his services need not be used in the future and the goods in question can be bought elsewhere from better qualified suppliers. Given the necessity for the facilities, however, and the fact that they have increasingly fewer alternative civilian uses, the freedom of the government to buy or not to buy from a given contractor is often fictitious. This inflexible situation is frequently compounded by political pressures from the geographical areas in which the large contractors are located.

4. Private Benefit vs. the Public Interest. The problems discussed so far are at their most severe in the areas where private benefit and public interest conflict. Such public goals as cost control, the insurance of competition, and protection for small business all come into conflict with the profit motive.

A good instance of the general problem caused by the quasi-governmental character of many of the defense contractors is the case of Space Technology Laboratories, a wholly-owned subsidiary of Thompson Ramo Wooldridge, which was technical director of the Air Force's ballistic-missile program. STL was barred from manufacturing activities related to its role as technical director, since these activities would have involved clear conflict of interest with its managerial responsibilities. Nevertheless, its status as a profit-making organization caused conflict between its public responsibility as technical director and its private interests, and because of conflict of interest with other firms involved, militated against its full effectiveness as coordinator of the missile program. The General Accounting Office in May 1960 recommended that STL be absorbed within the Air Force on a number of grounds, most particularly the

two we have pointed out. The GAO commented that, "As STL's know-how grows through continued systems engineering and technical direction, it would appear that the financial incentive to withdraw from the program would become increasingly dependent on the capability acquired by STL." The government could only hope that the possibilities for increased profit would not cause STL to leave the program. In addition, its effectiveness as coordinator was hamstrung by its profit-making nature, said the GAO. "The likelihood that the know-how being developed may be used by [STL] to compete for production in related fields and in future programs is a deterrent to full cooperation by the participating contractors." Manufacturers have "a natural reluctance" to make information that might lead to important patents available to a potential competitor.

Many prime contractors for weapons systems seem to be in a position where similar problems would arise, and there is some evidence that they do. On the question of "make or buy" — to subcontract or not to subcontract — there seem to have been clear cases of conflict between the profit motive and "public responsibility" in instances where the guidelines were not at all clear. The prime contractor's private interests (be they profit or merely the desire for a quiet life) may lead him to rely on a relatively small number of subcontractors, without encouraging the fullest possible competition. As Representative Curtis recently phrased it, "one of the things that the Small Business Committee is concerned about is this mother sow process where one big prime gets its favorite little piglets and that is a closed family party that keeps going on." In addition, small subcontractors have complained that the large primes are "proselyting the engineering and design know-how of the subcontractors, who after obtaining all the engineering and manufacturing know-how needed, proceed to build the products in their own shops."

To some, the solution for this conflict between private and public interest is quite clear: the management function should be returned to the Defense Department. In particular, the GAO made this recommendation with respect to Space Technology Laboratories. Similar recommendations were made with respect to weapons systems from a small business point of view:

> The only way . . . to genuinely increase small business participation in [weapons-system procurement] which is increasingly becoming the preponderant defense activity, is by eliminating the single-manager concept and giving the coordinating responsibility and contracting authority back to the Defense Department where it really belongs.

The question of returning greater managerial responsibility to the military departments may be purely academic as long as the salary differential between public and private employment remains as large as it is. In the absence of marked salary differentials, there would still be problems: for many purposes, private organizations can act more flexibly than those bound by civil service procedures. But under present arrangements, government contributes to salary differentials through the funds it provides to contractors. Current proposals for making civil service salaries at executive levels competitive with those paid for comparable private jobs might enable the military departments to assume a greater portion of managerial functions. Nonetheless, such functions will continue to be shared by government and business to a certain extent because private firms enjoy a greater degree of flexibility than public agencies.

This brings us back to our thesis that public and private functions have become intertwined. Business is no longer merely a supplier but a participant in the management and administration of a public function. Negotiation and cost reimbursement have channeled public money into the private sector without the use of the market mechanism. Business, like government, must then become subject to noneconomic checks to avoid abuses. If they are to shoulder public responsibilities, private firms must ultimately become accustomed to close supervision with the resulting investigations, audits and other paraphernalia that accompany the spending of taxpayers' money. Finally, large firms administering subcontracts find themselves with administrative responsibilities toward their subcontractors similar to those the government holds toward them, and of allocating contractual funds with regard to such public policy goals as the sponsorship of small business, the relief of unemployment, "Buy-American," and non-discrimination in hiring.

It is certainly tempting to read elements of federalism into this emerging system. This is particularly true if we think of the so-called "new federalism" of the last twenty-five years, under which federal grants have softened the traditionally emphasized legal distinctions of federalism in favor of federal-state cooperation in matters of broad public policy. Business retains its "autonomy" in the sphere of its purely commercial transactions, subject, of course, to existing regulations, just as the states have "autonomy" subject to the Constitution. But overall business performance (investment patterns and so on) is affected by the availability of federal funds, just as state functions are affected by federal grants. In the contractual area itself, the business firm is subject to audits and administrative control but still retains a wide sphere of independence in the allocation of funds (for instance, salaries), again presenting a situation analogous to that of the states. Finally, efforts to allocate funds to small business and to labor surplus areas present a problem quite similar to the question of "fiscal need" (diversion of grant funds to resource-poor states) in federal finance.

To be sure, there is great danger in pushing the federal analogy too far. One could with greater safety speak in terms of a partnership, or of the industrial "public-mindedness" so cherished by the American business creed. Nevertheless, the term "federalism" brings at least one important item to mind — the fact that tax money is being spent on a decentralized basis and that the spenders, both "grantor" and "grantee," are subject to public accountability. But the involvement of private firms as opposed to institutions like state governments presents a distinct complication. Business is still not government; it is by nature oriented toward its private interests.

A major problem of our defense establishment, then, is to find effective contracting methods to enable private business to cooperate in public administration without conflict with its private interests. The tools and skills of administration must be further developed to ensure controls which will approximate the results of the market mechanism.

18.

RACHEL CARSON: The "Control" of Nature

Humanity's organized effort to control or eliminate the natural forces it deems inimical to its welfare became the subject of debate in the United States in 1962 following the publication of Rachel Carson's well-publicized and controversial book, Silent Spring. *In the book Miss Carson asserted that man, with his imperfect knowledge of biological interrelationships and his inability to judge the future effects of present actions, was doing himself and all living things irreparable harm through massive programs of pest extermination. The book spurred widespread discussion and led to a reappraisal, on both local and federal levels, of the problems as well as the potentialities of such programs. The so-called third generation, or biological, pesticides were offered during the later 1960s as a solution of the problem of indiscriminate use of such agents, but ecological research continued and promised to become one of the most important activities of governments and chemical firms in the last third of the century. Portions of Miss Carson's book are reprinted here.*

Source: *Silent Spring,* New York, 1966, pp. 13-23, 261-262.

The sedge is wither'd from the lake,
   And no birds sing.   KEATS

I am pessimistic about the human race because it is too ingenious for its own good. Our approach to nature is to beat it into submission. We would stand a better chance of survival if we accommodated ourselves to this planet and viewed it appreciatively instead of skeptically and dictatorially.   E. B. WHITE

THERE WAS ONCE A TOWN in the heart of America where all life seemed to live in harmony with its surroundings. The town lay in the midst of a checkerboard of prosperous farms, with fields of grain and hillsides of orchards where, in spring, white clouds of bloom drifted above the green fields. In autumn, oak and maple and birch set up a blaze of color that flamed and flickered across a backdrop of pines. Then foxes barked in the hills and deer silently crossed the fields, half-hidden in the mists of the fall mornings.

Along the roads, laurel, viburnum, and alder, great ferns and wildflowers delighted the traveler's eye through much of the year. Even in winter the roadsides were places of beauty, where countless birds came to feed on the berries and on the seed heads of the dried weeds rising above the snow. The countryside was, in fact, famous for the abundance and variety of its bird life, and when the flood of migrants was pouring through in spring and fall people traveled from great distances to observe them. Others came to fish the streams, which flowed clear and cold out of the hills and contained shady pools where trout lay. So it had been from the days, many years ago, when the first settlers raised their houses, sank their wells, and built their barns.

Then a strange blight crept over the area and everything began to change. Some evil spell had settled on the community: mysterious maladies swept the flocks of chickens; the cattle and sheep sickened and died. Everywhere was a shadow of death. The farmers spoke of much illness among their families. In the town the doctors had become more and more puzzled by new kinds of sickness appearing among their patients. There had been several sudden and unexplained deaths, not only among adults but even among children, who would be stricken suddenly while at play and die within a few hours.

There was a strange stillness. The birds, for example — where had they gone? Many people spoke of them, puzzled and disturbed. The feeding stations in the backyards were deserted. The few birds seen anywhere were moribund; they trembled violently and could not fly. It was a spring without voices. On the mornings that had once throbbed with the dawn chorus of robins, catbirds, doves, jays, wrens, and scores of other bird voices there was now no sound; only silence lay over the fields and woods and marsh.

On the farms the hens brooded, but no chicks hatched. The farmers complained that they were unable to raise any pigs —

the litters were small and the young survived only a few days. The apple trees were coming into bloom but no bees droned among the blossoms, so there was no pollination and there would be no fruit.

The roadsides, once so attractive, were now lined with browned and withered vegetation as though swept by fire. These, too, were silent, deserted by all living things. Even the streams were now lifeless. Anglers no longer visited them, for all the fish had died.

In the gutters under the eaves and between the shingles of the roofs, a white granular powder still showed a few patches; some weeks before it had fallen like snow upon the roofs and the lawns, the fields and streams.

No witchcraft, no enemy action had silenced the rebirth of new life in this stricken world. The people had done it themselves.

This town does not actually exist, but it might easily have a thousand counterparts in America or elsewhere in the world. I know of no community that has experienced all the misfortunes I describe. Yet every one of these disasters has actually happened somewhere, and many real communities have already suffered a substantial number of them. A grim specter has crept upon us almost unnoticed, and this imagined tragedy may easily become a stark reality we all shall know.

What has already silenced the voices of spring in countless towns in America? . . .

THE HISTORY OF LIFE on earth has been a history of interaction between living things and their surroundings. To a large extent, the physical form and the habits of the earth's vegetation and its animal life have been molded by the environment. Considering the whole span of earthly time, the opposite effect, in which life actually modifies its surroundings, has been relatively slight. Only within the moment of time represented by the present century has one species — man — acquired significant power to alter the nature of his world.

During the past quarter century this power has not only increased to one of disturbing magnitude but it has changed in character. The most alarming of all man's assaults upon the environment is the contamination of air, earth, rivers, and sea with dangerous and even lethal materials. This pollution is for the most part irrecoverable; the chain of evil it initiates not only in the world that must support life but in living tissues is for the most part irreversible. In this now universal contamination of the environment, chemicals are the sinister and little-recognized partners of radiation in changing the very nature of the world — the very nature of its life. Strontium 90, released through nuclear explosions into the air, comes to earth in rain or drifts down as fallout, lodges in soil, enters into the grass or corn or wheat grown there, and in time takes up its abode in the bones of a human being, there to remain until his death. Similarly, chemicals sprayed on croplands or forests or gardens lie long in soil, entering into living organisms, passing from one to another in a chain of poisoning and death. Or they pass mysteriously by underground streams until they emerge and, through the alchemy of air and sunlight, combine into new forms that kill vegetation, sicken cattle, and work unknown harm on those who drink from once-pure wells. As Albert Schweitzer has said, "Man can hardly recognize the devils of his own creation."

It took hundreds of millions of years to produce the life that now inhabits the earth — eons of time in which that developing and evolving and diversifying life reached a state of adjustment and balance with its surroundings. The environment, rigorously shaping and directing the life it supported, contained elements that were hostile as well as supporting. Certain rocks gave out dangerous radiation; even within the light of the sun, from which all life draws its energy, there were short-wave radiations with

power to injure. Given time — time not in years but in millennia — life adjusts, and a balance has been reached. For time is the essential ingredient; but in the modern world there is no time.

The rapidity of change and the speed with which new situations are created follow the impetuous and heedless pace of man rather than the deliberate pace of nature. Radiation is no longer merely the background radiation of rocks, the bombardment of cosmic rays, the ultraviolet of the sun that have existed before there was any life on earth; radiation is now the unnatural creation of man's tampering with the atom. The chemicals to which life is asked to make its adjustment are no longer merely the calcium and silica and copper and all the rest of the minerals washed out of the rocks and carried in rivers to the sea; they are the synthetic creations of man's inventive mind, brewed in his laboratories, and having no counterparts in nature.

To adjust to these chemicals would require time on the scale that is nature's; it would require not merely the years of a man's life but the life of generations. And even this, were it by some miracle possible, would be futile, for the new chemicals come from our laboratories in an endless stream; almost 500 annually find their way into actual use in the United States alone. The figure is staggering and its implications are not easily grasped — 500 new chemicals to which the bodies of men and animals are required somehow to adapt each year, chemicals totally outside the limits of biologic experience.

Among them are many that are used in man's war against nature. Since the mid-1940s, over 200 basic chemicals have been created for use in killing insects, weeds, rodents, and other organisms described in the modern vernacular as "pests"; and they are sold under several thousand different brand names.

These sprays, dusts, and aerosols are now applied almost universally to farms, gardens, forests, and homes — nonselective chemicals that have the power to kill every insect, the "good" and the "bad," to still the song of birds and the leaping of fish in the streams, to coat the leaves with a deadly film, and to linger on in soil — all this though the intended target may be only a few weeds or insects. Can anyone believe it is possible to lay down such a barrage of poisons on the surface of the earth without making it unfit for all life? They should not be called "insecticides" but "biocides."

The whole process of spraying seems caught up in an endless spiral. Since DDT was released for civilian use, a process of escalation has been going on in which ever more toxic materials must be found. This has happened because insects, in a triumphant vindication of Darwin's principle of the survival of the fittest, have evolved super races immune to the particular insecticide used, hence a deadlier one has always to be developed — and then a deadlier one than that. It has happened also because . . . destructive insects often undergo a "flareback," or resurgence, after spraying, in numbers greater than before. Thus the chemical war is never won, and all life is caught in its violent crossfire.

Along with the possibility of the extinction of mankind by nuclear war, the central problem of our age has therefore become the contamination of man's total environment with such substances of incredible potential for harm — substances that accumulate in the tissues of plants and animals and even penetrate the germ cells to shatter or alter the very material of heredity upon which the shape of the future depends.

Some would-be architects of our future look toward a time when it will be possible to alter the human germ plasm by design. But we may easily be doing so now by inadvertence, for many chemicals, like radiation, bring about gene mutations. It is ironic to think that man might determine his own future by something so seemingly trivial as the choice of an insect spray.

All this has been risked — for what? Future historians may well be amazed by our distorted sense of proportion. How could intelligent beings seek to control a few unwanted species by a method that contaminated the entire environment and brought the threat of disease and death even to their own kind? Yet this is precisely what we have done. We have done it, moreover, for reasons that collapse the moment we examine them. We are told that the enormous and expanding use of pesticides is necessary to maintain farm production. Yet is our real problem not one of *overproduction?* Our farms, despite measures to remove acreages from production and to pay farmers *not* to produce, have yielded such a staggering excess of crops that the American taxpayer in 1962 is paying out more than one billion dollars a year as the total carrying cost of the surplus-food storage program. And is the situation helped when one branch of the Agriculture Department tries to reduce production while another states, as it did in 1958, "It is believed generally that reduction of crop acreages under provisions of the Soil Bank will stimulate interest in use of chemicals to obtain maximum production on the land retained in crops."

All this is not to say there is no insect problem and no need of control. I am saying, rather, that control must be geared to realities, not to mythical situations, and that the methods employed must be such that they do not destroy us along with the insects.

The problem whose attempted solution has brought such a train of disaster in its wake is an accompaniment of our modern way of life. Long before the age of man, insects inhabited the earth — a group of extraordinarily varied and adaptable beings. Over the course of time since man's advent, a small percentage of the more than half a million species of insects have come into conflict with human welfare in two principal ways: as competitors for the food supply and as carriers of human disease.

Disease-carrying insects become important where human beings are crowded together, especially under conditions where sanitation is poor, as in time of natural disaster or war or in situations of extreme poverty and deprivation. Then control of some sort becomes necessary. It is a sobering fact, however . . . that the method of massive chemical control has had only limited success, and also threatens to worsen the very conditions it is intended to curb.

Under primitive agricultural conditions the farmer had few insect problems. These arose with the intensification of agriculture — the devotion of immense acreages to a single crop. Such a system set the stage for explosive increases in specific insect populations. Single-crop farming does not take advantage of the principles by which nature works; it is agriculture as an engineer might conceive it to be. Nature has introduced great variety into the landscape, but man has displayed a passion for simplifying it. Thus he undoes the built-in checks and balances by which nature holds the species within bounds. One important natural check is a limit on the amount of suitable habitat for each species. Obviously then, an insect that lives on wheat can build up its population to much higher levels on a farm devoted to wheat than on one in which wheat is intermingled with other crops to which the insect is not adapted.

The same thing happens in other situations. A generation or more ago, the towns of large areas of the United States lined their streets with the noble elm tree. Now the beauty they hopefully created is threatened with complete destruction as disease sweeps through the elms, carried by a beetle that would have only limited chance to build up large populations and to spread from tree to tree if the elms were only occasional trees in a richly diversified planting.

Another factor in the modern insect problem is one that must be viewed against a background of geologic and human history: the spreading of thousands of different

Erich Hartmann from Magnum

Rachel Carson, photographed in 1962

kinds of organisms from their native homes to invade new territories. This worldwide migration has been studied and graphically described by the British ecologist Charles Elton in his recent book *The Ecology of Invasions*. During the Cretaceous Period, some hundred million years ago, flooding seas cut many land bridges between continents, and living things found themselves confined in what Elton calls "colossal separate nature reserves." There, isolated from others of their kind, they developed many new species. When some of the land masses were joined again, about 15 million years ago, these species began to move out into new territories — a movement that is not only still in progress but is now receiving considerable assistance from man.

The importation of plants is the primary agent in the modern spread of species, for animals have almost invariably gone along with the plants, quarantine being a comparatively recent and not completely effective innovation. The United States Office of Plant Introduction alone has introduced almost 200,000 species and varieties of plants from all over the world. Nearly half of the 180 or so major insect enemies of plants in the United States are accidental imports from abroad, and most of them have come as hitchhikers on plants.

In new territory, out of reach of the restraining hand of the natural enemies that kept down its numbers in its native land, an invading plant or animal is able to become enormously abundant. Thus it is no accident that our most troublesome insects are introduced species.

These invasions, both the naturally occurring and those dependent on human assistance, are likely to continue indefinitely. Quarantine and massive chemical campaigns are only extremely expensive ways of buying time. We are faced, according to Dr. Elton, "with a life-and-death need not just to find new technological means of suppressing this plant or that animal"; instead we need the basic knowledge of animal populations and their relations to their surroundings that will "promote an even balance and damp down the explosive power of outbreaks and new invasions."

Much of the necessary knowledge is now available but we do not use it. We train ecologists in our universities and even employ them in our governmental agencies but we seldom take their advice. We allow the chemical death rain to fall as though there were no alternative, whereas, in fact, there are many, and our ingenuity could soon discover many more if given opportunity.

Have we fallen into a mesmerized state that makes us accept as inevitable that which is inferior or detrimental, as though having lost the will or the vision to demand that which is good? Such thinking, in the words of the ecologist Paul Shepard,

idealizes life with only its head out of water, inches above the limits of toleration of the corruption of its own environment . . . Why should we tolerate a diet of weak poisons, a home in insipid surroundings, a circle of acquaintances

who are not quite our enemies, the noise of motors with just enough relief to prevent insanity? Who would want to live in a world which is just not quite fatal?

Yet such a world is pressed upon us. The crusade to create a chemically sterile, insect-free world seems to have engendered a fanatic zeal on the part of many specialists and most of the so-called control agencies. On every hand there is evidence that those engaged in spraying operations exercise a ruthless power. "The regulatory entomologists . . . function as prosecutor, judge, and jury, tax assessor and collector and sheriff to enforce their own orders," said Connecticut entomologist Neely Turner. The most flagrant abuses go unchecked in both state and federal agencies.

It is not my contention that chemical insecticides must never be used. I do contend that we have put poisonous and biologically potent chemicals indiscriminately into the hands of persons largely or wholly ignorant of their potentials for harm. We have subjected enormous numbers of people to contact with these poisons, without their consent and often without their knowledge. If the Bill of Rights contains no guarantee that a citizen shall be secure against lethal poisons distributed either by private individuals or by public officials, it is surely only because our forefathers, despite their considerable wisdom and foresight, could conceive of no such problem.

I contend, furthermore, that we have allowed these chemicals to be used with little or no advance investigation of their effect on soil, water, wildlife, and man himself. Future generations are unlikely to condone our lack of prudent concern for the integrity of the natural world that supports all life.

There is still very limited awareness of the nature of the threat. This is an era of specialists, each of whom sees his own problem and is unaware of or intolerant of the larger frame into which it fits. It is also an era dominated by industry, in which the right to make a dollar at whatever cost is seldom challenged. When the public protests, confronted with some obvious evidence of damaging results of pesticide applications, it is fed little tranquilizing pills of half truth. We urgently need an end to these false assurances, to the sugar coating of unpalatable facts. It is the public that is being asked to assume the risks that the insect controllers calculate. The public must decide whether it wishes to continue on the present road, and it can do so only when in full possession of the facts. In the words of Jean Rostand, "The obligation to endure gives us the right to know." . . .

A TRULY EXTRAORDINARY variety of alternatives to the chemical control of insects is available. Some are already in use and have achieved brilliant success. Others are in the stage of laboratory testing. Still others are little more than ideas in the minds of imaginative scientists, waiting for the opportunity to put them to the test. All have this in common: they are *biological* solutions, based on understanding of the living organisms they seek to control, and of the whole fabric of life to which these organisms belong. Specialists representing various areas of the vast field of biology are contributing — entomologists, pathologists, geneticists, physiologists, biochemists, ecologists — all pouring their knowledge and their creative inspirations into the formation of a new science of biotic controls. . . .

Through all these new, imaginative, and creative approaches to the problem of sharing our earth with other creatures there runs a constant theme, the awareness that we are dealing with life — with living populations and all their pressures and counterpressures, their surges and recessions. Only by taking account of such life forces and by cautiously seeking to guide them into channels favorable to ourselves can we hope to achieve a reasonable accommodation between the insect hordes and ourselves.

The current vogue for poisons has failed utterly to take into account these most fundamental considerations. As crude a weapon as the cave man's club, the chemical barrage has been hurled against the fabric of life — a fabric on the one hand delicate and destructible, on the other miraculously tough and resilient, and capable of striking back in unexpected ways. These extraordinary capacities of life have been ignored by the practitioners of chemical control who have brought to their task no "high-minded orientation," no humility before the vast forces with which they tamper.

The "control of nature" is a phrase conceived in arrogance, born of the Neanderthal Age of biology and philosophy, when it was supposed that nature exists for the convenience of man. The concepts and practices of applied entomology for the most part date from that Stone Age of science. It is our alarming misfortune that so primitive a science has armed itself with the most modern and terrible weapons, and that in turning them against the insects it has also turned them against the earth.

◆

The most unhappy thing about conservation is that it is never permanent. Save a priceless woodland or an irreplaceable mountain today, and tomorrow it is threatened from another quarter. Man, our most ingenious predator, sometimes seems determined to destroy the precious treasures of his own environment.
HAL BORLAND, *New York Times Book Review,* February 1964

19.

Senate Report on Urban Mass Transportation

One of the greatest difficulties facing millions of Americans in the 1960s was simply getting to work in the morning and getting home again in the evening. A number of factors had produced the problem, which reached staggering proportions as the decade wore on: the increasing number of privately owned automobiles, with resulting traffic jams; obsolescence of railroad and bus mass transportation; and the ever growing cost of obtaining right-of-ways and of building new facilities. It was normal for a man or woman to spend two hours a day in commuting, or approximately 7 percent of the total hours in a week; and higher figures were not uncommon. It almost seemed that all of the time gained by shorter working hours was being spent in getting to and from work. One solution was to do away with the central city altogether, and to disperse business and industry about the countryside. But this meant the end of the city as men had known it for more than 2,000 years, and most people were unwilling even to imagine such a totally new way of life. The Senate Committee on Banking and Currency held hearings in the early 1960s and on August 7, 1962, reported out a bill that summed up the problem as it then appeared and suggested a number of remedies. The majority report that accompanied the bill is reprinted here in part.

Source: 87 Congress, 2 Session, Senate Report No. 1852, pp. 3-11.

THE COMMITTEE BELIEVES that there is no doubt about the critical need for action on the urban transportation problems in our nation's cities. Every citizen who commutes to work is aware of the serious impact of inadequate and overcrowded existing facilities and the necessity for immediate action to improve and expand transportation systems.

The problem derives both from the rapidly increasing concentration of people and vehicles in the metropolitan and other urban areas of the nation and from a rapid decline and deterioration of mass-transportation services and facilities in those areas. The decline in mass-transportation service has coincided with the decline in riders which has taken place primarily during off-peak hours. This decline in passengers and the corresponding reduction in revenues, coupled with rising costs, has imperiled the ability of mass-transport carriers to continue providing adequate rush-hour service.

The loss, deterioration, and curtailment of such service has many profound adverse effects on the community. It deprives many people of an essential service, either because they are too young, too old, or too poor to drive, and, in many cases, because many families have two members who must work but have only one car. It also increases street and highway congestion, accentuates downtown parking problems, and lowers the values of residential property, to mention just some of the ill effects on the community.

Efficient and economical mass-transportation service is essential to the people who live in and around our urban centers. Unfortunately, it is not now available in many places, and the present conditions will grow worse in the years ahead unless prompt action is taken. The movement of families away from concentrated built-up areas into scattered suburban patterns and the shift to the use of private automobiles for commuting to and from work has taken many passengers away from public transportation.

In the last decade the number of private motor vehicles on the streets has been increasing faster than the population. The availability and convenience of this mode of transportation has put it into strong competition with mass transportation. Moreover, by filling up available street space, the increased automobile traffic has prevented the efficient and rapid operation of surface mass-transit vehicles which use the same rights-of-way.

The rate of the urbanization process in the United States in recent decades has been spectacular: 70 percent of the nation's population now live in urban areas. And transportation problems in urban areas have been complicated, not only by the tremendous population increase but by the changing pattern of urban growth. Economic prosperity, coupled with improved mobility, has enabled an increasing number of American families to move to suburban areas. In the last decade (1950-60), metropolitan-area growth constituted 85 percent of the total national population increase, but more than three-fourths of this growth in the metropolitan areas took place in the suburbs outside the central cities. This residential outflow from the central cities has been accompanied by extensive commercial and industrial decentralization, and, as a result, urban travel patterns have changed materially from those of former years.

These changes, in turn, have greatly affected modes of travel. Since World War II, automobile usage has been increasing while mass transit patronage has been declining steadily. From 1956 to 1960, the number of revenue passengers carried by buses and streetcars declined by about 22 percent. Today, in most urban areas, over 85 percent of the total daily travel is by automobile. On the other hand, at peak hours, 40 to 90 percent of the travel to the central business district in the larger cities continues to be made by public mass transportation.

By 1980 the total population of the United States is expected to reach 250 million, and it is anticipated that 3 out of every 4 persons will be living within urban areas. Occupying only about 2 percent of the nation's land area, the urban areas will contain not only a great concentration of the total population but of commerce and industry as well. Over half of the total population in 1980 — some 140 million people — are expected to be living in forty great urban complexes, each having a minimum population of 1 million. By the year 2000, less than forty years hence, the nation's total population may well reach 350 million. If present trends continue, 85 percent of these people will live in urban areas, and more than fifty urban complexes will have attained the million population mark.

It is clear from these present and expected future trends that a balanced urban transportation system, utilizing both highways and transit, is essential to help shape as well as serve future urban growth and to achieve optimum efficiency, economy, and effectiveness in meeting the transportation needs of the urban area.

One of the factors contributing to the deterioration of mass-transit service in many areas is the inability of the system to maintain an adequate level of capital investment in new facilities and equipment. Despite the tremendous growth of our cities and the future outlook for an even more intensive concentration of our people in and around urban areas, capital investment in urban transportation systems has declined rather than increased.

Many private bus, transit, and rail carriers are finding it extremely difficult to meet operating expenses of existing facilities and almost prohibitive to finance new capital improvements to meet expansion requirements. Caught in the squeeze of rising capital and operating costs, and declining patronage, many private bus and rail carriers must resort to raising fares, trimming service, and deferring maintenance, which simply drives away more riders and accelerates the downward spiral.

According to the American Transit Association, these declines in riding, with their resulting serious financial impact, have caused the sale or abandonment of many transit companies in recent years. The committee was informed that since the beginning of 1954, a total of 211 transit companies have been sold and an additional 152 have been abandoned. . . .

One regrettable consequence of this trend is that many communities have abandoned mass transit rights-of-way which are now urgently needed by an expanded population, but which can be redeemed or replaced only at heavy cost. Another result of the abandonment of transportation systems has been an increasingly critical congestion on all the main arteries of travel. Though federal aid programs have been keeping pace relatively well with the need for developing the interstate, primary, and secondary systems of highways, the cities and larger metropolitan areas have not been able to meet their increasing problems of congestion.

Total capital requirements for mass transportation in the next decade are estimated at $9.8 billion by the Institute of Public Administration in its report to the secretary of commerce and the housing administrator. The estimates are rough approximations and probably on the conservative side, but they are based on intensive study of published information and on-the-spot investigations in twenty-six urban regions. The $9.8 billion estimate is made up of the following: $2.8 billion for presently planned new systems; $1.7 billion for extensions of existing systems; $4.3 billion for rehabilitation and replacement; and $1 billion for new projects now being considered for initiation in the next decade. For all these purposes, the costs of rights-of-way and structures are estimated at $6.4 billion and rolling stock at $3.4 billion.

A large part of this total capital cost can be expected to be met from the fare box. However, a certain margin must be provided by public grants, without which much of the investment requirement will undoubtedly go unmet.

The cost of providing transportation is one which cannot be evaded. The committee believes that this bill will help solve this problem in the most economical and effective way. Traffic congestion exacts a heavy toll from the public. Testimony before the subcommittee pointed up the tremendous expenditures for roads which would be necessary if mass-transit service could not be maintained. For example, the American Municipal Association has estimated that if the five cities of New York, Chicago, Boston, Philadelphia, and Cleveland were to lose just their rail-commuter service, it would cost $31 billion, including financing costs, to build the highways necessary to serve a comparable number of people.

The heavy cost of acquiring new rights-of-way through congested city areas may suggest the abandonment of all efforts to provide adequate mass-transportation facilities for the central business districts of our cities in favor of complete reliance on business development in the suburbs. However, any objective appraisal of the needs of our cities will show this to be a wholly unrealistic and impractical approach.

Of course, new food stores, drugstores, and other residential service trades will continue to be provided near new housing developments in the suburbs. Also, many large manufacturing plants and some wholesale firms will continue to seek suburban locations free from the congestion of the central city and with land adequate to meet modern industrial planning standards.

On the other hand, the core of the city can satisfy requirements that cannot be met in any other location within the metropolitan area. In finance, real estate, and in the main and regional offices of large firms, there is a need for face-to-face contact through a whole series of business relationships. Many other businesses are dependent upon clustering in a central location to obtain the same advantage. Others must be reasonably accessible to the hotels which serve out-of-town customers and business relations. Still others, like printing and publishing, must have access to the complementary trades which serve them. Finally, the businesses occupying the great office centers and certain other centrally located industries are dependent upon a central location to bring together a sufficiently large work force. This is particularly true of those businesses and industries dependent upon white-collar female employment.

The central area of the city is the necessary locale for a large variety of small businesses, particularly manufacturers and wholesalers. These businesses must place a premium upon custom-designed products and rapid service. They need to be close to the common suppliers which can provide raw or semiprocessed materials for a large number of these small businesses. They need ready access to their customers and adequate space at reasonable rates. Typically, many small businesses can survive and prosper only in the central area of the large cities. The core area serves, in this respect, as a protector and incubator of small businesses lacking resources to operate, assemble a staff, and obtain the necessary materials and supplies in more peripheral locations.

The central business district and its environs provide a place for supplying goods and services of unusual or unique character such as the museums, the concert halls, and the opera stages which can be successful only if they are accessible to nearly all of the people who live in the metropolis. These functions cannot be subdivided or duplicated in the suburban shopping district. This is no less true of the private art galleries, of the dealers in objets d'art, of the vast array of top-quality restaurants, and, on the other hand, of some stores serving the mass market of low-cost goods for the lower middle class. The same argument applies in lesser measure to our expanding urban universities and hospitals.

There is a new and emerging concept of the downtown which sees the basic purpose of downtown as providing those unusual and unique services and goods which cannot be economically supported in suburban locations. It should mean for all of the people in the area access to a more diverse and livelier life through improved employment opportunities and shopping facilities, through the cultural institutions of the area, and through numerous opportunities for amusement and entertainment. Many of these functions and opportunities will not be carried out and will not be available unless they can survive in the core of the city.

The bulk of the population increase is occurring and will continue to occur in the outlying portions of the metropolitan areas. The population of the suburbs and the resulting commuter traffic are increasing much too fast for the central cities to cope with anything but a small fraction of it.

With proper planning, mass transit as well as highways can be as great a boon to the suburbs as to the central city. It can be a vital tool to help curb suburban sprawl, and help provide better patterns of suburban development.

An illustration of how this might work can be seen in the proposed year 2000 plan for the Washington metropolitan area. In an effort to curb the present haphazard sprawl that characterizes current development at the fringe of this metropolitan area, city planners have recommended a "corridor" plan, with future development radiating out from the present fringe in five or six corridors, separated by wedges of open space. More compact and economical development in the corridors would be encouraged by placing high-speed rapid transit and highways down the centers of the corridors, like spokes on a wheel, tying the suburbs to the central city. With this kind of development, suburban officials could provide necessary school, utility, police, and other community services at considerably less cost than would be possible under a pattern of widely scattered, low-density development. Also, industry locating out in the corridors would be assured of easy access to a labor market throughout the metropolitan area.

It would be a mistake to conclude that mass transportation is a problem of concern only to larger areas. The larger cities usually command more national publicity. However, a recent editorial from the Fairmont, W.Va., *Times* commenting on a fare increase by the local bus company noted that —

> . . . more than 100 bus companies have been forced out of business in West Virginia within a little more than ten years. Only 28 are still in operation, counting both city and suburban lines. Between 1955 and 1959 alone, the number of passengers hauled on West Virginia local lines dropped 35.3 percent.

What has happened in West Virginia has been happening throughout the country. The American Transit Association estimates that there are about sixty cities of 25,000 population or more which have no public transportation service at all. Many of our smaller cities and towns are experiencing rapid rates of growth, and they are begin-

ning to taste the first bitter fruits of traffic congestion. Testimony before the committee showed that growing rapidly or not, these cities and towns all have a sizable portion of their residents who have been seriously inconvenienced by the loss of public transportation service.

The proposed federal program is designed to help assist in the solution of mass transportation problems wherever they occur, in large cities or in small ones, and the committee believes the legislation can be extremely beneficial to both, but at the same time the committee recognizes that areas having the most critical needs, considering density of population and other factors, should have priority. . . .

The improvement of passenger transportation in urban areas is one of the major problems facing the country today. The need for federal assistance has long been recognized. Under the present $41-billion federal-aid highway program, approximately $20 billion will be spent for the Interstate System in urban areas. In addition, on the federal-aid primary and secondary systems, the expenditures for streets and expressways in urban areas runs into hundreds of millions of dollars every year. For example, Congress has authorized for this program $925 million for each of the fiscal years 1962 and 1963, 25 percent of which is earmarked specifically for urban portions.

When state or local governments begin searching for an answer to traffic problems, they are faced with the overwhelmingly powerful economic fact that in many cases they need put up only 10 percent of the cost for a highway solution, whereas they must bear 100 percent of the cost of a transit solution, whether it involves improving a rail line, buying a new fleet of buses, providing fringe-area parking, or establishing a downtown distributor system. Obviously this situation is not conducive to the establishment of a balanced urban-transportation system, utilizing transit where it is logically needed and using a highway where it is logically needed.

There are, of course, a number of other reasons why this problem involves a considerable measure of federal responsibility.

For one thing, the problem of providing adequate urban mass-transportation service has long ago spilled over the boundaries of many local political jurisdictions. In fact, it has spilled over a good many state boundaries. Some 53 of our 200-odd metropolitan areas either border on or cross over state lines. The financial difficulties of the state and local governments are even more acute than the jurisdictional difficulties. Most of our cities are faced with rising service costs and declining tax bases.

There is a very great burden to the national economy through congestion and inadequate urban transportation. It has been estimated that traffic jams cost the nation about $5 billion a year in time and wages lost, extra fuel consumption, faster vehicle depreciation, lower downtown commercial sales, and lower taxes, and so on. It is also clear that traffic congestion discourages private investment in central cities, and thereby makes the task of urban renewal much more difficult and costly.

The former mayor of Philadelphia, for example, has testified that Philadelphia businessmen would be willing to invest $500 million to $600 million over their present plans if they had some assurance that something would be done about traffic congestion. Officials of Downtown Progress, a nonprofit organization in Washington, D.C., which is attempting to revitalize the downtown area, have frequently stated that the key to their efforts is the construction of an adequate rapid transit system.

Traffic congestion also adds to the cost of moving interstate freight through metropolitan areas, because trucks have to compete for clogged street space with the automobile. Trucks are faced with incessant stops and starts, which are not only time consuming but extremely expensive.

Public safety is another factor to be considered when reviewing problems of traffic congestion. In some cities, traffic, during peak hours, has become so dense that it is extremely costly to provide a police force sufficiently large to unsnarl traffic congestion and to direct an efficient ingress and egress on urban arteries. Property damage caused by motor-vehicle accidents has reached such proportions that insurance companies are continually forced to increase rates in order to have adequate reserves to cover the cost of the damage.

The fumes from motor vehicles are contributing to smog problems which have become so acute in some areas as to present a real danger to the health of urban dwellers, as well as to those using the urban place for work, play, and worship. In fact, the committee was told that, in approximately 90 percent of the urban areas in the United States, there are air-pollution problems that need attention and that the automobile is a major contributor to air pollution in every urban area.

And, last but not least, an incalculable number of man-hours are lost by our people — from family life, from work, from recreation — because of having to commute through traffic congestion.

The President recently summarized the reasons for this program:

To conserve and enhance values in existing urban areas is essential. But at least as important are steps to promote economic efficiency and livability in areas of future development. In less than twenty years we can expect well over half of our expanded population to be living in forty great urban complexes. Many smaller places will also experience phenomenal growth. The ways that people and goods can be moved in these areas will have a major influence on their structure, on the efficiency of their economy, and on the availability for social and cultural opportunities they can offer their citizens. Our national welfare, therefore, requires the provision of good urban transportation, with the properly balanced use of private vehicles and modern mass transport to help shape as well as serve urban growth.

It is for these reasons that the leadership and financial assistance of the federal government is needed now to encourage solutions that are forward looking and generally applicable to urban areas regardless of size.

20.

CLEMENT GREENBERG: Action Painting — A Reprise

American painting in the 1950s and 1960s was strong and influential — so much so that it was able, as the critic Clement Greenberg observed in the article part of which is reprinted here, to "challenge the leadership of Paris." But, Greenberg said, criticism of American art — writing about it both by Americans and by others — lagged far behind and seemed largely irrelevant. He attempted to explain this and at the same time discussed the "Action Painting" that Harold Rosenberg had named and described several years before. The article by Greenberg, one of the best-known American art critics, appeared late in 1962.

Source: *Encounter*, December 1962: "How Art Writing Earns Its Bad Name."

TWENTY YEARS AGO who expected that the United States would shortly produce painters strong enough, and independent enough, to challenge the leadership of Paris? The more knowing you were about art, the more surprised you were when it happened. For a long while after it had actually happened, you refused to believe it. You were convinced only when confirmation arrived from, of all places, Paris itself.

Jackson Pollock had a show there in 1952, and it made such an impression that, though hardly a picture was sold, his art began to be taken more seriously in certain quarters of the Paris art world than anywhere else, including New York. And along with Pollock, the new American abstract painting in general began to be taken more seriously in the same quarters. As it then seemed to me, it was over a year before news of this effectively reached New York. From that time the success in America itself of the new American painting dates, at least as far as collectors and museums and art journalism are concerned.

But it is as though a fatality dogged the success: a fatality of misinterpretation that was also a fatality of nonsense. I call it a fatality — though it might be more proper to call it a comedy — because the misinterpretation and the nonsense have come, not from those who professed to reject the new American painting but from friends or supposed friends. It was as though the critics of modern art set out to justify everything that Philistines have said about them.

Late in the same year as Pollock's Paris show, an article by Harold Rosenberg appeared in *Art News* in New York under the title "Action Painting." Though it named no names, it was taken as a first attempt to throw real light, friendly or hostile, on the intentions of the new American painters. Transposing some notions from Heidegger's and Sartre's Existentialism, Mr. Rosenberg explained that these painters were not really seeking to arrive at art, but rather to discover their own identities through the unpremeditated and more or less uncontrolled acts by which they put paint to canvas. For them the picture surface was the "arena" of a struggle waged outside the limits of art in which "existence" strove as it were to become "essence." "Essence," or the identity of the painter, could be recognized by the painter himself only in the very act of painting, not in the result, it being presumed, apparently, that acts in themselves identified you as results or consequences could not. The painted "picture," having been painted, became an indifferent matter. Everything lay in the doing, nothing in the making. The covered canvas was left over as the unmeaning aftermath of an "event," the solipsistic record of purely personal "gestures," and belonging therefore to the same reality that breathing and thumbprints, love affairs and wars belonged to, but not works of art.

Mr. Rosenberg did not explain why the painted leftovers of "action," which were devoid of anything but autobiographical meaning in the eyes of their own makers, should be exhibited by them and looked at and even acquired by others. Or how the painted surface, as the by-product of acts of sheer self-expression ungoverned by the norms of any discipline, could convey anything but clinical data, given that such data is all that raw, unmediated personality has ever been able to convey in the past. Nor did Mr. Rosenberg explain why any one by-product of "action painting" should be valued more than any other. Since these things, and the action that "caused" them,

belonged to no discernible branch of social activity, how could they be differentiated qualitatively? There were still other things that Mr. Rosenberg's eloquence left unexplained, but they need not detain us here.

When his essay first appeared it was read by many people as an exposure of the new abstract painting. To those who could not make head or tail of Pollock's middle-period paintings, it offered a plausible explanation: if these things were not really art you had every right to be baffled by them. A corollary was that those who claimed to be able to tell the difference between good and bad "dripped" Pollocks (and Mr. Rosenberg, patently, did not so claim) were deluding themselves and others. Abstract art was under renewed attack in the early 1950s, and "Action Painting" was greeted — or resented — as a veiled blow at "extremist" art. As that, it was soon on its way to being forgotten, as movingly written as it was.

That it finally did not get forgotten was mainly the fault of a young English art critic named Lawrence Alloway. Almost two years after its original appearance it was Mr. Alloway who rescued Mr. Rosenberg's article and set its ideas and terms in effective circulation. Not that Mr. Alloway was an opponent of "extremist" art. On the contrary, he was an ardent champion of it, and especially of the new American kind — being, for that matter, an equally ardent, practically a sectarian champion of most things American. Mr. Rosenberg's notions seem to have struck him as offering the right kind of subversive and futurist explanation of the subversive and futurist and very American species of art that Pollock seemed to represent. The very flavor of the words, "action painting," had something racy and demotic about it — like the name of a new dance step — that befitted an altogether new and very American way of making art — a way that was all the newer, all the more avant-garde, and all the more American because the art itself was not really art, or at least not art in the way the stuffy past had known it. At the same time, it all sounded, in Mr. Rosenberg's rhetoric, so dramatically modernistic and opaquely profound — like Rimbaud and Sartre and Camus rolled into one — and avant-garde art critics have a special weakness for the opaquely profound.

Not only did Mr. Alloway take Mr. Rosenberg's amphigoric piece of art interpretation as a manifesto in favor of its subject (and he was but the first among many to do so); he also took it (again, as but the first among many) as a legitimate statement of the aims of "Pollock & Co." as professed by Pollock himself. There was just enough truth in this to make it ironic. Two or three painters close to Pollock in the early 1950s, but who painted in a quite different direction, did rant about "the act," and did say that what mattered was not to have your art appreciated and recognized but simply to perform the "act" of making *good* art; what happened after that was of small consequence; for all he cared, one of them is reported as saying, his finished pictures could be burned. The artists in question (every one of whom has since become renowned, and rightly so) were not making much headway in the world at that time, and it would not be unjust to characterize their talk in this vein as sour grapes. How much of it Mr. Rosenberg heard, I cannot say.

Pollock told me, very sheepishly, that some of the main ideas of the "Action Painting" article came from a half-drunken conversation he had had with Mr. Rosenberg on a trip between East Hampton and New York (if so, Pollock had been parroting in that conversation things he heard from his friends). Mr. Rosenberg has denied this in print, asserting that his *"literary discoveries* [were] outside his [Pollock's] range" (Mr. Rosenberg's italics). Be all this as it may, Pollock and his friends took Mr. Ro-

senberg's "literary discoveries," when they were made public, for a malicious representation of both their work and their ideas. After all, it was *good* art, and no other kind, that they were interested in. (If Pollock was the one least upset, though seeming the one most directly aimed at, it was because he could not help feeling that "Action Painting" was a big spoof; and he felt that all the more because he thought he was partly responsible for it.)

Mr. Alloway could not have been expected to know all this seven or eight years ago in London. But he still might have waited for some corroboration before proceeding on the assumption that "Action Painting" was a faithful statement of the intentions of the new American painters. As it was, he propagated Mr. Rosenberg's notions with such conviction and verve, and with such confidence, that "action painting" became current overnight in England as the authorized brand name and certified label of the new abstract painting from America. That it connoted a freakish, new-fangled way of applying paint to canvas made it seem all the more appropriate to what struck most people as being a freakish, new-fangled kind of art — or non-art. And though English art lovers joined Mr. Alloway (or were led by him into doing so) in reading Mr. Rosenberg's piece as sympathetic to its subject, they found a reassurance in it much like that which Americans had found on its first appearance. . . .

It was from England and nowhere else that Mr. Rosenberg's notions, with the prestige conferred upon them by Mr. Alloway, were exported to the Continent and back to the United States. That prestige seemed to grow with the prestige of the new American painting itself. What made it wonderful was that nobody stopped to ask what "action painting" could possibly be if it was not supposed to be art. Avant-garde art critics everywhere invoked and quoted Mr. Rosenberg's rhetoric — and not only with regard to American painting — and then went on to talk about art and artistic qualities to show that they had not grasped a single implication of his ideas. For Mr. Alloway as for everybody else who "dug" "action painting," there were superior and inferior exponents of it, superior and inferior examples of it. Just as if it had not been Mr. Rosenberg's point throughout his essay to exclude the possibility of such discriminations.

Yet this muddle attested precisely to the fact that the new American painting was making its way in the world on the basis of qualities more substantial than those allowed it by "Action Painting." It was making its way as art, unmistakable art, not as a super avant-garde stunt or as an interesting aberration. Its very real success, worldly and other, no less than the concurrent, if ironical, success of his article — or rather the muddled reading of his article — may be what now leads Mr. Rosenberg to talk as if it had been meant from the first as a wholly sympathetic treatment of the new American painting. He has also let it be known recently that it was mainly "de Kooning & Co." he had in mind, not Pollock. This last will confound, whether they admit it or not, all those art writers who took it for granted all along that Mr. Rosenberg had written about and for Pollock, and for whom de Kooning was, or is, too European (or "civilized") to qualify as an "action painter." But these writers deserve to be confounded for not having been confounded by Mr. Rosenberg's article in the first place.

Sense, the tortoise, usually overtakes nonsense, the hare, even in this not-quite-perfect world. It begins to dawn on art lovers here and there that they have not yet really seen any kind of painting that conforms to Mr. Rosenberg's description. Art turns out to be almost inescapable by now for any one dealing with a flat surface, even if it is mostly bad art. The works of the "gestural" painters, of the "action" athletes, down-

town in New York and elsewhere (I'm not referring to the artists originally aimed at by Mr. Rosenberg) reveal themselves as mannered with mannerisms borrowed from de Kooning for the most part, but also from Kline, Gorky, Pollock, and Still, and more lately from Monet too, and maybe even from Magnasco; and their main trouble is disclosed to be a want, not an excess, of spontaneity.

It is discovered that flung paint can be as thoroughly controlled and as carefully manipulated as patted or stroked paint. And now that the accidental has been completely assimilated to the tradition of the painterly, even the donkey's tails and the painting chimpanzees and parrots expose themselves as abjectly derivative — and we no longer have to know what artists their owners or keepers admire. Like the wildest painter on 10th Street or in the 14th *arrondissement,* they can't get out of their systems, moreover, the habit of being guided by the shape of the support.

Pollock's art turns out at the same time to rely far less on the accidental than had been thought. It turns out, in fact, to have an almost completely Cubist basis, and to be the fruit of much learning and much discipline. The same is true, perhaps excessively true, of de Kooning's art. It was the first look of the new American painting, and only the first look, that led Harold Rosenberg to take it for a mystification beyond art on to which he could safely graft another mystification. (That his "literary discoveries" could seem to anyone to throw light on anything is explained only by the supposition that the blind actually prefer being led by the blind. . . .)

What is there about art writing that encourages this sort of thing? What is there in the people who read art writing that makes them tolerate it? Why is art writing the only kind of writing in English that has lent itself to Existentialist and Phenomenological rhetoric? What is there about modern art itself that leads minds like Herbert Read's and Harold Rosenberg's astray? The answer is not one, I think, that reflects on modern art. It has to do with the speed with which modernist painting and sculpture have outrun the common categories of art criticism, invalidating them not only for the present or future but also for the past. (This has not been a revolution; it has been a clarification.) The widening of the gap between art and discourse solicits, as such widenings will, perversions and abortions of discourse: pseudo-description, pseudo-narrative, pseudo-exposition, pseudo-history, pseudo-philosophy, pseudo-psychology, and — worst of all — pseudo-poetry (which last represents the abortion, not of discourse but of intuition and imagination). The pity, however, is not in the words; it is in the fact that art itself has been made to look silly.

21.

Principles of the John Birch Society

The John Birch Society rose to national prominence in the late 1950s as one of the leading manifestations of the revival at that time of conservative political thought. Founded by a Boston businessman, Robert H. W. Welch, Jr., the organization was named after a U.S. intelligence officer who was killed by Chinese Communists shortly after World War II. During its first years the society was most influential in southern California, but it had chapters in many states and, in later years, greatly increased its membership. The movement's basic manual was The Blue Book of the John Birch Society, *supplemented by a monthly magazine,* American Opinion. *Its general position was that communism is a gigantic conspiracy to enslave mankind and that its main threat to the United States is not from Soviet military power but from internal subversion. The following statement of principles of the society was printed in the* Congressional Record *on June 12, 1962, at the request of Congressman John H. Rousselot, Republican of California.*

Source: *Record, App.,* 87 Cong., 2 Sess., pp. A4292-A4293.

I

WITH VERY FEW EXCEPTIONS the members of the John Birch Society are deeply religious people. A member's particular faith is entirely his own affair. Our hope is to make better Catholics, better Protestants, better Jews — or better Moslems — out of those who belong to the society. Our never-ending concern is with morality, integrity, and purpose. Regardless of the differences between us in creed and dogma, we all believe that man is endowed by a Divine Creator with an innate desire and conscious purpose to improve both his world and himself. We believe that the direction which constitutes improvement is clearly visible and identifiable throughout man's known history, and that this God-given upward reach in the heart of man is a composite conscience to which we all must listen.

II

WE BELIEVE THAT the Communists seek to drive their slaves and themselves along exactly the opposite and downward direction, to the Satanic debasement of both man and his universe. We believe that communism is as utterly incompatible with all religion as it is contemptuous of all morality and destructive of all freedom. It is intrinsically evil. It must be opposed, therefore, with equal firmness, on religious grounds, moral grounds, and political grounds. We believe that the continued coexistence of communism and a Christian-style civilization on one planet is impossible. The struggle between them must end with one completely triumphant and the other completely destroyed. We intend to do our part, therefore, to halt, weaken, rout, and eventually to bury, the whole international Communist conspiracy.

III

WE BELIEVE THAT means are as important as ends in any civilized society. Of all the falsehoods that have been so widely and deliberately circulated about us, none is so viciously untrue as the charge that we are willing to condone foul means for the sake of achieving praiseworthy ends. We think that communism as a way of life, for instance, is completely wrong; but our ultimate quarrel with the Communists is that they insist on imposing that way of life on the rest of us by murder, treason, and cruelty rather than by persuasion. Even if our own use of force ever becomes necessary and morally acceptable because it is in self-defense, we must never lose sight of the legal, traditional, and humanitarian considerations of a compassionate civilization. The

Communists recognize no such compulsions, but this very ingredient of amoral brutishness will help to destroy them in the end.

IV

WE BELIEVE IN PATRIOTISM. Most of us will gladly concede that a parliament of nations, designed for the purpose of increasing the freedom and ease with which individuals, ideals, and goods might cross national boundaries, would be desirable. And we hope that in some future decade we may help to bring about such a step of progress in man's pursuit of peace, prosperity, and happiness. But we feel that the present United Nations was designed by its founders for the exactly opposite purpose of increasing the rigidity of government controls over the lives and affairs of individual men. We believe it has become, as it was intended to become, a major instrumentality for the establishment of a one-world Communist tyranny over the population of the whole earth. One of our most immediate objectives, therefore, is to get the United States out of the United Nations, and the United Nations out of the United States. We seek thus to save our own country from the gradual and piecemeal surrender of its sovereignty to this Communist-controlled supergovernment, and to stop giving our support to the steady enslavement of other people through the machinations of this Communist agency.

V

WE BELIEVE THAT a constitutional republic, such as our founding fathers gave us, is probably the best of all forms of government. We believe that a democracy, which they tried hard to obviate, and into which the liberals have been trying for fifty years to convert our republic, is one of the worst of all forms of government. We call attention to the fact that up to 1928 the U.S. Army Training Manual still gave our men in uniform the following quite accurate definition, which would have been thoroughly approved by the Constitutional Convention that established our republic. "Democracy: A government of the masses. Authority derived through mass meeting or any form of direct expression results in mobocracy. Attitude toward property is communistic — negating property rights. Attitude towards law is that the will of the majority shall regulate, whether it be based upon deliberation or governed by passion, prejudice, and impulse, without restraint or regard to consequences. Results in demagogism, license, agitation, discontent, anarchy." It is because all history proves this to be true that we repeat so emphatically: "This is a republic, not a democracy; let's keep it that way."

VI

WE ARE OPPOSED to collectivism as a political and economic system, even when it does not have the police-state features of communism. We are opposed to it no matter whether the collectivism be called socialism or the welfare state or the New Deal or the Fair Deal or the New Frontier, or advanced under some other semantic disguise. And we are opposed to it no matter what may be the framework or form of government under which collectivism is imposed. We believe that increasing the size of government, increasing the centralization of government, and increasing the functions of government all act as brakes on material progress and as destroyers of personal freedom.

VII

WE BELIEVE THAT even where the size and functions of government are properly limited, as much of the power and duties of government as possible should be retained in the hands of as small governmental units as possible, as close to the people served by such units as possible. For the tendencies of any governing body to waste, expansion, and despotism all increase with the distance of that body from the people governed; the more closely any governing body can be kept under observation by those who pay its bills and provide its delegated authority, the more honestly responsible it will be. And the diffusion of governmental power and functions is one of the greatest safeguards against tyranny man has yet devised. For this reason it is extremely important in our case to keep our township, city, county and state governments from being bribed and coerced into coming under one direct chain of control from Washington.

VIII

WE BELIEVE THAT for any people eternal vigilance is the price of liberty far more as against the insidious encroachment of internal tyranny than against the danger of subjugation from the outside or from the prospect of any sharp and decisive revolution. In a republic we must constantly seek to elect and to keep in power a government we can trust, manned by people we can trust, maintaining a currency we can trust, and working for purposes we can trust (none of which we have today). We think it is even more important for the government to obey the laws than for the people to do so. But for thirty years we have had a steady stream of governments which increasingly have regarded our laws and even our Constitution as mere pieces of paper, which should not be allowed to stand in the way of what they, in their omniscient benevolence, considered to be "for the greatest good of the greatest number." (Or in their power-seeking plans pretended so to believe.) We want a restoration of a "government of laws, and not of men" in this country; and if a few impeachments are necessary to bring that about, then we are all for the impeachments.

IX

We believe that in a general way history repeats itself. For any combination of causes, similar to an earlier combination of causes, will lead as a rule to a combination of results somewhat similar to the one produced before. And history is simply a series of causes which produced results, and so on around cycles as clearly discernible as any of the dozens that take place elsewhere in the physical and biological sciences. But we believe that the most important history consists not of the repetitions but of the changes in these recurring links in the series. For the changes mark the extent to which man has either been able to improve himself and his environment, or has allowed both to deteriorate, since the last time around. We think that this true history is largely determined by ambitious individuals (both good and evil) and by small minorities who really know what they want. And in the John Birch Society our sense of gratitude and responsibility (to God and to the noble men of the past), for what we have inherited makes us determined to exert our influence, labor, and sacrifice for changes which we think will constitute improvement.

Ernest Reshovsky — Pix from Publix

Robert Welch, retired Boston candymaker and founder of the John Birch Society

X

In summary, we are striving, by all honorable means at our disposal and to the limits of our energies and abilities, to bring about less government, more responsibility, and a better world. Because the Communists seek, always and everywhere, to bring about more government, less individual responsibility, and a completely amoral world, we would have to oppose them at every turn, even on the philosophical level. Because they are seeking through a gigantically organized conspiracy to destroy all opposition, we must fight them even more aggressively on the plane of action. But our struggle with the Communists, while the most urgent and important task before us today, is basically only incidental to our more important long-range and constructive purposes. For that very reason we are likely to be more effective against the Communists than if we were merely an ad hoc group seeking to expose and destroy so huge and powerful a gang of criminals. In organization, dedication, and purpose we offer a new form of opposition to the Communists which they have not faced in any other country. We have tried to raise a standard to which the wise and the honest can repair. We welcome all honorable allies in this present unceasing war. And we hope that once they and we and millions like us have won a decisive victory at last, many of these same allies will join us in our long look toward the future.

22.

ARCHIBALD MACLEISH AND MARK VAN DOREN: Dialogue on the American Dream

Archibald MacLeish and Mark Van Doren were old friends with many rich conversations behind them when, during the summer of 1962, they engaged in a series of discussions at MacLeish's home in Massachusetts — like Van Doren's in Connecticut, an abandoned but now partly resuscitated farm — for the benefit of television cameras that followed them wherever they went and for microphones that picked up everything they said. They talked about many things, wending this way and that through their ideas and impressions and experiences, for more than eight hours all told. The television show that was the result ran for one hour and was a considerable success. The show's producer, Warren V. Bush, feeling that much of value had been left out, asked the two poets for permission to publish the transcript of their talks, which, after minimum editing on their part, was done in 1964. In the part of the conversation reprinted here MacLeish and Van Doren discuss a subject to which they returned over and over again in the course of their long conversation: the American dream, or idea, or ideal, and what has become of it in these latter days.

Source: *The Dialogues of Archibald MacLeish and Mark Van Doren,* Warren V. Bush, ed., New York, 1964, pp. 206-233.

MacLeish: The Greek dream. You know, Mark, we in America may not honor strangers, but we have a dream of our own, the dream we were talking about on the way up from the village this morning. Where did the American dream come from, if not Greece? Not from our own landscape certainly. I can't help believe that the American dream to the first settlers was a nightmare.

Van Doren: It was not a dream.

MacLeish: It was not a dream, it was a nightmare. They were surrounded by danger. The trees were their enemies. They had to cut, hew, break up, pull out roots. Stones were their enemies. The Indians were their enemies. And it was a brutal and bitter struggle. I suppose there was hope,

hope of making a good living. Certainly in New England agriculture did provide a good living well down to the beginning of the last century, well down to the opening of the West.

Van Doren: Yes.

MacLeish: But where does the American dream begin, Mark? Do you have to wait for Jefferson? Is it as late as that?

Van Doren: I would think so. You have to wait until the vision extended almost indefinitely West, and you thought of the country as something that was going to be huge.

MacLeish: When you knew you could master the land, when you moved out into the prairies, when you moved into the high lands, the high plains, when you went over the mountains and into California, it was then that the dream began to become promise. Isn't that it?

Van Doren: Yes, I believe so.

MacLeish: Well, if that's true, then it raises a very interesting question about the concept of America now. If the American dream is related — as some sardonic historians say — to the material possibilities of the opening of the continent, what happens to it now that the continent is fully occupied? Does the sense of promise die with the hope of material fulfillment, or is there still that thing that Lincoln talked about when he said that the essence of the Declaration of Independence was that it gave all men everywhere the hope that the weights would some day be lifted from their shoulders? Have we lost that, or haven't we? I think that's the most grievous question that men of our generation have to face.

Van Doren: Well, you know, I often wonder what it means now to say that we should love our country. I certainly think we should.

MacLeish: You know that you do.

Van Doren: Yes, I know I do, and maybe everybody does, but it's a very different thing from what it used to be.

MacLeish: Exactly! What is this object you love?

Van Doren: Is it a single thing?

MacLeish: Yes, is it a single thing?

Van Doren: I think it has to remain single. You know I often look back with a certain kind of nostalgia to Greece of the fifth century. I get the impression that every young Greek knew what he lived in. He was born into a going thing. He knew what it was. Maybe he couldn't find words for it, but he was proud to belong to it, was prepared to make any sacrifice to perpetuate it. And I'd say, Archie, that the same is true here now. You see it during our national party conventions. Here are the delegates from the various states, getting up and bellowing forth their identifications: "the great

State of Montana," "the great State of Florida," "the great State of Georgia," "the great State of Illinois." All of them are assuming, are they not, that there's one thing here with fifty parts. There's no assumption that it isn't one thing.

MacLeish: Then, the possibility of the breaking up of this whole is no longer a real possibility, it's no longer conceivable in anybody's mind?

Van Doren: I think not.

MacLeish: But still, if the country is more firmly than ever before an economic, an industrial, a political whole, is it creatively *itself*? Does it have the kind of impulse it had at the time of the early settlers — that America is the beginning of the future, that the future *is* America?

Van Doren: Yes, I would think so.

MacLeish: Does it still have a central idea? You know, Mark, there's only one central idea, that ever was America, as I see it. That central idea was human freedom. It is the idea that all men are created equal, an idea which the wiseacres have sneered at and laughed at for so long: "Of course, they're not created equal." But of course they are! I continue to hold that this central idea is the only idea that ever was America, but I ask to what extent is it still an American idea?

During the McCarthy time, for example, it seemed to me that a great part of the country was frightened, including the so-called conservatives and particularly the well-to-do. And a great part of the country was thus lost to this central idea which is America. They were trying to build walls around what they had, instead of opening out the fences toward freedom. What that situation is now is anybody's guess. I can't help believing that the idea of freedom still exists.

Van Doren: Neither can I.

MacLeish: The difficulty is how to measure to what extent it still exists. How can anybody know the temper of America?

Usually when you have somebody reporting on the temper of America in the *New York Times Magazine,* which is a good reporter on the temper of America, or when you have somebody reporting through various forms of testing, samples, averages, and so forth, usually what you have is a mathematical attempt to find out what it is that people think. For example, you get reporters moving around before an election, talking to political leaders here, there, and elsewhere. Then they tell you that Kennedy is going to win or Nixon is going to win.

Van Doren: Or, as they say, a sampling; they've taken a sampling.

MacLeish: Yes, yes. Or you have professional opinion samplers, people who have made a reputation out of their ability to do this. Do any of their findings persuade you? Are you persuaded, are you convinced, that you are really listening to an account of, a representation of, the temper of America?

Van Doren: No, because they've never asked me.

MacLeish (LAUGHING): If they did ask you, would you think so?

Van Doren: Well, I would tell them.

MacLeish: You'd tell them what you think, but . . .

Van Doren: What my answer means is that they have to ask everybody before they know.

MacLeish: But even if they asked everybody, would a mathematical summary, so many *yeses* and so many *noes,* give you the answer?

I do think that when you're talking about the temper of a country, which means not only how people are going to vote on a given issue but what the general orientation is, what the tilt of the continent is, how the world feels, you're not going to measure that by asking questions, because nobody has the brains to ask the kind of question which will elicit the kind of answer you need.

Van Doren: Obviously you couldn't know about the temper of America that way. It isn't mathematical. It isn't statistical. You can't poll it. And certainly, above all, it can't be sampled. No, the question how one finds that out fascinates me, too. I'm reminded of certain foreign observers who have been here in the past. De Tocqueville was one of them.

MacLeish: De Tocqueville somehow or other seems to have made some sort of electrical connection, doesn't he?

Van Doren: Yes.

MacLeish: History seems to indicate he did.

Van Doren: People keep on reading his books and finding out what they wouldn't know for themselves. Of course, there were other travelers, sometimes friendly, sometimes hostile: Dickens, Mrs. Trollope, and others.

And then you remember later in the nineteenth century, there was James Bryce who came as an outsider, as an Englishman, a very sober, responsible old English liberal. He looked at the American scene and decided such things as are implied by the title of one of his chapters in *The American Commonwealth* — "Why Great Men Are Never Elected President." What an appalling idea! It really makes your blood run cold, doesn't it? Well, maybe sometimes an observer from the other side is in a better position to see what we can't see for ourselves.

MacLeish: Certainly they're in a better position to observe the American scene than the people inside the country who estimate temper by mathematical means. But, you know, Mark, I believe there are those who have been able to know the true temper of the country. Two examples have occurred to me: looking back with a hundred years' perspective, it now appears that Lincoln, whose adult life had been spent on the frontier, and who was regarded by everyone who knew him as a rather unsophisticated, uncouth man . . .

Van Doren: A country lawyer.

MacLeish: . . . a country lawyer, had a better sense of the temper of the United States, not only North, but North and South, than any man of his time. And a nearer example that I would offer you, not knowing whether you would agree or not, is Sandburg in *The People, Yes.* At a time of great doubt and skepticism in the country, Sandburg somehow had a sense of an optimistic temper, a temper of belief and assertion which later demonstrated itself.

Van Doren: Of course, Carl Sandburg is particularly convincing because, among other things, he is humorous. You see, humor is an essential part of it, just as for Lincoln it was an essential part of it.

MacLeish: It's a unique aspect of the American temper. Anybody who takes the Americans too seriously certainly can't catch their temper, which is why the Marxists were always wrong. . . .

MacLeish: Well, assuming all the necessary humilities in the way of coming to any sort of conclusion, and agreeing on the impossibility of doing it mathematically, or saying the American people are moving this way or that way because 745 people out of a sample of 1,230 say *no* to this and *yes* to that — excepting all that, have you a sort of sense of what the temper of the country is now, in terms of its confidence in itself, which is, I think, the essential question?

Van Doren: Well, I wonder to what extent those are right who say that too many of us are afraid to speak our minds. I'm sure that the most important American tradition is the tradition of the individual speaking his mind, regardless of how many people he thinks may disagree with him, and regardless of any danger in which he may put his reputation.

I think we've always honored those who, as we say, spoke out. It might seem to be an unpopular thing to speak out. It often turns out to have been a popular thing. Because, eventually, the American people do not respect a politician who never says anything. They want him to say something, even though they're going to disagree with it. They'd rather he'd say it — say something — than say nothing.

MacLeish: Yes, I agree, and though I'm not debating this with you, I really would like to know, I'd like to know in myself — and I don't really know — is it a fear of talking out, or something else?

Take the present wave that many observers have observed, the wave of childish criticism of the President of the United States on the part of American business. Or put it the other way around if you want. But I'm concerned here, primarily, with the attitude toward the President.

Now, certainly there's no basic fear of talking out against the President. People have long said idiotic and ridiculous things without any fear or apprehension, but have they really *said* anything? Have they been expressing more than a temporary irritation or a personal disappointment in relation to a given situation? Are they really expressing a view on the basis of which you could say: "This is what America is like"? I myself doubt it very much. Because a considerable number of American businessmen have a certain attitude toward Kennedy at the present time, I doubt that it means that the American community is pro-business or anti-government. These are more or less expressions of a temporary irritation or, perhaps, even a permanent irritation. But they're personal expressions, and they are not wise; they are childish.

So what you are left with is to wonder how far and how deeply men are really thinking and speaking out boldly on their country's situation? It seems to me, when you are talking about the temper of a country, you must say something about the orientation of the country in relation to its own destiny, what it thinks it is, and what it thinks it's going to become. Perhaps my example is a bad example.

Van Doren: No, it's a very interesting example, I would say.

MacLeish: You see, Mark, it seems to me, when you're talking about the temper of a country, how deeply it believes in itself and in its own destiny, the irritations are not important. I think certain people miss the whole point when they say, I no longer believe in the American destiny, because I think such and such things are going on in Washington; and there are such and such trends in the Congress; and legislation is moving this way and moving that way. This, incidentally, is the kind of mind which says "they," the mysterious "they" with quotation marks around it. "They" are against it. "They" are going to do this or that. This means, in a sense, that "you" don't really believe much in "us" any more. "You" are more concerned about "they" than "you" are about "us."

Van Doren: A very good point.

MacLeish: You may recall at the beginning of this century the American business community wasn't so much concerned about "they." Now you may argue that "they," at that point, hadn't yet begun to throw "their" weight around. But still the American business community, America as a business operation, was much more concerned at that time with what *it* was going to do. And maybe if one were going to generalize about the temper of the country today, one would have to say that these very protestations, these very complaints, testify to a certain lack of confidence, not in the country, but in business.

Van Doren: What you're really saying is that you think more persons or more groups of persons should make a conscious effort to address themselves to the question of what the common good is, what the good for us all might be, if it ever existed.

MacLeish: I think what I'm after, Mark, is within what we were talking about earlier; that insofar as America is something new, it is an idea; that this idea is an idea which had its essential expression in the Declaration of Independence, which had a reexpression in Lincoln's speech in Philadelphia on his way to his inauguration, which has had reexpression in generation after generation since. It's an idea which is relatively easy to state, but can only be stated in the greatest language, as in the Declaration.

It is an idea which affirms the supreme worth of the human individual and, through an act of faith, believes in him, and believes that, given the opportunity, he will make for himself a good life.

Now, if this is what America is, if America is that idea, the only real question that anybody ought to be talking about when they talk about the temper of this country is the question of whether or not we're still committed to that idea. I don't think the whining, the complaining, the fearsome talk on the public side, or perhaps the bullying on the government side, really goes to the heart of that question.

It would take another Lincoln to know what our temper is in that regard, and I don't think there's another Lincoln on the political scene now.

Van Doren: Well, there's one long perspective to take upon this: the doctrine of equality has what as its source? I would say it has religion as its source, it has the Bible as its source. I believe there's no other book which so completely states, and which so completely justifies, the doctrine of equality, where all men are equal because they're all sons of the same father. I think the Bible is the only thing that makes sense: "Love thy neighbor as thyself," as the Old Testament keeps on saying over and over and over again.

All persons were to have sanctity because they were persons. Then the talk was not so much about the *dignity* of the individual — that's a fairly gray phrase for me — but the *sanctity of the person*. You see, that gives the idea of equality greater depth, I should say. I don't know whether this is true, but you know, Archie, someone has said that democracy has never existed in any place where the Bible didn't exist.

MacLeish: But is this an historical accident, the fact that democracy developed in the West . . .

Van Doren: Yes, it could be.

MacLeish: Or is it the other way around?

Van Doren: I don't know.

MacLeish: Well, I certainly agree with you that it's only within the frame of the world as seen through the window of the Bible that it's possible to conceive of a man, any man, as having the kind of importance that in the founding of this country it was assumed that he had.

Van Doren: Yes, and I think we must still somehow or other continue to be able to assume that every man has this kind of importance. If not, we're lost. I think what you and I are saying today we should say at the tops of our voices.

MacLeish: Yes, certainly at the tops of our voices, but still, Mark, if one is inquiring about the temper of one's country one is bound to ask whether there is *evidence* that the country has made the supreme commitment to the sanctity of every person that it ought to have made.

Van Doren: The fact that it's difficult to see the signs doesn't necessarily mean that they don't exist. The signs are there to be seen, if we could understand them. It's difficult because the face of the country changes every minute, and young people, in particular, are being asked to consider a different transformation every year of their lives.

MacLeish: Maybe this accounts for some of the rather cynical, snotty young reactionaries who tear down these beliefs, who make liberalism a fabricated enemy for themselves, regarding as liberals all men who really believe in the concept we're talking about. This kind of young man is a man who is really fearful at heart. He's also a man with an extraordinary poverty of spiritual power.

Van Doren: I don't need to remind you, Archie, that this reached a critical stage not long ago when word came to us of the brainwashing of American prisoners in Korea. It appeared then, at least so it was said, that some of our men in Korea who were put under a strain, and under that strain were asked to remember what this country was about, and what they were for, couldn't do it.

MacLeish: One wonders, Mark, whether this incapacity was the result of brainwashing, or whether it was the result of the fact that very little grafting into a man of the fundamental tree of human liberty took place in their childhood.

Van Doren: That's right; that's what was said by many people. These boys had not somehow or other ever been told, nor had they ever defined from their own observation, what the American experience was all about.

MacLeish: I've seen criticisms of the curricula of the American high schools, which indicate that because individual civil liberties, fundamental American concepts, are now controversial in certain areas where McCarthyism left its hairy touch, or where the John Birch Society is now leaving its rather dirty bird tracks, that the basic American concept is barely touched on, is passed over lightly, or is taught by uninspired teachers who themselves don't understand what they're talking about. Whether this sort of criticism is justified I don't know. I've never made such an examination myself, but I'll bet you anything it is.

Van Doren: You mean that the criticism is valid?

MacLeish: I think the criticisms are valid, that only in the best high schools do the teachers really deal at all with the fundamental American concept.

Van Doren: Well, maybe everyone should begin self-examination at home. Do you and I have this faith to the limit? If the answer is yes, and I think it is, if we have this faith to the limit, that's all we can do, plus say so. We should say so whenever we can, and wherever we can.

You see, Archie, I don't think it's a question of what other people think; more importantly it's what *we* think. And maybe that's what saves the society; every member in it looking within himself and saying, "Who am I? What do *I* think?" Not, "What does my neighbor think?" If he believes in what *he* thinks, and says so, his neighbor is probably changed.

MacLeish: And yet in the American conception of the place of man in the universe, the person that one values isn't oneself. The person that one values most is those other selves with which one has to do in one's life. Isn't that so?

Van Doren: Yes, but I think we can have faith in others, which I think we must have, only when we have faith in ourselves, when we have no doubt about ourselves. You see, maybe this incessant search, this burrowing and buzzing into the beliefs of others comes from a lack of conviction in our beliefs; we don't know what we think, so we don't want to know what anyone thinks.

MacLeish: I thought you were going to say the opposite. Maybe one of the results of burrowing into the depths and interstices of the self — which comes out of the development of Freudian psychology — is an increasing doubt as to the integrity and wholeness of other human beings.

Van Doren: Put it this way, Archie. You know the famous paradox, that whenever you have written an entirely personal poem or piece of prose, whenever you have really delivered the goods so far as you yourself are concerned, and said what you thought, what happened? You found that everybody else understood you, didn't you?

MacLeish: I wish I could say yes to that; at least, I hope so.

Van Doren: It's been my experience. Whenever I have been afraid that my work was so personal that no one could understand it, everybody did understand it. When I tried to speak for others, they didn't know what I was talking about.

MacLeish: That's very wise. That's wise and well said, and I really think it's true. But I don't draw the same conclusion from this very wise saying of yours that you do. I don't think that one can search one's own heart to find if one holds the conviction which is fundamental to this republic. I don't find that it is in the searching of oneself that that realization comes.

I think the realization comes when you arrive at a point in your life — which some men do earlier, some later, and some not at all — a point at which you cannot look into any other human face without seeing there everything that you value in yourself. You see something there that you respect as much as you could possibly respect yourself, something that can't be hurt, can't be limited, and can't be obstructed.

Van Doren: Well, now I'm going to be stubborn about this, only because you are. For instance, what is courtesy? Courtesy consists in assuming that everyone else is a gentleman, not in wondering whether he is or not, but in just assuming that he is. To be a gentleman is to be nothing, I say, except a man who thinks all other men are gentlemen. Now, it may seem naïve sometimes to make this assumption, but it's astonishing how many gentlemen you create by making such an assumption, and how many ladies you can create by assuming that all women are ladies.

Lincoln made us all political philosophers by being a political philosopher in our presence. He paid us the supreme compliment of believing we could understand him, and you know he said very closely reasoned things. It took lots of attention, and we gave it to him.

MacLeish: Perhaps the essence of agreement, for me, is to say that I think you have demonstrated exactly what I am trying to say.

Van Doren: Yes. I don't think we're really disagreeing.

MacLeish: It does seem to me that we

agree, except that I am taking two steps, two bites of the cherry.

Van Doren: Maybe I'm missing a step here.

MacLeish: Well, the first bite of this cherry — the essential thing — is to realize what you are as a "person." This you can learn only in yourself. You learn it in yourself in relation to others. You learn it in relation to your mother, your father, your brothers, your sisters, your friends. But you learn it *in* yourself, and sooner or later, if the process of your education proceeds far enough so that you become mature, you realize that you are a person, for better or for worse, with all your faults upon you, and that you have a kind of value which is not limited by the fact that you're going to die. You're a mortal, but you're valuable nevertheless. That, I think, is the first bite in the cherry. You have to feel what a human being is, know what a human being is.

The second bite of the cherry, and the really important one so far as the political organization goes, is the realization that if you are a "person," then so is he and he, and he and he.

Van Doren: That's right. I think that is an act of faith too. I think that is something you must be able to believe, because it's true. I pity those who can't believe it, who despise others because they're not the same as themselves.

You see, what turns out to be true, I think, is this: although we're all different from one another so that no one of us is mistaken for another, yet the resemblances among us are probably more important than the differences.

You know, we are the same in many, many respects. The fact that you and I are talking, using the English language with each other, implies that we think we have the same mind.

MacLeish: Well, the miraculous thing is that it's possible for two human beings to talk with each other in words about what to them is simply impressions or depths of feeling so that somehow or other agreement does become possible.

Van Doren: But the third thing out there, what we're really talking about, is more important than either one of us.

MacLeish: Yes, that's true. I think the reason why America is of such tremendous and fundamental importance to you and me is not that you or I are patrioteers who feel we're only dressed when we have a flag wrapped around us; the reason it's so important is that America *is* that third thing out there.

America is a concept of what life could be like if you had an understanding of the human self in yourself, a respect for the human self in others, and a political mechanism which would make it work. And the word *freedom,* I think, is a word which simply describes the viability of this kind of relationship. It describes a man not free simply of government supervision, of policemen, of bullying Southern cops, of any of the other tyrants who gag the world. It means that a man is free of the constant attrition of other people's suspicion and denigration, and this achieved is what America is. And from that point of view, America is something worth any man's belief and any man's passionate loyalty!

23.

WILLIAM J. BRENNAN, JR.: *Baker v. Carr*

While the Constitution provides for the apportionment of congressional representatives among states, it does not determine whether the representatives apportioned to each state shall be elected from districts or by the state at large. The custom of electing representatives by district is now universal, but the state legislatures have wide discretion in drawing district boundary lines; for example, many legislatures use county and town boundaries in determining the districts, while others use weighted ratios to give additional representation to certain areas. The delineation of congressional districts frequently allows one party to gain a definite plurality, and in most cases the state legislatures are reluctant to redistrict at all if doing so would jeopardize the political future of incumbent members. One prevalent charge directed at rural-dominated state legislatures is that of drawing boundary lines for congressional districts in such a way as to deprive urban and suburban areas of full representation. Metropolitan areas had no legal redress for this practice until 1962, when the Supreme Court, in Baker v. Carr, *ruled that the federal courts could hear complaints in cases where voters alleged that they had been deprived of proper representation by gross malapportionment of legislative districts. Justice William J. Brennan, Jr., delivered the Court's opinion, part of which is reprinted here, on March 26, 1962.*

Source: 369 U.S. 186.

THIS CIVIL ACTION was brought under 42 U.S.C. Sections 1983 and 1988 to redress the alleged deprivation of federal constitutional rights. The complaint, alleging that by means of a 1901 statute of Tennessee apportioning the members of the General Assembly among the state's ninety-five counties, "these plaintiffs and others similarly situated are denied the equal protection of the laws accorded them by the Fourteenth Amendment to the Constitution of the United States by virtue of the debasement of their votes," was dismissed by a three-judge court convened under 28 U.S.C. Section 2281 in the Middle District of Tennessee. The court held that it lacked jurisdiction of the subject matter and also that no claim was stated upon which relief could be granted. . . . We noted probable jurisdiction of the appeal. . . . We hold that the dismissal was in error, and remand the cause to the District Court for trial and further proceedings consistent with this opinion.

The General Assembly of Tennessee consists of the Senate with thirty-three members and the House of Representatives with ninety-nine members. The Tennessee Constitution provides in Article II as follows:

Section 3. Legislative authority — Term of office. — The legislative authority of this state shall be vested in a General Assembly, which shall consist of a Senate and House of Representatives, both dependent on the people; who shall hold their offices for two years from the day of the general election.

Section 4. Census. — An enumeration of the qualified voters, and apportionment of the representatives in the General Assembly, shall be made in the year 1871, and within every subsequent term of ten years.

Section 5. Apportionment of representatives. — The number of representatives shall, at the several periods of making the enumeration, be apportioned among the several counties or districts, according to the number of qualified voters in each; and shall not exceed seventy-five, until the population of the state shall be one million and a half, and shall never exceed ninety-nine; *Provided*, that any county having two-thirds of the ratio shall be entitled to one member.

Section 6. Apportionment of senators. — The number of senators shall, at the several periods of making the enumeration, be apportioned among the several counties or districts according to the number of qualified electors in each, and shall not exceed one-third the number of representatives. In apportioning the senators among the different counties, the fraction that may be lost by any county or counties, in the apportionment of members to the House of Representatives, shall be made up to such county or counties in the Senate, as near as may be practicable. When a district is composed of two or more counties, they shall be adjoining; and no county shall be divided in forming a district.

Thus, Tennessee's standard for allocating legislative representation among her counties is the total number of qualified voters resident in the respective counties, subject only to minor qualifications.

Decennial reapportionment in compliance with the constitutional scheme was effected by the General Assembly each decade from 1871 to 1901. The 1871 apportionment was preceded by an 1870 statute requiring an enumeration. The 1881 apportionment involved three statutes: the first authorizing an enumeration; the second enlarging the Senate from twenty-five to thirty-three

members and the House from seventy-five to ninety-nine members; and the third apportioning the membership of both Houses. In 1891 there were both an enumeration and an apportionment. In 1901 the General Assembly abandoned separate enumeration in favor of reliance upon the federal census and passed the Apportionment Act here in controversy. In the more than sixty years since that action, all proposals in both houses of the General Assembly for reapportionment have failed to pass.

Between 1901 and 1961, Tennessee has experienced substantial growth and redistribution of her population. In 1901 the population was 2,020,616, of whom 487,380 were eligible to vote. The 1960 federal census reports the state's population at 3,567,089, of whom 2,092,891 are eligible to vote. The relative standings of the counties in terms of qualified voters have changed significantly. It is primarily the continued application of the 1901 Apportionment Act to this shifted and enlarged voting population which gives rise to the present controversy.

Indeed, the complaint alleges that the 1901 statute, even as of the time of its passage, "made no apportionment of representatives and senators in accordance with the constitutional formula . . . but instead arbitrarily and capriciously apportioned representatives in the Senate and House without reference . . . to any logical or reasonable formula whatever." It is further alleged that "because of the population changes since 1900 and the failure of the legislature to reapportion itself since 1901," the 1901 statute became "unconstitutional and obsolete." Appellants also argue that, because of the composition of the legislature effected by the 1901 Apportionment Act, redress in the form of a state constitutional amendment to change the entire mechanism for reapportioning, or any other change short of that, is difficult or impossible.

The complaint concludes that "these

plaintiffs and others similarly situated, are denied the equal protection of the laws accorded them by the Fourteenth Amendment to the Constitution of the United States by virtue of the debasement of their votes." They seek a declaration that the 1901 statute is unconstitutional and an injunction restraining the appellees from acting to conduct any further elections under it. They also pray that unless and until the General Assembly enacts a valid reapportionment, the District Court should either decree a reapportionment by mathematical application of the Tennessee constitutional formulae to the most recent federal census figures, or direct the appellees to conduct legislative elections, primary and general, at large. They also pray for such other and further relief as may be appropriate. . . .

In light of the District Court's treatment of the case, we hold today only (a) that the court possessed jurisdiction of the subject matter; (b) that a justiciable cause of action is stated upon which appellants would be entitled to appropriate relief; and (c) because appellees raise the issue before this Court, that the appellants have standing to challenge the Tennessee apportionment statutes. Beyond noting that we have no cause at this stage to doubt the District Court will be able to fashion relief if violations of constitutional rights are found, it is improper now to consider what remedy would be most appropriate if appellants prevail at the trial.

The District Court was uncertain whether our cases withholding federal judicial relief rested upon a lack of federal jurisdiction or upon the inappropriateness of the subject matter for judicial consideration — what we have designated "nonjusticiability." The distinction between the two grounds is significant. In the instance of nonjusticiability, consideration of the cause is not wholly and immediately foreclosed; rather, the Court's inquiry necessarily proceeds to the point of deciding whether the duty asserted can be judicially identified and its breach judicially determined, and whether protection for the right asserted can be judicially molded.

In the instance of lack of jurisdiction the cause either does not "arise under" the federal constitution, laws, or treaties (or fall within one of the other enumerated categories of Article III, Section 2), or is not a "case or controversy" within the meaning of that section; or the cause is not one described by any jurisdictional statute. Our conclusion . . . that this cause presents no nonjusticiable "political question" settles the only possible doubt that it is a case or controversy. Under the present heading of "Jurisdiction of the Subject Matter" we hold only that the matter set forth in the complaint does arise under the Constitution and is within 28 U.S.C. Section 1343.

Article III, Section 2, of the federal Constitution provides that "The judicial power shall extend to all cases in law and equity arising under this Constitution, the laws of the United States, and treaties made, or which shall be made, under their authority. . . ." It is clear that the cause of action is one which "arises under" the federal Constitution. The complaint alleges that the 1901 statute effects an apportionment that deprives the appellants of the equal protection of the laws in violation of the Fourteenth Amendment. Dismissal of the complaint upon the ground of lack of jurisdiction of the subject matter would, therefore, be justified only if that claim were "so attenuated and unsubstantial as to be absolutely devoid of merit" . . . or "frivolous." . . . That the claim is unsubstantial must be "very plain." . . . Since the District Court obviously and correctly did not deem the asserted federal constitutional claim unsubstantial and frivolous, it should not have dismissed the complaint for want of jurisdiction of the subject matter. And of course no further consideration of the merits of the claim is relevant to a determination of the court's jurisdiction of the subject matter. . . .

Since the complaint plainly sets forth a case arising under the Constitution, the subject matter is within the federal judicial power defined in Article III, Section 2, and so within the power of Congress to assign to the jurisdiction of the District Courts. Congress has exercised that power in 28 U.S.C. Section 1343 (3):

> The district courts shall have original jurisdiction of any civil action authorized by law to be commenced by any person . . . [t]o redress the deprivation, under color of any state law, statute, ordinance, regulation, custom or usage, of any right, privilege or immunity secured by the Constitution of the United States. . . .

An unbroken line of our precedents sustains the federal courts' jurisdiction of the subject matter of federal constitutional claims of this nature. . . .

A federal court cannot "pronounce any statute, either of a state or of the United States, void, because irreconcilable with the Constitution, except as it is called upon to adjudge the legal rights of litigants in actual controversies." . . . Have the appellants alleged such a personal stake in the outcome of the controversy as to assume that concrete adverseness which sharpens the presentation of issues upon which the court so largely depends for illumination of difficult constitutional questions? This is the gist of the question of standing. It is, of course, a question of federal law.

The complaint was filed by residents of Davidson, Hamilton, Knox, Montgomery, and Shelby counties. Each is a person allegedly qualified to vote for members of the General Assembly representing his county. These appellants sued "on their own behalf and on behalf of all qualified voters of their respective counties, and further, on behalf of all voters of the State of Tennessee who are similarly situated. . . ." The appellees are the Tennessee secretary of state, attorney general, coordinator of elections, and members of the State Board of Elections; the members of the State Board are sued in their own right and also as representatives of the County Election Commissioners whom they appoint.

We hold that the appellants do have standing to maintain this suit. Our decisions plainly support this conclusion. Many of the cases have assumed rather than articulated the premise in deciding the merits of similar claims. And *Colegrove* v. *Green* . . . squarely held that voters who allege facts showing disadvantage to themselves as individuals have standing to sue. A number of cases decided after *Colegrove* recognized the standing of the voters there involved to bring those actions.

These appellants seek relief in order to protect or vindicate an interest of their own, and of those similarly situated. Their constitutional claim is, in substance, that the 1901 statute constitutes arbitrary and capricious state action, offensive to the Fourteenth Amendment in its irrational disregard of the standard of apportionment prescribed by the state's constitution or of any standard, effecting a gross disproportion of representation to voting population. The injury which appellants assert is that this classification disfavors the voters in the counties in which they reside, placing them in a position of constitutionally unjustifiable inequality *vis-à-vis* voters in irrationally favored counties. A citizen's right to a vote free of arbitrary impairment by state action has been judicially recognized as a right secured by the Constitution, when such impairment resulted from dilution by a false tally . . . or by a refusal to count votes from arbitrarily selected precincts . . . or by a stuffing of the ballot box. . . .

It would not be necessary to decide whether appellants' allegations of impairment of their votes by the 1901 apportionment will, ultimately, entitle them to any relief, in order to hold that they have standing to seek it. If such impairment does produce a legally cognizable injury, they are among those who have sustained it. They are asserting "a plain, direct and adequate interest in maintaining the effectiveness of their votes" . . . not merely a claim of "the right, possessed by every citizen, to require that the Government be administered according to law. . . ." They are entitled to a hearing and to the District Court's decision on their claims. "The very essence of civil liberty certainly consists in the right of every individual to claim the protection of the laws, whenever he receives an injury." *Marbury* v. *Madison*, 1 Cranch 137, 163.

In holding that the subject matter of this suit was not justiciable, the District Court relied on *Colegrove* v. *Green, supra,* and subsequent *per curiam* cases. The court stated: "From a review of these decisions there can be no doubt that the federal rule . . . is that the federal courts . . . will not intervene in cases of this type to compel legislative reapportionment." . . . We understand the District Court to have read the cited cases as compelling the conclusion that since the appellants sought to have a legislative apportionment held unconstitutional, their suit presented a "political question" and was therefore nonjusticiable. We hold that this challenge to an apportionment presents no nonjusticiable "political question." The cited cases do not hold the contrary.

Of course the mere fact that the suit seeks protection of a political right does not mean it presents a political question. Such an objection "is little more than a play upon words." . . . Rather, it is argued that apportionment cases, whatever the actual wording of the complaint, can involve no federal constitutional right except one resting on the guaranty of a republican form of government, and that complaints based on

that clause have been held to present political questions which are nonjusticiable.

We hold that the claim pleaded here neither rests upon nor implicates the Guaranty Clause and that its justiciability is therefore not foreclosed by our decisions of cases involving that clause. The District Court misinterpreted *Colegrove* v. *Green* and other decisions of this Court on which it relied. Appellants' claim that they are being denied equal protection is justiciable, and if "discrimination is sufficiently shown, the right to relief under the equal protection clause is not diminished by the fact that the discrimination relates to political rights." . . .

It is apparent that several formulations which vary slightly according to the settings in which the questions arise may describe a political question, although each has one or more elements which identify it as essentially a function of the separation of powers. Prominent on the surface of any case held to involve a political question is found a textually demonstrable constitutional commitment of the issue to a coordinate political department; or a lack of judicially discoverable and manageable standards for resolving it; or the impossibility of deciding without an initial policy determination of a kind clearly for nonjudicial discretion; or the impossibility of a court's undertaking independent resolution without expressing lack of the respect due coordinate branches of government; or an unusual need for unquestioning adherence to a political decision already made; or the potentiality of embarrassment from multifarious pronouncements by various departments on one question.

Unless one of these formulations is inextricable from the case at bar, there should be no dismissal for nonjusticiability on the ground of a political question's presence. The doctrine of which we treat is one of "political questions," not one of "political cases." The courts cannot reject as "no law suit" a bona-fide controversy as to whether some action denominated "political" exceeds constitutional authority. The cases we have reviewed show the necessity for discriminating inquiry into the precise facts and posture of the particular case, and the impossibility of resolution by any semantic cataloguing.

But it is argued that this case shares the characteristics of decisions that constitute a category not yet considered, cases concerning the Constitution's guaranty, in Article IV, Section 4, of a republican form of government. A conclusion as to whether the case at bar does present a political question cannot be confidently reached until we have considered those cases with special care. We shall discover that Guaranty Clause claims involve those elements which define a "political question," and for that reason and no other, they are nonjusticiable. In particular, we shall discover that the nonjusticiability of such claims has nothing to do with their touching upon matters of state governmental organization. . . .

We come, finally, to the ultimate inquiry whether our precedents as to what constitutes a nonjusticiable "political question" bring the case before us under the umbrella of that doctrine. A natural beginning is to note whether any of the common characteristics which we have been able to identify and label descriptively are present. We find none. The question here is the consistency of state action with the federal Constitution. We have no question decided, or to be decided, by a political branch of government coequal with this Court. Nor do we risk embarrassment of our government abroad or grave disturbance at home if we take issue with Tennessee as to the constitutionality of her action here challenged. Nor need the appellants, in order to succeed in this action, ask the Court to enter upon policy determinations for which judicially manageable standards are lacking. Judicial standards under the Equal Protection Clause are well developed and familiar, and it has been open to courts since the enactment of the Fourteenth Amendment to determine, if on the particular facts they must, that a discrimination reflects *no* policy, but simply arbitrary and capricious action.

This case does, in one sense, involve the allocation of political power within a state, and the appellants might conceivably have added a claim under the Guaranty Clause. Of course, as we have seen, any reliance on that clause would be futile. But because any reliance on the Guaranty Clause could not have succeeded, it does not follow that appellants may not be heard on the equal protection claim which in fact they tender. True, it must be clear that the Fourteenth Amendment claim is not so enmeshed with those political question elements which render Guaranty Clause claims nonjusticiable as actually to present a political question itself. But we have found that not to be the case here. . . .

We conclude that the complaint's allegations of a denial of equal protection present a justiciable constitutional cause of action upon which appellants are entitled to a trial and a decision. The right asserted is within the reach of judicial protection under the Fourteenth Amendment.

The judgment of the District Court is reversed and the cause is remanded for further proceedings consistent with this opinion.

All the ills of democracy can be cured by more democracy.
ALFRED E. SMITH

24.

On the School Prayer Decision

*The Board of Education of Union Free School District No. 9, in New Hyde Park,
New York, began in the late 1950s to require that all of the children in the schools
of the district repeat each morning the following prayer: "Almighty God, we
acknowledge our dependence upon Thee, and we beg Thy blessings upon us, our
parents, our teachers, and our country." The State Board of Regents, which originally
composed and recommended the prayer, thought that it was a proper part of the moral
training that all students should receive, and stated that "we believe that this statement
will be subscribed to by all men and women of good will." Nevertheless, the statement
was objected to, and the issue finally reached the Supreme Court, which, in a 6 to 1
decision handed down in 1962* (Engel v. Vitale), *ruled that the New York prayer was
illegal under the First Amendment to the Constitution. The decision, which was a
precedent for later rulings concerning the reading of the Bible and the reciting of the
Lord's Prayer in public schools, was vociferously criticized, and the Senate Committee
on the Judiciary held hearings in the summer of 1962 on a number of bills proposing
amendments to the Constitution that would make such school prayers legal. Criticism
was not unanimous, however, as is indicated by the following statement of July 26
by Protestants and Other Americans for the Separation of Church and State.*

Source: *Prayers in Public Schools and Other Matters, Hearings Before the Committee on the
Judiciary, U.S. Senate*, 87 Congress, 2 Session, Washington, 1963, pp. 230-232.

THE ATTEMPT BY A GROUP of New York public officials to prescribe a prayer for schoolchildren in that state has been pronounced unconstitutional by a 6 to 1 decision of the U.S. Supreme Court. All persons who believe in prayer as the authentic thrust of the human spirit toward its Maker should welcome this decision. We predict that when the current wave of emotion has subsided the Court's decision in *Engel v. Vitale* will loom as a landmark of religious freedom.

The decision strikes down a law under which public officials in New York state sought to use the coercive processes of government to make a prayer of their own composing required for an important segment of the population. It is a rebuke to official religion in whatever form it may be imposed upon the American people. The Court did not outlaw prayer; it merely made prayer free of political limitation and control.

The principle enunciated by the Court in this opinion is eminently sound. It reiterates the deeply cherished American principle of the separation of church and state. As Justice Black correctly notes: ". . . In this country it is no part of the business of government to compose official prayers for any group of the American people to recite as part of a religious program carried on by government."

Is the Court wrong? If so, then must we not concede that government officials do have authority to compose prayers and require their repetition? If we concede them that authority, does it not follow that we must be prepared to accept the kind of prayers they may formulate? What is to prevent them or their successors from prescribing a kind of prayer which, while highly pleasing to a large segment of the population, would be offensive to other groups? We repeat that if these officials are in their proper function when they formulate and require prayers, then the public will be stuck with the particular prayers which they formulate and require. What resentment and bedlam await to be unleashed?

A careful analysis of the regents' prayer would probably indicate that no religious group could be entirely satisfied with it. Prayers composed by politicians and governments have never been satisfactory to deeply religious people. Christians are not offended by this prayer, but they do not find it satisfying because it contains no mention of Christ. Members of other faiths are, likewise, not offended. But they are no better satisfied with it. What is the regents' prayer, basically? It is an empty salute to religion, a gesture which falsely parades as something real. The regents' prayer achieves acceptability by being vapid. A truly religious person ought not to lament its passing.

The regents' prayer and the public school religion of which it is an example are a religion of the least common denominator. This is the standard brand of religion that public officials could be counted on to provide if this matter were placed in their domain. The objection to their product is not that it is too religious but that it is not religious enough. We are not convinced that there has been such a collapse of the church and the home as to necessitate a transfer of religious responsibility to public officials. The fact that such a transfer has been seriously proposed and urged, and to some extent accepted, is in itself a symptom of spiritual sickness which only a genuine spiritual revival can cure. Surely government intervention is not the answer here. The state's edict cannot produce the sincere seeker and the contrite heart.

The Court's decision is a blow to the totalitarian concept of government. There are those among us who want government to take over everything. Now, this thinking invades the most intimate and personal realm known to man — that of religious experience. Public school children in New York state have been, in effect, required by law to pray and have been regimented in their prayers. To establish such a religious exercise upon these citizens is an unconstitutional use of government authority. So the Supreme Court has wisely held. The decisive point of difference between a free government and a Communist or Fascist government is this — that the free government does not try to run everything. Certain matters are deliberately left to the personal conscience and decision of the people themselves. Religion is eminently one of these matters and the Supreme Court has now enabled us to keep it so.

Believers in church-state separation will be heartened by this decision in their endeavor to hold the "money line" between state and church. Those who had hoped to advance public money for parochial schools by legislating a government-composed prayer will be disappointed. The attempt failed. Justice Black, speaking for the Court, gives every evidence not of relaxing but rather of tightening the ban on state aid to church institutions, which he has repeatedly asserted in other opinions.

This matter receives even sharper articulation in the concurring opinion of Justice Douglas which stresses the unconstitutionality of money involvement between state and church. It is the expenditure of public funds to support a religious exercise, he declares, which provides the decisive constitutional test. If the miniscule expenditure of public funds involved in the preparation and implementation of the regents' prayer renders this program unconstitutional, then surely the channeling of many millions of dollars of public funds into church schools would be unconstitutional as well.

We come now to the question of a constitutional amendment which would have the effect of giving public officials certain authority in the religious field which the Court has now held they lack. Focusing our attention on the specific issue here, we may say that the proposed amendment would be designed to give the New York authorities in question authority to compose prayers and impose them upon schoolchildren.

We wish to register our opposition to any such amendment which might well open the door to further government intrusions in this area. We believe we speak for millions of our people and for a respected tradition of this country when we respectfully say to our government: "The realm of religious experience is personal and private; please keep out."

25.

Lloyd W. Lowrey: For Strengthening the States in the Federal System

As twentieth-century problems grew more and more complex, there existed also a growing tendency to take them to the courts. Even liberal members of the federal judiciary voiced concern at the popular view, as Supreme Court Justice John Marshall Harlan put it, that "all deficiencies in our society which have failed of correction by other means should find a cure in the courts," and that the courts have "blanket authority to step into every situation where the political branch may be thought to have fallen short." Conservatives and states' rights advocates tended to go further, and a program for radical constitutional change was proposed in December 1962 by the Council of State Governments. The program included reversing the 1962 Baker v. Carr *decision on judicial review of legislative apportionment, permitting state legislatures to amend the federal Constitution without appeal to any national forum, and setting up a court composed of the chief justices of the fifty states, with power to review and overrule certain Supreme Court decisions. Lloyd W. Lowrey, a California legislator and chairman of the National Legislative Conference, urged adoption of the program in the following Statement of Principles, published in 1963.*

Source: *State Government*, Winter 1963, pp. 10-15.

The characteristic of our constitutional government which has contributed most to the development of democratic processes and the preservation of human rights is the division of the powers of government between the nation and the states, on the one hand, and between the executive, legislative, and judicial departments of both state and federal governments, on the other.

Over the years we have escaped the evils of despotism and totalitarianism. It is only when each division of the whole governmental structure insists upon the right to exercise its powers, unrestrained by any other division, that the proper balance can be maintained and constitutional government, as we understand it, preserved.

It is the responsibility of the central government to protect the people from invasion by the states of those rights which are guaranteed to them by the federal Constitution. It is equally the obligation of the states to initiate and to prosecute to fruition the necessary procedures to protect the states and the people from unwarranted assumption of power by any department of the federal government.

The most sacred duty of all public officials, whether state or federal, and the highest patriotic responsibility of all citizens is to preserve, protect, and defend the Constitution, including that portion of the Constitution intended to guarantee a government of dual sovereignty. When it becomes apparent that purposely or inadvertently, any department or agency of government has embarked upon a course calculated to destroy the balance of power essential to our system, it behooves all other departments and agencies acting within their respective spheres of jurisdiction to take all steps within their power necessary to avert the impending evil. We believe that grave imbalance now exists.

Some federal judicial decisions involving powers of the federal and state governments carry a strong bias on the federal side, and consequently are bringing about a strong shift toward the extension of federal powers and the restraint of state powers. This shift tends to accelerate as each decision forms the basis and starting point for another extension of federal domination.

A greater degree of restraint on the part of the United States Supreme Court can do much, but experience shows that it is not likely to be sufficient. The basic difficulty is that the Supreme Court's decisions concerning the balance between federal and state power are final and can be changed in practice only if the states can muster sufficient interest in Congress, backed by a three-fourths majority of the states themselves to amend the Constitution. While the founding fathers fully expected and wished the words of the Constitution to have this degree of finality, it is impossible to believe that they envisaged such potency for the pronouncements of nine judges appointed by the President and confirmed by the Senate. The Supreme Court is, after all, an organ of the federal government. It is one of the three branches of the national government, and in conflicts over federal and state power, the Court is necessarily an agency of one of the parties in interest. As such, its decisions should not be assigned the same finality as the words of the Constitution itself. There is need for an easier method of setting such decisions straight when they are unsound.

To amend the federal Constitution to correct specific decisions of the federal courts on specific points is desirable, but it will not necessarily stop the continuing drift toward more complete federal domination. The present situation has taken a long time to develop and may take a long time to remedy. Accordingly, some more fundamental and far-reaching change in the federal Constitution is necessary to preserve and protect the states.

We appeal most earnestly to all branches of the federal government, and particularly to the highest federal court, to take diligent and impartial reflection upon the dangers to the nation inherent in the trends herein described. We urge them to evaluate the possibilities of an all-powerful central government with unlimited control over the lives of the people, the very opposite of self-government under a federal system.

It is the ultimate of political ingenuity to achieve a vigorous federal system in which dynamic states combine with a responsible central government for the good of the people. Your committee is dedicated to this objective.

26.

JOHN F. KENNEDY: Soviet Missiles in Cuba

On Sunday, October 14, 1962, a U.S. surveillance flight over Cuba took photographs furnishing incontrovertible evidence that Soviet medium-range missiles were already in place on the island and that sites for more advanced missiles were under construction. President Kennedy received the information on October 16 and immediately assembled a group of key government personnel to determine a course of action for the United States. For five days the group discussed various alternatives; surveillance of Cuba was intensified and strict security measures were implemented. In the interim, on October 18, Soviet Foreign Secretary Andrei Gromyko told Kennedy and Secretary of State Dean Rusk in the course of a conversation that Soviet aid to Cuba was for defense purposes only; Kennedy did not reveal that he had evidence to the contrary. On Saturday the 20th, a naval quarantine of Cuba was decided on and letters were drafted to the heads of forty-three allied governments, to all Latin-American governments, and to Soviet Premier Nikita Khrushchev. On Monday the 22nd, Kennedy delivered a televised address to the nation, part of which is reprinted here, explaining the situation and outlining the American government's course of action. Within forty-eight hours, twelve of twenty-five Russian ships carrying cargoes to Cuba turned around, and on Sunday, October 28, Moscow Radio broadcast what was obviously an official response to the American position, accepting Kennedy's assurance that no invasion of Cuba was contemplated by the U.S. and announcing that construction of military sites on the island would be discontinued and that those already in existence would be dismantled. Secretary Rusk summed up the tensions of that unforgettable week in a later remark: "We're eyeball to eyeball, and I think the other fellow just blinked."

Source: *Bulletin*, November 12, 1962, pp. 715-720.

THIS GOVERNMENT, as promised, has maintained the closest surveillance of the Soviet military buildup on the island of Cuba. Within the past week unmistakable evidence has established the fact that a series of offensive missile sites is now in preparation on that imprisoned island. The purpose of these bases can be none other than to provide a nuclear strike capability against the Western Hemisphere.

Upon receiving the first preliminary hard information of this nature last Tuesday morning [October 16] at 9 A.M., I directed that our surveillance be stepped up. And having now confirmed and completed our evaluation of the evidence and our decision on a course of action, this government feels obliged to report this new crisis to you in fullest detail.

The characteristics of these new missile sites indicate two distinct types of installations. Several of them include medium-range ballistic missiles capable of carrying a nuclear warhead for a distance of more than

1,000 nautical miles. Each of these missiles, in short, is capable of striking Washington, D.C., the Panama Canal, Cape Canaveral, Mexico City, or any other city in the south-eastern part of the United States, in Central America, or in the Caribbean area. . . .

This action also contradicts the repeated assurances of Soviet spokesmen, both publicly and privately delivered, that the arms buildup in Cuba would retain its original defensive character and that the Soviet Union had no need or desire to station strategic missiles on the territory of any other nation.

The size of this undertaking makes clear that it has been planned for some months. Yet only last month, after I had made clear the distinction between any introduction of ground-to-ground missiles and the existence of defensive antiaircraft missiles, the Soviet government publicly stated on September 11 that, and I quote, "The armaments and military equipment sent to Cuba are designed exclusively for defensive purposes," and, and I quote the Soviet government, "There is no need for the Soviet government to shift its weapons for a retaliatory blow to any other country, for instance Cuba," and that, and I quote the government, "The Soviet Union has so powerful rockets to carry these nuclear warheads that there is no need to search for sites for them beyond the boundaries of the Soviet Union." That statement was false.

Only last Thursday, as evidence of this rapid offensive buildup was already in my hand, Soviet Foreign Minister Gromyko told me in my office that he was instructed to make it clear once again, as he said his government had already done, that Soviet assistance to Cuba, and I quote, "pursued solely the purpose of contributing to the defense capabilities of Cuba," that, and I quote him, "training by Soviet specialists of Cuban nationals in handling defensive armaments was by no means offensive," and that "if it were otherwise," Mr. Gromyko went

on, "the Soviet government would never become involved in rendering such assistance." That statement also was false.

Neither the United States of America nor the world community of nations can tolerate deliberate deception and offensive threats on the part of any nation, large or small. We no longer live in a world where only the actual firing of weapons represents a sufficient challenge to a nation's security to constitute maximum peril. Nuclear weapons are so destructive and ballistic missiles are so swift that any substantially increased possibility of their use or any sudden change in their deployment may well be regarded as a definite threat to peace. . . .

Acting, therefore, in the defense of our own security and of the entire Western Hemisphere, and under the authority entrusted to me by the Constitution as endorsed by the resolution of the Congress, I have directed that the following *initial* steps be taken immediately:

First, to halt this offensive buildup, a strict quarantine on all offensive military equipment under shipment to Cuba is being initiated. All ships of any kind bound for Cuba from whatever nation or port will, if found to contain cargoes of offensive weapons, be turned back. This quarantine will be extended, if needed, to other types of cargo and carriers. We are not at this time, however, denying the necessities of life as the Soviets attempted to do in their Berlin blockade of 1948.

Second, I have directed the continued and increased close surveillance of Cuba and its military buildup. The Foreign Ministers of the OAS [Organization of American States] in their communiqué of October 3 rejected secrecy on such matters in this hemisphere. Should these offensive military preparations continue, thus increasing the threat to the hemisphere, further action will be justified. I have directed the Armed Forces to prepare for any eventualities; and I trust that, in the interest of both the Cuban people and the Soviet technicians at the sites, the hazards to all concerned of continuing this threat will be recognized.

Third, it shall be the policy of this nation to regard any nuclear missile launched from Cuba against any nation in the Western Hemisphere as an attack by the Soviet Union on the United States, requiring a full retaliatory response upon the Soviet Union.

Fourth, as a necessary military precaution I have reinforced our base at Guantanamo, evacuated today the dependents of our personnel there, and ordered additional military units to be on a standby alert basis.

Fifth, we are calling tonight for an immediate meeting of the Organ of Consultation, under the Organization of American States, to consider this threat to hemisphere security and to invoke Articles 6 and 8 of the Rio Treaty in support of all necessary action. The United Nations Charter allows for regional security arrangements — and the nations of this hemisphere decided long ago against the military presence of outside powers. Our other allies around the world have also been alerted.

Sixth, under the Charter of the United Nations, we are asking tonight that an emergency meeting of the Security Council be convoked without delay to take action against this latest Soviet threat to world peace. Our resolution will call for the prompt dismantling and withdrawal of all offensive weapons in Cuba, under the supervision of UN observers, before the quarantine can be lifted.

Seventh and finally, I call upon Chairman Khrushchev to halt and eliminate this clandestine, reckless, and provocative threat to world peace and to stable relations between our two nations. I call upon him further to abandon this course of world domination and to join in an historic effort to end the perilous arms race and transform the history of man. He has an opportunity now to move the world back from the abyss of destruction — by returning to his govern-

ment's own words that it had no need to station missiles outside its own territory, and withdrawing these weapons from Cuba — by refraining from any action which will widen or deepen the present crisis — and then by participating in a search for peaceful and permanent solutions.

This nation is prepared to present its case against the Soviet threat to peace, and our own proposals for a peaceful world, at any time and in any forum — in the OAS, in the United Nations, or in any other meeting that could be useful — without limiting our freedom of action.

We have in the past made strenuous efforts to limit the spread of nuclear weapons. We have proposed the elimination of all arms and military bases in a fair and effective disarmament treaty. We are prepared to discuss new proposals for the removal of tensions on both sides — including the possibilities of a genuinely independent Cuba, free to determine its own destiny. We have no wish to war with the Soviet Union, for we are a peaceful people who desire to live in peace with all other peoples. . . .

My fellow citizens, let no one doubt that this is a difficult and dangerous effort on which we have set out. No one can foresee precisely what course it will take or what costs or casualties will be incurred. Many months of sacrifice and self-discipline lie ahead — months in which both our patience and our will will be tested, months in which many threats and denunciations will keep us aware of our dangers. But the greatest danger of all would be to do nothing.

The path we have chosen for the present is full of hazards, as all paths are; but it is the one most consistent with our character and courage as a nation and our commitments around the world. The cost of freedom is always high — but Americans have always paid it. And one path we shall never choose, and that is the path of surrender or submission.

1963

27.

Martin Luther King, Jr.: Letter from Birmingham Jail

The "Negro Revolution" of the 1950s and early 1960s, which in the public mind had its beginning in the 1954 Supreme Court decision desegregating public schools, generally followed two paths: lawsuits pressed in state and federal courts, and the direct action programs of such organizations as the National Association for the Advancement of Colored People (NAACP), Congress of Racial Equality (CORE), and the Southern Christian Leadership Conference (SCLC). The Reverend Martin Luther King, Jr., who urged the tactic of passive resistance — Negroes, he said, should meet "physical force with an even stronger force, namely, soul force" — assumed the presidency of the SCLC and leadership of the new nonviolent protest movement. King and his followers chose Birmingham, Alabama, as the target of their antisegregation drive of 1963. King explained the choice: "If Birmingham could be cracked, the direction of the entire nonviolent movement in the South could take a significant turn." While King's group was pressing a boycott that crippled business and forced Birmingham businssmen to negotiate a desegregation agreement, Attorney General Robert F. Kennedy acted to secure the immediate registration of more than 2,000 Birmingham Negroes previously denied voting rights. Federal courts upheld the right of Negroes to nonviolent protest in Birmingham and elsewhere, but not before King had been arrested and jailed. The following letter (reprinted here in part), written from his cell on April 16, 1963, contained King's answer to charges by a group of eight Birmingham clergymen that he was in their city as an "outside agitator."

Source: *Christian Century*, June 12, 1963.

My Dear Fellow Clergymen:

While confined here in the Birmingham City Jail, I came across your recent statement calling my present activities "unwise and untimely." Seldom do I pause to answer criticism of my work and ideas. If I sought to answer all the criticisms that cross my desk, my secretaries would have little time for anything other than such correspondence in the course of the day, and I would have no time for constructive work. But since I feel that you are men of genuine goodwill and that your criticisms are sincerely set forth, I want to try to answer your statement in what I hope will be patient and reasonable terms.

I think I should indicate why I am here in Birmingham, since you have been influenced by the view which argues against "outsiders coming in." I have the honor of serving as president of the Southern Christian Leadership Conference, an organization operating in every Southern state, with headquarters in Atlanta, Georgia. We have some eighty-five affiliate organizations across the South, and one of them is the Alabama Christian Movement for Human Rights. Frequently, we share staff, educational, and financial resources with our affiliates. Several months ago the affiliate here in Birmingham asked us to be on call to engage in a nonviolent direct-action program if such were deemed necessary. We readily consented, and when the hour came we lived up to our promise. So I, along with several members of my staff, am here because I was invited here. I am here because I have organizational ties here.

But more basically, I am in Birmingham because injustice exists here. Just as the prophets of the 8th century B.C. left their villages and carried their "thus saith the Lord" far afield, and just as the apostle Paul left his village of Tarsus and carried the gospel of Jesus Christ to the far corners of the Greco-Roman world, so am I compelled to carry the gospel of freedom beyond my own hometown. Like Paul, I must constantly respond to the Macedonian call for aid.

Moreover, I am cognizant of the interrelatedness of all communities and states. I cannot sit idly by in Atlanta and not be concerned about what happens in Birmingham. Injustice anywhere is a threat to justice everywhere. We are caught in an inescapable network of mutuality, tied in a single garment of destiny. Whatever affects one directly affects all indirectly. Never

again can we afford to live with the narrow, provincial "outside agitator" idea. Anyone who lives inside the United States can never be considered an outsider anywhere within its bounds.

You deplore the demonstrations taking place in Birmingham. But your statement, I am sorry to say, fails to express a similar concern for the conditions that brought about the demonstrations. I am sure that none of you would want to rest content with the superficial kind of social analysis that deals merely with effects and does not grapple with underlying causes. It is unfortunate that demonstrations are taking place in Birmingham, but it is even more unfortunate that the city's white power structure left the Negro community with no alternative. . . .

You may well ask, "Why direct action? Why sit-ins, marches, etc.? Isn't negotiation a better path?" You are quite right in calling for negotiation. Indeed, this is the very purpose of direct action. Nonviolent direct action seeks to foster such a tension that a community which has constantly refused to negotiate is forced to confront the issue. It seeks so to dramatize the issue that it can no longer be ignored. My citing the creation of tension as part of the work of the nonviolent resister may sound rather shocking. But I readily acknowledge that I am not afraid of the word "tension." I have earnestly opposed violent tension, but there is a type of constructive, nonviolent tension which is necessary for growth. Just as Socrates felt that it was necessary to create a tension in the mind so that individuals could shake off the bondage of myths and half-truths and rise to the realm of creative analysis and objective appraisal, so must we see the need for nonviolent gadflies to create the kind of tension in society that will help men rise from the dark depths of prejudice and racism to the majestic heights of understanding and brotherhood.

The purpose of our direct-action program

is to create a situation so crisis-packed that it will inevitably open the door to negotiation. I therefore concur with you in your call for negotiation. Too long has our beloved Southland been bogged down in a tragic effort to live in monologue rather than dialogue. . . .

We have waited for more than 340 years for our constitutional and God-given rights. The nations of Asia and Africa are moving with jetlike speed toward gaining political independence, but we still creep at horse-and-buggy pace toward gaining a cup of coffee at a lunch counter. Perhaps it is easy for those who have never felt the stinging darts of segregation to say "Wait." But when you have seen vicious mobs lynch your mothers and fathers at will and drown your sisters and brothers at whim; when you have seen hate-filled policemen curse, kick, and even kill your black brothers and sisters with impunity; when you see the vast majority of your 20 million Negro brothers smothering in an air-tight cage of poverty in the midst of an affluent society; when you suddenly find your tongue twisted as you seek to explain to your six-year-old daughter why she can't go to the public amusement park that has just been advertised on television, and see tears welling up when she is told that Funtown is closed to colored children, and see ominous clouds of inferiority beginning to form in her little mental sky, and see her beginning to distort her personality by unconsciously developing a bitterness toward white people; when you have to concoct an answer for a five-year-old son asking, "Daddy, why do white people treat colored people so mean?"; when you take a cross-country drive and find it necessary to sleep night after night in the uncomfortable corners of your automobile because no motel will accept you; when you are humiliated day in and day out by nagging signs reading "white" and "colored"; when your first name becomes "nigger," your middle name becomes

"boy" (however old you are), and your last name becomes "John," and your wife and mother are never given the respected title "Mrs."; when you are harried by day and haunted by night by the fact that you are a Negro, never quite knowing what to expect next, and are plagued with inner fears and outer resentments; when you are forever fighting a degenerating sense of "nobodiness" — then you will understand why we find it difficult to wait. There comes a time when the cup of endurance runs over, and men are no longer willing to be plunged into an abyss of injustice where they experience the bleakness of corroding despair. I hope, sirs, you can understand our legitimate and unavoidable impatience.

You express a great deal of anxiety over our willingness to break laws. This is certainly a legitimate concern. Since we so diligently urge people to obey the Supreme Court's decision of 1954 outlawing segregation in the public schools, at first glance it may seem rather paradoxical for us consciously to break laws. One may well ask, "How can you advocate breaking some laws and obeying others?" The answer lies in the fact that there are two types of laws: just and unjust. I agree with St. Augustine that "an unjust law is no law at all.". . .

Let us consider some of the ways in which a law can be unjust. A law is unjust, for example, if the majority group compels a minority group to obey the statute but does not make it binding on itself. By the same token, a law in all probability is just if the majority is itself willing to obey it. Also, a law is unjust if it is inflicted on a minority that, as a result of being denied the right to vote, had no part in enacting or devising the law. Who can say that the legislature of Alabama which set up that state's segregation laws was democratically elected? Throughout Alabama all sorts of devious methods are used to prevent Negroes from becoming registered voters, and there are some counties in which, even though Negroes constitute a majority of the population, not a single Negro is registered. Can any law enacted under such circumstances be considered democratically structured?

Sometimes a law is just on its face and unjust in its application. For instance, I have been arrested on a charge of parading without a permit. Now there is nothing wrong in having an ordinance which requires a permit for a parade. But such an ordinance becomes unjust when it is used to maintain segregation and to deny citizens the First Amendment privilege of peaceful assembly and protest.

I hope you are able to see the distinction I am trying to point out. In no sense do I advocate evading the law, as would the rabid segregationist. That would lead to anarchy. One who breaks an unjust law must do so *openly, lovingly,* and with a willingness to accept the penalty. I submit that an individual who breaks a law that conscience tells him is unjust and who willingly accepts the penalty of imprisonment in order to arouse the conscience of the community over its injustice is in reality expressing the highest respect for law. . . .

I must make two honest confessions to you, my Christian and Jewish brothers. First, I must confess that over the past few years I have been gravely disappointed with the white moderate. I have almost reached the regrettable conclusion that the Negro's great stumbling block in his stride toward freedom is not the White Citizen's Counciler or the Ku Klux Klanner but the white moderate who is more devoted to "order" than to justice; who prefers a negative peace which is the absence of tension to a positive peace which is the presence of justice; who constantly says "I agree with you in the goal you seek, but I cannot agree with your methods"; who paternalistically believes he can set the timetable for another man's freedom; who lives by a mythical concept of time and who constantly advises the Negro

to wait for a "more convenient season." Shallow understanding from people of goodwill is more frustrating than absolute misunderstanding from people of ill will. Lukewarm acceptance is much more bewildering than outright rejection.

I had hoped that the white moderate would understand that law and order exist for the purpose of establishing justice and that when they fail in this purpose they block social progress. I had hoped that the white moderate would understand that the present tension in the South is a necessary phase of the transition from an obnoxious negative peace, in which the Negro passively accepted his unjust plight, to a substantive and positive peace, in which all men will respect the dignity and worth of human personality. Actually, we who engage in nonviolent direct action are not the creators of tension. We merely bring to the surface the hidden tension that is already alive. We bring it out in the open where it can be seen and dealt with. Like a boil that can never be cured so long as it is covered up but must be opened with all its pus-flowing ugliness to the natural medicines of air and light, injustice must be exposed, with all the tension its exposure creates, to the light of human conscience and the air of national opinion before it can be cured. . . .

You speak of our activity in Birmingham as extreme. At first I was rather disappointed that fellow clergymen would see my nonviolent efforts as those of an extremist. I began thinking about the fact that I stand in the middle of two opposing forces in the Negro community. One is a force of complacency made up of Negroes who, as a result of long years of oppression, are so completely drained of self-respect and a sense of "somebodiness" that they have adjusted to segregation, and of a few middle-class Negroes who, because of a degree of academic and economic security and because in some ways they profit by segregation, have unconsciously become insensitive to the problems of the masses. The other force is one of bitterness and hatred, and it comes perilously close to advocating violence. It is expressed in the various black nationalist groups that are springing up across the nation, the largest and best-known being Elijah Muhammad's Muslim movement. Nourished by the Negro's frustration over the continued existence of racial discrimination, this movement is made up of people who have lost faith in America, who have absolutely repudiated Christianity, and who have concluded that the white man is an incorrigible "devil."

I have tried to stand between these two forces, saying that we need emulate neither the "do-nothingism" of the complacent nor the hatred of the black nationalist. For there is the more excellent way of love and nonviolent protest. I am grateful to God that, through the influence of the Negro church, the way of nonviolence became an integral part of our struggle.

If this philosophy had not emerged, by now many streets of the South would, I am convinced, be flowing with blood. And I am further convinced that if our white brothers dismiss as "rabble-rousers" and "outside agitators" those of us who employ nonviolent direct action and if they refuse to support our nonviolent efforts, millions of Negroes will, out of frustration and despair, seek solace and security in black nationalist ideologies — a development that would inevitably lead to a frightening racial nightmare. . . .

Let me take note of my other major disappointment. Though there are some notable exceptions, I have also been disappointed with the white church and its leadership. I do not say this as one of those negative critics who can always find something wrong with the church. I say this as a minister of the gospel, who loves the church; who was nurtured in its bosom; who has been sustained by its spiritual

blessings and who will remain true to it as long as the cord of life shall lengthen.

When I was suddenly catapulted into the leadership of the bus protest in Montgomery, Alabama, a few years ago, I felt we would be supported by the white church. I felt that the white ministers, priests, and rabbis of the South would be among our strongest allies. Instead, some have been outright opponents, refusing to understand the freedom movement and misrepresenting its leaders; all too many others have been more cautious than courageous and have remained silent and secure behind stained-glass windows.

In spite of my shattered dreams I came to Birmingham with the hope that the white religious leadership of this community would see the justice of our cause and with deep moral concern would serve as the channel through which our just grievances could reach the power structure. But again I have been disappointed.

I have heard numerous Southern religious leaders admonish their worshipers to comply with a desegregation decision because it is the *law,* but I have longed to hear white ministers declare, "Follow this decree because integration is morally *right* and because the Negro is your brother." In the midst of blatant injustices inflicted upon the Negro I have watched white churchmen stand on the sideline and mouth pious irrelevancies and sanctimonious trivialities. In the midst of a mighty struggle to rid our nation of racial and economic injustice I have heard many ministers say, "Those are social issues with which the gospel has no real concern," and I have watched many churches commit themselves to a completely otherworldly religion which makes a strange, unbiblical distinction between body and soul, between the sacred and the secular.

We are moving toward the close of the twentieth century with a religious community largely adjusted to the status quo — a taillight behind other community agencies rather than a headlight leading men to higher levels of justice. . . .

But the judgment of God is upon the church as never before. If today's church does not recapture the sacrificial spirit of the early church, it will lose its authenticity, forfeit the loyalty of millions, and be dismissed as an irrelevant social club with no meaning for the twentieth century. Every day I meet young people whose disappointment with the church has turned into outright disgust.

Perhaps I have once again been too optimistic. Is organized religion too inextricably bound to the status quo to save our nation and the world? Perhaps I must turn my faith to the inner spiritual church, the church within the church, as the true *ecclesia* and the hope of the world. But again I am thankful to God that some noble souls from the ranks of organized religion have broken loose from the paralyzing chains of conformity and joined us as active partners in the struggle for freedom. They have left their secure congregations and walked the streets of Albany, Georgia, with us. They have gone down the highways of the South on torturous rides for freedom. Yes, they have gone to jail with us. Some have been kicked out of their churches, have lost the support of their bishops and fellow ministers. But they have acted in the faith that right defeated is stronger than evil triumphant. Their witness has been the spiritual salt that has preserved the true meaning of the gospel in these troubled times. They have carved a tunnel of hope through the dark mountain of disappointment.

I hope the church as a whole will meet the challenge of this decisive hour. But even if the church does not come to the aid of justice, I have no despair about the future. I have no fear about the outcome of our struggle in Birmingham, even if our motives are at present misunderstood. We will reach the goal of freedom in Birmingham and all over the nation, because the goal of America is freedom. . . .

Before closing I feel impelled to mention one other point in your statement that has troubled me profoundly. You warmly commended the Birmingham police force for keeping "order" and "preventing violence." I doubt that you would have so warmly commended the police force if you had seen its angry dogs sinking their teeth into six unarmed, nonviolent Negroes. I doubt that you would so quickly commend the policemen if you were to observe their ugly and inhuman treatment of Negroes here in the City Jail; if you were to watch them push and curse old Negro women and young Negro girls; if you were to see them slap and kick old Negro men and young boys; if you were to observe them, as they did on two occasions, refuse to give us food because we wanted to sing our grace together. I cannot join you in your praise of the Birmingham Police Department.

It is true that the police have exercised discipline in handling the demonstrators. In this sense they have conducted themselves rather "nonviolently" in public. But for what purpose? To preserve the evil system of segregation. Over the past few years I have consistently preached that nonviolence demands that the means we use must be as pure as the ends we seek. I have tried to make clear that it is wrong to use immoral means to attain moral ends. But now I must affirm that it is just as wrong, or perhaps even more so, to use moral means to preserve immoral ends. Perhaps Mr. Connor and his policemen have been rather nonviolent in public, as was Chief Pritchett in Albany, Georgia, but they have used the moral means of nonviolence to maintain the immoral end of racial injustice. As T. S. Eliot has said, there is no greater treason than to do the right deed for the wrong reason.

I wish you had commended the Negro sit-inners and demonstrators of Birmingham for their sublime courage, their willingness to suffer and their amazing discipline in the midst of great provocation. One day the South will recognize its real heroes. . . . One day the South will know that when these disinherited children of God sat down at lunch counters they were in reality standing up for what is best in the American dream and for the most sacred values in our Judeo-Christian heritage, thereby bringing our nation back to those great wells of democracy which were dug deep by the founding fathers in their formulation of the Constitution and the Declaration of Independence.

28.

JAMES BALDWIN: My Dungeon Shook

The 100th anniversary of the Emancipation Proclamation was ambiguously observed in the United States. Some Negroes and many whites marked the date — January 1, 1963 — as of vast importance in American history, and paid homage to the men — mainly one man, Abraham Lincoln — who a century before had stated officially, and for the first time, that slavery was not only immoral but also illegal. Others were not in a celebrating mood. One of them was the noted Negro novelist James Baldwin, who may have summed up the feelings of a large number of Americans, both white and black, in the remark: "You know, and I know, that the country is celebrating one hundred years of freedom one hundred years too soon." The remark closed a letter that Baldwin wrote to his nephew and published in December 1962. The letter, slightly revised, appeared in a collection of essays published the following year.

Source: *The Fire Next Time*, New York, 1963.

Dear James:

I have begun this letter five times and torn it up five times. I keep seeing your face, which is also the face of your father and my brother. Like him, you are tough, dark, vulnerable, moody — with a very definite tendency to sound truculent because you want no one to think you are soft. You may be like your grandfather in this, I don't know, but certainly both you and your father resemble him very much physically. Well, he is dead, he never saw you, and he had a terrible life; he was defeated long before he died because, at the bottom of his heart, he really believed what white people said about him. This is one of the reasons that he became so holy. I am sure that your father has told you something about all that. Neither you nor your father exhibit any tendency towards holiness: you really *are* of another era, part of what happened when the Negro left the land and came into what the late E. Franklin Frazier called "the cities of destruction." You can only be destroyed by believing that you really are what the white world calls a *nigger*. I tell you this because I love you, and please don't you ever forget it.

I have known both of you all your lives, have carried your Daddy in my arms and on my shoulders, kissed and spanked him and watched him learn to walk. I don't know if you've known anybody from that far back; if you've loved anybody that long, first as an infant, then as a child, then as a man, you gain a strange perspective on time and human pain and effort. Other people cannot see what I see whenever I look into your father's face, for behind your father's face as it is today are all those other faces which were his. Let him laugh and I see a cellar your father does not remember and a house he does not remember and I hear in his present laughter his laughter as a child. Let him curse and I remember him falling down the cellar steps, and howling, and I remember, with pain, his tears, which my hand or your grandmother's so easily wiped away. But no one's hand can wipe away those tears he sheds invisibly today, which one hears in his laughter and in his speech and in his songs. I know what the world has done to my brother and how narrowly he has survived it. And I know, which is much worse, and this is the crime of which I accuse my country and my countrymen, and for which neither I nor time nor history will ever forgive them, that they have destroyed and are destroying hundreds of thousands of lives and do not know it and do not want to know it. One can be, indeed one must strive to become, tough and philosophical concerning destruction and death, for this is what most of mankind has been best at since we have heard of man. (But remember: *most* of mankind is not *all* of mankind.) But it is not permissible that the authors of devastation should also be innocent. It is the innocence which constitutes the crime.

Now, my dear namesake, these innocent and well-meaning people, your countrymen, have caused you to be born under conditions not very far removed from those described for us by Charles Dickens in the London of more than a hundred years ago. (I hear the chorus of the innocents screaming, "No! This is not true! How *bitter* you are!" — but I am writing this letter to *you,* to try to tell you something about how to handle *them,* for most of them do not yet

really know that you exist. I *know* the conditions under which you were born, for I was there. Your countrymen were *not* there, and haven't made it yet. Your grandmother was also there, and no one has ever accused her of being bitter. I suggest that the innocents check with her. She isn't hard to find. Your countrymen don't know that *she* exists, either, though she has been working for them all their lives.)

Well, you were born, here you came, something like fourteen years ago; and though your father and mother and grandmother, looking about the streets through which they were carrying you, staring at the walls into which they brought you, had every reason to be heavyhearted, yet they were not. For here you were, Big James, named for me — you were a big baby, I was not — here you were: to be loved. To be loved, baby, hard, at once, and forever, to strengthen you against the loveless world. Remember that: I know how black it looks today, for you. It looked bad that day, too, yes, we were trembling. We have not stopped trembling yet, but if we had not loved each other none of us would have survived. And now you must survive because we love you, and for the sake of your children and your children's children.

This innocent country set you down in a ghetto in which, in fact, it intended that you should perish. Let me spell out precisely what I mean by that, for the heart of the matter is here, and the root of my dispute with my country. You were born where you were born and faced the future that you faced because you were black and *for no other reason.* The limits of your ambition were, thus, expected to be set forever. You were born into a society which spelled out with brutal clarity, and in as many ways as possible, that you were a worthless human being. You were not expected to aspire to excellence: you were expected to make peace with mediocrity. Wherever you have turned, James, in your short time on this earth, you have been told where you could go and what you could do (and *how* you could do it) and where you could live and whom you could marry. I know your countrymen do not agree with me about this, and I hear them saying, "You exaggerate." They do not know Harlem, and I do. So do you. Take no one's word for anything, including mine — but trust your experience. Know whence you came. If you know whence you came, there is really no limit to where you can go. The details and symbols of your life have been deliberately constructed to make you believe what white people say about you. Please try to remember that what they believe, as well as what they do and cause you to endure, does not testify to your inferiority but to their inhumanity and fear.

Please try to be clear, dear James, through the storm which rages about your youthful head today, about the reality which lies behind the words *acceptance and integration*. There is no reason for you to try to become like white people and there is no basis whatever for their impertinent assumption that *they* must accept *you*. The really terrible thing, old buddy, is that *you* must accept *them*. And I mean that very seriously. You must accept them and accept them with love. For these innocent people have no other hope. They are, in effect, still trapped in a history which they do not understand; and until they understand it, they cannot be released from it. They have had to believe for many years, and for innumerable reasons, that black men are inferior to white men. Many of them, indeed, know better, but, as you will discover, people find it very difficult to act on what they know. To act is to be committed, and to be committed is to be in danger. In this case, the danger, in the minds of most white Americans, is the loss of their identity.

Try to imagine how you would feel if you woke up one morning to find the sun shining and all the stars aflame. You would

Marc Riboud from Magnum

James Baldwin, photographed in 1962

be frightened because it is out of the order of nature. Any upheaval in the universe is terrifying because it so profoundly attacks one's sense of one's own reality. Well, the black man has functioned in the white man's world as a fixed star, as an immovable pillar: and as he moves out of his place, heaven and earth are shaken to their foundations. You, don't be afraid. I said that it was intended that you should perish in the ghetto, perish by never being allowed to go behind the white man's definitions, by never being allowed to spell your proper name. You have, and many of us have, defeated this intention; and, by a terrible law, a terrible paradox, those innocents who believed that your imprisonment made them safe are losing their grasp of reality.

But these men are your brothers — your lost, younger brothers. And if the word *integration* means anything, this is what it means: that we, with love, shall force our brothers to see themselves as they are, to cease fleeing from reality and begin to change it. For this is your home, my friend, do not be driven from it; great men have done great things here, and will again, and we can make America what America must become. It will be hard, James, but you come from sturdy, peasant stock, men who picked cotton and dammed rivers and built railroads, and, in the teeth of the most terrifying odds, achieved an unassailable and monumental dignity. You come from a long line of great poets, some of the greatest poets since Homer. One of them said, *The very time I thought I was lost, My dungeon shook and my chains fell off.*

You know, and I know, that the country is celebrating one hundred years of freedom one hundred years too soon. We cannot be free until they are free. God bless you, James, and Godspeed.

Your uncle,
James

29.

John F. Kennedy: The Negro and the American Promise

On June 11, 1963, a momentous event occurred at the University of Alabama. Two Negro residents of Alabama, who were clearly qualified for studies at the state's highest institution of learning, had been refused admittance on the grounds of their color. They had appealed this refusal to a federal court, which had demanded that they be admitted. Governor George Wallace promised to "stand in the schoolhouse door" to keep them out, but at the last moment he stepped aside as the two young Negroes, protected by federal guardsmen, entered. That night President Kennedy discussed the Alabama situation in a radio and television address to the American people, in the course of which he declared that the issue of the Negro's position in American life was no longer merely economic and political, but also moral.

Source: *Record*, 88 Cong., 1 Sess., pp. 10965-10966.

THIS AFTERNOON, following a series of threats and defiant statements, the presence of Alabama National Guardsmen was required on the University of Alabama to carry out the final and unequivocal order of the U.S. District Court of the Northern District of Alabama. That order called for the admission of two clearly qualified young Alabama residents who happened to have been born Negro.

That they were admitted peacefully on the campus is due in good measure to the conduct of the students of the University of Alabama, who met their responsibilities in a constructive way.

I hope that every American, regardless of where he lives, will stop and examine his conscience about this and other related incidents. This nation was founded by men of many nations and backgrounds. It was founded on the principle that all men are created equal and that the rights of every man are diminished when the rights of one man are threatened.

Today we are committed to a worldwide struggle to promote and protect the rights of all who wish to be free, and when Americans are sent to Vietnam or West Berlin, we do not ask for whites only. It ought to be possible, therefore, for American students of any color to attend any public institution they select without having to be backed up by troops.

It ought to be possible for American consumers of any color to receive equal service in places of public accommodation, such as hotels and restaurants and theaters and retail stores, without being forced to resort to demonstrations in the street; and it ought to be possible for American citizens of any color to register and to vote in a free election without interference or fear of reprisal.

It ought to be possible, in short, for every American to enjoy the privileges of being American without regard to his race or his color. In short, every American ought to have the right to be treated as he would wish to be treated, as one would wish his children to be treated. But this is not the case.

The Negro baby born in America today, regardless of the section of the nation in which he is born, has about one-half as much chance of completing a high school as a white baby born in the same place on the same day, one-third as much chance of completing college, one-third as much chance of becoming a professional man, twice as much chance of becoming unemployed, about one-seventh as much chance of earning $10,000 a year, a life expectancy which is seven years shorter, and the prospects of earning only half as much.

This is not a sectional issue. Difficulties over segregation and discrimination exist in every city in every state of the Union, producing in many cities a rising tide of discontent that threatens the public safety. Nor is this a partisan issue in a time of domestic crisis. Men of goodwill and generosity should be able to unite regardless of party

Matt Heron from Black Star

State trooper seizes an American flag being carried by a five-year-old boy at a civil rights demonstration in Mississippi

or politics. This is not even a legal or legislative issue alone. It is better to settle these matters in the courts than on the streets, and new laws are needed at every level, but law alone cannot make men see right.

We are confronted primarily with a moral issue. It is as old as the Scriptures and is as clear as the American Constitution.

The heart of the question is whether all Americans are to be afforded equal rights and equal opportunities, whether we are going to treat our fellow Americans as we want to be treated. If an American, because his skin is dark, cannot eat lunch in a restaurant open to the public, if he cannot send his children to the best public school available, if he cannot vote for the public officials who represent him, if, in short, he cannot enjoy the full and free life which all of us want, then who among us would be content to have the color of his skin changed and stand in his place? Who among us would then be content with the counsels of patience and delay?

One hundred years of delay have passed since President Lincoln freed the slaves, yet their heirs, their grandsons, are not fully free. They are not yet freed from the bonds of injustice. They are not yet freed from social and economic oppression, and this nation, for all its hopes and all its boasts, will not be fully free until all its citizens are free.

We preach freedom around the world, and we mean it, and we cherish our freedom here at home; but are we to say to the world, and much more importantly, to each other that this is a land of the free except for the Negroes; that we have no second-class citizens except Negroes; that we have no class or caste system, no ghettoes, no master race except with respect to Negroes?

Now the time has come for this nation to fulfill its promise. The events in Birmingham and elsewhere have so increased the cries for equality that no city or state or legislative body can prudently choose to ignore them. The fires of frustration and discord are burning in every city, North and South, where legal remedies are not at hand. Redress is sought in the streets, in demonstrations, parades, and protests, which create tensions and threaten violence and threaten lives.

We face, therefore, a moral crisis as a country and as a people. It cannot be met by repressive police action. It cannot be left to increased demonstrations in the streets. It cannot be quieted by token moves or talk. It is a time to act in the Congress, in your state and local legislative body and, above all, in all of our daily lives.

It is not enough to pin the blame on others, to say this is a problem of one section of the country or another, or deplore the fact that we face. A great change is at hand, and our task, our obligation, is to make that revolution, that change, peaceful and constructive for all. Those who do nothing are inviting shame as well as violence. Those who act boldly are recognizing right as well as reality.

Next week I shall ask the Congress of the United States to act, to make a commitment it has not fully made in this century to the proposition that race has no place in American life or law. The federal judiciary has upheld that proposition in a series of forthright cases. The executive branch has adopted that proposition in the conduct of its affairs, including the employment of federal personnel, the use of federal facilities, and the sale of federally financed housing.

But there are other necessary measures which only the Congress can provide, and they must be provided at this session. The old code of equity law under which we live commands for every wrong a remedy, but in too many communities, in too many parts of the country, wrongs are inflicted on Negro citizens as there are no remedies at law. Unless the Congress acts, their only remedy is in the street.

I am therefore asking the Congress to enact legislation giving all Americans the right to be served in facilities which are open to the public — hotels, restaurants, theaters, retail stores, and similar establishments. This seems to me to be an elementary right. Its denial is an arbitrary indignity that no American in 1963 should have to endure, but many do.

I have recently met with scores of business leaders urging them to take voluntary action to end this discrimination and I have been encouraged by their response; and in the last two weeks over seventy-five cities have seen progress made in desegregating these kinds of facilities. But many are unwilling to act alone, and for this reason nationwide legislation is needed if we are to move this problem from the streets to the courts.

I am also asking Congress to authorize the federal government to participate more fully in lawsuits designed to end segregation in public education. We have succeeded in persuading many districts to desegregate voluntarily. Dozens have admitted Negroes without violence. Today a Negro is attending a state-supported institution in every one of our fifty states, but the pace is very slow.

Too many Negro children entering segregated grade schools at the time of the Supreme Court's decision nine years ago will enter segregated high schools this fall, having suffered a loss which can never be restored. The lack of an adequate education denies the Negro a chance to get a decent job. The orderly implementation of the Supreme Court decision, therefore, cannot be left solely to those who may not have the economic resources to carry the legal action or who may be subject to harassment.

Other features will be also requested, including greater protection for the right to vote. But legislation, I repeat, cannot solve this problem alone. It must be solved in the homes of every American in every community across our country.

In this respect, I want to pay tribute to those citizens North and South who have been working in their communities to make life better for all. They are acting not out of a sense of legal duty but out of a sense of human decency. Like our soldiers and sailors in all parts of the world, they are meeting freedom's challenge on the firing line, and I salute them for their honor and their courage.

My fellow Americans, this is a problem which faces us all — in every city of the North as well as the South. Today there are Negroes unemployed two or three times as many compared to whites, inadequate in education, moving into the large cities, unable to find work, young people particularly out of work without hope, denied equal rights, denied the opportunity to eat at a restaurant or lunch counter or go to a movie theater, denied the right to a decent education, denied almost today the right to attend a state university even though qualified. It seems to me that these are matters which concern us all, not merely Presidents or congressmen or governors, but every citizen of the United States.

This is one country. It has become one country because all of us and all the people who came here had an equal chance to develop their talents. We cannot say to ten percent of the population that you can't have that right; that your children can't have the chance to develop whatever talents they have; that the only way that they are going to get their rights is to go into the streets and demonstrate. I think we owe them and we owe ourselves a better country than that. Therefore, I am asking for your help in making it easier for us to move ahead and to provide the kind of equality of treatment which we would want ourselves; to give a chance for every child to be educated to the limit of his talents.

As I have said before, not every child has an equal talent or an equal ability or an equal motivation, but they should have the equal right to develop their talent and their ability and their motivation to make something of themselves. We have a right to expect that the Negro community will be responsible, will uphold the law, but they have a right to expect that the law will be fair; that the Constitution will be color blind, as Justice Harlan said at the turn of the century.

This is what we are talking about and this is a matter which concerns this country and what it stands for, and in meeting it I ask the support of all of our citizens.

———◆———

Segregation is on its deathbed — the question now is, how costly will the segregationists make the funeral.

MARTIN LUTHER KING, JR.

30.

MARTIN LUTHER KING, JR.: I Have a Dream

*In Washington, D.C., on August 28, 1963, more than 200,000 persons participated in
a "march for jobs and freedom" at the Lincoln Memorial — one hundred years and
eight months after the Emancipation Proclamation. The march was intended to prod
Congress to deal at last with the issues of civil rights and poverty. (No legislation
was in fact forthcoming until after President Kennedy's assassination.) The marchers
came from all walks of life: labor leaders, politicians, show business figures,
clergy, students and teachers, rich and poor, Negroes and whites. The ten speakers
included Eugene Carson Blake, Walter Reuther, A. Philip Randolph, Roy Wilkins,
Floyd McKissick (who delivered James Farmer's address), and Whitney M. Young, Jr.
But it was generally conceded that Martin Luther King, Jr., president of the Southern
Christian Leadership Conference, most effectively articulated the meaning of the great
demonstration in the speech reprinted below. James Reston of the* New York Times
*described King's speech as "a peroration that was an anguished echo from all the
old American reformers, Roger Williams calling for religious liberty, Sam Adams
calling for political liberty, old man Thoreau denouncing coercion, William Lloyd
Garrison demanding emancipation, and Eugene V. Debs crying for economic
equality — Dr. King echoed them all. . . . He was full of the symbolism of Lincoln
and Gandhi, and of the cadences of the Bible." The words with which King closed his
remarks were inscribed on his tombstone after his assassination on April 4, 1968.*

Source: *The SCLC Story in Words and Pictures*, Atlanta, 1964, pp. 50-51.

FIVE SCORE YEARS AGO, a great American, in whose symbolic shadow we stand, signed the Emancipation Proclamation. This momentous decree came as a great beacon light of hope to millions of Negro slaves who had been seared in the flames of withering injustice. It came as a joyous daybreak to end the long night of captivity.

But one hundred years later, we must face the tragic fact that the Negro is still not free. One hundred years later, the life of the Negro is still sadly crippled by the manacles of segregation and the chains of discrimination. One hundred years later, the Negro lives on a lonely island of poverty in the midst of a vast ocean of material prosperity. One hundred years later, the Negro is still languished in the corners of American society and finds himself an exile in his own land. So we have come here today to dramatize an appalling condition.

In a sense we have come to our nation's Capital to cash a check. When the architects of our republic wrote the magnificent words of the Constitution and the Declaration of Independence, they were signing a promis-

U.P.I. — Compix

Martin Luther King, Jr. (center front) heading the march on Washington, 1963

sory note to which every American was to fall heir. This note was a promise that all men would be guaranteed the unalienable rights of life, liberty, and the pursuit of happiness.

It is obvious today that America has defaulted on this promissory note insofar as her citizens of color are concerned. Instead of honoring this sacred obligation, America has given the Negro people a bad check; a check which has come back marked "insufficient funds." But we refuse to believe that the bank of justice is bankrupt. We refuse to believe that there are insufficient funds in the great vaults of opportunity of this nation. So we have come to cash this check — a check that will give us upon demand the riches of freedom and the security of justice.

We have also come to this hallowed spot to remind America of the fierce urgency of *now.* This is no time to engage in the luxury of cooling off or to take the tranquilizing drug of gradualism. *Now* is the time to make real the promises of democracy. *Now* is the time to rise from the dark and desolate valley of segregation to the sunlit path of racial justice. *Now* is the time to open the doors of opportunity to all of God's children. *Now* is the time to lift our nation from the quicksands of racial injustice to the solid rock of brotherhood.

It would be fatal for the nation to overlook the urgency of the moment and to underestimate the determination of the Negro. This sweltering summer of the Negro's legitimate discontent will not pass until there is an invigorating autumn of freedom and equality. Nineteen sixty-three is not an end, but a beginning. Those who hope that the Negro needed to blow off steam and will now be content will have a rude awakening if the nation returns to business as usual. There will be neither rest nor tranquillity in America until the Negro is granted his citizenship rights. The whirlwinds of revolt will continue to shake the foundations of our nation until the bright day of justice emerges.

But there is something that I must say to my people who stand on the warm threshold which leads into the palace of justice. In the process of gaining our rightful place we must not be guilty of wrongful deeds. Let us not seek to satisfy our thirst for freedom by drinking from the cup of bitterness and hatred. We must forever conduct our struggle on the high plane of dignity and discipline. We must not allow our creative protest to degenerate into physical violence. Again and again we must rise to the majestic heights of meeting physical force with soul force.

The marvelous new militancy which has engulfed the Negro community must not lead us to a distrust of all white people, for many of our white brothers, as evidenced by their presence here today, have come to realize that their destiny is tied up with our destiny and their freedom is inextricably bound to our freedom. We cannot walk alone.

And as we walk, we must make the pledge that we shall march ahead. We cannot turn back. There are those who are asking the devotees of civil rights, "When will you be satisfied?"

We can never be satisfied as long as the Negro is the victim of the unspeakable horrors of police brutality.

We can never be satisfied as long as our bodies, heavy with the fatigue of travel, cannot gain lodging in the motels of the highways and the hotels of the cities.

We cannot be satisfied as long as the Negro's basic mobility is from a smaller ghetto to a larger one.

We can never be satisfied as long as a Negro in Mississippi cannot vote and a Negro in New York believes he has nothing for which to vote.

No, no, we are not satisfied, and we will not be satisfied until justice rolls down like waters and righteousness like a mighty stream.

I am not unmindful that some of you have come here out of great trials and tribulations. Some of you have come fresh from narrow jail cells. Some of you have come from areas where your quest for freedom left you battered by the storms of persecution and staggered by the winds of police brutality. You have been the veterans of creative suffering. Continue to work with the faith that unearned suffering is redemptive.

Go back to Mississippi, go back to Alabama, go back to South Carolina, go back to Georgia, go back to Louisiana, go back to the slums and ghettos of our Northern cities, knowing that somehow this situation can and will be changed. Let us not wallow in the valley of despair.

I say to you today, my friends, that in spite of the difficulties and frustrations of the moment I still have a dream. It is a dream deeply rooted in the American dream.

I have a dream that one day this nation will rise up and live out the true meaning of its creed: "We hold these truths to be self-evident; that all men are created equal."

I have a dream that one day on the red hills of Georgia the sons of former slaves and the sons of former slaveowners will be able to sit down together at the table of brotherhood.

I have a dream that one day even the state of Mississippi, a desert state sweltering with the heat of injustice and oppression, will be transformed into an oasis of freedom and justice.

I have a dream that my four little children will one day live in a nation where they will not be judged by the color of their skin but by the content of their character.

I have a dream today.

I have a dream that one day the state of Alabama, whose governor's lips are presently dripping with the words of interposition and nullification, will be transformed into a situation where little black boys and black girls will be able to join hands with little white boys and white girls and walk together as sisters and brothers.

I have a dream today.

I have a dream that one day every valley shall be exalted, every hill and mountain shall be made low, the rough places will be made plain, and the crooked places will be made straight, and the glory of the Lord shall be revealed, and all flesh shall see it together.

This is our hope. This is the faith with which I return to the South. With this faith we will be able to hew out of the mountain of despair a stone of hope. With this faith we will be able to transform the jangling discords of our nation into a beautiful symphony of brotherhood.

With this faith we will be able to work together, to pray together, to struggle together, to go to jail together, to stand up for freedom together, knowing that we will be free one day.

This will be the day when all of God's children will be able to sing with new meaning, "My country 'tis of thee, sweet land of liberty, of thee I sing. Land where my fathers died, land of the Pilgrims' pride, from every mountainside, let freedom ring."

And if America is to be a great nation, this must become true. So let freedom ring from the prodigious hilltops of New Hampshire. Let freedom ring from the mighty mountains of New York. Let freedom ring from the heightening Alleghenies of Pennsylvania!

Let freedom ring from the snowcapped Rockies of Colorado! Let freedom ring from the curvaceous peaks of California! But not only that; let freedom ring from Stone Mountain of Georgia! Let freedom ring from Lookout Mountain of Tennessee!

Let freedom ring from every hill and molehill of Mississippi. From every mountainside, let freedom ring.

When we let freedom ring, when we let it ring from every village and every hamlet, from every state and every city, we will be able to speed up that day when all of God's children, black men and white men, Jews and Gentiles, Protestants and Catholics, will be able to join hands and sing in the words of the old Negro spiritual, "Free at last! Free at last! Thank God Almighty, we are free at last!"

31.

Songs of the Civil Rights Movement

*From time immemorial men and women engaged in a common cause have sung together.
This is likely to be all the more true of rebels and revolutionaries, who, lacking the
physical force of those in authority, must discover emotional and moral forces within
themselves. It was true, at any rate, of the Negro civil rights movement in the
United States, at least until 1965 or 1966. The songs sung by civil rights marchers
were in many cases very old ones. "Oh Freedom" was a Negro marching song in
the Civil War; "Which Side Are You On?" is a labor song that dates from the early
1930s in Harlan County, Kentucky; "We Shall Not Be Moved" is one of the most widely
known labor songs in both the United States and Canada, and also dates from the 1930s;
"We Shall Overcome," perhaps the most famous of all modern civil rights songs, is at
least a half century old and may be a good deal older. (The other four songs reprinted
here, on the other hand, may be quite recent in origin.) But even though the tunes
were old, and some of the words meaningful in other traditions of economic and social
protest, all of the songs, old and new, gained new currency and new power when they
were sung by white men and black men alike, in North and South, in Birmingham and
Selma, Alabama, in Watts (Los Angeles), and in Chicago. Watts, which saw the
movement take another turn, may have been the last place, and 1965 the last year, in
which they were sung with full effect.*

Source: *We Shall Overcome!*, compiled by Guy and Candie Carawan, New York, 1963.

OH FREEDOM

Oh Freedom, Oh Freedom,
Oh Freedom over me, over me —

Chorus:
And before I'll be a slave
I'll be buried in my grave
And go home to my Lord and be free.

No segregation, no segregation,
No segregation over me, over me —

No more weeping, no more weeping,
No more weeping over me, over me —

No burning churches, no burning
churches,
No burning churches over me, over
me —

No more Jim Crow, no more Jim Crow,
No more Jim Crow over me, over me —

No more Barnett, no more Barnett,
No more Barnett over me, over me —

No more Pritchett, no more Pritchett,
No more Pritchett over me, over me.

❧ WHICH SIDE ARE YOU ON?

Come all you freedom lovers and listen while I tell
Of how the freedom riders came to Jackson to dwell.

Chorus:
Oh which side are you on, boys,
Which side are you on? (Tell me)
Which side are you on, boys,
Which side are you on?

My daddy was a freedom fighter and I'm a freedom son —
I'll stick right with this struggle until the battle's won.

Don't "Tom" for "Uncle Charlie," don't listen to his lies,
'Cause black folks haven't got a chance until they organize.

They say in Hinds County, no neutrals have they met —
You're either for the Freedom Ride or you "Tom" for Ross Barnett.

Oh, people, can you stand it, oh tell me how you can?
Will you be an Uncle Tom or will you be a man?

Cap'n Ray'll holler "move on!" but the Freedom Riders won't budge,
They'll stand there in the terminals and even before the judge.

❧ WE SHALL NOT BE MOVED

We are fighting for our freedom,
    We shall not be moved;
We are fighting for our freedom,
    We shall not be moved —

Chorus:
Just like a tree
Planted by the water,
    We shall not be moved.

We are black and white together, etc.

We will stand and fight together, etc.

Our parks are integrating, etc.

We're sunning on the beaches, etc.

🎵 KEEP YOUR EYES ON THE PRIZE

Paul and Silas, bound in jail,
Had no money for to go their bail.

Chorus:
  Keep your eyes on the prize,
  Hold on, hold on,
  Hold on, hold on —
  Keep your eyes on the prize,
    Hold on, hold on.

Paul and Silas begin to shout,
The jail door opened and they walked out.

Freedom's name is mighty sweet —
Soon one of these days we're going to meet.

Got my hand on the Gospel plow,
I wouldn't take nothing for my journey now.

The only chain that a man can stand
Is that chain of hand in hand.

The only thing that we did wrong —
Stayed in the wilderness too long.

But the one thing we did right
Was the day we started to fight.

We're gonna board that big Greyhound,
Carryin' love from town to town.

We're gonna ride for civil rights,
We're gonna ride, both black and white.

We've met jail and violence too,
But God's love has seen us through.

Haven't been to Heaven but I've been told
Streets up there are paved with gold.

🎵 WOKE UP THIS MORNING WITH MY MIND STAYED ON FREEDOM

Woke up this morning with my mind stayed on freedom,
Woke up this morning with my mind stayed on freedom,
Woke up this morning with my mind stayed on freedom,
    Hallelu, hallelu, hallelu, hallelu, hallelujah.

Ain't no harm to keep your mind stayed on freedom, etc.

Walkin' and talkin' with my mind stayed on freedom, etc.

Singin' and prayin' with my mind stayed on freedom, etc.

Doin' the twist with my mind stayed on freedom, etc.

🎵 AIN'T GONNA LET NOBODY TURN ME ROUND

Ain't gonna let nobody, Lordy, turn me round,
  Turn me round, turn me round.
Ain't gonna let nobody, Lordy, turn me round.

Chorus:
  I'm gonna keep on a-walkin', Lord,
  Keep on a-talkin', Lord,
  Marching up to freedom land.

Ain't gonna let Nervous Nelly turn me round, etc.

Ain't gonna let Chief Pritchett turn me round, etc.

Ain't gonna let Mayor Kelly turn me round, etc.

Ain't gonna let segregation turn me round, etc.

Ain't gonna let no jailhouse turn me round, etc.

Ain't gonna let no injunction turn me round, etc.

THIS LITTLE LIGHT OF MINE

This little light of mine, I'm gonna let it shine;
This little light of mine, I'm gonna let it shine;
This little light of mine, I'm gonna let it shine;
   Let it shine, let it shine, let it shine.

The light that shines is the light of love,
Lights the darkness from above.
It shines on me and it shines on you,
And shows what the power of love can do.
I'm gonna shine my light both far and near,
I'm gonna shine my light both bright and clear.
Where there's a dark corner in this land,
I'm gonna let my little light shine.

We've got the light of freedom, we're gonna let it shine;
We've got the light of freedom, we're gonna let it shine;
We've got the light of freedom, we're gonna let it shine;
   Let it shine, let it shine, let it shine.

Deep down in the South, we're gonna let it shine, etc.

Down in Birmingham, we're gonna let it shine, etc.

All over the nation, we're gonna let it shine, etc.

Everywhere I go, I'm gonna let it shine, etc.

Tell Chief Pritchett, we're gonna let it shine, etc.

All in the jailhouse, we're gonna let it shine, etc.

On Monday he gave me the gift of love;
Tuesday peace came from above;
Wednesday he told me to have more faith;
Thursday he gave me a little more grace;
Friday he told me just to watch and pray;
Saturday he told me just what to say;
Sunday he gave me the power divine —
To let my little light shine.

❧ WE SHALL OVERCOME

We shall overcome,
 we shall overcome,
We shall overcome some day.
Oh, deep in my heart, I do believe,
We shall overcome some day.

We are not afraid,
 we are not afraid,
We are not afraid today.
Oh, deep in my heart, I do believe,
We shall overcome some day.

We are not alone,
 we are not alone,
We are not alone today.
Oh, deep in my heart, I do believe,
We shall overcome some day.

The truth will make us free,
 the truth will make us free,
The truth will make us free some day.
Oh, deep in my heart, I do believe,
We shall overcome some day.

We'll walk hand in hand,
 we'll walk hand in hand,
We'll walk hand in hand some day.
Oh, deep in my heart, I do believe,
We shall overcome some day.

The Lord will see us through,
 the Lord will see us through,
The Lord will see us through today.
Oh, deep in my heart, I do believe,
We shall overcome some day.

32.

Howard Morgan: On the Staffing of Regulatory Agencies

*The number of federal regulatory agencies greatly increased during and after
the New Deal era, and with increasing numbers went increasing power and influence
on the national scene. But the benefits of such agencies and commissions were often
less than they might have been owing to the inability of various Presidents — and
sometimes their unwillingness — to obtain the best men and women for these
important jobs. Howard Morgan, a member of the Federal Power Commission, wrote a
letter to President Kennedy early in 1963 explaining why he would refuse to be
reappointed when his term ran out in June 1963. The letter, which touched on
compelling but little publicized problems confronting democratic government in our time,
was published in March.*

Source: *Progressive*, March 1963: "A Letter to the President."

IT IS WITH CONSIDERABLE REGRET that I now convey to you my firm decision not to accept a further appointment to this Commission after expiration of my present term of office on June 22, 1963. I respectfully request that a nomination to replace me be made in time to permit confirmation by the Senate prior to that date.

There are a number of reasons for my decision, but I am sure I should be considered less than gracious if I were to list them all. Besides, several of them are clearly visible to those who have read the dissenting opinions which I have been obliged to write during my service here.

I should, however, like to make a general comment concerning the regulatory agencies which may be of some small help to you, to my successors, and to the public interest. My study and work in the regulatory field cover a period of twenty-five years, and the strongest convictions produced by that experience are those I am setting forth in this letter.

Standing as it does midway between the extremes of unbridled monopoly and undiluted state ownership, public-utility regulation has been perhaps as noble, hopeful, and challenging a concept as any in our democratic framework of government. The passage of laws establishing this concept required all the courage, self-sacrifice, and tenacity of men like George Norris, Hiram Johnson, Gifford Pinchot, and many, many more of the same caliber.

Ordinary men could not possibly have secured the enactment of those laws against the almost overwhelming forces opposed to them. Ordinary men cannot administer those laws today in the face of pressures generated by huge industries and focused with great skill on and against the sensitive areas of government. Ordinary men yield too quickly to the present-day urge toward conformity, timidity, and personal security.

Under our laws the great natural monopolies which form our utility industries are granted almost priceless protections and privileges. The industries and individual companies are keenly alert to their rights, as they should be, and properly insist before the commissions, the courts, and the Congress upon prompt and full enjoyment of those rights. But those unusual rights —

rights not enjoyed by unregulated industry — are accompanied by unusual obligations and responsibilities. Or are supposed to be. There is the rub. If our regulatory laws are not administered by men of the same character, courage, and outlook as the men who enacted the laws, we will surely find the regulated industries and companies successful in postponing, or evading entirely, the responsibilities which are supposed to accompany their rights. When this happens, utility regulation ceases to be, or never becomes, a protection to the consuming public. Instead it can easily become a fraud upon the public and a protective shield behind which monopoly may operate to the public detriment.

The big problem in the regulatory field is not *ex parte* communications, influence peddling, and corruption as that word is commonly understood, though where these problems exist they can be serious. In my experience as a regulatory official I have been approached only once with a veiled intimation that money or stock was available in return for a favorable decision, and that was at the state level, not here in Washington. But abandonment of the public interest can be caused by many things, of which timidity and a desire for personal security are the most insidious, the least detectable, and, once established in a regulatory agency, the hardest to eradicate.

This Commission, for example, must make hundreds and even thousands of decisions each year, a good many of which involve literally scores and hundreds of millions of dollars in a single case. Without the needed sense of public responsibility, a commissioner can find it very easy to consider whether his vote might arouse an industry campaign against his reconfirmation by the Senate, and even easier to convince himself that no such thought ever crossed his mind. And if he can fool himself, whom can he not fool?

The big problem is to find men of ability, character, courage, and broad vision who have the same viewpoint as the authors of the legislation they will be called on to administer; men who would feel at ease while working with a Pinchot or a Norris; men who don't become neurotic with worry after having cast a vote for the public interest.

Admittedly there is no oversupply of such men these days. There never was. But such men, and only such men, make great regulatory commissioners. It is only when a commission is staffed by men, for example, like Eastman, Aitchison, Splawn, and Mahaffie of the old Interstate Commerce Commission, that the public gets protection instead of platitudes; principle instead of puff-jobs and image building; hard work instead of "streamlining" and wall-chart juggling.

As you well know, there has been a great deal of study of regulatory agencies lately, and with good reason. All of the studies I have seen mention the matters I have discussed in this letter, but only in passing, and then proceed to make detailed suggestions of an organizational and administrative character. I am sure the agencies will continue to benefit from these studies and suggestions, but I am equally convinced that the main problem is in the area of personnel selection, which I have discussed.

Regulatory agencies have extraordinary problems and responsibilities, and they operate under extraordinary pressures. They require — and they cannot operate successfully without — extraordinary men.

Let me emphasize that these comments have been general in nature and apply equally to all regulatory agencies. With the exception of the persons named herein, they are not intended to depict or describe any individual, including my colleagues and myself.

Service on the Commission has been an immensely stimulating and educational experience for me, for which I shall remain grateful to you. Please let me extend all good wishes for the continued success of your administration.

Brandenburg Gate seen through a roll of barbed wire, the Soviets' first version of the Berlin Wall

COLD WAR STALEMATE

It became apparent during the 1960s that the East-West conflict had undergone major changes. While the rhetoric of the Cold War continued, the nature of U.S.-Russian relations had altered rather drastically; the arms race of nuclear weapons and missiles, based on chronic overestimations of the other side's strength — the "missile gap" — led quickly to a balance of total destructive capability known as nuclear detente. The increased reliance on missile-oriented offensive and defensive systems effectively precluded face-to-face confrontations except in situations where one side or the other had clearly overextended itself, as in Cuba or the U-2 incident. Furthermore, the gradual assumption of power by European nations, the coming to national consciousness of many undeveloped and hitherto ignored nations, and the Sino-Soviet split made Cold War rhetoric and strategy even more dangerously simplistic than it had been.

Tass from Sovfoto

(Above) U-2 pilot Francis Gary Powers on trial in Moscow, 1960; (below) Khrushchev blasts America at the Moscow exhibit of evidence relating to the capture of the U-2

"Paris Match" from Pictorial Parade

(Above) West Berlin woman attempts to ask favor of an East German soldier patroling the wall; (below) cartoonist's view of the Vienna meeting between John F. Kennedy and Nikita Khrushchev

A period of U.S.-Russian cordiality followed Khrushchev's visit in 1959; the tension of the Berlin situation eased, and there was some hope of progress at the summit conference planned for May 1960 in Paris. On May 5, shortly before the conference began, Russia announced it had shot down an American aircraft deep in Soviet territory; the U.S., relying on the auto-destruct mechanisms built into the U-2, claimed that the plane was engaged in weather research and that no spying had been intended. The flimsy cover story was shattered by Russia's announcement that the plane, the pilot, the cameras, and film had been captured. The U.S. was forced to admit the reconnaissance missions of four years. Khrushchev refused to enter the Paris discussions.

(Above) U.S. patrol plane and destroyer (foreground) keep watch on Soviet freighter removing missiles from Cuba; (below) President Kennedy addressing the people of West Berlin, 1963

(Above) Signing the Nuclear Test Ban Treaty in Moscow, August 1963; (below) cartoon by Hugh Haynie relating to the installation of a direct telephone line between Washington and Moscow

In June 1961 President Kennedy, Macmillan of Great Britain, and De Gaulle of France met and reaffirmed the Allied stand on Berlin; predictably, Khrushchev revived his ultimatum of 1958 by threatening to sign a separate peace with East Germany if the Allies did not evacuate West Berlin by the end of the year. A period of sabre-rattling ensued with large arms build-ups announced by both sides. In August East Berlin authorities erected the Berlin Wall, restricting passage between the East and West sectors and re-establishing the stalemate in its most extreme position. In October 1962 Kennedy disclosed the presence of Russian missile bases in Cuba and ordered a U.S. blockade of the island; threats of war were exchanged, and world tension mounted until Soviet ships bound for Cuba turned back. A Russian proposal to trade the Cuban bases for U.S. bases in Turkey was rejected; on October 28 Khrushchev agreed to a unilateral withdrawal.

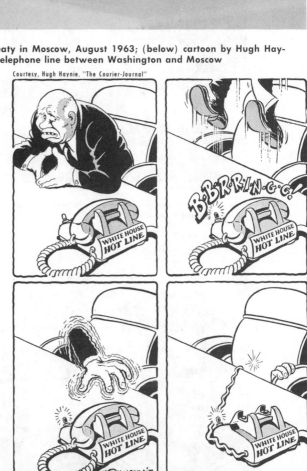

(Above) Hats of various generals on a table outside a conference room at SHAPE Headquarters; (below) sailors from seven NATO countries serving as the combined crew of a U.S. destroyer

Cornell Capa from Magnum

A NATO supply point in West Germany

The NATO alliance had been the mainstay of the West's Cold War military front and it had provided a political framework for Western European cooperation; both aspects of the alliance had been largely U.S.-directed, with American arms, money, and goals as the tools. During the 1960s, however, with Europe fully recovered and relatively prosperous, a dissatisfaction with American domination of NATO developed. Beyond resurgent nationalism and disenchantment with Cold War romance was a growing doubt about the real depth of the U.S. commitment to NATO. A real break in the Atlantic community came in March 1966 when French President De Gaulle announced the withdrawal of French forces from the NATO command.

Final lowering of flags at Rocquencourt as the NATO headquarters are transferred from Paris

Dalmas — Pix from Publix

(Above) French President Charles de Gaulle, 1962; (below) mushroom cloud from the first nuclear device detonated by France on the island of Muruora, French Polynesia, 1966

Charles de Gaulle became the leading force for an independent, united Europe. Long before taking France out of NATO he had pursued foreign policy often contrary to U.S.-NATO goals. Since 1960 France had developed an independent nuclear striking force which broke the Russian-Anglo-American monopoly; refused to admit Great Britain to the European Common Market because of its special relations with the Commonwealth and with the U.S.; and granted recognition to Communist China. Gaulism aimed at creating a third power center in the world as a means of breaking the U.S.-Russian deadlock and thus establishing an atmosphere for change. American reaction to De Gaulle's policies was, naturally, rather negative. Following the removal of NATO military facilities from France, a token blow was struck at De Gaulle with the further removal of the NATO political apparatus; the greatly diminished importance of NATO as a whole, however, made the attempt to isolate France entirely futile.

(Above) Long freight train transporting Belgian cars into Holland as a part of the Common Market trade agreements; (below) Coca-Cola truck in Belgium

Henri Cartier-Bresson from Magnum

Courtesy, Edward Kuekes, "Cleveland Plain Dealer"

"Sign now, talk later!"

(Above) Tanks of the Red Chinese Army pass in review at the Tenth Anniversary parade in Peking, 1959; (left) cartoon by Kuekes in the "Cleveland Plain Dealer," 1963; (right) Buddhist priest blesses American troops at the opening of a new Air Force base in U-Tapao, Thailand, 1966

The uneasiness within the NATO community had been matched in many respects by a growing independence among the Communist nations of Eastern Europe. Both NATO and the Warsaw Pact were being looked upon as at least badly in need of revision. The total stalemate in Europe and the mutual loss of influence led to a shift of interest to other areas by both the U.S. and Russia. Attention was directed to the undeveloped areas of the world and the competition for power and influence continued, though on modified terms. The Russian-Chinese split emphasized the growing degree of U.S. and Russian accord on vital issues as the direct confrontation in Europe ended.

Ebba Freund — Pix from Publix

(Top left) A Syrian peasant stands guard along the frontier border near Israel; (top right) remains of an Egyptian soldier killed fighting Israel, June 1967; (left) Gamal Abd-al Nasser, President of the United Arab Republic

The Middle East was a popular area for the new conflict-by-proxy method adopted by the U.S. and Russia. The impossibility of forcing regional and nationalist problems into simple Cold War terms, however, kept the area in a confused and fluid situation. American money and arms poured into the oil kingdoms and into the Western state, Israel. Communist aid was concentrated on the independent Arab nationalist states, notably Egypt and Syria. When Israel launched the lightning war of June 1967, the forced coalition of pro-Nasser and pro-Western Arab states kept both the U.S. and Russia in an attitude of mild and distant support for their respective sides.

33.

R. Sargent Shriver: Two Years of the Peace Corps

The Peace Corps was proposed by President Kennedy in a speech on November 2, 1960, late in the presidential campaign of that year. The response of young people the country over was immediate and enthusiastic, and the Peace Corps was formally established early the next year, and placed under the direction of Sargent Shriver, the President's brother-in-law. Shriver described the agency's first two years of operation in an article, part of which is reprinted here, that was published in the summer of 1963.

Source: Reprinted by special permission from *Foreign Affairs*, July 1963.

Oscar Wilde is said to have observed that America really was discovered by a dozen people before Columbus, but it was always successfully hushed up. I am tempted to feel that way about the Peace Corps; the idea of a national effort of this type had been proposed many times in past years. But in 1960 and 1961 for the first time the idea was joined with the power and the desire to implement it. On Nov. 2, 1960, Sen. John F. Kennedy proposed a "peace corps" in a campaign speech at the Cow Palace in San Francisco. Thirty thousand Americans wrote immediately to support the idea; thousands volunteered to join.

The early days of the Peace Corps were like the campaign days of 1960, but with no election in sight. My colleagues were volunteer workers and a few key officials loaned from other agencies. "I use not only all the brains I have but all I can borrow," Woodrow Wilson said. So did we. Letters cascaded in from all over the country in what one writer described as "paper tornadoes at the Peace Corps." The elevators to our original two-room office disgorged constant sorties of interested persons, newspaper reporters, job seekers, academic figures, and generous citizens offering advice. Everywhere, it seemed, were cameras, coils of cable, and commentators with questions.

An organization, we know, gains life through hard decisions, so we hammered out basic policies in long, detailed discussions in which we sought to face up to the practical problems and reach specific solutions before we actually started operations. We knew that a few wrong judgments in the early hours of a new organization's life, especially a controversial government agency, can completely thwart its purposes — even as a margin of error of a thousandth of an inch in the launching of a rocket can send it thousands of miles off course. And we knew the Peace Corps would have only one chance to work. As with the parachute jumper, the chute had to open the first time. We knew, too, that a thousand suspicious eyes were peering over our shoulders. Some were the eyes of friendly critics, but many belonged to unfriendly skeptics. The youthfulness of the new administration, particularly the President, enhanced the risk; an older leadership would have had greater immunity from charges of "sophomorism." . . .

Would enough qualified Americans be willing to serve? Even if they started, would they be able to continue on the job despite frustration, dysentery, and boredom? Could Americans survive overseas without special foods and privileges, special housing, automobiles, television, and air conditioners? Many Americans thought not. The Washington correspondent of the respected *Times of India* agreed with them in these words:

When you have ascertained a felt local need, you would need to find an American who can exactly help in meeting it. This implies not only the wherewithal (or what you inelegantly call the "know how") but also a psychological affinity with a strange new people who may be illiterate and yet not lack wisdom, who may live in hovels and yet dwell in spiritual splendor, who may be poor in worldly wealth and yet enjoy a wealth of intangibles and a capacity to be happy. Would an American young man be in tune with this world he has never experienced before? I doubt it. . . .

One also wonders whether American young men and tender young girls, reared in air-conditioned houses at a constant temperature, knowing little about the severities of nature (except when they pop in and out of cars or buses) will be able to suffer the Indian summer smilingly and, if they go into an Indian village, whether they will be able to sleep on unsprung beds under the canopy of the bejeweled sky or indoors in mud huts, without writing home about it.

At a time when many were saying that Americans had gone soft and were interested mainly in security, pensions, and suburbia, the Peace Corps could have been timorous. Possible ways of hedging against an anticipated shortage of applicants could have included low qualification standards, generous inducements to service, cautious programming, a period of duty shorter than two years, an enforced period of enlistment such as the "hitch" in the armed forces, or draft exemption for volunteer service in the Peace Corps. We deliberately chose the risk rather than the hedge in each case and created an obstacle course. The applicant could remove himself any time he realized his motive was less than a true desire for service. This method of self-selection has by

now saved us from compounded difficulties abroad.

Our optimism about sufficient recruits was justified. More than 50,000 Americans have applied for the Peace Corps. In the first three months of this year, more Americans applied for the Peace Corps than were drafted for military service. This happened notwithstanding the fact that young men who volunteer for the Peace Corps are liable to service on their return. . . .

We debated hotly the question of age and whether or not older people should be eligible. We listened to proposals for an age limit in the thirties and then in the sixties and finally decided to set no upper age limit at all. Our oldest volunteer today happens to be seventy-six, and we have more grandparents than teenagers in the Peace Corps. Some older volunteers have turned out to be rigid and cantankerous in adapting to a standard of living *their* parents took for granted, but the majority of them make a lot of us in the New Frontier look like stodgy old settlers. . . .

Some of my colleagues proposed that Peace Corps volunteers act as technical helpers to ICA technicians, "extra hands" for the more experienced older men. Peace Corps practice has moved in another direction. A natural distinction between the AID adviser at a high level in government and the Peace Corps volunteer making his contribution as a "doer" or "worker" at the grass roots soon became apparent. It also became clear that the Peace Corps volunteer had a new and perhaps unique contribution to make as a person who entered fully into host-country life and institutions, with a host-country national working beside him and another directing his work. This feature of the Peace Corps contributed substantially to its early support abroad.

Discussion of the possibility that the Peace Corps might be affiliated with the ICA led into the question of its relationship to U.S. political and information establishments overseas. The Peace Corps in Wash-

Dennis Stock from Magnum

R. Sargent Shriver, director and chief organizer of the Peace Corps

ington is responsible to the secretary of state. Volunteers and staff abroad are responsible to the American ambassador. Nevertheless, the Peace Corps maintains a distinction between its functions and those of embassies, AID and USIA offices. There was a design to this which Secretary Rusk has aptly described: "The Peace Corps is not an instrument *of* foreign policy, because to make it so would rob it of its contribution *to* foreign policy."

Peace Corps volunteers are not trained diplomats; they are not propagandists; they are not technical experts. They represent our society by what they are, what they do, and the spirit in which they do it. They steer clear of intelligence activity and stay out of local politics. Our strict adherence to these principles has been a crucial factor in the decision of politically uncommitted countries to invite American volunteers into their midst, into their homes, and even into their classrooms and schoolyards to teach future generations of national leaders. In an era of sabotage and espionage, intelligence and counterintelligence, the Peace Corps and its volunteers have earned a priceless yet simple renown: they are trustworthy. . . .

The involvement of private organizations and universities has been crucial to the Peace Corps' success. America is a pluralistic society and the Peace Corps expresses its diversity abroad by demonstrating that the public and private sectors can work cooperatively and effectively. We consciously seek contracts with private organizations, colleges, and universities to administer our programs. We gain the advantage of expert knowledge, long experience, tested working relationships, and often even private material resources. For example, CARE has contributed more than $100,000 worth of equipment to the Peace Corps in Colombia. Initially, there was suspicion by some of these agencies that the Peace Corps, with the resources of the United States taxpayer behind it, would preempt their own work abroad. Suspicion has turned into understanding, however, as the United States government, through the Peace Corps, has facilitated the work of private organizations and has focused new attention on the needs and opportunities for service abroad.

In our "talent search" we went to government, academic life, business, the bar, the medical profession, and every other walk of life where leadership was available.

We deliberately recruited as many Negroes and representatives of other minority groups as possible for jobs in every echelon. We knew that Negroes would not ordinarily apply for high-level policy jobs, so we decided to seek them out. Today 7.4 percent of our higher echelon positions are filled by Negroes as compared to .8 percent for other government agencies in similar grades; 24 percent of our other positions are filled by Negroes, compared to a figure for government agencies in general of 5.5 percent.

How big should the Peace Corps be? Everyone was asking this question and everyone had an answer. Advice ranged from 500 to 1 million. There were strong voices raised in support of "tentative pilot projects," looking to a Peace Corps of less than 1,000. However, Warren W. Wiggins, an experienced foreign-aid expert, took a broader view. He pointed out that ultracautious programming might produce prohibitive per capita costs, fail even to engage the attention of responsible foreign officials (let alone have an impact), and fail to attract the necessary American talent and commitment. Furthermore, when the need was insatiable, why should we try to meet it with a pittance?

There were also arguments in those early days about "saturation" of the foreign country, either in terms of jobs or the psychological impact of the American presence. I have since noticed that the same arguments made about a 500-1,000-man program in 1961 were also made about our plans to expand to 5,000 volunteers (March 1963), to 10,000 volunteers (March 1964), and to 13,000 (September 1964). I am not suggesting that the Peace Corps should continue to grow indefinitely. But I am proposing that much time and energy are wasted in theoretical musings, introspections, and worries about the future. Peace Corps volunteers are a new type of overseas American. Who is to say now how many of them will be welcome abroad next year, or in the next decade? Our country and our

times have had plenty of experience with programs that were too little, too late. . . .

Many of the original doubts and criticisms of the Peace Corps have not materialized. On the other hand, substantive problems have emerged which were little discussed or expected two years ago. One of the most difficult is the provision of adequate language training. This was foreseen, but most observers thought that the exotic languages such as Thai, Urdu, Bengali, and Twi would give us our main problem, while Spanish and French speakers could be easily recruited or quickly trained. The opposite has been true. The first volunteers who arrived in Thailand in January 1962 made a great impression with what observers described as "fluent" Thai. As the volunteers were the first to point out, their Thai was not actually fluent, but their modest achievement was tremendously appreciated. Since then, of course, a large proportion of the volunteers there have become truly fluent.

On the other hand, a considerable number of volunteers going to Latin America and to French Africa have been criticized for their mediocre language fluency. Expectations are high in these countries and halting Spanish or French is not enough. We have learned that America contains rather few French-speaking bus mechanics, Spanish-speaking hydrologists, or math-science teachers who can exegete theorems in a Latin-American classroom. Can we devise more effective and intensive language training, particularly for farmers, craftsmen, construction foremen, well drillers, and other Americans who never before have needed a second language? Should we take skilled people and teach them languages, or take people with language abilities and teach them skills?

We still need more volunteers, especially those who combine motivation and special skills. The person with a ready motivation for Peace Corps service tends to be the liberal arts student in college, the social scientist, the person with "human relations" interests. The developing countries need and want a great many Americans with this background, but they also want engineers, agronomists, lathe operators, and geologists. We cannot make our maximum contribution if we turn down requests for skills which we have difficulty finding. There are presently 61 engineers in the Peace Corps, 30 geologists, and 236 nurses, respectable numbers considering the ready availability of generously paying jobs in the domestic economy. But requests still far outnumber the supply. . . .

We face increasingly difficult choices as we grow. Should we concentrate in the future on the countries where we now have programs and resist expanding to new areas? We are already committed to programs in forty-seven nations. Should we favor a program where there are relatively stable social conditions, good organization, and effective leadership? Or should we take greater risks and commit our resources in a more fluid and disorganized situation, usually in a poorer country, where the Peace Corps might make a crucial difference or find a great opportunity? Where should we draw the line between adequate material support to the volunteers and the perils of providing them with too many material goods? Where is the equilibrium between safeguarding the volunteer's health and morale and protecting the Peace Corps' declared purpose that he should live as does his co-worker in the host country, without special luxury or advantage?

When is a particular program completed? In Nigeria the answer is relatively easy. That country's coordinated educational development plan projects a need for 815 foreign teachers in 1965, 640 in 1966, 215 in 1968, and none in 1970. By then enough Nigerians will have been trained to fill their own classrooms. Progress may not follow so fine a plan, but the Peace Corps can look ahead to a day when its academic, teaching work in Nigeria will be done.

The answer is not so simple in Colombia, where volunteers are working on community development in ninety-two rural towns. There is no lack of change and progress: the Colombian government has trebled its own commitment of resources and staff to this progressive community development program. Scores of individual communities have already learned how to organize to transform their future. When volunteer John Arango organized the first town meeting in Cutaru almost two years ago, for example, not one soul showed up. Twenty months later almost every citizen turns out for these meetings. The townsmen have changed an old jail into a health clinic; they have drained the nearby swamps; they have rebuilt wharves on the river; they have cleared stumps out of the channel to make it navigable; and they are now building the first eighteen of seventy-two do-it-yourself houses designed by the volunteer.

John Arango's Colombian co-worker is equally responsible for the results in Cutaru. In community development, particularly, the ability of the host organization to provide able counterparts is crucial to a program's success. I might also mention that host countries have in every case made voluntary contributions to the Peace Corps programs. In Africa, alone, they have supported the program to the value of $2.5 million. During and after the Puerto Rico conference, three countries in Latin America announced plans to establish home-grown Peace Corps organizations; when implemented, these will help solve the shortage of counterparts. We believe North American and Latin-American volunteers will complement one another and increase the total effectiveness.

The first "replacement group" in the Peace Corps is about to complete training for service in Colombia. Should we send these volunteers to fill the shoes of their predecessors in the villages which are now moving ahead, albeit shakily? Or should we send the volunteers to new communities where nothing has been done? We know that more is needed than two years of work by a North American and his Colombian co-workers to effect self-perpetuating change. On the other hand, we do not want the volunteer to become a crutch in a community's life. Some of the new volunteers in Colombia will, therefore, try to follow through with their predecessor's work, but others will take on villages where no American has served. In the meantime we are planning to study what happens in those towns where volunteers are not replaced.

Earlier I mentioned there has been a change in the nature of comment and criticism about the Peace Corps. In the beginning, the doubters worried about the callowness of youth and the ability of mortals to make any good idea work. The more recent criticism is more sophisticated and more substantive. Eric Sevareid recently observed: "While the Corps has something to do with spot benefits in a few isolated places, whether in sanitizing drinking water, or building culverts, its work has, and can have, very little to do with the fundamental investments, reorganizations, and reforms upon which the true and long-term economic development of backward countries depends." Mr. Sevareid acknowledges that "giving frustrated American youth a sense of mission and adding to our supply of comprehension of other societies fatten the credit side of the ledger." He adds: "If fringe benefits were all the Corps' originators had in mind, then this should be made clear to the country."

I do not agree with him that the second and third purposes of the Peace Corps Act — representing America abroad in the best sense and giving Americans an opportunity to learn about other societies — are "fringe benefits." Fulton Freeman, the United States ambassador in Colombia, believes the whole Peace Corps program could be justified by its creation of a new American resource in the volunteers who are acquiring language skills and intensive understanding

of a foreign society. Former volunteers will be entering government service (150 have already applied to join USIA), United Nations agencies, academic life, international business concerns, and a host of other institutions which carry on the business of the United States throughout the world. Others will return to their homes, capable of exerting an enlightened influence in the communities where they settle. Many trite euphemisms of the ignorant and ready panaceas of the uninformed will clash immediately with the harsh facts that volunteers have learned to live with abroad.

Is the second purpose of the Peace Corps Act — to be a good representative of our society — a "fringe benefit"? Peace Corps volunteers are reaching the people of foreign countries on an individual basis at a different level from the influence of most Americans abroad. The Peace Corps volunteer lives under local laws, buys his supplies at local stores, and makes his friends among local people. He leaves to the diplomat and the technicians the complex tools which are peculiarly their own while he sets out to work in the local environment. . . .

Although I disagree with Mr. Sevareid's emphasis in dismissing two of the three purposes of the Peace Corps Act as "fringe benefits," he does get to the heart of an important question when he compares the direct economic impact of the Peace Corps to fundamental investments, reorganizations, and economic development. The Peace Corps' contribution has been less in direct economic development than in social development — health, education, construction, and community organization. We are convinced that economic development directly depends on social development. In his valedictory report this past April as head of the Economic Commission for Latin America, Raul Prebisch observed that there are *not* "grounds for expecting that economic development will take place first and be followed in the natural course of events by social development. Both social and economic development must be achieved in measures that require the exercise of rational and deliberate action. . . . There can be no speed-up in economic development without a change in the social structure."

While they have their differences, Theodore W. Schultz and J. Kenneth Galbraith have no disagreement on the essential role of social development in economic progress. In contrast, some who argue from the European-North American experience overlook the vital need for social development which had already been substantially achieved in the countries of the Atlantic community. This is the basic difference between the problem of the Marshall Plan, which was concerned with economic reconstruction in societies with abundant social resources, and the problem of forced-draft economic development in much of Asia, Africa, and Latin America. . . .

The Peace Corps is not a "foreign aid" agency. Two of the three purposes of the Peace Corps as defined in the Act deal with understanding, not economic assistance. Moreover, our financial investment is in the volunteer who brings his skills and knowledge home with him. Seventy-five percent of the Peace Corps' appropriated funds enters the economy of the United States; of the remaining 25 percent, more than half (57 percent) is spent on American citizens, the Peace Corps volunteers themselves.

A Jamaican radio commentator recently asserted that "a great distance between people is the best creator of goodwill. Jumble people up together on a sort of temporary basis of gratitude on one side and condescension on the other, and you'll have everyone at each other's throat in no time." If I believed this were inevitable, regardless of the attitude, preparation, and mode of life of volunteers, I would advocate disbanding the Peace Corps — as well as most other programs overseas. But I have greater faith in the universality of men's aspirations and of men's ability to respect each other when they know each other. It is the American

who lives abroad in isolation and the thoughtless tourist who create distrust and dislike.

I believe the Peace Corps is also having more impact than we may realize on our own society and among our own people. . . .

Our own Peace Corps volunteers are being changed in other ways than in the acquisition of languages and expertise. They will be coming home more mature, with a new outlook toward life and work. Like many other Americans, I have wondered whether our contemporary society, with its emphasis on the organizational man and the easy life, can continue to produce the self-reliance, initiative, and independence that we consider to be part of our heritage. We have been in danger of losing ourselves among the motorized toothbrushes, tranquilizers, and television commercials. Will Durant once observed that nations are born stoic and die epicurean; we have been in danger of this happening to us. The Peace Corps is truly a new frontier in the sense that it provides the challenge to self-reliance and independent action which the vanished frontier once provided on our own continent. Sharing in the progress of other countries helps us to rediscover ourselves at home.

The influence of the Peace Corps idea might be described as a series of widening circles, like the expanding rings from a stone thrown into a pond. The inner, most sharply defined circle represents the immediate effect of the program — accomplishments abroad in social and economic development, skills, knowledge, understanding, institution-building, a framework for cooperative effort with private organizations, research and experiment in "overseas Americanship," language training, and improvements in health.

The second ring moving outward on the water might be the Peace Corps' influence on our society, on institutions and people, on the creation of a new sense of participation in world events, an influence on the national sense of purpose, self-reliance, and an expanded concept of volunteer service in time of peace.

There is still a wider circle and, being farthest from the splash, the hardest to make out clearly. Perhaps I can explain it by describing the relationships I see between the Peace Corps and our American Revolution. The Revolution placed on our citizens the responsibility for reordering their own social structure. It was a triumph over the idea that man is incompetent or incapable of shaping his destiny. It was our declaration of the irresistible strength of a universal idea connected with human dignity, hope, compassion, and freedom. The idea was not simply American, of course, but arose from a confluence of history, geography, and the genius of a resolute few at Philadelphia.

We still have our vision, but our society has been drifting away from the world's majority: the young and raw, the colored, the hungry, and the oppressed. The Peace Corps is helping to put us again where we belong. It is our newest hope for rejoining the majority of the world without at the same time betraying our cultural, historic, political, and spiritual ancestors and allies. As Pablo Casals, the renowned cellist and democrat, said of the Peace Corps last year:

This is new, and it is also very old. We have come from the tyranny of the enormous, awesome, discordant machine, back to a realization that the beginning and the end are man — that it is man who is important, not the machine, and that it is man who accounts for growth, not just dollars and factories. Above all, that it is man who is the object of all our efforts.

34.

Jerome B. Wiesner: Science in the Affluent Society

Jerome Wiesner, special assistant for science and technology to President Kennedy and, according to knowing commentators, one of the most influential members of the American "scientific establishment" in the 1960s, summed up the circumstances surrounding the following speech in its first paragraph. The general interest in science was, in 1963, greater than ever before, he said; but the uncritical praise that had been the norm in the past had been replaced by an attitude of doubt and concern — a concern that Wiesner seemed to share at the same time that he attempted to identify its underlying causes. The speech, reprinted here in part, was delivered during the Centennial Celebration of the National Academy of Sciences, in Washington, on October 23, 1963.

Source: *Where Science and Politics Meet*, New York, 1965, pp. 54-65.

THE GENERAL INTEREST IN SCIENCE is greater now than ever before. It is evidenced in the newspapers and other publications and in Congress too. There are at the moment several congressional committees examining the purposes and methods of government-financed scientific and technological activities. While such interest is not new, the point of view seems to be. Until recently, most discussions of science consisted of uncritical praise. Now the situation is changed. Serious questions are being asked, and many of them reflect deep-seated concern about the character and purposes of the nation's scientific and technological undertakings, reflecting a clear desire to become more familiar with these processes.

Why has the mood changed so? Has science changed, or was too much expected from science in the past, or have the nation's needs changed? I don't believe that the answers really lie in this direction. What has changed, I believe, is the scope of the motivation for supporting research through the federal government. There has been a broadening of emphasis from a primary need to support military development to a wider purpose encompassing the entire spectrum of social needs. The military objective is still of great significance, to be sure, but now this is only one of many reasons for the new research and development activities.

To be specific: While the level of spending for military research and development has remained almost constant during the past three years, total federal expenditures for all research and development have continued to rise at an exponential rate and have doubled every four to five years. The last doubling involved an increment of approximately $7 billion. Military research and development is still the largest single component of the federal technical budget, amounting to approximately $8 billion of the almost $14-billion fiscal year 1963 budget.

When the increases in the budget were primarily for improved military security, they were easier to understand and therefore easier to justify than they are today. In retrospect, the country was very fortunate — I hope this is not misunderstood — that this incentive for research support did exist following World War II. I doubt if there was at that time a sufficient appreciation of the general importance of scientific research

to have made possible the creation of our present large and very competent scientific establishment on the basis of needs for the general welfare.

In reviewing the political scene, President Kennedy once observed that there are cycles in the affairs of men. And in science, too, we can observe this phenomenon. We have experienced a heady period of growth, and it is time to review objectives, assess accomplishments, and adjust stressed institutional arrangements to present needs.

The country has been through these periods of growth and integration, stocktaking and reorientation before — many times — during its history as a nation. Starting with the Constitutional Convention, the American people have had a concern for science. And it has always presented a problem to the government. Science has contributed steadily to the development of the nation, and, at every step, the needs of the federal government and federal funds have been a major incentive in its achievements. At some point in every historical period, the question of the role of the federal government in science and the search for the proper form of science organization within the federal establishment have been a burning issue. Though the research efforts involved may appear minuscule by our standards, they were as important to their times as our much bigger programs are to ours. Physical surveys, exploration, standards of time and measure, geological surveys, patent incentives to spur invention, navigation, agricultural science, and public health were among the early issues that involved the government in scientific endeavors.

Most interesting to the contemporary scene is the violent debate which took place over a Department of Science in the 1880s. This argument was resolved by the Allison Commission, a joint congressional committee, which concluded that the government's scientific establishment and the scientific community in the universities had already grown too complex for such a change in organizational structure. The recommendation for a Department of Science came from a committee of the National Academy of Sciences. It thus appears that committee work for scientists is not a new invention, or for that matter are government consultants, who figure prominently in the early history of federal science.

When I came to Washington in 1961, I encountered considerable pressure for the creation of a stronger coordination and science-policy mechanism at the presidential level. There were then, and still are, strong proponents of a Department of Science — complete with Cabinet-level secretary — both in the Congress and among members of the scientific community. The President's Science Advisory Committee studied the question for approximately a year and concluded that a Department of Science, bringing together many research activities now found in the individual agencies of the government, was not advantageous, and that it would, in fact, reduce the effectiveness of the programs to take them out of agencies to which they were relevant. But they did say that a need existed for more effective and more comprehensive supervision of the federal scientific and technological activities.

One characteristic stands out above all others in connection with science in the federal government, and that is its continued growth. In periods of national emergency and of enthusiasm for science, the rate of growth has been fast; during periods of reassessment or preoccupation with other problems, such as the great depressions, it has been slow; but the average slope continues upward. I have examined manpower data which go back about forty years, and this steady rate of growth is clear. During this interval, the number of scientists and engineers has doubled every twelve years. If one assumes that the same rate of growth has persisted since 1800, there would have had to be about one hundred individuals

Cornell Capa from Magnum
Jerome B. Wiesner

then engaged in scientific and technical activities, a not too unreasonable number for the size and character of the society at that time.

I don't cite this history to absolve us of the need to deal with our current problems, but rather to give us some perspective and to indicate that any solutions which we devise today will undoubtedly not be adequate a few years hence.

Not many years ago in his provocative book, *The Affluent Society*, Kenneth Galbraith illuminated the new problems of transition when he attributed many of the economic and social ills of the United States to its failure to appreciate the fundamental changes that technology had made in the industrial society. He pointed out that modern machinery and automation had made it possible to produce all of the consumer goods which the American people would ever want, using a fraction of the total labor force; that following the conventional wisdom existing among economists, we still practised an economy of scarcity in a society where scarcities need not exist. To use his words:

> The final problem of the productive society is what it produces. This manifests itself in an implacable tendency to provide an opulent supply of some things and a niggardly yield of others. This disparity carries to the point where it is a cause of social discomfort and social unhealth. The line which divides our area of wealth from our area of poverty is roughly that which divides privately produced and marketed goods and services from publicly rendered services. Our wealth in the first is not only in startling contrast with the meagerness of the latter, but our wealth of privately produced goods is, to a marked degree, the cause of the crisis in the supply of public services. For we fail to see the importance, indeed the urgent need, of maintaining a balance between the two.

There is obviously no simple, or even single, answer to the question of how to make the best use of our available resources. Public support of science has, until now, largely been exempted from this debate because funds for it were a small part of the very large sums of money provided to insure military security. The only substantial sums provided for any other purpose in recent times were those related to health needs. The existence of unfulfilled social and economic needs, coupled with a significant fact — the leveling off of research and development in relation to gross national product — suggest that the country faces an era of reevaluation. This process of leveling off is the reason for many of the current questions. It indicates that confusions which were of no consequence ten years ago must be gotten straight today. To the extent that federally supported research and development is justified for social purposes other than national security, it will be judged by different standards, less well-defined, and more controversial as well.

There is concern about waste of funds and imbalances in the federal programs. There is concern about distortion of our federal activities and our universities. There is worry that the unanticipated but inevitable side effects of new technology are causing more and more difficult problems which then require further, expensive remedial actions. Agricultural surpluses, air and water pollution are good examples. The unpredictable consequences of the widespread effects of the use of pesticides is another. Technological unemployment is yet another. There is some feeling that federal research and development expenditures are responsible for unbalanced economic development between geographic areas of the country and between different industries. There is fear also that too large a fraction of the ablest youngsters are being attracted into science and engineering. Underlying it all is the belief that the whole activity is beyond the comprehension of the individuals in the government who are responsible for it, be they in the executive branch or in the Congress.

Some of these worries stem from real problems, involve the need for policy actions and should be considered and deliberated. Others stem from misunderstandings which we should strive to eliminate. First of all, research activities and development are frequently not distinguished. They are mixed together and called science. Even most engineers and scientists fail to make a clear enough distinction between activities carried out solely for the purpose of adding to existing scientific knowledge and work that is performed because it may be able to satisfy some practical need. And this confusion is at the root of much misunderstanding among non-scientists who are called upon to make decisions or pass judgments about technical matters. It isn't that most people fail to recognize that there is a spectrum of activities with pure research at one end and hardware development at the other. The problem is rather a failure to understand that the methods and motivations of each are different, and that often research, new knowledge, is necessary in order to achieve a practical goal.

Not only are research activities quite different from development work, but so are their costs. We have estimated that the fiscal year 1963 obligations for basic research by the federal government are approximately $1.4 billion out of the approximately $15 billion devoted to research and development, and of this $1.4 billion, one-half billion are funds for space science and include the cost of boosters and launching operations. I quoted this figure during a congressional hearing and was later told by Congressman Pucinski that he hadn't realized that basic research was so small a portion of the total. "Maybe," he said, "we were focusing on the wrong problem when we focused our inquiry on basic research expenditures rather than on those for development."

In my view, development activities, the creation of useful new devices, should only be undertaken if there is a clear-cut requirement for a new product after it has been developed. This is reasonable, for it is ordinarily possible to make satisfactory predictions about the probable cost and performance of a proposed new device, whether it is an aircraft, a computer, a chemical-processing apparatus, or a nuclear power plant. It is also possible to make a decision about the desirability of a given development. Furthermore, because development efforts are generally much more costly than research, one should apply rigorous tests of need before starting new efforts.

In the case of exploratory development and applied research, there is reason to be more venturesome. Here the search is to see if practical applications of new knowledge are possible. For example, there is an effort today to explore possible new uses of the laser, the source of coherent light developed recently, and elements of this work should

be carried to the point of demonstrating the feasibility of underlying concepts. Here, too, work beyond that point should be permitted only if the ultimate capability is needed. These criteria are applicable to all but the basic research segment of the research and development effort. In other words, a basis exists by which administrators and legislators could establish the need for most items of the more than 90 percent of the federal expenditures for research and development. I am not saying that they could or should pass on the technical validity of proposals or judge between competing ways of accomplishing a given objective. This must still be the function of experts, but then the experts will be passing on means, not ends. Corporation executives, government budget officers, and department heads and members of Congress have traditionally made such decisions with confidence and with access to scientific and engineering advice; there is no reason why they cannot continue to successfully.

But the choices in the field of basic research must be left to the scientists. This is why I place so much emphasis on the matter of distinctions. Even here, others will need to make decisions regarding the overall level of effort, and if that level is less than is required to support all of the worthwhile research that scientists want to do at any given time, it will be necessary for the scientists to make decisions regarding the support for the different disciplines. Not that this would be easy either. I could write an entertaining book about our efforts to make decisions in the field of high-energy accelerators.

I am very frequently asked whether there are no limits to the growth of research activities, and I find it impossible to give a simple answer to the question. There is no foreseeable limit to the amount of productive scientific research that can be done. Clearly, a lack of interesting and important work is not in sight. Many more people have the potential to do effective, creative research than are currently engaged in such work or are studying to become scientists. It appears then that the amount of research will be set by the willingness of the country to pay for it. Though we have not passed the point where we can fail to reap increased benefits from increased expenditures on basic research, we have reached the point in time where the rate of growth for the total research and development effort will probably be diminished.

Though the actual level of federal research and development obligations rose from $11.2 billion in fiscal year 1962 to $14.5 billion in 1963, the percentage of the gross national product for the given years represented by these figures remained constant at approximately 2 percent. In this climate our basic research activities should be carefully scrutinized. Marginal activities should not be tolerated. Here considerable assistance is needed from the academic institutions and from individual scientists, for it would be extremely difficult and very undesirable for the government to set standards for academic research and even worse for it to try to police them.

The interrelationships of institutions and individuals in the scientific community make the United States' scientific enterprise today a complex one, involving many different associations among universities, industries, government, and individual scientists. It is a many-faceted organism with little defined structure. . . .

To me, the most perplexing problem of all is that of reconciling our present system for awarding research grants, which is based solely on scientific quality, with the need and desire to build up academic and scientific excellence in many parts of the country where it has not previously existed. There is a widely held view that the present system discriminates against areas with modest scientific establishments; that federal funds are used to attract scientists and students from such areas to the large centers and, so, in effect, the rich get richer and the poor get poorer. With the growing realization that economic well-being will be ever more closely linked to technologically based industry, which in turn depends upon scientific activities in local universities, most areas of the country not already so endowed are determined to create a strong scientific base. Hence, the growing resentment and criticism of the manner in which the federal funds for research are allocated. . . .

These issues and many others will undoubtedly be examined by the House committees investigating research and development. The future for all of science will be significantly affected by the outcome.

Many individuals and many organizations will inevitably be party to the present inquiry about science that will be undertaken by the entire nation, for the entire nation. Under these circumstances, the National Academy of Sciences could give invaluable service by leading the discussion which would contribute to a broader comprehension by all sectors of the society — the scientific community included — of the emerging implications and opportunities of science in our affluent society.

Science is a great game. It is inspiring and refreshing. The playing field is the universe itself.

I. I. Rabi

35.

JOHN F. KENNEDY: The Nuclear Test-Ban Treaty

Negotiations between the U.S., Great Britain, and the U.S.S.R. on a nuclear test-ban treaty began in Geneva in 1955 and informal talks had been conducted before that, but as late as 1963 little or no progress had been made. On June 10, 1963, President Kennedy, in an attempt to break the deadlock, delivered an address at the American University in Washington, D.C., on the "strategy of peace," in which he declared that despite long-standing differences the time had come when the great powers must "direct our attention to our common interests and the means by which those differences can be resolved." The President then announced that the three major nuclear powers had agreed to meet in Moscow for further talks, and he promised that the U.S. would halt atmospheric nuclear testing so long as other nations did so. The Moscow conference resulted in a treaty that was signed on August 5 by the foreign ministers of the three nations. The treaty had been introduced to the American people on July 26 by the President in the television address reprinted here. A conservative faction charged that the treaty was a threat to U.S. security, but the Senate nevertheless ratified it on September 24 by a vote of 80 to 19. The treaty was ratified by the Soviet Union the next day and shortly thereafter by Great Britain.

Source: *Record,* 88 Cong., 1 Sess., pp. 13453-13455.

I SPEAK TO YOU tonight in a spirit of hope. Eighteen years ago the advent of nuclear weapons changed the course of the world as well as the war. Since that time, all mankind has been struggling to escape from the darkening prospects of mass destruction on earth. In an age when both sides have come to possess enough nuclear power to destroy the human race several times over, the world of communism and the world of free choice have been caught up in a vicious circle of conflicting ideology and interests. Each increase of tension has produced an increase in arms; each increase in arms has produced an increase in tension.

In these years, the United States and the Soviet Union have frequently communicated suspicions and warnings to each other, but very rarely hope. Our representatives have met at the summit and at the brink; they have met in Washington and in Mos-

cow, at the United Nations and in Geneva. But too often these meetings have produced only darkness, discord, or disillusion.

Yesterday a shaft of light cut into the darkness. Negotiations were concluded in Moscow on a treaty to ban all nuclear tests in the atmosphere, in outer space and underwater. For the first time, an agreement has been reached on bringing the forces of nuclear destruction under international control — a goal first sought in 1946 when Bernard Baruch submitted our comprehensive plan to the members of the United Nations.

That plan, and many subsequent disarmament plans, large and small, have all been blocked by those opposed to international inspection. A ban on nuclear tests, however, requires on-the-spot inspection only for underground tests. This nation now possesses a variety of techniques to detect the nuclear tests of other nations which are conducted in the air or underwater. For such tests produce unmistakable signs which our modern instruments can pick up.

The treaty initiated yesterday, therefore, is a limited treaty which permits continued underground testing and prohibits only those tests that we ourselves can police. It requires no control posts, no on-site inspection, and no international body.

We should also understand that it has other limits as well. Any nation which signs the treaty will have an opportunity to withdraw if it finds that extraordinary events related to the subject matter of the treaty have jeopardized its supreme interest; and no nation's right to self-defense will in any way be impaired. Nor does this treaty mean an end to the threat of nuclear war. It will not reduce nuclear stockpiles; it will not halt the production of nuclear weapons; it will not restrict their use in time of war.

Nevertheless, this limited treaty will radically reduce the nuclear testing which would otherwise be conducted on both sides; it will prohibit the United States, the United Kingdom, the Soviet Union, and all others who sign it from engaging in the atmosphere tests which have so alarmed mankind; and it offers to all the world a welcome sign of hope.

For this is not a unilateral moratorium, but a specific and solemn legal obligation. While it will not prevent this nation from testing underground, or from being ready to resume atmospheric tests if the acts of others so require, it gives us a concrete opportunity to extend its coverage to other nations and later to other forms of nuclear tests.

This treaty is in part the product of Western patience and vigilance. We have made clear — most recently in Berlin and in Cuba — our deep resolve to protect our security and our freedom against any threat or aggression. We have also made clear our steadfast determination to limit the arms race. In three administrations, our soldiers and diplomats have worked together to this end, always with the support of Great Britain. Prime Minister Macmillan joined with President Eisenhower in proposing a limited test-ban treaty in 1959, and again with me in 1961 and 1962.

But the achievement of this goal is not a victory for one side — it is a victory for mankind. It reflects no concessions either to or by the Soviet Union. It reflects simply our common recognition of the dangers in further testing.

This treaty is not the millennium. It will not resolve all conflicts, or cause the Communists to forgo their ambitions, or eliminate the dangers of war. It will not reduce our need for arms or allies or programs of assistance to others. But it is an important first step — a step toward peace — a step toward reason — a step away from war.

Here is what this step can mean to you and your children and your neighbors.

First, this treaty can be a step toward reduced world tensions and broader areas of agreement. The Moscow talks reached no agreement on any other subject, nor is this treaty conditioned on any other matter. Undersecretary Harriman made it clear that any nonaggression arrangements across the division in Europe would require full consultation with our allies and full attention to their interests. He also made clear our strong preference for a more comprehensive treaty banning all tests everywhere, and our ultimate hope for general and complete disarmament. The Soviet government, however, is still unwilling to accept the inspections such goals require.

No one can predict with certainty, therefore, what further agreements, if any, can be built on the foundations of this one. They could include controls on preparations for surprise attack, or on numbers and types of armaments. There could be further limitations on the spread of nuclear weapons. The important point is that efforts to seek new agreements will go forward.

But the difficulty of predicting the next

Ben Roth Agency

"Feel Safe Enough?"; cartoon by Liederman for the "Long Island Press" in reaction to the inability to include all the nuclear powers in the nuclear test-ban pact of 1963

step is no reason to be reluctant about this one. Nuclear test-ban negotiations have long been a symbol of East-West disagreement. If this treaty can also be a symbol — if it can symbolize the end of one era and the beginning of another — if both sides can by this treaty gain confidence and experience in peaceful collaboration — then this short and simple treaty may well become a historic mark in man's age-old pursuit of peace.

Western policies have long been designed to persuade the Soviet Union to renounce aggression, direct or indirect, so that their people and all peoples may live and let live in peace. The unlimited testing of new weapons of war cannot lead toward that end — but this treaty, if it can be followed by further progress, can clearly move in that direction.

I do not say that a world without aggression or threats of war would be an easy world. It will bring new problems, new challenges from the Communists, new dangers of relaxing our vigilance or of mistaking their intent.

But those dangers pale in comparison to those of the spiraling arms race and a collision course toward war. Since the beginning of history, war has been mankind's constant companion. It has been the rule, not the exception. Even a nation as young and peace-loving as our own has fought through eight wars. And three times in the last two and one-half years I have been required to report to you as President that this nation and the Soviet Union stood on the verge of direct military confrontation — in Laos, in Berlin, and in Cuba.

A war today or tomorrow, if it led to nuclear war, would not be like any war in history. A full-scale nuclear exchange, lasting less than sixty minutes, could wipe out more than 300 million Americans, Europeans, and Russians, as well as untold numbers elsewhere. And the survivors, as Chairman Khrushchev warned the Communist Chinese, "would envy the dead." For they would inherit a world so devastated by explosions and poison and fire that today we cannot even conceive of all its horrors.

So let us try to turn the world from war. Let us make the most of this opportunity and every opportunity, to reduce tension, to slow down the perilous nuclear arms race, and to check the world's slide toward financial annihilation.

Second, this treaty can be a step toward freeing the world from the fears and dangers of radioactive fallout. Our own atmospheric tests last year were conducted under conditions which restricted such fallout to an absolute minimum. But over the years the number and yield of weapons tested have rapidly increased — and so have the radioactive hazards from such testing. Continued unrestricted testing by the nuclear powers, joined in time by other nations which may be less adept in limiting pollution, will increasingly contaminate the air that all of us must breathe.

Even then, the number of children and grandchildren with cancer in their bones, with leukemia in their blood, or with poison in their lungs might seem statistically small to some, in comparison with natural health hazards. But this is not a natural health hazard — and it is not a statistical issue. The loss of even one human life, or the malformation of even one baby — who may be born long after we are gone — should be of concern to us all. Our children and grandchildren are not merely statistics toward which we can be indifferent.

Nor does this affect the nuclear powers alone. These tests befoul the air of all men and all nations, the committed and the uncommitted alike, without their knowledge and without their consent. That is why the continuation of atmospheric testing causes so many countries to regard all nuclear powers as equally evil; and we can hope that its prevention will enable those countries to see the world more clearly, while enabling all the world to breathe more easily.

Third, this treaty can be a step toward preventing the spread of nuclear weapons to nations not now possessing them. During the next several years, in addition to the four current nuclear powers, a small but significant number of nations will have the intellectual, physical and financial resources to produce both nuclear weapons and the means of delivering them. In time, it is estimated, many other nations will have either this capacity or other ways of obtaining nuclear warheads, even as missiles can be commercially purchased today.

I ask you to stop and think for a moment what it would mean to have nuclear weapons in many hands — in the hands of countries large and small, stable and unstable, responsible and irresponsible, scattered throughout the world. There would be no rest for anyone then, no stability, no real security, and no chance of effective disarmament. There would only be increased chances of accidental war, and an increased necessity for the great powers to involve themselves in otherwise local conflicts.

If only one thermonuclear bomb were to

be dropped on any American, Russian, or other city — whether it was launched by accident or design, by a madman or an enemy, by a large nation or small, from any corner of the world — that one bomb could release more destructive force on the inhabitants of that one helpless city than all the bombs dropped during World War II.

Neither the United States, nor the Soviet Union, nor the United Kingdom, nor France can look forward to that day with equanimity. We have a great obligation — all four nuclear powers have a great obligation — to use whatever time remains to prevent the spread of nuclear weapons, to persuade other countries not to test, transfer, acquire, possess, or produce such weapons.

This treaty can be the opening wedge in that campaign. It provides that none of the parties will assist other nations to test in the forbidden environments. It opens the door for further agreements on the control of nuclear weapons. And it is open for all nations to sign. For it is in the interest of all nations — and already we have heard from a number of countries who wish to join with us promptly.

Fourth, and finally, this treaty can limit the nuclear arms race in ways which, on balance, will strengthen our nation's security far more than the continuation of unrestricted testing. For, in today's world, a nation's security does not always increase as its arms increase, when its adversary is doing the same. And unlimited competition in the testing and development of new types of destructive nuclear weapons will not make the world safer for either side.

Under this limited treaty, on the other hand, the testing of other nations could never be sufficient to offset the ability of our strategic forces to deter or survive a nuclear attack and to penetrate and destroy an aggressor's homeland. We have, and under this treaty we will continue to have, all the nuclear strength that we need.

It is true that the Soviets have tested nuclear weapons of a yield higher than that which we have thought to be necessary; but the 100-megaton bomb of which they spoke two years ago does not and will not change the balance of strategic power. The United States has deliberately chosen to concentrate on more mobile and more efficient weapons, with lower but entirely sufficient yield; and our security is not, therefore, impaired by the treaty I am discussing.

It is also true, as Mr. Khrushchev would agree, that nations cannot afford in these matters to rely simply on the good faith of their adversaries. We have not, therefore, overlooked the risk of secret violations. There is at present a possibility that deep in outer space, that hundreds and thousands and millions of miles away from the earth, illegal tests might go undetected. But we already have the capability to construct a system of observation that would make such tests almost impossible to conceal, and we can decide at any time whether such a system is needed in the light of the limited risk to us and the limited reward to others of violations attempted at that range. For any tests which might be conducted so far out in space, which cannot be conducted more easily and efficiently and legally underground, would necessarily be of such a magnitude that they would be extremely difficult to conceal. We can also employ new devices to check on the testing of smaller weapons in the lower atmosphere. Any violation, moreover, involves, along with the risk of detection, the end of the treaty and the worldwide consequence for the violator.

Secret violations are possible and secret preparations for a sudden withdrawal are possible, and, thus, our own vigilance and strength must be maintained, as we remain ready to withdraw and to resume all forms of testing, if we must. But it would be a mistake to assume that this treaty will be quickly broken. The gains of illegal testing are obviously slight compared to their cost and the hazard of discovery, and the nations which have initialed and will sign this treaty prefer it, in my judgment, to unrestricted testing as a matter of their own self-interest, for these nations, too, and all nations, have a stake in limiting the arms race, in holding the spread of nuclear weapons, and in breathing air that is not radioactive. While it may be theoretically possible to demonstrate the risks inherent in any treaty, and such risks in this treaty are small, the far greater risks to our security are the risks of unrestricted testing, the risk of a nuclear arms race, the risk of new nuclear powers, nuclear pollution, and nuclear war.

This limited test ban, in our most careful judgment, is safer by far for the United States than an unlimited nuclear arms race. For all these reasons, I am hopeful that this nation will promptly approve the limited test-ban treaty. There will, of course, be debate in the country and in the Senate. The Constitution wisely requires the advice and consent of the Senate to all treaties, and that consultation has already begun. All this is as it should be. A document which may mark a historic and constructive opportunity for the world deserves a historic and constructive debate. It is my hope that all of you will take part in that debate, for this treaty is for all of us. It is particularly for our children and our grandchildren, and they have no lobby here in Washington. This debate will involve military, scientific, and political experts, but it must be not left to them alone. The right and the responsibility are yours.

If we are to open new doorways to peace, if we are to seize this rare opportunity for progress, if we are to be as bold and farsighted in our control of weapons as we have been in their invention, then let us now show all the world on this side of the wall and the other that a strong America also stands for peace. There is no cause for complacency.

We have learned in times past that the spirit of one moment or place can be gone in the next. We have been disappointed more than once, and we have no illusions now that there are short cuts on the road to peace. At many points around the globe the Communists are continuing their efforts to exploit weakness and poverty. Their concentration of nuclear and conventional arms must still be deterred.

The familiar contest between choice and coercion, the familiar places of danger and conflict are still there, in Cuba, in Southeast Asia, in Berlin, and all around the globe, still requiring all the strength and the vigilance that we can muster. Nothing could more greatly damage our cause than if we and our allies were to believe that peace has already been achieved and that our strength and unity were no longer required.

But now for the first time in many years the path of peace may be open. No one can be certain what the future will bring. No one can say whether the time has come for an easing of the struggle. But history and our own conscience will judge us harsher if we do not now make every effort to test our hopes by action, and this is the place to begin. According to the ancient Chinese proverb, "A journey of a thousand miles must begin with a single step."

My fellow Americans, let us take that first step. Let us, if we can, get back from the shadows of war and seek out the way of peace. And if that journey is 1,000 miles or even more, let history record that we, in this land, at this time, took the first step.

36.

John F. Kennedy: Undelivered Dallas Speech

The theme of the address President Kennedy planned to deliver at a luncheon in the Dallas Trade Mart on November 22, 1963, was similar to that of earlier addresses, notably those at the University of Washington in November 1961 and at the American University in June 1963. The American people, the President had said before and intended to say again, did not have unlimited power to control the affairs of the world, but must instead learn to live with the reality of what he had earlier called "a long twilight struggle." Kennedy's choice of this theme of moderation seemed to some people later to have ironic significance. Long before the Texas journey began Kennedy had been warned by such men as Arkansas Senator J. W. Fulbright and UN Ambassador Adlai Stevenson that a mood of deep, perhaps even violent, hostility prevailed in Dallas; and only a few weeks before the assassination Stevenson, after a speech in support of the United Nations, had been jeered, struck, and spat upon in the city's streets.

Source: *Record*, 88 Cong., 1 Sess., pp. 22823-22824.

I AM HONORED to have this invitation to address the annual meeting of the Dallas Citizens Council, joined by the members of the Dallas Assembly — and pleased to have this opportunity to salute the Graduate Research Center of the Southwest. It is fitting that these two symbols of Dallas' progress are united in the sponsorship of this meeting, for they represent the best qualities, I am told, of leadership and learning in this city — and leadership and learning are indispensable to each other.

The advancement of learning depends on community leadership for financial and political support; and the products of that learning, in turn, are essential to the leadership's hopes for continued progress and prosperity. It is not a coincidence that those communities possessing the best in research and graduate facilities — from M.I.T. to Cal Tech — tend to attract the new and growing industries. I congratulate those of you here in Dallas who have recognized these basic facts through the creation of the unique and forward-looking Graduate Research Center.

This link between leadership and learning is not only essential at the community level. It is even more indispensable in world affairs. Ignorance and misinformation can handicap the progress of a city or a company; but they can, if allowed to prevail in foreign policy, handicap this country's security. In a world of complex and continuing problems, in a world full of frustrations and irritations, America's leadership must be guided by the lights of learning and reason, or else those who confuse rhetoric with reality and the plausible with the possible will gain the popular ascendancy with their seemingly swift and simple solutions to every world problem.

There will always be dissident voices heard in the land, expressing opposition without alternatives, finding fault but never favor, perceiving gloom on every side and seeking influence without responsibility. Those voices are inevitable. But today other voices are heard in the land — voices preaching doctrines wholly unrelated to reality, wholly unsuited to the sixties, doctrines which apparently assume that words will suffice without weapons, that vituperation is as good as victory and that peace is a sign of weakness.

At a time when the national debt is steadily being reduced in terms of its burden on our economy, they see that debt as the greatest single threat to our security. At a time when we are steadily reducing the number of federal employees serving every thousand citizens, they fear those supposed hordes of civil servants far more than the actual hordes of opposing armies.

We cannot expect that everyone, to use the phrase of a decade ago, will "talk sense to the American people." But we can hope that fewer people will listen to nonsense. And the notion that this nation is headed for defeat through deficit, or that strength is but a matter of slogans, is nothing but just plain nonsense.

I want to discuss with you today the status of our strength and our security because this question clearly calls for the most responsible qualities of leadership and the most enlightened products of scholarship. For this nation's strength and security are not easily or cheaply obtained — nor are they quickly and simply explained.

There are many kinds of strength and no one kind will suffice. Overwhelming nuclear strength cannot stop a guerrilla war. Formal pacts of alliance cannot stop internal subversion. Displays of material wealth cannot stop the disillusionment of diplomats subjected to discrimination.

Above all, words alone are not enough. The United States is a peaceful nation. And where our strength and determination are clear, our words need merely to convey conviction, not belligerence. If we are strong, our strength will speak for itself. If we are weak, words will be no help.

I realize that this nation often tends to identify turning points in world affairs with the major addresses which preceded them. But it was not the Monroe Doctrine that kept all Europe away from this hemisphere — it was the strength of the British Fleet and the width of the Atlantic Ocean. It was not General Marshall's speech at Harvard which kept communism out of Western Europe — it was the strength and stability made possible by our military and economic assistance.

In this administration also it has been necessary at times to issue specific warnings that we could not stand by and watch the Communists conquer Laos by force, or intervene in the Congo, or swallow West Berlin, or maintain offensive missiles on Cuba.

But while our goals were at least temporarily obtained in those and other instances, our successful defense of freedom was due not to the words we used but to the strength we stood ready to use on behalf of the principles we stand ready to defend. This strength is composed of many different elements, ranging from the most massive deterrents to the most subtle influences. And all types of strength are needed — no one kind could do the job alone. Let us take a moment, therefore, to review this nation's progress in each major area of strength.

First, as Secretary McNamara made clear in his address last Monday, the strategic nuclear power of the United States has been so greatly modernized and expanded in the last 1,000 days by the rapid production and deployment of the most modern missile systems that any and all potential aggressors are clearly confronted now with the impossibility of strategic victory — and the certainty of total destruction — if by reckless attack they should ever force upon us the necessity of a strategic reply.

In less than three years, we have increased by 50 percent the number of Polaris submarines scheduled to be in force by the next fiscal year; increased by more than 70 percent our total Polaris purchase program; increased by 50 percent the portion of our strategic bombers on fifteen-minute alert; and increased by 100 percent the total number of nuclear weapons available in our strategic alert forces. Our security is further enhanced by the steps we have taken regarding these weapons to improve the speed and certainty of their response, their readiness at all times to respond, their ability to survive an attack, and their ability to be carefully controlled and directed through secure command operations.

But the lessons of the last decade have taught us that freedom cannot be defended by strategic nuclear power alone. We have, therefore, in the last three years accelerated the development and deployment of tactical nuclear weapons, and increased by 60 percent the tactical nuclear forces deployed in Western Europe.

Nor can Europe or any other continent rely on nuclear forces alone, whether they are strategic or tactical. We have radically improved the readiness of our conventional forces; increased by 45 percent the number of combat-ready Army divisions; increased by 100 percent the procurement of modern Army weapons and equipment; increased by 100 percent our ship construction, conversion, and modernization program; increased by 100 percent our procurement of tactical aircraft; increased by 30 percent the number of tactical air squadrons; and increased the strength of the Marines.

As last month's Operation Big Lift — which originated here in Texas — showed so clearly, this nation is prepared as never before to move substantial numbers of men in surprisingly little time to advanced positions anywhere in the world. We have increased by 175 percent the procurement of airlift aircraft — and we have already achieved a 75 percent increase in our existing strategic airlift capability. Finally, moving beyond the traditional roles of our military forces, we have achieved an increase of nearly 600 percent in our special forces — those forces that are prepared to work with our allies and friends against the guerrillas, saboteurs, insurgents, and assassins who threaten freedom in a less direct but equally dangerous manner.

But American military might should not and need not stand alone against the ambitions of international communism. Our security and strength, in the last analysis, directly depend on the security and strength of others — and that is why our military and economic assistance plays such a key role in enabling those who live on the periphery of the Communist world to maintain their independence of choice.

Our assistance for these nations can be painful, risky, and costly, as is true in Southeast Asia today. But we dare not weary of the task; for our assistance makes possible the stationing of 3.5 million allied troops along the Communist frontier at one-tenth the cost of maintaining a comparable number of American soldiers. A successful Communist breakthrough in these areas, necessitating direct U.S. intervention, would cost us several times as much as our entire foreign-aid program, and might cost us heavily in American lives as well.

About 70 percent of our military assistance goes to nine key countries located on or near the borders of the Communist bloc; nine countries confronted directly or indirectly with the threat of Communist aggression — Vietnam, Free China, Korea, India, Pakistan, Thailand, Greece, Turkey, and Iran. No one of these countries possesses on its own the resources to maintain the forces which our own chiefs of staff think needed in the common interest. Reducing our efforts to train, equip, and assist their armies can only encourage Communist penetration and require in time the increased oversea deployment of American combat forces. And reducing the economic help needed to bolster these nations that undertake to help defend freedom can have the same disastrous result. In short, the $50 billion we spend each year on our own defense could well be ineffective without the $4 billion required for military and economic assistance.

Our foreign-aid program is not growing in size; it is, on the contrary, smaller now than in previous years. It has had its weaknesses, but we have undertaken to correct them, and the proper way of treating weaknesses is to replace them with strength, not to increase those weaknesses by emasculating essential programs. Dollar for dollar, in or out of government, there is no better form of investment in our national security than our much abused foreign-aid program. We cannot afford to lose it. We can afford to maintain it. We can surely afford, for example, to do as much for our nineteen needy neighbors of Latin America as the Communist bloc is sending to the island of Cuba alone.

I have spoken of strength largely in terms of the deterrence and resistance of aggression and attack. But, in today's world, freedom can be lost without a shot being fired, by ballots as well as bullets. The success of our leadership is dependent upon respect for our mission in the world as well as our missiles — on a clearer recognition of the virtues of freedom as well as the evils of tyranny. That is why our information agency has doubled the shortwave broadcasting power of the Voice of America and increased the number of broadcasting hours by 30 percent, increased Spanish-language broadcasting to Cuba and Latin American readers, and taken a host of other steps to carry our message of truth and freedom to all the far corners of the earth.

And that is also why we have regained the initiative in the exploration of outer space — making an annual effort greater than the combined total of all space activities undertaken during the Fifties — launching more than 130 vehicles into earth orbit; putting into actual operation valuable weather and communications satellites; and making it clear to all that the United States of America has no intention of finishing second in space.

This effort is expensive but it pays its own way, for freedom and for America. For there is no longer any fear in the free world that a Communist lead in space will become a permanent assertion of supremacy and the basis of military superiority. There is no longer any doubt about the strength and skill of American science, American industry, American education, and the American free enterprise system. In short, our national space effort represents a great gain in, and a great resource of, our national strength — and both Texas and Texans are contributing greatly to this strength.

Finally, it should be clear by now that a nation can be no stronger abroad than she is at home. Only America, which practises what it preaches about equal rights and social justice, will be respected by those whose choice affects our future. Only an America which has fully educated its citizens is fully capable of tackling the complex problems and perceiving the hidden dangers of the world in which we live. And only an America which is growing and prospering economically can sustain the worldwide defense of freedom while demonstrating to all concerned the opportunities of our system and society.

It is clear, therefore, that we are strengthening our security as well as our economy by our recent record increases in national income and output — by surging ahead of most of Western Europe in the rate of business expansion. And the margin of corporate profits — by maintaining a more stable level of prices than almost any of our oversea competitors — and by cutting personal and corporate income taxes by some $11 billion, as I have proposed, to assure this nation of the longest and strongest expansion in our peacetime economic history.

This nation's total output — which three years ago was at the $500 billion mark —

will soon pass $600 billion, for a record rise of over $100 billion in three years. For the first time in history we have 70 million men and women at work. For the first time in history average factory earnings have exceeded $100 a week. For the first time in history corporation profits after taxes — which have risen 43 percent in less than three years — have reached an annual level of $27.4 billion.

My friends and fellow citizens, I cite these facts and figures to make it clear that America today is stronger than ever before. Our adversaries have not abandoned their ambitions — our dangers have not diminished — our vigilance cannot be relaxed. But now we have the military, the scientific, and the economic strength to do whatever must be done for the preservation and promotion of freedom. That strength will never be used in pursuit of aggressive ambitions — it will always be used in pursuit of peace. It will never be used to promote provocations — it will always be used to promote the peaceful settlement of disputes.

We in this country, in this generation, are — by destiny rather than choice — the watchmen on the walls of world freedom. We ask, therefore, that we may be worthy of our power and responsibility, that we may exercise our strength with wisdom and restraint, and that we may achieve in our time and for all time the ancient vision of peace on earth, goodwill toward men. That must always be our goal — and the righteousness of our cause must always underlie our strength. For as was written long ago, "Except the Lord keep the city, the watchman waketh but in vain."

———◆———

Assassination is the extreme form of censorship.
GEORGE BERNARD SHAW

37.

MIKE MANSFIELD: Eulogy for John F. Kennedy

Few Americans who lived through it will ever forget that long weekend at the end of November 1963 — from Friday the 22nd, when the young, handsome, vigorous President was shot down in the streets of Dallas, to Monday the 25th, when his coffin was lowered into the grave on the hillside of Arlington Cemetery, overlooking the capital of the United States. Everyone has his special memory — for example, of the place where he was, and of the activity in which he was engaged, when he first heard the terrible news — but some memories are shared by millions. One of these is the somber ceremony in the Capitol Rotunda on Sunday afternoon. The President's body lay in state; the widow and her two charming children stood together to one side; and the Senate majority leader, the chief justice of the Supreme Court, and the speaker of the House paid homage in short, moving eulogies to their departed leader. Chief Justice Warren and Speaker McCormack spoke well and memorably, but Senator Mansfield's address, reprinted here, had a special and rather surprising eloquence, coming as it did from a man not widely known for poetry of language. It was later learned that Mrs. Kennedy had not in fact placed her wedding ring in her dead husband's hand, as Mansfield supposed at the time.

Source: *Record*, 88 Cong., 1 Sess., p. 21592.

THERE WAS A SOUND OF LAUGHTER; in a moment, it was no more. And so she took a ring from her finger and placed it in his hands.

There was a wit in a man neither young nor old, but a wit full of an old man's wisdom and of a child's wisdom, and then, in a moment it was no more. And so she took a ring from her finger and placed it in his hands.

There was a man marked with the scars of his love of country, a body active with the surge of a life far, far from spent and, in a moment, it was no more. And so she took a ring from her finger and placed it in his hands.

There was a father with a little boy, a little girl, and a joy of each in the other. In a moment it was no more, and so she took

a ring from her finger and placed it in his hands.

There was a husband who asked much and gave much, and out of the giving and the asking wove with a woman what could not be broken in life, and in a moment it was no more. And so she took a ring from her finger and placed it in his hands, and kissed him and closed the lid of a coffin.

A piece of each of us died at that moment. Yet, in death he gave of himself to us. He gave us of a good heart from which the laughter came. He gave us of a profound wit, from which a great leadership emerged. He gave us of a kindness and a strength fused into a human courage to seek peace without fear.

He gave us of his love that we, too, in turn, might give. He gave that we might give of ourselves, that we might give to one another until there would be no room, no room at all, for the bigotry, the hatred, prejudice, and the arrogance which converged in that moment of horror to strike him down.

In leaving us — these gifts, John Fitzgerald Kennedy, President of the United States, leaves with us. Will we take them, Mr. President? Will we have, now, the sense and the responsibility and the courage to take them?

38.

LYNDON B. JOHNSON: Let Us Continue

Lyndon Johnson's first formal address as President of the United States, delivered on November 27, 1963, before a joint session of Congress with the members of the Supreme Court and of the Cabinet in attendance, emphasized the theme of continuity in national leadership and pledged that the dead President's program would be carried forward to completion. Johnson did in fact succeed in carrying through Congress such Kennedy-sponsored measures as a tax cut, the 1963 foreign aid bill, several education bills, and a broad civil rights law.

Source: *Record*, 88 Cong., 1 Sess., pp. 22838-22839.

Mr. Speaker, Mr. President, Members of the House, Members of the Senate, My Fellow Americans:

All I have I would have given gladly not to be standing here today.

The greatest leader of our time has been struck down by the foulest deed of our time. Today John Fitzgerald Kennedy lives on in the immortal words and works that he left behind. He lives on in the mind and memories of mankind. He lives on in the hearts of his countrymen.

No words are sad enough to express our sense of loss. No words are strong enough to express our determination to continue the forward thrust of America that he began.

The dream of conquering the vastness of space — the dream of partnership across the Atlantic, and across the Pacific as well — the dream of a Peace Corps in less de-

veloped nations — the dream of education for all of our children — the dream of jobs for all who seek them and need them — the dream of care for our elderly — the dream of an all-out attack on mental illness — and, above all, the dream of equal rights for all Americans, whatever their race or color — these and other American dreams have been vitalized by his drive and by his dedication.

Now the ideas and the ideals which he so nobly represented must and will be translated into effective action.

Under John Kennedy's leadership, this nation has demonstrated that it has the courage to seek peace and it has the fortitude to risk war. We have proved that we are a good and reliable friend to those who seek peace and freedom. We have shown that we can also be a formidable foe to those who reject the path of peace and those who seek to impose upon us or our allies the yoke of tyranny.

This nation will keep its commitments from South Vietnam to West Berlin. We will be unceasing in the search for peace; resourceful in our pursuit of areas of agreement, even with those with whom we differ, and generous and loyal to those who join with us in common cause.

In this age when there can be no losers in peace and no victors in war, we must recognize the obligation to match national strength with national restraint. We must be prepared at one and the same time for both the confrontation of power and the limitation of power. We must be ready to defend the national interest and to negotiate the common interest. This is the path that we shall continue to pursue. Those who test our courage will find it strong and those who seek our friendship will find it honorable. We will demonstrate anew that the strong can be just in the use of strength — and the just can be strong in the defense of justice. And let all know we will extend no special privilege and impose no persecution.

We will carry on the fight against poverty and misery, ignorance and disease — in other lands and in our own. We will serve all of the nation, not one section or one sector, or one group, but all Americans. These are the United States — a united people with a united purpose.

Our American unity does not depend upon unanimity. We have differences; but now, as in the past, we can derive from those differences strength, not weakness, wisdom, not despair. Both as a people and as a government we can unite upon a program, a program which is wise, just, enlightened, and constructive.

For thirty-two years Capitol Hill has been my home. I have shared many moments of pride with you — pride in the ability of the Congress of the United States to act; to meet any crisis; to distill from our differences strong programs of national action.

An assassin's bullet has thrust upon me the awesome burden of the presidency. I am here today to say I need your help, I cannot bear this burden alone. I need the help of all Americans in all America. This nation has experienced a profound shock and in this critical moment it is our duty — yours and mine — as the government of the United States — to do away with uncertainty and doubt and delay and to show that we are capable of decisive action — that from the brutal loss of our leader we will derive not weakness but strength, that we can and will act and act now.

From this chamber of representative government let all the world know, and none misunderstand, that I rededicate this government to the unswerving support of the United Nations, to the honorable and determined execution of our commitments to our allies, to the maintenance of military strength second to none, to the defense of the strength and stability of the dollar, to the expansion of our foreign trade, to the reinforcement of our programs of mutual assistance and cooperation in Asia and Africa, and to our Alliance for Progress in this hemisphere.

On the 20th day of January, in 1961, John F. Kennedy told his countrymen that our national work would not be finished "in the first thousand days, nor in the life of this administration, nor even perhaps in our lifetime on this planet. But" — he said — "let us begin." Today in this moment of new resolve, I would say to my fellow Americans, let us continue.

This is our challenge — not to hesitate, not to pause, not to turn about and linger over this evil moment but to continue on our course so that we may fulfill the destiny that history has set for us. Our most immediate tasks are here on this Hill.

First, no memorial oration or eulogy could more eloquently honor President Kennedy's memory than the earliest possible passage of the Civil Rights Bill for which he fought so long. We have talked

Wide World

Lyndon Johnson is sworn in as President on the presidential plane, Nov. 22, 1963

long enough in this country about equal rights. We have talked for 100 years or more. It is time now to write the next chapter — and to write it in the books of law.

I urge you again, as I did in 1957 and again in 1960, to enact a civil rights law so that we can move forward to eliminate from this nation every trace of discrimination and oppression that is based upon race or color. There could be no greater source of strength to this nation both at home and abroad.

And, second, no act of ours could more fittingly continue the work of President Kennedy than the early passage of the tax bill for which he fought all this long year. This is a bill designed to increase our national income and federal revenues, and to provide insurance against recession. That bill, if passed without delay, means more security for those now working, more jobs for those now without them, and more incentive for our economy.

In short, this is no time for delay. It is time for action — strong, forward-looking action on the pending education bills to help bring the light of learning to every home and hamlet in America; strong, for-

ward-looking action on youth employment opportunities; strong, forward-looking action on the pending foreign aid bill, making clear that we are not forfeiting our responsibilities to this hemisphere or to the world, nor erasing executive flexibility in the conduct of our foreign affairs; and strong, prompt, and forward-looking action on the remaining appropriation bills.

In this new spirit of action, the Congress can expect the full cooperation and support of the executive branch. And in particular I pledge that the expenditures of your government will be administered with the utmost thrift and frugality. I ask your help. I will insist that the government get a dollar's value for a dollar spent. The government will set an example of prudence and economy. This does not mean that we will not meet our unfilled needs or that we will not honor our commitments. We will do both.

As one who has long served in both houses of the Congress, I firmly believe in the independence and the integrity of the legislative branch. I promise you that I shall always respect this. It is deep in the marrow of my bones. With equal firmness, I believe in the capacity and I believe in the ability of the Congress, despite the divisions of opinion which characterize our nation, to act — to act wisely, to act vigorously, to act speedily when the need arises.

The need is here. The need is now.

We meet in grief; but let us also meet in renewed dedication and renewed vigor. Let us meet in action, in tolerance, and in mutual understanding.

John Kennedy's death commands what his life conveyed — that America must move forward. The time has come for Americans of all races and creeds and political beliefs to understand and to respect one another. So let us put an end to the teaching and preaching of hate and evil and violence. Let us turn away from the fanatics of the far left and the far right, from the apostles of bitterness and bigotry, from those defiant of law and those who pour venom into our nation's bloodstream.

I profoundly hope that the tragedy and the torment of these terrible days will bind us together in new fellowship, making us one people in our hour of sorrow. So let us here highly resolve that John Fitzgerald Kennedy did not live — or die — in vain. And on this Thanksgiving Eve, as we gather together to ask the Lord's blessing and give Him our thanks, let us unite in those familiar and cherished words:

America, America,
　　God shed His grace on thee,
And crown thy good
　　With brotherhood
From sea to shining sea.

39.

J. WILLIAM FULBRIGHT: Violence in the American Character

President Kennedy's assassination revived an old American concern that the very liberty essential to the existence of a free society may ultimately lead to the destruction of that society by fostering violence in thought and action. Historian Henry Steele Commager, in the wake of Kennedy's death, was led to observe that "out of all this, the tradition of frontier violence, the special saturation of race relations in the South, the double standard of morality, the assumption that the ordinary rules did not apply to us, that we were exempt from the laws and the processes of history — out of all this has come that bigotry and arrogance and vanity and violence which so deeply shocks us today." Arkansas Senator J. W. Fulbright dealt with the same theme in the Rockefeller Public Service Award Address, delivered at Washington on December 5, 1963, and reprinted here in part.

Source: *Record*, 88 Cong., 1 Sess., pp. 23726-23728.

As WE MOURN THE DEATH of President Kennedy, it is fitting that we reflect on the character of our society and ask ourselves whether the assassination of the President was merely a tragic accident or a manifestation of some deeper failing in our lives and in our society.

It may be that the tragedy was one which could have occurred anywhere at any time to any national leader. It may be that the cause lies wholly in the tormented brain of the assassin. It may be that the nation as a whole is healthy and strong and entirely without responsibility for the great misfortune which has befallen it. It would be comforting to think so.

I for one do not think so. I believe that our society, though in most respects decent, civilized, and humane, is not, and has never been, entirely so. Our national life, both past and present, has also been marked by a baleful and incongruous strand of intolerance and violence. It is in evidence all around us. It is in evidence in the senseless and widespread crime that makes the streets of our great cities unsafe. It is in evidence in the malice and hatred of extremist political movements. And it is in evidence in the cruel bigotry of race that leads to such tragedies as the killing of Negro children in a church in Alabama.

We must ask ourselves many questions about this element of barbarism in a civilized society. We must ask ourselves what its sources are, in history and in human nature. We must ask ourselves whether it is the common and inevitable condition of man or whether it can be overcome. And if we judge that it can be overcome, we must ask ourselves why we Americans have not made greater progress in doing so. We must ask ourselves what, if anything, all this has to do with the death of our President. Finally, and most important, we must ask ourselves what we must do, and how and when, to overcome hatred and bigotry and to make America as decent and humane a society as we would like it to be.

I do not pretend to be able to answer these questions. I do suggest, however, that the conditions of our time call for a national self-examination although the process may be a long and difficult and painful one. I further suggest, and most emphatically, that if such a national self-examination is to be productive it must be conducted in a spirit of tolerance rather than anger, serenity rather than guilt, and Christian charity rather than crusading moralism.

We might begin our reflections about ourselves by an examination of the effects of crusading self-righteousness in the history of Western civilization and in our own society.

Moral absolutism — righteous, crusading, and intolerant — has been a major force in the history of Western civilization. Whether religious or political in form, movements of crusading moralism have played a significant, and usually destructive, role in the evolution of Western societies. Such movements, regardless of the content of their doctrines, have all been marked by a single characteristic: the absolute certainty of their own truth and virtue. Each has regarded itself as having an exclusive pipeline to heaven, to God, or to a deified concept of history — or whatever is regarded as the ultimate source of truth. Each has regarded itself as the chosen repository of truth and virtue and each has regarded all nonbelievers as purveyors of falsehood and evil.

Absolutist movements are usually crusading movements. Free as they are from any element of doubt as to their own truth and virtue, they conceive themselves to have a mission of spreading the truth and destroying evil. They consider it to be their duty to regenerate mankind, however little it may wish to be regenerated. The means which are used for this purpose, though often harsh and sometimes barbaric, are deemed to be wholly justified by the nobility of the end. They are justified because the end is absolute and there can be no element of doubt as to its virtue and its truth. . . .

The strand of fanaticism and violence has been a major one in Western history. But it has not been the only one, nor has it been the dominant one in most Western societies. The other strand of Western civilization, conceived in ancient Greece and Rome and revived in the European age of reason, has been one of tolerance and moderation, of empiricism and practicality. Its doctrine has been democracy, a radically different kind of doctrine whose one "absolute" is the denial of absolutes and of the messianic spirit. The core of the democratic idea is the element of doubt as to the ability of any man or any movement to perceive ultimate truth. Accordingly, it has fostered societies in which the individual is left free to pursue truth and virtue as he imperfectly perceives them, with due regard for the right of every other individual to pursue a different, and quite possibly superior, set of values.

Democratic societies have by no means been free of self-righteousness and the crusading spirit. On the contrary, they have at times engaged in great crusades to spread the gospel of their own ideology. Indeed, no democratic nation has been more susceptible to this tendency than the United States, which in the past generation has fought one war to "make the world safe for democracy," another to achieve nothing less than the "unconditional surrender" of its enemies, and even now finds it possible to consider the plausibility of "total victory" over communism in a thermonuclear war.

It is clear that democratic nations are susceptible to dogmatism and the crusading spirit. The point, however, is that this susceptibility is not an expression but a denial of the democratic spirit. When a free nation embarks upon a crusade for democracy, it is caught up in the impossible contradiction of trying to use force to make men free. The dogmatic and crusading spirit in free societies is an antidemocratic tendency, a lingering vestige of the strand of dogmatism and violence in the Western heritage. . . .

By the time of the establishment of the English colonies in the New World, the evolution toward constitutional democracy was well advanced. The process quickly took hold in the North American colonies and their evolution toward democracy outpaced that of the mother country. This was the basic heritage of America — a heritage of tolerance, moderation, and individual liberty that was implanted from the very beginnings of European settlement in the New World. America has quite rightly been called a nation that was born free.

There came also to the New World the Puritans, a minor group in England who became a major force in American life. Their religion was Calvinism, an absolutist faith with a stern moral code promising salvation for the few and damnation for the many. The intolerant, witch-hunting Puritanism of 17th-century Massachusetts was not a major religious movement in America. It eventually became modified and as a source of ethical standards made a worthy contribution to American life. But the Puritan way of thinking, harsh and intolerant, permeated the political and economic life of the country and became a major secular force in America. Coexisting uneasily with our English heritage of tolerance and moderation, the Puritan way of thinking has injected an absolutist strand into American thought — a strand of stern moralism in our public policy and in our standards of personal behavior.

The Puritan way of thinking has had a powerful impact on our foreign policy. It is reflected in our traditional vacillation between self-righteous isolation and total involvement and in our attitude toward foreign policy as a series of idealistic crusades rather than as a continuing defense of the national interest. It is reflected in some of the most notable events of our history: in the unnecessary war with Spain, which was spurred by an idealistic fervor to liberate Cuba and ended with our making Cuba an American protectorate; in the war of 1917, which began with a national commitment to "make the world safe for democracy" and ended with our repudiation of our own blueprint for a world order of peace and law; in the radical pacifism of the interwar years which ended with our total involvement in a conflict in which our proclaimed objective of "unconditional surrender" was finally achieved by dropping atomic bombs on Hiroshima and Nagasaki.

Throughout the 20th century American foreign policy has been caught up in the inherent contradiction between our English heritage of tolerance and accommodation and our Puritan heritage of crusading righteousness. This contradiction is strikingly illustrated by the policy of President Wilson in World War I. In 1914 he called upon the American people to be neutral in thought as well as in their actions; in early 1917, when the United States was still neutral, he called upon the belligerents to compromise their differences and accept a "peace without victory"; but in the spring of 1918, when the United States had been involved in the war for a year, he perceived only one possible response to the challenge of Germany in the war: "Force, force to the utmost, force without stint or limit, the righteous and triumphant force which shall make right the law of the world and cast every selfish dominion down in the dust."

The danger of any crusading movement issues from its presumption of absolute truth. If the premise is valid, then all else follows. If we know, with absolute and unchallengeable certainty, that a political leader is traitorous, or that he is embarked upon a course of certain ruin for the nation, then it is our right, indeed our duty, to carry our opposition beyond constitutional means and to remove him by force or even murder. The premise, however, is not valid. We do not know, nor can we know, with absolute certainty that those who disagree with us are wrong. We are human and therefore fallible, and being fallible, we cannot escape the element of doubt as to our own opinions and convictions. This, I believe, is the

core of the democratic spirit. When we acknowledge our own fallibility, tolerance and compromise become possible and fanaticism becomes absurd.

Before I comment on recent events, it is necessary to mention another major factor in the shaping of the American national character. That factor is the experience of the frontier, the building of a great nation out of a vast wilderness in the course of a single century. The frontier experience taught us the great value of individual initiative and self-reliance in the development of our resources and of our national economy. But the individualism of the frontier, largely untempered by social and legal restraints, has also had an important influence on our political life and on our personal relations. It has generated impatience with the complex and tedious procedures of law and glorified the virtues of direct individual action. It has instilled in us an easy familiarity with violence and vigilante justice. In the romanticized form in which it permeates the television and other mass media, the mythology of the frontier conveys the message that killing a man is not bad as long as you don't shoot him in the back, that violence is only reprehensible when its purpose is bad, and that in fact it is commendable and glorious when it is perpetrated by good men for a good purpose.

The murder of the accused assassin of President Kennedy is a shocking example of the spirit of vigilante justice. Compounding one crime with another, this act has denied the accused individual of one of the most basic rights of a civilized society: the right to a fair trial under established procedures of law. No less shocking are the widespread expressions of sympathy and approval for the act of the man who killed the accused assassin. Underlying these expressions of approval is an assumption that it is not killing that is bad but only certain kinds of killing, that it is proper and even praiseworthy for a citizen to take justice into his own hands when he deems his purpose to be a just one or a righteous act of vengeance. This attitude is a prescription for anarchy. Put into general practice, it would do far more to destroy the fabric of a free society than the evils which it purports to redress.

The mythology of the frontier, the moral absolutism of our Puritan heritage, and of course other factors which I have not mentioned, have injected a strand of intolerance and violence into American life. This violent tendency lies beneath the surface of an orderly, law-abiding democratic society, but not far beneath the surface. When times are normal, when the country is prosperous at home and secure in its foreign relations, our violent and intolerant tendencies remain quiescent and we are able to conduct our affairs in a rational and orderly manner. But in times of crisis, foreign or domestic, our underlying irrationality breaks through to become a dangerous and disruptive force in our national life.

Since World War II, times have not been normal; they are not normal now, nor are they likely to be for as far into the future as we can see. In this era of nuclear weapons and cold war, we live with constant crises and the continuing and immediate danger of incineration by hydrogen bombs. We are a people who have faced dangers before but we have always been able to overcome them by direct and immediate action. Now we are confronted with dangers vastly greater than we or any other nation has ever before known and we see no end to them and no solutions to them. Nor are there any solutions. There are only possibilities, limited, intermittent, and ambiguous, to alleviate the dangers of our time. For the rest, we have no choice but to try to live with the unsolved problems of a revolutionary world.

Under these conditions, it is not at all surprising that the underlying tendencies toward violence and crusading self-righteous-

ness have broken through the surface and become a virulent force in the life and politics of the postwar era. They have not thus far been the dominant force because the nation has been able to draw on the considerable resources of wisdom, patience, and judgment which are the core of our national heritage and character. The dominance of reason, however, has been tenuous and insecure and on a number of occasions in these years of crisis we have come close to letting our passions shape critical decisions of policy.

American politics in the postwar period has been characterized by a virulent debate between those who counsel patience and reason and those who, in their fear and passion, seem ever ready to plunge the nation into conflict abroad and witchhunts at home. As the years of crisis have gone on, the politics of the nation have been poisoned by the increasingly irresponsible charges of those zealots who, as President Kennedy would have said in his undelivered Dallas speech, assume that "words will suffice without weapons, that vituperation is as good as victory, and that peace is a sign of weakness."

The voices of suspicion and hate have been heard throughout the land. They were heard a decade ago when statesmen, private citizens, and even high-ranking members of the armed forces were charged with treason, subversion, and communism because they had disagreed with or somehow displeased the senator from Wisconsin, Mr. McCarthy. They are heard today when extremist groups do not hesitate to call a former President or the chief justice of the United States a traitor and a Communist. They are heard in the mail which U.S. senators receive almost daily charging them with communism or treason because they voted for the Foreign Aid Bill or for the Nuclear Test-Ban Treaty. . . .

It was in this prevailing atmosphere of suspicion and hate that the murder of the

President was spawned, whatever its immediate causes may have been. In an atmosphere in which dissent can be regarded as treason, in which violence is glorified and romanticized, in which direct action is widely preferred to judicial action as a means of redressing grievances, assassination is not really a radical departure from acceptable behavior. As Chief Justice Warren said in his eulogy of President Kennedy:

> What moved some misguided wretch to do this horrible deed may never be known to us, but we do know that such acts are commonly stimulated by the forces of hatred and malevolence, such as today are eating their way into the bloodstream of American life.

What is to be done? What must we do to overcome hatred and bigotry in our national life?

For a start, we can call forth the basic decency of America in the wake of the tragedy which has befallen us. Again, in the words of the chief justice:

> If we really love this country; if we truly love justice and mercy; if we fervently want to make this nation better for those who are to follow us, we can at least abjure the hatred that consumes people, the false accusations that divide us, and the bitterness that begets violence. Is it too much to hope that the martyrdom of our beloved President might even soften the hearts of those who would themselves recoil from assassination, but who do not shrink from spreading the venom which kindles thoughts of it in others?

It is to be hoped, profoundly to be hoped, that there will be some redemption for the death of our President. That redemption could issue from a national revulsion against extremism and violence, from a calling forth of the basic decency and humanity of America to heal the wounds of divisiveness and hate. We will, and should, continue to have controversy and debate in our public life. But we can reshape the character of our controversies and conduct them as the honest differences of honest men in quest of a consensus. We can come to recognize that those who disagree with us are not necessarily attacking us but only our opinions and ideas. Above all, we must maintain the element of doubt as to our own convictions, recognizing that it was not given to any man to perceive ultimate truth and that, however unlikely it may seem, there may in fact be truth or merit in the views of those who disagree with us. . . .

Furthermore, if we are to overcome violence and bigotry in our national life, we must alter some of the basic assumptions of American life and politics. We must recognize that the secular Puritanism which we have practised, with its principles of absolute good, absolute evil, and intolerance of dissent, has been an obstacle to the practice of democracy at home and the conduct of an effective foreign policy. We must recognize that the romanticized cult of the frontier, with its glorification of violence and of unrestrained individualism, is a childish and dangerous anachronism in a nation which carries the responsibility of the leadership of the free world in the nuclear age.

Finally, we must revive and strengthen the central core of our national heritage, which is the legacy of liberty, tolerance, and modernization that came to us from the ancient world through a thousand years of English history and three centuries of democratic evolution in North America. It is this historic legacy which is the best and the strongest of our endowments. It is our proper task to strengthen and cultivate it in the years ahead. If we do so, patiently and faithfully, we may arrive before too long at a time when the voices of hate will no longer be heard in our land and the death of our President will be redeemed.

1964

40.

LYNDON B. JOHNSON: The War on Poverty

President Johnson's relations with the Congress were extremely friendly during the first year or so after Kennedy's death. Both Johnson and the legislators seemed to sense a widespread desire in the country to carry through on the deceased President's program, and indeed to go beyond in significant respects what Kennedy probably could have done if he had lived. One of the most important such cooperative endeavors was the so-called war on poverty, inaugurated by Johnson in a message to Congress of March 16, 1964, that is reprinted here in part.

Source: 88 Congress, 2 Session, Senate Document No. 86.

WE ARE CITIZENS of the richest and most fortunate nation in the history of the world. One hundred and eighty years ago we were a small country struggling for survival on the margin of a hostile land. Today we have established a civilization of freemen which spans an entire continent.

With the growth of our country has come opportunity for our people — opportunity to educate our children, to use our energies in productive work, to increase our leisure — opportunity for almost every American to hope that through work and talent he could create a better life for himself and his family.

The path forward has not been an easy one. But we have never lost sight of our goal — an America in which every citizen shares all the opportunities of his society, in which every man has a chance to advance his welfare to the limit of his capacities. We have come a long way toward this goal. We still have a long way to go.

The distance which remains is the measure of the great unfinished work of our society. To finish that work I have called for a national war on poverty. Our objective: total victory.

There are millions of Americans — one-fifth of our people — who have not shared in the abundance which has been granted to most of us, and on whom the gates of opportunity have been closed. What does this poverty mean to those who endure it? It means a daily struggle to secure the necessities for even a meager existence. It means that the abundance, the comforts, the opportunities they see all around them are beyond their grasp. Worst of all, it means hopelessness for the young.

The young man or woman who grows up without a decent education, in a broken home, in a hostile and squalid environment, in ill health or in the face of racial injustice — that young man or woman is often trapped in a life of poverty. He does not have the skills demanded by a complex society. He does not know how to acquire those skills. He faces a mounting sense of despair which drains initiative and ambition and energy.

Our tax cut will create millions of new jobs — new exits from poverty. But we must also strike down all the barriers which keep many from using those exits. The war on poverty is not a struggle simply to support people, to make them dependent on the generosity of others. It is a struggle to give people a chance. It is an effort to allow them to develop and use their capacities, as we have been allowed to develop and use ours, so that they can share, as others share, in the promise of this nation.

We do this, first of all, because it is right that we should. From the establishment of public education and land-grant colleges through agricultural extension and encouragement to industry, we have pursued the goal of a nation with full and increasing opportunities for all its citizens. The war on poverty is a further step in that pursuit. We do it also because helping some will increase the prosperity of all. Our fight against poverty will be an investment in the most valuable of our resources — the skills and strength of our people. And in the future, as in the past, this investment will return its cost manyfold to our entire economy.

If we can raise the annual earnings of 10 million among the poor by only $1,000 we will have added $14 billion a year to our national output. In addition we can make important reductions in public-assistance payments, which now cost us $4 billion a year, and in the large costs of fighting crime and delinquency, disease and hunger.

This is only part of the story. Our history has proved that each time we broaden the base of abundance, giving more people the chance to produce and consume, we create new industry, higher production, increased earnings, and better income for all. Giving new opportunity to those who have little will enrich the lives of all the rest.

Because it is right, because it is wise, and because, for the first time in our history, it is possible to conquer poverty, I submit, for the consideration of the Congress and the country, the Economic Opportunity Act of 1964. The act does not merely expand old programs or improve what is already being done. It charts a new course. It strikes at the causes, not just the consequences of poverty. It can be a milestone in our 180-year search for a better life for our people.

This act provides five basic opportunities: It will give almost half a million underprivileged young Americans the opportunity to develop skills, continue education, and find useful work; it will give every American community the opportunity to develop a comprehensive plan to fight its own poverty — and help them to carry out their plans; it will give dedicated Americans the opportunity to enlist as volunteers in the war against poverty; it will give many workers and farmers the opportunity to break through particular barriers which bar their escape from poverty; it will give the entire nation the opportunity for a concerted attack on poverty through the establishment, under my direction, of the Office of Economic Opportunity, a national headquarters for the war against poverty.

This is how we propose to create these opportunities:

First, we will give high priority to helping young Americans who lack skills, who have not completed their education, or who cannot complete it because they are too poor. The years of high school and college age are the most critical stage of a young person's life. If they are not helped then, many will be condemned to a life of poverty which they, in turn, will pass on to their children.

I therefore recommend the creation of a Job Corps, a work-training program, and a work-study program. A new national Job Corps will build toward an enlistment of 100,000 young men. They will be drawn from those whose background, health, and education make them least fit for useful work. Those who volunteer will enter more than 100 camps and centers around the country. Half of these young men will work, in the first year, on special conservation projects to give them education, useful work experience, and to enrich the natural resources of the country. Half of these young men will receive, in the first year, a blend of training, basic education, and work experience in job-training centers.

These are not simply camps for the underprivileged. They are new educational institutions, comparable in innovation to the land-grant colleges. Those who enter them will emerge better qualified to play a productive role in American society.

A new national work-training program operated by the Department of Labor will provide work and training for 200,000 American men and women between the ages of sixteen and twenty-one. This will be developed through state and local governments and nonprofit agencies. Hundreds of thousands of young Americans badly need the experience, the income, and the sense of purpose which useful full or part-time work can bring. For them such work may mean the difference between finishing school or dropping out. Vital community activities from hospitals and playgrounds to libraries and settlement houses are suffering because there are not enough people to staff them. We are simply bringing these needs together.

A new national work-study program op-

erated by the Department of Health, Education, and Welfare will provide federal funds for part-time jobs for 140,000 young Americans who do not go to college because they cannot afford it. There is no more senseless waste than the waste of the brainpower and skill of those who are kept from college by economic circumstance. Under this program they will, in a great American tradition, be able to work their way through school. They and the country will be richer for it.

Second, through a new community-action program we intend to strike at poverty at its source — in the streets of our cities and on the farms of our countryside among the very young and the impoverished old. This program asks men and women throughout the country to prepare long-range plans for the attack on poverty in their own local communities.

These are not plans prepared in Washington and imposed upon hundreds of different situations. They are based on the fact that local citizens best understand their own problems and know best how to deal with those problems. These plans will be local plans striking at the many unfilled needs which underlie poverty in each community, not just one or two. Their components and emphasis will differ as needs differ. These plans will be local plans calling upon all the resources available to the community — federal and state, local and private, human and material.

And when these plans are approved by the Office of Economic Opportunity, the federal government will finance up to 90 percent of the additional cost for the first two years.

The most enduring strength of our nation is the huge reservoir of talent, initiative, and leadership which exists at every level of our society. Through the community-action program we call upon this, our greatest strength, to overcome our greatest weakness.

Third, I ask for the authority to recruit and train skilled volunteers for the war against poverty. Thousands of Americans have volunteered to serve the needs of other lands. Thousand more want the chance to serve the needs of their own land. They should have that chance.

Among older people who have retired, as well as among the young, among women as well as men, there are many Americans who are ready to enlist in our war against poverty. They have skills and dedication. They are badly needed. If the state requests them, if the community needs and will use them, we will recruit and train them and give them the chance to serve.

Fourth, we intend to create new opportunities for certain hard-hit groups to break out of the pattern of poverty. Through a new program of loans and guarantees we can provide incentives to those who will employ the unemployed. Through programs of work and retraining for unemployed fathers and mothers we can help them support their families in dignity while preparing themselves for new work. Through funds to purchase needed land, organize cooperatives, and create new and adequate family farms we can help those whose life on the land has been a struggle without hope.

Fifth, I do not intend that the war against poverty become a series of uncoordinated and unrelated efforts — that it perish for lack of leadership and direction. Therefore this bill creates, in the Executive Office of the President, a new Office of Economic Opportunity. Its director will be my personal chief of staff for the war against poverty. I intend to appoint Sargent Shriver to this post. He will be directly responsible for these new programs. He will work with and through existing agencies of the government. . . .

What you are being asked to consider is not a simple or an easy program. But poverty is not a simple or an easy enemy. It

America's "Sampan Dwellers"; cartoon by Reg Manning for the "Arizona Republic"

cannot be driven from the land by a single attack on a single front. Were this so we would have conquered poverty long ago. Nor can it be conquered by government alone.

For decades American labor and American business, private institutions and private individuals have been engaged in strengthening our economy and offering new opportunity to those in need. We need their help, their support, and their full participation.

Through this program we offer new incentives and new opportunities for cooperation, so that all the energy of our nation, not merely the efforts of government, can be brought to bear on our common enemy. Today, for the first time in our history, we have the power to strike away the barriers to full participation in our society. Having the power, we have the duty.

The Congress is charged by the Constitution to "provide . . . for the general welfare of the United States." Our present abundance is a measure of its success in fulfilling that duty. Now Congress is being asked to extend that welfare to all our people.

The President of the United States is

President of all the people in every section of the country. But this office also holds a special responsibility to the distressed and disinherited, the hungry and the hopeless of this abundant nation. . . .

On similar occasions in the past we have often been called upon to wage war against foreign enemies which threatened our freedom. Today we are asked to declare war on a domestic enemy which threatens the strength of our nation and the welfare of our people. If we now move forward against this enemy — if we can bring to the challenges of peace the same determination and strength which has brought us victory in war — then this day and this Congress will have won a secure and honorable place in the history of the nation and the enduring gratitude of generations of Americans yet to come.

41.

Lyndon B. Johnson: The Great Society

*The programs of most twentieth-century American Presidents have been given
slogan-nicknames, either by the Presidents themselves or by the press, which
prefers short phrases that fit headlines. Thus Theodore Roosevelt had his Square
Deal, Woodrow Wilson his New Freedom, FDR his New Deal, Harry Truman his
Fair Deal, JFK his New Frontier; Lyndon Johnson outlined his own program in a
speech at the University of Michigan on May 22, 1964, naming it the Great Society.*

Source: White House Press Release.

I HAVE COME TODAY from the turmoil of your Capitol to the tranquility of your campus to speak about the future of our country. The purpose of protecting the life of our nation and preserving the liberty of our citizens is to pursue the happiness of our people. Our success in that pursuit is the test of our success as a nation. For a century we labored to settle and to subdue a continent. For half a century we called upon unbounded invention and untiring industry to create an order of plenty for all of our people. The challenge of the next half century is whether we have the wisdom to use that wealth to enrich and elevate our national life and to advance the quality of our American civilization.

Your imagination, your initiative, and your indignation will determine whether we build a society where progress is the servant of our needs or a society where old values and new visions are buried under unbridled growth. For, in your time, we have the opportunity to move not only toward the rich society and the powerful society but upward to the Great Society.

The Great Society rests on abundance and liberty for all. It demands an end to poverty and racial injustice, to which we are totally committed in our time. But that is just the beginning. The Great Society is a place where every child can find knowledge to enrich his mind and to enlarge his talents. It is a place where leisure is a welcome chance to build and reflect, not a feared cause of boredom and restlessness. It is a place where the city of man serves not only the needs of the body and the demands of commerce but the desire for beauty and the hunger for community.

It is a place where man can renew contact with nature. It is a place which honors creation for its own sake and for what it adds to the understanding of the race. It is a place where men are more concerned with the quality of their goals than the quantity of their goods. But, most of all, the Great Society is not a safe harbor, a resting place, a final objective, a finished work; it is a challenge constantly renewed, beckoning us toward a destiny where the meaning of our lives matches the marvelous products of our labor.

So I want to talk to you today about three places where we begin to build the Great Society — in our cities, in our countryside, and in our classrooms. Many of you will live to see the day, perhaps fifty years from now, when there will be 400 million Americans, four-fifths of them in urban areas. In the remainder of this century, urban population will double, city land will double, and we will have to build homes, highways, and facilities equal to all those built since this country was first settled. So, in the next forty years, we must rebuild the entire urban United States.

Aristotle said, "Men come together in cities in order to live, but they remain together in order to live the good life." It is harder and harder to live the good life in American cities today. The catalog of ills is long: there is the decay of the centers and the despoiling of the suburbs. There is not enough housing for our people or transportation for our traffic. Open land is vanishing and old landmarks are violated. Worst of all, expansion is eroding the precious and time-honored values of community with neighbors and communion with nature. The loss of these values breeds loneliness and boredom and indifference. Our society will never be great until our cities are great. Today the frontier of imagination and innovation is inside those cities, and not beyond their borders. New experiments are already going on. It will be the task of your generation to make the American city a place

where future generations will come, not only to live but to live the good life.

I understand that if I stay here tonight I would see that Michigan students are really doing their best to live the good life. This is the place where the Peace Corps was started. It is inspiring to see how all of you, while you are in this country, are trying so hard to live at the level of the people.

A second place where we begin to build the Great Society is in our countryside. We have always prided ourselves on being not only America the strong and America the free but America the beautiful. Today that beauty is in danger. The water we drink, the food we eat, the very air that we breathe are threatened with pollution. Our parks are overcrowded. Our seashores overburdened. Green fields and dense forests are disappearing.

A few years ago we were greatly concerned about the Ugly American. Today we must act to prevent an Ugly America. For once the battle is lost, once our natural splendor is destroyed, it can never be recaptured. And once man can no longer walk with beauty or wonder at nature, his spirit will wither and his sustenance be wasted.

A third place to build the Great Society is in the classrooms of America. There your children's lives will be shaped. Our society will not be great until every young mind is set free to scan the farthest reaches of thought and imagination. We are still far from that goal. Today, 8 million adult Americans, more than the entire population of Michigan, have not finished five years of school. Nearly 20 million have not finished eight years of school. Nearly 54 million, more than one-quarter of all America, have not even finished high school.

Each year more than 100,000 high-school graduates, with proved ability, do not enter college because they cannot afford it. And if we cannot educate today's youth, what will we do in 1970 when elementary-school enrollment will be 5 million greater than 1960? And high-school enrollment will rise by 5 million? College enrollment will increase by more than 3 million? In many places, classrooms are overcrowded and curricula are outdated. Most of our qualified teachers are underpaid, and many of our paid teachers are unqualified. So we must give every child a place to sit and a teacher to learn from. Poverty must not be a bar to learning, and learning must offer an escape from poverty.

But more classrooms and more teachers are not enough. We must seek an educational system which grows in excellence as it grows in size. This means better training for our teachers. It means preparing youth to enjoy their hours of leisure as well as their hours of labor. It means exploring new techniques of teaching, to find new ways to stimulate the love of learning and the capacity for creation.

These are three of the central issues of the Great Society. While our government has many programs directed at those issues, I do not pretend that we have the full answer to those problems. But I do promise this: We are going to assemble the best thought and the broadest knowledge from all over the world to find those answers for America. I intend to establish working groups to prepare a series of White House conferences and meetings on the cities, on natural beauty, on the quality of education, and on other emerging challenges. And from these meetings and from this inspiration and from these studies we will begin to set our course toward the Great Society.

The solution to these problems does not rest on a massive program in Washington, nor can it rely solely on the strained resources of local authority. They require us to create new concepts of cooperation, a creative federalism, between the national Capitol and the leaders of local communities.

Woodrow Wilson once wrote: "Every man sent out from his university should be a man of his nation as well as a man of his time." Within your lifetime powerful forces, already loosed, will take us toward a way of life beyond the realm of our experience, almost beyond the bounds of our imagination. For better or for worse, your generation has been appointed by history to deal with those problems and to lead America toward a new age. You have the chance never before afforded to any people in any age. You can help build a society where the demands of morality and the needs of the spirit can be realized in the life of the nation.

So will you join in the battle to give every citizen the full equality which God enjoins and the law requires, whatever his belief, or race, or the color of his skin? Will you join in the battle to give every citizen an escape from the crushing weight of poverty? Will you join in the battle to make it possible for all nations to live in enduring peace as neighbors and not as mortal enemies? Will you join in the battle to build the Great Society, to prove that our material progress is only the foundation on which we will build a richer life of mind and spirit?

There are those timid souls who say this battle cannot be won, that we are condemned to a soulless wealth. I do not agree. We have the power to shape the civilization that we want. But we need your will, your labor, your hearts if we are to build that kind of society.

Those who came to this land sought to build more than just a new country. They sought a free world. So I have come here today to your campus to say that you can make their vision our reality. Let us from this moment begin our work so that in the future men will look back and say: It was then, after a long and weary way, that man turned the exploits of his genius to the full enrichment of his life.

42.

Herbert Harris: Why Labor Lost the Intellectuals

The American labor movement has undergone many vicissitudes. Born, at least in its modern dress, in the period after the Civil War, it was at first violent and was subjected to severe pressures as well as criticism from the country at large. Fending off the temptation to become radical or left wing in the 1890s and again in the 1930s, it continued to grow and to gain economic and political power until after World War II. Then, for reasons that Herbert Harris discusses in the following selection, it began to lose its effectiveness, seeming by the 1960s to speak for fewer and fewer of the citizens of the United States. Journalist and editor Harris was the author of several books on labor and its problems, and he served on various government boards and commissions. The article from which the selection is taken was published in the summer of 1964.

Source: *Harper's*, June 1964.

THE AMERICAN LABOR MOVEMENT is sleep-walking along the corridors of history. At every step it is failing to adapt effectively to the innovations which science and technology daily impose upon our ways of work. Lacking boldness in social invention, it clings on the whole to precepts which run the gamut from static to archaic.

Typical are its responses to automation. Labor spokesmen keep pressing for the shorter work week. But this dubious palliative tends to raise labor costs and thus makes the new robotism more attractive than ever to management. Then to console the displaced worker who can rarely find anything else to do, union negotiators concentrate on larger lump sums in severance pay. This emphasis, in effect, turns the labor movement into a mortician preoccupied with arrangements for his own funeral.

In no small degree this state of affairs derives from the fact that the labor movement has been losing its minds. Ever since World War II, it has been estranging the people who produce, distribute, and conspicuously consume ideas. Intellectuals have been in-creasingly disengaged as labor activists and disenchanted as sympathizers. Many of them no longer regard the labor movement as protector of the underdog, pioneer of social advance, keeper of the egalitarian conscience. Merely to ask whether the labor movement has "failed" the intellectuals, or the other way round, is to start a donny-brook at any national union headquarters or university conference on industrial relations. The point may be moot and is still obscured by feelings of mutual guilt.

But there is no doubt that the cleavage between labor and the intellectuals accounts, more than anything else, for the present crisis in the labor movement, the erosion of its vitality and its membership rolls, and its prickly defensiveness toward even the friendliest critics. . . .

"MORE AND MORE
AND MORE NOW"

CONSERVATIVE INTELLECTUALS, of course, have always been hostile toward the labor movement. During the entire nineteenth century they scolded it for getting born and trying to stay alive. And they have since kept whacking it for its refusal to comply with their misinterpretations of Adam Smith. But their animosity has been less important than the aid and amity of liberal and/or radical intellectuals. They have traditionally helped the labor movement to define and articulate its aspirations. They have also — at various times — explained, needled, split, glorified, and whitewashed it. Their number has included middle-class and patrician reformers as well as self-taught workingmen.

One such, for example, was the learned blacksmith Elihu Burritt, who had mastered all Europe's languages and enraptured nineteenth-century audiences with lectures on the noble need for education. After the Civil War, a former theological student and teacher turned tailor, Uriah S. Stephens, founded the Knights of Labor, which was to serve as sounding board for advocates of an industrial brotherhood that would, in effect, make every man his own employer. The Knights established some two hundred producer-consumer cooperatives in shoes, cooperage, and mining. All of them succumbed to lack of horse sense or the ungentle competition of Robber Baron capitalism. The Knights also espoused such political shortcuts to salvation as the single tax and the nationalizing of public utilities.

But when the American Federation of Labor was formed in 1886 it soon discarded all such utopianism. It plumped instead for a bread-and-butter unionism, with a minimal involvement in politics and government. Determined to depend for its gains upon its own economic strength of strike and boycott, the AFL had no ultimate aims. It embraced the existing order, striving only to obtain from it "more and more and more now" in income and respectability.

The AFL majority therefore resisted far-reaching plans of political action and the formation of a labor party — proposals regularly put forward by such insider Socialists as Max Hayes of the Typographers and John Fitzpatrick of the building trades and by such outsider Socialists as authors Upton Sinclair and William English Walling. Equating socialism with intellectualism and both with "governmentalism," the AFL excoriated all three as subversive. As late as 1930, the AFL was so fearful of becoming a "ward of the state" that it opposed unemployment insurance.

From four million in 1920, AFL membership tumbled to two million in the early thirties. Then the AFL finally began to welcome massive federal help. It even turned cordial toward such vanguard thinkers as the young lawyer-economist Leon H. Keyserling, who drafted major provisions of Labor's Magna Carta, the Wagner Act. It was passed in 1935. In the same year a dissident faction, the Committee (later Congress) of Industrial Organizations (CIO) broke away from the AFL. The split centered ostensibly around the issue of industrial (plant-wide and vertical) vs. craft (skill-narrow and horizontal) union structure. But the cleavage also reflected profound differences as to labor's role in politics and government's role in labor affairs. Determined to go beyond AFL business unionism, the CIO was eager to extend the social and economic reforms of President Roosevelt's first term. With this agenda it became home and hunting ground for left-of-center intellectuals. (Some of their enthusiasm spilled over to the AFL in its subsequent rivalry with the CIO.)

The CIO had need for intellectuals to write, speak, proselytize, plead in the courts, organize, and administer as it sought to channel into orderly unionism hundreds of thousands of rebellious workers in automobiles, steel, meat-packing, and other mass-production industries. The intellectuals responded with religious intensity.

Many were Marxists of varying hues. There were some Stalinists among these, carefully instructed to infiltrate the burgeoning CIO. Often they fought valiantly. But they remained the agents of a foreign power. And when union interests collided with Party-line vagaries, the union always lost out. Many more were Socialists (more accurately, Social Democrats) and non-Marxist liberals in the Populist tradition. Whether on the CIO staff, or as volunteers, they prepared the pamphlets, composed the songs, collected funds, and ran the mimeograph machines turning out the endless bulletins, instructions, notices. On picket lines, they braved the cops, sheriffs, private police, the mobsters hired by employers to smash strikes, and they were rewarded with broken heads, jaws, and arms. And everywhere they talked — at faculty teas and radio forums, at dinner parties and from loading platforms. Some served as brain-trusters for young leaders coming up from the shop and others developed into union officials themselves.

During the 1920s the Communists had originated a new cult, the Adoration of the Worker. The stereotype mesmerized many intellectuals. It was visually based on drawings in the *New Masses,* which showed a larger-than-life-size wage earner, his eyes fixed on the far horizon. His martial jaw proclaimed a proletarian toughness armoring a heart that bled for all humanity. His muscular neck and bulging biceps suggested a spectacular virility. He was portrayed in effect as a combination of St. Augustine, Paul Bunyan, and a stud bull.

ABRASIVE "INSIDERS"

It was not until the 1940s that the mystique of the worker began to evaporate. The intellectuals discovered by means of personal contact that he was pretty much like everybody else; that, indeed, the son of toil they had romanticized at a distance could be anti-Catholic, anti-Semitic, a white supremacist, a rancorous xenophobe; that

his favorite reading was the sports page, comic books, and detective magazines, and that this diet did not endow him with a profound grasp of national and international issues.

They discovered also that the CIO and AFL (they did not merge until 1955) were concentrating on business or market unionism, intent on taking care of their own, and downgrading social or national-interest unionism.

Critical reports and articles began to appear as labor's intellectual friends found, for example, that union "democracy" was not always of the New England town-meeting variety and that the corruptions of commercialism were infecting unions. Perhaps they were naïve. But above all, these intellectuals did not want the labor movement to become merely the mirror of a society in which everybody sells out to everybody else. Workers, they believed, should use some of their new ease and leisure to pursue things of the mind and spirit.

Within the labor movement the new criticism was more sophisticated. It was spearheaded by two of the foremost union-made intellectuals of the century. The first was J. B. S. Hardman, a former editor of *The Advance,* official organ of the clothing workers, and a man whose incorrigible optimism is tempered by a wry and even mordant wit. Under CIO auspices he established in 1946 a "Union Institute for Labor and Democracy." His right hand in this venture was Solomon Barkin, then research director of the Textile Workers (CIO) and perhaps the most incisive and even abrasive "insider" analyst of the modern labor scene. The Institute and its publication, the bimonthly *Labor and Nation,* were created to foster candid and independent examination of the labor movement and its missions.

But after six years this enterprise foundered for lack of support. Mr. Hardman observed that the place of the intellectual in the labor movement was to make a philosophy of no philosophy and went on to co-edit with Professor Maurice Neufield of Cornell the symposium *The House of Labor*. Mr. Barkin kept warning the labor movement that it faced stagnation unless it became the champion not just of its own adherents but of slum dwellers, migrant workers, and other Americans in the lower depths. Mr. Barkin left the Textile Workers last year to join the Office of Economic Cooperation and Development.

His counsels have been largely ignored. Indeed, the labor movement stopped listening to such apostasy in the first few years after World War II when it was riding high and enjoying unprecedented growth. During the 1935-45 decade alone, union membership rose from a scant 4 million to a staggering 14.3 million. For this achievement union chieftains quite humanly credited their own perspicacity and sweat.

They conveniently forgot how much the unions owed to the intellectuals in general and in particular to the great wartime innovators in management-labor affairs. Among them were the lawyer J. Warren Madden, chairman of the National Labor Relations Board (NLRB), and its chief economist David J. Saposs; patent attorney William H. Davis, chairman of the War Labor Board (WLB), and his colleague Senator Wayne Morse, then dean of the Law School at the University of Oregon; Professor George W. Taylor, the Edison of modern collective bargaining, who is now chairman of the Department of Industry at the Wharton School of the University of Pennsylvania; and Clark Kerr, WLB West Coast director and now president of the University of California.

Nor did the union chieftains recognize that special circumstances of depression and war had enabled them to fashion a new design for union living out of the economic autarchy of Samuel Gompers and the political favoritism of Franklin D. Roosevelt. They had forgotten, too, that the labor movement, in bringing to millions of workers a new sense of economic self-determination and psychological self-respect, had performed as a vehicle of social reconstruction; that it was to this image of its function that it owed public acceptance and support, without which it would lose its thrust. But the intellectuals who said this were arguing against success, with its heady aroma. And since there are limits even to their masochism, they began, one after the other, to give up and slip away. As early as 1948 the union protagonist and Columbia sociologist, the late C. Wright Mills, pointed out that union leaders as "new men of power" were proving to be either unwilling or unable to cooperate with the "men of intellect" on any viable basis.

"OUT IN LEFT FIELD"

WHY HAS THE LATTER-DAY labor movement been largely impervious to the critiques and recommendations of intellectuals? The answer lies in the character of the typical labor leader, his background, his style, the way he sees his job. He is a blend of political boss, evangelist, military chieftain, and salesman. Above all, he is a self-made man. He is the Siamese twin of the versatile entrepreneur who has built the business from scratch, is reluctant to delegate authority, and yearns for the old days when he could call everybody in the shop by his first name. Moreover, the labor leader has had to claw his way up in a bruising competition that makes even the high-tension cabals of the executive suite seem genteel. He is manipulative and practical in all his dealings and it is in accord with these criteria that he measures the extent to which the intellectuals are useful to him.

Among the latter are the staff economist who prepares a presentation to justify a wage increase; the lawyer who argues the union case before labor-relations boards and commissions, and in the courts; the industrial engineer who figures out how the union can benefit from a new time study for production norms; the publicist who puts together a speech or Congressional testimony; the actuary familiar with the intricacies of pension funds.

All these assist the labor leader to crystallize, express, dress up what he wants to do. (The Michigan professor, Harold L. Wilenski, who a decade ago conducted the only full-scale sociological survey of union intellectuals, thinks that their overriding function is that of "verbalizers.") The labor leader thinks it is up to him to create and coordinate policy while the experts implement it, rather than do much to formulate it. He regards such aides as his men just as he regards the union as an extension of his psyche. Even though he may respect the abilities and attainments of intellectuals, his attitude remains ambivalent, especially toward the university scholar, the foundation researcher, the writer turned social critic who concerns himself with union affairs. Labor leaders usually refer to the member of this genus as "pedantic," "an ivory tower guy," or as "out in left field, hell, further, out in space," or as a "pipe-smoking long-hair" (labor leaders cherish their cigars only more than their barbers).

Labor leaders are not impressed by the intellectual's inclination toward objective inquiry; they have felt too long beleaguered for that. They are even less impressed by his individualistic propensity to dissent from the prevailing values and mores of "the system." For the labor leader is gregarious, one of the boys, regards himself as chief of a tribe for whom he gets what he can out of the system which he accepts more than it accepts him.

THREATENED BY BRAINPOWER

WITHIN THE LABOR MOVEMENT there is still a tiny handful of intellectuals who play a key role in formulating and initiating union pol-

icy. . . . But this dwindling remnant can scarcely begin to meet the labor movement's need for brainpower at a time when leadership in our society is being everywhere transferred to people with intellectual training and capability. The labor leader who in most cases has only a high-school education is not unaware that the intellectual may one day threaten his own ascendancy. This fear explains his insistence that intellectuals be kept in their place and his lack of pronounced grief when they depart. He can then more comfortably rely on the old concepts and techniques of which he is master and which hasten labor's decline.

Today trade unions have not only stopped growing; as a percentage of the total labor force they are not even holding their own. Between 1960 and 1962, they lost nearly half a million members, and the rate is accelerating. Only a few years ago, one out of four persons who had a job or was looking for employment belonged to a union; now the ratio is edging toward one out of five and all indications are pointing downward.

Some apologists absolve the labor movement from responsibility for this predicament. They blame, among other factors, technological change; the guile of employers who forestall union organization by pretending to offer union-won benefits "for free"; the restrictions imposed by Taft-Hartley, Landrum-Griffin, and the state right-to-work laws; the unfriendliness of the press, radio, TV; the extent to which the McClellan disclosures on labor racketeering and corruption have been falsified into national folklore; the lavish antiunion propaganda and lobbying of the National Association of Manufacturers and the John Birch Society.

Yet it seems almost comic to ascribe all of labor's troubles to external conditions. After all, union members with their families still comprise nearly a fifth of the entire population of the United States, hardly a fragile potentiality in terms of economic and political strength.

The labor movement in fact is in a bad way chiefly because the bulk of intellectuals are not affirmatively on its side, and because it is no longer making use of that theoretical-pragmatic "mix" demanded by the ecology of the space age.

The discourse between analyst and administrator produced during the past generation our finest achievement in domestic policy, the Tennessee Valley Authority, and perhaps our finest achievement in foreign policy, the Marshall Plan.

Similarly, the State Department can hardly begin to function until its policy-planning staff has sifted the reports, the insights, the proposals of both the "pros" and the "professors" in international relations. The Pentagon's adroit use of its "military intellectuals" explains, in no small degree, the readiness of our defense posture.

Industry, likewise, regularly has its judgments checked by management consultants, the freelance intelligentsia of the business community. And within many companies the intellectual who was formerly regarded only as specialist is being brought closer to the policy center. The word has gone out to business recruiters on campus to search for fewer conformist organization men and more independent eggheads.

But the labor movement has little truck with such newfangled notions. The AFL-CIO headquarters has no policy-planning staff. It has no clearinghouse for the regular exchange of views between intellectuals and labor leaders. It has no equivalent, in terms of its own requirements, of alternative position papers, gaming theory, operations or market research and analysis. Among its affiliated unions, only a handful have management training and development programs.

There are, of course, research, legislative, legal, editorial, and public-relations people. All are overworked. All are immersed in immediacies, and play little part in basic decision making.

Yet the practical men who, by and large, are leaders of labor cannot by themselves reverse the movement's downward slide. It is not a question of intelligence. In native sagacity, or at least shrewdness, they are the equal of any comparable group in industry, government, the professions. But today's issues transcend their lore of collective bargaining, of building and running a union, of grasping intimately the problems of a particular company or industry. The dominant issues are now matters of national policy.

To blame automation as they do for causing unemployment, for example, is like blaming armaments for causing war. The answer to automation will be found in a national policy which can modify the socioeconomic framework to enable the computer to create more jobs than it destroys. And similar considerations of national policy on prices, wages, taxes, investment, manpower retraining, foreign trade are intertwined with any attempts to organize the unorganized, blue-collar or white-collar; to educate the unionized; to improve channels of communication between leaders and rank and file; to determine whether the labor movement should be politically something more than the tail of the Democratic party kite; whether the very structural forms of unionism should be revised.

In all these areas the labor movement has no logical choice but to draw, more positively and consistently than ever before, upon the talents and disciplines of intellectuals. In no other way can Big Labor test prevailing assumptions, explore new directions, and adjust to pivotal developments in Big Business and Big Government.

43.

J. WILLIAM FULBRIGHT: Old Myths and New Realities

The wedding of foreign policy to domestic politics has, in the view of some, made of U.S. foreign policy in the twentieth century an unworkable set of maxims designed more to please the voters at home than to provide sound guidelines for national action. George Kennan condemned this tendency when he said: "History does not forgive us our national mistakes because they are explicable in terms of our domestic politics. . . . A nation which excuses its own failure by the sacred untouchableness of its own habits can excuse itself into complete disaster." In a speech before the Senate on March 25, 1964, a portion of which is reprinted here, Arkansas Senator J. William Fulbright challenged what he called an American myth: the idea that in a world dominated by two powers, all other nations were inexorably allied with one side or the other and thereby committed either to Communism or freedom.

Source: *Record*, 88 Cong., 2 Sess., pp. 6227-6232.

THERE IS AN INEVITABLE DIVERGENCE, attributable to the imperfections of the human mind, between the world as it is and the world as men perceive it. As long as our perceptions are reasonably close to objective reality, it is possible for us to act upon our problems in a rational and appropriate manner. But when our perceptions fail to keep pace with events, when we refuse to believe something because it displeases or frightens us, or because it is simply startlingly unfamiliar, then the gap between fact and perception becomes a chasm, and action becomes irrelevant and irrational.

There has always — and inevitably — been some divergence between the realities of foreign policy and our ideas about it. This divergence has in certain respects been growing rather than narrowing; and we are handicapped, accordingly, by policies based on old myths rather than current realities. This divergence is, in my opinion, dangerous and unnecessary — dangerous, because

it can reduce foreign policy to a fraudulent game of imagery and appearances; unnecessary, because it can be overcome by the determination of men in high office to dispel prevailing misconceptions by the candid dissemination of unpleasant, but inescapable, facts.

Before commenting on some of the specific areas where I believe our policies are at least partially based on cherished myths rather than objective facts, I should like to suggest two possible reasons for the growing divergence between the realities and our perceptions of current world politics. The first is the radical change in relations between and within the Communist and the free world; and the second is the tendency of too many of us to confuse means with ends and, accordingly, to adhere to prevailing practices with a fervor befitting immutable principles.

Although it is too soon to render a definitive judgment, there is mounting evidence that events of recent years have wrought profound changes in the character of East-West relations. In the Cuban missile crisis of October 1962, the United States proved to the Soviet Union that a policy of aggression and adventure involved unacceptable risks. In the signing of the test-ban treaty, each side in effect assured the other that it was prepared to forgo, at least for the present, any bid for a decisive military or political breakthrough. These occurrences, it should be added, took place against the background of the clearly understood strategic superiority — but not supremacy — of the United States.

It seems reasonable, therefore, to suggest that the character of the cold war has, for the present, at least, been profoundly altered by the drawing back of the Soviet Union from extremely aggressive policies; by the implicit repudiation by both sides of a policy of "total victory"; and by the establishment of an American strategic superiority which the Soviet Union appears to have tacitly accepted because it has been accompanied by assurances that it will be exercised by the United States with responsibility and restraint. These enormously important changes may come to be regarded by historians as the foremost achievements of the Kennedy administration in the field of foreign policy. Their effect has been to commit us to a foreign policy which can accurately — though perhaps not prudently — be defined as one of "peaceful coexistence." . . .

These astonishing changes in the configuration of the postwar world have had an unsettling effect on both public and official opinion in the United States. One reason for this, I believe, lies in the fact that we are a people used to looking at the world, and indeed at ourselves, in moralistic rather than empirical terms. We are predisposed to regard any conflict as a clash between good and evil rather than as simply a clash between conflicting interests. We are inclined

to confuse freedom and democracy, which we regard as moral principles, with the way in which they are practised in America — with capitalism, federalism, and the two-party system, which are not moral principles but simply the preferred and accepted practices of the American people. . . .

Our national vocabulary is full of "self-evident truths," not only about "life, liberty, and happiness" but about a vast number of personal and public issues, including the cold war. It has become one of the "self-evident truths" of the postwar era that just as the President resides in Washington and the Pope in Rome, the devil resides immutably in Moscow. We have come to regard the Kremlin as the permanent seat of his power and we have grown almost comfortable with a menace which, though unspeakably evil, has had the redeeming virtues of constancy, predictability, and familiarity. Now the devil has betrayed us by traveling abroad and, worse still, by dispersing himself, turning up now here, now there, and in many places at once, with a devilish disregard for the laboriously constructed frontiers of ideology. . . .

The master myth of the cold war is that the Communist bloc is a monolith composed of governments which are not really governments at all but organized conspiracies, divided among themselves perhaps in certain matters of tactics, but all equally resolute and implacable in their determination to destroy the free world. I believe that the Communist world is indeed hostile to the free world in its general and long-term intentions but that the existence of this animosity in principle is far less important for our foreign policy than the great variations in its intensity and character, both in time and among the individual members of the Communist bloc.

Only if we recognize these variations, ranging from China, which poses immediate threats to the free world, to Poland and Yugoslavia, which pose none, can we hope to act effectively upon the bloc and to turn its internal differences to our own advantage and to the advantage of those bloc countries which wish to maximize their independence. It is the responsibility of our national leaders, both in the executive branch and in Congress, to acknowledge and act upon these realities, even at the cost of saying things which will not win immediate widespread enthusiasm.

For a start, we can acknowledge the fact that the Soviet Union, though still a most formidable adversary, has ceased to be totally and implacably hostile to the West. It has shown a new willingness to enter mutually advantageous arrangements with the West and, thus far at least, to honor them. It has, therefore, become possible to divert some of our energies from the prosecution of the cold war to the relaxation of the cold war and to deal with the Soviet Union, for certain purposes, as a normal state with normal and traditional interests.

If we are to do these things effectively, we must distinguish between communism as an ideology and the power and policy of the Soviet state. It is not communism as a doctrine, or communism as it is practised within the Soviet Union or within any other country, that threatens us. How the Soviet Union organizes its internal life, the gods and doctrines that it worships, are matters for the Soviet Union to determine. It is not Communist dogma as espoused within Russia but Communist imperialism that threatens us and other peoples of the non-Communist world. . . .

Important opportunities have been created for Western policy by the development of "polycentrism" in the Communist bloc. The Communist nations, as George Kennan has pointed out, are, like the Western nations, currently caught up in a crisis of indecision about their relations with countries outside their own ideological bloc. The choices open to the satellite states are limited but by no means insignificant. They can

Dennis Brack from Black Star

J. William Fulbright, head of the Senate Foreign Relations Committee

adhere slavishly to Soviet preferences or they can strike out on their own, within limits, to enter into mutually advantageous relations with the West.

Whether they do so, and to what extent, is to some extent at least within the power of the West to determine. If we persist in the view that all Communist regimes are equally hostile and equally threatening to the West, and that we can have no policy toward the captive nations except the eventual overthrow of their Communist regimes, then the West may enforce upon the Communist bloc a degree of unity which the Soviet Union has shown itself to be quite incapable of imposing — just as Stalin in the early postwar years frightened the West into a degree of unity that it almost certainly could not have attained by its own unaided efforts. If, on the other hand, we are willing to reexamine the view that all Communist regimes are alike in the threat which they pose for the West — a view which had a certain validity in Stalin's time —

then we may be able to exert an important influence on the course of events within a divided Communist world.

We are to a great extent the victims, and the Soviets the beneficiaries, of our own ideological convictions and of the curious contradictions which they involve. We consider it a form of subversion of the free world, for example, when the Russians enter trade relations or conclude a consular convention or establish airline connections with a free country in Asia, Africa, or Latin America — and to a certain extent we are right. On the other hand, when it is proposed that we adopt the same strategy in reverse — by extending commercial credits to Poland or Yugoslavia, or by exchanging ambassadors with a Hungarian regime which has changed considerably in character since the revolution of 1956 — then the same patriots who are so alarmed by Soviet activities in the free world charge our policymakers with "giving aid and comfort to the enemy" and with innumerable other categories of idiocy and immorality. . . .

There are numerous areas in which we can seek to reduce the tensions of the cold war and to bring a degree of normalcy into our relations with the Soviet Union and other Communist countries — once we have resolved that it is safe and wise to do so. We have already taken important steps in this direction: the Antarctic and Austrian treaties and the nuclear test-ban treaty, the broadening of East-West cultural and educational relations, and the expansion of trade.

On the basis of recent experience and present economic needs, there seems little likelihood of a spectacular increase in trade between Communist and Western countries, even if existing restrictions were to be relaxed. Free-world trade with Communist countries has been increasing at a steady but unspectacular rate, and it seems unlikely to be greatly accelerated because of the limited ability of the Communist countries to pay for increased imports. A modest increase in East-West trade may nonetheless serve as a modest instrument of East-West detente — provided that we are able to overcome the myth that trade with Communist countries is a compact with the devil and to recognize that, on the contrary, trade can serve as an effective and honorable means of advancing both peace and human welfare.

Whether we are able to make these philosophic adjustments or not, we cannot escape the fact that our efforts to devise a common Western trade policy are a palpable failure and that our allies are going to trade with the Communist bloc whether we like it or not. . . .

There is little in history to justify the expectation that we can either win the cold war or end it immediately and completely. These are favored myths, respectively, of the American right and of the American left. They are, I believe, equal in their unreality and in their disregard for the feasibilities of history. We must disabuse ourselves of them and come to terms, at last, with the realities of a world in which neither good nor evil is absolute and in which those who move events and make history are those who have understood not how much but how little it is within our power to change. . . .

Latin America is one of the areas of the world in which American policy is weakened by a growing divergency between old myths and new realities. . . . I think the time is overdue for a candid reevaluation of our Cuban policy, even though it may also lead to distasteful conclusions.

There are and have been three options open to the United States with respect to Cuba: first, the removal of the Castro regime by invading and occupying the island; second, an effort to weaken and ultimately bring down the regime by a policy of political and economic boycott; and, finally, acceptance of the Communist regime as a disagreeable reality and annoyance but one which is not likely to be removed in the near future because of the unavailability of acceptable means of removing it.

The first option, invasion, has been tried in a halfhearted way and found wanting. It is generally acknowledged that the invasion and occupation of Cuba, besides violating our obligations as a member of the United Nations and of the Organization of American States, would have explosive consequences in Latin America and elsewhere and might precipitate a global nuclear war. I know of no responsible statesman who advocates this approach. It has been rejected by our government and by public opinion, and I think that, barring some grave provocation, it can be ruled out as a feasible policy for the United States.

The approach which we have adopted has been the second of those mentioned, an effort to weaken and eventually bring down the Castro regime by a policy of political and economic boycott. This policy has taken the form of extensive restrictions against trade with Cuba by United States citizens, of the exclusion of Cuba from the inter-American system and efforts to secure Latin-American support in isolating Cuba politically and economically, and of diplomatic efforts, backed by certain trade and aid sanctions, to persuade other free-world countries to maintain economic boycotts against Cuba.

This policy, it now seems clear, has been a failure, and there is no reason to believe that it will succeed in the future. Our efforts to persuade our allies to terminate their trade with Cuba have been generally rebuffed. The prevailing attitude was perhaps best expressed by a British manufacturer who, in response to American criticisms of the sale of British buses to Cuba, said: "If America has a surplus of wheat, we have a surplus of buses." . . .

The boycott policy has not failed because of any "weakness" or "timidity" on the part of our government. This charge, so fre-

quently heard, is one of the most pernicious myths to have been inflicted on the American people. The boycott policy has failed because the United States is not omnipotent and cannot be. The basic reality to be faced is that it is simply not within our power to compel our allies to cut off their trade with Cuba, unless we are prepared to take drastic sanctions against them, such as closing our own markets to any foreign company that does business in Cuba, as proposed by Mr. Nixon. We can do this, of course, but if we do, we ought first to be very sure, as apparently Mr. Nixon is, that the Cuban boycott is more important than good relations with our closest allies. In fact, even the most drastic sanctions are as likely to be rewarded with defiance as with compliance. . . .

The prospects of bringing down the Castro regime by political and economic boycott have never been very good. Even if a general free-world boycott were successfully applied against Cuba, it is unlikely that the Russians would refuse to carry the extra financial burden and thereby permit the only Communist regime in the Western Hemisphere to collapse. We are thus compelled to recognize that there is probably no way of bringing down the Castro regime by means of economic pressures unless we are prepared to impose a blockade against nonmilitary shipments from the Soviet Union. Exactly such a policy has been recommended by some of our more reckless politicians, but the preponderance of informed opinion is that a blockade against Soviet shipments of nonmilitary supplies to Cuba would be extravagantly dangerous, carrying the strong possibility of a confrontation that could explode into nuclear war.

Having ruled out military invasion and blockade, and recognizing the failure of the boycott policy, we are compelled to consider the third of the three options open to us with respect to Cuba: the acceptance of the continued existence of the Castro regime as a distasteful nuisance but not an intolerable danger so long as the nations of the hemisphere are prepared to meet their obligations of collective defense under the Rio Treaty. . . .

We would do well, while continuing our efforts to promote peaceful change through the Alliance for Progress, to consider what our reactions might be in the event of the outbreak of genuine social revolution in one or more Latin-American countries. Such a revolution did occur in Bolivia, and we accepted it calmly and sensibly. But what if a violent social revolution were to break out in one of the larger Latin-American countries? Would we feel certain that it was Cuban or Soviet inspired? Would we wish to intervene on the side of established authority? Or would we be willing to tolerate or even support a revolution if it was seen to be not Communist but similar in nature to the Mexican revolution or the Nasser revolution in Egypt?

These are hypothetical questions and there is no readily available set of answers to them. But they are questions which we should be thinking about because they have to do with problems that could become real and urgent with great suddenness. We should be considering, for example, what groups in particular countries might conceivably lead revolutionary movements, and if we can identify them, we should be considering how we might communicate with them and influence them in such a way that their movements, if successful, will not pursue courses detrimental to our security and our interests.

The Far East is another area of the world in which American policy is handicapped by the divergence of old myths and new realities. Particularly with respect to China, an elaborate vocabulary of make-believe has become compulsory in both official and public discussion. We are committed, with respect to China and other areas in Asia, to inflexible policies of long standing from which we hesitate to depart because of the attribution to these policies of an aura of mystical sanctity. It may be that a thorough reevaluation of our Far Eastern policies would lead us to the conclusion that they are sound and wise, or at least that they represent the best available options. It may be, on the other hand, that a reevaluation would point up the need for greater or lesser changes in our policies. The point is that, whatever the outcome of a rethinking of policy might be, we have been unwilling to undertake it because of the fear of many government officials, undoubtedly well-founded, that even the suggestion of new policies toward China or Vietnam would provoke a vehement public outcry.

I do not think the United States can, or should, recognize Communist China, or acquiesce in its admission to the United Nations under present circumstances. It would be unwise to do so because there is nothing to be gained by it so long as the Peiping regime maintains its attitude of implacable hostility toward the United States. I do not believe, however, that this state of affairs is necessarily permanent. As we have seen in our relations with Germany and Japan, hostility can give way in an astonishingly short time to close friendship; and, as we have seen in our relations with China, the reverse can occur with equal speed. It is not impossible that in time our relations with China will change again — if not to friendship then perhaps to "competitive coexistence." It would therefore be extremely useful if we could introduce an element of flexibility, or, more precisely, of the capacity to be flexible, into our relations with Communist China.

We would do well, as former Assistant Secretary Hilsman has recommended, to maintain an "open door" to the possibility of improved relations with Communist China in the future. For a start, we must jar open our minds to certain realities about China, of which the foremost is that there really are not "two Chinas," but only one — mainland China; and that it is ruled by Communists, and is likely to remain so for the indefinite future. Once we accept this fact, it becomes possible to reflect on the conditions under which it might be possible for us to enter into relatively normal relations with mainland China. . . .

In the immediate future, we are confronted with possible changes in the Far East resulting from recent French diplomacy. French recognition of Communist China, although untimely and carried out in a way that can hardly be considered friendly to the United States, may nonetheless serve a constructive long-term purpose, by unfreezing a situation in which many countries, none more than the United States, are committed to inflexible policies by long-established commitments and the pressures of domestic public opinion. One way or another, the French initiative may help generate a new situation in which the United States, as well as other countries, will find it possible to reevaluate its basic policies in the Far East.

The situation in Vietnam poses a far more pressing need for a reevaluation of American policy. Other than withdrawal, which I do not think can be realistically considered under present circumstances, three options are open to us in Vietnam: First, continuation of the antiguerrilla war within South Vietnam, along with renewed American efforts to increase the military effectiveness of the South Vietnamese Army and the political effectiveness of the South Vietnamese government; second, an attempt to end the war, through negotiations for the neutralization of South Vietnam, or of both North and South Vietnam; and, finally, the expansion of the scale of the war, either by the direct commitment of large numbers of American troops or by equipping the South

Vietnamese Army to attack North Vietnamese territory, possibly by means of commando-type operations from the sea or the air.

It is difficult to see how a negotiation, under present military circumstances, could lead to termination of the war under conditions that would preserve the freedom of South Vietnam. It is extremely difficult for a party to a negotiation to achieve by diplomacy objectives which it has conspicuously failed to win by warfare. The hard fact of the matter is that our bargaining position is at present a weak one; and until the equation of advantages between the two sides has been substantially altered in our favor, there can be little prospect of a negotiated settlement which would secure the independence of a non-Communist South Vietnam. . . .

It seems clear that only two realistic options are open to us in Vietnam in the immediate future: the expansion of the conflict in one way or another, or a renewed effort to bolster the capacity of the South Vietnamese to prosecute the war successfully on its present scale. The matter calls for thorough examination by responsible officials in the executive branch; and until they have had an opportunity to evaluate the contingencies and feasibilities of the options open to us, it seems to me that we have no choice but to support the South Vietnamese government and Army by the most effective means available. Whatever specific policy decisions are made, it should be clear to all concerned that the United States will continue to meet its obligations and fulfill its commitments with respect to Vietnam.

These, I believe, are some, although by no means all, of the issues of foreign policy in which it is essential to reevaluate long-standing ideas and commitments in the light of new and changing realities.

44.

Louis Lasagna: Problems of Drug Development

The 1950s and 1960s were marked, among other things, by acrimonious discussions about the problem of drug development. Congressional hearings — most notably that of the Kefauver Committee in 1959-1960 — brought the problem to the front pages, but it had been lying dormant since World War II and continued to trouble legislators, physicians, and, of course, patients even after the furor created by the hearings died down. The problem, stated very simply, was that the drug industry seemed from one point of view to be a kind of public utility, and from another a private business. Should it be controlled like any public-service business — or should it be allowed to operate like other private enterprises? These and other questions were discussed by Louis Lasagna, associate professor of pharmacology and experimental therapeutics at Johns Hopkins University, in an article in Science *in 1964. Part of the article is reprinted here.*

Source: *Science*, July 24, 1964.

THERE ARE ALMOST DAILY complaints about some aspect of drug usage in our society. The academicians are constantly berating industry for its motivations and promotional excesses. When not so engaged, they are lambasting Congress for inadequate support of clinical pharmacology or for adding to the headaches of researchers by passing "patient consent" laws. The personnel of the Food and Drug Administration (FDA) are rarely allowed to rest quietly in their foxholes: on one day they are bombed for pusillanimity, on the next for high-handedness. (If a specific issue is lacking, it is considered good form to brand them as generally inept.)

The drug industry, in its turn, is bitter about the unreasonableness and extravagance of the professional attacks. The pharmaceutical folk are understandably annoyed when their substantial scientific contributions are ignored, or when they are asked for funds to support research or scientific societies by the same academicians who have berated them. Government is constantly a threat to the industry, the nature of the danger ranging from possible patent restrictions to "arbitrariness" or "ignorance" on the part of specific FDA staffers determined to prevent a drug's being marketed or to snatch a profitable pharmaceutical off the market.

The government, for its part, must be confused by scientists who won't "stand still" ideologically. Just when a senator or representative thinks he has done a creditable job in following up on the suggestion of some distinguished scientists, they turn on him for going too far. The FDA is perpetually spending time justifying to the press, Congress, the drug industry, or the medical profession some action it took two years ago, or didn't take last week. There is, then, no paucity of strong sentiment about the handling of drug matters. What is lacking is rapport between the various forces responsible for the health of the public. . . .

The search for new drugs has been criticized as a sort of blindman's buff, a groping for precious jewels hidden in a vast desert. And so it is, in part. The science of pharmacology is not sufficiently precise or profound to permit the rational design of wondrous new agents. Pharmaceutical research has of necessity, therefore, to spend a good part of its effort in "screening" and in testing chemicals related to older drugs found — usually by luck — to be effective. This kind of search, which includes testing of soils for antibiotics, scouring the world for effective folk remedies, and synthesizing congeners, is not without rationale, and occasionally it yields a fine new product. It is nonetheless expensive and inefficient. Usually, for example, the testing of congeners fails to provide a dramatic breakthrough, and the result is a "me-too" drug which it is hard to justify putting into man at all, let alone on the market.

From the drug house's viewpoint, on the other hand, it may be simply a matter of capitalizing on someone else's serendipity so as to assure a satisfactory sales volume and thus satisfy stockholders and support the entire organization, including the research staff. As one drug house physician put it to me: "With our firm's fine reputation and large detail force, we can put out a thiazide diuretic that is no better or worse than any of those already available from other firms and capture 15 percent of a huge market. Why shouldn't we?" In such a situation there may be a serious conflict between good business decisions and the needs of the physician and his patient. (It is true, to be sure, that a "me-too" drug may still turn out to be uniquely useful for *some* patients, and the existence of competing products may occasionally have a salubrious effect on drug prices. Such a matter is rarely black-and-white.)

There is another aspect of new drug development which gives rise to conflicts: the pressure of time. Time is a precious commodity for us all, and it is especially precious in a market characterized by rapid obsolescence and fierce competition. If a drug house is working in a field known to be tilled by other firms, there will of necessity be pressures to market at the earliest opportunity. There are considerable market advantages in being the "first firm in the territory," and even if there is no worry about the emergence of similar drugs from other firms, someone else may be working on a completely different kind of drug which may soon toll the commercial death knell for the earlier product.

This is not to say that the result is invariably inadequate documentation, or excessive and premature claims for safety and efficacy, but it would be unrealistic not to admit that pressures are exerted in these directions by the ticking of the clock.

A paradox also emerges from the very pace of industrial activity. I believe that the drug industry generates certain anxieties in physicians in direct proportion to the rate at which it introduces new drugs on the market. Such anxieties do not require that these drugs be worthless or "me-too" products; indeed I suspect that the greatest unrest would derive from the marketing of large numbers of unique and excellent drugs!

Let me explain. The incorporation of new drugs, like new tests or new surgical treatments, into one's medical bag of tricks creates serious trouble for today's busy practitioner. The doctor's life was simplest when he needed only to concern himself with a small number of proven remedies. Such slogans as "It isn't the anesthetic that's important; it's the man who uses it," and "Learn to use one digitalis preparation well, rather than many poorly" are in part sound principle, but in part also a reflection of the turmoil created by the need to master a large pharmacopeia. It is on such anxieties and frustrations that the success of *Consumer Reports*-type periodicals like *The Medical Letter* and how-to-do-it books like *Drugs of Choice* or *Current Therapy* is built. No doctor is capable of expert judgment on all drugs, and he must increasingly seek quick, authoritative, "unbiased" advice regarding new agents. Such expert and reliable advice is obviously desirable, provided the physician does not accept ex cathedra statements as Eternal and Infallible Truth.

The productivity of the drug industry also compounds the difficulties in another area. There are thousands of chemists and pharmacologists and technicians busily at work trying to come up with new drugs. The budgets supporting such research are astronomical. The success of these research programs demands the elaboration of a certain number of useful products. To put even a small number of drugs on the market requires that a much larger number be evaluated in man. Unfortunately, but a handful of investigators in the country are trained to evaluate drugs in man, and the number of industrial products requiring accurate and careful study is extremely large.

If the supply of first-rate investigators is short in general, it becomes shorter with respect to drugs that do not look intellectually exciting. As a result the help of second-rate investigators (who may be first-rate physicians) is solicited. The resultant level of drug investigation is thus suboptimal and serves to promote erroneous decisions in regard to marketing, and to accumulate poor data, inadequate to support advertising claims for new drugs.

Whereas drug advertising is better than it was, some of it continues to be lacking in taste, intelligence, or truth. The inadequacies in clinical pharmacology already mentioned and the frenetic pace of industrial activity contribute to the problems. The marketing of drugs that are not world-beaters or that are "me-too" products automatically makes for trouble, since the existence of such drugs presents the advertising man with the necessity to choose between distortion and not selling. No one can sell a chemical by saying, "Peppo is not really very good for depression and fatigue, but it's pretty safe," or "Salo is not much better or worse than any of the eight other related diuretics that you've been using for years."

When the decision is made to market a drug, there can be no wishy-washy approach to its promotion. Either the firm believes in the drug's potential, or it will not try to sell it. But when a drug is first put on sale — no matter what the amount of experience to date has been — there will be uncertainties about its true capacity for good and harm. It takes years for a drug to settle into its proper niche (and some never do). A common pattern of evolution is for therapeutic and safety claims to be tempered with the passage of time. If a new drug turns out to be a superb agent, then everyone is better off if the advertising campaign is wildly successful. If the new drug turns out to be a dud, or unpredictably toxic, the public is best served if the ads miss the mark.

While a drug firm does not wish to make profits at the price of harming people, it is not unreasonable to believe that a firm would not feel badly about sales of a drug to patients who didn't need the drug at all or who didn't respond as well to the drug as they might have to some other agent. Most drug ads do not really qualify as "educational," but as "persuaders." There is thus a certain conflict between the goals of advertising and the goals of the physician and his patient, and no amount of wishful thinking can alter this fact.

Obviously drug houses must make money. No one but a fool would want them out of business. Yet many drugs do seem expensive to many people, and there is no evidence in the yearly earnings reports of individual firms that the industry is perched on the brink of financial disaster. It is furthermore difficult to convince the consumer that he should use trade brands rather than generic products if considerable savings can be had by using generic products of apparently equal quality.

The problem is not a simple one. The small house that capitalizes on other people's discoveries is, in a sense, parasitic. A society with nothing but such firms would be in a sad fix. Patents have been infringed upon in other countries, and manufacturing secrets are occasionally stolen. The aims of these small houses are less humanitarian than profit-minded. . . .

On the other hand, much of the attack by the ethical houses on generic drugs has been below the belt. Many such drugs are perfectly satisfactory products and not the sort of hopelessly inferior junk pictured in campaigns against them. An occasional preparation, to be sure, is sufficiently off the mark to interfere with medical care, but the same can be said of the products of large firms. It would seem important, rather, for techniques and standards to be developed which insure that no substandard drugs are sold by anyone.

The untoward effects of drugs constitute another source of discontent. Many physicians are convinced that there is too much prescribing of drugs (by *other* physicians, of course). The incidence of toxicity is probably directly related to the number of drugs a patient takes. While admitting the physician's complicity, critical academicians point the accusing finger at the firms "overpromoting" these drugs. In addition, there is often friction between the physicians reporting new and serious side effects and the manufacturers involved.

A common pattern of action is the following: A drug has been on the market for some time, apparently doing its job well with a minimum of trouble. Suddenly, the drug is alleged to cause serious toxicity or even death. The cases are reported. The firm examines the cases critically and points out that it is less than certain that the agent in question was the only cause. As the reports accumulate, there is a clear-cut difference of opinion: Several responsible clinicians become convinced that mischief from the drug is occurring with some frequency; the firm is convinced that most or all of the reported cases can be explained away. Retrospective analyses by the firm are begun, and they often "show" that the drug not only doesn't *cause* cataracts, jaundice, or strokes, but actually *prevents* these troubles, since there are fewer *reported* instances of trouble in patients taking the drug than are shown in the public-health figures available for the general population. Eventually, however, it is demonstrated that the toxicity is produceable at will in animals, or that it occurs conclusively in man, and the drug is taken off the market.

The FDA staff, meanwhile, can't win in such a situation. If they don't whisk the drug off the market at the first report, they are considered slothful, or gutless, by some doctors. If they do, they are accused of bureaucratic, impetuous, and dictatorial action by the manufacturers. If they take the drug off the market after due deliberation, they may be attacked by both the manufacturer and some physicians who have gotten to like the drug.

It is too little appreciated that the FDA has a fantastically difficult tightrope to walk, and that public-health decisions can't be made separately for this physician or that, this patient or that, but that (as FDA Commissioner Larrick has pointed out) "the government must make a judgment as to the hazards likely to be encountered when the drug is employed by physicians of varying skills . . . in patients with a multitude of disease processes . . . and in patients incorrectly diagnosed or inadequately tested. . . ."

The very existence of the FDA is a thorny irritant to some. An agency which can delay or block the marketing of a drug, cause warnings to be put on labels or to be sent out to doctors, or remove a profitable and useful drug from the market will of necessity be resented by the drug industry and, on occasions, by members of the medical profession. The policeman is welcome when you're being attacked or robbed but not when he's giving you a speeding ticket.

In addition, the FDA has made enemies in the past by the ineptitude of some of its procedures: by long delays in answering the simplest of queries, by peremptorily demanding voluminous data from firms within a short period of time and then postponing action on such data for many months, by assigning untalented and inexperienced scientists or physicians to discuss matters with drug-house experts who felt "insulted" at the quality of their interrogators and their questions.

At times the lack of insight into the attitudes of investigators has been amazing. One highly placed FDA staff member once stated: "It is difficult to understand why any conscientious and experienced clinical investigator would object to supplying detailed reports of his work." Such a statement is explainable only by the numbing tolerance to paper work that is developed by those whose every working day is occupied with the weary filing of forms in quadruplicate.

Some of the discomfort and pained surprise experienced by industry, government, and segments of the medical profession arises from a fundamental lack of appreciation of the guiding principles of the academic scientist. One hears complaints from the drug industry, for example, about "lack of moderation," "ingratitude," "faulty perspective," and "partiality.". . . It might help if the industry remembered that a university scientist can get highly incensed over one bad ad, no matter how many other, unobjectionable ads he encounters and accepts as a matter of course. He can take a drug-house grant or fellowship with one hand, while the other hand is busily clubbing the drug house about a shoddy product. He is concerned with what he considers principle and with the eradication of what he perceives to be error. He often looks upon himself as the keeper of the flame. It is unwise to expect him to be a compromiser or a diplomat, as his colleagues, dean, or university president know all too well. The academician, then, is likely to be a scientific boat-rocker. . . .

The recent struggle over the banning of some antibiotic mixtures is a case in point. An extraordinarily distinguished and experienced panel of scientists recommended to the FDA that oral "cold remedies" which combined antibiotics with analgesics, antihistamines, decongestants, and caffeine be removed from the market. The uproar that followed was intense, but predictable. The drug industry resented the move because it would have eliminated a lucrative market. Many physicians objected because they thought the mixtures useful.

Most academic scientists, on the other hand, regard the preparations as irrational and of little value. Furthermore, it is almost certain that the "experts" do not subscribe to the AMA's democratic notion that "only the medical profession, after widespread usage, can determine the true effectiveness of a drug." Scientific truth is not arrived at by majority vote. There is too much evidence that the medical profession, like the rest of us, can be misled by "practical experience" to encourage the testing of truth by referendum. Our "experience" tells us that the earth is flat, and that we are not spinning around in space, but neither of these happens to be true. . . .

For some years now the FDA has been under recurrent scrutiny. Some recommendations of past investigating committees have been heeded in the Drug Industry Act of 1962. Other suggestions have not been followed. It is difficult to know how to proceed now. The Bureau of Medicine has a new director, and his comments to date have been reassuring. Perhaps he should be given time to set his shop in order without sniping from critics. After a reasonable period of time, it would be helpful if a new non-HEW committee were to inquire from the director and his staff what their needs were, and what further reorganization is required. To outsiders, there still seems a lack of close liaison within the FDA. It is still thought by some that there is not adequate collaboration between the FDA pharmacologists and its medical people, for example.

In the meantime, it is to be hoped that the FDA will call increasingly on the academic community for help, for sharing in decisions and in responsibility. There is a large untapped reservoir of friendly academic talent. For example, I suspect that in regard to problems of drug advertising and toxicity reporting, the FDA would find strong allies in the medical-school faculties.

Most academicians with whom I speak believe firmly in the principle espoused by the government that indications and contraindications for a drug should be presented in fair balance in advertising, and our medical students agree. In regard to the reporting of drug toxicity, most of my colleagues would back the request that "*any* deaths associated with the use of a drug, whether or not it is attributable to the drug," be reported to the FDA. Many of us have had experiences which suggest that it is unwise to require the reporting only of cases where the firm involved considers that "there was adequate reason to believe that use of the drug may have contributed to the cause of death." I have no objection to an opinion to this effect from the firm, but reported deaths should not be buried in a firm's files because someone there doesn't agree with the suggestion by a physician that the drug *may* have been implicated.

Another example of talent which could be used by the FDA resides in the pharmacy departments of drug houses and in schools of pharmacy. There is now a growing body of knowledge indicating that too little attention has been paid in the past to the physicochemical aspects of pharmaceutical formulation. Obviously old-fashioned ideas about "disintegration-time" are no longer adequate, and USP and FDA specifications for drugs may require considerable revision. In this, as in other matters, there is much to be gained in the long run by all of us if the FDA operates at the highest possible level of intellectual and technical competence.

The PMA would do the drug industry a great service if it could diminish the number of objectionable ads run by its member firms. Much valuable information along these lines is already available, if member firms were willing to share at least a fraction of their hard-earned knowledge with each other. At the very least, it would help if continuing attempts were made to scrutinize drug ads to find those that irritate the physician-consumer. It would be educational to have these criticized ads made available to all firms, plus rebuttal commentaries by the ad men responsible. In the other direction, why not give awards for *excellence* in drug ads? It is done already for other kinds of advertising — why not for medical ads? It should also be remembered that one firm's or agency's objectionable ads are likely to reflect — unfairly — on all firms and agencies.

It is tragic that education in pharmacology is declining at a time when it is most needed. In an era of therapeutic explosiveness, one finds medical schools wondering whether pharmacology should exist as a separate discipline. The formal teaching of therapeutics to students is either considered an impossibility or explained away by the statement that "it is taken care of by each individual clinical department." The education of physicians in practice is left pretty much to the drug houses, the medical journals (including *The Medical Letter*), and a few medical meetings each year. How many medical schools are doing a good job of keeping the doctors in their communities up-to-date on drug therapy?

We must face the fact that the practice of medicine is getting more, not less, difficult because of the many powerful drugs put into our hands. There is an urgency to the situation which is not being heeded. Mean-while the ill suffer daily from errors of omission and commission.

Our society's handling of the problems created by the pharmacological revolution of the last quarter century leaves much to be desired. Equitable solutions are not likely to be evolved without the full cooperation of the medical profession, the medical schools, the drug industry, and the government.

45.

The Integrity of Science

The traditional American faith in science was tried more severely in the years after World War II than probably ever before. The scientists had produced the atomic bomb and thereby, as many people felt, had won the war — but testing of new and larger bombs created dangerous problems of fallout. Potent new drugs saved lives — but the specter of malformed and defective infants cast doubt on the use of some of them. Pesticides helped produce a revolution in agriculture — but they also seemed to threaten the balance of nature. These and similar problems were discussed in 1964 in a report prepared by the Committee on Science in the Promotion of Human Welfare of the American Association for the Advancement of Science, under the chairmanship of Barry Commoner. Part of the report is reprinted here.

Source: *Science and Culture*, Gerald Holton, ed., Boston, 1965, pp. 291-315.

I. THE PROBLEM

SCIENCE HAS SYSTEMATICALLY CREATED a powerful and rapidly growing body of knowledge. From this basic knowledge have come the spectacular feats of modern technology: space vehicles, nuclear explosives, and power plants, new substances and electronic machines, and a significant increase in human longevity. This record of growth and achievement creates a widespread impression that science is a strong, well-established human enterprise. Confidence that science can continue to fulfill human needs is a distinctive characteristic of modern society.

But the ultimate source of the strength of science will not be found in its impressive products or in its powerful instruments. It will be found in the minds of the scientists and in the system of discourse which scientists have developed in order to describe what they know and to perfect their understanding of what they have learned. It is these internal factors — the methods, procedures, and processes which scientists use to discover and to discuss the properties of the natural world — which have given science its great success.

We shall refer to these processes and to the organization of science on which they depend as the *integrity of science*. The term is a useful one, for it connotes the importance of a unified internal structure to the success of science, as well as its guiding imperative — the search for objective knowledge. On the integrity of science depends our understanding of the enormous powers which science has placed at the disposal of society. On this understanding, and therefore ultimately on the integrity of science, depends the welfare and safety of mankind. . . .

II. EXPERIMENTS IN SPACE

SYMBOLIC OF THE IMMENSE GROWTH and power of modern science is the exploration of space. With the development of powerful rockets for military purposes it has become possible in the last decade to send vehicles and human passengers beyond the earth's atmosphere. With the concurrent development of highly efficient sensing devices and methods of communication, these vehicles have also served as important means of gathering scientific information. Elaborate basic research, a vastly expensive technology, and strong political and military motivation unite in nearly every venture into space.

The "Starfish" Experiment. One of the earliest discoveries of space research was the existence of belts of atomic particles surrounding the earth and trapped by its magnetic field in arcs between the North and South poles. Hardly had this "magnetosphere" been noticed and named for its discoverer, Van Allen, than *experiments*, rather than mere observations, were under way there.

On April 30, 1962, the U.S. government announced its intention to conduct nuclear explosions at high altitudes in order to ascertain the effects of artificially-injected electrons on the natural belts of the magnetosphere. The immediate motivation was military interest in the disruptive effects on radio communication of atomic particles produced by a high altitude nuclear explosion.

The experiment — "Starfish" — was also of interest to scientists because its effects might reveal significant data about the magnetosphere itself.

Three high-altitude tests had been set off secretly in August 1958 over the South Atlantic. When they were made public some six months later, scientists in this country and abroad protested vigorously. The announcement of the new test brought renewed protests from scientists, especially radio-astronomers. Some scientists predicted that the experiment would cause large-scale, persistent changes and hamper further study of the still poorly understood Van Allen belts, but others disagreed. Resolution of these disagreements was difficult, for secrecy restrictions limited the exchange of information among the disputants.

The U.S. government then announced that it had called together a group of leading scientists to consider whether the proposed tests would substantially prejudice astrophysical and geophysical science or create a radiation hazard to manned space flights. On May 28, 1962, the U.S. government announced that this committee was convinced that the effects of the Starfish experiment would "disappear within a few weeks to a few months," and that there "is no need for concern regarding any lasting effects on the Van Allen belts and associated phenomena."

The Starfish explosion took place on July 9, 1962, when a 1.4-megaton hydrogen bomb was detonated 250 miles above Johnson Island in the Pacific. Despite early confusion regarding the physical consequences of this explosion, it is now clear that it generated a long-lived belt of atomic particles in the magnetosphere and that it has obscured the properties of the natural radiation belts. According to a review of the experiment by McIlwain,

. . . it may be necessary to wait more than thirty years before the natural electron fluxes in the region around 1.5

earth radii can be measured with complete freedom from artificial effects.

Several satellites, *Transit VIB, Traac,* and *Ariel,* were extensively damaged by the new radiation belt. *Ariel* is especially noteworthy as it was launched by the United States in order to carry British instruments, as a cooperative venture. *Telstar,* on the other hand, rode out the high radiation levels successfully for some time after the test, but radiation damage was noted in later reports.

The Starfish experiment is a spectacular demonstration of present capabilities for human intervention into natural phenomena in space. It also reveals serious inadequacies in our present ability to predict the consequences of such interventions and in the attendant experimental procedures. . . .

Properly executed, the Starfish experiment would have been preceded by a survey of natural bands followed by general scientific discussion of the observations. Had this been done, the data derived from particles artificially injected by the explosion could have added to scientific knowledge without precluding information about the natural phenomenon. Instead, the Starfish experiment was carried out in the absence of adequate knowledge of the natural belts. By artificially injecting subatomic particles into the unique and worldwide magnetosphere, the experiment has limited the information which can be derived from inquiries into this aspect of nature. . . .

III. EXPLORATION OF THE MOON: PROJECT "APOLLO"

A CONSIDERABLE PART OF THE U.S. space program is devoted to a particular mission, *Apollo,* which is designed to land one or more men on the moon and return them to earth. The Apollo project is a technological enterprise in that it requires the application of basic scientific knowledge to the solution of a given problem — the accomplishment of a manned landing on the moon. However, since the project is to be achieved in an environment which is new to science, it requires the acquisition of certain basic knowledge about the moon and interplanetary space: for example, the gross physical character of the moon's surface, chemical properties and radioactivity of surface materials, intermittent changes in cosmic ray intensity in interplanetary space.

The chief independent body which has advised the government on the scientific aspects of space research is the Space Science Board (SSB) established by the National Academy of Sciences in 1958. In the scientific considerations developed by the specialists serving on committees reporting to the Space Science Board, the scientific values to be derived from the manned exploration of the moon have been given relatively little importance, as compared with a number of other investigations of the moon which do not involve a manned landing. . . .

A timetable for manned lunar exploration was established for the first time by the decision of President Kennedy, announced on May 25, 1961, which concluded that ". . . this nation should commit itself to achieving the goal, before this decade is out, of landing a man on the moon and returning him safely to earth." The controlling reasons given for this decision by President Kennedy and by his scientific adviser, Dr. Jerome B. Wiesner, were not scientific, but social and political. Thus, in response to a question regarding his agreement with President Kennedy's decision to establish the project as a national goal, Dr. Wiesner stated:

Yes. But many of my colleagues in the scientific community judge it purely on its scientific merit. I think if I were being asked whether this much money should be spent for purely scientific reasons, I would say emphatically "no." I think they fail to recognize the deep military implications, the very important political significance of what we are doing and the other important factors that influenced the President when he made his decision. . . .

In general, scientific observations required for the planning of the manned landing are now assigned higher priorities than other studies which are of greater scientific interest but not essential to the development of the technology needed for the Apollo project. Therefore, the pattern for development of scientific research in space has been altered significantly by the essentially political decision to undertake the Apollo program.

This procedure is seriously at variance with important precepts of scientific experimentation and technology. The preferable order of events is: basic scientific investigation, technological application based on the resultant basic knowledge, social use of the technological innovations. In the Apollo program this sequence has been reversed, so that a program for a particular technological achievement has been committed, even as to the date of its accomplishment, in advance of the orderly acquisition of the related basic knowledge. The Apollo program, in its present form, does not appear to be based on the orderly, systematic extension of basic scientific investigation.

The Apollo program is extremely costly in funds and in required personnel. The total projected budget for space research, a large part of which is devoted to the Apollo project, represents a considerable part of the nation's entire expenditures for research. . . .

The demand of the space program for scientific personnel, which is in large part due to the Apollo program, has been the subject of some confusion. In 1962, Dr. Hugh L. Dryden, deputy director of NASA, stated:

It has been estimated that by 1970 as many as one-fourth of the nation's trained scientific and engineering manpower will be engaged in space activities, although I cannot confirm the accuracy of this estimate.

NASA testimony before the Senate Committee on Aeronautical and Space Sciences in November 1963 reduced this estimate to 5.9 percent of the total supply of scientists and engineers in 1970. Nevertheless a questionnaire sent to 2,000 randomly selected members of the AAAS in July 1964 showed that the percentage of those answering who receive direct or indirect federal support in connection with space activities had already reached the level of 12 percent.

A recent analysis of scientific manpower utilization by a committee of the National Academy of Sciences reported that

. . . the NASA program will accentuate the shortage of personnel with specialties such as systems technology, stability and control, guidance systems, and internal flow dynamics. Furthermore there will be a pronounced effect on the market for less experienced mechanical, electrical, and aeronautical engineers and for physicists and mathematicians.

Thus, the NASA basic research program erects, in parallel with the NSF program, a new national system of scientific support, which, in contrast to that of NSF, is mission-oriented rather than science-oriented. Its major program, Apollo, which is justified by a social rather than scientific purpose, will significantly influence the direction of basic scientific research in the United States. . . .

Finally, we find reason for concern in the confusion regarding the social and scientific justification of the Apollo project. In the scientific considerations of the Apollo program, we have found several instances in which scientific advisory groups assert, in their reports, that the Apollo program is justified by such nonscientific motivations as "man's innate drive to explore unknown regions," or "national prestige." We believe that such appeals, which are made by scientists who are acting in their professional capacities, or are closely attached to professional scientific judgments, are inherently dangerous both to the democratic process and to science.

If a scientist, as an individual citizen, wishes to promulgate a particular political course, he is of course free to do so. However, in our view, when such advocacy is associated with his organized professional scientific activity, the political or social intent acquires a wholly unwarranted cloak of scientific objectivity. This tends to obscure the fact that the political issue, despite its association with science, is, like all matters of public policy, open to debate. Such action on the part of scientists is likely to inhibit the free public discussion of the issue, and delay the development of an independent judgment by citizens generally.

IV. LARGE SCALE TECHNOLOGY AND THE ENVIRONMENT

Detergents and Insecticides. In the last twenty-five years there has been a dramatic improvement in the capability of chemical technology to produce commercially important quantities of a large number of useful new synthetic compounds: plastics, pesticides, herbicides, food additives, medical drugs, detergents, and a great many products for specialized industrial applications. This development reflects basic scientific advances in organic chemistry and chemical engineering. It is the basis of new heavily capitalized industries that have yielded important economic and social benefits.

These advances have resulted in the dispersal into the biosphere of numerous synthetic organic compounds, some in the amounts of millions of pounds annually. Some of these substances are not immediately degraded on entry into the biosphere. As a result, living things, including man, have absorbed varying amounts of newly synthesized substances with which they have had no previous contact.

A number of problems have arisen recently which are characterized by the appearance of undesirable side effects incidental to the application of some of the new products. Examples are: killing of animals and fish by insecticides, increasingly troublesome pollution of water supplies by agricultural chemicals and by industrial wastes, accumulation of synthetic detergents in water supplies. Two informative examples of these problems are experiences with synthetic detergents and insecticides.

Within a few years after the large-scale introduction of new synthetic detergents in the early 1940s, untoward effects, especially foaming, were noted in water supplies in various parts of the country. It was then discovered that the new detergents, unlike soap, were not degraded by the biological processes in sewage disposal plants. As a result, in certain areas detergents began to appear in streams and rivers and in potable water supplies derived from these sources. Questions — as yet unanswered — arose concerning the possibly hazardous effects of ingestion of detergents by human beings.

It was then discovered that the resistance of detergents to degradation in sewage disposal processes was due to a particular chemical attribute — branched structure of the detergent molecule. Bacterial enzymes that degrade hydrocarbons are incapable of acting on branched molecules. (In contrast, common soap is a straight-chain molecule and is degradable.) The chemical industry is now making an intensive effort to develop economical, degradable, synthetic detergents. Legislation preventing sale of nondegradable detergents has been introduced into Congress, and the industry has announced plans to replace the nondegradable types.

The problems arising from the large-scale dissemination of pesticides, particularly insecticides, during the last twenty years are exceedingly complex and diverse. . . . In 1957 the first extensive spraying with the then relatively new pesticide endrin, a chlorinated hydrocarbon, began in the Mississippi Valley. It has since been used extensively by sugarcane and cotton farmers to control insects attacking these crops.

Between 1954 and 1958, investigators reported several instances in which dieldrin (an insecticide closely related to endrin and produced metabolically from the latter) was found to cause killing of fish following application of the insecticide to nearby land. In March 1964, the U.S. Public Health Service and officials of the state of Louisiana announced that "water pollution involving toxic synthetic organic materials appears to be the cause" of fish-kills in the Mississippi River. The fish, the river waters, and the river mud were found to contain endrin and dieldrin, as well as several unidentified organic compounds.

The Mississippi River fish-kills have had significant economic effects. A long-established fishing industry in the bayou country of Louisiana has been reported to be seriously hampered by the problem. Investigations are under way to determine if levels harmful to humans have occurred, but little detailed information about chronic toxic effects in humans is available as yet. Fish containing measurable amounts of insecticide have reportedly reached the market in some Louisiana towns, and health officials have expressed concern about possible hazards from drinking water of Louisiana cities which is taken from contaminated rivers.

The sources of the insecticides found in Mississippi River fish are not firmly established at this time. Possible sources are runoff from farmlands routinely treated with insecticides and industrial wastes from insecticide manufacturing plants. . . .

The introduction of synthetic detergents and insecticides into the biosphere represents a serious human intervention into natural processes. The evidence cited shows that this intervention was not based on an orderly, disciplined development of all the requisite basic scientific information. The full biological significance of the large-scale introduction of synthetic detergents and insecticides could have been discovered much sooner if there had been planned systematic studies of their effects on the water supply in small-scale field trials.

In the absence of such studies there was a large economic commitment in the production of these contaminants before their crucial faults were discovered. There has been inadequate contact between the scientific considerations operative in the development of these substances — their chemical structure and synthesis, and their efficiency as detergents or insecticides — and the equally well-known biological phenomena into which they are to intervene. In the development of these new products there has been a serious gap between the relevant branches of science.

Fallout. Experience with nuclear testing provides a further insight into these problems. Since 1948, nuclear explosions carried out for purely experimental purposes (that is, for the technological improvement of weapons) by China, France, Great Britain, the United States, and the U.S.S.R. have disseminated millions of curies of radioactive materials over the planet as fallout. Considerable amounts of these materials have been absorbed by plants, animals, and man. Because radiation causes important damage to biological processes, this burden of radioactivity — added to radiation from natural sources and from medical procedures — increases the total risk of harm to man. The problem of estimating this medical risk has resulted in considerable confusion and controversy. . . .

It would appear that nuclear tests, like other recent interventions into the biosphere, were undertaken without an adequate understanding of their possible biological hazards. As massive experimental effects on the biosphere, nuclear explosions therefore represent operations which have not been carried out in keeping with disciplined scientific procedures.

An important cause for this technological failure is that discussion of the fallout problem by the general scientific community was hampered by secrecy. Until 1954, nearly all data about fallout were unavailable to the scientific community because of security restrictions. Following the declassification of these data, when the general scientific community had an opportunity to consider the problem, a number of important changes in the understanding of the fallout problem took place through contributions made by the general scientific community. The corrective effects that followed partial declassification testify to the importance of an independent community of scientists to the effectiveness of science as a source of knowledge.

The problem of evaluating environmental hazards, which is particularly exemplified by experience with fallout, reveals another issue for the integrity of science. By 1958-59, sufficient evidence had accumulated to convince most scientists that there is a linear relationship between radiation dose and biological damage. This viewpoint has been adopted by the Federal Radiation Council (FRC), which has the responsibility of establishing standards for radiation exposure in the U.S. . . . Since the FRC is presumably a scientific body, an unresolved challenge to the validity of its conclusions will tend to be regarded — especially by the public — as a reflection on the ability of science to elucidate the problem.

Similar difficulties have occurred with disturbing frequency in the recent controversies regarding the effects of fallout, of nuclear war, and of environmental contamination in general. In a number of instances, individual scientists, independent scientific committees, and scientific advisory groups to the government have stated that a particular hazard is "negligible," "acceptable," or "unacceptable" — without making it clear that the conclusion is *not a scientific conclusion, but a social judgment.* Nevertheless, it is natural that the public should assume that such pronouncements are scientific conclusions. Since such conclusions, put forward by individual scientists, or by groups of scientists, are often contradictory, a question which commonly arises among the public is

"How do we know which scientists are telling the truth?" Regardless of its origin, such a doubt erodes the confidence of the public in the capability of the scientific community to develop objective knowledge about scientific issues of crucial importance to public policy. To arrogate to the science that which belongs to the judgment of society or to the conscience of the individual inevitably weakens the integrity of science.

V. THE INTEGRITY OF MODERN SCIENCE

THE FOREGOING EXAMPLES TESTIFY to the striking success of modern science. They show that science has developed powers of unprecedented intensity and worldwide scale. The entire planet can now serve as a scientific laboratory. . . .

It is a major responsibility of science to provide society with a proper guide to its interaction with nature. Apparently, in modern circumstances, science has not adequately met this responsibility, and it becomes important to inquire into the possible reasons for this defect.

There is a common tendency in the execution of large-scale experimentation and technological operations to neglect the principles of disciplined experimentation, of consideration for experimental controls, and of open disclosure and discussion of results. These erosions in the integrity of science reflect important changes in the relationships between the acquisition of new scientific knowledge and its use for the satisfaction of social needs. . . .

Under these conditions, the laboratory of basic science inevitably loses much of its isolation from cultural effects and becomes subject to strong social demands for particular results. This new relationship has, of course, greatly reduced the delays which previously intervened between discovery and application. However, the new relationship has also had a less fortunate effect: *It has resulted in technological application before the related basic scientific knowledge was sufficiently developed to provide an adequate understanding of the effects of the new technology on nature. . . .*

Another source of present weakness in the integrity of science is that the social agencies which are responsible for the pattern of research support — especially Congress — do not yet appreciate the hazards involved in developing support for science on the basis of immediate demands for particular results. Support for science which does not permit the free and balanced development of all aspects of a problem tends to narrow the range of available scientific information and dangerously unbalances our control of new interventions into natural phenomena. . . .

The scientist's position in society has changed considerably in the last decade and some of these changes have influenced the integrity of science. Because of the rapid increase in the importance of science to major national needs (military, economic, international), scientists have been drawn into extensive participation in business, government agencies, and public affairs generally. The public has become willing to accept, with the respect accorded scientific conclusions, the scientist's views on numerous topics that have nothing to do with his special area of competence or with science as a whole.

The scientist now often finds himself, by virtue of being a scientist, in a powerful position to influence social decisions which are not solely matters of science. For example, most major policy decisions about the space program require social judgments. Although scientists, as a group, have no greater competence or rights than other citizens in such matters, their close association with the space program has afforded them opportunities to exert disproportionate influence on these decisions. Scientists have also played a major role in advising the government on the development of the nation's military strength and on important international negotiations. Since such advice almost always involves nonscientific matters, which are not subject to the self-correcting effects of scientific discourse, there are often serious disagreements on these issues among different scientists and groups of scientists.

When scientists serve as advisers to a governmental or private agency which is committed to a particular point of view on a public issue, questions also arise concerning the influence of the parent agency's viewpoint on the advice given to it. Where such advisory bodies operate under rules of secrecy, or for some other reason do not make their deliberations accessible to the scrutiny of the scientific community, the normal self-correcting procedures of scientific discourse cannot be brought to bear. Conflicts may develop between the advisory group and other members of the scientific community regarding scientific matters or the significance of nonscientific considerations. Such disagreements are difficult to resolve because, in the absence of open discussion, they do not become explicitly stated.

The growing interaction between science and public policy requires considerable attention to the problem of distinguishing scientific problems from those issues which ought to be decided by social processes. An example of the tendency to confuse scientific evaluation with social judgment is the matter of radiation standards. Here a scientific body, the Federal Radiation Council, is engaged in setting standards of acceptability which are basically social judgments regarding the balance between the hazards and benefits of nuclear operations. These judgments are, or ought to be, wholly vulnerable to political debate, but their appearance in the guise of a scientific decision may shield them from such scrutiny.

46.

Conclusion of the Warren Commission Report

On November 29, 1963, seven days after the murder of President Kennedy, a
commission to investigate the circumstances surrounding the assassination was
appointed by President Johnson. In his executive order establishing the commission,
Johnson charged the group with the duty of satisfying itself "that the truth is known
so far as it can be discovered and to report its findings . . . to him [the President], to
the American people, and to the world." The chairman of the commission was the
chief justice of the Supreme Court, Earl Warren; other members were two
U.S. senators, Richard B. Russell of Georgia and John Sherman Cooper of Kentucky;
two members of the House of Representatives, Hale Boggs of Louisiana and
Gerald R. Ford of Michigan; and two private citizens, Allen W. Dulles, former
director of the CIA, and John J. McCloy, former president of the International Bank
for Reconstruction and Development. From its first meeting on December 5, 1963,
to September 24, 1964, when its findings were submitted to the President, the
commission received more than 3,100 reports from the Secret Service and FBI and
took the testimony of 552 witnesses; it received the assistance of 10 major departments
of the federal government, 14 independent agencies, and 4 congressional committees.
The report — which ran to 888 pages — was released to the public immediately after
being submitted to President Johnson, and the commission's working papers were
deposited in the National Archives.

Source: *Report of the President's Commission on the Assassination of President John F. Kennedy,*
Washington, 1964.

THIS COMMISSION WAS CREATED to ascertain the facts relating to the preceding summary of events and to consider the important questions which they raised. The Commission has addressed itself to this task and has reached certain conclusions based on all the available evidence. No limitations have been placed on the Commission's inquiry; it has conducted its own investigation, and all government agencies have fully discharged their responsibility to cooperate with the Commission in its investigation. These conclusions represent the reasoned judgment of all members of the Commission and are presented after an investigation which has satisfied the Commission that it has ascertained the truth concerning the assassination of President Kennedy to the extent that a prolonged and thorough search makes this possible.

1. The shots which killed President Kennedy and wounded Governor Connally were fired from the sixth-floor window at the southeast corner of the Texas School Book Depository. This determination is based upon the following:

a. Witnesses at the scene of the assassination saw a rifle being fired from the sixth-floor window of the Depository Building, and some witnesses saw a rifle in the window immediately after the shots were fired.

b. The nearly whole bullet found on Governor Connally's stretcher at Parkland Memorial Hospital and the two bullet fragments found in the front seat of the presidential limousine were fired from the 6.5-millimeter Mannlicher-Carcano rifle found on the sixth floor of the Depository Building, to the exclusion of all other weapons.

c. The three used cartridge cases found near the window on the sixth floor at the southeast corner of the building were fired from the same rifle which fired the above-described bullet and fragments, to the exclusion of all other weapons.

d. The windshield in the presidential limousine was struck by a bullet fragment on the inside surface of the glass but was not penetrated.

e. The nature of the bullet wounds suffered by President Kennedy and Governor Connally and the location of the car at the time of the shots establish that the bullets were fired from above and behind the presidential limousine, striking the President and the Governor as follows:

(1) President Kennedy was first struck by a bullet which entered at the back of his neck and exited through the lower front portion of his neck, causing a wound which would not necessarily have been lethal. The President was struck a second time by a bullet which entered the right-rear portion of his head, causing a massive and fatal wound.

(2) Governor Connally was struck by a bullet which entered on the right side of his back and traveled downward through the right side of his chest, exiting below his right nipple. This bullet then passed through his right wrist and entered his left thigh, where it caused a superficial wound.

f. There is no credible evidence that the shots were fired from the Triple Underpass, ahead of the motorcade, or from any other location.

2. The weight of the evidence indicates that there were three shots fired.

3. Although it is not necessary to any essential findings of the Commission to determine just which shot hit Governor Connally, there is very persuasive evidence from the experts to indicate that the same bullet which pierced the President's throat also caused Governor Connally's wounds. However, Governor Connally's testimony and certain other factors have given rise to some difference of opinion as to this probability, but there is no question in the mind of any member of the Commission that all the shots which caused the President's and Governor Connally's wounds were fired from the sixth-floor window of the Texas School Book Depository.

4. The shots which killed President Kennedy and wounded Governor Connally were fired by Lee Harvey Oswald. This conclusion is based upon the following:

a. The Mannlicher-Carcano 6.5-millimeter Italian rifle from which the shots were fired was owned by and in the possession of Oswald.

b. Oswald carried this rifle into the Depository Building on the morning of November 22, 1963.

c. Oswald, at the time of the assassination, was present at the window from which the shots were fired.

d. Shortly after the assassination, the Mannlicher-Carcano rifle belonging to Oswald was found partially hidden between some cartons on the sixth floor, and the improvised paper bag in which Oswald brought the rifle to the Depository was found close by the window from which the shots were fired.

e. Based on testimony of the experts and their analysis of films of the assassination, the Commission has concluded that a rifleman of Lee Harvey Oswald's capabilities could have fired the shots from the rifle used in the assassination within the elapsed time of the shooting. The Commission has concluded further that Oswald possessed the capability with a rifle which enabled him to commit the assassination.

f. Oswald lied to the police after his arrest concerning important substantive matters.

g. Oswald had attempted to kill Maj. Gen. Edwin A. Walker (Resigned, U.S.

Army) on April 10, 1963, thereby demonstrating his disposition to take human life.

5. Oswald killed Dallas Police Patrolman J. D. Tippit approximately forty-five minutes after the assassination. This conclusion upholds the finding that Oswald fired the shots which killed President Kennedy and wounded Governor Connally and is supported by the following:

a. Two eyewitnesses saw the Tippit shooting and seven eyewitnesses heard the shots and saw the gunman leave the scene with revolver in hand. These nine eyewitnesses positively identified Lee Harvey Oswald as the man they saw.

b. The cartridge cases found at the scene of the shooting were fired from the revolver in the possession of Oswald at the time of his arrest, to the exclusion of all other weapons.

c. The revolver in Oswald's possession at the time of his arrest was purchased by and belonged to Oswald.

d. Oswald's jacket was found along the path of flight taken by the gunman as he fled from the scene of the killing.

6. Within eighty minutes of the assassination and thirty-five minutes of the Tippit killing, Oswald resisted arrest at the theater by attempting to shoot another Dallas police officer.

7. The Commission has reached the following conclusions concerning Oswald's interrogation and detention by the Dallas police:

a. Except for the force required to effect his arrest, Oswald was not subjected to any physical coercion by any law-enforcement officials. He was advised that he could not be compelled to give any information and that any statements made by him might be used against him in court. He was advised of his right to counsel. He was given the opportunity to obtain counsel of his own choice and was offered legal assistance by the Dallas Bar Association, which he rejected at that time.

b. Newspaper, radio, and television reporters were allowed uninhibited access to the area through which Oswald had to pass when he was moved from his cell to the interrogation room and other sections of the building, thereby subjecting Oswald to harassment and creating chaotic conditions which were not conducive to orderly interrogation or the protection of the rights of the prisoner.

c. The numerous statements, sometimes erroneous, made to the press by various local law-enforcement officials, during this period of confusion and disorder in the police station, would have presented serious obstacles to the obtaining of a fair trial for Oswald. To the extent that the information was erroneous or misleading, it helped to create doubts, speculations, and fears in the mind of the public which might otherwise not have arisen.

8. The Commission has reached the following conclusions concerning the killing of Oswald by Jack Ruby on November 24, 1963:

a. Ruby entered the basement of the Dallas Police Department shortly after 11:17 A.M. and killed Lee Harvey Oswald at 11:21 A.M.

b. Although the evidence on Ruby's means of entry is not conclusive, the weight of the evidence indicates that he walked down the ramp leading from Main Street to the basement of the Police Department.

c. There is no evidence to support the rumor that Ruby may have been assisted by any members of the Dallas Police Department in the killing of Oswald.

d. The Dallas Police Department's decision to transfer Oswald to the County Jail in full public view was unsound. The arrangements made by the Police Department on Sunday morning, only a few hours before the attempted transfer, were inadequate. Of critical importance was the fact that news media representatives and others were not excluded from the basement even after the police were notified of threats to Oswald's life. These deficiencies contributed to the death of Lee Harvey Oswald.

9. The Commission has found no evidence that either Lee Harvey Oswald or Jack Ruby was part of any conspiracy, domestic or foreign, to assassinate President Kennedy. The reasons for this conclusion are:

a. The Commission has found no evidence that anyone assisted Oswald in planning or carrying out the assassination. In this connection it has thoroughly investigated, among other factors, the circumstances surrounding the planning of the motorcade route through Dallas, the hiring of Oswald by the Texas School Book Depository Co. on October 15, 1963, the method by which the rifle was brought into the building, the placing of cartons of books at the window, Oswald's escape from the building, and the testimony of eyewitnesses to the shooting.

b. The Commission has found no evidence that Oswald was involved with any person or group in a conspiracy to assassinate the President, although it has thoroughly investigated, in addition to other possible leads, all facets of Oswald's associations, finances, and personal habits, particularly during the period following his return from the Soviet Union in June 1962.

c. The Commission has found no evidence to show that Oswald was employed, persuaded, or encouraged by any foreign government to assassinate President Kennedy or that he was an agent of any foreign government, although the Commission has reviewed the circumstances surrounding Oswald's defection to the Soviet Union, his life there from October of 1959 to June of 1962 so far as it can be reconstructed, his known contacts with the Fair Play for Cuba Committee, and his visits to the Cuban and Soviet embassies in Mexico City during his trip to Mexico from September 26 to October 3, 1963, and his known contacts with the Soviet Embassy in the United States.

Camera Press — Pix from Publix

Earl Warren, chief justice of the Supreme Court and head of the team investigating the assassination of President Kennedy

d. The Commission has explored all attempts of Oswald to identify himself with various political groups, including the Communist Party, U.S.A., the Fair Play for Cuba Committee, and the Socialist Workers Party, and has been unable to find any evidence that the contacts which he initiated were related to Oswald's subsequent assassination of the President.

e. All of the evidence before the Commission established that there was nothing to support the speculation that Oswald was an agent, employee, or informant of the FBI, the CIA, or any other governmental agency. It has thoroughly investigated Oswald's relationships prior to the assassination with all agencies of the U.S. government. All contacts with Oswald by any of these agencies were made in the regular exercise of their different responsibilities.

f. No direct or indirect relationship between Lee Harvey Oswald and Jack Ruby has been discovered by the Commission, nor has it been able to find any credible evidence that either knew the other, although a thorough investigation was made of the many rumors and speculations of such a relationship.

g. The Commission has found no evidence that Jack Ruby acted with any other person in the killing of Lee Harvey Oswald.

h. After careful investigation the Commission has found no credible evidence either that Ruby and Officer Tippit, who was killed by Oswald, knew each other, or that Oswald and Tippit knew each other.

Because of the difficulty of proving negatives to a certainty, the possibility of others being involved with either Oswald or Ruby cannot be established categorically, but if there is any such evidence it has been beyond the reach of all the investigative agencies and resources of the United States and has not come to the attention of this Commission.

10. In its entire investigation the Commission has found no evidence of conspiracy, subversion, or disloyalty to the U.S. government by any federal, state, or local official.

11. On the basis of the evidence before the Commission, it concludes that Oswald acted alone. Therefore, to determine the motives for the assassination of President Kennedy, one must look to the assassin himself. Clues to Oswald's motives can be found in his family history, his education, or lack of it, his acts, his writings, and the recollections of those who had close contacts with him throughout his life. The Commission has presented with this report all of the background information bearing on motivation which it could discover. Thus, others may study Lee Oswald's life and arrive at their own conclusions as to his possible motives.

The Commission could not make any definitive determination of Oswald's motives. It has endeavored to isolate factors which contributed to his character and which might have influenced his decision to assassinate President Kennedy. These factors were:

a. His deep-rooted resentment of all authority which was expressed in a hostility toward every society in which he lived;

b. His inability to enter into meaningful relationships with people, and a continuous pattern of rejecting his environment in favor of new surroundings;

c. His urge to try to find a place in history and despair at times over failures in his various undertakings;

d. His capacity for violence as evidenced by his attempt to kill General Walker;

e. His avowed commitment to Marxism and communism, as he understood the terms and developed his own interpretation of them; this was expressed by his antagonism toward the United States, by his defection to the Soviet Union, by his failure to be reconciled with life in the United States even after his disenchantment with the Soviet Union, and by his efforts, though frustrated, to go to Cuba.

Each of these contributed to his capacity to risk all in cruel and irresponsible actions.

12. The Commission recognizes that the varied responsibilities of the President require that he make frequent trips to all parts of the United States and abroad. Consistent with their high responsibilities, presidents can never be protected from every potential threat. The Secret Service's difficulty in meeting its protective responsibility varies with the activities and the nature of the occupant of the Office of President and his willingness to conform to plans for his safety. In appraising the performance of the Secret Service it should be understood that it has to do its work within such limitations. Nevertheless, the Commission believes that recommendations for improvements in presidential protection are compelled by the facts disclosed in this investigation.

a. The complexities of the presidency have increased so rapidly in recent years that the Secret Service has not been able to develop or to secure adequate resources of personnel and facilities to fulfill its important assignment. This situation should be promptly remedied.

b. The Commission has concluded that the criteria and procedures of the Secret Service designed to identify and protect against persons considered threats to the President were not adequate prior to the assassination.

(1) The Protective Research Section of the Secret Service, which is responsible for its preventive work, lacked sufficient trained personnel and the mechanical and technical assistance needed to fulfill its responsibility.

(2) Prior to the assassination, the Secret Service's criteria dealt with direct threats against the President. Although the Secret Service treated the direct threats against the President adequately, it failed to recognize the necessity of identifying other potential sources of danger to his security. The Secret Service did not develop adequate and specific criteria defining those persons or groups who might present a danger to the President. In effect, the Secret Service largely relied upon other federal or state agencies to supply the information necessary for it to fulfill its preventive responsibilities, although it did ask for information about direct threats to the President.

c. The Commission has concluded that there was insufficient liaison and coordination of information between the Secret Service and other federal agencies necessarily concerned with presidential protection. Although the FBI, in the normal exercise of its responsibility, had secured considerable information about Lee Harvey Oswald, it had no official responsibility, under the Secret Service criteria existing at the time of the President's trip to Dallas, to refer to the Secret Service the information it had about Oswald. The Commission has concluded, however, that the FBI took an unduly restrictive view of its role in preventive intelligence work prior to the assassination. A more carefully coordinated treatment of the Oswald case by the FBI might well have resulted in bringing Oswald's activities to the attention of the Secret Service.

d. The Commission has concluded that some of the advance preparations in Dallas made by the Secret Service, such as the detailed security measures taken at Love Field and the Trade Mart, were thorough and well executed. In other respects, however, the Commission has concluded that the advance preparations for the President's trip were deficient.

(1) Although the Secret Service is compelled to rely to a great extent on local law-enforcement officials, its procedures at the time of the Dallas trip did not call for well-defined instructions as to the respective responsibilities of the police officials and others assisting in the protection of the President.

(2) The procedures relied upon by the Secret Service for detecting the presence of an assassin located in a building along a motorcade route were inadequate. At the time of the trip to Dallas, the Secret Service, as a matter of practice, did not investigate, or cause to be checked, any building located along the motorcade route to be taken by the President. The responsibility for observing windows in these buildings during the motorcade was divided between local police personnel stationed on the streets to regulate crowds and Secret Service agents riding in the motorcade. Based on its investigation, the Commission has concluded that these arrangements during the trip to Dallas were clearly not sufficient.

e. The configuration of the presidential car and the seating arrangements of the Secret Service agents in the car did not afford the Secret Service agents the opportunity they should have had to be of immediate assistance to the President at the first sign of danger.

f. Within these limitations, however, the Commission finds that the agents most immediately responsible for the President's safety reacted promptly at the time the shots were fired from the Texas School Book Depository Building.

1965

47.

John R. Tunis: Laugh Off $11 Million?

*In the summer of 1964 the Columbia Broadcasting Company bought a controlling
interest in the New York Yankees Baseball Club for something over $11 million. The
event was the occasion for a lot of bad jokes; the biggest joke of all was that the
Yankees, perennial champions of the world, ended up last in the American League in
1966. But something else besides joking was involved, for the sale made more
evident than ever before the fact that sports in America were no longer "sport" at
all, but business, and pretty big business at that. John R. Tunis, long a sports
enthusiast, dealt with the changes in this important aspect of the national scene in an
article published early in 1965.*

Source: *New Republic*, January 2, 1965.

THE FOLLOWING ADVERTISEMENT appeared
last summer in the classified section of the
New York Times.

FOR SALE

The Yale Football Team
WXYZ Broadcasting Company
New Haven, Conn.

What did it mean? Simply that the station
was trying to line up sponsors for the
broadcasting and televising of the Yale elev-
en. Price was discreetly omitted. It is estimated at from $20,000 to $30,000 for the
eight home games.

Yale was the college of Walter Camp,
one of the founders of modern football. To-

day Yale is a better educational institution
than it was in 1900. The faculty is better.
The student body is more carefully chosen,
hence more intelligent. The endowment
runs to around $300 million. Why should
Yale sell out to the hucksters for the few
thousands? Perhaps the question should be
asked differently. What has happened to
American sport since the time of Walter
Camp?

First, one observes the advent of violence
in organized American athletics. Football,
say the coaches, is a rugged game. Knock
him down before he hits you; or else, don't
come out for the team.

As far back as 1810, William Hazlitt remarked that:

Men do not become what by nature they were meant to be, but what society makes them. The generous feelings, the high propensities of the soul are, as it were, seared, violently wrenched, and amputated to fit us for intercourse with the world.

Following the three wars of the present century, violence permeates every game we play. The adhesive-bound fist of the football linesman, the hockey forward who ruptures his opponent's spleen (two minutes in the penalty box), the beanball and the spitball thrown by big-league pitchers, the elbow under the chin of the halfback poised to throw and unable to protect himself — these violences did not exist at the time of Walter Camp. As Coach Jim (Jumbo) Elliott of the Villanova track team suggested, when watching his men fouled in a meet: "It looks as though we should supply our runners with knives." Coach Darrel Royal of the 1963 championship University of Texas eleven put it more succinctly: "The big ones always eat up the little ones." Sport breeds an aggressiveness that has infected the whole American scene.

Another difference one notices today is the increased booty attached to victory. Mark McCormick, business manager for Arnold Palmer, Jack Nicklaus, and Gary Player, estimates in *Sports Illustrated* that a victory in the Masters is worth more than $1 million. This has been true of course for many years. What is new are the sums involved. For, because of the skills of a few athletes, a kind of vested interest in sport has arisen. This interest is represented by persons who do not in the least care for sport — only for the money. They have corrupted our games and confused our thinking about their values.

Last summer the Columbia Broadcasting System, presumably with one eye to shutting pay television out of Manhattan, bought the New York Yankee Baseball Club for $11.2 million. It was an example of the acquisitive system in all its naked purity. CBS of course will sell the Yankees for several times that sum to the makers of toothpaste and cars, for the Yankees are still the biggest and most profitable baseball factory in the country. True, ever since Cy Young and Connie Mack, baseball has been a business, based on profits. What's different is the size of the sums involved. Winning is more important than ever.

In 1964, CBS also paid $28 million for television rights to the fourteen games of the National Football League. Since Columbia made $41.8 million in its last fiscal year, this was no great strain. The sums are smaller in college sport, yet not so small either. At Ohio State, football gate receipts in 1963 were $2 million, the total taken in through sport almost $3 million. Nobody asks what a tax-free, publicly supported institution of learning is doing in the entertainment business. Or why Yankee Stadium in New York is owned by Rice Institute in Houston, Texas, nor yet what place tournament basketball has in a high-school sport program.

The sense of fun, a kind of high elation, has disappeared. When youngsters discover that sport champions need business managers, that Osuna, Emerson, and Santana, three leading amateur tennis players, are paid salaries by cigarette companies, the wonder of sport vanishes. Kids hear about it, read of it. The mystery is gone from our games. This sense of mystery was there in the first World Series at the Huntington Avenue Grounds in Boston, the Pilgrims of the American League against the Pittsburgh Pirates of the National League. My brother and I, nippers of ten and eleven, watched the special trains pour in from all over New England, and the "Loyal Rooters," that column of men, each with a ticket stuck in the hatband of his derby and a blue rosette on his chest. At the head was "Nuff Sed" McGreevy, a 250-pound saloonkeeper; up front was the band of the First Corps Cadets playing "Tessie." No, it wasn't heaven, but as we watched the "Loyal Rooters" parade on the field, and the crowd rise cheering, we were one of them. Jimmy Breslin said it best: "Did you ever watch a kid coming up out of the subway to go to a ball game? The whole wonderful thing of being young is there. Eyes shining, feet running, pushing through those adults to get the first look at the ball park."

Now money comes first. Sports are better now, but the bigger they get the further you are from the field. I was part of that first World Series, watched the face of every player, saw his anxiety and emotion.

But aren't there more persons playing games and sports than ever before? There are, indeed. (There are more persons with money and more leisure in this country than during Walter Camp's life, too.) But as Herbert Warren Wind remarked: "Today the ordinary game of golf and tennis or the informal sailing race has become . . . less a path of recreation than an expressway for releasing frustration in a display of superiority. Friendly competition has given way to purposeful gamesmanship." From the top down, sport is aggressive. No, not always, not with everyone. But too often and with too many.

One change in our sport, and a good one, is that sport has opened to everyone. Maybe you need to be a millionaire to be President, yet, in organized sport, the man or woman who delivers reaches the top. Since the arrival of Jackie Robinson at Ebbets Field in Brooklyn in 1947, the barriers have fallen fast, and increasing numbers of Negroes have come into sport. Here, let me hazard a guess. In ten or fifteen years, most of our professional and much amateur sport will be dominated by Negroes and Puerto Ricans. Not only are they natural athletes, with unusual coordination. More important, they are hungry.

Another great difference in sport today and six years ago is the growth of watching.

Millions of Americans sit entranced every week before the Derby, a Rose Bowl game, a World Series, the Masters, or the Open. This audience is so important that the television industry has supplanted the Amateur Athletic Union, the Baseball Commissioner (a feebly frustrated individual named Ford Frick), the United States Golf Association, as well as the two football leagues. Television in its new role is the owner and dictator of American sport. As a result, our sport is run by the entertainment industry for its own profit. Sport is on sale to the highest bidder. It is a weapon in the hands of the network presidents, as Sylvester Weaver, head of Subscription Television in Los Angeles, is discovering. Had the Los Angeles Dodgers won the National League pennant, the Yanks controlled by CBS could have refused Weaver broadcasting rights for his pay television on the coast.

To raise doubts about American sport and the path it has taken during the present century is spitting on the flag. Proceed at your own risk, because sport in recent times has become our universal religion. Everyone is a true believer. American men are, at any rate. Go to a party the night the Bears play the Packers, and the room will soon be empty of males. They are all in the den watching the game.

If it wasn't sacrilegious (and if we had a sense of humor) we'd laugh at the dog-bores, the horse-bores, the golf- and football-bores to whom their particular pastime is the vital thing of all human existence. But how can an American laugh off $11 million? Besides, if there were any humor in our games, or if we were able to survey our sporting scene as it appears to the English, the Japanese, or the Europeans, we wouldn't be true-blue, red-blooded, white American sportsmen. Nor top dog in about every sport on earth, either.

That's important, too. It surely is to the program director of the Columbia Broadcasting Company.

48.

Corporate Support for the Performing Arts

The performing arts have suffered serious financial troubles during the last two or three decades. Production costs of plays and musical and dance programs have increased like everything else, but "live" theater and allied activities have lost much of their audience to television, so that as ticket prices go up the number of potential buyers goes down. In order to regain the broad audience support that they once enjoyed, it is obviously necessary for the performing arts to be subsidized. The federal and state governments have given something but not much, and the Rockefeller Brothers Fund therefore assessed the degree and amount of corporate support for these arts — and found that here, too, the level of support was not encouraging.

Source: *The Performing Arts: Problems and Prospects*, New York, 1965, pp. 81-93.

THE ARTS CAN BE A MAJOR SOURCE of strength for the business community. They provide cultural resources increasingly recognized as essential to a suitable environment for business enterprise. Their presence or absence in a community frequently plays a role in the decision of personnel to join or stay with a company. Their availability certainly encourages new firms to locate in a city and helps attract tourists and conventions. They help make the increased leisure with which our greater productivity has rewarded us a boon rather than a dangerous emptiness. They constitute a growing market and provide expanding avenues for employment. There are, therefore, compelling reasons why, in the interest of his community and, indeed, in his own self-interest, a businessman and his firm should be concerned with the cultural and artistic life of his community.

Yet the typical American corporation has so far shown very little enthusiasm for financial support of the performing arts. Indeed, its contribution to philanthropy of all sorts is surprisingly small.

In applying corporate income tax, which takes about half of net corporate income, the federal government permits deductions of up to 5 percent of this income for contributions to charitable and educational organizations, which are construed to include nonprofit arts organizations. The purpose is to provide an incentive for contributions.

It has been the practice of American corporations in recent years to use only a little over one-fifth of the allowable tax exemption. For example, in 1963, the latest year for which complete figures are available, their contributions totaled $536 million, or 1 percent of their taxable income of $51.3 billion. There remained a total of over $2 billion of business income that would have had the government as an equal partner in giving if it had been contributed to eligible nonprofit organizations. Business corporations are an important potential source of financial support for the arts.

TRENDS IN SUPPORT

ALTHOUGH THE AMOUNTS remain small, corporations during the past quarter of a century have increased their support of philanthropic activities, and there is some evidence of growing interest in the arts. For instance, during 1962, according to a survey of 465 companies by the National Industrial Conference Board, corporate funds allotted to civic and cultural activities were 5.3 cents of each contribution dollar. This was a substantial increase above the average of 3 cents in 1959. The Conference Board found that companies having their own foundations gave more in the civic and cultural category (5.7 percent) than those without foundations (4.9 percent). Larger companies seem to direct less of their contribution budgets for civic and cultural activities than do smaller. The range was from 4.45 percent for companies with over 10,000 employees to as much as 12.11 percent for those with only 500 to 999 employees.

Recently the Rockefeller Brothers Fund surveyed 100 corporations of varying sizes. It learned that 55 percent gave something to the arts. But about half of these gave less than 1 percent of their total contributions to the arts. In some instances in which large grants had been made, the range was from 3 to 7 percent, and one bank allocated 22 percent.

In a 1963 survey by the American Society of Corporate Secretaries, with 346 companies responding, 48 percent reported their companies contributing from 1 to 9 percent of total contributions to cultural activities. Only 5 percent gave more (one company gave nearly 80 percent of its total in support of cultural projects, another reported 50 percent), while 47 percent of the responding companies replied that they make no contributions whatever to the arts, approximately the same as indicated in the Rockefeller Brothers Fund survey.

In summary, it can be estimated that only slightly over half of all corporations in the United States give anything to the arts. Of the total contributions made by all corporations, only a tiny fraction — at most 3 to 4 percent, or some $16 million to $21 million in 1963 — goes to the arts.

A LEAD BY ARTS ORGANIZATIONS

IF THE PRESENT TRICKLE of corporate support for the arts is to be expanded, both arts organizations and corporate managements have mutual responsibilities to fulfill. As a practical matter, broad recognition of the importance of the arts by the business community will depend primarily on the initiative of arts organizations. There is a tendency on the part of leaders of arts organizations to assume that anyone who is moderately perceptive will understand the significance of the arts. This is a poor assumption.

It is not even safe, as a matter of fact, for an arts organization to assume that the direct economic contribution of the arts to the business community is fully appreciated. The Stanford Research Institute has calculated that in 1960 the arts market, exclusive of books and expenditures for education, was a $2.5 billion market, with 50 million people involved, and by 1970 may approach $7 billion. By 1970, $4 billion will have been spent on new construction of arts centers in the United States and Canada. But these facts are not fully known or appreciated by business.

The contributions of a thriving cultural life to increasing tourist and convention business, attracting new industry, recruiting personnel — particularly when professional people are being transferred to a new location — also need to be stressed. Corporations find that an important consideration in determining the willingness of executive and scientific personnel to move to a new community is the quality of artistic resources offered.

The arts can also help business in coping constructively with the increased leisure created by the shorter work week, earlier retirements, and greater longevity. Business concerns have an interest in seeing that increased leisure is a source of satisfaction — not boredom and frustration.

There has been a growing appreciation

that the success of business enterprise is in part measured by its contribution to a better life in the community. As this sense of corporate citizenship has developed, the emphasis in giving has moved from health and welfare to education. The importance of corporate support of the arts, as a matter of civic responsibility, is just beginning to be recognized by business executives. But much remains to be done to make the arts widely regarded as an appropriate object of corporate support — an acceptance that is important in achieving a firm financial underpinning.

A DEMONSTRATION OF GOOD PLANNING

IN REQUESTING CORPORATE SUPPORT, arts organizations should recognize that although corporations have the pursuit of profit as a common purpose, they also have a wide variety of individual attributes. Some are national in scope, some are regional, and many are strictly local. Some make extensive use of intellectual and artistic talent, others make relatively little. The products and services of some go largely to youngsters, the products of others to adults. (The toy company is much more likely to contribute to a youth concert than it is to a concert planned for adults.) As a matter of practical strategy, arts organizations should accept responsibility for relating their requests for corporate support to the "personality" of the corporation from which they seek it.

Arts organizations owe it to themselves and to business to make well-reasoned and well-documented cases for corporate support. The most generous and farsighted corporation still expects the organization seeking its help to prove that it has competent management and a realistic budget, that it is developing other sources of support, and that it has plans to attain both immediate objectives and long-range goals. Responses received in the Rockefeller Brothers Fund

survey underlined the importance of responsible planning and good management.

One way arts organizations can improve their managements and sharpen their objectives is to encourage corporate executives to assist them. Mastering the management of a business corporation is no guarantee that a man can automatically transfer his skill to an arts organization. But, given careful orientation, the business executive can be a great help, and he can be particularly effective in making the case for corporate and community financial support.

CORPORATE RESPONSIBILITY

THE CORPORATION HAS TO TAKE the initiative in setting its own priorities in giving. Balances shift according to need and in keeping with the corporate interest and understanding. In 1962, for instance, company gifts to education were for the first time greater than those to health and welfare — 41.9 percent as against 40.9. Funds allotted to civic and cultural enterprises, which until a few years ago seldom appeared as a budget item, are more in evidence than ever before.

Clearly, it is impractical to set priorities without knowledge and information. Yet the Rockefeller Brothers Fund survey showed only 3 out of 100 corporations had studied, directly or through company foundations, the possible role of corporate giving to the arts. . . .

WHAT THEY HAVE DONE

CONTRIBUTIONS for operating expenses — either direct or through united arts funds — are extremely helpful and are the most frequent means of support. The Detroit Symphony Orchestra was revived by gifts totaling $412,400, of which $260,000 was donated by twenty-six corporations, with pledges of continued aid over two additional years. A substantial portion of the $120,000 given to cultural activities by the United States Steel Foundation in 1962 was for operating needs of various orchestras and opera companies. Corporations also contributed 44.2 percent of the $433,858 raised in 1963-1964 by the United Fine Arts Fund of Cincinnati for support of the symphony orchestra, the art museum, the Taft Museum, and the summer opera.

As well as support for general operations, there have been significant contributions to community development projects. A group of Connecticut insurance companies donated about $450,000 to the capital development campaign of the Hartford cultural center. Both Lincoln Center and the John F. Kennedy Center for the Performing Arts have received substantial support from the business community. In addition to actual dollars given, corporate executives who are involved in urban renewal and other municipal development projects can assure that adequate facilities for the performing arts are considered in urban planning.

Other valuable support of the arts includes making business facilities available to arts groups, encouraging executives to participate in the cultural life of the community, and giving management advice and assistance to arts organizations.

Some corporations are helping to build audiences for the arts through special employee concerts and subsidized tickets for employees. The Archer-Daniels-Midland Company subsidizes a fixed amount of the purchase price of Minneapolis Symphony tickets, and the employee pays the difference, which varies according to location of seats. The Monsanto Company held a concert by Van Cliburn in 1961 for its St. Louis employees, in addition to making annual contributions to some fourteen arts organizations throughout the country. Republic Steel sponsors a "Republic Night" once or twice a year at the Cleveland Play House and a summer concert of the Cleveland Orchestra. The company buys large quantities of tickets at a discount and resells them to the employees at cost.

Sponsorship of the arts on radio and television is another important way corporations can contribute to audience building. Conspicuous examples include the "Bell Telephone Hour," sponsored by the American Telephone and Telegraph Company, Texaco's sponsorship of radio broadcasts of the Metropolitan Opera, and the Standard Oil Company of New Jersey's success with "The Play of the Week," "The Age of Kings," "The Festival of Performing Arts," and "Esso World Theatre." "Esso Theatre, U.S.A.," featuring performances by permanent professional theatres throughout the country, is the most recent in this series.

Commissioning presentation of special works — often beyond the regular operating budget of an arts organization — can significantly enhance the quality of production provided. An outstanding example in 1963 was the gift to the Metropolitan of a new production of "Aïda" by the American Export and Isbrandtsen Lines. In making this gift, a hardheaded business board reasoned, in the words of its chairman, John M. Will:

> Our line carries opera stars and other artists who spend a great part of their lives in travel; furthermore, we feel that others in all fields may be induced to travel. We're in close contact with the lands that have produced great art since ancient times — Egypt, Greece, Spain, Italy. It seemed a natural.

The enthusiastic response of press and public alike appeared to adequately justify the board's action in terms of prestige and public relations alone.

A unique type of corporate support for the arts is the work of the Recording Industries Music Performance Trust Funds, created as part of the settlement of the American Federation of Musicians' strike against the recording industry in 1948. The Funds receive from recording companies a payment of 1 to 1.5 percent of the total dollar volume of record sales at "suggested retail price" levels. The Funds are administered by an independent trustee named by the recording companies. In recent years the Trust Funds have received payments exceeding $5 million a year, which must be expended currently. Since establishment of the Funds in 1949, the money has been used for single-engagement free concerts in all parts of the country. Beginning in 1964, the receipts from new production will be divided in half, one half continuing to be used for free concerts and the other half going directly to the musicians who played the original recordings.

Business support for the arts is important in preserving a healthy balance between private and government support. The arts now receive public assistance, particularly at the local level, and more is anticipated. But strong private support is just as essential to the economic structure of the arts as it is to our system of higher education, which receives massive public aid. . . .

Leadership in investing in the artistic life of a free society, based on reasoned policy, is the opportunity now afforded the corporation. *Corporate dollars are important dollars, capable of making the difference between life or death for an arts organization. If business corporations have not done so, as most of them have not, the panel urges that they look carefully at the arts and their place in the community. Support for the arts is a part of community responsibility, and a healthy cultural environment is clearly in the self-interest of the business community.*

49.

Mississippi Accepts the Civil Rights Law

Southern resistance to federal programs extending civil rights to Negroes in the late 1950s and in the 1960s seemed to a casual observer to be monolithic and total. But in fact there were cracks in the wall of the South's distrust of measures that it considered punitive rather than just. Desegregation of schools did not proceed quickly, but some schools were integrated; public services throughout much of the region were opened to all; and in a few Southern cities official desegregation was adopted across the board. Mississippi remained perhaps the most firm in its opposition to the federal civil rights program and the following statement of the Mississippi Economic Council was therefore all the more surprising when it was made public in early 1965. Issued by MEC president Balmer Hill, Jr., following a special meeting of the organization's Board of Directors in Jackson, Mississippi, on February 3, the statement was front page news in many newspapers across the country.

Source: Press Release of the Mississippi Economic Council.

THE MISSISSIPPI ECONOMIC COUNCIL, since it was organized in 1949, has been concerned with the economic and social well-being of our state. This means that it is concerned with the peace and tranquillity of our state.

The recent passage of certain federal legislation creates monumental problems for Mississippians. The Council opposed passage of the Civil Rights Act, but as a leadership organization it cannot bury its head in the sand and ignore its existence.

In the past, the MEC has faced up to its responsibility in dealing with major public problems. It has also spoken out for principles in the field of federal affairs. For instance, it has repeatedly declared its position:

1. For constitutional government and states' rights and in opposition to any legislation which would destroy the constitutional foundation of our state and federal governments.

2. For the proposition that education for all citizens is indispensable and that education provided by public schools is essential.

3. For the right to control public schools as guaranteed to states by the Constitution of the United States and to finance them without additional federal funds.

4. That public schools, colleges, and universities must remain open and maintain their integrity, quality instructional standards, and full accreditation.

Today, the Council's Board of Directors, in a special session, reviewed these developments and adopted the following statement:

As concerned Mississippians aware of the monumental problems facing our state, we advance with pride the fact that Mississippi is not an island unto itself but is an integral and responsible part of the United States.

We recognize that the Civil Rights Act of 1964 has been enacted by the Congress as law. It cannot be ignored and should not be unlawfully defied. Resistance to the law should be through established procedures in the American tradition of resort to enlightened public opinion, the ballot boxes, and the courts. We should adjust ourselves to the impact of this legislation regardless of personal feelings and convictions and limit our resistance to the stated methods.

For the purpose of furthering justice, harmony, and continued development in Mississippi, we respectfully urge the following:

1. Order and respect for the law must be maintained. Lawless activities in the state by individuals and organizations cannot be tolerated. The penalty for law violation should be fairly and equitably applied to all law violators.

2. Communications must be maintained between the races within the state.

3. Registration and voting laws should be fairly and impartially administered for all.

4. Support of public education must be maintained and strengthened.

Mississippians have the capacity and courage to face the problems of this state and to create conditions favorable to their solution. We call upon all Mississippians to take positive action toward these ends.

50.

Nathan Glazer: The Peoples of the U.S.A.

"America for Americans," "the 100% American," "the hyphenated American," "the Melting Pot" — all of these are terms or slogans that have marked the history of immigration and ethnic assimilation in the United States. The problems of immigration have been largely solved, owing to the modern restrictions on immigrants (if in fact they can really be said to have solved the problems), but the problems of assimilation remain, particularly those of the "unwilling immigrants" — the Negroes — who a century after emancipation have still not been absorbed fully into the mainstream of American life.

Source: *Nation*, 100th Anniversary Issue, September 20, 1965: "The Peoples of America."

THE HISTORY OF ETHNICITY and ethnic self-consciousness in this country has moved in waves; we are now in a trough between two crests, and the challenge is to describe the shape and form of the next crest. That there will be another crest it is hardly possible to doubt. Since the end of European mass immigration to this country forty years ago we have waited for the subsidence of ethnic self-consciousness, and often announced it, and it has returned again and again. But each time it has returned in so different a form that one could well argue it was not the same thing returning at all, that what we saw was not the breakthrough of the consciousness of common origin and community among the groups that made America, but rather that ethnicity was being used as a cover for some other more significant force, which was borrowing another identity.

During the early years of the Depression, ethnicity withdrew as a theme in American life. Both those who had urged the "Americanization" of the immigrant and the creation of "cultural pluralism" now had more important concerns. Immigration was matched by a counter-emigration back to the countries of origins; one episode of American history it seemed had come to an end. Then, with the rise of Hitler, the ethnic texture of American life began to reassert itself. First Jews; then Germans; then Czechs, Poles, Italians, and even the "old Americans," remembering their origins in England, all were spurred to action and organization by Hitler and the great war that he began. Samuel Lubell has traced how the support for Franklin D. Roosevelt in the great cities shifted from class to ethnicity as the international conflict developed and various groups responded to, or against, Roosevelt, as he displayed his sentiments and allegiances.

In 1945 this great crest began to withdraw. True, there was the continuing impact on ethnic groups of the confrontation with Russia and communism, but with the passage of time this began to lose its ethnic coloration. Catholics in general were more anti-Communist than others, Poles still more so, Jews much less so. But the international conflict was so sharply colored by ideology rather than national antagonism, that with the passage of time it no longer served to set group against group (as it had in the Hitler years). Soviet opposition to Israel and Soviet anti-Semitism; the rise of a measure of cautious Polish independence; de-Stalinization in Russia — all these developments softened the sharp conflicts which had created a powerful resonance among immigrants and their children in this country.

The Eisenhower period marked thus a new trough, and it was possible to conclude that the workings of the melting pot had been retarded only slightly by the neolithic tribal ferocity of Hitler and the counterreactions he evoked. But now a new wave began to gather force, a wave that had nothing to do with international affairs. Will Herberg interpreted the increased religious activity of the postwar years as a half-embarrassed means of maintaining group identity in a democratic society which did not look with favor on the long-continued maintenance of sharply distinguished ethnic groups. The "triple melting pot" theory of Ruby Jo Reeves Kennedy, along with her data on intermarriage, suggested that old ethnic lines were being replaced by new religious lines.

The chameleon-like force of ancestral connection, one could argue, was being transmuted into the forms of religion. Those who were concerned for religion could of course take no comfort in this analysis, even if the religious denominations benefited from higher collections and new buildings. If our major religions are replacing ethnic groups, one could not yet herald the creation of a homogeneous and undivided American group consciousness in America, but at least our divisions no longer paralleled those of old Europe — something which had deeply troubled our leaders from Washington to Woodrow Wilson — but the more acceptable divisions of religion, which ostensibly had an older and more respectable lineage and justification. Thus, if Herberg could still discern the forces of ethnic identity at work in the new clothes of religious denominationalism, at least they no longer expressed themselves openly.

But once again an unabashed ethnicity reasserted itself in the campaign of John F. Kennedy and his brief presidency. In his Cabinet, for the first time, there sat a Jew of East European origin, an Italian-American, a Polish-American. If the Jews were no longer being appointed primarily to represent a group, there was no question that this was the explanation for the appointment of an Italian-American and a Polish-American. The Catholic President was reminded by everyone that he was an Irish President. He was the first President to be elected from an immigrant group that had suffered discrimination and prejudice, and that still remembered it — and those of us from later immigrant groups, who had experienced the lordly position of the Irish in the cities of the East, discovered only with some surprise that the Irish did remember their days as a degraded minority. Those who stemmed from the new immigration now realized that the Irish shared very much the same feelings of resentment at past treatment, of gratification in present accomplishment and recognition.

But the old Americans too responded to the realization that they had an Irish President, as well as a Democratic, Catholic, and intellectual President. Certainly it is hard to explain otherwise the mutual antagonism that rapidly sprang up between the new administration and such a large part of the big business establishment, the seat of the old Americans, the "WASP" power. The administration's policies were not antagonistic to big business. There was of course the President's violent response to the steel price rise, but was not that, too, a reflection

— at least in part — of old ethnic images and conflicts? No one who spoke to anyone close to those events could doubt it.

I would suggest a gentle recession, if not a trough, in the period since President Kennedy's assassination. Two events to my mind suggest the retreat of an open and congratulatory ethnic self-assertiveness, and they are related. One is the new concern with the poor, which complementarily marks all the nonpoor as members of the same group, with the same social task laid upon them; and the second is the steady radicalization of the civil rights movement and Negro opinion, and this increasingly places all the whites in the same category, without distinction. And once again a symbolic political event marks the recession of ethnic self-consciousness: the accession of President Johnson, who, like President Eisenhower, comes from a part of America that was relatively unaffected by European immigration.

I have marked recurrent crests and troughs of ethnic self-consciousness by political events, but the political events have of course paralleled social events. The crisis of the Depression erased for the moment ethnic memories and allegiances. The agony of the European peoples reawakened it. Prosperity and the rapid rise of the new immigrant groups to upper working-class and middle-class status again reduced their sense of difference. The security that came with long-sustained prosperity made it possible for the descendants of despised immigrants to again take pleasure in their origins and their differences. One of the less observed effects of affluence is that it leads people to their real or hopefully reconstructed origins. In Europe and among Americans who look to the European upper classes, this may mean acquiring crests, forebears, and antiques. Among the American descendants of European peasants and artisans, it meant, in a surprising number of cases, a new interest

in the culture of the old country. But in the most recent period, the rise of the joint problems of poverty and the assimilation of the Negro raises a new set of questions. For the moment, ethnic self-assertiveness is in eclipse and even in bad odor. And the eclipse is directly related to the new problems.

Michael Harrington put the matter quite directly when he said in a recent speech that the accumulated wisdom of the great European immigrant groups in this country has become irrelevant, for it will not help the current poor and it will not help the Negroes. In varying degrees, we are hearing the same from Louis Lomax, from James Baldwin, from Nat Hentoff, and from other supporters and defenders of Negro militancy. Inevitably the next wave of ethnic self-consciousness must reflect one of the most remarkable and least expected consequences of the Negro revolution — the growing estrangement between European ethnic groups and the Negroes.

Its beginnings were studied by Samuel Lubell in the early postwar period, and we have seen the estrangement develop to the point where the fear of the white backlash — and this meant generally the backlash from recent white immigrant groups in the cities — became one of the major issues of the Goldwater-Johnson campaign. The separation, first the barest of lines, has deepened through conflicts over the adoption and administration of fair employment laws, fair housing laws, measures to combat *de facto* school segregation. The patterns under which and through which the European ethnic groups have lived — the trade unions and branches of industry dominated by one or a few ethnic groups, the ethnically concentrated neighborhood with its distinctive schools and churches and organizations — all have come under increasing attack. And thus the distinctive social patterns of the North and West, which the immigrant and the ethnic groups helped create, are now being slowly but surely turned into a Southern-like confrontation of white and black. The varied, more balanced, and more creative ethnic conflicts of the North are now in danger of being transformed into the monolithic confrontation of the South.

In the South, Northern variety never developed. One great division dominated and smothered all others, the division between black and white. In this area, the European immigrant of the later 19th and early 20th century never penetrated. All he had to offer generally was unskilled labor, and in the South the unskilled labor was the work of Negroes. The white immigrant laborer refused to enter an area in which the laborer was degraded, not only by his work but by a caste system, where wages were low and racial conflict hindered trade-union development and social legislation. The immigrant worked in the parts of the country where work had greater respect and was better rewarded. If he entered the South, it was more often as a merchant than as a worker.

But in the Northern cities, where almost half the Negroes now live, it was not inevitable that the same line of division should be imported from the South. The entry of the Negro into the Northern cities in great numbers during and after World War I and again during and after World War II raised a critical question: Was he the last of the great immigrant groups? Would his experience parallel that of the Irish and the Poles and the Jews who had arrived as exploited and unskilled workers and had moved upward, at varying speeds, into middle-class occupations, the professions, business? How would those who were themselves children and grandchildren of recent immigrant waves view him? How would he view himself and his prospects? Against whom would he measure his circumstances? And would the inevitable conflicts between the poorer and the more prosperous resemble the conflicts between Yankees and Irish,

Irish and Italians — or would they take the form of the far more deadly and longer established conflict between black and white? I feel the answers are still not given. They will be shaped both by the established ethnic groups and the Negro migrant. But I fear the answer from both sides will be . . . yes, the Negro is different.

It is impossible for the history of ethnic self-consciousness to escape from the impact of Negro urban migration, for all the waves of immigration have affected the self-consciousness of waves that came before. The old Americans reacted to the first great waves of immigrants of the '40s and '50s of the 19th century with an exaggerated sense of their own high status and aristocratic connections. The early immigrants from each group withdrew from later immigrants, but were generally forced together with them because the old Americans imposed a common identity on them. The history of ethnic self-consciousness, it is clear, has not worked itself out independently of social and economic and political events. If anything, it has been a reaction to these events: the rise of one group, the occupancy of the bottom by another, the political conflicts of Europe, the sequence of immigration in each town and city and section. All these have helped mold ethnic self-consciousness, and its reflection in social activity, in political choice, in economic history.

But on the whole this self-consciousness, whatever its stages, has been marked by optimism and hope. I have described the Kennedy mood among the more recent and more sharply defined American ethnic groups as self-congratulation. Indeed it was that, though each of the groups might have found some basis for resentment rather than pride. The Irish had reached the heights of political success, and the Jews were prosperous, but both were still in large measure excluded from the pinnacles of economic power — the great banks, insurance companies, corporations. The Italians still were remarkably poorly represented in high political posts, and had a much smaller share in every establishment — economic, political, cultural — than the Jews, who had come at the same time and were less numerous. The Poles were even poorer.

And yet such invidious comparisons — which the census made clear — were rarely made. All the new groups seem to have escaped from the difficult period of second generation self-depreciation and exaggerated Americanism. All seemed to wear ethnic connection with self-assurance. Certainly the growing prosperity of Europe, the increased trade with Europe, the wide acceptance of its consumer goods here, the large influence of European culture, all made the acceptance of one's ethnic connections easier — for by doing so, after all, one was no longer acknowledging poor relations. It was fascinating to remark upon the change in the image of the homeland among the more self-conscious and better educated descendants of the immigrants. Ireland was no longer the home of potatoes and cabbage, but of Joyce and the Abbey Theatre, good Irish whiskey and Georgian architecture, horseracing and tweeds. Italy became the land of chic, while Israel and Poland, if they could not compete in the arts of affluent consumption, became now paragons of political independence and heroism. Every group fortunately found something to admire in the old (or new) country, and found it easy to acknowledge the connection that had once been obscured.

But if this characterizes the most recent mood of ethnic self-consciousness, it is now challenged by the new Negro militancy and the theory on which it is reared. The self-congratulatory expressions are strangled in the throat. For a while, in the '40s and '50s, when Jewish and Catholic groups worked effectively with Urban League and NAACP, with Negroes proud of having achieved middle-class status, the older ethnic groups and their representatives could

present themselves as models and elder brothers — in community organization, group defense work, in cultural and political activity. But the radical Negro mood, and its growing reflection among intellectuals, turns all whites into exploiters, with old Americans, old immigrants, and new immigrants lumped together. The success of the ethnic groups — limited as it is for many — now becomes a reproach. Their very history, which each group has been so busy writing and reconstructing, now becomes an unspoken (and sometimes spoken) criticism of the Northern Negro. Both sides see it and rush to explain themselves.

What after all is the history of the American ethnic groups but a history of group and individual adaptation to difficult circumstances? All the histories move in the same patterns. The immigrants arrive; they represent the poorest and least educated and most oppressed of their countries in Europe and Asia. They arrive ignorant of our language and customs, exploited and abused. They huddle together in the ghettos of the cities, beginning slowly to attend to their most immediate needs — organization for companionship, patterns of self-aid in crisis, churches for worship, schools to maintain the old culture. American society and government is indifferent to their needs and desires; they are allowed to do what they wish, but neither hindered nor aided.

In this amorphous setting where no limits are set to group organization, they gradually form a community. Their children move through the public schools and perhaps advance themselves — if not, it may be the grandchildren who do. The children are embarrassed by the poverty and ignorance of the parents. Eventually they, or the grandchildren, learn to accept their origins as poverty and ignorance are overcome. They move into the spheres of American life in which many or all groups meet — the larger economy, politics, social life, education. Eventually many of the institutions created by the immigrants become a hindrance rather than a necessity; some are abandoned, some are changed. American society in the meantime has made a place for and even become dependent on some of these institutions, such as old-age homes and hospitals, adoption services and churches — these survive and perhaps flourish. More and more of these institutions become identified with the religious denomination, rather than the ethnic group as such.

Note one element of this history: demand on government plays a small role; response by government plays a small role. There is one great exception, the labor movement. But even the labor movement, which eventually found support in public law and government administrative structure, began its history as voluntary organization in the amorphous structure of American society and achieved its first triumphs without, or even against, government.

Does this history have any meaning for the American Negro? This is the question that Jews and Japanese, Irish and Italians, Poles and Czechs ask themselves. Some new immigrant groups — Puerto Ricans and Mexicans — think it does have a meaning for them. They try to model their institutions on those of earlier immigrant groups. They show the same uncertainties and confusions over what to do with the culture and language they have brought with them.

The militant Negro and his white allies passionately deny the relevance or even the truth of this history. It is white history; as white history it is also the history of the exploitation of the Negro, of the creation of privilege on the basis of his unpaid and forced labor. It is not history he can accept as having any meaning for him. His fate, he insists, has been far more drastic and frightful than any other, and neither Irish famines nor Jewish pogroms make the members of these groups brothers in understanding. The hatred with which he is looked upon by whites, he believes, has nothing in common with the petty prejudices that European immigrant groups have met. And the America of today, in which he makes his great and desperate effort for full equality, he asserts, has little in common with the America of mass immigration.

A subtle intervention of government in every aspect of social life, of economy, of culture, he insists, is necessary now to create justice. Every practice must now be scrutinized anew for its impact on this totally unique and incomparable group in American life. The neighborhood school, the civil service system, the personnel procedures of our corporations, the practices of small business, the scholarship systems of our states, the composition and character of our churches, the structure of neighborhood organization, the practices of unions — all, confronted with this shibboleth, fail. The Negro has not received his due, and the essence of all of them is therefore discrimination and exclusion, and the defense of privilege. It is no wonder that ethnic self-consciousness, after its brief moment of triumph, after its legitimization in American life, now turns upon itself in confusion. After all, it is these voluntary churches, organizations, hospitals, schools, and businesses that have become the pride of ethnic groups and the seat of whatever distinctiveness they possess. It is by way of this participation that they have become part of the very fabric of American life. But the fabric is now challenged. And looked at from another perspective, the Negro perspective, the same structure that defends some measure of uniqueness by the same token defends some measure of discrimination and exclusion.

It is impossible for the ethnic groups in America, who have already moved through so many protean forms, to be unaffected by the civil rights revolution. For this raises the question of the status of the largest of American minority groups, the one most closely bound up with American history from its very beginnings. Chinese and Japanese, perhaps Puerto Ricans and Mexican-Americans can accept the patterns of development and gradual assimilation into American society that are exhibited in the history of the great European immigrant groups. For a while, some of us who studied this history and saw in its variety and flexibility some virtues for a mass, industrial society, which suppresses variety and flexibility in so many areas, hoped that the American Negro, as he entered the more open environments of Northern cities, could also move along the paths the European immigrant groups had followed.

We now wonder whether this hope was illusory. Whether it was the infection of Europeans with the virus of American racial prejudice; or the inability to confine the direct and violent conflict in the South; or the impact of slavery and Southern experience on the American Negro — it is clear, whatever the causes, that for one of the major groups in American life, the idea of pluralism, which has supported the various developments of other groups, has become a mockery. Whatever concrete definition we give to pluralism, it means a limitation of government power, a relatively free hand for private and voluntary organizations to develop their own patterns of worship, education, social life, residential concentration, and even their distinctive economic activity. All of these inevitably enhance the life of one group; from the perspective of the American Negro they are inevitably exclusive and discriminatory.

The general ideas that have justified the development of the ethnic group in America have never been too well explicated. We have tended to obscure the inevitable conflicts between individual group interest and national interest, even when they have occurred, rather than set down sharp principles to regulate the ethnic groups. If an ethnic group interest clashed with a national interest, we have been quite ruthless and even extreme in overriding the group interest. Thus two world wars radically diminished the scale and assertiveness of German-American group life. But we have never fully developed what is permitted and what is not. Now a new national interest is becoming defined — the final liquidation of Negro separation, in all areas of our life: the economic, the social, the cultural, the residential.

In every area, Negro separation, regardless of its causes, is seen as unbearable by Negroes. Inevitably this must deeply mark the future development of American ethnic groups, whose continuance contributes, in some measure, to this separation. Recently in this country there has been a positive attitude to ethnic distinctiveness. Oscar Handlin and others have argued that it does not divide the nation or weaken it in war; rather it helps integrate the immigrant groups and adds a rich strand of variety to American civilization. Now a new question arises: What is its effect on the Negro?

Perhaps, ironically, the final homogenization of the American people, the creation of a common nationality replacing all other forms of national connection, will now come about because of the need to guarantee the integration of the Negro. But I believe the group character of American life is too strongly established and fits too many individual needs to be so completely suppressed. Is it not more likely that as Negro demands are in varying measure met, the Negro too will accept the virtues of our complex society, in which separation is neither forbidden nor required, but rather tolerated? Perhaps the American Negro will become another ethnic group, accepted by others and accepting himself.

51.

JAMES RIDGEWAY: More Lost Indians

After 100 or 200 years — or 473, if one counts from Columbus' discovery up to the publication of this article by James Ridgeway — the Indian problem is still unsolved. Government policies have changed from time to time, and a handful of more vigorous and ambitious Indians leave the reservation and take their place, not without difficulty, in the mainstream of American life. But most of the original lords of this land continue, and will continue for a long time, to live the kind of life that Ridgeway described in 1965.

Source: *New Republic*, December 11, 1965.

PINE RIDGE RESERVATION is a 5,000-square-mile expanse of rolling prairie and badlands along the bottom tier of South Dakota where the Oglala Sioux were finally penned up after battling the U.S. Cavalry across the Plains. It is one of the biggest reservations in the country. Ten thousand Sioux live spread out along the creek bottoms or in one of the half-dozen little settlements. The largest of these is the village of Pine Ridge, which has a population of 2,000. Most of the people still live in one- or two-room shacks, or, if they are lucky, in one of the frame houses built by public housing. This is the seat of the superintendent of the Bureau of Indian Affairs, which runs a large school. Up on the hill, the Public Health Service maintains a free hospital.

There are no regular restaurants or motels at Pine Ridge, but you can get a meal at the Red Wing Cafe. The jukebox there can be made to play "Heart Break Tepee" or the "Sioux Anthem." The older Indians, who mostly dress as cowboys, creak into town in their beaten-up cars in the early morning and hang around the Indian Bureau or the headquarters of the Oglala Sioux tribe, where Enos Poorbear, the president, has his office. Sometimes a tribal council is in session, which provides enter-tainment, but more likely they will wander into the tribal court, where minor crimes are tried. Major crimes are tried in federal court.

The day I stumbled into this narrow courtroom (it smells heavily of lavatory disinfectant and the windows are obscured by barbed wire), Judge Wop Ladeau, a short, white-haired man who appeared to be missing most of his teeth, was sprawled out across the top of his bench. His mouth was wide open and he listened in fascination as Betty Fire Thunder described how Ella Thunder Bull created disorder at the Allen School where Betty had peacefully been popping popcorn one night prior to a dance. Ella suddenly burst from the kitchen where she had been drinking, accused Betty of making faces at her, and then yelled, "I am going to knock the shit out of you." But Ella got sidetracked and tried to beat up Agnes Bad Wound instead, and the worst that happened was that the women were made to dance with people they did not like.

The court spent the better part of the afternoon pondering this matter and was in recess when I left. Numerous defense attorneys were wandering around the place, although, as it turned out, anyone could be a defense attorney, and it was a good way to pick up $8, the fee for taking a case. The main idea was to trick the prosecuting attorney, a harried-looking woman, by getting rid of her material witnesses. Both the court and the tribal council are conducted in English and Lakota, the native tongue.

The Indians have a certain fondness for the late President Kennedy and his brother Robert. They have letters of the former which they would like to sell, the price being right. And they are sure that when the documentary evidence of bungled management is laid before the latter, he will clean everything up. (They apparently are referring to his role as attorney general.)

The Oglala Sioux are regarded as the great masters of passive resistance. They pay no attention to foolish ideas coming from outside. A local schoolteacher took charge of the local civil defense effort and tried to get the Indians to build bomb shelters; they paid little heed. In a fury, he put around the story that while one in every seventeen Americans was a Communist, the rate at the reservation was considerably higher. His efforts ended in failure.

The government still views the Indians on reservations as wards who one day will improve themselves enough to manage their own affairs. This is a goal which amuses the older Sioux, since to them the government people are servants; the goods and services dispensed are part of the price paid for land taken away in the wars of the last century. They act like exiled European aristocrats, in this case, waiting to leave the prairie and go back into the Black Hills — the prized possession that was granted them in 1868 in return for a promise to live on reservations and stop molesting white settlers.

Then gold was discovered in the hills, and they were taken away in 1877. A claim for their return was begun with Charles Evans Hughes in the 1920s and endures still in the Indian Claims Commission, where after perhaps another five years of argument

it may be decided. At best, each member of the different Sioux tribes could hope for not much more than a few thousand dollars, and even that is an uncertain prospect.

Since the turn of the century, the government sought first to drive the younger and talented Indians off the reservations, and then, more recently, to lure them away, in the hope of intermingling them with white people and thereby getting rid of this unpleasant problem altogether. A residue, however, remained, and it has now sprouted into a sort of inexperienced and uneducated middle class that is trying to govern a population of old people and little children. The fortunes of its leaders are decided in the elected tribal council. They teeter constantly on the brink of despair, represented by the whisky bottle; what energy and hope for the future they may have is generated largely through Richard Schifter, the tribe's Washington lawyer, who helped them get through a public-housing project, and more recently brought in half a million dollars of poverty funds.

GOING AWAY TO SCHOOL

THE BUREAU OF INDIAN AFFAIRS pursues a policy of improving education and at the same time developing the economic base of the reservations. While the Bureau maintains elementary day schools in various settlements scattered around the reservation that are accessible to most of the students, it runs only one high school at Pine Ridge. The school bus only goes out nine miles from town, and therefore a good many of the thousand or so students board. The school is modern and the dormitories look pleasant enough, a lot pleasanter than the little shacks out on the prairie; nonetheless, the Bureau school is a hangover from a policy pursued at the turn of the century when the government decided the best way to deal with the Indians would be to take the children away, put them in boarding schools, and civilize them that way.

This did not stop Indians from being Indians, but it did contribute to the breakdown of the Indian family. One teacher told me the main difference in dealing with Indian children was the family's absolute dread of education. They knew it was meant to break up the family. Large numbers of children now drop out of eighth grade rather than go away to high school. Children at Pine Ridge are above the national level in achievement at the fourth-grade level, hold their own up to the eighth grade, and then abruptly slide downhill. This is the time when they must go on to high school and when the bleakness of their chance in life dawns on them. There is no school board so that the parents have little reason to take an interest in education.

An increasing number of youngsters are finishing high school, however, and are going on to vocational training or to college. The Bureau has a relocation program, and last year it assisted 215 people to get out to West Coast cities, usually Los Angeles or Oakland, finding them lodging, getting them into job training, and practically guaranteeing them jobs. Most of the trainees are between eighteen and twenty-five. Still the ties to the reservations are strong and about 40 percent come back.

The reservation school system may have improved some in recent years, but teachers complain that their graduates cannot express themselves very well. Last year seventeen- and eighteen-year-olds were put to reading the New York Times, but it was over their heads, and the project was dropped.

The Indian Bureau's economic development policies at Pine Ridge are fairly recent and as of now have not produced much new enterprise. About half the work force is unemployed. Families are large. The mean annual family income is below $900. In the lean months of February and March, one-third of the reservation population is on welfare.

Much of the reservation is rangeland. Indians always have been good at herding cattle but poor as business managers. They have ranched off and on, and by the end of the last war a large cattle association flourished. Then the members got greedy and broke up the common cattle herd for individual gain. The enterprise floundered. About half the rangeland now is rented to white ranchers. Small portions of farmlands are mostly leased out. Periodically there is talk of starting ranching again in a big way but the costs are high and the profits slender. The Sioux also have worked in the past as migrant laborers, but machinery has cut back this employment. A fishhook factory came on the reservation in 1960, and while the labor turnover was heavy during the first two years, workers have now settled down and have proved to be adept. But at peak periods it employs only 240 people.

One out of every four tourists who come through South Dakota is supposed to tow a trailer behind his car, and the Indian Bureau has been working to build campsites to attract them. There are no restaurants or motels on the reservation. William Nye, the man who runs the Economic Development office at Pine Ridge, has a master plan for capturing a big share of the tourist business that is bringing South Dakota $170 million a year; and by 1970 is expected to produce revenues of $700 million. Nye hit on the idea of building a replica of old Fort Phil Kearney, which in 1866 was put up on the Bozeman Trail in what is now Wyoming. The great Sioux chief, Red Cloud, burned it two years later.

Nye has the plans for the fort, and when the replica is finished, the old cavalry headquarters will be a restaurant; the guests can stay in the officers' and enlisted men's quarters, which will be a motel. The old trading center will become a museum and an arts and crafts center. And the supply sheds will house a factory where the arts and crafts can be made. Each summer a Sioux pageant will be put on to entertain the guests. This project, Nye estimates, might cost half a million dollars. It might be supplemented later on by a dude ranch.

A perhaps more plausible scheme involves making use of the large clay deposits on the reservation. Clay can be used to make pipes that can be used in diversion projects underway along the Missouri River. Richard Schifter in Washington is talking with businessmen about setting up an operation under the new Economic Development Administration, which makes cheap loans.

A major difficulty at Pine Ridge is to keep what little money there now is on the reservation from flowing off. The tribe insists on prohibition on the reservation, thereby guaranteeing profits for saloonkeepers at nearby White Clay, Nebraska. When lease money is paid, the Nebraska State Highway Patrol has been known suddenly to appear and throw up roadblocks outside the reservation, just across state lines. Indians arrested and fined on drunk charges help to swell the community coffers, so the story goes. The tribe now is building a supermarket complex, but many Bureau employees like to shop in Nebraska where there is no sales tax and where they can get away from Pine Ridge for a few hours Saturday.

Indians are heavily in debt to merchants outside the reservation. The tribe at present is suing a store owner in White Clay for unusual lending practices. He gave an Indian credit on purchases, but first made him sign a blank check on a bank where he did not have an account. The store owner then would exact small payments when he could, or in lieu of that let his debtor work it off. At last, the Indian insisted he had paid off the debt. But the store owner said no. He filled in the check and put it through the bank. The check bounced. The sheriff was called in and brought a criminal charge against the Indian, threatening to throw him in jail.

THE LOST COMMUNITIES

OUT ON THE PRAIRIE there are a handful of little settlements, each one dominated by an elementary school with an adjacent row of neat frame houses where the teachers live. There is apt to be a general store run by a white. The rest of the buildings are one- or two-room log houses, surrounded by rusting heaps of old cars that have been abandoned and stripped of spare parts. Some people still live in tents. Beyond these settlements, along the creek beds and down the gullies, are the lost communities: Blackeyes, Red Shirt Table, Lower Medicine Root Community, and Potato Creek. Here the people often are old and sickly. At Potato Creek, a cluster of seven or eight shacks on a creek bottom fifty-five miles north and east of Pine Ridge, I met a man and his wife who were living with three children, and until recently the woman's diabetic mother, in a log shack about twenty feet long by twelve feet wide. The husband had once made a living on a sheep farm in Nebraska, but then he got tuberculosis. The family came back to the free hospital on the reservation. None of them works.

The main electric lines run close by, but the woman said they could not pay the bills and thus didn't have electricity. Fortunately, there was a spring nearby so they did not have to drink water from the dirty creek bottom. The aged mother had been to the hospital at various times, being sent home with instructions on what to eat. The family lives off surplus commodities, which made the old woman constantly sick. She finally had a stroke and now was back in the hospital. For a while the man and his wife talked about the good days in Nebraska, and then the woman launched into a description of what went on at the Native American Church, a rather larger shack on a nearby hill.

People came from miles around Saturday and stayed all night reading the Bible, beating drums, and shaking gourds, and chewing peyote. The peyote itself was no good unless you had faith. If you had faith, it could work incredible miracles. One time, there was an old woman with sores all over her face; they washed her face with a peyote solution and the sores disappeared. Another time, a child had been born blind. Its eyelids were gray and all stuck together. The mother prayed hard and then put a peyote mixture into an eyedropper. She squirted a drop down behind the eyelid and miraculously the eyes opened and the child could see. People had come from Washington and were so impressed that they were going back to make sure peyote was used all over the country.

NO POWER OR WATER

PRACTICALLY NONE OF THE HOUSES on the reservation has electricity. Half of the houses are without wells nearby; Poverty-Program workers are discovering people hauling water fifteen miles. Indoor plumbing or telephone service is rare.

The Public Health Service, which runs the hospital and is in charge of a sanitation program, lumbers along under the Indian Sanitation Act, which is meant to provide free waterworks to Indian communities. But each project for each tiny settlement must go through Congress, which means it takes three years to get approval, and no appropriations have been forthcoming recently, so the program is now at a standstill.

There is a great deal of illness at Pine Ridge, and, according to the sanitation experts, the quickest way to cut down on the disease rate is to get a toilet and a sink indoors. The infant mortality rate is twice that of the nation's, and infectious diseases among small children are a major problem. The incidence of tuberculosis is seventeen times that for the rest of the country. The life expectancy for a person at Pine Ridge is thirty-eight years, compared with sixty-two

years nationally. Because of the lack of bathing, the children commonly have bad sores on their faces.

Part of this may also be due to poor nutrition. Many live on surplus commodities which are low in proteins. (For instance, only enough dried milk is allotted per person to make four quarts of milk per month.) Sometimes the free commodities are not eaten. A Vista worker said she was babysitting one night for a white family outside of Kyle, one of the small communities, when an Indian woman came to the door. She wanted to sell some commodities to get money for gas to take a child to Pine Ridge, to the hospital. She apparently made a practice of this.

The birthrate is one-third higher than for the rest of the nation. Dr. Michael Ogden, the man in charge of the hospital at Pine Ridge, explained that if a married woman asks about birth control, she will be told, and, if she wants one, will be given an intrauterine device. The PHS does not inform people about birth control on its own. The intrauterine device is prescribed only where the woman has had one child. As a general practice, Dr. Ogden was leery of dealing with unmarried women (the illegitimate birthrate is high), but he said each case would have to be decided on its own merits.

Although the hospital has what looks to be a fairly new operating room and there is a surgeon on the staff, Dr. Ogden said the room had not been used since March because of the shortage of nurses. There were sixteen positions, and he had only nine nurses on duty. People are flown to Omaha when an operation is necessary. The hospital maintains two station wagons, which in the past were used as ambulances, but Dr. Ogden claims he does not have the drivers, and the Indians so badly abused the service, using it as a ruse for getting a free lift into Pine Ridge, that he is unsympathetic to their demands it be resumed.

Leo Vocu, an assistant director of the local Poverty Program, bitterly assails the PHS on this account. He says a middle-aged man died recently of dehydration and diarrhea because the hospital refused to heed a Public Health nurse's pleas to bring him in. When they did finally go out, Vocu says, it was too late; he died on the way to the hospital.

The policy of developing the economic potential of Indian reservations began with Secretary Stewart Udall. It has run for only five years, and the results are bound to be slow in coming. Steering the course is tricky business, since what Udall wants to do is curiously contradictory. The talented young people whom the Bureau tries to educate and then help make a go of it in the outside world are the very ones needed most at home to bring off economic development. The solution to the Indian problem still is dimly seen to lie in pouring the Indians into the big cities where they will intermingle with everyone else. But the city planners are trying to figure out how to get people out of the cramped city and back into the countryside. If the administration does not pull hard to redevelop these rural areas, it will end up merely fanning the flames in the cities.

52.

Edmund K. Faltermayer: The Half-Finished Society

The social problems resulting from rapid industrialization were recognized early in this century, and have been partially dealt with though in halting, inadequate steps, since the New Deal. But the serious environmental problems resulting from scientific and technological advance have only lately begun to be recognized at all, and when recognized have received only token attention by federal, state, and local authorities. Indeed, current problems have become so complex and interrelated that those who write about them must adopt what has been called an ecological tone. Such an approach was taken by Edmund K. Faltermayer, associate editor of Fortune, *in the article from which the following selection is drawn.*

Source: *Fortune,* March 1965.

OUR AMERICAN CIVILIZATION is only half built. From the standpoint of per capita consumption of goods, home ownership, education, and social mobility, the U.S. leads the world and the American Dream is now largely fulfilled. But that dream, which spurred on frontiersmen clearing the wilderness and inspired immigrants to break out of the slums, was never really a blueprint for a mature society. It emphasized the individual's demand for material comfort, privacy, and the education needed to obtain them. But it largely ignored the other half of civilized life: a whole spectrum of human needs that can be met only through communal action.

The society we have built fulfills the lopsided American Dream with a vengeance. Our immaculate homes are crowded with gleaming appliances and our refrigerators are piled high with convenience foods. But beyond our doorsteps lies a shamefully neglected social and physical environment. Foreigners who come to these shores expecting to find splendid countryside and magnificent cities discover other things instead: noise, vandalism, polluted air, befouled streams, filthy streets, forests of ugly telegraph poles and wires, decrepit mass-transit systems, and parks that are unkempt and unsafe. They also see: a countryside being devoured by housing subdivisions and by shopping centers whose graceless buildings are little more than merchandise barns; highways splattered with enormous billboards and hideous drive-ins that shriek for the passing motorist's attention; central cities that, except for a rather insignificant amount of reconstruction at the core, are sprawling wastelands of decayed speculative construction left over from yesteryear. The only places where Americans have extensively beautified their country, visitors soon discover, are certain upper-middle-class suburbs — fine for those who can afford them — and some college campuses. Otherwise, there is little relief from what the English magazine *Architectural Review* a decade ago called "the mess that is man-made America."

The archvillain in the despoliation of our landscape, it sometimes seems, is American capitalism. To one returning here after a long sojourn abroad, the impression gained is one of pathologically profit-minded enterprises striving to outdo each other in the creation of eyesores. You see the results everywhere: the exhausted gravel pit that was never replanted, the porcelain gasoline station that brutally shoulders up against the village church, the speculative office tower that has all the aesthetic appeal of a throwaway container, which is basically what it is in the eyes of its tax-motivated builders. A rather disturbing question naturally arises: is public ugliness the price America must pay for its incredibly high level of private consumption?

The answer is no. Western Europe is

managing to retain its beauty amid rapidly rising consumption. Blaming it all on American capitalism is about as logical as criticizing plants for wanting to grow toward the sun. If there is chaos, it is the community's fault for failing to exercise its role as gardener. European countries, governed by men with a pride in appearances rarely encountered here, have never lost control of their environment. America has yet to *gain* control of its environment. Because of this the American free-enterprise system, whose efficiency and command of technology could have created the tidiest-looking country in the world, has tended to produce an overpowering disorder.

The U.S. therefore has gigantic tasks before it. The whole place needs to be done over. The cost will be staggering: trillions of dollars, over and above the equally enormous investment needed to accommodate the doubling of urban population expected by the year 2000. But given the country's unprecedented wealth, the result could be a transformation on the scale of the Italian Renaissance. In view of this opportunity, it is surprising that two current patterns of thinking — the prognostications of economists and President Johnson's Great Society program — fail to see all of the possibilities in the situation.

Many economists are somewhat worriedly predicting a slowdown in the country's economic growth rate about a year from now and calling for fiscal remedies like tax cuts and stepped-up federal spending. While both measures may prove desirable, neither one would necessarily stimulate activity where it is needed most — not in raising the quantity of goods consumed but in lifting the *quality* of American life by renovating the environment. Because economic forecasting does not take account of quality, as perhaps it cannot, we have become obsessed with the need for more quantitative output and more innovations to provide jobs for the growing labor force.

Thus, we are biting our nails wondering whether more families will buy backyard swimming pools or whether industry will come up with a wrist television set — which we will probably get anyway — when all about us is enough urgent unfinished business to occupy the labor force for years to come.

President Johnson's Great Society program is a step in the right direction. But some of the proposals that have been transmitted to Congress imply a heavy reliance on federal spending to remedy society's ills. Some money will unquestionably be needed from Washington. But there is a danger that the Great Society *vision* — which some have derided as utopian — could turn out to be a rather narrow one tailored to political and budgetary considerations. The sums available to the federal government for additional nondefense spending are unlikely to exceed $3 billion or $4 billion a year, if social-security increases are excluded. When measured against the cost of completing our half-finished civilization, this is an absolutely trifling amount. Far more money will have to come from state and local governments, and the biggest contributor of all will have to be the private economy. Washington's primary role is not to spend but to lead. President Johnson, to be sure, realizes this and has said as much. But it remains to be seen whether the Great Society program will turn out to be a collection of federally financed patches on the present model, or a true national renovation sustained by the vision of the highest officials in the land.

Fortunately, the elements of a larger vision are very much in the air these days. Though the tangible accomplishments are modest to date, most of our cities are now consciously trying to rejuvenate themselves, and business leaders have provided much of the momentum. The middle class is trickling back from the suburbs. Alarmed citi-

Courtesy, Reg Manning from McNaught Syndicate, Inc.

"Start by lifting a calf —"; cartoon by Reg Manning in the "Arizona Republic," 1966

zens' groups are pushing through ordinances to save landmarks from the wrecking ball. Architects are "in" at the better cocktail parties, and corporations are beginning to demand something better than glass boxes for their headquarters. The Great Society speech — as distinguished from the legislative program now unfolding — may have been a major turning point. "It is harder and harder to live the good life in American cities today," the President declared, and he went on to catalogue all the ills in unflattering terms. "Our society will never be great until our cities are great." Never has an American President spoken in quite this way. The mere fact that someone at the top *cares* about junkyards has given new drive to the movement to raise the quality of American life. The prospects for action raised by that speech, says one city planner, are "absolutely stupendous."

But we must get busy. First, the American capitalist system, for all its efficiency, presents a rather shabby image to the outside world. "An important test of an economy is how it looks," says conservationist William H. Whyte, a former *Fortune* editor. Ours, for the most part, looks like hell. Reaching the moon will gain us little, in worldwide acclaim, if we cannot build habitable cities. Second, we are in an era of onrushing technological change. If we cannot create a more harmonious environment to mitigate the effects of this change, our nerves may get awfully taut.

Third, we are running out of living space. Superficially, this statement sounds absurd, for the urban portions of the forty-eight contiguous states use up only 2 percent of the total land area. But the best job opportunities today are in the major metropolitan regions, where the surrounding countryside is rapidly being gobbled up by haphazard real-estate development. In one region, the so-called "megalopolis" that stretches from Boston to Washington between the Appalachian ridges and the sea, the population density is already greater than in such crowded foreign lands as Britain and West Germany. The arc that extends from Pittsburgh through Chicago and Milwaukee is almost as densely peopled as Western Europe, and the corridor between San Francisco and San Diego will be before long.

The vast national parks and wilderness areas in the hinterlands are of significance only during vacations; half of America's people spend most of their lives in crowded little "countries" like megalopolis. It is precisely in these areas that the coming population increase will be concentrated. In fifty years, President Johnson forecasts, America will have a population of 400 million, four-fifths of it urban. If we do not establish intelligent controls over land use, most Americans will soon be spending 95 percent of their lives in huge blighted zones, hundreds of miles long, that are neither city nor country, but one vast, dispiriting Nowhere. . . .

A SURVEY OF THE NATIONAL SCENE demonstrates that we have not only the governmental tools, but the technology and the wealth to complete the unfinished business of America:

Public safety: The approximately $2.5 billion a year our municipalities spend on police and fire protection is obviously inadequate. Even a 50 percent increase would not unduly strain a $650-billion economy, especially since the money would be repaid through lower crime and fire rates. A few figures suggest that in police protection, as in other things, you get what you pay for. New York City has 25,861 policemen, counting plainclothesmen, enforcing the law in an area inhabited by about 8 million people. London, with a population about 2 percent larger, has 31 percent more policemen — and had 42 percent fewer serious crimes in the last reported year (1963). Paris, which is more heavily policed than London, has even fewer crimes.

Noise: For more than a decade a ban against automobile horn tooting, except in real emergencies, has been effectively enforced in Paris, where the population is supposedly more temperamental than our own. Cars are not the only villains, of course. An expert quoted in the book *Sick Cities,* by Mitchell Gordon, estimates that New York City could easily reduce its noise level 80 percent by requiring homeowners to use plastic containers for trash, installing rubber pads on garbage-collection trucks, and, most important of all, requiring more effective mufflers on buses and trucks.

Pollution: Sewage is our major river pollutant, and the cost of making good the arrears in the construction of treatment plants will, of course, fall on taxpayers. According to the U.S. Public Health Service, municipalities could easily spend a total of $8 billion on treatment plants by 1975, and this would require them to boost their current spending rate by about one-third. In addition, older cities could spend $20 billion to $30 billion to provide separate sanitary and storm sewer lines. Corporations, too, will have to spend heavily to reduce both air and water pollution. Most industrial processes can now be made clean, or nearly so, but many municipalities and states are reluctant to pass strict anti-pollution laws for fear of driving companies away. Strong federal legislation, which President Johnson has requested in the case of water pollution, may therefore be the only answer.

The cost of the long-overdue industrial cleanup might well result in slightly higher product prices, but competition and increased productivity will undoubtedly prompt many companies to hold the line. In the Los Angeles area seven large petroleum refineries have spent $68,200,000 on pollution-control equipment during the past fifteen years, plus $72,600,000 more for operation and maintenance. Emissions into the atmosphere have been reduced 90 percent. But the costly cleanup effort has had no noticeable effect on the price of gasoline at the pump. The bigger air polluters now are the cars themselves, and the new exhaust-control devices will not eliminate all the irritating emissions.

The federal government should prod the automotive industry to develop a cleaner-burning engine or, failing that, to find a substitute. Yardney Electric Co., a maker of batteries for cordless power tools, already has a prototype of a small battery-operated car that will run 100 miles on a single charge, and a spokesman asserts that a car with twice this range and a top speed of seventy-five miles per hour could be brought to market in three to five years. While even the second vehicle would not match today's standard-sized car in size or power, it might supplant smaller cars, which are popular in urban areas where air pollution is most serious.

Eyesores: Junkyards, utility poles, bill-boards, and weird-looking hamburger stands produce a type of "scenery pollution" we should not tolerate in our once lovely land. Junkyards, which the Johnson Administration is studying, are the least of our difficulties, for they can be screened. Electric and other utility wires are already underground in most European urban areas, and this is where they belong. "Undergrounding" is more costly here because our sprawling suburbs necessitate longer trenches. But advances in cable design now make it possible to do the job in new subdivisions for as little as $150 per household. Elsewhere the cost can run as high as $1,000 or more. Taking a rough average of $600, and assuming that two-thirds of the nation's 58 million dwelling units could stand such treatment, the cost comes to about $23 billion — somewhat less than the country spends on electricity and telephone bills in one year. If the project were spaced over twenty years, therefore, it would raise rates only by a few percentage points. Meanwhile it would provide plenty of employment.

In terms of its ability to ruin everybody's view at minimum expense, the billboard is perhaps the most efficient device ever invented by man. You see relatively few of the big ones in Europe, and this is not just happenstance. They are rigorously controlled, and banned outright in scenic areas; nearly a third of England is completely off limits. Only twenty states have taken advantage of a small federal inducement (an added half-percent support of construction costs) and curbed billboards on the new interstate highways. President Johnson has indicated, in his special message to Congress on natural beauty, that he wants stronger authority to control billboards. The proposed curbs would apply to all interstate highways and other new federally aided roads, but they would be of no help on other roads. A few states, such as Oregon and Hawaii, have passed more comprehensive laws to limit billboards, but progress in the state capitals is slow. A possible future lever here is the fact that Washington supports some 870,000 miles of existing conventional roads. Together with the interstate system, they account for 65 percent of all motor-vehicle traffic and undoubtedly contain most of the billboards.

The ugly "strip commercial" developments that grace the entrances to our cities present an even more serious problem. After all, people need to eat, shop, and fuel their cars. President Johnson's new highway-beautification program will probably be of little help in areas already lined with drive-ins. But we need not live with these atrocities until the end of time. Again, using the leverage of its highway-aid program, the federal government could move states and localities to condemn some of the more ghastly structures and regroup the enterprises into shopping centers.

As some tastefully designed shopping centers show, commercial activity need not uglify the nation. The same holds true of industry, particularly heavy industry, which in its proper setting has a special grandeur all its own. Even a Henry Thoreau might be moved by the complex of chimneys and blast furnaces south of Chicago. Much of our industry, to be sure, needs major cosmetic treatment. But we need not feel ashamed of living in an industrial age.

Mass transit. Real city life, in most cases, is impossible without mass transit. The sums needed to provide good mass-transit systems in all major cities tower above the $375 million recently provided by Congress. The New York metropolitan region could easily spend $3 billion merely to modernize existing commuter lines and extend some subways, and the national investment could run to ten times that figure. We also need to extend the mass-transit principle to intercity travel. High-speed trains in the Boston-Washington corridor, now being studied by the Commerce Department, should be only the beginning.

In West Germany, 45 percent of intercity travel is by train, and business executives are among the most enthusiastic rail passengers. In the U.S., 90 percent is by private automobile and only 2.3 percent by train (airlines and buses share most of the rest). We have the know-how — or soon will have — for operating 200-mph trains between New York and Chicago, thus cutting the journey to five hours from the present minimum of fifteen and a half. That would be almost as fast as the downtown-to-downtown time by jet, and the service would be weatherproof and easier on the nerves of those who hate flying.

Some public initiative will undoubtedly be needed to break the vicious circle we are now in: declining use of trains because of poor service, which leads to further curtailments. The individual's travel options — and thus his freedom of movement — are being abridged. If necessary, a public authority will have to be formed, outside the regular federal budget, to finance new high-speed railroads and lease them to concessionaires.

Cities. The task of renovating our cities is the biggest one of all, but we have no choice. As architect Victor Gruen remarks in his book *The Heart of Our Cities*, "There is a whole generation of Americans who have known the city only at its worst and who have not experienced the pleasures and advantages of true urban life." Some idea of the job ahead can be gleaned from the fact that slum-clearance and urban-renewal projects to date have involved only sixty-five square miles of land, or less than one-thousandth of the urban territory in the U.S. The job obviously gets cheaper as you move away from the core, where many of the projects have been concentrated until now. But one conclusion is inescapable. Governments cannot finance or even subsidize the rebuilding of all our urban areas;

private enterprise will have to do most of the job. The main task of government is to bring about an orderly pattern in the private construction — *i.e.*, to play the role of gardener. Fortunately, most American cities now have planning commissions because Washington wisely has made their existence a precondition for urban-renewal grants. But only a few, notably Philadelphia and Boston, have drafted truly comprehensive plans. . . .

Regions. Planning, of course, cannot stop at the city limits. Most metropolitan areas have regional planning bodies of some sort, since the newer federal programs make these, too, a condition for aid. But they have barely got off the ground. In New York City, the place that needs metropolitan planning the most, the Regional Plan Association has no official status. Regional planning can do much to define the areas for suburban housing construction, which is pushing the true countryside farther and farther from city centers, and to stimulate the more efficient use of space within existing metropolitan areas.

There is no question that the existing urban areas could absorb a lot more people. Victor Gruen, who has worked out a theoretical plan for cities, figures that the present population of many American metropolitan regions could be fitted into a fraction of their present territory. Gruen's scheme would provide low-density "suburban" living for those who want it, but half of his metropolitan area would consist of public open space — far more than in most new subdivisions. (There is a town in California with one baseball diamond for 85,000 people.)

The best way to "contain" and define metropolitan areas is to surround them with "greenbelts." Since the late 1940s an area of farms, parks, and woodlands twenty miles wide has been formed around London. The Dutch have also acted to preserve the rural landscape on the urban fringe, and

so have such cities as Honolulu, Toronto, and Ottawa. Similar zones should be set up, while there is still time, to keep cities such as Baltimore and Washington from fusing into a single formless mass. So far, the new federal and state "open space" programs have concentrated mainly on acquiring land for recreational use. But public moneys cannot possibly buy all the green space needed, least of all the operating farms, which represent a type of scenery desperately needed near big cities.

Several solutions to this problem, none of them revolutionary, are emerging. One, of course, is better planning by metropolitan regions or by the counties that adjoin urban areas; they can simply zone land for agricultural use. Another approach, where the local authorities drag their feet, is to institute statewide zoning, as Hawaii has done. A third method, considered most effective of all by some, is for state or local governments to buy "easements." For a fraction of the cost of buying land outright, the government acquires control over its future use; the procedure has been employed to protect the view from parkways. In some places such as Monterey County, California, property owners anxious to protect their investment have donated such easements to the county.

WE CAN LEARN MUCH from Western Europe, and in many ways we can improve upon it. By gaining control of our environment we can also preserve portions of our uniquely American heritage that now face obliteration. Some may ask whether a national renovation is politically feasible; defeatist voices are often heard among those who have long fought for planning and conservation in the face of public indifference. But the tide is turning, and tourism may be one of the reasons. This has been pointed out by Christopher Tunnard and Boris Pushkarev, the principal authors of a remarkable study of our environment entitled *Man-*

Made America: Chaos or Control? "Even the New York taxi driver, the owner of the small corner store, and the lowliest paid schoolteacher," they write, "has saved enough to make a trip to Europe and come back with the image of beautiful communities and a more gracious way of life than his own." Given an aroused public opinion and political leadership at the highest level, what looked impossible can suddenly become possible.

The impending population surge places us at an important crossroads. Either we will be forced by it to gain mastery over the world we move about in, or we will ignore the opportunity and pile new chaos upon the old. The U.S., as the authors of Man-Made America put it, must define once and for all the purpose of its highly efficient, free economic system. Is it "freedom for making the richest country the ugliest in the world? Or freedom, among other freedoms, for shaping an environment worthy of man?"

53.

Ben J. Wattenberg and Richard M. Scammon: A Prophecy

The U.S. census of 1960 filled about ninety volumes of statistics and closely written analysis, and revealed to a handful of courageous readers that extraordinary changes were occurring under Americans' very eyes. Believing that the tale the census reports had to tell should be made available to a large audience, journalist Ben J. Wattenberg collaborated with Census Director Richard M. Scammon in a one-volume popularization of the massive work that appeared in 1965. A chapter of their book is reprinted here.

Source: *This U.S.A.*, Garden City, N.Y., 1965, pp. 298-304: "Past, Present, Prophecy."

Carriages without horses shall go,
And accidents fill the world with woe.
Around the world thoughts shall fly
In the twinkling of an eye.
Under water men shall walk
Shall ride, shall sleep, and talk.
In the air men shall be seen
In white, in black and in green.
                    "Mother" Shipton
                    1488-1561

Prophecy is not always as hard a trade as one might suppose. By 1925, many of the changes that this country would see by 1965 were already noticeable — although not always noticed. Indeed, most of the great changes that were to occur in the

world at large were also noticeable — and perhaps even less noticed.

In this country in 1925, it took no Mother Shipton to see that the automobile was becoming an ever more popular device and that it would continue to grow in popularity. It took no Nostradamus to know that airplanes were here to stay, that child labor was on its way out, that infant mortality was being drastically lowered, that America was electrifying, that suburban residence was the wave of the future, or that Dr. Einstein's theories were, at the least, important, at the most, epochal.

On the world scene — if one cared to look — a communist dictatorship was already installed in Russia, and fascism was a growing power in continental Europe. Gandhi was inviting the British to leave India, Zionists were asking them to leave Palestine, and Egyptians wanted them out of Egypt — and, again, it took no particular punditry to know that the forces of communism, fascism, and nationalism would wield mighty influence in the next decades.

These things were there to be seen — but they were not always noticed, and because they were not our world has been the worse for it. The forces that shape human existence often give fair warning. To be sure, not all things are predictable forty years in advance. Who, for example, was to know that Robert Goddard's rocket experiments in the thirties would lead so quickly to orbital and space flights; who was to know in 1925, or 1935, that television would be in so many homes in less than thirty years? The lesson here only seems to be a redundancy: predictable things are predictable. But many things are predictable.

Forty years would seem to be as good a span to forecast as any. It is long enough into the future to allow for fancifulness, and yet near enough so that a majority of Americans alive today will be alive then. This book was published in 1965. Forty years later, the calendar will read 2005.

What kind of America will we have then? What will the analysts of the twenty-second Decennial Census be talking about, and what will we all be talking about between now and then?

Here . . . is what we can expect.

Demography. Certain demographical conclusions are the easiest to reach; we *know*, for example, that the percentage of old persons in the total population will *decline* because of the comparatively low birth rates from 1925-45 (unless immigration policies are changed drastically). We *know* that within the next decade or so population will go up even if the birth rates keep going down — because the "baby-boom" chil-

dren will be reaching reproductive age. We *know* that colleges will be crowded over the next decade particularly as the post-war babies and the fifties babies become young people headed for higher learning. We know too that even if population doubles from 1960 to 2000 (to 360 million people) the nation has the land and resources to house, clothe, feed, and entertain them, for by world standards America is both richly endowed and sparsely populated and could support such a population *today.*

We do not know, of course, what the birth rate will be in the future. Our guess is that it will decline, say, to 105 per 1000 females of childbearing age, and then level off. We *do not know* what the life expectancy rates will be, but current indications are that the rate will advance only very slowly through the ensuing decades now that infant mortality has been reduced so drastically.

We also do not know what the immigration rate will be, but if it is not increased, there will be precious few persons of foreign birth in America in the year 2000. What effect this, in turn, will have remains to be seen. It may provide increased cultural homogeneity among the nation as a whole. It may make for cultural drabness. In any event, it will be different from the America of the 1960s.

Residence and Mobility. There seems little doubt that we will continue suburbanizing for years to come and, indeed, by the year 2000 this may well have become a nation whose majority lives in the suburbs — that is, "near but not in a big central city." Gradually, the areas between central cities are filling up. In the northeast today the growth of what has been called "megalopolis" is before us. The megalopolitan growth structure is occurring elsewhere as well — a slow process but one that will continue for the remaining decades of this century.

There is every indication that the farm population will continue to decline. An inordinately large number of farmers today are older persons, and the farms they work are often small. Many of these farms are marked for extinction, although in fertile areas much of the land itself will be used up by larger farm operators. The decrease in the number of farms and farmers has been going on since 1920 and will in all likelihood continue. It cannot, however, go on forever. The 3.5 million farmers and farm laborers in 1960 may be reduced by 1 million or even more by, say, 1970 or 1980. Eventually, the numbers may reverse themselves and start climbing again as the marginal farmer is eliminated and the increasing populations demand more from farm labor than increased productivity-per-man can achieve.

If the rate of farm migration is self-reversing, the rates of two other major mobility trends are not. There is no immediate reason to believe that Negroes will stop leaving the South or that Americans of all races will stop migrating to Florida and the western states.

Over 1.5 million Negroes left the southlands during the 1950-60 decade, and yet, because of the high birth rate, the number of southern Negroes actually increased slightly. At that rate the pool of Negroes left in the South as still-prime candidates for out-migration remains inexhaustible. They can keep leaving but there will still be more to leave at a later date. It is a point to ponder the next time the statement is heard that Negro education in the South is a matter for southern states alone to be concerned with. Ours is a mobile nation, and the Negroes who may be under-educated or poorly educated in the South may well end up on relief rolls in northern states because they are ill-trained. Their early education, then, is of prime concern to non-southern states.

There is little doubt that growth will continue in California, Nevada, Arizona, and Florida, and that the center of population will continue to move southwestward from Mr. Kleiboeker's farm near Centralia, Illinois. But if anyone looks for a prediction that California, by virtue of its "largest-state" distinction will become the real core of America by the year 2000 or even by the year 2100, no such prophecy will be made here. New York City is the real capital of the world, insofar as the world has one, and the real capital of American business. New York's megalopolitan suburb — Washington, D.C. — is the political capital of both the nation and the free world. By comparison, California is the trans-desert republic: a golden home for 20 or 30 or 40 million American citizens a full continent away from the action, from the seats of power. There seem to be few indications that this will change.

Another area destined for healthy population growth are the urban areas of the South. The racial ferment has slowed the movement and development of industry in a few southern localities, while others, free from such problems, have been booming. The continued development of the urban South will progress despite the Negro exodus — and, indeed, if greater racial harmony comes to the South, the increased industrialization may be the one factor that would tend to keep down the rates of Negro out-migration.

Again, for all the growth the South and the West may see, the great center of the America of the future should remain where it is today: in that rectangle that stretches from Boston to Minneapolis to Kansas City to Washington and back up to Boston.

Education. The trigger to the ongoing revolution in America will continue to be education. By the year 2000, perhaps graduate degrees will be as common as college degrees today and college degrees as normal as high school diplomas, although such speedy progress would seem to be at least a little over-optimistic. One key change will involve the educational attainment figures for the population as a whole. It stands today at 10.3 years — and 12.1 years for the young 25-29 age group. In the Census of the year 2000, today's young group will be aged 65-69, and the younger cohorts, presumably, will be even better educated. It is thus not particularly daring to suggest that by 2000 our national attainment median will reach, say, 14.0 years — or the equivalent of an "average" education through the sophomore year of college. What this will mean is anybody's guess. There is no reason to suspect that a nation whose typical citizen is college-educated will behave in the same way as a high school-educated nation. Politics is just one of the more obvious elements that will perforce be changed. For politics and politicians in America, however it may appear at times, are directly reflective of the society. As a frontier nation we had a vogue of frontier politicians, as a rural nation our politicians turned rural, as an urban nation our leaders reflected big-city values. Appealing in the future to an ever more highly educated populace, our new politicians will increasingly be educated politicians.

Hopefully, educated politicians serving an educated electorate will pass enlightened legislation for the betterment of all. There is, of course, no such guarantee nor even conclusive evidence that this will happen. Hitler's Germany was one of the best-educated nations in Europe, certainly in 1939 better-educated than the Poland it was preparing to butcher. It has been remarked that only an educated man — like Goebbels or Himmler — can be a true sadist, and it should be remembered forever that the perpetrators of Auschwitz and Bergen-Belsen were neither illiterate nor ill-educated — only immoral and insane.

So then, increased education provides only the conditions in which a better or bettering society can flourish. Education in itself offers no ironclad guarantees against fascism, communism, or any other threat. We may hope that education will bolster the citizenry, and indeed, as the future unrolls we feel this will happen — but it will

not happen strictly as cause and effect, nor will it happen if everyone relaxes and thinks that it will automatically occur.

Income. Real incomes have been going up steadily for many decades — actually centuries. By the year 2000 median family income in America will certainly surpass the $10,000 per year mark, and even $15,000 is not too wild a guess, for after all, real family income climbed by 37 percent in the one decade from 1950 to 1960. If that rate should continue, the figure by the year 2000 would be well over $25,000 per year. At first glance this would seem to be enough so that our "needs" would be satiated — but don't bet on it. A three-month vacation on Venus will cost plenty and the 1999 electrodynamic Chevrolet may well have automatic controls, superb safety features, and whiz along a few feet above the ground. However it rides, it will not be cheap by any means. Education will cost more and last longer. Whether the dollars come from taxes or directly from private pocketbooks is of little relevance. Medical care is another cost item that is headed ever upward. One prediction seems safe: there will be plenty of goods and services to spend our money on. A second: most of us will not have quite enough to live the kind of lives we want to live.

Occupation. The question that haunts many today is this: what will we do? We already hear that society's next major problem is to "produce consumers" who will be able to loll around creatively while glistening automated machines do all the work. Do not believe it.

It is true that automation eliminates many jobs, but it is also true that society, in its relentless march, sometimes rolling, sometimes limping, creates jobs as it eliminates others. When the dropout rate falls, more high school teachers are needed; as the typical high school student becomes the typical college student, more college teachers are needed; as open-heart surgery becomes an everyday remedy, teams of ten medical people are needed to operate on a single stricken individual who used to provide work for only one — the undertaker. Above and beyond all that, if we continue to say we want to go to the moon, the price tag is 30 billion dollars in jobs and materials. And if the moon costs 30 billion dollars for the first ride, how many jobs is it going to cost to go to Venus, for we'll be headed for Venus and Mars within forty years, just as fifty years after the invention of the airplane we were in orbit.

Here, under the moon, are things that must be done on earth. Take, for example, 1 billion uneducated earthlings and teach them to read, write, add, and know the history of their own planet. That, at the rate of twenty students per teacher, would require 50 million new teachers, all of whom will pay taxes in order to send other earthlings to the floors of the ocean and to explore the inner secrets of life itself. What will we do? Why, we're just beginning to really do things.

Unemployment and automation are both question marks and as problems could become more grievous before they get better. But these are problems of faulty labor distribution and are not the same as a lack of things to do or of too many people to do them. We must (and will) learn to produce millions of teachers and to distribute them where they are needed. We may eventually cut to a thirty-hour work week or a four-day work week, and then again we may not; we may give adults instead of school children a two-month vacation, but if we do, it will be a long way from a tragedy. These developments will come to us only when and if our society has earned them, when we can produce a healthy enough fraction of what we need without working five days a week to do it. The early retirement at the end of a day, a week, or a career will not come as a punishment meted out by machines whose production we are unable to control. We will continue to have

things to do because society is an organic, responsive mechanism, and men want to do things: men want to fly to the moon, to cure cancer, to sell vacuum cleaners and to build skyscrapers.

Will a four-day week or a six-hour work day provoke an enforced leisure that will madden men with inactivity? Doubtful. Those who cannot abide coming home from work at four instead of five or six or seven will find some other ways to keep busy for another hour or two a day, just as today our more compulsive citizens are more than able to keep themselves busy seven days a week. The rest of us will welcome the extra hours for all manner of activities.

"Things." The past forty years brought spacecraft, television, dishwashers, air conditioners, penicillin, fluorescent lights, computers, synthetic fibers, polio vaccines, and atomic bombs. What new things the next forty years will see is anybody's guess, but this much can be postulated without much fear of going wrong: we face an America of new, newer, newest things, a profusion and abundance of new things that will continue to transform life.

Some form of limited space travel seems a surety. So does increased use of peaceful atomic power. What about the things that are not as sure? Genetic control of human beings? Anti-sleep pills? Beard depilatories? And beards? Will there be facsimile machines to reproduce printed matter electronically in your living room or office, cooking devices to produce entire meals at the press of a button, walls, floors, and ceilings that clean themselves, automatic secretaries, monorail, private one-man helicopters, and a brief treatment to eliminate tooth decay? What about practical robots? Will people live to age 150?

All these things and more are possibilities to contend with in a still better America. They will be preceded, no doubt, by yet more dishwashers, air conditioners, and clothes dryers, unless of course we can come up with other remedies for dishes, hot weather, and used wet clothes. Some of the "revolutionary" new things may last only for a comparative moment in time — the revolutionary pony express lasted for seven years, the revolutionary silent movie for about twenty, and the heyday of the revolutionary river steamboat lasted for less than fifty. Today, the car, television, the printing press, electricity, and the wheel all seem well entrenched — but so did the steamboat and the trolley car.

This much we all know: it will be an exciting future. One thing the nation cannot do is stand still, nor will it. Nearly every pointer from census statistics shows progress. We have just begun, and the best is yet to come. There is an America in the future that will make present accomplishments seem like the early adolescent flexings of a human body that will one day high-jump eight feet, run the hundred in eight seconds, and put the shot eighty feet. We, and along with us the rest of the world, are approaching a Golden Age.

54.

Eric Larrabee: Automation, Jobs, and Leisure

Probably no word in modern economic life is more fraught with consequences than the word "automation." The replacement of human labor by machines is not only necessary for the continued existence of the industrial economy of the United States, and is not only the source of the unexampled ease and comfort of life as enjoyed by most of America's citizens; it also holds out the promise of realizing an age-old dream of man: a situation in which all men, not just a few, may seek the good life, and none have to sweat and strive for their subsistence. At the same time automation, partly because it has this dreamlike quality, is held by many to be the most dangerous development of our time. Indeed, many questions that arise when automation is thought about have not yet been answered — the most pressing being this: Will human beings actually seek the good life, and will they find it, when they have the opportunity; or will they turn into "sorcerer's apprentices," unable to stop the machines they have started, finally aware that they have become the servants of their own servants? These and other questions were discussed by Eric Larrabee, a former associate editor of Harper's *and the author of a book on the subject, in an article published in 1965.*

Source: *Nation*, 100th Anniversary Issue, September 20, 1965: "Time to Kill: Automation, Leisure and Jobs."

THE PARABLE OF AUTOMATION and leisure is that of the sorcerer's apprentice. Half-educated man, lured by the prospect of relief from toil, mechanizes and eliminates his work. The chores get done, idleness is achieved, but the would-be wizard finds

that he is drawn into a nightmare where the machines will not stop and his fate is to be their victim.

Man of his nature is a tool-using animal, but a machine — as Lewis Mumford was pointing out thirty years ago in *Technics and*

Civilization — is something different from a tool. It is a tool which can function independently of its operator's skill or expended energy. The difference, Mumford wrote, "lies primarily in the degree of automatism. . . ." Mechanization implies automation, and all self-controlling mechanisms are to some extent uncanny. The dancing brooms and mops of the sorcerer's workshop are only the extreme case; all machines hold possibilities for awe and terror.

Mumford's argument, in his pioneering book, was that humanity had to mechanize itself before it was ready for the machine. People had to be willing to constrict their lives, to adapt themselves to regularity and repetitiveness, before the machine would unloose its power on their behalf. For Mumford the turning point was the introduction of the mechanical clock into Western Europe about the 13th century, since the clock is the type case of automatized precision and order, and since no other machine so permeates and controls our daily lives. The history of mechanization, as Mumford, Siegfried Giedion, and others have told it, is one in which man increasingly makes himself the machine's servant and fears his master.

Automation is the currently fashionable object of that recurrent fear. In the past fifteen years, with the application of electronic computers to commercial and industrial tasks, true automation — or what some writers, following Donald N. Michael, prefer to call cybernation — has become a reality. Vast domains of hitherto human handicraft in farm, factory, office, and even executive suite can now be invaded and occupied by machines. While the depth and meaning of this invasion are still in dispute, the fears which it arouses are many and natural, most of them deriving from a fundamental fear of being dehumanized: being deprived of identity, deprived of function, deprived of meaning — that is, the fears of bureaucracy, of unemployment, and of empty leisure.

The fear of losing identity is the most individual and immediate. One is vividly made aware of becoming a punched card and a number by one's inability to communicate with institutions except through a screen of coded responses, often inappropriate and always impersonal. Though every number is in fact unique, the sense of being treated as a number is one of being reduced to a common denominator. A mechanized economy, on the face of it, seems to produce nothing but interchangeable objects and demand nothing but interchangeable men and women to operate it. The characteristic posture of youthful revolt, in an incipient age of automation, is understandably one of revulsion and flight from the prospect of stereotyped lives: identical jobs, identical cars and consumer goods, identical houses, and virtually identical spouses and children — like a row of little boxes, in the words of the modern folk song, all made out of ticky-tacky and looking just the same.

The fear of unemployment is the most general and traditional. It is general in that a threat of vanishing jobs produces the only organized response to automation, that of organized labor, whether in defiant resistance to all change or in grudging accommodation to the inevitable. It is traditional in that the arrival of automatic machinery in the textile industries of Germany, Holland, and England caused riots and brought on prohibitory edicts as early as the 17th century, and eventually reached a symbolic climax in Yorkshire with the Luddite riots of 1812, which have given their name to an attitude of hatred for machines and the desire to smash them. So deeply does this history permeate the world of learning that C. P. Snow, in his *Two Cultures and the Scientific Revolution*, was constrained to describe all humanistic intellectuals as "natural Luddites."

The fear of leisure participates in these other fears, but it is neither so impingent nor specific. It is, by comparison, a fear one feels on behalf of others. Leisure is a recent arrival on the agenda of officially defined "problems"; as long as there was not enough of it to go round, it could be regarded as an undoubted good, as indeed the rare but indispensable ingredient of art and high culture. Leisure in this context is not merely inactivity or time free from labor, like the unoccupied but unusable time of the prisoner or the peon sleeping in the sun. It is disposable time, time paid for by work, whether your own or someone else's. Leisure is the luxury and the burden of conscious choice; it compels a statement of what you would do if left to your own devices — a definition, for yourself and others, of who and what you are. The machine has democratized this type of leisure, making gifts of it to many who never before possessed it, until one can now legitimately speak of Mass Leisure, an unprecedented phenomenon in which enormous numbers of people have not only free time but the resources to do with it what they will.

The fear of leisure is at base the fear of boredom, of what the medieval monks called *acedia* or what Robert M. MacIver has called "the great emptiness," the restlessness that comes upon us when we have time and nothing to do with it, or when we look inward and find nothing there. Modern experiments in sensory deprivation (in which the subject spends as much time as he can tolerate at rest in a sightless, soundless cubicle) have emphasized the obvious: that if you force a man to do literally nothing he will eventually go mad. Deprived of variety, the mind begins to oscillate and empty itself until a new message, whether in brainwashing or a mystical conversion, comes to it radiant with ineffable truth. Multiply individual boredom by the millions and you have all the unattractive attributes of mass culture: the worst of the mass media and the ever present possibility of mass hysteria. "When men and women find nothing within themselves but emptiness," in the words of the *Report of the Commission on the Humanities* last year, "they turn to trivial and narcotic amusements, and the society of which they are a part becomes socially delinquent and politically unstable."

When leisure was limited to a minority class, the burden of it could be borne, so to speak, vicariously. What Veblen called conspicuous consumption by that minority had to be conspicuous in order to allow the majority to watch, to derive that paradoxical pleasure the employed multitudes have always seemed to get from the spectacle of the idle rich being ostentatiously unemployed. Envy is not eliminated, to be sure, so that people at any given level of social stratification — given the chance — tend to adopt the leisure styles of the strata immediately above them, with the regrettable consequence that the 20th century middle class exhausts itself (and strains the available facilities) trying to behave like the landed aristocracy of the 19th. Also, it is a question whether vacations for recreation (which is to say, recovery from work) can properly be defined as leisure at all, and the frantic exhaustion which characterizes them is a telling weapon in the debating armory of those to whom mass leisure is a contradiction in terms.

Old-fashioned optimism about the indolent paradise which automation will bring, as you might expect, is more likely to flourish today in the Soviet Union than in the United States. Mihajlo Mihajlov, a Yugoslav teacher of literature, who published in the Belgrade monthly *Delo* an account of his visit to Moscow during the summer of 1964 (reprinted in translation in *The New Leader*), tells of how surprised he was to find even a Westernized intellectual like Ilya Ehrenburg completely doctrinaire and inflexible about the coming future in which machines will liberate mankind from work and "people will read a lot, listen to music, conduct intelligent conversations. . . ."

The American experience with a declining work week (from sixty-six hours in the mid-19th century down nearly to forty by the mid-20th) has already been extensive enough to induce profound doubts and, where an even shorter work week has been tried for any length of time — in Akron, Ohio, for example, as described for *The Nation* by Harvey Swados in 1958 — the most notable result is moonlighting, an increase in the number of men who hold two jobs at once. Perhaps the only reasonable balance between naïve hope and premature despair is the point so clearly and forehandedly made by the Canadians E. W. Leaver and J. J. Brown in their *Fortune* article, "Machines Without Men," in 1946, one of the earliest announcements of automation's imminent arrival. "The new machines," they wrote, "will force the issue, force society to find better use for men than to make them the mechanical operators of machines."

But what are the alternatives? The potentiality of leisure for self-cultivation is one that, historically, no more than a minority has been allowed to exploit. Though no evidence exists that this limitation is ordained by natural law, since lifting it has not been tried, writers of an elitist persuasion have traditionally maintained that it was — that culture of necessity had to be supported by a few, and those happy few supported by the rest. "On inequality," as Clive Bell bluntly put it in his little book *Civilization* (1928), "all civilizations have stood." Now that such outright snobbery is no longer respectable, this view is less often heard, but similar reservations about mass leisure are entertained by those to whom true leisure seems unattainable in a society organized around work, as ours still is.

Leisure in a civilized sense is a form of inner equilibrium and grace which cannot simply be ordered up as part of a three-week holiday package. As long as people define themselves in terms of their work, in work will their deepest satisfactions lie; and the image of unlimited leisure will be insep-

arable from a threat of self-deprivation and loss. "What we require," as Michael Harrington has said, "and this is particularly difficult for English-speaking countries, is an end to the Protestant Ethic that a man establishes his worth in the eyes of his neighbor and his God, and works out his eternal salvation by doing drudgery and engaging in saving."

It is no accident, if the phrase may be used, that Michael Harrington is the author of an influential book on contemporary American poverty and that he spoke these words (over the Chicago radio station WFMT) as a member of the Ad Hoc Committee on the Triple Revolution, a private group which is trying to generate public concern over automation (along with civil rights and thermonuclear war) as part of an interlocked crisis for our times. Members of the committee vary in the emphasis they put on one aspect or another, but in outline they hold that automation is coming on a great deal faster than any preparations being made to meet it, and that a major social disaster is implicit in the efforts of the dispossessed minorities, especially the Negroes, to move upward into those very jobs which automation will destroy just before they get there. The economist Robert Theobald, one of the committee members, took the extreme position on the same radio program that within the present decade "most of the new factories, the new public works, will employ machines rather than men and that it will be absolutely impossible to give everybody a job."

The consequences would be so far-reaching, if this conclusion were accepted as a base for public policy, that the conclusion itself is naturally being challenged. Charles E. Silberman, in a *Fortune* magazine series on "Technology and the Labor Market," has said of the Ad Hoc Committee's predictions that "nothing of the sort is happening," that no fully automated process for any major product exists anywhere in the

United States, and that employment of manufacturing production workers has actually increased by one million in the past three and a half years. At a national conference on automation in March 1965, sponsored by the American Bankers Association, the popular viewpoint seemed to be that no one really knew how many jobs had been destroyed by automation since those industries which had automated the most had also been expanding the most in employment. Yet Charles Silberman himself willingly agrees with his adversaries about the long-term trend. "Sooner or later," he writes, "of course, we will have the technical capability to substitute machines for men in most of the functions men now perform" — a confession which carries weight, coming from this quarter, even if it seems to imply that the future is clearer than the present.

The conclusion Robert Theobald draws from this minimal possibility, and from the economy which secular increases in productivity have already brought about, is that we must immediately start reconciling ourselves to the inevitability of paying people merely to exist. Theobald's latest book, *Free Men and Free Markets,* ends with a ringing demand for what he calls "an absolute constitutional right to an income." This concept, he says, "would guarantee to every citizen of the United States, and to every person who has resided within the United States for a period of five consecutive years, the right to an income from the federal government sufficient to enable him to live with dignity."

Theobald's proposal has the qualities of clarity and excess. As Leaver and Brown said of automation, it forces the issue; there could hardly be a more concrete reduction to cases of what it means to substitute a Keynesian doctrine of consumption for the Protestant Ethic. Anyone who wants to argue with Theobald has got to propose some better solution of what to do with econom-

ically no-longer-necessary people, or else propound some competitive morality to the mild humanitarianism which has shaped the present, almost worldwide welfare state. One can take the position that humanity is simply not ready yet to stop working, that it has not yet found anything remotely suitable as a substitute. As William Faulkner told an interviewer from the *Paris Review* in 1956, "One of the saddest things is that the only thing a man can do eight hours a day, day after day, is work. You can't eat eight hours a day nor drink for eight hours a day nor make love for eight hours — all you can do for eight hours is work. Which is the reason why man makes himself and everybody else so miserable and unhappy." But to differ with Theobald one has to be as categorical, if perhaps not so ironic, as Faulkner.

To be sure, when Faulkner spoke of work he spoke as an artist, knowing full well that what he did as an artist for eight hours a day was in fact hard work. In principle, there is no reason why the challenge and satisfaction he derived from the craft of novelist could not be found by the multitudes in similarly uneconomic activities, from the arts as such to the more mundane and less honorific arts of daily living. For the individual's well-being it is the struggle rather than the goal which matters, provided only the goal is defined as admirable by one's own standard and that of one's peers. Theoretically, again, we can conceive of a society superficially not too different from our own in which self-respect could be based on personal achievement of a purely aesthetic or even spiritual kind, but the word "achievement" itself is a booby trap packed explosively tight with traditional Western assumptions about virtue and individuality.

A truly Keynesian aesthetic would be built around the ephemeral experience, since this is the only thing we can all consume indefinitely, and it would therefore put as high a value on a dew-tipped blade of grass as on Beethoven's Ninth. There is just not room enough, either physically or psychologically, for everyone to be Beethoven all at once; we would have to be seeking fulfillment in self-expression while denying ourselves permanence, and to say as much is to ask for a reversal of inherited criteria in art as wrenching to individual ego and integrity as the economic idea of becoming a permanently depauperized ward of the government.

The consequences of denying mankind the one thing it can do eight hours a day are not likely to be manifest immediately, since they are so various and interrelated as to resemble a generalized psychic malnutrition of the body social rather than the onslaught of any single disease. But certainly it requires no tight certainty about cause and effect to observe that industrial democracy needs a number of incentives spread through the population in order to function properly, and that it functions very poorly without them.

For one thing, the whole machinery of upgrading deprived social classes, such as the immigrants to America, has called for ambition and discipline on their part which today's deprived, for good and evident reasons, no longer share. Character is hard enough to come by even in the awareness that it generally profits a white, upper-middle-class male to apply himself and behave decently; take away that awareness and a decay of morale sets in, spreading inescapably into education and the formation of coming generations. The sense of hopelessness which pervades the New York Public School system, as Martin Mayer has described it in the *New York Times Magazine*, is but the mirror image of hopelessness in its pupils' future. "We have just got to accept the fact," a junior-high-school principal told Mayer, gesturing at an assembly of 900 Negro and Puerto Rican students, "that half

of these children will never hold a job in their lives."

Their misfortune is to have been born into an overdeveloped society engaged in the headlong pursuit of economic goals it has long since left behind; all of its habits are organized around the struggle for material sufficiency and it doesn't know how to break them. These several hundred children are not useless by any objective measure; they are merely classified as useless by contrast with the energy and sophistication of a world metropolis. In any other surroundings there would be plenty for them to do. Remove them to a South Sea island or Siberia and they would reveal all the motivations and resources which New York City has bred in them but will presently deny them the scope to exercise. They learn as victims what it means to belong to an insufficiently utopian society. The fault is not in Manhattan Island's dynamism but in the failure of its aspirations to keep up with its capabilities, so that surplus human energies are left unengaged — surplus, that is, in the sense of being the most convenient to disregard. In an unequal race for a previously awarded prize, most of the contestants are superfluous, and the vulnerable minorities — in pain, in public disgrace, and mainly in ignorance — have but the honor of being first to make the discovery.

For it is absurd to suppose, given the amount of ugliness and suffering the world still affords, that we have run out of work; what we have run out of is a set of organized connections between purposes crying out to be achieved and people crying out for purpose. Utopianism is one of the names for a connection between aims and efforts. It has to be a serious fantasy in that means must exist for pursuing it, but it must nonetheless remain fantastic to the extent of picturing a future worth extravagant risks to win. Automation is not the villain of this parable but only the occasion for it;

there is so far no disequilibrium caused by increased productivity which could not be restored to balance by raising social goals. Automation forces the issue, as Leaver and Brown might have said, by compelling a given society to decide what its goals are going to be. It is a weapon put in man's hand like the dagger of the Gurkha: once drawn, it must be used.

If a reversal of the Protestant Ethic seems too much to ask, or an America given over to culture and contemplation is unrecognizable, then the reader should at least remember that utopianism is a national habit of long standing, and that the nation was in part created by men who expected sound institutions to nourish prosperity, and prosperity in turn to nourish art. "I must study politics and war," wrote one of them, "that my sons may have liberty to study mathematics and philosophy. My sons ought to study mathematics and philosophy, geography, natural history and naval architecture, navigation, commerce, and agriculture, in order to give their children a right to study painting, poetry, music, architecture. . . ." The prophecy was John Adams', and the last portion of it has yet to be realized.

55.

RALPH NADER: Unsafe Automotive Design

The relation between Americans and the automobile is nothing other than a love affair. (The citizens of other nations seem to feel the same way; they adopt cars with the same enthusiasm as soon as they become available.) But like most love affairs, this one is dangerous, and as Ralph Nader points out in the selection reprinted here, the automobile has caused a vast amount of suffering as well as providing immense pleasure and utility. When Nader's Unsafe at Any Speed *appeared in 1965, there were already rumblings of discontent about the automobile's disadvantages — traffic jams and air pollution as well as accidents — but this book seemed to crystallize the feelings of many persons and almost singlehandedly resulted in pressure on Detroit and on the federal government to devise adequate safety standards for the American automobile. The following selection comprises the preface to Nader's book and a portion of its concluding chapter.*

Source: *Unsafe at Any Speed,* New York, 1966.

FOR OVER HALF A CENTURY the automobile has brought death, injury, and the most inestimable sorrow and deprivation to millions of people. With Medea-like intensity, this mass trauma began rising sharply four years ago, reflecting new and unexpected ravages by the motor vehicle. A 1959 Department of Commerce report projected that 51,000 persons would be killed by automobiles in 1975. That figure will probably be reached in 1965, a decade ahead of schedule.

A transportation specialist, Wilfred Owen, wrote in 1946, "There is little question that the public will not tolerate for long an annual traffic toll of 40,000 to

Logos — Pix from Publix

Ralph Nader, Washington lawyer, writer, and critic
of the automotive industry

50,000 fatalities." Time has shown Owen
to be wrong. Unlike aviation, marine, or
rail transportation, the highway-transport
system can inflict tremendous casualties and
property damage without in the least affecting the viability of the system. Plane
crashes, for example, jeopardize the attraction of flying for potential passengers and
therefore strike at the heart of the air-
transport economy. They motivate preventative efforts. The situation is different on
the roads.

Highway accidents were estimated to
have cost this country, in 1964, $8.3 billion
in property damage, medical expenses, lost
wages, and insurance overhead expenses.
Add an equivalent sum to comprise roughly
the indirect costs and the total amounts to
over 2 percent of the gross national product. But these are not the kind of costs
which fall on the builders of motor vehicles
(excepting a few successful law suits for
negligent construction of the vehicle) and
thus do not pinch the proper foot. Instead,
the costs fall to users of vehicles, who are in

no position to dictate safer automobile designs.

In fact, the gigantic costs of the highway
carnage in this country support a service industry. A vast array of services — medical,
police, administrative, legal, insurance, automotive repair, and funeral — stand
equipped to handle the direct and indirect
consequences of accident-injuries. Traffic accidents create economic demands for these
services running into billions of dollars. It is
in the post-accident response that lawyers
and physicians and other specialists labor.
This is where the remuneration lies and this
is where the talent and energies go. Working in the area of prevention of these casualties earns few fees. Consequently our society has an intricate organization to handle
direct and indirect aftermaths of collisions.
But the true mark of a humane society
must be what it does about *prevention* of
accident injuries, not the cleaning up of
them afterward.

Unfortunately, there is little in the dynamics of the automobile accident industry
that works for its reduction. Doctors, lawyers, engineers, and other specialists have
failed in their primary professional ethic: to
dedicate themselves to the prevention of accident-injuries. The roots of the unsafe-
vehicle problem are so entrenched that the
situation can be improved only by the forg-
ing of new instruments of citizen action.
When thirty practicing physicians picketed
for safe auto design at the New York International Automobile Show on April 7,
1965, their unprecedented action was the
measure of their desperation over the inaction of the men and institutions in government and industry who have failed to provide the public with the vehicle safety to
which it is entitled. The picketing surgeons,
orthopedists, pediatricians, and general practitioners marched in protest because the
existing medical, legal, and engineering organizations have defaulted.

A great problem of contemporary life is

how to control the power of economic interests which ignore the harmful effects of their applied science and technology. The automobile tragedy is one of the most serious of these man-made assaults on the human body. The history of that tragedy reveals many obstacles which must be overcome in the taming of any mechanical or biological hazard which is a by-product of industry or commerce. Our society's obligation to protect the "body rights" of its citizens with vigorous resolve and ample resources requires the precise, authoritative articulation and front-rank support which is being devoted to civil rights.

This country has not been entirely laggard in defining values relevant to new contexts of a technology laden with risks. The postwar years have witnessed an historic broadening, at least in the courts, of the procedural and substantive rights of the injured and the duties of manufacturers to produce a safe product. Judicial decisions throughout the fifty states have given living meaning to Walt Whitman's dictum, "If anything is sacred, the human body is sacred." Mr. Justice Jackson in 1953 defined the duty of the manufacturers by saying,

> Where experiment or research is necessary to determine the presence or the degree of danger, the product must not be tried out on the public, nor must the public be expected to possess the facilities or the technical knowledge to learn for itself of inherent but latent dangers. The claim that a hazard was not foreseen is not available to one who did not use foresight appropriate to his enterprise.

It is a lag of almost paralytic proportions that these values of safety concerning consumers and economic enterprises, reiterated many times by the judicial branch of government, have not found their way into legislative policy-making for safer automobiles. Decades ago legislation was passed changing the pattern of private business investments to accommodate more fully the safety value on railroads, in factories, and more recently on ships and aircraft. In transport, apart from the motor vehicle, considerable progress has been made in recognizing the physical integrity of the individual. There was the period when railroad workers were killed by the thousands and the editor of *Harper's* could say late in the last century: "So long as brakes cost more than trainmen, we may expect the present sacrificial method of car-coupling to be continued." But injured trainmen did cause the railroads some operating dislocations; highway victims cost the automobile companies next to nothing and the companies are not obliged to make use of developments in science technology that have demonstrably opened up opportunities for far greater safety than any existing safety features lying unused on the automobile companies' shelves.

A principal reason why the automobile has remained the only transportation vehicle to escape being called to meaningful public account is that the public has never been supplied the information nor offered the quality of competition to enable it to make effective demands through the marketplace and through government for a safe, nonpolluting, and efficient automobile that can be produced economically. The consumer's expectations regarding automotive innovations have been deliberately held low and mostly oriented to very gradual annual style changes. The specialists and researchers outside the industry who could have provided the leadership to stimulate this flow of information by and large chose to remain silent, as did government officials.

The persistence of the automobile's immunity over the years has nourished the continuance of that immunity, recalling Francis Bacon's insight: "He that will not apply new remedies must expect new evils, for time is the greatest innovator."

The accumulated power of decades of effort by the automobile industry to strengthen its control over car design is reflected today in the difficulty of even beginning to bring it to justice. The time has not come to discipline the automobile for safety; that time came over four decades ago. But that is not cause to delay any longer what should have been accomplished in the 1920s.

ONLY THE FEDERAL GOVERNMENT can undertake the critical task of stimulating and guiding public and private initiatives for safety. A democratic government is far better equipped to resolve competing interests and determine whatever is required from the vast spectrum of available science and technology to achieve a safer highway-transport environment than are firms whose all-absorbing aim is higher and higher profits. The public which bears the impact of the auto industry's safety policy must have a direct role in deciding that policy. The decision as to what an adequate standard of public responsibility in vehicle safety should be ought not to be left to the manufacturers regardless of their performance. But the extraordinarily low quality of that performance certainly accentuates the urgent need for publicly defined and enforced standards of safety.

Two industry policies are especially inimical to a rational quest for safer automobiles. First is the all-pervasive secrecy that obstructs freedom of communication in the scientific and engineering communities. Company engineers are happy to benefit from the work of university engineering professors, but in return the university engineers are offered excuses about proprietary data, however purely technical or related strictly to safety it may be. Not only does this industry secrecy impede the search for knowledge to save lives — presumably a common dedication for all men — but it shields the automobile makers from being called to account for what they are doing or not doing. Secrecy preserves their control

over how quickly safety innovations will be introduced.

The perfect illustration of this is the curtain Ford has kept over its numerous prototype safety cars during the past decade — not to mention industry opposition to the New York state prototype car project and to a similar bill on the federal level introduced by Senator Gaylord Nelson. Secrecy permits the industry to enjoy a double standard of proof. For example, Liberty Mutual Insurance Company's demonstration safety cars have been criticized by auto company representatives on the legitimate ground that they were never crash-tested. Liberty's cars were scheduled to be crash-tested in late 1965, with public recording of the data by Derwyn Severy's group at UCLA.

But the automobile industry had no plans to expose its vehicles to the same treatment. While it properly states that safety features have to be proven before adoption, it exempts from this stringent testing such features as sharp fins, glare-ridden chrome, hardtops, wraparound windshields, undersized tires, smaller brake drums, and front placement of fuel tanks in rear-engine cars (considered a dangerous collision hazard by many engineering authorities, whose findings are supported by mounting accident data).

The second policy inimical to the quest for safer automobiles is the industry's research and development commitment. Probably no other major manufacturing industry in this country devotes so few of its resources to innovations in its basic product. The automobile is not in line for any significant changes in the next two decades; this is the estimate of J. M. Bidwell of General Motors' research laboratories and is also the understanding that the Cornell Aeronautical Laboratory representatives carried away from extensive consultations with company executives and engineers.

Many scientists and engineers in government or outside the industry concur with William Stieglitz's observation: "It may well be that the evolutionary development of the automobile from the horseless carriage has gone as far as it can and that a totally fresh approach is required." This would mean innovation in an industry that has slowed innovation to a snail's pace, as shown by a glance at the list of "automotive highlights" since 1900 which *Automotive News* prints in its annual almanac issue.

George Romney pointed to this problem before the Kefauver subcommittee in 1958 when he declared, "All companies in the automobile industry have the benefit of the vast research organizations of the supplier industries and companies, and that area of research vastly outweighs the area of research and improvement that is occurring right in the motor-vehicle industry itself." Romney cited among other illustrations power steering and improved application of steel to automobiles as supplier contributions. The automobile industry has also adopted as its own a number of important advances that came from military transportation research.

An idea of how meager a sum the automobile industry spends for safety innovations was given in 1958 by Andrew Kucher, vice-president for engineering and research at the Ford Motor Company. His was the only public estimate given up to the summer of 1965. Speaking for the Automobile Manufacturers Association, Kucher told an audience of motor-vehicle administrators:

Because we are thoroughly sold on this philosophy, the motor-vehicle manufacturers spend between $5 million and $6 million each year in safety-oriented research programs. This expenditure is aimed at solving basic problems and also is a searching for new and better solutions to old problems. You may be interested to know how this research effort is budgeted. One company [Ford Motor Company], for example, estimates that about one-third of its annual safety research budget of $1 million is devoted to the problem of safely packaging passengers. Another third goes to safety control of vehicle components, and the last third to projects such as lighting and development of general safety equipment. In individual company organizations, brake development programs cost between $200,000 and $250,000 annually. Studies of vehicle controls and stability range from $150,000 to $350,000 in specific company budgets. Visibility and lighting problems each are accorded budgets in the $50,000-range.

Even granting Kucher a margin for exaggeration, the sum of $5 million amounted to less than one-twentieth of 1 percent of the industry's gross sales in vehicles that year. Ford was spending $333,000 on second-collision research and at that time was assumed to be in the vanguard of the industry in such work. There is no evidence that any greater sums were spent in succeeding years.

In July 1965, after refusing to tell the Ribicoff subcommittee how much it spends on second-collision safety research, General Motors released a statement saying that it spent $193 million in 1964 on "safety, durability, and reliability." . . . Not to be outdone, Ford and Chrysler followed by stating that they spent $138 million and $78 million respectively in the areas delimited by General Motors. Ford's breakdown was more specific and listed 1965 expenditures of $700,000 for its new automotive safety center and $300,000 for designing and building of prototype safety cars — indicating the outer limits of their research on crashworthiness. . . .

All these multi-million-dollar figures for safety and reliability did not fool anyone with any familiarity of the industry's actual commitments to the development and application of safety innovations. In 1965, General Motors' chief safety engineer, Kenneth Stonex, was still writing to individual physicians asking them if they could give him any data about maximum loads that a motorist can absorb should he strike the steering wheel or instrument panel. Ford was lending its new cars to Dr. Huelke to drive around for a week at a time so he could advise them that sharp edges or points inside the vehicle could hurt people. And Chrysler was dilatorily arguing that it was not getting enough police data on accident causation, while fully knowing that the Cornell data, the Harvard and Northwestern studies, and particularly the rapidly increasing variety and equality of human-simulation techniques, statistical and computer tools, and crash-testing permitted them many avenues for developing and evaluating safer designs.

Scientists in the Bureau of Public Roads estimate that the combined public and private support of highway traffic research (defined as the design and testing of safety measures and techniques) was $8 million at the most in 1964 — the highest to date. . . . At the $8-million level, this country is spending about $166 in research for every traffic fatality, without taking into account the more than 4 million injuries every year.

With some 1,200 or less fatalities annually in civil aviation, the federal government spent between $35 million and $64 million each year from 1960 to 1965 on research and development for greater air safety. This was in addition to what was spent for safety work by the aircraft industry itself. Expenditure of $64 million for 1,200 fatalities means over $53,000 spent in safety research per fatality. The Federal Aviation Agency and the Civil Aeronautics Board spent about $5 million to determine the cause of two Electra turboprop transport crashes in 1959 and 1960 and to find out how to correct the defect in other Electras.

Patently, such neglect of highway safety research is a rebuke to an affluent, technologically advanced society. The federal government's delay of decades in facing up to basic initiatives in vehicle safety is not without its price, for now the solution of the highway safety problem is fragmented and scattered among numerous federal agencies, each jealously guarding its presumed prerogatives and all either staunchly supporting or frightfully cowed by the automobile industry. . . .

The federal effort in highway safety in general and vehicle safety in particular suffers from the inadequate legislative authority of the groups that are required to administer it, from insufficient funds allocated to the effort, and from the lack of administrative consolidation that could launch a concrete program with a concrete purpose that would have the kind of high-level support that complex programs in atomic energy and space ventures have. But the highway safety effort has not received this high-level support (though President Johnson's highway beautification program did recently).

On February 20, 1957, when he was still a senator, Lyndon B. Johnson expressed on the Senate floor a thought that regrettably is still true. He called the "deadly toll of highway accidents" a problem whose "very familiarity has bred either contempt or indifference. . . . We cannot abolish the automobile, but neither can we ignore the problems that it brings to us. There is a responsibility here which we must face." The senator was proposing the establishment of an automobile and highway safety division in the Department of Health, Education, and Welfare that, among other objectives, would "promote research into improved designs for automobiles. . . ."

A federal research and development facility where problems of automobile safety could be comprehensively examined and solved is only the first stage of greater federal authority extending to the establishment and enforcement of safety standards and their continuous upgrading. This function in turn must form a part of a larger highway transport research and development program for more efficient and safe travel, by means of a more advanced integration of the functions of highway and vehicle. . . .

The advantages of taking the Bureau of Public Roads out of the Department of Commerce and making it into a separate entity (called, say, the Federal Highway Transportation Agency) directly responsible to the President should be seriously explored. It could be the first step toward creating an overall Department of Transportation.

If the government is to be made capable of securing continually safer automotive design, it will require a sharply focused supportive constituency that is dedicated and skilled in pursuing the interests of safety. For until sufficient engineers, lawyers, physicians, and other specialists whose income and skills are pertinent to the building of the automobile or to its post-collision problems — until these people assume the roles of leadership that their superior knowledge makes available to them, legislators and administrators will continue to display "contempt or indifference." . . .

The regulation of the automobile must go through three stages — the stage of public awareness and demand for action, the stage of legislation, and the stage of continuing administration. Since automobile safety ideally should keep pace with advancing technological capabilities, administrators have to do more than hold the line; they have to advance it. Without full disclosure, congressional review, and participation by a consumer-oriented constituency of professionally qualified citizens, obsolescence and bureaucratic inertia will stifle the purpose of even a properly drafted law. Motorists may

benefit from the efforts of dedicated and selfless champions performing this persistent vigilance, but these efforts will not be enough without a residual vigilance throughout the consumer public.

This vigilance can be kept up simply by understanding a few facts about automobile safety. First, safety measures that do not require people's voluntary and repeated cooperation are more effective than those that do. Second, the sequence of events that leads to an accident injury can be interrupted by effective measures even before there is a complete understanding of the causal chain. Apply these two cardinal principles of safety policy, proven in the control of epidemics and machine hazards, to highway safety and the spotlight turns on the engineering of the automobile. Furthermore, our society knows a good deal more about building safer machines than it does about getting people to behave safely in an almost infinite variety of driving situations that are overburdening the driver's perceptual and motor capacities. In the 20 or 40 million accidents a year, only a crashworthy vehicle can minimize the effects of the second collision. Vehicle deficiencies are more important to correct than human inadequacies simply because they are easier to analyze and to remedy. And whether motorists are momentarily careless or intoxicated, or are driving normally when they are struck by another vehicle, is entirely irrelevant to the responsibility of the automobile makers to build safe cars.

Dr. Bernard Fox, a distinguished psychologist in the Division of Accident Prevention, after spending many years in research on the "human factor," concludes that the most economically, administratively, and technically feasible safety measure, and the one with the quickest and greatest results in saving lives and preventing injuries, is a crashworthy automobile. This is not a startling observation, except that it comes finally from a federal researcher who has stated his candid judgment.

A leading crash researcher and biophysicist, Dr. Carl Clark of The Martin Co. states:

> Instead of the 40 mph barrier collision survival being a "spectacular accomplishment," it should be a routine requirement of proper car and restraint design. Indeed, without major modifications of car structure and size, by applying what we now know about crash protection, a fixed barrier impact of 45 mph should be experienced without injury, and crashes at higher speeds should be survivable.

(A 45 mph crash into a fixed barrier, like a tree or stone wall, generates, for example, the same forces as a car striking the rear end of a stationary vehicle at more than 75 mph.)

Engineers are not noted for making metaphors, but a safety engineer for one of the Big Three companies inadvertently offered an illuminating one to *Automotive News* (August 30, 1965) in describing his work: "It's like walking into a room in which there are a bunch of ping-pong balls on the floor. Then you throw another ball in the middle and try to keep track of what happens." That last ping-pong ball was safety. Dr. Donald Huelke, one of the few outsiders to be brought into the inner sanctums of design studios and given the confidence of the three or four safety engineers at General Motors and Ford, reported: "The auto industry has a small, dedicated group of individuals — almost a fifth column — working for car designs of greater safety."

One ping-pong ball among many presents a low order of probability. A fifth column indicates the activity is subversive of the dominant way.

At the basis of such symptoms and impressions is the unwillingness of the automobile companies to dedicate their engineering and investment energies to the kind of first-line research and development that will produce the innovations that can make the automobile responsive to the safety requirements of motorists. Over the past decade in particular, the possibilities for completely new approaches to be translated into mass-production hardware are almost programable given certain allocations of men and resources. The gap between existing design and attainable safety has widened enormously in the postwar period. As these attainable levels of safety rise, so do the moral imperatives to use them. For the tremendous range of opportunity of science-technology — by providing easier and better solutions — serves to clarify ethical choices and to ease the conditions for their exercise by the manufacturers.

There are men in the automobile industry who know both the technical capability and appreciate the moral imperatives. But their timidity and conformity to the rigidities of the corporate bureaucracies have prevailed. When and if the automobile is designed to free millions of human beings from unnecessary mutilation, these men, like their counterparts in universities and government who knew of the suppression of safer automobile development yet remained silent year after year, will look back with shame on the time when common candor was considered courage.

Marilyn Silverstone from Magnum

Crowd of schoolchildren in an Indian city

THE THIRD WORLD

The Cold War strategy of the balance of terror was, in its own terms, quite successful. After years of bloc-politics and arms-racing, the antagonists were essentially equal in influence and destructive capability. During the late 1950s and early 1960s, however, there emerged between the horns of the dilemma the Third World, a group of small African, Latin-American, and Asian nations, undeveloped, mostly of colonial heritage and consequently strongly nationalistic, and totally uncommitted in the major power struggle. A collection of nations forced into concert by circumstance and the realities of power, this Third World was primarily interested in economic and social self-development. Neither American capitalism nor communism was particularly relevant to its needs, and attempts by Russia and the U.S. to tie development assistance to political alignment and even domination were sharply resented.

Leaders of the nonaligned nations drink a toast to peace at the Belgrade Conference, 1961. Center figures are Sihanouk, Cambodia; Nasser, U.A.R.; Selassie, Ethiopia; Tito, Yugoslavia; Sukarno, Indonesia; Nehru, India

Though the Third World nations did not function as an integrated power bloc — the nationalistic springs of their position rendered this impossible — they were able to agree in their independence. Regional association was relatively successful, and in the United Nations the group did on occasion function as a single force. The nonaligned stance, firmly defended, forced a reassessment of American policy toward the undeveloped nations. Cold War foreign aid had generally been predicated on simple anti-communism; the U.S. was apparently willing to support any regime that proclaimed itself pro-West. With the spread of neutralism, however, American military and economic assistance became less and less overtly political in nature, and more directed to rational development of resources and peoples. The Peace Corps, created in the Kennedy administration, was the best example of non-political aid. Under this program, thousands of volunteers, trained in the language and customs of host nations, sought to bring education and technical progress to the people of undeveloped countries. The program was a major success, despite chronic underfunding.

OPPOSITE PAGE: (Bottom) U.S. wheat is used to pay Indians working on various local improvement projects in Rajasthan. (Below) Peace Corps volunteer teaching agriculture in Pakistan

Paul Conklin — Pix from Publix

John F. Kennedy in a televised press conference dealing with sending advisers to Vietnam, 1961

The increasingly authoritarian and repressive Diem regime in South Vietnam withstood popular unrest and the spectacular protests of Buddhist monks, but fell to an army coup in November 1963. A series of military governments succeeded and no political stability was achieved until June 1965 when Nguyen Cao Ky, commander of the Air Force, assumed leadership. American military aid continued through this period in an apparently fruitless effort to train and depoliticize the South Vietnamese Army and make it capable of combatting the NLF guerrilla forces.

U.S. adviser with a member of the Vietnamese Army

James Pickerell from Black Star

(Above) Saigon revolution overthrows Ngo
Dinh Diem, November 1963; (right) men in
the First Cavalry shipping out to Vietnam in
August 1965; (below) medics carrying out a
wounded G.I. under enemy fire

Vernon Merritt III from Black Star

Catherine LeRoy from Black Star

(Above) U.S. trooper puts his rifle to the head of a woman Viet Cong suspect being questioned by the Vietnamese national police

In 1961 the number of U.S. military advisers in South Vietnam passed the limit of 700 set by the 1954 Geneva agreements; by the time of Diem's fall, over 17,000 American troops were present and engaging in full combat. A huge escalation began in 1964; in response to an enigmatic incident in the Gulf of Tonkin, Congress approved a resolution empowering the President to use discretionary force to repel and prevent armed attacks on U.S. forces. Full-scale bombing of North Vietnam ensued, while U.S. forces in the South were increased to well over half a million. Military progress was doubtful; meanwhile the Ky regime resisted popular reform, and widespread corruption diverted U.S. economic aid from the displaced populace.

(Left) U.S. bombing of Phuc Yen airfield in North Vietnam; (below) jet creates a shock wave as it pulls away from a bomb drop

(Above) South Vietnamese farmer works in his rice paddy under the protection of an armored personnel carrier; (below) North Vietnamese soldiers using bicycles to transport supplies; (right) party boss Mao Tse-tung and Ho Chi Minh, leader of North Vietnam, attend a celebration honoring the tenth anniversary of communism's victory in China

¡Ni Yankis ni Rusos!
Ecuador

Costa Manos from Magnum

(Above) Sign on a wall in Riobamba, Ecuador, expressing anti-American and anti-Soviet sentiments of the people; (bottom left) boy gets water from well brought to his Colombian village through the aid of "Alianza"; (bottom right) scene along Zeppalar Beach in Chile

Costa Manos from Magnum

An optimistic proposal by President Kennedy grew into the Alliance for Progress, envisioned as a new approach to foreign aid within the hemisphere. Intended to be a cooperative effort at development and stabilization, it was seen as the best preventative for Castro-style revolution. Cuba was not included in the Alliance because of "Soviet domination" of the island. The Alliance failed to promote the reforms desperately needed in Latin America; society remained essentially feudal, government continued to be oligarchic, and little was done on either side to encourage change.

Sergio Larrain from Magnum

Fidel Castro, Communist leader of Cuba, speaking in Havana

Latin-American distrust of the United States, dating back to 19th-century interventionism and the days of gunboat- and dollar-diplomacy, had been somewhat allayed by the Good Neighbor Policy and the subsequent multilateral approach to hemisphere problems. Then in 1961 came the abortive Bay of Pigs invasion by Cuban exiles organized, financed, and trained by the CIA and the State Department. Most Latin-American governments grudgingly accepted the U.S. action on the grounds of anti-communism, but moderates and liberals were alienated both at home and abroad. The U.S. went even further and lost considerable prestige in 1965. The Dominican Republic, politically unstable since the assassination of dictator Trujillo in 1961, was at the time under a military junta; liberal elements and a portion of the Army revolted in April 1965 demanding a return to constitutional government and reinstatement of President Juan Bosch. U.S. Marines were landed, ostensibly to protect Americans in the country, and to prevent a "Communist" takeover. The occupation Marines were merged into an inter-American peace force created in May by the OAS.

(Above) Cuban exiles being trained by the United States at a camp in the Guatemalan jungle; (below) Castro's soldiers relax following their defeat of the invasion forces at the Bay of Pigs

Scenes in Santo Domingo during the intervention by the United States, 1965: (Top) Marine lines suspicious men against a wall to check them for hidden weapons; (bottom left) anti-U.S. poster in rebel zone; (bottom right) gun-carrying girls march in support of the rebels

(Top) India's first plutonium extraction plant, built at Trombay, near Bombay, with Canadian aid; (bottom left) Communist Party demonstration in New Delhi to protest U.S. bombing of North Vietnam; (bottom right) U.N. Trade and Development Conference meeting in Geneva, 1964

peace
in
butcher's
hand

American foreign policy toward the sensitive "emerging" nations of the world was complicated by several factors. It was, first of all, difficult to keep in mind the fact that terms like "democratic," "Communist," or "capitalist" had little real meaning in many areas of the world. Secondly, the heritage of the Cold War had made U.S. policy immediately suspicious of liberalizing or socially oriented movements as being possibly Communist-inspired. And, not the least, the deep involvement of American business in underdeveloped nations has created a predisposition toward the status quo.

56.

Baiting the Hook with Merchandise

*What has been called the consumer credit revolution of the twentieth century began
in the 1920s but did not explode into a social and economic problem for Americans
until the 1950s and 1960s. Basically, according to a certain view of the matter, the
revolution involved a shift from the selling of merchandise to the "selling" of debt;
and it was true enough that the credit charge on many purchases ended up by comprising
a large portion of the item's "price," and often made up all of the merchant's "profit"
on the transaction. In these circumstances it became customary to speak of "baiting
the hook with merchandise," to indicate that the retailer was more interested in getting
a customer to buy on credit than to buy for cash. Some of the practices used by "debt
merchants," as well as some of the serious dangers involved in them, were discussed
in an unsigned article in* Consumer Reports *in 1965, part of which is reprinted here.*

Source: *Consumer Reports*, September 1965: "Bait the Hook with Merchandise."

THE PLUNGE OF THE STOCK MARKET early in
the summer threw a searchlight over consumer credit for a brief period of time —
brief because both business and government
appeared to prefer focusing public attention
on other, steadier aspects of the current
economy. Even when things are shipshape,
consumer debt is an uneasy source of economic stimulation because it is cursed by a
dilemma: it must continue to grow even
larger in order to maintain its stimulating
power, and yet, as it grows, it threatens to
pierce a ceiling of safety beyond which further growth would be dangerous.

When people promise tomorrow's income to pay for today's purchases, the market for goods today is stimulated. But tomorrow is right on today's heels; and in
that early tomorrow, today becomes yesterday, and yesterday's credit purchases do
not, of course, stimulate today's demand.
On the contrary, debt for yesterday's buying limits today's demand for goods by the
amount of current purchasing power that is
tied up in debt repayments. Thus, to continue functioning as a market stimulator,
consumer credit must build up bigger and
bigger debt; and when it happens, as it can
and has, that new debts fall short of repayments on old debts, then consumer credit
reverses its economic role and becomes a
market drag rather than a stimulator. In the
terms of the trade, when debt repayments
outrun new credit extensions, consumer
credit becomes a deflationary force.

Consumer credit was not a deflationary
force, however, when the stock market fell
this past summer. On the contrary, during
the first half of 1965, consumer debt had
grown at a record rate — at such a rate, in
fact, that a slowdown in the future seemed
inevitable. The fear was that, when it came,
such a slowdown would be apt to result in
debt repayments that would exceed new extensions and that whatever deflationary
trends in the economy were being reflected
by the stock market drop would be deepened by the heavy repayment demands to
come. The *Wall Street Journal* summed up
the situation as follows:

The debt-loaded individuals would naturally be in a tight spot if their earnings declined in a recession, as would be the lenders if they couldn't get repayment. In fact, some economists believe the debt burden would intensify a downturn. As one of them . . . puts it: "When the earnings of consumers and corporations start to fall, the pinch is obviously worse if a considerable amount of debt must be paid off."

The amount of debt that has been piled up for consumers to repay is more than considerable. It is mountainous. Moreover, it has built up rapidly in the past twenty years. Back in the fall of 1945, people were just beginning to satisfy their war-starved appetites for homes and things, and especially for cars. Savings were at an all-time high then, and debt was low. Mortgage debt for urban homes was around $20 billion, and short-term debt — debt for goods and services scheduled for repayment in five years or less — was just over $5½ billion. Ten years later, in 1955, mortgage debt had grown to $88 billion, more than four times what it had been. Short-term debt had grown to $39 billion, about seven times what it had been. In another ten years, by the late summer of 1965, mortgage debt had become nearly $200 billion, ten times its 1945 level. Short-term debt had multiplied about twelve times to a total of around $80 billion.

INSTALLMENT DEBT IS DIFFERENT

SINCE THE SHORT-TERM DEBT is the more volatile, it is more worrisome. Most of it is installment debt for goods. And this kind of debt differs significantly from other kinds of debt in that the proceeds of the loans do not produce income out of which debt repayments might be made, as is the case with business or farm loans, for example. And short-term debt differs from mortgage

debt in that an equity in a house and lot can be considered as an asset, whereas the goods and services purchased on short-term credit, except for automobiles, have no substantial market value. They cannot be turned into cash to meet debt demands. Thus, short-term loans for consumption purposes are scarcely more than promises to pay, and most consumers making the promises count on future earnings to liquidate these debts. So the ratio of such debt to income is an important factor in evaluating the burden of consumer credit.

Here again the record of the past twenty years is startling. Between 1945 and 1965, disposable income tripled. During that same period, short-term consumer debt increased twelve times. Currently, according to the Federal Reserve Board, 14 percent of disposable income is tied up in debt repayments. But that is not even half the story. Not everybody has such debt. And among those who have, the distribution of debt is not even. Although who is and who isn't in debt and by how much is a controversial matter among the experts in this field, most informed commentators assume that about half the nation's families owe all the debt. On the basis of that assumption, the 14 percent figure has to be doubled before it provides a meaningful comment on the debt-income ratio, because the debt must be repaid out of the incomes of the 50 percent who owe it.

Much the same goes for personal savings figures, to which those who counsel complacency about consumer debt are fond of pointing. The Federal Reserve Board, for example, wrote in its June *Bulletin* that while most consumers rely on current income to pay debts, consumer savings were high and those with savings would be able to draw upon them should the need arise. But data on the distribution of savings are sparse, to say the least. Although some people with debt no doubt have savings too, there is little reason to believe that a significant part of the savings is in the hands of those owing most of the consumer debt.

What is involved in these calculations of the ratio of debt to income and to savings is an attempt to determine what lenders refer to as the quality of consumer debt, by which they mean simply the chance that the debt is going to be paid back without causing trouble — trouble to lenders. When a family's debt burden is so heavy that relatively small decreases in income, or small increases in demand on income (an illness, new tires, an auto repair bill, etc.) could interrupt debt repayments, the quality of that family's debt is questionable. In other words, poor-quality credit means overcommitted families, families in trouble as well as lenders.

THE VANISHING PRUDENCE OF LENDERS

OVERCOMMITMENT has long been recognized as a hazard attending the use of debt to finance consumption. The human tendency to discount the future for the present has been noted over the ages by philosophers, poets, economists, and fable makers. In contrast to present urgent desire, possible future need pales. But the promoters of consumer credit have maintained that this hazard was small because, they said, lenders would see to it that consumer loans were solid. The prudence of lenders would protect both the economy and the borrower against human frailty. At hand for the lender in the performance of his social duty, so this notion ran, were two controls: (1) the terms of the loan could be so calculated that the goods sold would constitute security for the debt; and (2) loans could be made only to people whose circumstances and character were such that repayment was practically assured.

The only trouble with this reasonable and persuasive argument is that in reality lenders simply do not behave that way — at least not in the mid-20th century in the U.S.A. Even the automobile, the one consumer durable whose resale value might constitute security for the debt, is often sold on 36-month, low-down-payment terms, and under these terms the market value of the car is below the balance due on the contract for a good part of the contract time. As for the rest of the goods and services sold on credit, lenders no longer even pretend to exercise prudence in setting credit terms. It is all a fly-now, pay-later deal.

There is still a pretense, however, that consumer debt is based on character. As a public relations stance, the claim that lenders seek their security in character is a good one. It conjures up the figure of a firm but friendly banker looking deep into the eyes of a suppliant for a loan and recognizing the sturdiness of a Horatio Alger, Jr., hero in the would-be debtor. In reality, however, lenders seldom look into a borrower's eyes. They look at his handwriting. And the signatures of buyers, which give value to the contracts, are generally executed, not in a bank, but on auto lots or in retail stores, where a salesman on commission supplies first the sales pressure and then the pen.

THE FARCE OF THE "CREDIT CHECK"

WHAT LENDERS REALLY MEAN when they talk about a borrower's character is his credit rating, a report of the borrower's current debt and income ratio together with his payment record — a credit check that is available to lenders and sellers from commercial, or industry-supported cooperative credit-rating bureaus. In today's huge urban, impersonal marketplace, debtor-character is nothing but a euphemism for credit checking, and credit checking, as anyone familiar with trade reports is aware, is staggering into ineffectualness. The burden of trying to keep tabs on the ability to pay of some 30 million borrowers, who frequently drive 60 to 100 miles to buy on credit and who are, month by month and day by day, at home and abroad, pursued by a veritable army of credit granters, has stumped tabulators even in this computer age.

Consider the chaotic mushrooming of credit now offered. In addition to installment credit for autos and other durables, for jewelry, tires, furniture, rugs, and home repairs, there are scads of credit cards for both goods and services; there is revolving credit for all soft goods; there is the combination of credit card plus revolving credit offered by commercial banks (this is sometimes called a check-credit plan); and more recently banks have expanded this idea by inaugurating billing services for small retailers that open up to every side-street shop facilities for selling goods on time. So the hardware store, drugstore, dress shop, florist, beauty shop, sporting-goods outlet, dry cleaner, toy store, TV repair shop, and stationer have joined the car dealer, discount house, furniture retailer, department store, appliance dealer, mail-order house, house-to-house distributor, jeweler, gasoline station, book club, record club, hotel, restaurant, bus line, railroad, funeral parlor, and airplane company in the business of creating interest-bearing debt. Food is almost the only significant exemption from this onrush. Nearly all other goods and services, displayed from millions of counters and promoted by billions of advertising dollars, provide eagerly promoted opportunities to borrow as you buy.

In addition to the burden of the volume of sources to be checked, credit checking is further hampered by the lenders and sellers themselves, many of whom withhold credit information on their own accounts from credit-rating bureaus. Small-loan companies in a number of communities, for example, don't exchange borrower-delinquency information with each other because, as each knows all too well, one small loan leads to another, and lender A does not want to make it easy for lender B, a competitor, to horn in on A's delinquent debtor ripening for a second loan to pay off the first. And a retailer, depending on credit from the suppliers of his stock, is not apt to rush bad news about his revolving credit accounts out to a gossipy trade through the credit bureau. So lenders themselves undermine their own ability to determine borrower character and circumstances. Thus the second control against overcommitment, like the first, is more fiction than fact.

BUT THE LENDERS TAKE CARE OF THEMSELVES

This does not mean, however, that banks and sales finance companies, who hold the lion's share of the consumer paper, do not exercise cautions on their own behalf. They do. These lenders depend, in part at least, on an ingeniously devised hedge against losses on consumer loans. It is known in the business as a dealer reserve. It works this way. An auto dealer, for example, sells the installment contracts consumers have signed when they bought cars from him to a bank or sales finance company. (This is, by the way, what happens to all but a fraction of the contracts consumers sign when they buy goods on time.) The bank or sales finance company makes a deal with the car dealer about how much he (the lender) will charge for the car loan. This is not the amount, however, that the car buyer pays. He pays more.

If the lender's agreed-upon take from the loan is, say, 12 percent true annual interest, the dealer may write up a contract calling for 14, 18, 24, or even 35 percent. The difference between the lender's interest rate and the charges in the contract is known as the dealer's kickback or, in more polite terms, the dealer's reserve. It is his share of the finance charges. Whatever that amount may be, it is credited at the bank to his (the dealer's) account. But, although the money is the dealer's — he pays income tax on it — the lender controls it, and all or a part of these funds is held by the lender as insurance against losses on the consumer contracts bought from the dealer. Thus, when a car buyer fails to make his payments, the lender takes the balance due out of the dealer's reserve. . . .

The dealer reserve hides poor credit performance because, when the delinquent contract is charged to the reserve, it appears on the lender's books as paid up. Hence those optimistic reports from lenders about how low the losses are on consumer paper are more revealing about the adequacy of dealer reserves than about the quality of consumer credit. The delinquent buyer still owes the debt, of course, and the dealer, to whom the bank turns over the contract, proceeds against the consumer to collect.

ALL ROADS LEAD TO DEBT-SELLING

THE DEALER-RESERVE SYSTEM obviously invites retailers to charge what the traffic will bear by providing kickbacks based on what can be packed into a contract. And the lure of that opportunity is well nigh irresistible to dealers of cars and other durables who are under heavy pressure from manufacturers to take and move an ever larger quota of products. Under these circumstances the sale of goods on credit tends to become a gamble in which a dealer stands to win, if he is lucky, better returns from poor credit risks than he could earn from a cash sale.

In addition to high credit charges, called an interest pack, a credit contract offers other opportunities for profitable charges. A number of consumer contracts now carry credit life insurance, credit accident insur-

ance, credit disability insurance, etc. The commissions on the sale of this kind of insurance are apt to be high. So, too, are the dividends. Both the commissions and the dividends go to the lender, although the borrower pays the premium. Still other sources of earnings on consumer credit are late charges, collection fees, prepayment charges, and increased interest earnings to be had by refinancing the loans. In short, an installment contract is a bundle of possibilities for sellers and lenders. It is hardly surprising that whether it be cars, television sets, furniture, rugs, washing machines, refrigerators, aluminum siding, you name it, cash sales have become merchandising's Orphan Annie.

Sellers have made no secret of the fact that they make more on the credit than on the goods, and even such sellers and lenders as department stores and small-loan companies, which have no dealer reserves as a hedge, sell debt vigorously. These latter sellers and lenders, however, share with banks and finance companies access to police power to assure the repayment of delinquent balances. Before they resort to court action, they try various collection procedures, including the services of independent collection agencies. But fairly early in the game threats of legal action become a part of the collection process; and, finally, either wage garnishments or other attachments and judgments are the inevitable fate for the debtor who does not or cannot pay.

Few buyers signing the contract papers that make them debtors are aware of how directly they have pledged their total resources, present and future, when they give in to sales pressure. The lenders and sellers are aware, of course. They not only know how the law reads, but have practically dictated it in session after legislative session throughout the fifty states in the Union. The lenders' lobby is always a busy one at the state level, and what their lobbying efforts have achieved, among other things, is a public subsidy for debt collection. The county sheriff has become a backstop for the salesman.

The tricks and stratagems of the debt-collecting process can produce almost as many snares and pitfalls for the borrower as those used by the salesman to induce buyers to become borrowers. Even among sophisticated buyers, only a few are aware of how a debt can be, and is, escalated through the debt collection process; of how, for example, through a $196.73 debt a man can, as was reported to CU not long ago, lose an equity of several thousands of dollars in his home. Here is an area of present-day living about which little is known. . . . There are, however, some indications that the time is overripe for making a careful inquiry into this whole problem of overcommitment.

SOME SIGNS OF TROUBLE

NOT ONLY HAS THE NUMBER of bankruptcies increased at an astonishing and puzzling rate during the last twenty years of our great prosperity but the percentage of those bankruptcies that are family (as opposed to business) financial failures has risen steadily. Today more than 90 percent of the bankruptcies are consumer bankruptcies; the debts listed for the courts are debts for consumption purposes.

Among the creditors to be found in nearly every bankrupt's record are three, and sometimes more, personal loan companies. Usually these debts are for consolidation loans, installment personal loans at high interest rates (from 20 to 42 percent), used to pay up other interest-bearing debt for goods. Consolidation loans tend to be desperation borrowing that leads down a steep path to one after another loan in which interest on interest escalates the indebtedness at a tragic rate. Although not all personal loans are taken out for consolidation purposes, most of the advertisers in the person-

al loan field emphasize this use in their commercials. Since installment personal loans now account for about 25 percent of the consumer credit total, and are the most rapidly rising form of consumer debt today, these borrowings are an indication of trouble. . . .

AN EMPHASIS ON SECOND MORTGAGES

THE RESORT TO REFINANCING, or to second mortgages, for needed cash has been promoted by a segment of both sellers and lenders for a number of years. These inducements to liquidate savings in home equities, especially through second mortgages, have been stepped up sharply in the recent past. Unlike the refinanced first mortgage, which usually runs twenty to even thirty years, the second deed, or second mortgage, is generally a short-term debt running from thirty-six to sixty months. Although the rates on these loans are quoted to borrowers at 6 to 12 percent simple interest (depending on state real estate laws), the actual cost of such borrowing is much higher because other charges such as brokerage fees, finder's fees, investigation costs, etc., are charged against the loan before it is paid out. The result is that the borrower may receive an amount that is as much as 30 to 40 percent less than the face of the note he signs. A *New York Herald Tribune* (January 8, 1965) report of the rapid growth of second-mortgage financing cited the example of one debtor who, in return for $4,892 cash, had signed a second mortgage note for $9,525. . . .

How many homeowners have liquidated their equities through second mortgages, and what their remaining debt burden may be even after so drastic a sacrifice of savings, is a matter about which there is only speculation. But about one thing no speculation is called for. To the extent that such withdrawals of equity are made to get cash to meet obligations incurred through previous installment buying, this new development in consumer credit is yet another indicator pointing to a burden of debt growing heavy. . . .

Consumer credit in the Middle Ages was understood to be an evil exploitation of need, and for centuries usurers were condemned to the hottest spots in hell. Later, in the 19th and early 20th centuries, consumer credit was understood to be a financial device used to promote the sale of high-cost durable goods. Today, however, the emphasis has been reversed and the promotion of goods has become a device for the sale of debt. As a trade paper put it a number of years ago, the slogan is "Bait the hook with merchandise."

Thus consumer credit is no longer a sales tool. It has become the sales object. Debt is promoted with all the skill and ingenuity that American advertising and sales promotion can muster. And debt is sold by precisely the same ethical standards as those that characterize the promotion of the cold cure, the headache remedy, the weight reducer, the cigarette, the detergent, and the hair ointment. . . .

Here is a social and moral problem of perhaps more significance than the economic hazards attending consumer credit. What is called for is not such a passing concern as the stock market decline provided but a serious and careful investigation at the highest federal level into the human as well as the financial, the ethical as well as the economic, aspects of this credit game in which the cards are so heavily stacked by the strong against the weak, by the cunning against the trusting.

57.

ADLAI E. STEVENSON: The Meaning of the United Nations

Supporters of Adlai Stevenson, who had had their hopes for a third Stevenson candidacy dashed at the Democratic convention in 1960, were by and large pleased when President Kennedy nominated his onetime rival as U.S. ambassador to the United Nations. Stevenson served in the post with distinction, loyally supporting Kennedy's foreign policy through thick and thin, and President Johnson kept him in the position. Ambassador Stevenson delivered the following address in Chicago on June 23, 1965. He died in London three weeks later.

Source: VSD, August 1, 1965: "The Fundamental Meaning of the United Nations."

I AM DELIGHTED TO BE AT HOME — and to be here with you tonight to participate in this celebration of an important event in Chicago's history. And I am grateful and honored that my old friend and former law partner, Jim Oates, invited me.

A bonfire celebration is very much in order when we take note that a new building of the magnificence of Equitable's Pioneer Court now graces Chicago's skyline with another imposing silhouette.

I would also like to say that this handsome structure seems to me a mighty symbol of Equitable's foresight and progress in the public service, and of the imaginative and vigorous leadership of its chief executive officer. It is evidence of this great company's credo, so eloquently expressed by Jim Oates when he said: "We choose to serve the goal of excellence with humility."

And this brings me to what I want to say to you tonight, for excellence with humility is a sound national goal in this turbulent world.

All of us know that space and time have been annihilated on this small, small spaceship we call "planet earth." We can blow it up. We can annihilate the thin envelope of soil on which our nourishment depends, and contaminate the thin layer of air we breathe. This apocalyptic risk exists simply because our modern means of science have made neighbors of us all.

But this absolute propinquity comes at a time when the chances of conflict are uniquely high. We live in a twilight of power systems with few settled frontiers. We live in a time of growing misery for the many amid affluence for the few, and hence a time of potential international class war. We live in a time of acute ideological struggle.

Each of these has caused crisis in the past. Together, they threaten catastrophe.

What can we do about our triple crisis? Can we do anything about it? I will confess that I am an optimist — not, I trust, of the Pollyanna type, but as one who draws confidence from facts as well as from hopes. For the fact is that while our crises are in some measure old — as old as human living and striving — some of our means of dealing with them are new — as new as our new environment of political freedom and scientific advance.

For political freedom is new. It is only in the last two centuries that we have tried to practise it even on a continental scale. Now we have at least made a start in applying some of its principles on a global scale. Make no mistake about it. For all its frus-trations, muddles, and inconsistencies, international organization is an attempt to apply democratic principles to our planetary society.

Hitherto in the whole history of man, it has been the role of small nations both to put up and to shut up — to put up with alien domination and to shut up about resentment and discontent. Only since the American and French revolutions have peoples — even small peoples — felt they had a right to run their own affairs. Only since President Wilson has that right been formalized as part of a world philosophy of freedom. Only in the United Nations has it been realized over the face of the globe on such a flood tide of freedom that scores of new nations have been precipitated into sovereignty in one short decade.

The whole basis of the United Nations is the right of all nations — great or small — to have weight, to have a vote, to be attended to, to be a part of the 20th century. And because it is all this — because in the past twenty years it has demonstrated that out of the germ of international cooperation can flower a world of life and hope and growth, there has been much understandable concern over the UN's current difficulties.

I am now enroute to San Francisco where twenty years ago the architects of peace met to build a new dwelling place for the family of man. It was the twilight of the war and the dawn of a new era, and for those of us who were involved in that historic conference — and there are still some of us around — the memories are still fresh and green.

The anniversary we celebrate in the next few days is filled with meaning for all Americans, for it is the anniversary of an audacious dream come to fulfillment. President Johnson and the ambassadors of 114 member nations will come to San Francisco to mark it.

I mention this because an aura of gloom

and doom about the United Nations has of late pervaded the thinking of many people. Indeed, there were some who thought the twentieth anniversary meeting would not be a birthday party but a wake.

But the spirits of all who believe in a world of peace and justice ruled by law are rising again. In announcing that he would participate in the San Francisco ceremony, the President has made it clear how much this institution means to us. He will have more to say on this at San Francisco. But let me say now that never in history has a nation been more devoted to the multilateral ideal and to the concept of collective security and action than the United States during the twenty years since the world war ended.

It is because of this devotion to the concept of collective security enshrined in the United Nations Charter that we, like so many other nations, felt it shameful that the great peacekeeping institution must beg for the means to keep the peace. But I believe the financial troubles that gave rise to the anxiety may soon be over. The United Nations has been on a sickbed long enough. But it is not a deathbed. It is suffering not from death pangs but from growing pains. For the simple truth is that as long as the world is in crisis the United Nations will be in crisis. That's what it's there for. As long as there is global tension, there will be tension in the world headquarters. When it ceases to reflect the troubles of the world, then you can start worrying about its demise.

And it is well to remember that while the General Assembly, the parliamentary arm, has been temporarily paralyzed because of the deadlock over the financing of peacekeeping operations, the other organs of the United Nations have been in full operation — and in some respects on a scale greater than ever before. For two months I have been in almost continuous session in the Security Council on the Dominican Repub-

lic, Cyprus, and other peacekeeping problems. It is nice to be out for a few days at least!

But meanwhile UN troops and observers continue to patrol the uneasy borders of Kashmir and the Gaza Strip. The Blue Berets continue to keep peace between the Greek and Turkish communities in Cyprus. And in the sprawling, humming workshop of the world community international civil servants are busy improving soils . . . purifying water . . . harnessing rivers . . . eradicating disease . . . feeding children . . . caring for refugees . . . diffusing knowledge . . . training teachers . . . spreading technology . . . surveying resources . . . lending capital . . . probing the seas . . . studying the weather . . . improving diets . . . setting standards . . . developing law . . . and working away at a near infinitude of down-to-earth tasks — tasks for which science has given us the knowledge, and technology has given us the tools, and common sense has given us the wit to perceive that common interest impels us to common enterprise.

And while the search went on to find a new formula for the financing of peacekeeping operations, the Disarmament Commission met for six weeks to consider how to defuse the powder keg that threatens us all. This session of all 114 nations concluded with a call for a worldwide conference including perhaps Communist China. And it is clear now that most of the world is fully aware of the awful implications of further nuclear proliferation, and also the obstacles to arresting this death dance if the Communist Chinese or France, for example, won't cooperate.

So on the eve of the San Francisco anniversary, we can expect the United Nations to survive this crisis, as it has others, because it has long since demonstrated its indispensability, withstood all manner of criticism and cynicism, and dealt with the most stubborn problems of the postwar world in spite of all its imperfections and the frustrations of a divided world. Bear in mind that cases seldom come to the United Nations until all else has failed.

There are those who criticize the United Nations for doing too little, for being merely a debating society. And there are those who fear it is doing or trying to do too much; that it is more than a debating society and has the dangerous right to intervene in threatening situations and thereby to interfere with the full exercise of national sovereignty.

In recent months, for instance, some have complained that the United Nations has shown insufficient interest in Vietnam or the Dominican Republic; and others have complained that the United States has ignored the United Nations. While neither charge is true, my purpose tonight is not to review again the familiar details of our involvement in these countries, and all the efforts — now more than thirteen — we have made or agreed to with a view to unconditional negotiations for a peaceful settlement in Vietnam, or the continuing efforts of the Organization of American States to enable the Dominican people peacefully to choose their own government by free supervised elections.

Rather my purpose is to point out that the two views — the incapacity of the United Nations to do more and the fear that it can do too much — reveal the difficulty of the transition from nationalism to internationalism and from unilateralism to multilateralism.

We are still living in both worlds. We are not alone in this confused and violent voyage from a known past to an unknown future. We are all groping in the dark for something better than the lethal past. And I suspect we will all be groping for a long time to come. That is why I deposited a prophecy in the Pioneer Court's cornerstone box today that thirty-five years hence, in the year 2000, we would either have achieved coexistence or coextinction. I wish I were more confident that the decision to coexist would be reached by that time.

And another thing I wished to point out is that Vietnam and the Dominican Republic illustrate another problem astride our path that we did not have in mind at San Francisco twenty years ago. I refer, of course, to the new kind of aggression — clandestine and covert — and the "wars of national liberation," which the communists call "just" wars and which have nothing to do with nation or liberation or justice.

Small powers do not automatically preserve their rights and independence by seeing them subscribed in the United Nations Charter. They still have to cope with the problem of powerful neighbors who may or may not respect their autonomy and whom they have not the power to withstand alone. In need they will call for help where they can get it. In default of adequate and timely international peacekeeping power, they will ask for national power to come to the rescue — most likely the United States.

I believe that overt aggression against smaller neighbors is now unlikely. The world suffered too recently and directly from Hitler's aggressions to accept any longer armies crossing the frontiers in the full panoply of war. Two such open aggressions across frontiers — in Korea and at Suez — were checked by the near unanimous opposition and action of the world community. But we face today this more devious problem of covert aggression and subversion.

This is a far more delicate business. Since Cuba, we know how irrevocable a Communist takeover can be. And how little it is thereafter subject to popular control. Yet we know, too, how easy it is to mistake genuine local revolt for Communist subversion. For this opaque, uncertain type of crisis we have no adequate international machinery to ensure that if local disorder leads to civil war the frontiers can be sealed against external intervention, order can be restored, and free elections held.

I do not underestimate the difficulties of setting up such a policing system. But I believe it is the direction in which we must try to move. It could give greater security to the small powers living in the interstices between the great systems. It could restore order in the disorderly regions where power is disputed. It could point the way to the impartial police which one day must take the place of individual arms and the precarious "balance of terror."

But I doubt if there is any way to keep peace in a world mined by misery, hunger, and despair.

America can add $30 billion to an annual gross national product of some $630 billion in one year. And that, my friends, equals the entire gross national product of Latin America. These are the contrasts. One continent's almost casual surplus is as great as the whole apparatus of living among its neighbors.

The gap grows worse. Since 1960 the wealth of the wealthy has been growing at two and three times the speed of the national income of the poorest group. Yet this group covers half mankind and over 100 countries. The poor are caught fast in the ancient trap of poverty, and across the whole globe stretches the darkening shadow of injustice and despair.

What do we do about it? Pass by on the other side? There was almost a consensus in the middle of the 19th century that nothing much could be done about poverty. But such was not the case. Over the last century, the poorer classes inside our developed Western world have secured a larger share of the economy's steadily expanding production. And the richer members of society, by means of a progressive tax system, have shared more of their wealth with their less fortunate neighbors. And since tax money

went into better schooling and housing and health and skills, this in turn increased the capacities and abilities of the mass of the people, increased their productiveness, and so created yet more wealth to share.

If such changes can be brought about inside domestic society, we can repeat the success in the larger economy of the world. The proletarian nations of today are no more reckless, thoughtless, idle, and child-ridden — to quote a few of our current pessimisms — than were the proletarian classes of the day before yesterday. And the same strategies are available.

I would ask you to remember that it is not the active, reforming, liberal societies that have been swept into the discard of history. It is, on the contrary, those which were too proud, too rigid, too blind, and too complacent to change in time.

Let me end by recalling that we in this country are committed to narrowing the gap between promise and performance, between equality in law and equality in fact, between opportunity for the well-to-do and opportunity for the poor, between education for the successful and education for the whole people. But it is no longer a community or a nation or a continent but a whole generation of mankind for whom in the next two decades promises must be kept. If they are not kept for all, it will be less and less possible to keep them for some.

What promises? The promises, my friends, that science, that the ever more productive industrial machine, the ever more fertile and usable land, the computer, the wonder drug, the man in space have spread before us. The promises that the religions, the philosophies, the cultures, the wisdom that 5,000 years of hard-won civilization have finally distilled and confided to us. The promises of the abundant life and of the brotherhood of man.

It is a fragile heritage. A nuclear war would destroy it. Pride and arrogance could destroy it. Neglect and indifference could destroy it. Parochial nationalism or ideological intolerance could destroy it. Extremism of left or right could destroy it. To preserve it we must act together, act boldly, and act quickly to control and reduce armaments, to find the way as a community of nations, to keep the peace among us all, and to restrain by joint action any who place their ambitions or their dogmas or their prestige above the peace of the world.

We must reduce hunger and want and disease and the shocking difference between what life holds for a child in a developed country and what it holds for a child in an underdeveloped country. We must finish once and for all with the myth of inequality of races and peoples, with the scandal of discrimination, with the shocking violations of human rights and the cynical violations of political rights. We must stop preaching hatred, stop bringing up new generations to preserve and carry out the lethal fantasies of the old generation, stop believing that the gun or the bomb can solve anything, or that a revolution is any use if it closes doors and limits choices instead of opening both as wide as possible.

Every one of us — black, white, yellow, brown — faces extinction if we cannot ride our spaceship earth in safety and peace. There are no wars that we can afford to fight. Yet of all human institutions war is the oldest, the wickedest, the most tenacious. When we say "we cannot fight another war and survive," we speak the bare truth. But we have never been able — so far — to live without war. Must we then conclude that our enterprise is hopeless? That our doom is sure?

But for all our desperate dangers, I do not believe in the end of the human experiment. I do not believe, in the words of Winston Churchill, "that God has despaired of His children." For man in his civil society has learned how to live under the law with the institutions of justice, and with a controlled strength that can protect rich and poor, weak and strong alike. This has been done, I say, within domestic society. And in this century, for the first time in human history, we are attempting the same safeguards, the same framework of justice, the same sense of law and impartial protection in the whole wide society of man.

This is the profound, the fundamental, the audacious meaning of the United Nations. It is our only ultimate shield against disastrous war. Either we shall make it grow and flourish, arbitrator of our disputes, mediator of our conflicts, impartial protector against arbitrary violence, or I do not know what power or institution can save us.

But we have it. We have set it bravely up. We have taken the first giant step away from overriding national egoisms, away from the raw pretensions of imperial power, away from the unprotected weakness of little states.

So, let us resolve to go forward steadfastly on this new path toward peaceful settlement, toward the justice and neighborliness of a quiet world.

58.

Robert F. Kennedy: Counterinsurgency

In the twenty years between the end of World War II, and mid-1965, when Robert F. Kennedy delivered a speech to the graduating class of the International Police Academy in Washington, more than a score of guerrilla wars had broken out at various places in the world. These civil conflicts were a new kind of war, and every one of them was a source of trouble and distress to the United States. Not only were they necessarily fought in a way that put the vast military power of the U.S. at a disadvantage, but each was also capable of developing into a major war, even World War III. What to do about the problem of guerrilla wars hardly anyone knew, but Kennedy offered one proposal — he called it counterinsurgency — that he thought might work.

Source: VSD, August 15, 1965.

TODAY I WOULD LIKE TO SPEAK with you about a problem of common concern to all of us, a central concern to all the world: the question of revolutionary wars, sometimes called "wars of national liberation," or insurgency.

President Kennedy said in 1961 technology has made all-out war highly unlikely because if it comes it means the end of civilization as we know it. And we are faced, instead, he said, with

> another kind of war — new in its intensity, ancient in its origin — war by guerrillas, subversives, insurgents, assassins, war by ambush instead of by combat, by infiltration instead of aggression, seeking victory by eroding and exhausting the enemy instead of engaging him.

This war has worn many faces. It has been a war for independence from external domination, as in Algeria and Cyprus and Hungary. It has been a war for regional or tribal identity, as in Burma or Iraq or in the Naga Hills of India. And it has been a war for communism, as in Malaya or Venezuela or South Vietnam.

All these wars, of which there have been more than a score since World War II, offer us lessons for the future, for the decades of revolutionary war which are the challenge ahead.

At the moment, our most prominent problem is in Vietnam. We must realize, however, that Vietnam has become more and more an open military conflict as well, in which military action on our part is essential just to allow the government to act politically.

What I say today is in the hope that the lessons of the last twenty years will be applied in other places — so that we are able to win these wars before they reach the stage of all-out military conflict now apparent in South Vietnam.

I am a citizen of a nation which itself was born in a war for national liberation. It would be against our deepest traditions to oppose any genuine popular revolution. But acts of aggression, masquerading as national revolutions, pose a difficult problem. Revolutionary wars carried on with the outside support of the Soviet Union, or of China,

Henri Cartier-Bresson from Magnum

Robert F. Kennedy, attorney general, in his office

or of others of their allies, offer the greatest threat to the world order of free and independent states to which all nations pledged themselves in the charter of the United Nations.

But if these conflicts are called wars and have deep international consequences, they are at the same time not wars — and their outcome is determined by internal factors. For their essence is political — a struggle for the control of government, a contest for the allegiance of men. Allegiance is won as in any political contest — by an idea and a faith, by promise and performance. Governments resist such challenges only by being effective and responsive to the needs of their people.

Effective and representative government can, of course, take many forms. What is right for the United States may not be right for your countries, and others would have still other convictions on the precise form government should take — on own-

ership and control of the means of production, on the distribution of riches and the level of taxation, on the range of domestic and international policy. These questions must always be for each nation and people to decide for itself. So long as their choice is their own, not imposed from outside or by dictatorship of left or right, it must be respected by all others. If we wish to encourage the spread of democracy and freedom, primary reliance must be on the force of our example — on the qualities of the societies we build in our own countries — what we stand for at home and abroad.

In the 1960s, it should not be necessary to repeat that the great struggle of the coming decades is one for the hearts and minds of men. But too often, of late, we have heard instead of the language of gadgets — of force-ratios and oil-blots, techniques and technology, of bombs and grenades which explode with special violence, of guns which shoot around corners, of new uses for helicopters and special vehicles.

Men's allegiance, however, and this kind of war, are not won by superior force, by the might of numbers or by the sophistication of technology. On the tiny island of Cyprus, the British Army had 110 soldiers and policemen for every member of EOKA, which never numbered more than a few hundred terrorists; yet Britain had to surrender control of the island within five years after the rebellion began. In the Philippines, by contrast, Ramon Magsaysay had an army of only 50,000 to fight 15,000 Huks who were at the gates of Manila when he took office as defense minister. His forces had no special modern armament; yet within four years the Huk rebellion was crushed and its leaders had surrendered.

But why are mere numbers, or the possession of advanced weapons, not conclusive? And how can these conflicts be won without such force, or modern technology?

One answer lies in the character of military force itself. Conventional military force

— and all our advanced weapons technology — is useful only to destroy. But a government cannot make war on its own people, cannot destroy its own country. To do so is to abandon its reason for existence — its responsibility to its people — and its claim to their allegiance. Suppose, for example, that a government force is fired upon from a village, or that rebels have forced the village to fly the insurgent flag. A government which attacks that village from the air, or with heavy artillery, abandons all pretense of protecting the people of the village — abandons the first duty of any government worthy of the name.

There is another side to this coin. When an insurgent uprising threatened to unseat Jerome Bonaparte, his brother Napoleon told him, "Use your bayonets." Jerome replied, "Brother, you can do anything with bayonets — except sit on them." That is still true today.

Guns and bombs cannot build, cannot fill empty stomachs or educate children, cannot build homes or heal the sick. But these are the ends for which men establish and obey governments; they will give their allegiance only to governments which meet these needs.

In the Philippines, for example, Magsaysay pursued the Huks vigorously. But he offered much more than conflict to the people. First, he insured an honest election throughout the country; Gen. Edward Lansdale has said that this election marked the turning point of the war. Second, a thorough land reform was begun; and it was enforced through such devices as special landlord-tenant courts which were held from Jeeps so that the judges would be available to peasants in isolated rural areas. There followed many other reforms directed at the welfare of the people.

We all know the necessity for this political dimension to our actions. Too often, however, it is not given the priority it demands, for . . . we allow the military dimension to become more urgent and insistent. But reform and the hope it brings cannot be postponed; for insurgents of the modern variety continually institute at least a facsimile of such reforms in every area they control. In Vietnam, in China, in Cuba, to name but three, Communist insurgents have abolished landlordism, organized adult-education classes, established courts, and in all areas they occupied — even in many which they controlled only at night. They have thus entered into direct competition with the established government. When the defenders have ignored reform, the hopes of the people could only center on the insurgents. And when a victorious government army is followed by landlords collecting back rents from the peasants, we should not wonder that the insurgents often attract the allegiance of the peasants. It does little good to warn that the end result of communism will be dictatorship and exploitation; the deeds of today speak most loudly — if not most truly — on whose promises will be kept tomorrow.

A second reason for the inadequacy of military action is that it can give no hope. Force is neutral, it has no program. Every insurgent movement lives not primarily on force but on a dream — of independence, of justice, of progress, of a better life for one's children. For such dreams men will undergo great hardship and sacrifice — as we have done for our dream, as you have done and are doing for your own. Without a vision of the future to offer, a government can demand no sacrifice, no resistance to insurgent terror or blandishments.

Not only is the military approach deficient in itself. More dangerously, it tends to obscure and prevent essential political action. In conventional war the aim is to kill the enemy. But the essence of successful counterinsurgency is not to kill but to bring the insurgent back into the national life. In Malaya the British achieved great success by distributing photographs of prisoners —

half-starved and ragged when captured — well-fed and smiling after internment. Bonuses were given for arms turned into the government, with no questions asked; amnesty was offered to rebels who would surrender. Such devices were carried further in the Philippines; there, Huks who surrendered were settled with their families on newly cleared agricultural land of their own. George Marshall once said, "Let's not talk about this matter too much in military terms; to do so might make it a military problem." Too often we forget that wisdom.

Another central need of counterinsurgency effort is for adherence to fundamental rules of law and fair dealing. It may seem strange to assert that a legal government should bind itself by restrictions, such as the Geneva Convention, in the midst of an assault on its existence. But the government is competing with a rival administration, which often ruthlessly enforces its own rules of fair dealing with the people: no excessive taxation, no stealing (except from the rich), no physical maltreatment (except of those who aid the government). The government must match and overmatch the insurgents in this respect, punishing and rewarding wisely and consistently — as in Malaya, where villages were carefully graded on their help to the rebels, and food and equipment were distributed accordingly. Such a precise system of rewards and penalties is characteristic of civilian and political action — not of military force.

Actions such as these are necessary to success. But they are not the kind of measures which follow from thinking of insurgency as conventional war; rather they assume that the insurgents are fellow citizens who can be and should be returned to the political process. President Kennedy once said that the peace we must seek is

not the peace of the grave or the security of the slave [but] genuine peace, the kind of peace that makes life on earth worth

living, the kind that enables men and nations to grow and to hope and to build a better life for their children.

That is what we must offer insurgents as well.

It is sometimes said that political methods are ineffective against terrorists — as in Vietnam, where the Vietcong have cruelly assassinated over 16,000 local officials. But even the use of terror is limited by political considerations — and can be sharply limited by political action. Surely it is significant that unprotected Americans of the International Volunteer Service — who work for the direct benefit of the people — have not been molested even in the Vietcong areas, and that of several thousand AID officials who have served in the countryside there, less than a dozen have been harmed. Similarly, terrorist action in the last Venezuelan election failed because public reaction was unfavorable; and it was abandoned.

It has also been said that an insurgency cannot be put down as long as it is supplied from, and can seek sanctuary in, a neighboring country. No matter what assistance they receive from outside, however, insurgents stand or fall on their political success. Without popular support, they become conventional invaders — and can be dealt with by conventional means.

I think the history of the last twenty years demonstrates beyond doubt that our approach to revolutionary war must be political — political first, political last, political always. Where the needs and grievances of the people begin to be met by the political process, insurgency loses its popular character and becomes a police problem — as it did in Venezuela and Colombia, in the Philippines and Malaya. . . .

Most important, we must impart hope — hope for progress, fulfilled as quickly as circumstances permit. In many countries, land reform is the essential need of the vast majority of the people; it must receive central priority. Education is always vital — not just for the cities, not even only for children, but for every peasant who can learn to read, or drive a tractor, or even use a hoe instead of a forked stick. For what we must build, after all, is a nation — a nation in which, as in the Scriptures, "Your old men shall dream dreams, your young men shall see visions." And where there is no vision, life shall perish from the earth.

We must also build all the other structures that help to make up a stable society — such as labor unions and farmer cooperatives for those who work with their hands and their backs; student groups for the nation's new emerging leaders; political parties to give all men a voice in the councils of government. The political coloration of these groups is less important than the fact of their existence; simply by being organized, by being there, they add stability and permanence. Thus the British in Malaya did not attempt to break up the Communist labor-union movement so long as it did not engage in active subversion.

Moreover, these groups can be a great force for reform, progress — and action. The truce in the Bolivian tin miners' strike, for example, was arranged by two student leaders. Major social-action programs in rural Peru are being undertaken by students from the cities, as are similar programs in India. These student activities are especially important because as much as one-half the population of the nations concerned is under the age of twenty-five, and the young are often the progressive and dynamic leaders. Magsaysay, Mboya, Nyerere, Belaunde — and Castro and Nkrumah as well — were leaders of national stature in their thirties. These young men must have the scope to act within the society — or else they may turn to action outside the established order. . . .

But one last word of caution: No less than military action, political action in an unjust cause is lost. It is not enough to stand for anticommunism — or for stability — or for order. We all have a responsibility to stand with the people for justice, for understanding, for progress. If we meet that obligation, we need have no fear for the future, no worry over wars of revolution. I think you will meet that obligation — that you will have the fortitude and wisdom and patience to "bear the burden," as President Kennedy said, of the "long twilight struggle, year in and year out, 'rejoicing in hope, patient in tribulation' " — and I am proud, as much as I can, to share that burden with you.

The export of revolution is nonsense. Every country makes its own revolution, if it wants to, and if it does not want to, there will be no revolution.
                                                    JOSEPH STALIN, 1936

59.

W. Averell Harriman: The Challenges to Peace and Freedom

The son of one of the great American railroad magnates of the nineteenth century, Averell Harriman devoted most of his life to government service. After holding several administrative posts under the New Deal, he was named ambassador to the Soviet Union in 1943. He served in that important post throughout the war, and beginning in 1946 was named in quick succession ambassador to Great Britain, secretary of commerce, and director of the Mutual Security Agency, by President Truman. Governor of New York from 1954 to 1958, he served Presidents Kennedy and Johnson in a series of diplomatic posts after 1960. Perhaps no American in his time had greater experience in dealing with the Communist world. The following speech on America's relations with the emerging nations of the Far East was delivered in Tucson, Arizona, on October 31, 1965, when Harriman was ambassador at large.

Source: *Bulletin,* November 29, 1965, pp. 863-867.

THE VALUE OF THE UNITED NATIONS in restoring peace among nations has recently been reaffirmed by its success in bringing about a cease-fire in the India-Pakistan conflict. . . . The discordant note in this situation has been the threat of Red China to renew its attack on India, based on trumped-up charges of Indian violation of their frontier. This incident has further discredited the Peiping regime in thoughtful public opinion throughout the world. It is a useful reminder of the aggressive and troublemaking policies of the Peiping regime at a time when the United Nations General Assembly is preparing once again to debate the question of Communist China's admission to the United Nations.

People who favor Communist Chinese membership in the United Nations argue that it would provide an opportunity to talk with the Chinese. But the fact is that there are already many opportunities. We talk to the Communist Chinese on a continuing basis in Warsaw. And our experience is that the only thing they ever want to talk about is our handing Taiwan over to them. Furthermore, it is naïve to suppose that one can moderate Chinese Communist aggressiveness merely by talking with them. The British have been talking with them since 1949 and have not yet even been able to get them to agree on an exchange of ambassadors.

But the most compelling example is the Soviet Union. The Soviet Union is a Communist state which for years gave substantial assistance and support to Communist China. And yet now the Russians themselves cannot talk to the Chinese Communists.

If Communist China were to join the United Nations, the effect would be to disrupt the organization. If we doubt that, all we need do is listen to what Peiping itself has to say on this point. Peiping has made its views unmistakably clear.

Last month the Foreign Minister of Communist China, Mr. Chen Yi, held an outspoken news conference. Nearly 300 newsmen were present, including many foreign correspondents. For reasons of its own, Peiping itself did not publish the text of the news conference until a week later. However, we now have an official Chinese version of what was said, a transcript reviewed and approved by the regime. So there can be no doubt as to the authenticity of Peiping's views.

Chen Yi was emphatic about the conditions Communist China poses before it will join the United Nations. He said:

> The United Nations must rectify its mistakes and undergo a thorough reorganization and reform. It must admit and correct all its past mistakes. Among other things, it should cancel its resolution condemning China and the Democratic People's Republic of Korea as aggressors, and adopt a resolution condemning the United States as the aggressor; the UN Charter must be reviewed and revised jointly by all countries, big and small; all independent states should be included in the United Nations; and all imperialist puppets should be expelled.
>
> If [he continues] the task of reforming the United Nations cannot be accomplished, conditions will no doubt gradually ripen for the establishment of a revolutionary United Nations.

The revolutionary concept of the Chinese Communists has been clearly defined by an exceptionally important Chinese Communist document that appeared less than two months ago. It was written by Lin Piao, the minister of national defense of Communist China. He is also the vice-chairman of the Central Committee of the Chinese Communist Party and a vice-premier of Communist China. The article is 18,000 words long, but, despite its length, was published in full

David Moore from Black Star

Ambassador-at-Large Averell Harriman

in all the Peiping papers, was carried in all the provincial and municipal newspapers throughout China, was broadcast over both the domestic and international services of Peiping radio, was published as a pamphlet by the People's Publishing House of China and translated into many languages. There can be no doubt that the Communist Chinese themselves regard it as a document of the highest importance.

It spells out in unmistakable clarity and detail the Communist Chinese doctrine of world revolution. Its significance is similar to that of *Mein Kampf*. It states unequivocally what the intentions of Communist China are, what sort of world it wants, and how that world is to be created. It is a document that everyone should read but particularly those who disagree with our government's policy toward Communist China or are critical about our policy in Vietnam.

Lin Piao begins with a detailed analysis

of the Communist revolution in China and goes on to state:

It was on the basis of the lessons derived from the people's wars in China that Comrade Mao Tse-tung, using the simplest and most vivid language, advanced the famous thesis that "political power grows out of the barrel of a gun." He clearly pointed out: The seizure of power by armed force, the settlement of the issue by war is the central task and highest form of revolution. This Marxist-Leninist principle of revolution holds good universally, for China and for all other countries.

He then explains that the Chinese Communist Revolution had one essential difference from the Russian Revolution. The Russian Revolution, Lin notes,

. . . began with armed uprisings in the cities, and then spread to the countryside; while the Chinese Revolution won nationwide victory through the encirclement of the cities from the rural areas, and the final capture of the cities.

This leads Lin to his central theme. The "rural areas of the world" today, he states, are Asia, Africa, and Latin America. The "cities of the world" are Western Europe and North America. Hence, he concludes, just as communism in China succeeded by capturing first the countryside, and then encircling and defeating the cities, so the world Communist movement will succeed by first capturing Asia, Africa, and Latin America — thereby encircling Western Europe and North America — and then by finally and decisively defeating the United States and its Western allies.

And how is the countryside of the world — Asia, Africa, and Latin America — to be captured? It is to be captured, says Lin, by waging "wars of national liberation."

"In the last analysis," says Lin Piao bluntly, "the Marxist-Leninist theory of proletarian revolution is the theory of the seizure of state power by revolutionary violence, the theory of countering war against the people by people's war." "Today," he adds, "the conditions are more favorable than ever before for the waging of people's wars by the revolutionary peoples of Asia, Africa, and Latin America."

Thus the blueprint of Communist China is unmistakable. Win Asia, Africa, and Latin America through "wars of national liberation," and the United States and its Western allies will be encircled and eventually overwhelmed.

And the whole "focus" of the revolutionary movement against the United States today, he states, is in Vietnam. No matter what decision America may take in Vietnam, the Communist Chinese determination "to support and aid the Vietnamese people" is "unshakable"; and "the Chinese people will do everything in their power to support the Vietnamese people until every single one of the U.S. aggressors is driven out of Vietnam." . . .

My talks with Chairman Kosygin this summer left me convinced that, whatever changes may be occurring in Soviet society, Soviet objectives remain the same. Mr. Kosygin is pragmatic rather than dogmatic when it comes to improving methods of production, but he and his colleagues are faithful believers in communism. They remain convinced that communism is the way of the future, the inevitable trend of history.

However, Communist China's challenge to the Soviet Union for leadership of the world Communist movement has driven Moscow to attempt to outdo Peiping in promoting and supporting revolution abroad, particularly in the underdeveloped countries. The Soviets, directly and through Castro's Cuba, are especially active in Latin America.

In an important communiqué published simultaneously in Moscow and Havana earlier this year reporting the results of a conference of the Latin-American Communist parties in Havana it was stated:

Active aid should be given to those who are subjected at present to cruel repressions — for instance, the freedom fighters in Venezuela, Colombia, Guatemala, Panama, and others.

An editorial in *Pravda* that appeared at about the same time stated, in part,

The Soviet people have regarded, and still regard it, as their sacred duty to give support to the peoples fighting for their independence. True to their international duty, the Soviet people have been and will remain on the side of the Latin-American patriots.

Despite their concentrated efforts in Latin America, I am glad to say the Communists have not done well there in recent years. In the Dominican Republic, President Johnson's prompt decision and the effective action taken by the OAS [Organization of American States] in assuming responsibility in the political and internal security fields averted widespread bloodshed and prevented a Communist takeover. The Communists have also suffered setbacks in Chile, Venezuela, and Brazil. It remains to be seen whether their relative lack of success in encouraging so-called liberation movements to spread in Latin America will cause the Soviet leaders to change their tactics.

60.

The Sonic Boom

The airplane largely replaced the railroad train in the twenty years after World War II as the mainstay of long distance, intercity transportation in the United States, and at the same time replaced the ocean liner in intercontinental travel. Travel time decreased steadily, and by the mid-1960s it took only five hours or so to fly from New York to San Francisco, and little more to fly from New York to London or Paris. Even these speeds, however, were not felt to be adequate to the needs of modern life, and several countries, the U.S. among them, announced plans to build supersonic planes that would fly at speeds from 1,200 to 2,000 miles per hour. Some of the disadvantages of the decision were discussed in the following New Yorker *editorial in 1965.*

Source: *New Yorker*, December 18, 1965.

WE REMEMBER READING not long ago that the great majority of Americans have never been up in an airplane of any sort. In the consciousness of this deprived multitude, we gather, the entire grand march of progress in aviation enjoys no more than a derivative and hearsay existence. From the first vague flapping at Kitty Hawk to the latest in-flight movie, the thunderous course of aeronautical empire has rocked and rumbled on its way without awakening a single echo among these unthinking groundlings. It comes as a distinct satisfaction, therefore, to report that the Federal Aviation Agency, by a recent decision, has contrived to bring the latest advance in aviation literally home to virtually every householder in the land. The agency has approved the construction of a supersonic airliner that will whisk the impatient airborne minority from New York to

Los Angeles in two hours and a half, and will treat the earthbound majority to the phenomenon called "sonic boom."

When an airplane is flying faster than sound, it continuously produces a shock wave in the atmosphere, and this shock wave makes itself felt on the ground in a variety of ways, some of them downright brusque. For pointed example, there was the fate of a "test village" that had been built by the Federal Aviation Agency in the New Mexican desert with an eye to discovering the effects of sonic boom upon architecture. A jet fighter plane that was darting about to provide a note of technological color while the press inspected the village accidentally exceeded the speed of sound on a low-level pass, thereby smashing a greenhouse, shattering a storefront, and heavily damaging the plaster in seventeen test buildings.

A layman, thinking of the probable gruesome consequences of such an aerial contretemps in the vicinity of, say, the United Nations Secretariat Building, might suppose that this test was definitive, but the FAA, it appears, chose to discount it, possibly because none of its 110 recording instruments were turned on at the time of the occurrence. Besides, the agency had discovered a strongly countervailing, beneficent effect of the sonic boom. It increases the birthrate of chickens. Eggs that are exposed to the boom turn out to have a higher hatching rate than those incubated in relative tranquillity.

Homeowners who find themselves living along one of the major airline routes will doubtless be interested in the advice of Mr. Jack Huntress, an FAA engineer for structures. "Plate glass and plaster are most vulnerable, so I would go to smaller windowpanes, and sheetrock or plasterboard for the inside walls and ceilings," he said.

Modern shells, especially thin shells, and dome-shaped roofs and cantilever designs are highly susceptible. If I were building a home, I would put more money into the foundation, go a few feet deeper to prevent moisture from getting under the house, especially in areas subject to alternate dry-wet spells and great temperature changes. If water gets under the foundation, then dries up, it sets up a rocking stress that can strain joints and even crack them. Then the home is vulnerable to the boom. Joining dissimilar materials is also bad. In frame houses, I would use extra stiffening members, such as collar beams in the rafters and a stiff back over the ceiling joists. In most cases, I would recommend using an electric drill and screws instead of nails that come loose with moisture changes.

Mr. Huntress apparently sees the territory under the airline routes as the natural abode of the rich, who can afford the extra measures he suggests, such as having their houses constructed with screws, presumably by skilled cabinetmakers.

With the best will in the world, however, we cannot bring ourself to accept this extraordinary vision of self-sacrificing millionaires neatly arranged in transcontinental rows and all cringing away from their small windows and listening to the sky go bump. As it happens, we can think of a house that is much better suited to the age of supersonic flight than Mr. Huntress's deep-dug and well-buttressed structure. We mean the tepee. This ingenious shelter is one that can be knocked flat and set up again a dozen times in a day, with no more serious consequence than, perhaps, a certain amount of ill temper on the part of the owner.

As aviation continues to advance and existing houses are shaken into ruin, as chickens multiply and farmers depart, we may see the American Indian come into his own once more. At the expense of some slight deafness, he might occupy the abandoned land below the airline routes, and, with all his ancient craft, pursue chickens of unparalleled fecundity through a vast and reverberating forest.

1966

61.

Harry M. Caudill: Paradise Is Stripped

The Tennessee Valley Authority, with its control of disastrous floods and its cheap power for the multitudes, was one of the great achievements of the New Deal. But TVA is also the nation's biggest coal consumer, and its voracious appetite for coal is not so well controlled as the floods that used to ravage the valley but do so no longer. The country around Paradise, Kentucky, which had been turned into a wasteland by TVA's strip-mining operation, was described by Harry Caudill in 1966. But Paradise was only a symbol of a much larger problem; Americans are still despoiling their land and its plants and animals, and polluting their air and water; and they seem to do it all the more effectively, and perhaps irretrievably, as time goes on.

Source: *New York Times Magazine*, March 13, 1966.

DESCENDANTS OF THE PEOPLE who settled in the shallow valley of the Green River founded a small hamlet called Paradise, Ky. It was well-named, for the countryside was green and pleasant and the stream teemed with fish. Game abounded and a man could live an unworried life, the tedium broken by an occasional visit to the county seat to listen to trials and swap yarns with friends from other parts of Muhlenberg County.

But times have changed. There is still a dot called Paradise on the map of Kentucky but last year Muhlenberg produced 17.6 million tons of coal — more than any other county in America — and the production record was achieved at a staggering cost. Paradise is isolated and shrunken, huddled in an appalling waste. Thousands of acres of earth are piled high into ghastly ridges,

sometimes black with coal, sometimes brown with sulfur. The streams that wind through this dead landscape are devoid of life.

Here in western Kentucky, part of America's Eastern Interior coalfield, the mineral lies near the surface, and the region has fallen prey to strip mining on an immense scale. Strip mining is as easy as it is ruthless. It simply tears the earth apart stratum by stratum in order to rip out the minerals. Conventional tunnel and pillar mining leaves the surface relatively undisturbed, but stripping totally disrupts the land and its ecology.

In a typical Appalachian operation the development may proceed in two or more seams of coal at different levels in a mountain. The uppermost seam may be laid bare by the violent expedient of blasting away the entire overlying crest — a process known to the industry as "casting the overburden." Lower down, the seam is exposed, or "faced," by bulldozing and dynamiting the timber and soil away from the coal. The uprooted trees, loose dirt, and shattered stone are pushed down the slope. The coal is loosened by light explosive charges, scooped up with power shovels, and loaded onto giant trucks for hauling to the nearest railroad loading docks.

Where the terrain is level or gently rolling, the bulldozers and power shovels scrape away the dirt to expose the rock layer roofing the coal. The stone is then shattered with dynamite and lifted by immense shovels or draglines onto the spoil heaps, accumulations that sometimes rise almost sheer to a height of 200 feet. Several acres of the fuel may be bared in this manner before smaller shovels begin loading it onto the trucks. One gigantic shovel owned by the Peabody Coal Company is as tall as a 17-story building and has become a major tourist attraction. Thousands of people drive out of their way to watch it devastate the American land.

A traveler comes in along the new Kentucky Turnpike from The Bluegrass, where the lawns and fields are manicured and the miles of wooden fences gleam with fresh white paint. There the influence of the early German immigrants lives on, and in the counties around Lexington it is easy to conclude that the nation's heritage in its land is being safely guarded.

The turnpike carries the traveler through a line of lovely low hills into the west Kentucky plain. The land thins as it flattens. Muhlenberg County was never high-quality farmland, but it was adequate, and with constructive farm practices and enlightened forestry it had a substantial and permanent potential. By no stretch of the imagination did it warrant the destruction to which it has been subjected.

Aggravating the shock that accompanies one's visit to Paradise is the realization that this is TVA country and TVA is the nation's bench mark in land conservation. Two billion dollars have gone into TVA projects and a vast amount of favorable propaganda has accompanied its every venture. Millions of Americans assume that the TVA territory is in good hands.

At Paradise, TVA assumes tangible form in an enormous coal-burning electric power plant, built at a cost of $183 million. It consumes 12,000 tons of coal daily. Modern, automated, gigantic, the plant towers above a desolation created by its insatiable appetite for fuel. Just beyond the steel fences which surround it the desert begins. Within sight of the plant Peabody's machines rip the tortured earth while gargantuan trucks rush the coal to the voracious "cyclone" furnaces.

TVA has two faces. One is composed of the green hills around Knoxville, enriched with cheap government fertilizer and green with pines planted with government subsidies. It sparkles with TVA lakes and hums with profits from a multitude of new industries attracted by a pleasant climate, abundant water, flood control, and dirt-cheap electricity. But TVA's other face is less pleasing to contemplate. The agency generates much more electricity from coal than from its hydroelectric dams, and fuel-buying policies have long been the subject of bitter controversy. By insisting on rock-bottom coal prices for its growing string of huge steam plants, it has stimulated strip mining enormously.

TVA is the nation's biggest coal consumer and its purchasing policies have set the pace for the market elsewhere. Despite a general inflation, coal prices have remained stationary for fifteen years. Squeezed by rising costs of machines and labor, countless underground pits have been forced to close. Strip mines have been able to hold the price line and meet TVA's bid requirements. Therein lies the tragedy of Paradise. And therein lies similar tragedy for hundreds of other communities elsewhere in America — and, ultimately, enduring tragedy for all Americans.

A few years ago, oil and gas interests confidently assumed that theirs were the modern fuels. Coal was "old-fashioned." In burning, it left a residue of ashes, soot, and grit. The industry was archaic — fragmented into hundreds of small companies, undercapitalized and plagued with labor troubles. Obviously the future belonged to other fuels. But coal has staged an amazing comeback. The demand for electricity has grown enormously — and for most of America coal is the best fuel for generating it. The most optimistic proponents of atomic power estimate that nuclear generating plants will be able to meet no more than 20 percent of the nation's electric needs by the end of the century.

From a post-Depression low in 1954, coal production had climbed 5 percent by 1960. Then the market zoomed another 5 percent in 1961 and nearly as much in 1962. In 1963, the gain was 6.5 percent, and in 1964 it was more than 7 percent. Economists now predict that by 1970 the coal industry will be producing at 100 percent of present capacity.

According to the United States Bureau of Mines, more than 1.3 billion tons of coal, valued at about $6 billion, have been mined in Appalachia alone in the past three years. This year production is expected to reach 500 million tons. New pits are being opened, and most of the new production will come from "surface mining" — a euphemism dreamed up by the industry's public-relations firm.

The Appalachian coalfield extends through Pennsylvania, West Virginia, eastern Kentucky, western Virginia, eastern Tennessee, and northern Alabama. This mountain range is one of the richest resource areas in the continent — rich with coal, oil, natural gas, sandstone, limestone, low-grade iron ore, water, timber-growing potential, and marvelous scenery. The hunters and wilderness scouts who first penetrated the gaps never beheld a land more enchantingly beautiful than the wooded Appalachian hills and hollows on a misty morning.

With wise management of its resources, Appalachia could have been the richest part of America today. Instead, it has become synonymous with poverty of land and people. But Appalachian destitution did not occur by accident. It is the result of nearly a century of remorseless exploitation. The timber stands were bought by Eastern lumber companies, and the forests were cut down, sawed up, and shipped away in a barbarous manner which totally disregarded the capacity of the land to regenerate the stands. Few healthy seed trees were spared, and today the woods consist mainly of low-grade stock which the lumbermen have culled many times. . . .

The coal industry's lack of responsibility has culminated in today's strip mining. A flight along the Appalachian crest from Pennsylvania to Alabama reveals the awesome scope of the depredations. For hundreds of miles one passes over lands churned into darkening death.

In Pennsylvania alone, 250,000 acres have been left as bleak and barren as the Sahara. . . . In Ohio, 202,000 acres in a half-dozen counties have been churned by the machines. Ohio's Senator Frank Lausche, a stanch friend of business, has repeatedly denounced the strippers who are ruining so much of his state. . . . In Wise County, Virginia, the coal lies near the hilltops and many mountains have been decapitated — turned into flat-topped mesas. In eastern Tennessee, where the seams are thin and the mountains a bit less steep, the damage subsides somewhat. . . . In the Eastern Interior coalfield the creeping ruin has spread across western Kentucky and far into

Indiana and Illinois. Seventy-five thousand acres in Indiana have been ravaged. In Illinois, 105,000 acres embracing some of the world's best cornland have been turned upside down.

And the ravages of strip mining are spreading to other coalfields farther west. In North Dakota, the Truax-Traer Coal Company is strip mining 3 million tons of lignite coal annually for the giant new power plant of the Basin Electric Power Cooperative. Using an ingenious device called the "launch-hammer mining wheel," the operation is incredibly swift and efficient. With the growing demand for electricity on the West Coast and the spread of extra-high-voltage transmission lines to carry the product from generator to consumer, the vast lignite fields in the Dakotas are likely to be wrecked on a gigantic scale in the next two or three decades.

In addition, there is talk of cooking Colorado shales for their petroleum. If this occurs, the shales will be recovered by strip mining, and the beautiful hills of Colorado will face the extinction that now threatens so much of the Appalachian Range.

What kind of corporations commit this murder of the landscape? One might suppose them to be obscure entities whose managers have not yet learned that in the 20th century it is good business to preserve that which cannot be replaced.

Not so. Many of the great strippers are subsidiaries of well-known American corporations — Bethlehem Steel, Republic Steel, Inland Steel, Interlake Steel, Weirton Steel, Youngstown Sheet and Tube, and United States Steel. Their advertisements proclaim an enlightened concern for the perpetuation of the American way of life, but in Appalachian valleys they ruthlessly kill the land on which future generations of Americans must depend. The most brutal example of corporate irresponsibility lies on the Poor Fork of the Cumberland River in Harlan County, Kentucky, where the United States Coal

and Coke Company has shattered the Big Black Mountain for more than twenty miles, reducing much of this noble terrain feature to a rubble heap. . . .

And what of the people whose communities are shredded for cheap coal? Obviously, ruined lands must be abandoned, and the strip-mined counties all have shown sharp population declines. A million people have moved out of Appalachia in the past ten years, and the Eastern Interior field has fared little better. As subterranean mining declined, thousands of families passed onto the public assistance rolls. Today, welfare, not mining, provides most of the money spent by families in the nation's coalfields.

In Appalachia, exploitation has reduced a once proud and even violent people to the most passive and trampled-upon part of the American population. Passivity has reached its ultimate depths in eastern Kentucky where whole communities have been impoverished and debased with scarcely a protest. There, coal companies often own the minerals underlying the lands of farmers, and the state's highest court has ruled that the companies have the right to destroy the land in order to get out the minerals.

With this license to wreck, many operators have proceeded with complete abandon. They have rolled rocks through some homes and have pushed others off their foundations. Many have been demolished by avalanches from the spoil banks. In Knott County, a one-armed coal miner came home from a retraining program conducted as a part of the war on poverty to find his house and all its contents buried beneath a mammoth landslide.

When a group of mountaineers calling themselves The Appalachian Group to Save the Land and People visited Gov. Edward T. Breathitt of Kentucky last June, an eighty-year-old woman told him that she had stood on the front porch of her little home and watched the bulldozers invade her family cemetery. She said: "I thought my heart would break when the coffins of my children come out of the ground and went over the hill." This situation prompted one mountaineer to comment that the coal industry digs up the dead and buries the living. . . .

Early this year, conservationists all over America watched with admiration the efforts of Kentucky's young Governor Breathitt to tighten his state's reclamation law. The act, as amended, authorizes the Kentucky enforcement agency to require strippers in mountainous eastern Kentucky to drag part of the soil off the spoil banks and use it to cover the perpendicular highwalls, reducing them to a slope not exceeding forty-five degrees. In western Kentucky, the mined land must be shaped so that it can be traversed by farm machinery. All disturbed lands must be seeded to a prescribed vegetative cover or, in the mountains, planted with approximately 800 seedling trees for each acre.

To these modest and reasonable requirements the coal industry responded with outraged bellows. Scores of lobbyists descended on the State House. Huge funds were collected from operators and their suppliers for the avowed purpose of defeating the bill. Governor Breathitt spoke out against improper pressures upon legislators and the bill passed by a comfortable margin — the severest public setback ever suffered by any segment of the coal industry in Kentucky.

While Breathitt remains governor, strict enforcement is to be expected, but his administration is likely to be exceptional. The state has had a reclamation statute since 1954, but it has been generally ignored, and it is to be feared that future state administrations will emulate this leniency.

Elsewhere in Appalachia, Virginia, Tennessee, and Alabama have never bothered even to enact reclamation statutes. In the Eastern Interior field, only Illinois has any sort of reclamation law. In the Western field, such legislation has never been seriously considered.

If governmental power is to save the American land, it must be federal power backed by a strong national will and conscience. The American population is growing rapidly; estimates of the United States Bureau of the Census indicate a population of 300 million by the year 2000. The nation's land base cannot grow by a single inch, but it can be effectively diminished by industrial processes which include not only strip mining for coal but quarrying, borrow pits, open-cast iron mining, and similar operations. Under any enlightened philosophy, the present occupants of the land hold it in trust for future generations and are under a positive obligation to pass it on in a tolerable state.

The blight of strip mining does not stop at the edge of the spoil banks. When freshly exposed, the soil is hot with sulfuric acid: for years nothing can grow on it. In the meantime, the sulfur and mud wash into streams, killing aquatic life and piling up in horrible weed-grown banks. The long-range cost of dredging the Mississippi and its tributaries of this coal-flecked debris will be astronomical — a burden all federal taxpayers will share.

In my opinion, the Great Society should enunciate a clear-cut policy relative to extractive industry and its distorted practices of social accounting. Based on need and historical experience, strip mining should be permitted in those areas where terrain and weather permit complete reclamation — that is, in flat or gently rolling country. In West Kentucky, Illinois, Indiana, Ohio, and most of Pennsylvania, coal can be extracted cheaply and efficiently by this method, and the same machines which rip the earth can heal the scars. Following British practice, the land can be restored to its original condition and, perhaps, even improved. If funds are made available for the purpose, and if the state and federal governments make certain it occurs, intensive treatment with fertilizers, limestone, and leguminous plants and trees can restore the land to beauty and usefulness. Such costs should be borne by industry as part of the price of coal. . . .

The technology of subterranean mining has made fabulous strides in the last two decades. Continuous mining machines, roof-bolting devices, battery-powered coal cars, improved ventilating techniques, and strict enforcement of the federal mine safety code have not only made the miner's life easier and safer but increased his productivity more than twofold. Coal from tunneled mines must sell for a little more per ton than that from strip mines, but the difference is a small price to pay for the preservation of the land. . . .

The hour is late and the agony of the land is intense. Most Americans have long assumed that the waste of resources was curbed and that victory over greed and wantonness was achieved in the days of Theodore Roosevelt. Nothing could be farther from the truth. Shocking as were the mass slaughters of the American bison and the passenger pigeon, they were no more grotesque than the present destruction.

As wealth multiplies, hordes of Americans will purchase country retreats and seek quiet areas for recreation and leisure. Someday, every acre will be needed for its food and fiber. Unless we act now our grandchildren may inherit vast man-made deserts, devoid of life, polluted with acids, hideous to the eye, baked by the sun, and washed by the rains. If this is their heritage, they will curse us so long as the deserts remain to monumentalize our greed and folly.

Continued silence by the national administration on this urgent issue is inconsistent with the dream of a Great Society. It is, in fact, inconsistent with simple patriotism and basic common sense, for unless the land lives the people must perish.

62.

Frank L. Whitney: The Total Redevelopment of Cities

The immense problems — as well as the great opportunities — faced by city planners as a result of the changes in the modern American city were the subject of numerous books, pamphlets, and magazine articles throughout the 1960s. That more than professional city planners were involved was emphasized by Frank L. Whitney in the speech part of which is reprinted here. Whitney, head of one of the country's leading construction and engineering firms, delivered the speech in Cleveland on March 21, 1966.

Source: VSD, April 15, 1966: "The Impact of the Total Redevelopment of Cities."

How are we going to save our cities? Let's face it, gentlemen, we are not, at least not in the sense of returning them to their exalted status of a generation or more past.

Megalopolis is here to stay. Call it what you will — urban sprawl, slums of tomorrow, ticky-tack houses. It is here and it will be expanded. It will not change the texture of our communities. Certainly it is the ware of the future.

This will make many politicians unhappy — those who like a large but neatly packaged constituency. It will make many planners and architects unhappy — those who can relate only to the structure that is tall and thin or to the glory that was Rome. And it will make a lot of pseudo-intellectuals unhappy — those who Dr. David Riesman calls the "groupism cult," who like their subjects pigeonholed and stacked.

But this is what's happening and it will continue at flood. We live in an electronic age — an age of automation and instant communication. Electronics and automation have fractured our existing industrial patterns. They disperse industries to every corner of our country. Like it or not, this permits each of us to dictate our environment — and the exodus from the city is well underway.

This is not because of poor city government, although in many cases it has been profoundly inept. It is not because of high city taxes, although taxes within the city area will continue to increase. It is not because of crime or poor educational facilities. These only accelerate the move. The basic cause is simply that more and more people are permitted a choice and their choice is based on two fundamental factors — living near their work and, increasingly important, expanded opportunities and time for recreation. . . .

Before we can consider the effect of the electronic age on our patterns of living, let's first examine some of the primary forces that shaped cities as they now exist. Until the Industrial Revolution, the European city existed for essentially one reason — protection. People had to come in from the fields at night to keep from getting killed. Today we leave the city at night for the same reason. With the Industrial Revolution, the city entered its major period of growth. Industry and commerce were centered in the city, close to its marketplace and close to the available forms of power and transportation.

These basic criteria for locating industry and commerce in our cities — marketplace,

power, transportation — are no longer valid. Thus, industry continues to move out. The political climate today is committed to the philosophy that industry must move out. And no matter how hard a Lindsay or a Cavanagh or a Rockefeller or a Romney may try, it is politically impossible in a major city to provide the kind of incentives that would hold industry to the metropolitan center. And as industry moves out, people move out because people live where they work — and, more importantly, where they play. Call this a trend if you will, but it is basic and it will continue.

The city's long-time function as a communications center influences much of today's architectural and ecological thought about urban redevelopment. Thus, a Lewis Mumford, speaking out against the exodus from the city by business and institutions, can say,

> The positive values that are so achieved — open spaces, better residential quarters, ample recreation areas, contact with nature, all are genuine ones. But these improvements need rather to be brought back into the heart of the city to provide a sound basis for the challenging human variety and diversity that only the city can supply.

Along the same lines, architect Theo Crosby can write that his book *City Sense* is based on the assumption that "city life is desirable and exciting" and that this is an assumption "shared by most of the human race." Well, this is not shared by most of the human race. I don't think many of you share that assumption. But this is the type of wishful thinking we are subjected to every day. We are told, in effect, to feel guilty about deserting the city.

While I'm quoting people, let me toss one in from Frank Lloyd Wright. He was visiting the West Coast and his companion asked him, "What do you think about Los Angeles, Mr. Wright?" And the reply was, "I don't think about Los Angeles and, from the looks of it, apparently neither does anyone else."

Most of those who praise urban living do it with some particular city in mind. Too frequently, it is the same city. I've heard it said that most New Yorkers — and I am a New Yorker — think the sun rises over the East River and sets on the Hudson River and everything that happens in between is endlessly important to the whole world. This certainly colors the entire fabric of urban thinking.

At this point in time, we can say Manhattan Island was a poor site for a city in the first place. As bad as Pittsburgh. But too many of our so-called urban planners think in terms of New York and Los Angeles. I wish they'd gear their thinking a little more to the Jersey Citys and Tacomas and Chattanoogas and Tulsas.

The planners and politicians of our cities today are caught up in an enormous round of building projects. Many are praiseworthy in themselves, but most fail to reflect any recognition of the changing texture of our lives.

Our cities will not reduce the level of crime by construction of public housing for people who remain unable to get jobs. They will not retain existing business and draw business by creating vast new highway systems that are immediately clogged with traffic. And they will not encourage the return or the retention of that vast tax base known as the middle class by isolating in ghettolike centers the cultural facilities that are a city's last remaining drawing card, no matter how magnificent in concept and execution those ghettos of culture may be.

Today, in 1966, we are entering a critical growth period. The postwar baby boom of the late '40s is about to become the marriage and family boom of the late '60s. Where do you think these new families — most of them middle class — will live? In the urban redevelopment areas? No.

Our population growth will not be in the center cities. The Committee for Economic Development estimates that in just twenty years we will have 180 million people — as much as our total population in 1960 — living in metropolitan areas. That's 54 million more than today.

Nothing the city planners or the city politicians can do will keep these people in today's city. We saw a clue to this a few years ago when we prepared a study for our own guidance in serving clients who were planning industrial research facilities. A key part of this study involved an examination of the nature of industrial researchers, who have a great influence on locating research facilities because a primary goal of these facilities is to attract and then stimulate these people.

The researcher is, of course, very much an individual. He is highly trained, extremely intelligent, and generally has a wide range of interests beyond his own specialty. He is, I like to think, the typical man of tomorrow. Surely he is the perfect nominee for the so-called "exciting, desirable, challenging, and diverse" life the city offers.

Well, the researcher is not buying city life. Our study showed that he considers local education the most important community factor, not only because he is concerned about his children's schooling but because he believes the local school system's character is an accurate index of the community's cultural level. And this is the clincher — his own desire to identify himself with the entire educational process. Also important is easy access to a university, preferably less than fifteen minutes travel time. Other factors include availability of good housing, attractiveness of the community, taxes, local recreational and cultural facilities, churches, medical facilities, and convenient shopping. Far down the list is the distance to a metropolitan center. . . .

Too much of our thinking on city planning is mired in the 1930s. Of course, people and businesses and institutions need to communicate, but the city need not continue to exist as a communications center.

In New York City the mayor proposes new taxes, including a tax on stock transactions. So the New York Stock Exchange — very predictably, since this has happened before — promptly threatens to move out of the city. Is the Stock Exchange bluffing? Will the mayor back down on his taxes? New Yorkers are caught up in episode after episode of "Wall Street versus City Hall."

What a lot of nonsense! For, as now structured, there is no real justification for the existence of a stock exchange in its present physical form in New York City or anywhere else. Imagine — in the "highly sophisticated" financial centers of our "highly sophisticated" major cities, men still transact huge amounts of business by waving their hands and shaking their fingers. There's nostalgia here, but not a very sophisticated form of communications. This is just one example of the way our progress in the physical sciences has far outpaced our thinking in the social sciences.

That recent epic failure, the New York World's Fair, is another example. No one stopped to think that the same kind of Fair that made people perk up and say "Gee whiz" in 1939 would generate only yawns and "Oh yeahs" twenty-five years later. The difference, of course, was television.

For all its shortcomings, television has brought the culture of the world to every corner of the country. And we are only at the beginning. David Sarnoff, who has a pretty good track record in predicting these things, recently said that we "are on the brink of a Communications Revolution that will change the patterns of life as did the Industrial Revolution of the 19th century." Before the end of this century, we will have achieved instantaneous sight and sound communication anywhere in the world, among people and among computers. We will send and receive business documents, scientific data, blueprints and photographs — all electronically. You and I will attend and participate in meetings like this one without ever leaving our offices. Maybe we'll all just sit at home and project our work, our questions, our information, and our decisions to some vast network of computers.

Where does this leave our cities? It doesn't. Perhaps we won't, but our children will certainly see the day when the New Yorks and the Chicagos and the Los Angeles will cease to be dominant factors as living and working centers. We will change our whole definition of cities. Our gathering places will be an infinite variety of communications centers, from which we will control the tools of production and marketing and finance. Our cities as we know them today will evolve into civic centers for the government's social, health, and welfare activities and for the arts. But few will live there.

Nothing can stop this evolution — neither you nor I nor all the city planners, politicians, and sociologists combined. For even if today we would eliminate all the tax and transit and crime and education problems of the city, we could still not induce people to return in any appreciable numbers. Man has a basic desire for individuality — that's why teen-agers wear their hair long — and he welcomes the option of not living on top of his neighbor.

Where does all this leave us today? How will our cities evolve toward the communications centers and civic centers of tomorrow?

One of our most crucial battles is to escape the stranglehold of the automobile. It is a battle we cannot afford to lose, but it is also a battle we cannot really win within our existing cities.

For 1966, *Engineering News-Record* forecasts a total of $6.1 billion of construction contracts for transportation facilities. More than 70 percent of that — $4.5 billion — will be spent on our highways; less than 3 percent — $150 million — on our railroads. Do you think we are going wild in our race to conquer space? Don't worry. In 1966, we'll contract more money to build parking garages than space and missile bases. . . .

Beyond housing and transportation, the construction industry will, for the next five to ten years, be greatly influenced by — whether you like it or not — the direction of the Great Society. In my own company, our marketing forecasts indicate that by 1970, 80 percent of the business available to us — that excludes housing, utilities, and heavy chemical plants — will be in the field of health, education, and welfare. The remaining 20 percent will be industrial and commercial. And this does not indicate any dropoff in our industrial and commercial activity.

These then are the areas available to us as architects, engineers, and builders in the near future and, perhaps for many of us, during the entire remaining span of our professional activity.

But we must not look upon these next five, ten, even fifteen years as anything more than a period of transition in our ways of living and working with each other. For better or for worse, we — the architects, engineers, and builders — are the natural leaders in determining the character of the environment in which our children will live. This is why we are here today. Need I add that our record to date is something less than perfect?

One of the most encouraging signs of progress in our thinking today is the move by leading universities to revamp their architectural education programs. Our schools are recognizing that architecture must deal not simply with the physical design of structures, but with all the problems of the environment within which those structures must function. . . . But this horizon-broadening should not be limited to architectural education. It is desperately needed in the engineering disciplines as well. Our studies and our work in sanitation, air pollution, water supply, and transit must all be conducted, not as individual projects but within the broad framework of man and his environment.

Such changes in educational directions may well be the first steps into a tremendously exciting day after tomorrow, where we will develop the knowledge and the capability to successfully relate man to a far better environment than any of us have today. We are all deeply involved in this, whether we live in New York or Chicago or Cleveland or Hickman, Kentucky, because it is up to us to provide the leadership and encourage the atmosphere within which true innovation in environmental design can replace simple modification. Let's not continue to have this mantle of leadership simply thrust on us. Let's welcome it. Let's reach for it.

America is now an overdeveloped urban nation with an underdeveloped system for dealing with its city problems.

JAMES RESTON, 1966

63.

Charles F. Powers and Andrew Robertson: The Aging Great Lakes

The Great Lakes and their connecting waterways constitute the largest body of fresh water on earth and are of inestimable importance for the development of the region in the United States and in Canada that surrounds them. When the first white men saw the Great Lakes only four centuries ago their water was pure and cold. What men have done to these beautiful and valuable natural objects during those two centuries is told in the following article, which appeared in Scientific American.

Source: *Scientific American*, November 1966. Reprinted with permission.

THE FIVE GREAT LAKES in the heartland of North America constitute the greatest reservoir of fresh water on the surface of the earth. Lake Superior, with an area of 31,820 square miles (nearly half the area of New England), is the world's largest freshwater lake; Lake Huron ranks 4th in the world, Lake Michigan 5th, Lake Erie 11th, and Lake Ontario 13th. Together the five lakes cover 95,200 square miles and contain 5,457 cubic miles of water. They provide a continuous waterway into the heart of the continent that reaches nearly 2,000 miles from the mouth of the St. Lawrence River to Duluth at the western tip of Lake Superior.

The Great Lakes are obviously an inestimable natural resource for the development of the U.S. and Canada. They supply vast amounts of water for various needs: drinking, industrial uses, and so forth. They serve as a transportation system linking many large inland cities to one another and to the sea. Their falls and rapids generate huge supplies of hydroelectric power. Their fish life is a large potential source of food. And finally, they serve as an immense playground for human relaxation, through boating, swimming, and fishing.

The settlements and industries that have grown up around this attractive resource are already very substantial. Although less than 3.5 percent of the total U.S. land area lies in the Great Lakes basin, it is the home of more than 13.5 percent of the nation's population (and about a third of Canada's population). In the southern part of the basin, from Milwaukee on the west to Quebec on the east, is a string of cities that is approaching the nature and dimensions of a megalopolis. Many economists believe the Great Lakes region is likely to become the fastest-growing area in the U.S. Their forecast is based mainly on the fact that whereas most other regions of the country are experiencing increasing shortages of water, the Great Lakes area enjoys a seemingly inexhaustible supply.

Unfortunately the forecast is now troubled by a large question mark. The viability of this great water resource is by no means assured. Even under natural conditions the life of an inland lake is limited. It is subject to aging processes that in the course of time foul its waters and eventually exhaust them. The Great Lakes are comparatively young, and their natural aging would not be a cause for present concern, since the natural processes proceed at the slow pace of the geological time scale. The aging of these lakes is now being accelerated tremendously, however, by man's activities. Basically the destructive agent is pollution. The ill effect of pollution is not limited to the circumstance that it renders the waters unclean. Pollution also hastens the degeneration and eventual extinction of the lakes as bodies of water.

These conclusions are based on recent extensive studies of the Great Lakes by a number of universities and governmental agencies in the U.S. and Canada. Employing various research techniques, including those of oceanography, the studies have produced new basic knowledge about the natural history and ecology of the Great Lakes and recent major changes that have occurred in them.

The natural aging of a lake results from a process called "eutrophication," which means biological enrichment of its water. A newly formed lake begins as a body of cold, clear, nearly sterile water. Gradually, streams from its drainage basin bring in nutrient substances, such as phosphorus and nitrogen, and the lake water's increasing fertility gives rise to an accumulating growth of aquatic organisms, both plant and animal. As the living matter increases and organic deposits pile up on the lake bottom, the lake becomes smaller and shallower, its waters become warmer, plants take root in the bottom and gradually take over more and more of the space, and their remains accelerate the filling of the basin. Eventually the lake becomes a marsh, is overrun by vegetation from the surrounding area and thus disappears.

As a lake ages, its animal and plant life changes. Its fish life shifts from forms that prefer cold water to those that do better in a warmer, shallower environment; for example, trout and whitefish give way to bass, sunfish, and perch. These in turn are succeeded by frogs, mud minnows, and other animals that thrive in a marshy environment.

The natural processes are so slow that the lifetime of a lake may span geological eras. Its rate of aging will depend on physical and geographic factors such as the initial size of the lake, the mineral content of the basin, and the climate of the region. The activities of man can greatly accelerate this process. Over the past fifty years it has become clear that the large-scale human use of certain lakes has speeded up their aging by a considerable factor. A particularly dramatic example is Lake Zurich in Switzerland: the lower basin of that lake, which receives large amounts of human pollution, has gone from youth to old age in less than a century. In the U.S., similarly rapid aging has been noted in Lake Washington at Seattle and the Yahara lake chain in Wisconsin.

When the European explorers of North America first saw the Great Lakes, the lakes were in a quite youthful stage: cold, clear, deep, and extremely pure. In the geological sense they are indeed young — born of the most recent Ice Age. Before the Pleistocene their present sites were only river valleys. The advancing glaciers deepened and enlarged these valleys; after the glaciers began to retreat some 20,000 years ago the scoured-out basins filled with the melting water. The succeeding advances and retreats of the ice further deepened and reshaped the lakes until the last melting of the ice sheet left them in their present form.

The land area drained by the Great Lakes (194,039 square miles) is relatively small: it is only about twice the area of the lakes themselves, whereas the ratio for most other large lakes is at least six to one. The drainage alone is not sufficient to replace the water lost from the Great Lakes by evaporation and discharge into the ocean by way of the St. Lawrence. Thanks to their immense surface area, however, their capture of rainfall and snowfall, supplemented by inflow of groundwater, maintains the lakes at a fairly stable level. The level varies somewhat, of course, with the seasons (it is a foot to a foot and a half higher in summer than in winter) and with longer-range fluctuations in rainfall. Prolonged spells of abnormal precipitation or drought have raised or lowered the level by as much as ten feet, thereby causing serious flooding along the lake shores or leaving boat moorings high and dry.

The five lakes differ considerably from one another, not only in surface area but also in the depth and quality of their waters. Lake Superior averages 487 feet in depth, whereas shallow Lake Erie averages only 58 feet. There is also a large difference in the lakes' altitude: Lake Superior, at the western end, stands 356 feet higher above sea level than Lake Ontario at the eastern extreme. Most of the drop in elevation occurs in the Niagara River between Lake Erie and Lake Ontario. At Niagara Falls, where the river plunges over the edge of an escarpment, the drop is 167 feet. This escarpment, forming a dam across the eastern end of Lake Erie, is continuously being eroded away, and it is estimated that in 25,000 years it will be so worn down that Lake Erie will be drained and become little more than a marshy stream.

The lakes are all linked together by a system of natural rivers and straits. To this system man has added navigable canals that today make it possible for large oceangoing ships to travel from the Atlantic to the western end of Lake Superior. Hundreds of millions of tons of goods travel up and down the Great Lakes each year, and on the U.S. side alone there are more than sixty commercial ports. The Sault Ste. Marie Canal (the "Soo"), which connects Lake Superior and Lake Huron, carries a greater annual tonnage of shipping than the Panama Canal. Other major man-made links in the system are the Welland Canal, which bypasses the Niagara River's falls and rapids

to connect Lake Erie and Lake Ontario, and the recently completed St. Lawrence Seaway, which makes the St. Lawrence River fully navigable from Lake Ontario to the Atlantic Ocean.

One of the first signs that man's activities might have catastrophic effects on the natural resources of the Great Lakes came as an inadvertent result of the building of the Welland Canal. The new channel allowed the sea lamprey of the Atlantic, which had previously been unable to penetrate any farther than Lake Ontario, to make its way into the other lakes. The lamprey is a parasite that preys on other fishes, rasping a hole in their skin and sucking out their blood and other body fluids. It usually attacks the largest fish available. By the 1950s it had killed off nearly all the lake trout and burbot (a relative of the cod that is also called the eelpout) in Lake Huron, Lake Michigan, and Lake Superior. The lamprey then turned its attention to smaller species such as the whitefish, the chub (a smaller relative of the whitefish), the blue pike, the walleye, and the sucker. Its depredations not only destroyed a large part of the fishing industry of the Great Lakes but also brought radical changes in the ecology of these lakes.

Since the late 1950s, U.S. and Canadian agencies have been carrying on a determined campaign to eradicate the lamprey, using a specific larvicide to kill immature lampreys in streams where the species spawns. This program has succeeded in cutting back greatly the lamprey population in Lake Superior; it is now being applied to the streams feeding into Lake Michigan and will be extended next to Lake Huron. Efforts have already been started to reestablish a growing lake-trout population in Lake Superior.

Meanwhile, a second invader that also penetrated the lakes through the Welland Canal has become prominent. This fish is the alewife, a small member of the herring family. The alewife, which ranges up to about nine inches in length, does not attack adult fishes, but it feeds on their eggs and competes with their young for food. In the past decade it has multiplied so rapidly that it is now the dominant fish species in Lake Huron and Lake Michigan and seems to be on the way to taking over Lake Superior.

Recently, attempts have been made to convert the alewives from a liability to an asset. The Pacific coho, or silver salmon, has been introduced into Lake Superior and Lake Michigan on an experimental basis. This fish should thrive feeding on the alewife and yet be protected from its depredations, because the eggs and young of the coho are found in tributary streams the alewives do not frequent. Other fishes such as the Atlantic striped bass are being considered for introduction to supplement the coho.

The introduction of a new fish into a lake is always an unpredictable matter. It may, as in the accidental admission of the lamprey and the alewife, disrupt the ecological balance with disastrous results. Even when the introduction is made intentionally with a favorable prognosis, it frequently does not work out according to expectations. The carp, prized as a food fish in many countries of Europe, was stocked in the Great Lakes many years ago and has established itself in all the lakes except Lake Superior. Commercial and sport fishermen in these lakes, however, have come to regard the carp as a nuisance. North Americans generally consider it inedible, chiefly because they have not learned how to prepare and cook it properly. On the other hand, the smelt, introduced into the upper lakes from Lake Ontario early in this century, has become prized by fishermen and is taken in large numbers in the Great Lakes today. What effect it will eventually have on the ecology of the lakes remains to be seen.

The Great Lakes are so young that, biologically speaking, they must be considered in a formative stage. So far only a few species of fishes have been able to invade them and adapt to their specialized environment, particularly in their deep waters. As time goes on, more species will arrive in the lakes and evolve into forms specially adapted to the environmental conditions. Lake Baikal in Siberia, a very large and ancient body of fresh water, offers a good illustration of such a history: it has developed a well-diversified and distinctive population of aquatic animals, including a freshwater seal. As diversity in the Great Lakes increases, it will become less and less likely that the arrival or disappearance of one or two species (such as the lake trout and burbot) will result in any profound alteration of the ecological balance.

Pollution, however, is a decidedly different factor. Its effects are always drastic — and generally for the worse. This is clearly evident in Lake Erie, the most polluted of the Great Lakes. The catch of blue pike from this lake dropped from 18,857,000 pounds in 1956 to less than 500 pounds in 1965, and that of the walleye fell from 15,405,000 pounds in 1956 to 790,000 pounds in 1965. There was also a sharp decline in lake herring, whitefish, and sauger (a small relative of the walleye). While these most desirable fishes decreased, there were rises in the catch of sheepshead (the freshwater drum), carp, yellow perch, and smelt. Other signs in the lake gave evidence of an environment increasingly unfavorable for desirable fish; among these were the severe depletion of oxygen in the bottom waters, the disappearance of mayfly larvae (a fish food), which used to be extremely abundant in the shallow western end of the lake, and spectacular growths of floating algae — a certain sign of advanced age in a lake.

Lake Erie receives, to begin with, the grossly polluted water of the Detroit River, into which 1.6 billion gallons of waste are discharged daily from the cities and industries along the riverbanks. To this pollution an enormous amount is added by the great urban and industrial complex around the lake itself. A recent study of the Detroit River by the U.S. Public Health Service showed that its waters contain large quantities of sewage bacteria, phenols, iron, oil, ammonia, chlorides, nitrogen compounds, phosphates, and suspended solids. Similar waste materials are discharged into the lake by the steel, chemical, refining, and manufacturing plants along the lake. Pollution is particularly serious in Lake Erie because of the lake's shallowness; its volume of water is too small to dilute the pollutants effectively. Over the past fifty years the concentrations of major contaminants in the Lake Erie waters have increased sharply.

Many of the industrial wastes, notably phenols and ammonia, act as poisons to the fish and other animal life in the lake. Solid material settles to the bottom and smothers bottom-dwelling organisms. Moreover, some of the solids decompose and in doing so deplete the water of one of its most vital constituents: dissolved oxygen. Algae, on the other hand, thrive in the polluted waters, particularly since the sewage wastes contain considerable amounts of the plant-fertilizing elements nitrogen and phosphorus. The algae contribute to the depletion of oxygen (when they die and decay), give the lake water disagreeable tastes and odors and frustrate the attempts of water-purifying plants to filter the water.

In addition to Lake Erie, the southern end of Lake Michigan has also become seriously polluted. Interestingly the city of Chicago, the dominant metropolis of this area, apparently does not contribute substantially to the lake pollution; it discharges its sewage into the Mississippi River system instead of the lake. The main discharge into Lake Michigan comes from the large industrial concentration — steel mills, refineries, and other establishments — clustered along its southern shores. The Public Health Service has found that the lake water in this area contains high concentrations of inorganic nitrogen, phosphate, phenols, and ammonia.

Apart from the southern end, most of the water of Lake Michigan is still of reasonably good quality. In Lake Ontario, although it receives a considerable discharge of wastes, the situation is not yet as serious as in Lake Erie because Ontario's much larger volume of water provides a higher dilution factor. Lake Huron, bordered by a comparatively small population, so far shows only minor pollution effects, and Lake Superior almost none. Nevertheless, the growth of the entire region and the spreading pollution of the lakes and their tributary waters make the long-range outlook disquieting. Already the quality of the waters over a considerable portion of the lake system has greatly deteriorated, and many bathing beaches must be closed periodically because of pollution.

It is clear that in less than 150 years man has brought about changes in the Great Lakes that probably would have taken many centuries under natural conditions. These changes, shortening the usable life of the lakes, seem to be accumulating at an ever increasing rate. We still know far too little about the complicated processes that are under way or about what measures are necessary to conserve this great continental resource. Obviously the problem calls for much more study and for action that will not be too little and too late. No doubt the Great Lakes will be there for a long time to come; they are not likely to dry up in the foreseeable future. But it will be tragic irony if one day we have to look out over their vast waters and reflect bitterly, with the Ancient Mariner, that there is not a drop to drink. To realize that this is not an unthinkable eventuality we need only remind ourselves of the water crisis in New York City, where water last year had to be drastically rationed while billions of gallons in the grossly polluted Hudson River flowed uselessly by the city.

64.

Eleanor Garst: The A-Sexual Society

The most serious problem facing the human race at the beginning of the last third of the twentieth century was that there were too many human beings, or at least that there would be too many by the year 2000. Theoretically, the earth could provide subsistence for twice or thrice its present population, and practically it might be able to do this if there were enough time. But with the world's population growing at more than 2 percent a year it appeared that there would not be time, and that mankind was headed for a frightful reckoning. In the circumstances, the widespread efforts to produce a safe, cheap, and reliable birth-control device seemed to be the only solution. The contraceptive pill was the best known, if not necessarily the best, such device, and it occasioned much talk about the morals of America's youth. Of equal importance was the prospect that The Pill might finally emancipate women from their age-old dependent role. Eleanor Garst discussed this and other possibilities in an article published by the Center for the Study of Democratic Institutions late in 1966.

Source: *Center Diary: 15*, November-December 1966.

It seems logical to me to study the American housewife as the prototype for the new society. The analogy is apt. The American housewife already has a Guaranteed Annual Income: she married it. She has abundant leisure, except for the years of childbearing. Technically she has freedom, justice, equality; she is a person before the law. She has the vote and she has power; she has direct control of a substantial proportion of the nation's wealth. She has automated slaves to do her bidding.

As participating citizens and consumers, women could easily make the transition to abundance. It would not be too difficult for the housewife in the new society to learn to put up with having Himself underfoot twenty-four hours a day: early retirement, longer vacations, shorter work weeks, have conditioned her. She could even face having the young educated at home by TV.

It may be granted that women haven't yet produced much that is very important (except the human race — and that's debatable). Yet we might remember that it was the Athenian slaves who made possible our model democracy — and they weren't all males. Somebody had to provide the environment in which philosophers could contemplate infinity; somebody had to see that the species continued. Whether that involved settling the roving tribes into agriculture, or seeing that white and colored children are educated equally, women have seen the vacuum and filled it.

But tomorrow is all new. The biological revolution for the first time will truly free half the human race. None of us has yet begun to grasp the staggering implications.

Almost every individual now living would have lived quite differently if reproduction had been subject to free mutual choice.

Many of us would not be here. Will life be the same when every girl at the onset of puberty takes The Pill as routinely as she sees her dentist? — when the psychological separation of intercourse and reproduction has become as complete as the physical separation now can be?

What the Negro revolution has wrought in a few short years in this country, what the have-nots have wrought in a few short years on the world scene, pales by comparison with changes that will appear when women grasp the fact that not in some distant millennium, but *now*, they are truly free.

We are hurtling into, not a bisexual or a multisexual, but an asexual society: the boys grow long hair and the girls wear pants. (King Arthur's knights wore long hair and women in Asia have always worn pants; but Americans are horrified because nobody is staying in his place.) The girls take pills and the boys take LSD. When you can't tell who's who, it may be a joke, or a bad thing, or a good thing. But it does raise problems. Romance will disappear; in fact, it has almost disappeared now. No one will remember, either, what the equal-rights-for-women struggle was all about, which is probably just as well.

Given the Guaranteed Annual Income and The Pill, will women choose to marry? Why should they? Sex will be taken for granted when the possibility of accidental pregnancy is no longer omnipresent. It will be a pleasurable activity still, presumably, but not necessarily confined to one partner for life (how often is it now?). Heterosexual relationship will still be qualitatively different from homosexual relationship, but already, in cities where there are large concentrations of women, different kinds of communities are growing. Will society re-vert to dormitory arrangements? What social patterns will emerge? These, in turn, will affect the political climate, the economy, education, physical planning, environment. Will children be bred selectively as in some of the utopias? Will bonuses be paid for *not* having children? Will the heterosexual relationship be disapproved?

What of the time when the fertilized ovum can be implanted in the womb of a mercenary, and one's progeny selected from a sperm-bank? Will the lady choose to reproduce her husband, if there still are such things? If she's too busy feeding data to the computer, she can send her husband to select the desired model and arrange to have it cultivated under ideal conditions. No problems, no jealousy, no love-transference, no emotions. If there are any, they will at least be very different from those now experienced.

And what of the children, incubated perhaps under glass? (Shaw may have guessed well when he had them emerging from eggs at the age of 18.) Will they become the responsibility of the total community rather than of a set of parents? Will communal love develop the human qualities that we assume emerge from the present rearing of children? Will women under these conditions lose the survival drive and become as death-oriented as the present generation of American men?

I don't raise the questions in advocacy — I consider some of the possibilities horrifying. What disturbs me is the real possibility of the disappearance of our humane, life-giving qualities with the speed of developments in the life sciences, and the fact that no one seems to be discussing the alternative possibilities for good and evil in these developments.

Many waters cannot quench love, neither can the floods drown it.
Song of Solomon 8:7

65.

W. J. BRENNAN, JR., H. BLACK, AND W. O. DOUGLAS: *Ginzburg et al. v. United States*

Since March 1873, when Congress first legislated against sending obscene literature through the mails, American courts have had to deal with the issue of literary censorship. By and large, as public sentiment over the years has grown more tolerant, court decisions have also shown liberalizing tendencies, in spite of the fact that state and local censorship boards have remained rigid in their outlook. The U.S. Supreme Court, by liberal decisions, has opened the way for publication of hitherto banned books. But in the case from which the following selection is taken, the Supreme Court took a stricter view of the matter of obscenity and upheld a previous conviction of Ralph Ginzburg for sending obscene literature through the mail. The Court in this decision set new guidelines for the definition of obscenity by viewing the published materials in the larger context of the use of advertising, circumstances of publication, and sales technique and type of publicity, any of which taken alone could lead to the judgment that there was an intent at obscenity involved in publication. Reprinted below, in part, are the opinion of the Court by Justice William J. Brennan, Jr., and dissents by Justices Hugo Black and William O. Douglas, rendered March 21, 1966.

Source: 383 U.S. 463.

Mr. Justice Brennan. A judge sitting without a jury in the District Court for the Eastern District of Pennsylvania convicted petitioner Ginzburg and three corporations controlled by him upon all twenty-eight counts of an indictment charging violation of the federal obscenity statute. . . .[1] Each

1. The federal obscenity statute, 18 U.S.C. Section 1461, provides in pertinent part:
   "Every obscene, lewd, lascivious, indecent, filthy, or vile article, matter, thing, device, or substance; and . . . every written or printed card, letter, circular, book, pamphlet, advertisement, or notice of any kind giving information, directly or indirectly, where, or how, or from whom, or by what means any of such mentioned matters . . . may be obtained . . . is declared to be nonmailable matter and shall not be conveyed in the mails or delivered from any post office or by any letter carrier.
   "Whoever knowingly uses the mails for the mailing, carriage in the mails, or delivery of anything declared by this section to be nonmailable . . . shall be fined not more than $5,000 or imprisoned not more than five years, or both, for the first such offense. . . ."

count alleged that a resident of the Eastern District received mailed matter, either one of three publications challenged as obscene, or advertising telling how and where the publications might be obtained. . . .

We affirm. Since petitioners do not argue that the trial judge misconceived or failed to apply the standards we first enunciated in *Roth* v. *United States* . . . the only serious question is whether those standards were correctly applied.

In the cases in which this Court has decided obscenity questions since *Roth*, it has regarded the materials as sufficient in themselves for the determination of the question. In the present case, however, the prosecution charged the offense in the context of the circumstances of production, sale, and publicity and assumed that, standing alone, the publications themselves might not be obscene. We agree that the question of obscenity may include consideration of the setting in which the publications were presented as an aid to determining the question of obscenity, and assume without deciding that the prosecution could not have succeeded otherwise. . . .

We view the publications against a background of commercial exploitation of erotica solely for the sake of their prurient appeal. The record in that regard amply supports the decision of the trial judge that the mailing of all three publications offended the statute.

The three publications were *Eros,* a hardcover magazine of expensive format; *Liaison,* a biweekly newsletter; and *The Housewife's Handbook on Selective Promiscuity* (hereinafter the *Handbook*), a short book. The issue of *Eros* specified in the indictment, Vol. 1, No. 4, contains fifteen articles and photoessays on the subject of love, sex, and sexual relations. The specified issue of *Liaison,* Vol. 1, No. 1, contains a prefatory "Letter from the Editors," announcing its dedication to "keeping sex an art and preventing it from becoming a science." The remainder of the issue consists of digests of two articles concerning sex and sexual relations which had earlier appeared in professional journals and a report of an interview with a psychotherapist who favors the broadest license in sexual relationships. As the trial judge noted, "[w]hile the treatment is largely superficial, it is presented entirely without restraint of any kind. According to defendants' own expert, it is entirely without literary merit." . . .

The *Handbook* purports to be a sexual autobiography detailing with complete candor the author's sexual experiences from age three to age thirty-six. The text includes, and prefatory and concluding sections of the book elaborate, her views on such subjects as sex education of children, laws regulating private consensual adult sexual practices, and the equality of women in sexual rela-

tionships. It was claimed at trial that women would find the book valuable, for example, as a marriage manual or as an aid to the sex education of their children.

Besides testimony as to the merit of the material, there was abundant evidence to show that each of the accused publications was originated or sold as stock-in-trade of the sordid business of pandering — "the business of purveying textual or graphic matter openly advertised to appeal to the erotic interest of their customers." *Eros* early sought mailing privileges from the postmasters of Intercourse and Blue Ball, Pennsylvania. The trial court found the obvious, that these hamlets were chosen only for the value their names would have in furthering petitioners' efforts to sell their publications on the basis of salacious appeal; the facilities of the post offices were inadequate to handle the anticipated volume of mail, and the privileges were denied. Mailing privileges were then obtained from the postmaster of Middlesex, New Jersey. *Eros* and *Liaison* thereafter mailed several million circulars soliciting subscriptions from that post office; over 5,500 copies of the *Handbook* were mailed.

The "leer of the sensualist" also permeates the advertising for the three publications. The circulars sent for *Eros* and *Liaison* stressed the sexual candor of the respective publications, and openly boasted that the publishers would take full advantage of what they regarded as an unrestricted license allowed by law in the expression of sex and sexual matters. The advertising for the *Handbook,* apparently mailed from New York, consisted almost entirely of a reproduction of the introduction of the book, written by one Dr. Albert Ellis. Although he alludes to the book's informational value and its putative therapeutic usefulness, his remarks are preoccupied with the book's sexual imagery.

The solicitation was indiscriminate, not limited to those, such as physicians or psychiatrists, who might independently discern the book's therapeutic worth. Inserted in each advertisement was a slip labeled "GUARANTEE" and reading, "Documentary Books, Inc. unconditionally guarantees full refund of the price of *The Housewife's Handbook on Selective Promiscuity* if the book fails to reach you because of U.S. Post Office censorship interference." Similar slips appeared in the advertising for *Eros* and *Liaison;* they highlighted the gloss petitioners put on the publications, eliminating any doubt what the purchaser was being asked to buy.

This evidence, in our view, was relevant in determining the ultimate question of obscenity and, in the context of this record, serves to resolve all ambiguity and doubt. The deliberate representation of petitioners' publications as erotically arousing, for example, stimulated the reader to accept them as prurient; he looks for titillation, not for saving intellectual content. Similarly, such representation would tend to force public confrontation with the potentially offensive aspects of the work; the brazenness of such an appeal heightens the offensiveness of the publications to those who are offended by such material.

And the circumstances of presentation and dissemination of material are equally relevant to determining whether social importance claimed for material in the courtroom was, in the circumstances, pretense or reality — whether it was the basis upon which it was traded in the marketplace or a spurious claim for litigation purposes. Where the purveyor's sole emphasis is on the sexually provocative aspects of his publications, that fact may be decisive in the determination of obscenity. Certainly in a prosecution which, as here, does not necessarily imply suppression of the materials involved, the fact that they originate or are used as a subject of pandering is relevant to the application of the *Roth* test.

A proposition argued as to *Eros,* for example, is that the trial judge improperly found the magazine to be obscene as a whole, since he concluded that only four of the fifteen articles predominantly appealed to prurient interest and substantially exceeded community standards of candor, while the other articles were admittedly nonoffensive. But the trial judge found that "[t]he deliberate and studied arrangement of *Eros* is editorialized for the purpose of appealing predominantly to prurient interest and to insulate through the inclusion of nonoffensive material." . . . However erroneous such a conclusion might be if unsupported by the evidence of pandering, the record here supports it. *Eros* was created, represented, and sold solely as a claimed instrument of the sexual stimulation it would bring. Like the other publications, its pervasive treatment of sex and sexual matters rendered it available to exploitation by those who would make a business of pandering to "the widespread weakness for titillation by pornography." Petitioners' own expert agreed, correctly we think, that "[i]f the object [of a work] is material gain for the creator through an appeal to the sexual curiosity and appetite," the work is pornographic. In other words, by animating sensual detail to give the publication a salacious cast, petitioners reinforced what is conceded by the government to be an otherwise debatable conclusion. . . .

It is important to stress that this analysis simply elaborates the test by which the obscenity *vel non* of the material must be judged. Where an exploitation of interests in titillation by pornography is shown with respect to material lending itself to such exploitation through pervasive treatment or description of sexual matters, such evidence may support the determination that the material is obscene even though in other contexts the material would escape such condemnation.

Mr. Justice Black. Only one stark fact emerges with clarity out of the confusing welter of opinions and thousands of words written in this and two other cases today. That fact is that Ginzburg, petitioner here, is now finally and authoritatively condemned to serve five years in prison for distributing printed matter about sex which neither Ginzburg nor anyone else could possibly have known to be criminal. Since, as I have said many times, I believe the federal government is without any power whatever under the Constitution to put any type of burden on speech and expression of ideas of any kind (as distinguished from conduct), I agree with Part II of the dissent of my Brother Douglas in this case, and I would reverse Ginzburg's conviction on this ground alone. Even assuming, however, that the Court is correct in holding today that Congress does have power to clamp official censorship on some subjects selected by the Court, in some ways approved by it, I believe that the federal obscenity statute as enacted by Congress and as enforced by the Court against Ginzburg in this case should be held invalid on two other grounds.

Criminal punishment by government, although universally recognized as a necessity in limited areas of conduct, is an exercise of one of government's most awesome and dangerous powers. Consequently, wise and good governments make all possible efforts to hedge this dangerous power by restricting it within easily identifiable boundaries. Experience, and wisdom flowing out of that experience, long ago led to the belief that agents of government should not be vested with power and discretion to define and punish as criminal past conduct which had not been clearly defined as a crime in advance. To this end, at least in part, written laws came into being, marking the boundaries of conduct for which public agents could thereafter impose punishment upon people. In contrast, bad governments either wrote no general rules of conduct at all, leaving that highly important task to the unbridled discretion of government agents at the moment of trial, or sometimes, history tells us, wrote their laws in an unknown tongue so that people could not understand them or else placed their written laws at such inaccessible spots that people could not read them. It seems to me that these harsh expedients used by bad governments to punish people for conduct not previously clearly marked as criminal are being used here to put Mr. Ginzburg in prison for five years. . . .

It is obvious that the effect of the Court's decisions in the three obscenity cases handed down today is to make it exceedingly dangerous for people to discuss either orally or in writing anything about sex. Sex is a fact of life. Its pervasive influence is felt throughout the world and it cannot be ignored. Like all other facts of life it can lead to difficulty and trouble and sorrow and pain. But while it may lead to abuses, and has in many instances, no words need be spoken in order for people to know that the subject is one pleasantly interwoven in all human activities and involves the very substance of the creation of life itself. It is a subject which people are bound to consider and discuss, whatever laws are passed by any government to try to suppress it.

Though I do not suggest any way to solve the problems that may arise from sex or discussions about sex, of one thing I am confident, and that is that federal censorship is not the answer to these problems. I find it difficult to see how talk about sex can be placed under the kind of censorship the Court here approves without subjecting our society to more dangers than we can anticipate at the moment. It was to avoid exactly such dangers that the First Amendment was written and adopted. For myself, I would follow the course which I believe is required by the First Amendment; that is, recognize that sex at least as much as any other aspect of life is so much a part of our society that its discussion should not be made a crime.

I would reverse this case.

Mr. Justice Douglas. Today's condemnation of the use of sex symbols to sell literature engrafts another exception on First Amendment rights that is as unwarranted as the judge-made exception concerning obscenity. This new exception condemns an advertising technique as old as history. The advertisements of our best magazines are chock-full of thighs, ankles, calves, bosoms, eyes, and hair, to draw the potential buyer's attention to lotions, tires, food, liquor, clothing, autos, and even insurance policies. The sexy advertisement neither adds to nor detracts from the quality of the merchandise being offered for sale. And I do not see how it adds to or detracts one whit from the legality of the book being distributed. A book should stand on its own, irrespective of the reasons why it was written or the wiles used in selling it. I cannot imagine any promotional effort that would make Chapters 7 and 8 of the Song of Solomon any the less or any more worthy of First Amendment protection than does its unostentatious inclusion in the average edition of the Bible. . . . Certainly without the aura of sex in the promotion of these publications their contents cannot be said to be "utterly without redeeming social importance." . . .

One of the publications condemned today is *The Housewife's Handbook on Selective Promiscuity,* which a number of doctors and psychiatrists thought had clinical value. One clinical psychologist said:

I should like to recommend it, for example, to the people in my church to read, especially those who are having marital difficulties, in order to increase their tolerance and understanding for one another. Much of the book, I should

think, would be very suitable reading for teenage people, especially teen-age young women who could empathize strongly with the growing-up period that Mrs. Rey [Anthony] relates, and could read on and be disabused of some of the unrealistic notions about marriage and sexual experiences. I should think this would make very good reading for the average man to help him gain a better appreciation of female sexuality. . . .

Then there is the newsletter *Liaison.* One of the defendants' own witnesses, critic Dwight Macdonald, testified that while, in his opinion, it did not go beyond the customary limits of candor tolerated by the community, it was "an extremely tasteless, vulgar, and repulsive issue." This may, perhaps, overstate the case, but *Liaison* is admittedly little more than a collection of "dirty" jokes and poems, with the possible exception of an interview with Dr. Albert Ellis. . . . *Liaison's* appeal is neither literary nor spiritual. But neither is its appeal to a "shameful or morbid interest in nudity, sex, or excretion." The appeal is to the ribald sense of humor which is — for better or worse — a part of our culture. A mature society would not suppress this newsletter as obscene but would simply ignore it.

Then there is *Eros.* The Court affirms the judgment of the lower court, which found only four of the many articles and essays to be obscene. One of the four articles consisted of numerous ribald limericks, to which the views expressed as to *Liaison* would apply with equal force. Another was a photo essay entitled "Black and White in Color" which dealt with interracial love: a subject undoubtedly offensive to some members of our society. Critic Dwight Macdonald testified:

I suppose if you object to the idea of a Negro and a white person having sex together, then, of course, you would be horrified by it. I don't. From the artistic point of view, I thought it was very good. In fact, I thought it was done with great taste, and I don't know how to say it — I never heard of him before, but he is obviously an extremely competent and accomplished photographer. . . .

The very contrast in the color of the two bodies, of course, has presented him with certain opportunities that he would not have had with two models of the same color, and he has taken rather extraordinary and very delicate advantage of these contrasts.

The third article found specifically by the trial judge to be obscene was a discussion by Drs. Eberhard W. and Phyllis C. Kronhausen of erotic writing by women, with illustrative quotations. The worth of the article was discussed by Dwight Macdonald, who stated:

I thought [this was] an extremely interesting and important study with some remarkable quotations from the woman who had put down her sense of love-making, of sexual intercourse . . . in an extremely eloquent way. I have never seen this from the woman's point of view. I thought the point they made, the difference between the man's and the woman's approach to sexual intercourse, was very well-made and very important.

Still another article found obscene was a short introduction to and a lengthy excerpt from *My Life and Loves* by Frank Harris, about which there is little in the record. Suffice it to say that this seems to be a book of some literary stature. At least I find it difficult on this record to say that it is "utterly without redeeming social importance."

Some of the tracts for which these publishers go to prison concern normal sex, some homosexuality, some the masochistic yearning that is probably present in everyone and dominant in some. Masochism is a desire to be punished or subdued. In the broad frame of reference, the desire may be expressed in the longing to be whipped and lashed, bound and gagged, and cruelly treated. Why is it unlawful to cater to the needs of this group? They are, to be sure, some-

what offbeat, nonconformist, and odd. But we are not in the realm of criminal conduct, only ideas and tastes. Some like Chopin, others like "rock and roll." Some are "normal," some are masochistic, some deviant in other respects, such as the homosexual. Another group also represented here translates mundane articles into sexual symbols. This group, like those embracing masochism, are anathema to the so-called stable majority.

But why is freedom of the press and expression denied them? Are they to be barred from communicating in symbolisms important to them? When the Court today speaks of "social value," does it mean a "value" to the majority? Why is not a minority "value" cognizable? The masochistic group is one; the deviant group is another. Is it not important that members of those groups communicate with each other? Why is communication by the "written word" forbidden? If we were wise enough, we might know that communication may have greater therapeutical value than any sermon that those of the "normal" community can ever offer. But if the communication is of value to the masochistic community or to others of the deviant community, how can it be said to be "utterly without redeeming social importance"? "Redeeming" to whom? "Importance" to whom? . . .

Man was not made in a fixed mold. If a publication caters to the idiosyncrasies of a minority, why does it not have some "social importance"? Each of us is a very temporary transient, with likes and dislikes that cover the spectrum. However plebeian my tastes may be, who am I to say that others' tastes must be so limited and that other tastes have no "social importance"? How can we know enough to probe the mysteries of the subconscious of our people and say that this is good for them and that is not? Catering to the most eccentric taste may have "social importance" in giving that minority an opportunity to express itself rather than to repress its inner desires, as I suggest in my separate opinion in *Memoirs v. Massachusetts*. . . . How can we know that this expression may not *prevent* antisocial conduct?

I find it difficult to say that a publication has no "social importance" because it caters to the taste of the most unorthodox amongst us. We members of this Court should be among the last to say what should be orthodox in literature. An omniscience would be required which few in our whole society possess.

66.

Robert S. McNamara: Military Hardware, Economic Assistance, and Civic Action

In the midst of struggling with Congress over the Vietnam war policy as well as over the plans for a new bomber that Congress wanted but he did not, Defense Secretary Robert S. McNamara found time in May 1966 to deliver the following major address before a meeting of the American Society of Newspaper Editors in Montreal. The speech included a controversial suggestion that every young American give two years of service to his country, either in the armed forces, in the Peace Corps, in VISTA, or in some other voluntary work. But the speech was much more than that. In the course of it McNamara eloquently discussed most of the major problems that faced the United States at the time and offered solutions for many of them.

Source: VSD, June 1, 1966: "Voluntary Service for All Youth."

ANY AMERICAN would be fortunate to visit this lovely island city, in this hospitable land. But there is a special satisfaction for a secretary of defense to cross the longest border in the world — and realize that it is also the least armed border in the world. It prompts one to reflect how negative and narrow a notion of defense still clouds our century.

There is still among us an almost ineradicable tendency to think of our security problem as being exclusively a military problem, and to think of the military problem as being exclusively a weapons-system or hardware problem. The plain, blunt truth is that contemporary man still conceives of war and peace in much the same stereo-typed terms that his ancestors did. The fact that these ancestors — both recent and remote — were conspicuously unsuccessful at avoiding war, and enlarging peace, doesn't seem to dampen our capacity for cliches.

We still tend to conceive of national security almost solely as a state of armed readiness — a vast, awesome arsenal of weaponry. We still tend to assume that it is primarily this purely military ingredient that creates security. We are still haunted by this concept of military hardware.

But how limited a concept this actually is becomes apparent when one ponders the kind of peace that exists between the United States and Canada. It is a very cogent example. Here we are, two modern nations — highly developed technologically, each with immense territory, both enriched with great reserves of natural resources, each militarily sophisticated — and, yet, we sit across from one another, divided by an unguarded frontier of thousands of miles . . . and there is not a remotest set of circumstances, in any imaginable time-frame of the future, in which our two nations would wage war on one another. . . .

The decisive factor for a powerful nation, already adequately armed, is the character of its relationships with the world and groups of nations: first, those that are struggling to develop; second, those free nations that have reached a level of strength and prosperity that enables them to contribute to the peace of the world; and, finally, those nations who might be tempted to make themselves our adversaries. For each of these groups, the United States — to preserve its own intrinsic security — has to have distinctive sets of relationships.

First, we have to help protect those developing countries which genuinely need and request our help, and which — as an essential precondition — are willing and able to help themselves.

Second, we have to encourage and achieve a more effective partnership with those nations who can and should share international peacekeeping responsibilities.

Third, we must do all we realistically can to reduce the risk of conflict with those who might be tempted to take up arms against us.

Let us examine these three sets of relationships in detail.

First, the developing nations. Roughly, 100 countries today are caught up in the difficult transition from traditional to modern societies. There is no uniform rate of progress among them, and they range from primitive mosaic societies — fractured by tribalism and held feebly together by the slenderest of political sinews — to relatively sophisticated countries, well on the road to agricultural sufficiency and industrial competence. This sweeping surge of development, particularly across the whole southern half of the globe, has no parallel in history. It has turned traditionally listless areas of the world into seething cauldrons of change.

On the whole, it has not been a very peaceful process. In the last eight years alone there have been no less than 164 internationally significant outbreaks of violence — each of them specifically designed as a serious challenge to the authority, or the very existence, of the government in question. . . . Given the certain connection between economic stagnation and the incidence of violence, the years that lie ahead for the nations in the southern half of the globe are pregnant with violence.

This would be true even if no threat of Communist subversion existed — as it clearly does. Both Moscow and Peking — however harsh their internal differences — regard the whole modernization process as an ideal environment for the growth of communism. Their experience with subversive internal war is extensive; and they have developed a considerable array of both doctrine and practical measures in the art of political violence. What is often misunderstood is that Communists are capable of subverting, manipulating, and, finally, directing for their own ends, the wholly legitimate grievances of a developing society.

But it would be a gross oversimplification to regard communism as the central factor in every conflict throughout the underdeveloped world. Of the 149 serious internal insurgencies in the past eight years, Communists have been involved in only 58 of them — 38 percent of the total — and this includes 7 instances in which a Communist regime itself was the target of the uprising.

Whether Communists are involved or not, violence anywhere in a taut world transmits sharp signals through the complex ganglia of international relations; and the security of the United States is related to the security and stability of nations half a globe away.

But neither conscience nor sanity itself suggests that the United States is, should, or could be the global gendarme. . . . The United States has no mandate from on high to police the world, and no inclination to do so. There have been classic cases in which our deliberate nonaction was the wisest action of all. Where our help is not sought, it is seldom prudent to volunteer. . . .

But . . . the irreducible fact remains that our security is related directly to the security of the newly developing world. And our role must be precisely this: to help provide security to those developing nations which genuinely need and request our help, and which demonstrably are willing and able to help themselves.

The rub comes in this: We do not always grasp the meaning of the word security in this context. In a modernizing society, security means development. Security is not military hardware — though it may include it. Security is not military force — though it may involve it. Security is not traditional military activity — though it may encompass it. Security is development. Without development, there can be no security. A developing nation that does not in fact develop simply cannot remain "secure." It cannot remain secure for the intractable reason that its own citizenry cannot shed its human nature. If security implies anything, it implies a minimal measure of order and stability. Without internal development of at least a minimal degree, order and stability are simply not possible. They are not possible because human nature cannot be frustrated beyond intrinsic limits. It reacts because it must.

Now, that is what we do not always understand; and that is also what governments of modernizing nations do not always understand. But by emphasizing that security arises from development, I do not say that an underdeveloped nation cannot be subverted from within; or be aggressed upon from without; or be the victim of a combination of the two. It can. And to prevent any or all of these conditions, a nation does require appropriate military capabilities to deal with the specific problem. But the specific military problem is only a narrow facet of the broader security problem.

Military force can help provide law and order — but only to the degree that a basis for law and order already exists in the developing society: A basic willingness on the part of the people to cooperate. The law and order is a shield, behind which the central fact of security — development — can be achieved.

Now we are not playing a semantic game with these words. The trouble is that we have been lost in a semantic jungle for too long. We have come to identify "security" with exclusively military phenomena; and most particularly with military hardware. But it just isn't so. And we need to accommodate to the facts of the matter if we want to see security survive and grow in the southern half of the globe.

Development means economic, social, and political progress. It means a reasonable standard of living — and the word "reasonable" in this context requires continual redefinition. What is "reasonable" in an earlier stage of development will become "unreasonable" in a later stage.

As development progresses, security progresses; and when the people of a nation have organized their own human and natural resources to provide themselves with what they need and expect out of life — and have learned to compromise peacefully among competing demands in the larger national interest — then their resistance to disorder and violence will be enormously increased. Conversely, the tragic need of desperate men to resort to force to achieve the inner imperatives of human decency will diminish.

Now I have said that the role of the United States is to help provide security to these modernizing nations — providing they need and request our help; and are clearly willing and able to help themselves. But what should our help be? Clearly, it should be help toward development.

In the military sphere, that involves two broad categories of assistance. We should help the developing nation with such training and equipment as is necessary to maintain the protective shield behind which development can go forward. The dimensions of that shield vary from country to country; but what is essential is that it should be a shield and not a capacity for external aggression.

The second, and perhaps less understood category of military assistance in a modernizing nation, is training in civic action. "Civic action" is another one of those semantic puzzles. Too few Americans — and too few officials in developing nations — really comprehend what military civic action means.

Essentially, it means using indigenous military forces for nontraditional military projects — projects that are useful to the local population in fields such as education, public works, health, sanitation, agriculture — indeed, anything connected with economic or social progress. It has had some impressive results. In the past four years, the United States-assisted civic action program, worldwide, has constructed or repaired more than 10,000 miles of roads; built over 1,000 schools, hundreds of hospitals and clinics; and has provided medical and dental care to approximately 4 million people. What is important is that all this was done by indigenous men in uniform. Quite apart from the developmental projects themselves, the program powerfully alters the negative image of the military man, as the oppressive preserver of the stagnant status quo.

But assistance in the purely military sphere is not enough. Economic assistance is also essential. The President is determined that our aid should be hardheaded and rigorously realistic; that it should deal directly with the roots of underdevelopment and not merely attempt to alleviate the symptoms. His bedrock principle is that United States economic aid — no matter what its magnitude — is futile unless the country in question is resolute in making the primary effort itself. That will be the criterion, and that will be the crucial condition for all our future assistance.

Only the developing nations themselves can take the fundamental measures that make outside assistance meaningful. These measures are often unpalatable and frequently call for political courage and decisiveness. But to fail to undertake painful but essential reform inevitably leads to far more painful revolutionary violence. Our economic assistance is designed to offer a reasonable alternative to that violence. It is designed to help substitute peaceful progress for tragic internal conflict.

The United States intends to be compassionate and generous in this effort, but it is not an effort it can carry exclusively by itself. And thus it looks to those nations who have reached the point of self-sustaining prosperity to increase their contribution to the development — and, thus, to the security — of the modernizing world.

And that brings me to the second set of relationships that I underscored at the outset; it is the policy of the United States to encourage and achieve a more effective partnership with those nations who can, and should, share international peacekeeping responsibilities. . . .

If, for example, other nations genuinely believe — as they say they do — that it is in the common interest to deter the expansion of Red China's economic and political control beyond its national boundaries, then they must take a more active role in guarding the defense perimeter. . . .

The plain truth is the day is coming when no single nation, however powerful, can undertake by itself to keep the peace outside its own borders. Regional and international organizations for peacekeeping purposes are as yet rudimentary; but they must grow in experience and be strengthened by deliberate and practical cooperative action. . . .

The Organization of the American States in the Dominican Republic, the more than thirty nations contributing troops or supplies to assist the government of South Vietnam, indeed even the parallel efforts of the United States and the Soviet Union in the Pakistan-India conflict — these efforts, together with those of the United Nations, are the first attempts to substitute multinational for unilateral policing of violence. They point to the peacekeeping patterns of the future.

We must not merely applaud the idea. We must dedicate talent, resources, and hard practical thinking to its implementation.

In Western Europe — an area whose burgeoning economic vitality stands as a monument to the wisdom of the Marshall Plan — the problems of security are neither static nor wholly new. Fundamental changes are under way, though certain inescapable realities remain. The conventional forces of NATO, for example, still require a nuclear backdrop far beyond the capability of any Western European nation to supply, and the United States is fully committed to provide that major nuclear deterrent. However, the European members of the alliance have a natural desire to participate more actively in nuclear planning. A central task of the alliance today is, therefore, to work out the relationships and institutions through which shared nuclear planning can be effective. We have made a practical and promising start in the special committee of NATO defense ministers.

Common planning and consultation are essential aspects of any sensible substitute to the unworkable and dangerous alternative of independent national nuclear forces within the alliance. And even beyond the alliance, we must find the means to prevent the proliferation of nuclear weapons. That is a clear imperative.

There are, of course, risks in nonproliferation arrangements; but they cannot be compared with the indefinitely greater risks that would arise out of the increase in national nuclear stockpiles. In the calculus of risk, to proliferate independent national nuclear forces is not a mere arithmetical addition of danger. We would not be merely adding up risks. We would be insanely multiplying them. If we seriously intend to pass on a world to our children that is not threatened by nuclear holocaust, we must come to grips with the problem of proliferation. A reasonable nonproliferation agreement is feasible; for there is no adversary with whom we do not share a common interest in avoiding mutual destruction triggered by an irresponsible nth power.

That brings me to the third and last set of relationships the United States must deal with. Those with nations who might be tempted to take up arms against us. These relationships call for realism. But realism is not a hardened, inflexible, unimaginative attitude. The realistic mind is a restlessly creative mind — free of naïve delusions, but full of practical alternatives.

There are practical alternatives to our current relationships with both the Soviet Union and Communist China. A vast ideological chasm separates us from them and, to a degree, separates them from one another. There is nothing to be gained from our seeking an ideological rapprochement; but breaching the isolation of great nations like Red China, even when that isolation is largely of its own making, reduces the danger of potentially catastrophic misunderstandings and increases the incentive on both sides to resolve disputes by reason rather than by force.

There are many ways in which we can build bridges toward nations who would cut themselves off from meaningful contact with us. We can do so with properly balanced trade relations, diplomatic contacts, and, in some cases, even by exchanges of military observers.

We have to know where it is we want to place this bridge; what sort of traffic we want to travel over it; and on what mutual foundations the whole structure can be designed. There are no one-cliff bridges. If you are going to span a chasm, you have to rest the structure on both cliffs. Now, cliffs, generally speaking, are rather hazardous places. Some people are afraid even to look over the edge. But in a thermonuclear world, we cannot afford any political acrophobia.

President Johnson has put the matter squarely. By building bridges to those who make themselves our adversaries, "we can help gradually to create a community of interest, a community of trust, and a community of effort."

With respect to a "community of effort" let me suggest a concrete proposal for our own present young generation in the United States. It is a committed and dedicated generation. It has proven that in its enormously impressive performance in the Peace Corps overseas and in its willingness to volunteer for a final assault on such poverty and lack of opportunity that still remains in our own country. As matters stand, our present Selective Service System draws on only a minority of eligible young men. That is an inequity. It seems to me that we could move toward remedying that inequity by asking every young person in the United States to give two years of service to his country — whether in one of

the military services, in the Peace Corps, or in some other volunteer developmental work at home or abroad. We could encourage other countries to do the same; and we could work out exchange programs — much as the Peace Corps is already planning to do.

While this is not an altogether new suggestion, it has been criticized as inappropriate while we are engaged in a shooting war. But I believe precisely the opposite is the case. It is more appropriate now than ever, for it would underscore what our whole purpose is in Vietnam — and, indeed, anywhere in the world where coercion, or injustice, or lack of decent opportunity still holds sway. It would make meaningful the central concept of security: A world of decency and development, where every man can feel that his personal horizon is rimmed with hope.

Mutual interest, mutual trust, mutual effort — those are the goals. Can we achieve those goals with the Soviet Union, and with Communist China? Can they achieve them with one another?

The answer to these questions lies in the answer to an even more fundamental question. Who is man? Is he a rational animal? If he is, then the goals can ultimately be achieved. If he is not, then there is little point in making the effort.

All the evidence of history suggests that man is indeed a rational animal — but with a near infinite capacity for folly. His history seems largely a halting but persistent effort to raise his reason above his animality. He draws blueprints for utopia, but never quite gets it built. In the end, he plugs away obstinately with the only building material really ever at hand: His own part-comic, part-tragic, part-cussed but part-glorious nature.

I, for one, would not count a global free society out. Coercion, after all, merely captures man; freedom captivates him.

67.

J. WILLIAM FULBRIGHT: The Arrogance of Power

The following speech by Arkansas Senator J. William Fulbright should be viewed against the background of other statements by him on U.S. foreign policy. During televised hearings of the Senate Foreign Relations Committee early in 1966, Chairman Fulbright warned that the war in Vietnam might lead to armed conflict with China and urged that the United States halt the bombing of North Vietnam, review the entire military situation, and begin peace talks. In a Senate speech on March 1, 1966, he reiterated his warning and called for a "general accommodation" with China and for the "neutralization" of Southeast Asia. The administration paid little heed, and in the speech reprinted here in part, delivered at Johns Hopkins University School of Advanced International Studies on April 21, Fulbright emphasized the importance of responsible dissent. On June 20 he repeated his warning during his committee's hearings on NATO policy, again declaring that the U.S. could not act as "policeman for the world." Shortly after Fulbright's address at Johns Hopkins, President Johnson replied in a speech at Princeton on the obligation of power.

Source: *New York Times Magazine*, May 15, 1966: "The Fatal Arrogance of Power."

To CRITICIZE ONE'S COUNTRY is to do it a service and pay it a compliment. It is a service because it may spur the country to do better than it is doing; it is a compliment because it evidences a belief that the country can do better than it is doing.

Criticism may embarrass the country's leaders in the short run but strengthen their hand in the long run; it may destroy a consensus on policy while expressing a consensus of values. Woodrow Wilson once said that there was "such a thing as being too proud to fight." There is also, or ought to be, such a thing as being too confident to conform, too strong to be silent in the face of apparent error. Criticism, in short, is more than a right — it is an act of patriotism — a higher form of patriotism, I believe, than the familiar rituals of national adulation.

Thus, it is not pejorative but a tribute to say that America is worthy of criticism. If, nonetheless, one is charged with a lack of patriotism, I would reply with Albert Camus: "No, I didn't love my country, if pointing out what is unjust in what we love amounts to not loving, if insisting that what we love should measure up to the finest image we have of her amounts to not loving."

What is the finest image of America? To me it is the image of a composite — or, better still, a synthesis — of diverse peoples and cultures, come together in harmony but not identity, in an open, receptive, generous, and creative society.

We are an extraordinary nation, endowed with a rich and productive land and a talented and energetic population. Surely a nation so favored is capable of extraordinary achievement, not only in the area of producing and enjoying great wealth — where our achievements have indeed been extraordinary — but also in the area of human and international relations — in which area, it seems to me, our achievements have fallen short of our capacity and promise. The question that I find intriguing is whether a nation so extraordinarily endowed as the United States can overcome that arrogance of power which has afflicted, weakened, and, in some cases, destroyed great nations in the past.

The causes of the malady are a mystery but its recurrence is one of the uniformities of history: Power tends to confuse itself with virtue and a great nation is peculiarly susceptible to the idea that its power is a sign of God's favor, conferring upon it a special responsibility for other nations — to make them richer and happier and wiser, to remake them, that is, in its own shining image.

Power also tends to take itself for omnipotence. Once imbued with the idea of a mission, a great nation easily assumes that it has the means as well as the duty to do God's work. The Lord, after all, surely would not choose you as His agent and then deny you the sword with which to work His will. German soldiers in the First World War wore belt buckles imprinted with the words *"Gott mit uns."* It was approximately under this kind of infatuation — an exaggerated sense of power and an imaginary sense of mission — that the Athenians attacked Syracuse and Napoleon and then Hitler invaded Russia. In plain words, they overextended their commitments and they came to grief.

My question is whether America can overcome the fatal arrogance of power. My hope and my belief are that it can, that it has the human resources to accomplish what few, if any, great nations have ever accomplished before: to be confident but also tolerant and rich but also generous; to be willing to teach but also willing to learn; to be powerful but also wise. I believe that America is capable of all of these things; I also believe it is falling short of them. Gradually but unmistakably we are succumbing to the arrogance of power. In so doing we are not living up to our capacity and promise; the measure of our falling short is the measure of the patriot's duty of dissent.

The discharge of that most important duty is handicapped in America by an unworthy tendency to fear serious criticism of our government. In the abstract we celebrate freedom of opinion as a vital part of our patriotic liturgy. It is only when some Americans exercise the right that other Americans are shocked. No one, of course, ever criticizes the right of dissent; it is always this particular instance of it or its exercise under these particular circumstances or at this particular time that throws people into a blue funk. . . .

No one challenges the value and importance of national consensus, but consensus can be understood in two ways. If it is interpreted to mean unquestioning support of existing policies, its effects can only be pernicious and undemocratic, serving to suppress differences rather than to reconcile them. If, on the other hand, consensus is understood to mean a general agreement on goals and values, but not necessarily on the best means of realizing them, then it becomes a lasting basis of national strength.

It is consensus in this sense which has made America strong in the past. Indeed, much of our national success in combining change with continuity can be attributed to the vigorous competition of men and ideas within a context of shared values and generally accepted institutions. It is only through this kind of vigorous competition of ideas that a consensus of values can sometimes be translated into a true consensus of policy. . . .

A second great advantage of free discussion to democratic policymakers is its bringing to light of new ideas and the supplanting of old myths with new realities. We Americans are much in need of this benefit because we are severely, if not uniquely, afflicted with a habit of policy making by analogy: North Vietnam's involvement in South Vietnam, for example, is equated with Hitler's invasion of Poland and a parley with the Viet Cong would represent another Munich.

The treatment of slight and superficial resemblances as if they were full-blooded analogies — as instances, as it were, of history "repeating itself" — is a substitute for thinking and a misuse of history. . . .

There is a kind of voodoo about American foreign policy. Certain drums have to be beaten regularly to ward off evil spirits; for example, the maledictions which are regularly uttered against North Vietnamese aggression, the "wild men" in Peking, communism in general, and President de Gaulle. Certain pledges must be repeated every day lest the whole free world go to rack and ruin — for example, we will never go back on a commitment no matter how unwise; we regard this alliance or that as absolutely "vital" to the free world; and, of course, we will stand stalwart in Berlin from now until Judgment Day. Certain words must never be uttered except in derision — the word "appeasement," for example, comes as near as any word can to summarizing everything that is regarded by American policymakers as stupid, wicked, and disastrous.

I do not suggest that we should heap praise on the Chinese Communists, dismantle NATO, abandon Berlin, and seize every opportunity that comes along to appease our enemies. I do suggest the desirability of an atmosphere in which unorthodox ideas would arouse interest rather than horror, reflection rather than emotion. As likely as not, new proposals, carefully examined, would be found wanting and old policies judged sound; what is wanted is not change itself but the capacity for change.

Consider the idea of "appeasement." In a free and healthy political atmosphere it would elicit neither horror nor enthusiasm but only interest in what precisely its proponent had in mind. As Winston Churchill once said: "Appeasement in itself may be good or bad according to circumstances. . . . Appeasement from strength is magnanimous and noble and might be the surest and perhaps the only path to world peace."

In addition to its usefulness for redeeming error and introducing new ideas, free and open criticism has a third, more abstract but no less important function in a democracy. It is therapy and catharsis for those who are troubled or dismayed by something their country is doing; it helps to reassert traditional values, to clear the air when it is full of tension and mistrust.

There are times in public life as in private life when one must protest, not solely or even primarily because one's protest will be politic or materially productive but because one's sense of decency is offended, because one is fed up with political craft and public images, or simply because something goes against the grain. The catharsis thus provided may indeed be the most valuable of freedom's uses.

While not unprecedented, protests against a war in the middle of the war are a rare experience for Americans. I see it as a mark of strength and maturity that an articulate minority have raised their voices against the Vietnamese war and that the majority of Americans are enduring this dissent — not without anxiety, to be sure, but with better grace and understanding than would have been the case in any other war of the 20th century.

It is by no means certain that the relatively healthy atmosphere in which the debate is now taking place will not give way to a new era of McCarthyism. The longer the Vietnamese war goes on without prospect of victory or negotiated peace, the higher the war fever will rise. Past experience provides little basis for confidence that reason can prevail in such an atmosphere. In a contest between a hawk and a dove, the hawk has a great advantage, not because it is a better bird but because it is a bigger bird with lethal talons and a highly developed will to use them.

Without illusions as to the prospect of success, we must try nonetheless to bring reason and restraint into the emotionally charged atmosphere in which the Vietnamese war is now being discussed. Instead of trading epithets about the legitimacy of debate, we would do well to focus on the issue itself, recognizing that all of us make mistakes and that mistakes can be corrected only if they are acknowledged and discussed, and recognizing further that war is not its own justification, that it can and must be discussed unless we are prepared to sacrifice our traditional democratic processes to a false image of national unanimity.

In fact, the protesters against the Vietnamese war are in good historical company. On Jan. 12, 1848, Abraham Lincoln rose in the United States House of Representatives and made a speech about the Mexican War worthy of Senator Morse. Lincoln's speech was an explanation of a vote he had recently cast in support of a resolution declaring that the war had been unnecessarily and unconstitutionally begun by President Polk. "I admit," he said, "that such a vote should not be given in mere party wantonness, and that the one given is justly censurable if it had no other, or better, foundation. I am one of those who joined in that vote, and I did so under my best impression of the *truth* of the case."

That is exactly what the students and professors and politicians who oppose the Vietnamese war have been doing: They have been acting on their "best impression of the *truth* of the case." Some of our superpatriots assume that any war the United States fights is a just war, if not indeed a holy crusade, but history does not sustain their view. No reputable historian would deny that the United States has fought some wars which were unjust, unnecessary, or both — I would suggest the War of 1812, the Civil War, and the Spanish-American War as examples. In a historical frame of reference it seems to me logical and proper to question the wisdom of our present military involvement in Asia.

Protesters against the Vietnamese war have been held up to scorn on the ground that they wish to "select their wars," by which it is apparently meant that it is hypocritical to object to this particular war while not objecting to war in general. I fail to understand what is reprehensible about trying to make moral distinctions between one war and another — between, for example, resistance to Hitler and intervention in Vietnam. From the time of Grotius to the drafting of the United Nations Charter, international lawyers have tried to distinguish between "just wars" and "unjust wars." It is a difficult problem of law and an even more difficult problem of morality, but it is certainly a valid problem.

Under the American Constitution, the Congress — especially the Senate — has a particular responsibility in coping with such problems, yet in recent years the Congress has not fully discharged its obligations in the field of foreign relations. The reduced role of the Congress and the enhanced role of the President in the making of foreign policy are not the result merely of President Johnson's ideas of consensus; they are the culmination of a trend in the constitutional relationship between President and Congress that began in 1940 — that is to say, at the beginning of this age of crisis.

The cause of the change is crisis itself. The President has the authority and resources to make decisions and take actions in an emergency; the Congress does not. Nor, in my opinion, should it; the proper responsibilities of the Congress are to reflect and review, to advise and criticize, to consent and to withhold consent.

In the past twenty-five years, American foreign policy has encountered a shattering series of crises and inevitably — or almost inevitably — the effort to cope with these has been executive effort, while the Congress, inspired by patriotism, importuned by presidents and deterred by lack of information, has tended to fall in line. The result has been an unhinging of traditional constitutional relationships; the Senate's constitutional powers of advice and consent have atrophied into what is widely regarded — though never asserted — to be a duty to give prompt consent with a minimum of advice.

Two examples will illustrate the extent to which this trend has gone. On the afternoon of April 28, 1965, the leaders of Congress were called to an emergency meeting at the White House. We were told that the revolution that had broken out four days before in the Dominican Republic had got completely out of hand, that Americans and other foreigners on the scene were in great danger, and that American Marines would be landed in Santo Domingo that night for the sole purpose of protecting the lives of Americans and other foreigners. None of the congressional leaders expressed disapproval.

Four months later, after an exhaustive review of the Dominican crisis by the Senate Foreign Relations Committee, it was clear beyond reasonable doubt that, while saving American lives may have been a factor in the decision to intervene on April 28, the major reason had been a determination on the part of the United States government to defeat the rebel, or constitutionalist, forces whose victory at that time was imminent. Had I known in April what I knew in August, I most certainly would have objected to the American intervention in the Dominican Republic.

Almost nine months before the Domini-

can intervention, on Aug. 5, 1964, the Congress received an urgent request from President Johnson for the immediate adoption of a joint resolution regarding Southeast Asia. On August 7, after perfunctory committee hearings and a brief debate, the Congress, with only two senators dissenting, adopted the resolution, authorizing the President "to take all necessary steps, including the use of armed force," against aggression in Southeast Asia.

The joint resolution was a blank check signed by the Congress in an atmosphere of urgency that seemed at the time to preclude debate. Since its adoption, the administration has converted the Vietnamese conflict from a civil war in which some American advisers were involved to a major international war in which the principal fighting unit is an American army of 250,000 men. Each time that senators have raised questions about successive escalations of the war, we have had the blank check of Aug. 7, 1964, waved in our faces as supposed evidence of the overwhelming support of the Congress for a policy in Southeast Asia which, in fact, has been radically changed since the summer of 1964.

All this is very frustrating to some of us in the Senate, but we have only ourselves to blame. Had we met our responsibility of careful examination of a presidential request, had the Senate Foreign Relations Committee held hearings on the resolution before recommending its adoption, had the Senate debated the resolution and considered its implications before giving its overwhelming approval, we might have put limits and qualifications on our endorsement of future uses of force in Southeast Asia — if not in the resolution itself, then in the legislative history preceding its adoption. As it was, only Senators Morse and Gruening debated the resolution.

I myself, as chairman of the Foreign Relations Committee, served as floor manager of the Southeast Asia resolution and did all

I could to bring about its prompt and overwhelming adoption. I did so because I was confident that President Johnson would use our endorsement with wisdom and restraint. I was also influenced by partisanship: an election campaign was in progress and I had no wish to make any difficulties for the President in his race against a Republican candidate whose election I thought would be a disaster for the country. My role in the adoption of the resolution of Aug. 7, 1964, is a source of neither pleasure nor pride to me today — although I do not regret the outcome of the election.

The problem, then, is to find ways by which the Senate and individual senators can discharge their constitutional *duties* of advice and consent in an age in which the direction and philosophy of foreign policy are largely shaped by urgent decisions made at moments of crisis.

The Senate as a whole, I think, should undertake to revive and strengthen its deliberative function. Acting on the premise that dissent is not disloyalty, that a true consensus is shaped by airing our differences rather than suppressing them, the Senate should again become, as it used to be, an institution in which the great issues of American politics are contested with thoroughness, energy, and candor. . . .

I believe that the public hearings on Vietnam, by bringing before the American people a variety of opinions and disagreements pertaining to the war, and perhaps by helping to restore a degree of balance

between the executive and the Congress, have done far more to strengthen the country than to weaken it. The hearings have been criticized on the ground that they conveyed an "image" of the United States as divided over the war. Since the country obviously *is* divided, what was conveyed was a fact rather than an image. . . .

An individual senator, attempting to make a useful contribution to the country's foreign relations, faces some special problems. A senator who wishes to influence foreign policy must consider the probable results of communicating privately with the executive or, alternatively, of speaking out publicly. I do not see any great principle involved here; it is a matter of how one can better achieve what one hopes to achieve. For my own part, I have used both methods, with results varying according to circumstance. Other things being equal — which they seldom are — I find it more agreeable to communicate privately with Democratic Presidents and publicly with Republican Presidents. . . .

It is difficult to measure the effectiveness of a public statement by a senator — a speech, say — because its effect may be something *not* done rather than some specific action or change of policy by the executive. Generally speaking, it seems to me that a senator's criticism is less likely to affect the case in point than it is to affect some similar case in the future. . . . As to my criticisms — and those of my colleagues — regarding the Vietnamese war, their effect remains to be seen.

Early in life I had to choose between honest arrogance and hypocritical humility.
I chose honest arrogance, and have seen no occasion to change.

FRANK LLOYD WRIGHT

68.

Lyndon B. Johnson: The Obligation of Power

By 1966 the controversy caused by the war in Vietnam had produced a serious division
within the Democratic Party. Senator J. William Fulbright of Arkansas was a
leader of the attacks by some of his fellow Democrats on the President's policy. In
an address on April 21, 1966, at the Johns Hopkins University School of Advanced
International Studies, Fulbright had charged that the U.S. involvement in Vietnam
was largely the result of an exercise of executive authority, and had asserted that
America was succumbing to "that arrogance of power which has afflicted, weakened,
and, in some cases, destroyed great nations in the past." President Johnson replied
in the following speech at the Woodrow Wilson School of Public and International
Affairs of Princeton University, on May 11, 1966.

Source: VSD, June 1, 1966: "The Need for Scholars."

Governor Hughes, President Goheen, Trustees, Faculty and Students, Secretary Gardner, and Distinguished Guests of Princeton:

I am happy that I could come here today to help celebrate Princeton's continued growth. It is good that one of the nation's oldest universities is still young enough to grow.

This commitment to the increase of higher learning has deep roots in this country. Our forefathers had founded more than fifty colleges before the republic was a half a century old. With a sure sense that the pursuit of knowledge must be part and parcel of the pursuit of life, liberty, and happiness, they set in motion two forces which have helped to shape this land.

The first was that learning must erect no barriers of class or creed. The university was to nourish an elite to which all could aspire. Soon after our first colleges, came the first scholarships for worthy students who could not pay their own way.

The second idea was that the university would not stand as a lonely citadel isolated from the rest of the community. Its mission would be to search for truth and to serve mankind. As Woodrow Wilson later said: "It is the object of learning, not only to satisfy the curiosity and perfect the spirits of individual men but also to advance civilization."

We who work in Washington very much know the need for the vital flow of men and ideas between the halls of learning and the places of power. Each time my Cabinet meets I can call the roll of former professors — Humphrey and Rusk, McNamara and Wirtz, Katzenbach, another distinguished Princetonian, Gardner, and Weaver.

The 371 major appointments that I have made as President, in the two and a half years that I have occupied that office, collectively hold 758 advanced degrees. Two of my own White House counselors I borrowed from Princeton and they are here with me today — Dr. Donald Hornig and

Dr. Eric Goldman. And so many are the consultants called from behind the ivy that a university friend of mine recently said to me "at any given moment a third of the faculties of the United States are on a plane going somewhere to advise even if not always to consent."

While learning has long been the ally of democracy, the intellectual has not always been the partner of government. As recently as the early years of this century the scholar stood outside the pale of policy, with government usually indifferent to him. That, I'm glad to say, has changed. The intellectual today is very much an inside man. Since the 1930s our government has put into effect major policies which men of learning have helped to fashion. More recently, the 89th Congress passed bill after bill, measure after measure suggested by scholars from all over the country whom I had placed on task forces that were appointed in 1964. In almost every field of governmental concern from economics to national security the academic community has become a central instrument of public policy in these United States.

The affluence of power for an intellectual community that once walked on the barren fringes of authority has not been won without some pain. An uneasy conscience is the price any concerned man pays, whether politician or professor, for a share of power in this nuclear age. More than one scholar, thus, has learned how deeply frustrating it is to try to bring purist approaches to a highly impure problem. They have come to recognize how imperfect are the realities which must be wrestled with in this most complicated world. They have learned that criticism is one thing and that diplomacy is another. They have learned to fear dogmatism in the classroom as well as in the Capitol and to reject the notion that expertise acquired in a lifetime of study in one discipline brings expertise in all other subjects as well.

They have learned, too, that strident emotionalism in the pursuit of truth, no matter how disguised in the language of wisdom, is harmful to public policy, just as harmful as self-righteousness in the application of power, or, as Macaulay said, "the proof of virtue," and we might add, of wisdom, "is to possess boundless power without abusing it."

The responsible intellectual who moves between his campus and Washington knows above all that his task is, in the language of the current generation, "to cool it," to bring what my generation called "not heat but light" to public affairs. The man for whom this school is named always believed that to be the scope of real scholarship. He never doubted the interdependence of the intellectual community and the community of public service. The school, he said, must be the nation.

So, today we dedicate this building, not only to the man but to his faith that knowledge must be the underpinning of power and that public life is a calling that's worthy of the scholar as well as the politician.

There was once a time when knowledge seemed less essential to the process of government. Andrew Jackson held the opinion that the duties of all public offices were so plain and simple that any man of average intelligence could perform them. We are no longer so optimistic about our public servants. The public servant today moves along paths of adventure where he is helpless without the advanced tools of learning.

He seeks to chart the exploration of space, combining a thousand disciplines in an effort whose slightest miscalculation could have very fatal consequences. He is embarked on this planet on missions that are no less filled with risk and no less dependent on knowledge. He seeks to rebuild our cities and to reclaim the beauty of our countryside. He seeks to promote justice beyond our courtrooms, making education and health and opportunity the common birthright for every citizen; and he seeks to build peace based on man's hope rather than man's fears.

These goals will be the work of many men and of many years. We're still wrestling to provide a world safe for democracy, just as Wilson did more than fifty years ago. We're still fighting to gain the freedoms that Roosevelt talked about more than thirty years ago.

All of these will call for enormous new drafts of trained manpower that will be available for public service. Over the next four years the federal government will need 36,000 more scientists and engineers and 6,000 more specialists in health and technology and education. By 1970 our state governments, Governor Hughes, must grow by more than 600,000 to keep pace with the times.

Employment for state and local government will exceed 10 million persons. Each year over the next decade our nation will need 200,000 new public schoolteachers to keep up just with our growing population. The call for public service therefore cannot be met by professionals alone. We must revive the ancient ideal of citizen soldiers who answer their nation's call in time of peril. We need them on battlefronts where no guns are heard but freedom is no less tested.

So here at the Woodrow Wilson School you have done much to raise the sights of public service and I urge you to continue to promote its excellence at all levels. We intend to do the same in Washington, sparing no effort to assist those who select this as their life work.

I've asked chairman John Macy of the Civil Service Commission to head up a task force that will survey federal programs for career advancement. I've asked him to study an expanded program of graduate training which will help — which with the help of the universities can enlarge our efforts to develop the talents and broaden the horizons of our public service career officers.

I also intend next year to recommend to our Congress a program of expanding opportunities for those exceptionally talented who wish to go into training for our public service. And we will assist students that are planning careers in federal and state and local governments, colleges and universities that are seeking to enrich their own programs in this field, and local and state governments that are seeking to develop more effective career services for all of their employees.

Our concept of public service is changing to meet the demands of the hour. A new public servant has emerged. He may be the scholar who leaves his studies for the crucible of power in his state or national capital, or he may be the young man or woman who chooses public service but does not abandon at its doorstep the techniques of scholarship and the search for knowledge. These men and women will help us to answer the question that Franklin Roosevelt, our great American leader, asked more than thirty years ago: "Will it be said that democracy was a great dream but it could not do the job?"

President Roosevelt did not doubt the answer. Even as troubles mounted he took the starting steps to strengthen a federal structure capable of carrying this nation safely through its crisis. With his detractors and his debasers, with his dissenters and his doubters, just as Wilson had had to carry them a few decades before, he began to organize the modern office of the President and to bring American government into the mid-20th century.

Now, as we enter the final third of this century, we are engaged again today — yes, once again — with the question of whether democracy can do the job. Many fears of former years no longer seem so relevant. Neither Congress nor our Supreme Court indicate to me any signs of becoming rubber stamps to the executive. Moreover, the executive shows no symptoms of callous indifference to the ills that we must cure if we are to preserve our vitality. State and local governments are more alive and more involved than they were thirty years ago, and our nation's private enterprise has grown many times — many times over — in both size and vitality.

Some men, I remember vividly, said it was socialistic to consider enacting the Social Security measure. Some men said it was high-handed to favor the minimum wage when I first voted for it — 25 cents an hour. Some said it was the sign of an overbearing police state when I proposed the Voting Rights Bill only a short time ago.

Those who would change the status quo have been called many names, not only by the demagogue on the stump but on occasion by the intellectuals on the platform.

Forgotten now are the charges of socialism that were hurled at Social Security by the defenders of the status quo. Silent are the forces which cried "high-handed" at the minimum wage. Irrelevant today is the denunciation of the Voting Rights Law as an "overbearing act of a central authority, an act of a police state." The issue for this generation is a different kind. It has to do with the obligations of power in the world for a society that strives despite its worst flaws always to be just, fair, and human. Like almost every issue that we face, this is one in which scholars and public officials alike have a crucial stake.

Abroad we can best measure American involvement, whatever our successes and failures, by one simple proposition: not one single country where America has helped mount a major effort to resist aggression, from France, to Greece, to Korea, to Vietnam — not one single country where we have helped today has a government servile to outside interests.

There is a reason for this which I believe goes to the very heart of our society. The exercise of power in this century has meant for all of us in the United States not arrogance but agony. We have used our power

not willingly and recklessly ever but always reluctantly and with restraint. Unlike nations in the past with vast power at their disposal, the United States of America has never sought to crush the autonomy of her neighbors. We have not been driven by blind militarism down courses of devastating aggression, nor have we followed the ancient and conceited philosophy of the noble lie that some men are by nature meant to be slaves to others.

As I look upon America this morning from this great platform — this platform of one of her greatest universities — I see instead a nation whose might is not her master but her servant. I see a nation conscious of lessons so recently learned that security and aggression as well as peace and war must be the concerns of our foreign policy; that a great power influences the world just as surely when it withdraws its strength as when it exercises its strength; that aggression must be deterred where possible and met early when undertaken; that the application of military force when it becomes necessary must be for limited purposes and must be tightly controlled.

Surely it is not a paranoiac vision of America's place in the world to recognize that freedom is still indivisible, still has adversaries whose challenge must be answered. Today, of course, as we meet here, that challenge is sternest at the moment in Southeast Asia. Yet there, as elsewhere, our great power is also tempered by great restraint.

What nation has announced such limited objectives or such willingness to remove its military presence once those objectives are secured and achieved? What nation has spent the lives of its sons and vast sums of its fortune to provide the people of a small thriving country the chance to elect the course that we might not ourselves choose?

The aims for which we struggle are aims which in the ordinary course of affairs men of the intellectual world applaud and serve

— the principle of choice over coercion, the defense of the weak against the strong and the aggressive, the right — the right — of a young and frail nation to develop free from the interference of her neighbors, the ability of a people however inexperienced and however different and however diverse to fashion a society consistent with their own traditions and values and aspirations.

These are all at stake in that conflict. It is the consequences of the cost of their abandonment that men of learning must examine dispassionately, for, I would remind you, to wear the scholar's gown is to assume an obligation to seek truth without prejudice, and without clichés, even when the results of a search are sometimes at variance with one's own predilections and own opinions.

That is all that we expect from those who are troubled even as we are by the obligations of power the United States did not seek but from which the United States cannot escape.

It was twenty-six years ago that Archibald MacLeish asked of all scholars and writers and students of his generation what history would say of those who failed to oppose the forces of disorder then loose in Europe. We must ask of this generation the same question concerning Asia. MacLeish reminded that generation of the answer that was given by Leonardo when Michelangelo indicted him for indifference to the misfortunes of the Florentines. "Indeed," said Leonardo, "indeed the study of beauty has occupied my whole heart."

Other studies, no matter how important, must not now detract the man of learning from the misfortunes of freedom in Southeast Asia. While men may talk of the search for peace and the pursuit of peace, we really know that peace is not something to be discovered suddenly; it's not a thing to be caught and contained. Because peace must be built step by painful patient step. And the building will take the best work of the world's best men and women.

It will take men whose cause is not the cause of one nation but whose cause is the cause of all nations, men whose enemies are not other men but the historic foes of mankind. I hope that many of you will serve in this public service for our world.

Woodrow Wilson knew that learning is essential to the leadership that our world so desperately yearns for and needs today. Before he came to Princeton he attended a small college in North Carolina. He went to classes every day beneath a portal which bore the Latin inscription "Let Learning Be Cherished Where Liberty Has Arisen." Today this motto which served a President must also serve all mankind. Where liberty has arisen learning must be cherished or liberty itself becomes a very fragile thing.

We dedicate this building today not only to the man, not only to the nation's service, but to learning in the service of all mankind.

In the book of Egoism, it is written, Possession without obligation to the object possessed approaches felicity.

GEORGE MEREDITH, *The Egoist*

69.

STOKELY CARMICHAEL: Black Power

*What has been called the American Negro Revolution took many forms in the
twenty-two years between the end of World War II and 1967. At first a movement to
obtain such reforms as desegregation of the armed forces, it quickly concentrated
on school desegregation, an effort that won a legal victory with the Supreme Court
decisions of 1954 and 1955. Desegregation of public accommodations, especially in
the South, was the next goal, and although this too was largely achieved, the basic
problem remained unsolved. During the late 1950s and early 1960s the movement
was essentially nonviolent, despite occasional flareups, and its leaders were often
if not always clergymen like Martin Luther King. But as the 1960s wore on the
slogan changed from equal civil rights to Black Power, which expressed the Negro's
continuing frustration with the lack of real progress toward general social and
economic equality in the country. Stokely Carmichael, at the time the national
chairman of the Student Nonviolent Coordinating Committee, wrote the following article
for the* New York Review of Books *in September 1966. Entitled "What We Want,"
the article tried to sum up the feelings and desires of younger Negroes throughout the country.*

Source: *New York Review of Books,* September 22, 1966.

ONE OF THE TRAGEDIES of the struggle against racism is that up to now there has been no national organization which could speak to the growing militancy of young black people in the urban ghetto. There has been only a civil rights movement, whose tone of voice was adapted to an audience of liberal whites. It served as a sort of buffer zone between them and angry young blacks. None of its so-called leaders could go into a rioting community and be listened to. In a sense, I blame ourselves — together with the mass media — for what has happened in Watts, Harlem, Chicago, Cleveland, Omaha. Each time the people in those cities saw Martin Luther King get slapped, they became angry; when they saw four little black girls bombed to death, they were angrier; and when nothing happened, they were steaming. We had nothing to offer that they could see, except to go out and be beaten again. We helped to build their frustration.

For too many years, black Americans marched and had their heads broken and got shot. They were saying to the country, "Look, you guys are supposed to be nice guys and we are only going to do what we are supposed to do — why do you beat us up, why don't you give us what we ask, why don't you straighten yourselves out?" After years of this, we are at almost the same point — because we demonstrated from a position of weakness. We cannot be expected any longer to march and have our heads broken in order to say to whites: come on, you're nice guys. For you are not nice guys. We have found you out.

An organization which claims to speak for the needs of a community — as does the Student Nonviolent Coordinating Committee — must speak in the tone of that community, not as somebody else's buffer zone. This is the significance of black power as a slogan. For once, black people are going to use the words they want to use — not just the words whites want to hear. And they will do this no matter how often the press tries to stop the use of the slogan by equating it with racism or separatism.

An organization which claims to be working for the needs of a community — as SNCC does — must work to provide that community with a position of strength from which to make its voice heard. This is the significance of black power beyond the slogan.

Black power can be clearly defined for those who do not attach the fears of white America to their questions about it. We should begin with the basic fact that black Americans have two problems: they are poor and they are black. All other problems arise from this two-sided reality: lack of education, the so-called apathy of black men. Any program to end racism must address itself to that double reality.

Almost from its beginning, SNCC sought to address itself to both conditions with a program aimed at winning political power for impoverished Southern blacks. We had to begin with politics because black Americans are a propertyless people in a country where property is valued above all. We had to work for power, because this country does not function by morality, love, and nonviolence, but by power. Thus we determined to win political power, with the idea of moving on from there into activity that would have economic effects. With power, the masses could *make or participate in making* the decisions which govern their destinies, and thus create basic change in their day-to-day lives.

But if political power seemed to be the key to self-determination, it was also obvious that the key had been thrown down a deep well many years earlier. Disenfranchisement, maintained by racist terror, makes it impossible to talk about organizing for political power in 1960. The right to vote had to be won, and SNCC workers devoted their energies to this from 1961 to 1965. They set up voter registration drives in the Deep South. They created pressure for the vote by holding mock elections in Mississippi in 1963 and by helping to establish the Mississippi Freedom Democratic Party (MFDP) in 1964. That struggle was eased, though not won, with the passage of the 1965 Voting Rights Act. SNCC workers could then address themselves to the question: "Who can we vote for, to have our needs met — how do we make our vote meaningful?"

SNCC had already gone to Atlantic City for recognition of the Mississippi Freedom Democratic Party by the Democratic convention and been rejected; it had gone with the MFDP to Washington for recognition by Congress and been rejected. In Arkansas, SNCC helped thirty Negroes to run for School Board elections; all but one were defeated, and there was evidence of fraud and intimidation sufficient to cause their defeat. In Atlanta, Julian Bond ran for the state legislature and was elected — twice — and unseated — twice. In several states, black farmers ran in elections for agricultural committees which make crucial decisions concerning land use, loans, etc. Although they won places on a number of committees, they never gained the majorities needed to control them.

All of the efforts were attempts to win black power. Then, in Alabama, the opportunity came to see how blacks could be organized on an independent party basis. An unusual Alabama law provides that any group of citizens can nominate candidates for county office and, if they win 20 percent of the vote, may be recognized as a

county political party. The same then applies on a state level. SNCC went to organize in several counties such as Lowndes,
where black people — who form 80 percent of the population and have an average
annual income of $943 — felt they could
accomplish nothing within the framework
of the Alabama Democratic Party because
of its racism and because the qualifying fee
for this year's elections was raised from $50
to $500 in order to prevent most Negroes
from becoming candidates.

On May 3, five new county "freedom organizations" convened and nominated candidates for the offices of sheriff, tax assessor,
members of the school boards. These men
and women are up for election in November — if they live until then. Their ballot
symbol is the black panther: a bold, beautiful animal, representing the strength and
dignity of black demands today. A man
needs a black panther on his side when he
and his family must endure — as hundreds
of Alabamians have endured — loss of job,
eviction, starvation, and sometimes death,
for political activity. He may also need a
gun and SNCC reaffirms the right of black
men everywhere to defend themselves when
threatened or attacked.

As for initiating the use of violence, we
hope that such programs as ours will make
that unnecessary; but it is not for us to tell
black communities whether they can or cannot use any particular form of action to resolve their problems. Responsibility for the
use of violence by black men, whether in
self-defense or initiated by them, lies with
the white community.

This is the specific historical experience
from which SNCC's call for "black power"
emerged on the Mississippi march last July.
But the concept of "black power" is not a
recent or isolated phenomenon: It has
grown out of the ferment of agitation and
activity by different people and organizations in many black communities over the
years. Our last year of work in Alabama

added a new concrete possibility. In
Lowndes County, for example, black power
will mean that if a Negro is elected sheriff,
he can end police brutality. If a black man
is elected tax assessor, he can collect and
channel funds for the building of better
roads and schools serving black people —
thus advancing the move from political
power into the economic arena. In such
areas as Lowndes, where black men have a
majority, they will attempt to use it to exercise control. This is what they seek: control.

Where Negroes lack a majority, black
power means proper representation and
sharing of control. It means the creation of
power bases from which black people can
work to change statewide or nationwide
patterns of oppression through pressure
from strength — instead of weakness. Politically, black power means what it has always meant to SNCC: the coming-together
of black people to elect representatives and
*to force those representatives to speak to their
needs*. It does not mean merely putting
black faces into office. A man or woman
who is black and from the slums cannot be
automatically expected to speak to the
needs of black people. Most of the black
politicians we see around the country today
are not what SNCC means by black power.
The power must be that of a community,
and emanate from there.

SNCC today is working in both North
and South on programs of voter registration
and independent political organizing. In
some places, such as Alabama, Los Angeles,
New York, Philadelphia, and New Jersey,
independent organizing under the black
panther symbol is in progress. The creation
of a national "black panther party" must
come about; it will take time to build, and
it is much too early to predict its success.
We have no infallible master plan and we
make no claim to exclusive knowledge of
how to end racism; different groups will
work in their own different ways. SNCC
cannot spell out the full logistics of self-

Don Getsug from Rapho Guillumette
Stokely Carmichael speaking in Minneapolis, Minn.

area but the essential result has been the same — a powerful few have been maintained and enriched at the expense of the poor and voiceless colored masses. This pattern must be broken. As its grip loosens here and there around the world, the hopes of black Americans become more realistic. For racism to die, a totally different America must be born.

This is what the white society does not wish to face; this is why that society prefers to talk about integration. But integration speaks not at all to the problem of poverty, only to the problem of blackness. Integration today means the man who "makes it," leaving his black brothers behind in the ghetto as fast as his new sports car will take him. It has no relevance to the Harlem wino or to the cottonpicker making $3 a day. As a lady I know in Alabama once said, "The food that Ralph Bunche eats doesn't fill my stomach."

Integration, moreover, speaks to the problem of blackness in a despicable way. As a goal, it has been based on complete acceptance of the fact that *in order to have* a decent house or education, blacks must move into a white neighborhood or send their children to a white school. This reinforces, among both black and white, the idea that "white" is automatically better and "black" is by definition inferior. This is why integration is a subterfuge for the maintenance of white supremacy. It allows the nation to focus on a handful of Southern children who get into white schools, at great price, and to ignore the 94 percent who are left behind in unimproved all-black schools.

Such situations will not change until black people have power — to control their own school boards, in this case. Then Negroes become equal in a way that means something, and integration ceases to be a one-way street. Then integration doesn't mean draining skills and energies from the ghetto into white neighborhoods; then it

determination but it can address itself to the problem by helping black communities define their needs, realize their strength, and go into action along a variety of lines which they must choose for themselves. Without knowing all the answers, it can address itself to the basic problem of poverty; to the fact that in Lowndes County, eighty-six white families own 90 percent of the land. What are black people in that county going to do for jobs, where are they going to get money? There must be reallocation of land, of money.

Ultimately, the economic foundations of this country must be shaken if black people are to control their lives. The colonies of the United States — and this includes the black ghettoes within its borders, North and South — must be liberated. For a century, this nation has been like an octopus of exploitation, its tentacles stretching from Mississippi and Harlem to South America, the Middle East, southern Africa, and Vietnam; the form of exploitation varies from area to can mean white people moving from Beverly Hills into Watts, white people joining the Lowndes County Freedom Organization. Then integration becomes relevant.

Last April, before the furor over black power, Christopher Jencks wrote in a *New Republic* article on white Mississippi's manipulation of the antipoverty program:

> The war on poverty has been predicated on the notion that there is such a thing as *a community* which can be defined geographically and mobilized for a collective effort to help the poor. This theory has no relationship to reality in the Deep South. In every Mississippi county there are *two* communities. Despite all the pious platitudes of the moderates on both sides, these two communities habitually see their interests in terms of conflict rather than cooperation. Only when the Negro community can muster enough political, economic, and professional strength to compete on somewhat equal terms, will Negroes believe in the possibility of true cooperation and whites accept its necessity. En route to integration, the Negro community needs to develop greater independence — a chance to run its own affairs and not cave in whenever "the man" barks. . . . Or so it seems to me, and to most of the knowledgeable people with whom I talked in Mississippi. To OEO, this judgment may sound like black nationalism. . . .

Mr. Jencks, a white reporter, perceived the reason why America's antipoverty program has been a sick farce in both North and South. In the South, it is clearly racism which prevents the poor from running their own programs; in the North, it more often seems to be politicking and bureaucracy. But the results are not so different: In the North, non-whites make up 42 percent of all families in metropolitan "poverty areas" and only 6 percent of families in areas classified as not poor. SNCC has been working with local residents in Arkansas, Alabama, and Mississippi to achieve control by the poor of the program and its funds; it has

also been working with groups in the North, and the struggle is no less difficult. Behind it all is a federal government which cares far more about winning the war on the Vietnamese than the war on poverty; which has put the poverty program in the hands of self-serving politicians and bureaucrats rather than the poor themselves; which is unwilling to curb the misuse of white power but quick to condemn black power.

To most whites, black power seems to mean that the Mau Mau are coming to the suburbs at night. The Mau Mau are coming, and whites must stop them. Articles appear about plots to "get Whitey," creating an atmosphere in which "law and order must be maintained." Once again, responsibility is shifted from the oppressor to the oppressed. Other whites chide, "Don't forget — you're only 10 percent of the population; if you get too smart, we'll wipe you out." If they are liberals, they complain, "What about me? — don't you want my help any more?" These are people supposedly concerned about black Americans, but today they think first of themselves, of their feelings of rejection. Or they admonish, "You can't get anywhere without coalitions," when there is in fact no group at present with whom to form a coalition in which blacks will not be absorbed and betrayed. Or they accuse us of "polarizing the races" by our calls for black unity, when the true responsibility for polarization lies with whites who will not accept their responsibility as the majority power for making the democratic process work.

White America will not face the problem of color, the reality of it. The well-intended say: "We're all human, everybody is really decent, we must forget color." But color cannot be "forgotten" until its weight is recognized and dealt with. White America will not acknowledge that the ways in which this country sees itself are contradicted by being black — and always have been.

Whereas most of the people who settled this country came here for freedom or for economic opportunity, blacks were brought here to be slaves.

When the Lowndes County Freedom Organization chose the black panther as its symbol, it was christened by the press "the Black Panther Party" — but the Alabama Democratic Party, whose symbol is a rooster, has never been called the White Cock Party. No one ever talked about "white power" because power in this country *is* white. All this adds up to more than merely identifying a group phenomenon by some catchy name or adjective. The furor over that black panther reveals the problems that white America has with color and sex; the furor over "black power" reveals how deep racism runs and the great fear which is attached to it.

Whites will not see that I, for example, as a person oppressed because of my blackness, have common cause with other blacks who are oppressed because of blackness. This is not to say that there are no white people who see things as I do, but that it is black people I must speak to first. It must be the oppressed to whom SNCC addresses itself primarily, not to friends from the oppressing group.

From birth, black people are told a set of lies about themselves. We are told that we are lazy — yet I drive through the Delta area of Mississippi and watch black people picking cotton in the hot sun for fourteen hours. We are told, "If you work hard, you'll succeed" — but if that were true, black people would own this country. We are oppressed because we are black — not because we are ignorant, not because we are lazy, not because we're stupid (and got good rhythm), but because we're black.

I remember that when I was a boy, I used to go to see Tarzan movies on Saturday. White Tarzan used to beat up the black natives. I would sit there yelling, "Kill the beasts, kill the savages, kill 'em!"

I was saying: Kill *me*. It was as if a Jewish boy watched Nazis taking Jews off to concentration camps and cheered them on. Today, I want the chief to beat hell out of Tarzan and send him back to Europe. But it takes time to become free of the lies and their shaming effect on black minds. It takes time to reject the most important lie: That black people inherently can't do the same things white people can do, unless white people help them.

The need for psychological equality is the reason why SNCC today believes that blacks must organize in the black community. Only black people can convey the revolutionary idea that black people are able to do things themselves. Only they can help create in the community an aroused and continuing black consciousness that will provide the basis for political strength. In the past, white allies have furthered white supremacy without the whites involved realizing it — or wanting it, I think. Black people must do things for themselves; they must get poverty money they will control and spend themselves; they must conduct tutorial programs themselves so that black children can identify with black people. This is one reason Africa has such importance: The reality of black men ruling their own natives gives blacks elsewhere a sense of possibility, of power, which they do not now have.

This does not mean we don't welcome help or friends. But we want the right to decide whether anyone is, in fact, our friend. In the past, black Americans have been almost the only people whom everybody and his momma could jump up and call their friends. We have been tokens, symbols, objects — as I was in high school to many young whites, who liked having "a Negro friend." We want to decide who is our friend, and we will not accept someone who comes to us and says: "If you do X, Y, and Z, then I'll help you." We will not be told whom we should choose as allies.

We will not be isolated from any group or nation except by our own choice. We cannot have the oppressors telling the oppressed how to rid themselves of the oppressor.

I have said that most liberal whites react to "black power" with the question, What about me?, rather than saying: Tell me what you want me to do and I'll see if I can do it. There are answers to the right question. One of the most disturbing things about almost all white supporters of the movement has been that they are afraid to go into their own communities — which is where the racism exists — and work to get rid of it. They want to run from Berkeley to tell us what to do in Mississippi; let them look instead at Berkeley. They admonish blacks to be nonviolent; let them preach nonviolence in the white community. They come to teach me Negro history; let them go to the suburbs and open up freedom schools for whites. Let them work to stop America's racist foreign policy; let them press this government to cease supporting the economy of South Africa.

There is a vital job to be done among poor whites. We hope to see, eventually, a coalition between poor blacks and poor whites. That is the only coalition which seems acceptable to us, and we see such a coalition as the major internal instrument of change in American society. SNCC has tried several times to organize poor whites; we are trying again now, with an initial training program in Tennessee. It is purely academic today to talk about bringing poor blacks and whites together, but the job of creating a poor-white power bloc must be attempted. The main responsibility for it falls upon whites. Black and white can work together in the white community where possible; it is not possible, however, to go into a poor Southern town and talk about integration. Poor whites everywhere are becoming more hostile — not less — partly because they see the nation's atten-

tion focused on black poverty and nobody coming to them. Too many young middle-class Americans, like some sort of Pepsi generation, have wanted to come alive through the black community; they've wanted to be where the action is — and the action has been in the black community.

Black people do not want to "take over" this country. They don't want to "get whitey"; they just want to get him off their backs, as the saying goes. It was, for example, the exploitation by Jewish landlords and merchants which first created black resentment toward Jews — not Judaism. The white man is irrelevant to blacks, except as an oppressive force. Blacks want to be in his place, yes, but not in order to terrorize and lynch and starve him. They want to be in his place because that is where a decent life can be had.

But our vision is not merely of a society in which all black men have enough to buy the good things of life. When we urge that black money go into black pockets, we mean the communal pocket. We want to see money go back into the community and used to benefit it. We want to see the cooperative concept applied in business and banking. We want to see black ghetto residents demand that an exploiting storekeeper sell them, at minimal cost, a building or a shop that they will own and improve cooperatively; they can back their demand with a rent strike, or a boycott, and a community so unified behind them that no one else will move into the building or buy at the store.

The society we seek to build among black people, then, is not a capitalist one. It is a society in which the spirit of community and humanistic love prevail. The word "love" is suspect; black expectations of what it might produce have been betrayed too often. But those were expectations of a response from the white community, which failed us. The love we seek to encourage is within the black community, the only

American community where men call each other "brother" when they meet. We can build a community of love only where we have the ability and power to do so: among blacks.

As for white America, perhaps it can stop crying out against "black supremacy," "black nationalism," "racism in reverse," and begin facing reality. The reality is that this nation, from top to bottom, is racist; that racism is not primarily a problem of "human relations" but of an exploitation maintained — either actively or through silence — by the society as a whole. Camus and Sartre have asked, can a man condemn himself? Can whites, particularly liberal whites, condemn themselves? Can they stop blaming us, and blame their own system? Are they capable of the shame which might become a revolutionary emotion?

We have found that they usually cannot condemn themselves, and so we have done it. But the rebuilding of this society, if at all possible, is basically the responsibility of whites — not blacks. We won't fight to save the present society, in Vietnam or anywhere else. We are just going to work, in the way *we* see fit, and on goals *we* define, not for civil rights but for all our human rights.

70.

KIRK DOUGLAS: On Patriotism

President Eisenhower established the "Person-to-Person" program in the belief that international tensions, particularly with the U.S.S.R., might be relaxed if more Russian and American citizens met and came to know each other. Under the program, which was administered by the State Department, a number of Americans traveled about the world, speaking to groups of businessmen, students, and others. One of these unofficial ambassadors was the Hollywood actor Kirk Douglas, who reported on some of his experiences to a meeting at the Center for the Study of Democratic Institutions in Santa Barbara, California. The following remarks on patriotism were published by the Center in 1966.

Source: *Center Diary:* 14, September-October 1966: "That Kind of Corn."

I'VE BEEN GOING on these tours for six straight years, and I've been all around the world now — to Latin America and out in Asia and twice across Europe. I pay my own way, and I turn down all the chances to plug my films or go to film festivals or make deals for my production company because I don't think it's right to mix business in with this. Sometimes it's great, you've got the university audiences with you, and you have time to talk with a lot of those young people in small groups, and you feel you are learning something too. And sometimes it's an awful drag, and you come to the end of a trip behind the Iron Curtain and you're sitting around in some place like Rumania and you've been frozen out because you were sent out by the State Department and the Rumanians are particularly sore at the United States that week — well, then, I tell my wife I've had it and we're not going to go through this again. And then the State Department calls up and the next thing I know, here I go again, back on the annual Kirk Douglas farewell tour. . . .

One time after I'd made a tour it suddenly occurred to me that I had never talked at an American university. So I went up to Berkeley. And, boy! I was impressed! I thought, there's no need to worry about this country — this group of students could handle any group of students I run into anywhere around the world. Maybe some of this is because of our democratic system which permits so much more freedom. Anyway I found myself fencing all over the lot . . . I didn't know where I was going to get it! But it was stimulating! It was exciting! They were bright, and they were sharp.

I think there is a special value in this contact with young people. I try to invite the same kind of give-and-take abroad. Maybe you could say I am taking unfair advantage of the impact of American movies all around the world. It's much more tremendous than you might think. And it gives me, you know, the basis to attract young people and communicate with them. I'm not there as a politician, I'm not there as a big smart professor who might overwhelm them. I'm there as someone they may have seen in movies, and this gives me a chance to talk to them about anything and everything.

Certainly I don't think of myself as much of a hero. But I do have a peculiar, corny concept of patriotism. I know we've reached a time when anyone who says, "I'm patriotic," is suspect, because it's a kind of square thing. But, if I analyze myself, it's a kind of . . . I do these things, make what small contribution it may be, out of a kind of . . . almost a guilt, if you will, which I understand is true of a lot of people.

You know, I'm one of the typical examples of America at work. My parents came from Russia, and they were illiterate immigrants. I taught my mother how to sign her name. They come here, they work hard, we don't have enough to eat — all that kind of corn. I say corn because it happened to so many people it became ordinary, and if anybody gave it to me as a script for a movie, I'd never do it. It would make a lousy movie! Still it's true and who can say it's not a big part of what America is? You come out of a background like that, you manage to get a college education, then you go into the work that you wanted to do, and finally you make it big. But the more I travel, the more I see that this is the only country where you have that much of a chance to do it.

So OK, so after a while every saying gets corny — even that one of President Kennedy's about, "Don't ask what your country can do for you; ask what you can do for your country." But he stimulated a lot of us, including me. That corny statement was the beginning of one of the greatest contributions any President has made, the development of the Peace Corps. There was a lot of interest in doing something for your country for a while after that. And I think that many Americans, if they had the chance, would still do a lot more for their country if they weren't afraid of seeming corny. I guess that's why it took me all this time just to say, "Well, I do it because I'm patriotic."

71.

WALTER LIPPMANN: The University

The problems of the university, as Walter Lippmann pointed out in the article reprinted below, go beyond the raising of money, the appeasing of alumni, the acquiring of faculties, and the care and feeding of students. The great problems are educational in the highest sense — they are concerned, that is, with ends, not means, with what the universities should be trying to do rather than with how to do it. Lippmann addressed himself to such matters and proposed that universities in our time must recognize that they have a high destiny indeed, none other, in fact, than filling "the modern void, which results from the vast and intricate process of emancipation and rationalization." His article, published late in May 1966, was adapted from an address given in California earlier in the month.

Source: *New Republic,* May 28, 1966.

I AM FREE OF THE OBLIGATION to offer solutions of the problems which occupy so much of the time of the governing authorities in the academic world: how to raise money, how to appease the alumni, how to get around the trustees, the state legislatures, the foundations and the Pentagon, how to ingratiate themselves with the chamber of commerce, the board of trade, and the clergy, how to tranquilize the egos of the faculty, how to deal with the students in their academic lives, their ideological lives, and their sexual lives, how to be cheerful and good fellows with the excessively inquiring reporters. About all of these preoccupations I shall have nothing to say. This leaves open to me the broad, unrestricted field of the human condition and what the universities ought to be doing for it and about it.

The proposition with which I am starting is that as men become modern men, they are emancipated and thus deprived of the guidance and support of traditional and cus-

tomary authority. Because of this, there has fallen to the universities a unique, indispensable and capital function in the intellectual and spiritual life of modern society. I do not say that the universities today are prepared to perform this spiritual and intellectual function. What I do say is that a way will have to be found to perform these functions if the pursuit of the good life, to which this country is committed, is to continue and to be successful.

For modern men are living today amidst the consequences of emancipation from established authority. The dream of Franklin and Jefferson, as Mr. James A. Perkins describes it in his recent Stafford Little Lecture, was of "an open society, free of both ecclesiastical and civil control, with little to fear from the uninhibited search for truth and for experiments in the application of truth." The preponderant majority of our people in America today have arrived at such an open society. They have found, I submit, that as they are emancipated from established authority they are not successfully equipped to deal with the problems of American society and of their private lives. They are left with the feeling that there is a vacuum within them, a vacuum where there were the signs and guide posts of an ancestral order, where there used to be ecclesiastical and civil authority, where there was certainty, custom, usage and social status, and a fixed way of life. One of the great phenomena of the human condition in the modern age is the dissolution of the ancestral order, the erosion of established authority; and, having lost the light and the leading, the guidance and the support, the discipline that the ancestral order provided, modern men are haunted by a feeling of being lost and adrift, without purpose and meaning in the conduct of their lives. The thesis which I am putting to you is that the modern void, which results from the vast and intricate process of emancipation and rationalization, must be filled, and that the universities must fill the void because they alone can fill it.

It is a high destiny. But it must be accepted and it must be realized.

Before we can proceed, we must ask ourselves why, in the quest of a good life in a good society, we now turn to the universities rather than, let us say, to the churches or the government. We do that because the behavior of man depends ultimately on what he believes to be true, to be true about the nature of man and the universe in which he lives, to be true about man's destiny in historical time, to be true about the nature of good and evil and how to know the difference, to be true about the way to ascertain and to recognize the truth and to distinguish it from error.

In other times and in other places, the possessors and guardians of true knowledge have been held to be the appointed spokesmen of a universal and indisputable tradition and of divine revelation. In the Western society to which we belong the tradi-

tional guardians and spokesmen of true knowledge have in varying degrees lost or renounced their titles to speak with complete authority. The hierarchy of priests, the dynasties of rulers, the courtiers, the civil servants and the commissars have to give way . . . and there is left as the court of last resort when the truth is at issue, "the ancient and universal company of scholars."

Having said this, I have not forgotten how often the professors have been proved to be wrong, how often the academic judgment has been confounded by some solitary thinker or artist, how often original and innovating men have been rejected by the universities, only to be accepted and celebrated after they are dead. The universal company of scholars is not an infallible court of last resort. Not in the least. On the contrary, it is an axiom of modern thought that the very process of thinking evolves. In human affairs nothing is infallible, absolute and everlasting. There are no courts which can anticipate fully the course of events. There are none which can take account of the unpredictability of genius. Nevertheless, in the modern world there exists no court which is less fallible than the company of scholars, when we are in the field of truth and error.

This court, this universal company of scholars, comprises all who study and teach in all the universities and institutes of the world. The colleagues of each scholar are his peers, those who have qualified themselves in mastering and obeying the criteria by which, in a field of knowledge, truth and error are judged.

The company of scholars is all over the globe, and its members are duty-bound to hear one another.

Insofar as the communication among them is adequate, so that a physicist in California is aware of the experiments and criticisms of a physicist in Peking, there exists the best possible insurance available to mortal men against the parochialism, the stuffiness and the dogmatism which are the chronic diseases of academies.

I have said enough, I hope, to reassure anyone who might think that I am glorifying the professors and attributing to them more power and authority than they are entitled to have. I do not mean to do that. I have had my share of controversies with a good many professors. What I do say is that the community of professors is, in the modern world, the best available source of guidance and authority in the field of knowledge. There is no other court to which men can turn and find what they once found in tradition and in custom, in ecclesiastical and civil authority. Because modern man in his search for truth has turned away from kings, priests, commissars and bureaucrats, he is left, for better or worse, with the professors.

And while we must treat the verdicts of the professors with a vigilant skepticism, they do have a certain authority. It comes from the fact that they have vowed to accept the discipline of scholarship and to seek the truth by using the best intellectual methods at the time known to contemporary men.

To make sure that I am not overstating my thesis, let me repeat. The community of scholars is the court of last resort in those fields of inquiry and knowledge about which scholars, as scholars, are concerned. Thus, if a professor is charged with the murder of his colleague, the court of last resort is not the faculty of his university or the faculties of all the universities. It is the judiciary of the state in which he lives. For the scholar is a scholar only part of the time and in part of his activity. In the role of murderer he is outside the field of scholarship.

But if a professor is alleged to have murdered his colleague a hundred years ago, as in the case of Professor Webster at Harvard, the court of last resort *today* about his guilt or innocence a century ago is not the judiciary of Massachusetts. It is the historians who have studied the evidence now available and have been confronted with the findings of all the historians who have read the history of the case. After a hundred years, no one is more qualified than are the historians to judge the case.

Reflecting on this we come close, I think, to the essential principle of academic freedom. In his relations with the laws of the land, a professor is as subject as any other man to the laws against murder, robbery, cheating on the income tax, driving his automobile recklessly. The laws for him, as for all other men, are what the law-enforcing authorities say they are. The professor has no special privileges and no special immunity.

But in the field of truth and error about the nature of things, and of the history and future of the universe and of man, the state and its officials have no jurisdiction. When the scholar finds that two and two make four, no policeman, no judge, no governor, no legislator, no trustee, no rich alumnus, has any right to ordain that two and two make five. Only other scholars who have gone through a mathematical training equivalent to his, and are in one way or another qualified as his peers, can challenge his findings that two and two make four. Here, it is the community of scholars who are the court of last resort.

It follows that they are the court of last resort in determining the qualifications of admission to the community of scholars — that is to say, the criteria of appointment and the license to teach. No criterion can be recognized which starts somewhere else than in the canons of scholarship and scientific research. No criterion is valid here because it emanates from the chamber of commerce, or the trade union council, or the American Legion, or the clergy, or the newspapers, or the Americans for Democratic Action, or the John Birch Society or any political party. The selection and the tenure of the members of the community of scholars is subject to the criterion that scholars shall be free of any control except a stern duty to bear faithful allegiance to the truth they are appointed to seek.

A judgment as to whether a scholar has been faithful is one that only his peers can render. The supreme sin of a scholar, *qua* scholar, is to lie, not about where he spent the previous weekend, but about whether two and two make four.

If we say that the vocation of the scholar is to seek the truth, it follows, I submit, that he must seek the truth for the simple purpose of knowing the truth. The search for truth proceeds best if it is inspired by wonder and curiosity, if, that is to say, it is disinterested — if the scholar disregards all secondary considerations of how his knowledge may be applied, how it can be sold, whether it is useful, whether it is good or bad, respectable, fashionable, moral, popular and patriotic, whether it will work or whether it will make men happier or unhappier, whether it is agreeable or disagreeable, whether it is likely to win him a promotion or a prize or a decoration, whether it will get a good vote in the Gallup poll. Genius is most likely to expand the limits of our knowledge, on which all the applied sciences depend, when it works in a condition of total unconcern with the consequences of its own findings.

Believing this, I hold that the university must have at its core a sanctuary for excellence, where the climate is favorable to the pursuit of truth for its own sake. In our conglomerate and swarming society, the last best hopes of mankind lie in what is done, and in what example is set, in these sanctuaries.

I do not think of them as monastic establishments shut off from the struggles and strains of the human condition. I think of them as societies of fellows within the great corporate institutions that our universities have become, as societies where the rela-

Henri Cartier-Bresson from Magnum
Columnist Walter Lippmann

tively few who can pursue truth disinterestedly will find the support and sustaining fellowship of their peers.

Since man's whole knowledge of things is not inherited and must be acquired anew by every generation, there is in every human society a culture, a tradition of the true and the false, the right and the wrong, of the good which is desirable and the bad which is to be avoided. This culture is rooted in the accepted version of the nature of things and of man's destiny. The accepted version evolves and the encyclopedias become outdated and have to be revised.

Since the prevailing tradition rests on the prevailing science, it follows that modern men must look to the company of scholars in the universities to guard and to preserve, to refine and enrich the tradition of civility. They have to revise the curricula of studies and the encyclopedias of knowledge.

This does not mean, of course, that the scientists and the scholars are to be regarded, much less are to regard themselves, as a mysterious elite of the initiated who can lay down the law of right and wrong, of good and evil, in human affairs. It does mean that insofar as religion, government, art and personal living assume or imply that this or that is true or false, they are subject to the criticism and judgment of the company of scholars. The prevailing and accepted science of the time is the root from which grow the creations of poets and artists, of saints and prophets and heroes. The science of an age is the material with which inspiration and genius create.

I am more than a little concerned as I proceed, that you will think that I am erecting a very high tower on a very small base, that I am nominating the professors to carry too great a responsibility. All I can say is that the human condition in the modern age brings us to what I have been talking about. The dissolution of the ancestral order and the dethronement of usage and authority in modern society have left us dependent upon man's ability to understand and govern his own fate. Necessarily, therefore, we are in a high degree dependent upon the men whose lives are committed to the pursuit of truth.

The responsibility may be too great for the professors to carry. But somehow — since the responsibility must be met — we shall have to learn to find men who will tell us how to find the professors who can carry the responsibility. And if we are ever to find them, we must begin by realizing the need to find them. If they cannot be found, modern man is indeed adrift on a trackless sea.

So, I venture to proceed. There is still something more, still another great function which the universities and their scholars cannot neglect, indeed cannot escape.

For there is more to the task of learning than to discover more and more truths than have ever been known before. That something more, which may mark the difference

between mediocrity and excellence, is the practice of a kind of alchemy, the creative function of transmuting knowledge into wisdom.

Wisdom, says the Oxford English Dictionary, is "the capacity of judging rightly in matters relating to life and conduct." It is "soundness of judgment in choice of means and ends." The development of the capacity of judging rightly is something different from, and in some ways much more than, the capacity to know the truth in any particular field of knowledge, or to have mastered the art of applying this knowledge to some desired end. The capacity to judge rightly in a choice of both means and ends cuts across the specialties and the technologies, and it is, I dare to say, the hallmark of a liberal, as distinguished from a utilitarian or vocational, education.

We may say, I think, that knowledge is made into wisdom when what is true about the nature of things is reshaped to the human scale and oriented to the human understanding, to human need and to human hope. As this is done, the findings of scientists and scholars are transformed into the humanities, and the materials for a liberal education begin to appear.

The universities, therefore, are not only the depositories of wisdom. They are also laboratories where alchemists work, whose function it is to transmute knowledge into human wisdom. If the scholars do this, insofar as they do this, they transcend the sterile controversies about the two cultures, the scientific and the humanistic, and they learn to transcend the intellectual puzzle about specialism and generalism. For knowledge transmuted into wisdom places the sciences and the humanities within one universe of discourse.

Can it be done? There is no need to doubt that it can be done. The most revolutionary of all the intellectual achievements of the modern age has been man's increasing mastery of the art of discovery and invention. The reshaping and reorientation of knowledge, so that it is humanly accessible and viable, is the task of philosophers, of the master-minds in the special fields of learning, of the advanced students in the field of education, and of the great teachers themselves. It would be a feeble kind of defeatism to think that man, who is penetrating the secrets of matter and of life itself, is unable to make usable the knowledge he is able to acquire.

A liberal education is concerned with what Plato calls the "royal science," the science that needs to be possessed by the rulers of the state. The education of a prince who is destined to be the king has from time immemorial been the primary function of education. Now that we live in a time when, as Huey Long truly said, every man is a king, it is still the prime function of education to instruct and to train the future rulers of the state.

It cannot be said that there exists as yet an adequate royal science. It is the task of the scholars to invent and compile the royal science of the modern age, a science which can in some measure be absorbed by all who vote, and can educate the comparatively few who will actually govern.

The heart of this science will be a presentation of the history and the practice of judging rightly in a choice of means and ends. Such a body of wisdom must be composed and compiled and made communicable, if the supreme teaching function of the institutions of learning is to be successful. This is their necessary business if they are to be more than laboratories of research, institutes of technology and vocational centers for careers.

For they cannot neglect the highest function of education which is the education of the rulers of the state. Quite evidently, it is not easy to discover what should be taught to the future rulers of a modern state, how

they are to be made to acquire that capacity of judging rightly, which is the essence of wisdom. We are only at the frontier of modern, democratic education, within sight of the promised land. Those who come after us will have to make, out of the accumulating knowledge of the specialists, a body of available and usable wisdom. The political scientists and the educators of the coming times will have to explore what is as yet a largely unknown continent — this royal science for our age. They will have to extract from the infinite complexity of knowledge what it is that the rulers of the state need to know.

Quite evidently, the ruler of a state, the President of the United States for example, cannot master all the branches of knowledge which bear on the decisions he must make. Yet he must have enough knowledge of a kind which will enable him to judge rightly whose judgment among the specialists he should decide to accept. He must learn the art, which is not described in the textbooks as yet, of listening to experts and seeing through them and around them. The educators of the future will have to extract from the whole body of nuclear science, for example, what it is that the President and the Congress and the leaders of public opinion need to know about nuclear science and the behavior of great powers when they are confronted, let us say, with a treaty prohibiting the testing of nuclear weapons. Out of these extracts from the body of knowledge, the educators must design the curriculum of our own royal science.

I have been meditating out loud about one central theme: that in the modern age, as the ancestral order of usage and authority dissolves, there exists a spiritual and intellectual vacuum of discipline and guidance which, in the last analysis, can be filled only by the universal company of scholars, supported and protected and encouraged by their universities.

72.

James S. Coleman *et al.*: Equal Opportunity in Education

*When the Supreme Court in its landmark decision in 1954 called for the integration of
the nation's public schools, on the grounds that segregated schools were inherently
unequal, it seemed to some commentators that the problem of unequal educational
opportunity in the United States might be solved — not immediately, of course, but
within a reasonable period of time. Desegregation did proceed, if not at the speed
desired by some, at least fairly quickly in some parts of the country; and there were
sections where improvement was noted. But as time went on it began to be realized
that the problem went deeper than the mere segregation of schools, and that differences
in the early home environment were probably far more important. Such at least was
the conclusion, admittedly controversial, of James S. Coleman of Johns Hopkins
University, who in 1966 published a book based on studies done by him and by a panel
of educators for the U.S. Office of Education of the Department of Health, Education,
and Welfare. Portions of the book's Summary Report are reprinted here.*

Source: *Equality of Educational Opportunity*, Washington, 1966, pp. 3-34.

SEGREGATION IN THE PUBLIC SCHOOLS

The great majority of American children
attend schools that are largely segregated;
that is, where almost all of their fellow students are of the same racial background as
they are. Among minority groups, Negroes
are by far the most segregated. Taking all
groups, however, white children are most
segregated. Almost 80 percent of all white
pupils in 1st grade and 12th grade attend
schools that are from 90 to 100 percent
white. And 97 percent at grade 1 and 99
percent at grade 12 attend schools that are
50 percent or more white.

For Negro pupils, segregation is more
nearly complete in the South (as it is for
whites also), but it is extensive also in all
the other regions where the Negro population is concentrated: the urban North, Midwest, and West.

More than 65 percent of all Negro pupils
in the 1st grade attend schools that are between 90 and 100 percent Negro. And 87
percent at grade 1 and 66 percent at grade
12 attend schools that are 50 percent or
more Negro. In the South most students
attend schools that are 100 percent white or
Negro.

The same pattern of segregation holds,
though not quite so strongly, for the teachers of Negro and white students. For the
nation as a whole, the average Negro elementary pupil attends a school in which 65
percent of the teachers are Negro; the average white elementary pupil attends a school
in which 97 percent of the teachers are
white. White teachers are more predomi-
nant at the secondary level, where the corresponding figures are 59 and 97 percent.
The racial matching of teachers is most pronounced in the South, where by tradition it
has been complete. On a nationwide basis,

in cases where the races of pupils and teachers are not matched, the trend is all in one direction: white teachers teach Negro children but Negro teachers seldom teach white children; just as, in the schools, integration consists primarily of a minority of Negro pupils in predominantly white schools but almost never of a few whites in largely Negro schools.

In its desegregation decision of 1954, the Supreme Court held that separate schools for Negro and white children are inherently unequal. This survey finds that, when measured by that yardstick, American public education remains largely unequal in most regions of the country, including all those where Negroes form any significant proportion of the population. Obviously, however, that is not the only yardstick. The next section of the summary describes other characteristics by means of which equality of educational opportunity may be appraised.

THE SCHOOLS AND THEIR CHARACTERISTICS

THE SCHOOL ENVIRONMENT of a child consists of many elements, ranging from the desk he sits at to the child who sits next to him, and including the teacher who stands at the front of his class. A statistical survey can give only fragmentary evidence of this environment. . . .

Statistics, too, must deal with one thing at a time, and cumulative effects tend to be lost in them. Having a teacher without a college degree indicates an element of disadvantage, but in the concrete situation, a child may be taught by a teacher who is not only without a degree but who has grown up and received his schooling in the local community, who has never been out of the state, who has a 10th-grade vocabulary, and who shares the local community's attitudes.

One must also be aware of the relative importance of a certain kind of thing to a certain kind of person. Just as a loaf of bread means more to a starving man than to a sated one, so one very fine textbook or, better, one very able teacher, may mean far more to a deprived child than to one who already has several of both.

Finally, it should be borne in mind that in cases where Negroes in the South receive unequal treatment, the significance in terms of actual numbers of individuals involved is very great, since 54 percent of the Negro population of school-going age, or approximately 3.2 million children, live in that region.

All of the findings reported in this section of the summary are based on responses to questionnaires filled out by public-school teachers, principals, district school superintendents, and pupils. The data were gathered in September and October of 1965 from 4,000 public schools. All teachers, principals, and district superintendents in these schools participated, as did all pupils in the 3rd, 6th, 9th, and 12th grades. First-grade pupils in half the schools participated. More than 645,000 pupils in all were involved in the survey. . . .

Data for Negro and white children are classified by whether the schools are in metropolitan areas or not. The definition of a metropolitan area is the one commonly used by government agencies: a city of over 50,000 inhabitants including its suburbs. All other schools in small cities, towns, or rural areas are referred to as nonmetropolitan schools. . . . For metropolitan schools there are usually five regions defined as follows:

> Northeast — Connecticut, Maine, Massachusetts, New Hampshire, Rhode Island, Vermont, Delaware, Maryland, New Jersey, New York, Pennsylvania, District of Columbia. (Using 1960 census data, this region contains about 16 percent of all Negro children in the nation and 20 percent of all white children age 5 to 19.)

Midwest — Illinois, Indiana, Michigan, Ohio, Wisconsin, Iowa, Kansas, Minnesota, Missouri, Nebraska, North Dakota, South Dakota (containing 16 percent of Negro and 19 percent of white children age 5 to 19).

South — Alabama, Arkansas, Florida, Georgia, Kentucky, Louisiana, Mississippi, North Carolina, South Carolina, Tennessee, Virginia, West Virginia (containing 27 percent of Negro and 14 percent of white children age 5 to 19).

Southwest — Arizona, New Mexico, Oklahoma, Texas (containing 4 percent of Negro and 3 percent of white children age 5 to 19).

West — Alaska, California, Colorado, Hawaii, Idaho, Montana, Nevada, Oregon, Utah, Washington, Wyoming (containing 4 percent of Negro and 11 percent of white children age 5 to 19).

The nonmetropolitan schools are usually classified into only three regions:

South — As above (containing 27 percent of Negro and 14 percent of white children age 5 to 19).

Southwest — As above (containing 4 percent of Negro and 2 percent of white children age 5 to 19).

North and West — All states not in the South and Southwest (containing 2 percent of Negro and 17 percent of white children age 5 to 19). . . .

Facilities

For the nation as a whole, white children attend elementary schools with a smaller average number of pupils per room (29) than do any of the minorities (which range from 30 to 33). . . . In some regions the nationwide pattern is reversed: in the nonmetropolitan North and West and Southwest, for example, there is a smaller average number of pupils per room for Negroes than for whites. . . . Secondary-school whites have a smaller average number of pupils per room than minorities, except Indians.

Looking at the regional breakdown, however, one finds much more striking differences than the national average would suggest: In the metropolitan Midwest, for example, the average Negro has 54 pupils per room — probably reflecting considerable frequency of double sessions — compared with 33 per room for whites. Nationally, at the high-school level, the average white has 1 teacher for every 22 students and the average Negro has 1 for every 26 students. . . .

Nationally, Negro pupils have fewer of some of the facilities that seem most related to academic achievement: They have less access to physics, chemistry, and language laboratories; there are fewer books per pupil in their libraries; their textbooks are less often in sufficient supply. To the extent that physical facilities are important to learning, such items appear to be more relevant than some others, such as cafeterias, in which minority groups are at an advantage.

Usually greater than the majority-minority differences, however, are the regional differences. . . . Ninety-five percent of Negro and 80 percent of white high-school students in the metropolitan Far West attend schools with language laboratories, compared with 48 and 72 percent, respectively, in the metropolitan South, in spite of the fact that a higher percentage of Southern schools are less than 20 years old.

Finally, it must always be remembered that these statistics reveal only majority-minority average differences and regional average differences; they do not show the extreme differences that would be found by comparing one school with another.

Programs

Just as minority groups tend to have less access to physical facilities that seem to be related to academic achievement, so too they have less access to curricular and extracurricular programs that would seem to have such a relationship.

Secondary-school Negro students are less likely to attend schools that are regionally accredited; this is particularly pronounced in the South. Negro and Puerto Rican pupils have less access to college preparatory curriculums and to accelerated curriculums; Puerto Ricans have less access to vocational curriculums as well. Less intelligence testing is done in the schools attended by Negroes and Puerto Ricans. Finally, white students in general have more access to a more fully developed program of extracurricular activities, in particular those which might be related to academic matters (debate teams, for example, and student newspapers).

Again, regional differences are striking. For example, 100 percent of Negro high-school students and 97 percent of whites in the metropolitan Far West attend schools having a remedial reading teacher (this does not mean, of course, that every student uses the services of that teacher, but simply that he has access to them) compared with 46 percent and 65 percent, respectively, in the metropolitan South — and 4 percent and 9 percent in the nonmetropolitan Southwest. . . .

ACHIEVEMENT IN THE PUBLIC SCHOOLS

THE SCHOOLS BEAR many responsibilities. Among the most important is the teaching of certain intellectual skills, such as reading, writing, calculating, and problem solving. One way of assessing the educational opportunity offered by the schools is to measure how well they perform this task. Standard achievement tests are available to measure these skills, and several such tests were administered in this survey to pupils at grades 1, 3, 6, 9, and 12.

These tests do not measure intelligence, nor attitudes, nor qualities of character. Furthermore, they are not, nor are they intended to be, "culture free." Quite the reverse: they are culture bound. What they measure are the skills which are among the most important in our society for getting a good job and moving up to a better one, and for full participation in an increasingly technical world. Consequently, a pupil's test results at the end of public school provide a good measure of the range of opportunities open to him as he finishes school — a wide range of choice of jobs or colleges if these skills are very high; a very narrow range that includes only the most menial jobs if these skills are very low. . . .

With some exceptions — notably Oriental-Americans — the average minority pupil scores distinctly lower on these tests at every level than the average white pupil. The minority pupils' scores are as much as one standard deviation below the majority pupils' scores in the 1st grade. At the 12th grade, results of tests in the same verbal and nonverbal skills show that, in every case, the minority scores are farther below the majority than are the 1st-graders. For some groups, the relative decline is negligible; for others, it is large.

Furthermore, a constant difference in standard deviations over the various grades represents an increasing difference in grade level gap. For example, Negroes in the metropolitan Northeast are about 1.1 standard deviations below whites in the same region at grades 6, 9, and 12. But at grade 6 this represents 1.6 years behind; at grade 9, 2.4 years; and at grade 12, 3.3 years. Thus, by this measure, the deficiency in achievement is progressively greater for the minority pupils at progressively higher grade levels.

For most minority groups, then, and most particularly the Negro, schools provide little opportunity for them to overcome this initial deficiency; in fact they fall farther behind the white majority in the development of several skills which are critical to making a living and participating fully in modern society. Whatever may be the combination of nonschool factors — poverty, community attitudes, low educational level of parents — which put minority children at a disadvantage in verbal and nonverbal skills when they enter the first grade, the fact is the schools have not overcome it. . . .

RELATION OF ACHIEVEMENT TO SCHOOL CHARACTERISTICS

IF 100 STUDENTS within a school take a certain test, there is likely to be great variation in their scores. One student may score 97 percent, another 13; several may score 78 percent. This represents variability in achievement within the particular school.

It is possible, however, to compute the average of the scores made by the students within that school and to compare it with the average score, or achievement, of pupils within another school, or many other schools. These comparisons then represent variations between schools.

When one sees that the average score on a verbal achievement test in school X is 55 and in school Y is 72, the natural question to ask is: What accounts for the difference?

There are many factors that may be associated with the difference. This analysis concentrates on one cluster of those factors. It attempts to describe what relationship the school's characteristics themselves (libraries, for example, and teachers and laboratories and so on) seem to have to the achievement of majority and minority groups (separately for each group on a nationwide basis, and also for Negro and white pupils in the North and South).

The first finding is that the schools are remarkably similar in the way they relate to the achievement of their pupils when the socioeconomic background of the students is taken into account. It is known that socioeconomic factors bear a strong relation to academic achievement. When these factors are statistically controlled, however, it appears that differences between schools account for only a small fraction of differences in pupil achievement.

The schools do differ, however, in their relation to the various racial and ethnic groups. The average white student's achievement seems to be less affected by the strength or weakness of his school's facilities, curriculums, and teachers than is the average minority pupil's. To put it another way, the achievement of minority pupils depends more on the schools they attend than does the achievement of majority pupils. Thus, 20 percent of the achievement of Negroes in the South is associated with the particular schools they go to, whereas only 10 percent of the achievement of whites in the South is. Except for Oriental-Americans, this general result is found for all minorities.

The inference might then be made that improving the school of a minority pupil may increase his achievement more than would improving the school of a white child increase his. Similarly, the average minority pupil's achievement may suffer more in a school of low quality than might the average white pupil's. In short, whites and, to a lesser extent, Oriental-Americans are less affected one way or the other by the quality of their schools than are minority pupils. This indicates that it is for the most disadvantaged children that improvements in school quality will make the most difference in achievement.

All of these results suggest the next question: What are the school characteristics that are most related to achievement? In other words, what factors in the school seem to be most important in affecting achievement?

It appears that variations in the facilities and curriculums of the schools account for relatively little variation in pupil -achievement insofar as this is measured by standard tests. Again, it is for majority whites that the variations make the least difference; for minorities, they make somewhat more difference. Among the facilities that show some relationship to achievement are several for which minority pupils' schools are less well equipped relative to whites. For example, the existence of science laboratories showed a small but consistent relationship to achievement, and . . . minorities, especially Negroes, are in schools with fewer of these laboratories.

The quality of teachers shows a stronger relationship to pupil achievement. Furthermore, it is progressively greater at higher grades, indicating a cumulative impact of the qualities of teachers in a school on the pupil's achievements. Again, teacher quality seems more important to minority achievement than to that of the majority.

It should be noted that many characteristics of teachers were not measured in this survey; therefore, the results are not at all conclusive regarding the specific characteristics of teachers that are most important. Among those measured in the survey, however, those that bear the highest relationship to pupil achievement are first, the teacher's score on the verbal skills test, and then his educational background — both his own level of education and that of his parents. On both of these measures, the level of teachers of minority students, especially Negroes, is lower.

Finally, it appears that a pupil's achievement is strongly related to the educational backgrounds and aspirations of the other students in the school. Only crude measures of these variables were used (principally the proportion of pupils with encyclopedias in the home and the proportion planning to go to college). Analysis indicates, however, that children from a given family background, when put in schools of different social composition, will achieve at quite different levels. This effect is again less for white pupils than for any minority group other than Orientals. Thus, if a white pupil from a home that is strongly and effectively supportive of education is put in a school where most pupils do not come from such homes, his achievement will be little different than if he were in a school composed of others like himself. But if a minority pupil from a home without much educational strength is put with schoolmates with strong educational backgrounds, his achievement is likely to increase.

This general result, taken together with the earlier examinations of school differences, has important implications for equality of educational opportunity. . . . The principal way in which the school environments of Negroes and whites differ is in the composition of their student bodies, and it turns out that the composition of the student bodies has a strong relationship to the achievement of Negro and other minority pupils.

This analysis has concentrated on the educational opportunities offered by the schools in terms of their student body composition, facilities, curriculums, and teachers. This emphasis, while entirely appropriate as a response to the legislation calling for the survey, nevertheless neglects important factors in the variability between individual pupils within the same school; this variability is roughly four times as large as the variability between schools. For example, a pupil attitude factor, which appears to have a stronger relationship to achievement than do all the "school" factors together, is the extent to which an individual feels that he has some control over his own destiny. . . . Minority pupils, except for Orientals, have far less conviction than whites that they can affect their own environments and futures. When they do, however, their achievement is higher than that of whites who lack that conviction.

Furthermore, while this characteristic shows little relationship to most school factors, it is related, for Negroes, to the proportion of whites in the schools. Those Negroes in schools with a higher proportion of whites have a greater sense of control. This finding suggests that the direction such an attitude takes may be associated with the pupil's school experience as well as his experience in the larger community.

OTHER SURVEYS AND STUDIES

Relation of integration to achievement

An education in integrated schools can be expected to have major effects on attitudes toward members of other racial groups. At its best, it can develop attitudes appropriate to the integrated society these students will live in; at its worst, it can create hostile camps of Negroes and whites in the same school. Thus, there is more to "school integration" than merely putting Negroes and whites in the same building, and there may be more important consequences of integration than its effect on achievement.

Yet the analysis of school factors described earlier suggests that, in the long run, integration should be expected to have a positive effect on Negro achievement as well. An analysis was carried out to seek such effects on achievement which might appear in the short run. This analysis of the test performance of Negro children in integrated schools indicates positive effects of integration, though rather small ones. . . .

[A] table . . . was constructed to observe whether there is any tendency for Negro pupils who have spent more years in integrated schools to exhibit higher average achievement. Those pupils who first entered integrated schools in the early grades record consistently higher scores than the other groups, although the differences are again small. No account is taken in these tabulations of the fact that the various groups of pupils may have come from different backgrounds. . . . Thus, although the differences are small, and although the degree of integration within the school is not known,

there is evident, even in the short run, an effect of school integration on the reading and mathematics achievement of Negro pupils. . . .

Case studies of school integration

As part of the survey, two sets of case studies of school integration were commissioned. These case studies examine the progress of integration in individual cities and towns, and illustrate problems that have arisen not only in these communities but in many others as well. . . .

In the main report, excerpts from these case studies are presented to illustrate certain recurrent problems. A paragraph which introduces [some] of these excerpts is given below, showing the kinds of problems covered. . . .

Compliance in a small community. — Many large metropolitan areas, North and South, are moving toward resegregation despite attempts by school boards and city administrations to reverse the trend. Racial housing concentration in large cities has reinforced neighborhood school patterns of racial isolation, while, at the same time, many white families have moved to the suburbs and other families have taken their children out of the public-school system, enrolling them instead in private and parochial schools. Small towns and medium-sized areas, North and South, on the other hand, are to some extent desegregating their schools.

In the Deep South, where there has been total school segregation for generations, there are signs of compliance within a number of school systems. The emphasis on open enrollment and freedom-of-choice plans, however, has tended to lead to token enrollment of Negroes in previously white schools. In school systems integrated at some grade levels but not at others, the choice of high-school grades rather than elementary grades has tended further to cut down on the number of Negroes choosing to transfer because of the reluctance to take extra risks close to graduation. . . .

A voluntary transfer plan for racial balance in elementary schools. — The public schools are more rigidly segregated at the elementary level than in the higher grades. In the large cities, elementary schools have customarily made assignments in terms of neighborhood boundaries. Housing segregation has, therefore, tended to build a segregated elementary-school system in most cities in the North and, increasingly, in the South as well, where *de facto* segregation is replacing *de jure* segregation.

Various communities have been struggling to find ways to achieve greater racial balance while retaining the neighborhood school. Bussing, pairing, redistricting, consolidating, and many other strategies have been tried. Many have failed; others have achieved at least partial success. In New Haven, Conn., considerable vigor has been applied to the problem: Whereas pairing was tried at the junior-high level, introducing compulsory integration, a voluntary transfer plan was implemented at the elementary level. Relief of overcrowding was given as the central intent of the transfer plan, but greater racial balance was achieved, since it was the Negro schools that were overcrowded. With the provision of new school buildings, however, this indirect stimulus to desegregation will not be present. In New Haven the transfer plan was more effective than in many other communities because of commitment of school leadership, active solicitation of transfers by door-to-door visits, provision of transportation for those transferring, teacher cooperation, heterogeneous grouping in the classrooms, and other factors.

The original plan provided that a student could apply to any one of a cluster of several elementary schools within a designated "cluster district," and the application would be approved on the basis of availability of space, effect on racial balance and certain unspecified educational factors; that students "presently enrolled" at a particular school would be given priority; and that transportation would be provided where necessary.

Desegregation by redistricting at the junior high school level. — The junior high schools, customarily grades 7 to 9, have been the focus of considerable effort and tension in desegregation plans in many communities. With most areas clinging to the neighborhood school at the elementary level with resultant patterns of racial concentration, and with high schools already more integrated because of their lesser reliance upon neighborhood boundaries and their prior consolidation to achieve maximum resources, junior high schools have been a natural place to start desegregation plans. Like the elementary schools, they have in the past been assigned students on the basis of geography; but, on the other hand, they tend to represent some degree of consolidation in that children from several elementary schools feed one junior high school. Further, parental pressures have been less severe for the maintenance of rigid neighborhood boundaries than at the elementary level.

Pairing of two junior high schools to achieve greater racial balance has been tried in a number of communities. Redistricting or redrawing the boundaries of areas that feed the schools has been tried in other areas. In Berkeley, Calif., after considerable community tension and struggle, a plan was put into effect that desegregated all three junior high schools (one had been desegregated previously). All the 9th graders were sent to a single school, previously Negro, and the 7th and 8th graders were assigned to the other two schools. The new 9th-grade school was given a new name to signal its new identity in the eyes of the community. . . .

A plan for racial balance at the high-school level. — In a number of communities, students are assigned to high schools on the basis of area of residence and hence racial imbalance is continued. In Pasadena, Calif., a plan was initiated to redress this imbalance by opening places in the schools to allow the transfer of Negroes to the predominantly white high school. A measure of success was achieved but only after much resistance. Of interest particularly in this situation was the legal opinion that attempts to achieve racial balance were violations of the Constitution and that race could not be considered as a factor in school districting. Apparently previous racial concentration, aided by districting, had not been so regarded, yet attempts at desegregation were. The School Board found its task made more difficult by such legal maneuvering. . . .

Relation of a university to school desegregation. — Education is a continuum — from kindergarten through college — and, increasingly, public-school desegregation plans are having an impact on colleges in the same area, particularly those colleges which are city or state supported. Free tuition, as in the New York City colleges, has no meaning for members of minority groups who have dropped out of school in high school and little meaning for those whose level of achievement is too low to permit work at the college level. A number of colleges, through summer tutorials and selective admittance of students whose grades would otherwise exclude them, are trying to redress this indirect form of racial imbalance.

73.

Andrew Hacker: Corporate America

The issues of Big Business, as Andrew Hacker points out in the selection reprinted here, are as old as large corporations themselves. And the problems raised by modern corporations' very bigness are more pressing than ever. When Hacker wrote in 1966, General Motors employed more than 600,000 people, a figure exceeding the combined government payrolls of New York, California, Illinois, Pennsylvania, Texas, and Ohio. The annual sales of Standard Oil of New Jersey were over $10 billion, a total exceeding the tax collections of those six states, plus Wisconsin, Connecticut, and Massachusetts. In fact, the fifty largest corporations employed almost three times as many people as the fifty states of the union, and their combined sales were over five times greater than the taxes those fifty states collected. Such statistics led Hacker to discuss the problems of controlling the modern giant corporation in an article published in the summer of 1966, part of which is reprinted here.

Source: *New York Times Magazine,* July 3, 1966: "A Country Called Corporate America."

PROBLEMS LIKE POVERTY, civil rights, and juvenile delinquency may have been "discovered" only in the past few years, but such can hardly be said about the issue of bigness in American business. On and off, for the last three-quarters of a century, the question has been raised whether the nation's large corporations have reached the point where they can cut a swath through society without having to account for the consequences of their actions. . . .

If corporate size has a variety of yardsticks, corporate power is beyond precise measurement. It is not an overstatement to say that we know too much about the economics of big business and not nearly enough about the social impact of these institutions. Professional economists tend to focus on the freedom of large firms to set or manage prices, with the result that attention is deflected from the broader but less tangible role played by corporations in the society as a whole. . . . What calls for a good deal more thought and discussion is the general and pervasive influence of the large corporate entity in and on the society. For the decisions made in the names of these huge companies guide and govern, directly and indirectly, all of our lives.

The large corporations shape the material contours of the nation's life. While original ideas for new products may come from a variety of sources, it is the big companies that have the resources to bring these goods to the public. The argument that the consumer has "free will," deciding what he will and will not buy, can be taken just so far. (Too much can be made of the poor old Edsel.) For in actual fact we *do* buy much or even most of what the large corporations put on the shelves or in the showrooms for us.

To be sure, companies are not unsophisticated and have a fair idea of what the consumer will be willing to purchase. But the general rule, with fewer exceptions than we would like to think, is that if they make it we will buy it. Thus we air-condition our bedrooms, watch color television in our living rooms, brush our teeth electrically in the bathroom, and cook at eye-level in the kitchen. It is time for frankness on this score: the American consumer is not notable for his imagination and does not know what he "wants." Thus he waits for corporate America to develop new products and, on hearing of them, discovers a long-felt "need" he never knew he had.

And more than any other single force in society, the large corporations govern the character and quality of the nation's labor market. The most visible example of this process has been the decision of companies to introduce computers into the world of work, bringing in train an unmistakable message to those who must earn a living. Millions of Americans are told, in so many words, what skills they will have to possess if they are to fill the jobs that will be available. A company has the freedom to decide *how* it will produce its goods and services, whether its product happens to be power mowers or life insurance or air transportation. And having made this decision, it establishes its recruiting patterns accordingly. Individuals, in short, must tailor themselves to the job if they want to work at all. Most of us and all of our children, will find ourselves adjusting to new styles of work whether we want to or not.

The impact of corporate organization and technology on the American educational system deserves far closer attention than it has been given. . . . All American education, in a significant sense, is vocational. Liberal-arts students may enjoy a period of insulation but they are well aware that they will eventually have to find niches for themselves in offices or laboratories. . . . Even the liberal-arts college in which I teach has recently voted to establish within its precincts a department of "computer science." It is abundantly clear that while IBM and Sperry Rand did not command Cornell to set up such a department, the university cannot afford to be insensitive to the changing character of the job market.

Our large firms both have and exercise the power to decide where they will build their new factories and offices. And these decisions, in their turn, determine which regions of the country will prosper and which will stagnate. The new face of the South is, in largest measure, the result of corporate choices to open new facilities in what was hitherto a blighted area. Not only has this brought new money to the region but new kinds of jobs and new styles of work have served to transform the Southern mentality. The transition to the twentieth century has been most rapid in the communities where national corporations have settled. You cannot remain an unrepentant Confederate and expect to get on in du Pont.

By the same token, the regions which have not prospered in postwar years have been those where corporations have opted not to situate. Too much can be made of the New England "ghost towns." Actually, corporations have "pulled out" of very few places; more critical has been their failure to establish or expand facilities in selected parts of the country. Thus patterns of migration — from the countryside to the city and from the city to the suburb — are reflections of corporation decisions on plant and office location. If men adjust to machines, they also move their bodies to where the jobs are.

Related to this have been the corporate decisions to rear their headquarters in the center of our largest cities, especially the East Side of New York. Leaving aside the architectural transformation and the aesthetic investment with which we will have to live for many years, the very existence of these prestige-palaces has had the effect of drawing hundreds of thousands of people into metropolitan areas not equipped to handle them. Thus, not only the traffic snarls and the commuter crush but also the burgeoning of suburbs for the young marrieds of management and the thin-walled apartments for others in their twenties, fifties, and sixties.

Much — perhaps too much — has been made of ours being an age of "organization men." Yet there is more than a germ of truth in this depiction of the new white-collar class which is rapidly becoming the largest segment of the American population. The great corporations created this type of individual, and the habits and style of life of corporate employment continue to play a key role in setting values and aspirations for the population as a whole. Working for a large organization has a subtle but no less inevitable effect on a person's character. It calls for the virtues of adaptability, sociability, and that certain caution necessary when one knows one is forever being judged. . . .

The pervasive influence of the large corporations, in these and other areas, derives less from how many people they employ and far more from their possession of great wealth. Our largest firms are very well-off indeed, and they have a good deal of spare cash to spend as and where they like. These companies make profits almost automatically every year, and they find it necessary to give only a fraction of those earnings back to their stockholders in the form of dividends. . . . Thus the big firms have had the money to create millions of new white-collar jobs. Department heads in the large companies ask for and are assigned additional assistants, coordinators, planners, and programmers, who fill up new acres of office space every year. What is ironic, considering that this is the business world, is that attempts are hardly ever made to discover whether these desk-occupiers actually enhance the profitability or the productivity of the company. But everyone keeps busy enough: attending meetings and conferences, flying around the country, and writing and reading and amending memoranda.

White-collar featherbedding is endemic in the large corporation, and the spacious amenities accompanying such employment make work an altogether pleasant experience. The travel and the transfers and the credit-card way of life turn work into half-play and bring with them membership in a cosmopolitan world. That a large proportion of these employees are not necessary was illustrated about ten years ago when the Chrysler Corporation had its back to the wall and was forced to take the unprecedented step of firing one-third of its white-collar force. Yet the wholesale departure of these clerks and executives, as it turned out, had no effect on the company's production and sales. Nevertheless, Chrysler was not one to show that an empire could function half-clothed, and it hired back the office workers it did not need just as soon as the cash was again available.

If all this sounds a bit Alice-in-Wonderland, it would be well to ponder on what the consequences would be were all of our major corporations to cut their white-collar staffs to only those who were actually needed. Could the nation bear the resulting unemployment, especially involving so many people who have been conditioned to believe that they possess special talents and qualities of character?

Corporate wealth, then, is spent as a corporation wishes. If General Motors wants to tear down the Savoy-Plaza and erect a corporate headquarters for itself at Fifth Avenue and 59th Street, it will go ahead and do so. Quite obviously an office building could, at a quarter of the cost, have been located on Eleventh Avenue and 17th Street. But why should cost be the prime consideration? After all, the stockholders have been paid their dividends, new production facilities have been put into operation, and there is still plenty of money left over. Nor is such a superfluity of spare cash limited to the very largest concerns. Ford, which is generally thought of as General Motors' poor sister, was sufficiently well-heeled to drop a quarter of a billion dollars on its Edsel and still not miss a dividend.

If our large corporations are using their power to reshape American society, indeed to reconstruct the American personality, the general public's thinking about such concentrated influence still remains ambiguous.

There persists, for example, the ideology of antitrust and the fond place in American hearts still occupied by small business. Thus politicians can count on striking a resonant chord when they call for more vigorous prosecutions under the Sherman Law and for greater appropriations for the Small Business Administration. Most Americans, from time to time, do agree that our largest companies are too big and should somehow or other be broken up into smaller units. But just how strong or enduring this sentiment is is hard to say. No one really expects that Mobil Oil or Bethlehem Steel can or will be "busted" into ten or a dozen entirely new and independent companies. Thus, if the ideology that bigness equals badness lingers on, there is no serious impetus to translate that outlook into action.

Part of the problem is that if Americans are suspicious of bigness, they are not really clear about just what it is about large corporations that troubles them. Despite the periodic exposures of defective brake cylinders or profiteering on polio vaccine, the big story is not really one of callous exploitation or crass irresponsibility. Given the American system of values, it is difficult to mount a thoroughgoing critique of capitalism or to be "anti-business" in an unequivocal way. The result is that our commentaries in this area are piecemeal and sporadic in character. We have the vocabularies for criticizing both "big government" and "big labor" but the image of the large corporation is a hazy one, and despite its everyday presence in our midst, our reaction to its very existence is uncertain.

Take the question of who owns our big enterprises. In terms of legal title the owners are the stockholders, and management is accountable to that amorphous group. But it is well known that in most cases a company's shares are so widely dispersed that the managers of a corporation can run the firm pretty well as they please. Yet even assuming that the executives are acting with the tacit consent of their company's theoretical owners, it is worth inquiring just who these stockholders are.

Interestingly, a rising proportion of the stockholders are not people at all but rather investing institutions. Among these non-people are pension funds, insurance companies, brokerage houses, foundations, and universities. Thus some of the most significant "voters" at the annual meetings of the big companies are the Rockefeller Foundation, Prudential Life, and Princeton University. And these institutions, out of habit and prudence, automatically ratify management decisions. . . .

From these observations at least one answer is possible: yes, there is a "power élite" presiding over corporate America. Yet the problem with this term is that the "élite" in question consists not so much of identifiable personalities — how many of the presidents of our twenty largest corporations can any of us name? — but rather of the chairs in the top offices.

The typical corporation head stays at his desk for only about seven years. The power he exercises is less discretionary than we would like to believe, and the range of decisions that can be called uniquely his own is severely limited. (It is only in the small companies on the way up, such as the Romney days at American Motors, that the top men impress their personalities on the enterprise.) John Kenneth Galbraith once noted that when a corporation president retires and his successor is named, the price of the company's stock, presumably a barometer of informed opinion, does not experience a perceptible change.

Unfortunately, it is far easier to think in terms of actual individuals than of impersonal institutions. Therefore it must be underlined that the so-called "élite" consists not of Frederic Donner and Frederick Kappel and Fred Borch but rather of *whatever* person happens to be sitting in the top seat at General Motors and AT&T and General Electric. We are reaching the point where corporate power is a force in its own right, for all intents and purposes independent of the men who in its name make the decisions.

The modern corporation is not and cannot be expected to be a "responsible" institution in our society. For all the self-congratulatory handouts depicting the large firm as a "good citizen," the fact remains that a business enterprise exists purely and simply to make more profits — a large proportion of which it proceeds to pour back into itself. (True, the big companies do not seek to "maximize" their profits: their toleration of make-work and high living is enough evidence for this.)

But corporations, like all businesses whether large or small, are in the primary business of making money; indeed, they do not even exist to produce certain goods or services that may prove useful or necessary to society. If Eli Lilly or Searle and the other drug companies discovered that they could chalk up larger profits by getting out of vaccines and manufacturing frozen orange juice instead, they would have no qualms or hesitation about taking such a step.

A corporation, then, cannot be expected to shoulder the aristocratic mantle. No one should be surprised that in the areas of civil rights and civil liberties our large companies have failed to take any significant initiative. The men who preside over them are not philosopher-kings, and no expectation should be held out that they may become so. . . . And this is as it should be. Corporate power is great — in fact, far more impressive than corporation executives are willing to admit — and were large corporations to become "social-minded," their impact would be a very mixed blessing. For then the rest of us would have to let corporate management define just what constitutes "good citizenship," and we would have to accept such benefactions without an excuse for comment or criticism.

Therefore, when corporations, in the course of doing their business, create social dislocations, there is no point in chiding or exhorting them to more enlightened ways.

It would be wrong, of course, to lay the blame for all of our social ills at the doorsteps of the large firms. If the drug companies manufacture cheap and effective birth-control pills, it is a trifle presumptuous to take them to task for whatever promiscuity occurs as a consequence.

Nevertheless, the American corporation, in the course of creating and marketing new merchandise, presents us with temptations — ranging from fast cars to color television — to which we sooner or later succumb. There is nothing intrinsically wrong with color television. It is, rather, that the money we spend for a new set is money that can no longer be put aside for the college education of our children. (Thus, no one should be surprised when, fifteen years from now, there is a demand for full federal scholarships for college students. Not the least reason for such a demand will be that we were buying color TV back in 1966.)

Specific questions can be framed easily enough. It is the answers that are far from clear. We have unemployment: how far is it because corporations have not been willing or able to create enough jobs for the sorts of people who need them? We have a civil rights problem: how far is it because corporations have been reluctant to hire and train Negroes as they have whites? We have a shortage of nurses: how far is it because corporations outbid and undercut the hospitals by offering girls secretarial jobs at higher pay for less work? We have whole waves of unwanted and unneeded immigrants pouring into our large cities: how far is it because corporations have decided to locate in Ventura County in California rather than Woodruff County in Arkansas?

Questions like these may suggest differing answers but they do add up to the fact that a good measure of laissez-faire continues to exist in our corporate economy. For all their ritual protestations over government intervention and regulation, our large companies are still remarkably free: free to make and sell what they want, free to hire the people they want for the jobs they have created, free to locate where they choose, free to dispose of their earnings as they like — and free to compel the society to provide the raw materials, human and otherwise, necessary for their ongoing needs.

The task of picking up the pieces left by the wayside belongs to government. This is the ancient and implicit contract of a society committed to freedom of enterprise. But whether the agencies of government have the resources or the public support to smooth out the dislocations that have been caused to our economy and society is not at all clear. . . .

Corporate America, with its double-edged benefactions and its unplanned disruptions, is in fact creating new problems at a rate faster than our governmental bureaus can possibly cope with them. . . .

The American commitment to private property means, at least for the foreseeable future, that we will be living with the large corporation. On the whole, Americans seem vaguely contented with this development, unanticipated as it may have been.

Corporations cannot commit treason, nor be outlawed, or excommunicated, for they have no souls.

Sir Edward Coke, *Case of Sutton's Hospital*, 1612

74.

Tom C. Clark: *Sheppard v. Maxwell, Warden*

On June 6, 1966, the majority opinion (8 to 1) in Sheppard v. Maxwell, Warden, *delivered by Justice Clark and reprinted here in part, set aside the 1954 conviction for murder of Cleveland physician Samuel Sheppard. The ruling, which confirmed Sheppard's claim that prejudicial press coverage had made a fair trial impossible in 1954, reinforced the efforts of some judges to curb newspaper coverage of trials. Early in 1967 Chicago Judge Herbert Paschen laid down strict rules for newsmen covering the similarly notorious Richard Speck murder trial at Peoria, Illinois. The result of such rulings was a sharp controversy over the freedom of the press, in which the American Newspaper Publishers Association, for example, argued that "there are grave inherent dangers to the public in the restriction or censorship at the source of news, among them secret arrest and ultimately secret trial."*

Source: 384 U.S. 333.

MARILYN SHEPPARD, petitioner's pregnant wife, was bludgeoned to death in the upstairs bedroom of their lakeshore home in Bay Village, Ohio, a suburb of Cleveland. On the day of the tragedy, July 4, 1954, Sheppard pieced together for several local officials the following story:

He and his wife had entertained neighborhood friends, the Aherns, on the previous evening at their home. After dinner they watched television in the living room. Sheppard became drowsy and dozed off to sleep on a couch. Later, Marilyn partially awoke him saying that she was going to bed. The next thing he remembered was hearing his wife cry out in the early morning hours. He hurried upstairs and in the dim light from the hall saw a "form" standing next to his wife's bed. As he struggled with the "form," he was struck on the back of the neck and rendered unconscious.

On regaining his senses, he found himself on the floor next to his wife's bed. He rose, looked at her, took her pulse and "felt that she was gone." He then went to his son's room and found him unmolested. Hearing a noise, he hurried downstairs. He saw a "form" running out the door and pursued it to the lakeshore. He grappled with it on the beach and again lost consciousness. Upon his recovery he was lying face down with the lower portion of his body in the water.

He returned to his home, checked the pulse on his wife's neck, and "determined or thought that she was gone." He then went downstairs and called a neighbor, Mayor Houk of Bay Village. The mayor and his wife came over at once, found Sheppard slumped in an easy chair downstairs and asked, "What happened?" Sheppard replied: "I don't know, but somebody ought to try to do something for Marilyn." Mrs. Houk immediately went up to the bedroom. The mayor told Sheppard, "Get hold of yourself. Can you tell me what happened?" Sheppard then related the above-outlined events.

After Mrs. Houk discovered the body, the mayor called the local police, Dr. Richard Sheppard, petitioner's brother, and the Aherns. The local police were the first to arrive. They in turn notified the coroner and Cleveland police. Richard Sheppard then arrived, determined that Marilyn was dead, examined his brother's injuries, and removed him to the nearby clinic operated by the Sheppard family. When the coroner, the Cleveland police, and other officials arrived, the house and surrounding area were thoroughly searched, the rooms of the house were photographed, and many persons, including the Houks and the Aherns, were interrogated. The Sheppard home and premises were taken into "protective custody" and remained so until after the trial.

From the outset, officials focused suspicion on Sheppard. After a search of the house and premises on the morning of the tragedy, Dr. Gerber, the coroner, is reported — and it is undenied — to have told his men, "Well, it is evident the doctor did this, so let's go get the confession out of him." He proceeded to interrogate and examine Sheppard while the latter was under sedation in his hospital room. . . .

On July 7, the day of Marilyn Sheppard's funeral, a newspaper story appeared in which Assistant County Attorney Mahon — later the chief prosecutor of Sheppard — sharply criticized the refusal of the Sheppard family to permit his immediate questioning. From there on headline stories repeatedly stressed Sheppard's lack of cooperation with the police and other officials. Under the headline "Testify Now In Death, Bay Doctor Is Ordered," one story described a visit by Coroner Gerber and four police officers to the hospital on July 8. When Sheppard insisted that his lawyer be present, the coroner wrote out a subpoena and served it on him. Sheppard then agreed to submit to questioning without counsel and the subpoena was torn up. The officers questioned him for several hours.

On July 9, Sheppard, at the request of the coroner, reenacted the tragedy at his home before the coroner, police officers, and a group of newsmen, who apparently were invited by the coroner. The home was locked so that Sheppard was obliged to wait outside until the coroner arrived. Sheppard's performance was reported in detail by the news media, along with photographers. The newspapers also played up Sheppard's refusal to take a lie detector test and "the protective ring" thrown up by his family.

Front-page newspaper headlines announced on the same day that "Doctor Balks At Lie Test; Retells Story." A column opposite that story contained an "exclusive" interview with Sheppard headlined: "'Loved My Wife, She Loved Me,' Sheppard Tells News Reporter." The next day, another headline story disclosed that Sheppard had "again late yesterday refused to take a lie detector test" and quoted an assistant county attorney as saying that "at the end of a nine-hour questioning of Dr. Sheppard, I felt he was now ruling [a test] out completely." But subsequent newspaper articles reported that the coroner was still pushing Sheppard for a lie detector test. More stories appeared when Sheppard would not allow authorities to inject him with "truth serum."

On the 20th, the "editorial artillery" opened fire with a front-page charge that somebody is "getting away with murder." The editorial attributed the ineptness of the investigation to "friendships, relationships, hired lawyers, a husband who ought to have been subjected instantly to the same third-degree to which any other person under similar circumstances is subjected. . . ." The following day, July 21, another page-one editorial was headed: "Why No Inquest? Do It Now, Dr. Gerber." The coroner called an inquest the same day and subpoenaed Sheppard. It was staged the next day in a school gymnasium; the coroner presided with the county prosecutor as his adviser and two detectives as bailiffs.

In the front of the room was a long table occupied by reporters, television and radio personnel, and broadcasting equipment. The hearing was broadcast with live microphones placed at the coroner's seat and the witness stand. A swarm of reporters and photographers attended. Sheppard was brought into the room by police who searched him in full view of several hundred spectators. Sheppard's counsel were present during the three-day inquest but were not permitted to participate. When Sheppard's chief counsel attempted to place some documents in the record, he was forcibly ejected from the room by the coroner, who received cheers, hugs, and kisses from ladies in the audience. Sheppard was questioned for five and one-half hours about his actions on the night of the murder, his married life, and a love affair with Susan Hayes. At the end of the hearing the coroner announced that he "could" order Sheppard held for the grand jury, but did not do so.

Throughout this period the newspapers emphasized evidence that tended to incriminate Sheppard and pointed out discrepancies in his statements to authorities. At the same time, Sheppard made many public statements to the press and wrote feature articles asserting his innocence. During the inquest on July 26, a headline in large type stated: "Kerr [Captain of the Cleveland Police] Urges Sheppard's Arrest." In the story, Detective McArthur "disclosed that scientific tests at the Sheppard home have definitely established that the killer washed off a trail of blood from the murder bedroom to the downstairs section," a circumstance casting doubt on Sheppard's accounts of the murder. No such evidence was produced at trial.

The newspapers also delved into Shep-

pard's personal life. Articles stressed his extramarital love affairs as a motive for the crime. The newspapers portrayed Sheppard as a Lothario, fully explored his relationship with Susan Hayes, and named a number of other women who were allegedly involved with him. The testimony at trial never showed that Sheppard had any illicit relationships besides the one with Susan Hayes.

On July 28, an editorial entitled "Why Don't Police Quiz Top Suspect" demanded that Sheppard be taken to police headquarters. . . . A front-page editorial on July 30 asked: "Why Isn't Sam Sheppard in Jail?" It was later titled "Quit Stalling — Bring Him In." After calling Sheppard "the most unusual murder suspect ever seen around these parts" the article said that "[e]xcept for some superficial questioning during Coroner Sam Gerber's inquest he has been scot-free of any official grilling. . . ." It asserted that he was "surrounded by an iron curtain of protection [and] concealment."

That night, at 10 o'clock, Sheppard was arrested at his father's home on a charge of murder. He was taken to the Bay Village City Hall where hundreds of people, newscasters, photographers, and reporters were awaiting his arrival. He was immediately arraigned — having been denied a temporary delay to secure the presence of counsel — and bound over to the grand jury.

The publicity then grew in intensity until his indictment on August 17. Typical of the coverage during this period is a front-page interview entitled: "DR. SAM: 'I Wish There Was Something I Could Get Off My Chest — But There Isn't.'" Unfavorable publicity included items such as a cartoon of the body of a sphinx with Sheppard's head and the legend below: "'I Will Do Everything In My Power to Help Solve This Terrible Murder.' — Dr. Sam Sheppard." Headlines announced, inter alia, that: "Doctor Evidence Is Ready for Jury," "Corrigan Tactics Stall Quizzing," "Sheppard 'Gay Set' Is Revealed by Houk," "Blood Is Found in Garage," "New Murder Evidence Is Found, Police Claim," "Dr. Sam Faces Quiz at Jail on Marilyn's Fear of Him." . . .

We do not detail the coverage further. There are five volumes filled with similar clippings from each of the three Cleveland newspapers covering the period from the murder until Sheppard's conviction in December 1954. The record includes no excerpts from newscasts on radio and television, but, since space was reserved in the courtroom for these media, we assume that their coverage was equally large.

With this background the case came on for trial two weeks before the November general election, at which the chief prosecutor was a candidate for Common Pleas judge and the trial judge, Judge Blythin. was a candidate to succeed himself. . . .

Sheppard stood indicted for the murder of his wife; the state was demanding the death penalty. For months the virulent publicity about Sheppard and the murder had made the case notorious. Charges and countercharges were aired in the news media besides those for which Sheppard was called to trial. In addition, only three months before trial, Sheppard was examined for more than five hours without counsel during a three-day inquest which ended in a public brawl. The inquest was televised live from a high-school gymnasium seating hundreds of people. Furthermore, the trial began two weeks before a hotly contested election at which both Chief Prosecutor Mahon and Judge Blythin were candidates for judgeships.

While we cannot say that Sheppard was denied due process by the judge's refusal to take precautions against the influence of pretrial publicity alone, the court's later rulings must be considered against the setting in which the trial was held. In light of this

background, we believe that the arrangements made by the judge with the news media caused Sheppard to be deprived of that "judicial serenity and calm to which [he] was entitled" (*Estes* v. *Texas*). . . .

The fact is that bedlam reigned at the courthouse during the trial and newsmen took over practically the entire courtroom, hounding most of the participants in the trial, especially Sheppard. At a temporary table within a few feet of the jury box and counsel table sat some twenty reporters staring at Sheppard and taking notes. The erection of a press table for reporters inside the bar is unprecedented. . . .

Having assigned almost all of the available seats in the courtroom to the news media the judge lost his ability to supervise that environment. The movement of the reporters in and out of the courtroom caused frequent confusion and disruption of the trial. And the record reveals constant commotion within the bar. Moreover, the judge gave the throng of newsmen gathered in the corridors of the courthouse absolute free rein. Participants in the trial, including the jury, were forced to run a gauntlet of reporters and photographers each time they entered or left the courtroom. The total lack of consideration for the privacy of the jury was demonstrated by the assignment to a broadcasting station of space next to the jury room on the floor above the courtroom, as well as the fact that jurors were allowed to make telephone calls during their five-day deliberation.

There can be no question about the nature of the publicity which surrounded Sheppard's trial. . . . Indeed, every court that has considered this case, save the court that tried it, has deplored the manner in which the news media inflamed and prejudiced the public.

Much of the material printed or broadcast during the trial was never heard from the witness stand, such as the charges that

Sheppard had purposely impeded the murder investigation and must be guilty since he had hired a prominent criminal lawyer; that Sheppard was a perjurer; that he had sexual relations with numerous women; that his slain wife had characterized him as a "Jekyll-Hyde"; that he was "a bare-faced liar" because of his testimony as to police treatment; and, finally, that a woman convict claimed Sheppard to be the father of her illegitimate child. As the trial progressed, the newspapers summarized and interpreted the evidence, devoting particular attention to the material that incriminated Sheppard, and often drew unwarranted inferences from testimony. At one point, a front-page picture of Mrs. Sheppard's blood-stained pillow was published after being "doctored" to show more clearly an alleged imprint of a surgical instrument. Nor is there doubt that this deluge of publicity reached at least some of the jury. . . .

The court's fundamental error is compounded by the holding that it lacked power to control the publicity about the trial. . . . The carnival atmosphere at trial could easily have been avoided since the courtroom and courthouse premises are subject to the control of the court. . . .

Second, the court should have insulated the witnesses. All of the newspapers and radio stations apparently interviewed prospective witnesses at will, and in many instances disclosed their testimony. A typical example was the publication of numerous statements by Susan Hayes, before her appearance in court, regarding her love affair with Sheppard. Although the witnesses were barred from the courtroom during the trial, the full verbatim testimony was available to them in the press. . . .

From the cases coming here we note that unfair and prejudicial news comment on pending trials has become increasingly prevalent. Due process requires that the accused receive a trial by an impartial jury free from outside influences. Given the pervasiveness of modern communications and the difficulty of effacing prejudicial publicity from the minds of the jurors, the trial courts must take strong measures to ensure that the balance is never weighed against the accused. And appellate tribunals have the duty to make an independent evaluation of the circumstances.

Of course, there is nothing that proscribes the press from reporting events that transpire in the courtroom. But where there is a reasonable likelihood that prejudicial news prior to trial will prevent a fair trial, the judge should continue the case until the threat abates, or transfer it to another county not so permeated with publicity. In addition, sequestration of the jury was something the judge should have raised *sua sponte* with counsel. If publicity during the proceedings threatens the fairness of the trial, a new trial should be ordered.

But we must remember that reversals are but palliatives; the cure lies in those remedial measures that will prevent the prejudice at its inception. The courts must take such steps by rule and regulation that will protect their processes from prejudicial outside interferences. Neither prosecutors, counsel for defense, the accused, witnesses, court staff, nor enforcement officers coming under the jurisdiction of the court should be permitted to frustrate its function. Collaboration between counsel and the press as to information affecting the fairness of a criminal trial is not only subject to regulation but is highly censurable and worthy of disciplinary measures.

Since the state trial judge did not fulfill his duty to protect Sheppard from the inherently prejudicial publicity which saturated the community and to control disruptive influences in the courtroom, we must reverse the denial of the habeas petition.

F. D. Dandridge — Pix from Publix

BLACK AMERICA

The civil rights movement in the 1960s underwent a radical shift in emphasis from the rural South to the urban North. A second generation of Negro leaders came out of the new urban struggle, leaders whose concerns went further than the integration of Negroes into an otherwise undisturbed American system. The long-term effect of dispossession in America, they pointed out, was deeper than the poverty-poor education-high unemployment-poverty cycle; it generated a mass psychological debility. To be black and poor was also to feel actually inferior — or invisible — with only white models and values to work toward. The ghetto Negro was daily bombarded, via mass media, with images of the American dream, from Cadillacs to potions for having more fun as a blond. The model was pleasant, middle-class, eminently white, and completely impossible. These new leaders saw that simple integration would not suffice; self-awareness, racial pride, and a determined celebration of Negro culture were necessary for full working membership in world society. This broad program, which revolved around such concepts as self-determination, Black Nationalism, and even tactical separatism, was generally misunderstood by white America; its political and economic implications, under the "Black Power" slogan, met with outright hostility.

(Left) Student sitting-in at a drugstore lunch counter in Birmingham, Ala.; (right) training girl to ignore harassment during a sit-in; (below) Negro youths trying to enter a white theater

Freedom Riders take refuge in a bus ringed by National Guardsmen, Montgomery, Alabama

The sit-in as a direct-action tactic intended to challenge legal segregation spread rapidly throughout the South, and thousands of demonstrators were arrested. The sit-in was extended to the "Freedom Rides" in 1961 as civil-rights workers sought to test the ICC's 1955 nondiscrimination ruling. Freedom riders were arrested and attacked by mobs, and one bus was burned. The sit-in movement succeeded in desegregating public facilities but it could not begin to deal with the vastly more extensive informal and often unconscious discrimination practiced across the nation.

Leaders plot strategy at the "Freedom Fighters" headquarters in Montgomery, Alabama

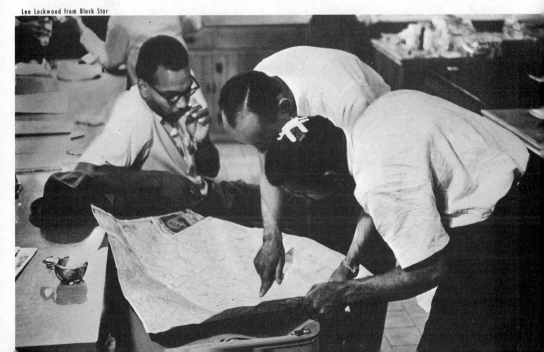

Frank Rockstroh — Pix from Publix

(Top) Stained glass window destroyed in an explosion in the 16th Street Baptist Church, Birmingham, Ala., which killed four girls; (below) car in which Viola Liuzzo, civil rights worker from Detroit, was slain; (right) Medgar Evers, fighter for civil rights in Mississippi; (bottom right) Mrs. Evers at her husband's funeral

Bruce Davidson from Magnum

Bill Shrout — Pix from Publix

London Daily Express — Pictorial Parade

(Above) Birmingham police using dogs to break up a civil rights demonstration in 1963; (right) Negro demonstrator who has been "subdued" by a fire hose during the Birmingham activities

Prompted by the revived Ku Klux Klan and by the quickly organized White Citizens Councils, the general reaction of the white South to the sit-in movement was violence. As court decisions and legislation opened public accommodations to black citizens, the emphasis of the Southern campaign turned more and more to gaining political strength commensurate with the numerical strength of Southern Negroes. Voter registration drives and community organization marked the high point of the Southern campaign and of the cooperative black-white coalition which had so far comprised the movement. Despite Congressional action in 1957, 1960, and 1964, strengthening and clarifying nondiscriminatory registration and voting procedures, regular political organizations in the South remained virtually all white.

Nine years after the Supreme Court's desegregation order of 1954, less than 8 percent of the Negro children in Southern and border states were attending integrated schools. In 1962 and 1963, however, public attention was focused on higher education; the governors of Mississippi and Alabama raised again the interposition doctrine to block the admission of Negro students to their respective state universities. Only the arrival of federal troops enabled the students to be registered.

(Top) Governor George Wallace blocks Nicholas Katzenbach and federal officials escorting two students into the University of Alabama, 1963; (left) James Meredith attends classes at the University of Mississippi escorted by U.S. marshals, 1962; (below) Negroes voting in Peachtree, Alabama, 1966

A.F.P. from Pictorial Parade

Martin Luther King, Jr., led a march on Washington in 1963 to unify support for a civil rights program

George W. Gardner

The climax of the program to register Negro voters in the South, and of the whole Southern campaign, came in early 1965 in Selma, Alabama. The drive was again met with violence; following the murder of Rev. James Reeb, a Boston minister, King led a protest march to the state capital. Brutal attacks by mobs and police ceased only when federal troops arrived. As demonstrators were dispersing, Mrs. Viola Liuzzo, a white marcher from Detroit, was shot and killed by Klansmen.

Scenes from the Selma to Montgomery march, 1965: (Above) Marchers en route to Montgomery under federal guard; (below) black and white demonstrators singing together in Selma; (opposite page) girl comforts demonstrator who was clubbed by a Selma sheriff's deputy

Charles Moore from Black Star

(Left) Bedroom of a wealthy Negro family in Atlanta, Ga.; (above) comfortable living room of a Negro white collar worker in New York City; (below) backyard of a New York tenement

(Above) Whites jeering open housing demonstrators in Gage Park, Ill.; (right) white parents demonstrating against proposed bussing of schoolchildren in New York City

The open discrimination of the South — the separate, labelled facilities, the Jim Crow statutes — had been an obvious and easy target for civil rights agitation. The North had comfortably watched and decried the mob violence and official antics in the South. Sometime in the period 1962-1964, however, the North itself became a target as Negro leaders began to point out to white America the urban ghetto. A new phrase, de facto segregation, was used to describe the informal, paralegal practices that resulted in closed neighborhoods, all-black schools of poor quality, and increasingly high unemployment in ghetto areas. The wide public sympathy shown by Northerners during the Southern campaign suddenly dried up, and violence became a national problem.

The civil rights movement now quickly broadened in a number of directions. The dominance of white value-models was repudiated and instead there developed a search for a genuine Afro-American culture. The significance of being black was explored by writers, artists, and musicians, and previous work of this sort took on a new importance. The emphasis was on affirmation: "Black is beautiful; it's beautiful to be black."

Four Negro writers of the twentieth century who focused on the Negro experience: (Top left) Langston Hughes; (top right) Richard Wright; (bottom left) Ralph Ellison; (bottom right) James Baldwin

To counter the injustice and futility that generally attended "urban renewal" projects, there gradually evolved from the ghetto the idea of community economic and political autonomy. "Black Power" was generally understood to mean such a reorganization of power relations in the city. Negro ownership of ghetto property and control of public facilities were seen as necessary for community betterment; full political and economic power within the ghetto would allow residents to grow with pride and responsibility into a true community. Integration, insofar as it remained a goal in itself, would no longer be a unilateral program.

(Right) Slogan scrawled on a wall in Detroit's east side neighborhood; (below) Malcolm X, a leader in the Black Muslim movement and an early advocate of a strong separate Negro community and a "back to Africa" program

Paul Conklin — Pix from Publix

Rizzoli Press — Pix from Publix

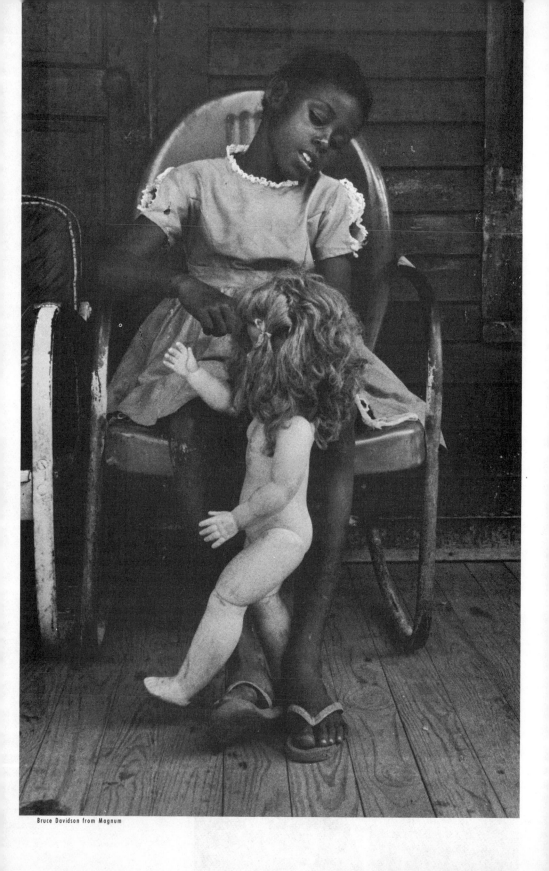

(Above) Ujama Shop, one of Harlem's several African culture shops; (left) suburban volunteers work to clean up slum street; (right) children attending a Freedom Day school in Chicago

(Above) Crowds take over the streets in Detroit, Mich., following outbreak of riots, 1967; (below) National Guardsmen standing guard amid ruins in Watts, 1965

National attention suddenly switched from the problems of the rural South to the urban ghetto of the North. Originally encouraged by apparent national concern, then quickly disillusioned by the reluctance of government to institute real reforms and progressive legislation, ghetto Negroes exploded into riots — the worst in Los Angeles in 1965 and Newark and Detroit in 1967 — in which stores and tenements were looted and burned. Negro-owned stores, identified by "Soul Brother" signs, were usually let alone; hardest hit were white-owned "credit" stores and run-down residences owned by absentee whites who refused to maintain the property. Riots typically were triggered by a minor incident, often involving the police, and developed spontaneously in response to pent-up tensions; that they were not strictly race- or poverty-motivated was demonstrated in Detroit where looting often appeared to be an integrated, middle-class affair.

Lee Balterman, "Life," © 1967, Time Inc.

(Above) Sign in the window of a Negro-owned store to prevent looting or burning during a riot; (below) aerial view of the buildings burning during the Detroit riots

"Detroit Free Press" — Black Star

(Above) Looter who failed to stop when ordered to do so by a policeman lies dead in Newark street; (below) police beating man during Harlem, New York, riots in 1965

National Guard tank in a street in Newark, New Jersey, 1967

Official reaction to riots in the cities was negative; Congress promptly dropped consideration of already underfunded poverty programs to pass hasty antiriot legislation. Police departments around the country began assembling riot-control arsenals. And when the President's Commission on Civil Disorders published its report in March 1968 and belied expectations of a simplistic crime report by placing primary responsibility on white racism, the Administration countered with a displeased silence.

Crowd taunting National Guardsman in Newark

In the wake of the summer of 1967 a large number of city police departments instituted training programs to meet further outbreaks of rioting. The need for some sort of training was clear, for police and even National Guardsmen in several cities had been demonstrably panicky and trigger-happy. The use of new antiriot weapons, however, raised a controversy; chemical sprays, armored personnel carriers and other military apparatus made descriptions of white police as "armies of occupation" begin to sound less and less distorted. Violence was given another and cruelly ironic expression on April 4, 1968. On that day, in Memphis, Tennessee, Martin Luther King, Jr., Nobel laureate and apostle of nonviolence, was shot and killed by an assassin.

(Left) Thousands march through streets of Atlanta, Ga., in funeral procession for Martin Luther King, Jr., April 1968; (below) demonstration staged for policemen attending an Army-sponsored course in riot-control, March 1968

Burk Uzzle from Magnum

Ken Regan — Camera 5

75.

Earl Warren and Byron R. White: *Miranda* v. *Arizona*

*In 1964 and 1966 the U.S. Supreme Court handed down opinions concerning the rights
of suspects held in custody by the police. It is probable that no two decisions of the
Court have aroused such adverse criticism from law enforcement agencies across
the nation as the majority opinions in* Escobedo v. *Illinois (1964) and* Miranda v.
Arizona *(1966). Police officials have faulted these decisions for giving undue protection
to criminals and making the work of investigation and conviction more difficult; they
have pointed to the 80-percent rise in the crime rate from 1960 to 1967 as evidence
that law enforcement procedures should be strengthened, not hampered. Other critics
have noted the need for countervailing measures to protect society at the same time
that the individual suspected of breaking the law is assured of his rights. The following
selection contains portions of Chief Justice Warren's majority opinion and of Associate
Justice White's dissent in the* Miranda *decision of June 13, 1966. The defendant,
Ernesto Miranda, had been arrested in Phoenix, Arizona, in connection with a rape
and robbery case. Under repeated questioning while in police custody, Miranda
produced a signed confession that was admitted as evidence at his trial and secured
a conviction.*

Source: 384 U.S. 436.

Mr. Chief Justice Warren. The cases before us raise questions which go to the roots of our concepts of American criminal jurisprudence: the restraints society must observe consistent with the federal Constitution in prosecuting individuals for crime. More specifically, we deal with the admissibility of statements obtained from an individual who is subjected to custodial police interrogation and the necessity for procedures which assure that the individual is accorded his privilege under the Fifth Amendment to the Constitution not to be compelled to incriminate himself. . . . Our holding . . . briefly stated . . . is this: the prosecution may not use statements, whether exculpatory or inculpatory, stemming from custodial interrogation of the defendant unless it demonstrates the use of procedural safeguards effective to secure the privilege against self-incrimination.

By custodial interrogation, we mean questioning initiated by law-enforcement officers after a person has been taken into custody or otherwise deprived of his freedom of action in any significant way. As for the procedural safeguards to be employed, unless other fully effective means are devised to inform accused persons of their right of silence and to assure a continuous opportunity to exercise it, the following measures are required:

Prior to any questioning, the person must be warned that he has a right to remain silent, that any statement he does make may be used as evidence against him, and that he has a right to the presence of an attorney, either retained or appointed. The defendant may waive effectuation of these rights, provided the waiver is made voluntarily, knowingly, and intelligently. If, however, he indicates in any manner and at any stage of the process that he wishes to consult with an attorney before speaking, there can be no questioning. Likewise, if the individual is alone and indicates in any manner that he does not wish to be interrogated, the police may not question him. The mere fact that he may have answered some questions or volunteered some statements on his own does not deprive him of the right to refrain from answering any further inquiries until he has consulted with an attorney and thereafter consents to be questioned.

The constitutional issue we decide in each of these cases is the admissibility of statements obtained from a defendant questioned while in custody and deprived of his freedom of action. In each, the defendant was questioned by police officers, detectives, or a prosecuting attorney in a room in which he was cut off from the outside world. In none of these cases was the defendant given a full and effective warning of his rights at the outset of the interrogation process. In all the cases, the questioning elicited oral admissions, and in three of them, signed statements as well which were admitted at their trials. They all thus share salient features — incommunicado interrogation of individuals in a police-dominated atmosphere, resulting in self-incriminating statements without full warnings of constitutional rights.

An understanding of the nature and setting of this in-custody interrogation is essential to our decisions today. The difficulty in depicting what transpires at such interrogations stems from the fact that in this country they have largely taken place incommunicado. From extensive factual studies undertaken in the early 1930s, including the famous Wickersham Report to Congress by a Presidential Commission, it is clear that police violence and the "third degree" flourished at that time. In a series of cases decided by this Court long after these studies, the police resorted to physical brutality — beating, hanging, whipping — and to sustained and protracted questioning incommunicado in order to extort confessions. . . . Unless a proper limitation upon custodial interrogation is achieved — such as these decisions will advance — there can be no assurance that practices of this nature will be eradicated in the foreseeable future. . . .

Again we stress that the modern practice of in-custody interrogation is psychologically rather than physically oriented. . . . Interrogation still takes place in privacy. Privacy results in secrecy and this in turn results in a gap in our knowledge as to what in fact goes on in the interrogation rooms. . . . To be alone with the subject is essential to prevent distraction and to deprive him of any outside support. The aura of confidence in his guilt undermines his will to resist. He merely confirms the preconceived story the police seek to have him describe. Patience and persistence, at times relentless questioning, are employed. To obtain a confession, the interrogator must "patiently maneuver himself or his quarry into a position from which the desired objective may be attained." When normal procedures fail to produce the needed result, the police may resort to deceptive stratagems, such as giving false legal advice. It is important to keep the subject off balance, for example, by trading on his insecurity about himself or his surroundings. The police then persuade, trick, or cajole him out of exercising his constitutional rights.

Even without employing brutality, the "third degree," or the specific stratagems described above, the very fact of custodial interrogation exacts a heavy toll on individual liberty and trades on the weakness of individuals. It is obvious that such an inter-

Courtesy, Joseph Parrish, "The Chicago Tribune"

"The Sentimental Prosecutor"; cartoon by Joseph Parrish in "The Chicago Tribune" drawn in reaction to the Supreme Court rulings on the rights of criminals

rogation environment is created for no purpose other than to subjugate the individual to the will of his examiner. This atmosphere carries its own badge of intimidation. To be sure, this is not physical intimidation, but it is equally destructive of human dignity. The current practice of incommunicado interrogation is at odds with one of our nation's most cherished principles — that the individual may not be compelled to incriminate himself. Unless adequate protective devices are employed to dispel the compulsion inherent in custodial surroundings, no statement obtained from the defendant can truly be the product of his free choice.

From the foregoing, we can readily perceive an intimate connection between the privilege against self-incrimination and police custodial questioning. . . .

Today, then, there can be no doubt that the Fifth Amendment privilege is available outside of criminal court proceedings and serves to protect persons in all settings in which their freedom of action is curtailed

from being compelled to incriminate themselves. We have concluded that without proper safeguards the process of in-custody interrogation of persons suspected or accused of crime contains inherently compelling pressures which work to undermine the individual's will to resist and to compel him to speak where he would not otherwise do so freely. In order to combat these pressures and to permit a full opportunity to exercise the privilege against self-incrimination, the accused must be adequately and effectively apprised of his rights and the exercise of those rights must be fully honored.

It is impossible for us to foresee the potential alternatives for protecting the privilege which might be devised by Congress or the states in the exercise of their creative rule-making capacities. Therefore, we cannot say that the Constitution necessarily requires adherence to any particular solution for the inherent compulsions of the interrogation process as it is presently conducted.

Our decision in no way creates a constitutional straitjacket which will handicap sound efforts at reform, nor is it intended to have this effect. We encourage Congress and the states to continue their laudable search for increasingly effective ways of protecting the rights of the individual while promoting efficient enforcement of our criminal laws. However, unless we are shown other procedures which are at least as effective in apprising accused persons of their right of silence and in assuring a continuous opportunity to exercise it, the following safeguards must be observed:

At the outset, if a person in custody is to be subjected to interrogation, he must first be informed in clear and unequivocal terms that he has the right to remain silent. For those unaware of the privilege, the warning is needed simply to make them aware of it — the threshold requirement for an intelligent decision as to its exercise. More important, such a warning is an absolute prerequisite in overcoming the inherent pressures of the interrogation atmosphere. It is not just the subnormal or woefully ignorant who succumb to an interrogator's imprecations, whether implied or expressly stated, that the interrogation will continue until a confession is obtained or that silence in the face of accusation is itself damning and will bode ill when presented to a jury. Further, the warning will show the individual that his interrogators are prepared to recognize his privilege should he choose to exercise it.

The Fifth Amendment privilege is so fundamental to our system of constitutional rule and the expedient of giving an adequate warning as to the availability of the privilege so simple, we will not pause to inquire in individual cases whether the defendant was aware of his rights without a warning being given. Assessments of the knowledge the defendant possessed, based on information as to his age, education, intelligence, or prior contact with authorities, can never be more than speculation; a warning is a clear-cut fact. More important,

whatever the background of the person interrogated, a warning at the time of the interrogation is indispensable to overcome its pressures and to insure that the individual knows he is free to exercise the privilege at that point in time.

The warning of the right to remain silent must be accompanied by the explanation that anything said can and will be used against the individual in court. This warning is needed in order to make him aware, not only of the privilege but also of the consequences of forgoing it. It is only through an awareness of these consequences that there can be any assurance of real understanding and intelligent exercise of the privilege. Moreover, this warning may serve to make the individual more acutely aware that he is faced with a phase of the adversary system — that he is not in the presence of persons acting solely in his interest. . . .

If the interrogation continues without the presence of an attorney and a statement is taken, a heavy burden rests on the government to demonstrate that the defendant knowingly and intelligently waived his privilege against self-incrimination and his right to retained or appointed counsel. . . . Whatever the testimony of the authorities as to waiver of rights by an accused, the fact of lengthy interrogation or incommunicado incarceration before a statement is made is strong evidence that the accused did not validly waive his rights. . . .

Our decision is not intended to hamper the traditional function of police officers in investigating crime (see *Escobedo* v. *Illinois*, 378 U. S. 478, 492). When an individual is in custody on probable cause, the police may, of course, seek out evidence in the field to be used at trial against him. Such investigation may include inquiry of persons not under restraint. General on-the-scene questioning as to facts surrounding a crime or other general questioning of citizens in the fact-finding process is not affected by our holding. It is an act of responsible citizenship for individuals to give whatever information they may have to aid in law enforcement. In such situations the compelling atmosphere inherent in the process of in-custody interrogation is not necessarily present.

In dealing with statements obtained through interrogation, we do not purport to find all confessions inadmissible. Confessions remain a proper element in law enforcement. Any statement given freely and voluntarily without any compelling influences is, of course, admissible in evidence. The fundamental import of the privilege while an individual is in custody is not whether he is allowed to talk to the police without the benefit of warnings and counsel, but whether he can be interrogated. There is no requirement that police stop a person who enters a police station and states that he wishes to confess to a crime, or a person who calls the police to offer a confession or any other statement he desires to make. Volunteered statements of any kind are not barred by the Fifth Amendment and their admissibility is not affected by our holding today.

Mr. Justice White. That the Court's holding today is neither compelled nor even strongly suggested by the language of the Fifth Amendment, is at odds with American and English legal history, and involves a departure from a long line of precedent does not prove either that the Court has exceeded its powers or that the Court is wrong or unwise in its present reinterpretation of the Fifth Amendment. It does, however, underscore the obvious — that the Court has not discovered or found the law in making today's decision, nor has it derived it from some irrefutable sources. What it has done is to make new law and new public policy in much the same way that it has in the course of interpreting other great clauses of the Constitution. This is what the Court

historically has done. Indeed, it is what it must do and will continue to do until and unless there is some fundamental change in the constitutional distribution of governmental powers.

But if the Court is here and now to announce new and fundamental policy to govern certain aspects of our affairs, it is wholly legitimate to examine the mode of this or any other constitutional decision in this Court and to inquire into the advisability of its end product in terms of the long-range interest of the country. . . .

First, we may inquire what are the textual and factual bases of this new fundamental rule. To reach the result announced on the grounds it does, the Court must stay within the confines of the Fifth Amendment, which forbids self-incrimination only if *compelled*. Hence, the core of the Court's opinion is that, because of the "compulsion inherent in custodial surroundings, no statement obtained from [a] defendant [in custody] can truly be the product of his free choice" . . . absent the use of adequate protective devices as described by the Court. However, the Court does not point to any sudden inrush of new knowledge requiring the rejection of seventy years' experience. Nor does it assert that its novel conclusion reflects a changing consensus among state courts . . . or that a succession of cases had steadily eroded the old rule and proved it unworkable. . . .

Rather than asserting new knowledge, the Court concedes that it cannot truly know what occurs during custodial questioning because of the innate secrecy of such proceedings. It extrapolates a picture of what it conceives to be the norm from police investigatorial manuals, published in 1959 and 1962 or earlier, without any attempt to allow for adjustments in police practices that may have occurred in the wake of more recent decisions of state appellate tribunals or this Court. But even if the relentless application of the described procedures could lead to involuntary confessions, it most assuredly does not follow that each and every case will disclose this kind of interrogation or this kind of consequence. . . .

Although in the Court's view in-custody interrogation is inherently coercive, the Court says that the spontaneous product of the coercion of arrest and detention is still to be deemed voluntary. An accused, arrested on probable cause, may blurt out a confession which will be admissible despite the fact that he is alone and in custody, without any showing that he had any notion of his right to remain silent or of the consequences of his admission. Yet, under the Court's rule, if the police ask him a single question, such as, "Do you have anything to say?" or "Did you kill your wife?" his response, if there is one, has somehow been compelled, even if the accused has been clearly warned of his right to remain silent. Common sense informs us to the contrary. While one may say that the response was "involuntary" in the sense the question provoked or was the occasion for the response and thus the defendant was induced to speak out when he might have remained silent if not arrested and not questioned, it is patently unsound to say the response is compelled.

Today's result would not follow even if it were agreed that to some extent custodial interrogation is inherently coercive. . . . But it has never been suggested, until today, that such questioning was so coercive and accused persons so lacking in hardihood that the very first response to the very first question following the commencement of custody must be conclusively presumed to be the product of an overborne will.

If the rule announced today were truly based on a conclusion that all confessions resulting from custodial interrogation are coerced, then it would simply have no rational foundation. . . . Even if one were to postulate that the Court's concern is not that all confessions induced by police interrogation are coerced but rather that some such confessions are coerced and present judicial procedures are believed to be inadequate to identify the confessions that are coerced and those that are not, it would still not be essential to impose the rule that the Court has now fashioned. Transcripts or observers could be required, specific time limits, tailored to fit the cause, could be imposed, or other devices could be utilized to reduce the chances that otherwise indiscernible coercion will produce an inadmissible confession.

On the other hand, even if one assumed that there was an adequate factual basis for the conclusion that all confessions obtained during in-custody interrogation are the product of compulsion, the rule propounded by the Court would still be irrational, for, apparently, it is only if the accused is also warned of his right to counsel and waives both that right and the right against self-incrimination that the inherent compulsiveness of interrogation disappears. But if the defendant may not answer without a warning a question such as, "Where were you last night?" without having his answer be a compelled one, how can the Court ever accept his negative answer to the question of whether he wants to consult his retained counsel or counsel whom the court will appoint? And why, if counsel is present and the accused nevertheless confesses, or counsel tells the accused to tell the truth, and that is what the accused does, is the situation any less coercive insofar as the accused is concerned?

The Court apparently realizes its dilemma of foreclosing questioning without the necessary warnings but at the same time permitting the accused, sitting in the same chair in front of the same policemen, to waive his right to consult an attorney. It expects, however, that not too many will waive the right; and if it is claimed that he has, the state faces a severe, if not impossible, burden of proof.

All of this makes very little sense in terms of the compulsion which the Fifth Amendment proscribes. That amendment deals with compelling the accused himself. It is his free will that is involved. Confessions and incriminating admissions, as such, are not forbidden evidence; only those which are compelled are banned. I doubt that the Court observes these distinctions today. By considering any answers to any interrogation to be compelled regardless of the content and course of examination and by escalating the requirements to prove waiver, the Court not only prevents the use of compelled confessions but for all practical purposes forbids interrogation except in the presence of counsel. That is, instead of confining itself to protection of the right against compelled self-incrimination the Court has created a limited Fifth Amendment right to counsel — or, as the Court expresses it, a "need for counsel to protect the Fifth Amendment privilege. . . ." The focus then is not on the will of the accused but on the will of counsel and how much influence he can have on the accused. Obviously there is no warrant in the Fifth Amendment for thus installing counsel as the arbiter of the privilege.

In sum, for all the Court's expounding on the menacing atmosphere of police interrogation procedures, it has failed to supply any foundation for the conclusions it draws or the measures it adopts.

Criticism of the Court's opinion, however, cannot stop at a demonstration that the factual and textual bases for the rule it propounds are, at best, less than compelling. Equally relevant is an assessment of the rule's consequences measured against community values. The Court's duty to assess the consequences of its action is not satisfied by the utterance of the truth that a value of our system of criminal justice is "to respect the inviolability of the human personality" and to require government to produce the evidence against the accused by its own independent labors. . . . More than the human dignity of the accused is involved; the human personality of others in the society must also be preserved. Thus the values reflected by the privilege are not the sole desideratum; society's interest in the general security is of equal weight.

The obvious underpinning of the Court's decision is a deep-seated distrust of all confessions. As the Court declares that the accused may not be interrogated without counsel present, absent a waiver of the right to counsel, and as the Court all but admonishes the lawyer to advise the accused to remain silent, the result adds up to a judicial judgment that evidence from the accused should not be used against him in any way, whether compelled or not. This is the not so subtle overtone of the opinion — that it is inherently wrong for the police to gather evidence from the accused himself. And this is precisely the nub of this dissent.

I see nothing wrong or immoral, and certainly nothing unconstitutional, in the police's asking a suspect whom they have reasonable cause to arrest whether or not he killed his wife or in confronting him with the evidence on which the arrest was based, at least where he has been plainly advised that he may remain completely silent. . . . Particularly when corroborated, as where the police have confirmed the accused's disclosure of the hiding place of implements or fruits of the crime, such confessions have the highest reliability and significantly contribute to the certitude with which we may believe the accused is guilty. Moreover, it is by no means certain that the process of confessing is injurious to the accused. To the contrary it may provide psychological relief and enhance the prospects for rehabilitation. . . .

The most basic function of any government is to provide for the security of the individual and of his property. . . . These ends of society are served by the criminal laws which for the most part are aimed at the prevention of crime. Without the reasonably effective performance of the task of preventing private violence and retaliation, it is idle to talk about human dignity and civilized values.

The modes by which the criminal laws serve the interest in general security are many. First, the murderer who has taken the life of another is removed from the streets, deprived of his liberty, and thereby prevented from repeating his offense. In view of the statistics on recidivism in this country and of the number of instances in which apprehension occurs only after repeated offenses, no one can sensibly claim that this aspect of the criminal law does not prevent crime or contribute significantly to the personal security of the ordinary citizen.

Second, the swift and sure apprehension of those who refuse to respect the personal security and dignity of their neighbor unquestionably has its impact on others who might be similarly tempted. That the criminal law is wholly or partly ineffective with a segment of the population or with many of those who have been apprehended and convicted is a very faulty basis for concluding that it is not effective with respect to the great bulk of our citizens or for thinking that without the criminal laws, or in the absence of their enforcement, there would be no increase in crime. Arguments of this nature are not borne out by any kind of reliable evidence that I have seen to this date.

Third, the law concerns itself with those whom it has confined. The hope and aim of modern penology, fortunately, is as soon as possible to return the convict to society a better and more law-abiding man than when he entered. Sometimes there is success, sometimes failure. But at least the effort is made, and it should be made to the very maximum extent of our present and future capabilities.

The rule announced today will measurably weaken the ability of the criminal law to perform in these tasks. It is a deliberate calculus to prevent interrogations, to reduce the incidence of confessions and pleas of guilty, and to increase the number of trials. Criminal trials, no matter how efficient the police are, are not sure bets for the prosecution, nor should they be if the evidence is not forthcoming. Under the present law, the prosecution fails to prove its case in about 30 percent of the criminal cases actually tried in the federal courts. . . .

But it is something else again to remove from the ordinary criminal case all those confessions which heretofore have been held to be free and voluntary acts of the accused and to thus establish a new constitutional barrier to the ascertainment of truth by the judicial process. There is, in my view, every reason to believe that a good many criminal defendants, who otherwise would have been convicted on what this Court has previously thought to be the most satisfactory kind of evidence, will now, under this new version of the Fifth Amendment, either not be tried at all or acquitted if the state's evidence, minus the confession, is put to the test of litigation.

I have no desire whatsoever to share the responsibility for any such impact on the present criminal process.

Let me remember, when I find myself inclined to pity a criminal, that there is likewise a pity due to the country.

SIR MATTHEW HALE, *History of the Pleas of the Crown*, (1685)

76.

Arnold L. Fein: The Warren Report and Its Critics

The Report of the Warren Commission on the assassination of President Kennedy appeared a year after Kennedy's death and was at first generally accepted as the last word on the matter. Shortly, however, people began to question both the Commission's methods and its conclusions, and a series of highly critical articles and books were published by men who believed that Chief Justice Warren and his colleagues had not, as they had promised to do, found out everything that should be known. In October 1966 Arnold Fein, a New York City judge and a former special counsel to the Kefauver Committee, published an article, reviewing the controversy, that is reprinted here in part. At the time, District Attorney Jim Garrison of New Orleans had not yet begun his investigation of the assassination, an investigation that offered the possibility that more, indeed, than the Warren Report had disclosed would eventually be revealed.

Source: *Saturday Review*, October 22, 1966: "JFK in Dallas."

As the war against the Warren Commission escalates, it is time to take stock. It is time to inquire into the supposed deficiencies of the Commission, its investigation, and its Report. It is time also to inquire into the possible deficiencies of the critics, their inquiries, and their conclusions. . . . Perhaps the greatest obstacle to an understanding of the investigation and the Report is the widespread public misconception about the nature of criminal trials and investigations. . . . It is expressly articulated only by Léo Sauvage, who remarks:

> The writer of detective stories who wants to keep his readers never lets question marks and unexplained clues linger after the words "The End." One would think the public would be no less demanding when confronted not by fiction but by a real-life investigation, and above all when the victim is the President of the United States.

If it is true, as this passage suggests, that life must conform to fiction in order to be credible, the Warren Commission was deficient. It did not answer all the questions nor did it explain all the clues. The Report so states at many points. Does this mean that we must reject the Report and the underlying investigation and accept the alternative theories of these critics who not only disagree with the Commission but with each other?

Only rarely does a trial, inquiry, or investigation — civil or criminal — present a tidy package fit for television dramas. More often than not there are loose ends. Guilt beyond a reasonable doubt does not mean beyond all doubt, and so criminal juries must be instructed. The perfect case is usually the fraudulent one.

It was obvious from the outset that there were so many conflicting clues and reports it would be impossible to reconcile them all. But this does not seem to deter our authors. Seizing these gaps or contradictions, some of which were inevitable and many of which the Commission could have avoided or explained, each of these critics has launched an attack on the motives of the

Commission, varying in intensity from the professorial tone of Edward Jay Epstein in *Inquest* to the staccato drumbeat of Harold Weisberg in *Whitewash*. Each implies or states that the Commission assumed at the outset that Oswald alone was guilty and then set out to demonstrate or prove it. Perhaps this is so, but these gentlemen have not made the case. It is more easily demonstrable that it is they who have sought to prove their own predisposition.

Although *Inquest* is written in a sober and scholarly law-school style with a remarkable economy of expression, the book is patently tendentious. Its essence is that the Commission was engaged not in the pursuit of facts but of "political truth," that its "dominant purpose" was "to protect the national interest by dispelling rumors" about "conspiracy" and to "lift the cloud of doubts . . . over American institutions," because "the nation's prestige was at stake." This "implicit purpose," deduced by Epstein from newspaper reports and comments taken out of context, is compared with the Commission's explicit purpose stated in the President's directive "to ascertain, evaluate, and report on the facts" including "its findings and conclusions."

Epstein then argues:

> These two purposes were compatible so long as the damaging rumors were untrue. But what if a rumor damaging to the national interest proved to be true? The Commission's explicit purpose would dictate that the information be exposed regardless of the consequences, while the Commission's implicit purpose would dictate that the rumor be dispelled regardless of the fact that it was true. In a conflict of this sort, one of the Commission's purposes would emerge as dominant.

Mark Lane makes the same point in *Rush to Judgment*, although not so precisely. The others state it more crudely.

Why? Is it naïve to suggest that the truth is the best way to dispel a rumor? What rumor was so damaging to the nation that the truth could not be told? In *The Second Oswald*, Richard H. Popkin suggests:

> The Western European critics can only see Kennedy's assassination as part of a subtle conspiracy, involving perhaps some of the Dallas Police, the FBI, the right-wing lunatic fringe in Dallas, or perhaps even (in rumors I have often heard) Kennedy's successor.

This paragraph is perhaps the best critique on Professor Popkin's theories and his book. What further commentary is necessary about an inquiry which will repeat without further explanation, clarification, or comment — critical or otherwise — that complicity in the assassination might be attributable to "perhaps even (in rumors I have often heard) Kennedy's successor"?

How could or should the rumor — repeated and undispelled by this its latest circulator, without any suggestion of basis — be dealt with or investigated? The repetition circulates. It neither justifies, explains, nor dispels. . . .

When the doctors at Parkland Hospital ascertained that the President was indeed dead, the need for an autopsy was evident. The Dallas hospital officials insisted that the law required it to be performed there before the body was moved. This would of course take some time. Federal intervention was questionable, the assassination of a President not then being a federal crime. Nonetheless, Kenneth O'Donnell was determined that the body be taken immediately to Washington, largely, he said, because Mrs. Kennedy insisted on staying with her husband. By bluff, persistence, and a threat of force, O'Donnell, aided by Secret Service Agent Roy Kellerman and others, removed the body from the hospital, took it to the airport, and caused it to be flown to Washington without waiting for a local autopsy.

The use of this incident in some of these books is curiously revealing. Sauvage explores it in some detail as an event of "political significance," which established a basis for federal jurisdiction over the investigation of the assassination. He cites it as evidence that the Justice Department legally could and should have taken over the entire inquiry. This is part of his rather complicated and murky argument that the Justice Department delayed intervention or avoided it in order not to embarrass the state of Texas, and his contention that the Texas officials were determined to establish Oswald's sole guilt before such federal intervention. Why is not apparent. Everything is grist to this mill. Sauvage glides over the whole complex question of federal-state relations and ignores the fact that the Justice Department's investigation did continue and that the Warren Commission is in fact a species of federal intervention.

Sylvan Fox at no little length uses the incident to demonstrate the pettiness and "ghastly ineptitudes . . . displayed by the Dallas authorities."

Contrast Weisberg's description of it as "an abuse of the Texas authorities." This in a paragraph in which he also declines to "embarrass" the "public servants" who "forcibly removed the President's body," but is critical of the Report for failing to do so and for not noting whether a Texas official was invited to observe or participate in the autopsy. Sauvage, however, quotes O'Donnell as suggesting that a Dallas doctor "accompany the body and take charge of the autopsy."

Weisberg goes on to defend the rights of the state of Texas, thus disrespected. He then suggests that had the autopsy been performed in Texas "there might have been no questions" — but a few lines later he indicates that had a Texas doctor or official been present "it is doubtful if the results would have differed."

Thus these authors use the same facts to infer what they will, however contradictory.

Weisberg's hints and speculations are the launching pad for his criticism of the autopsy reports and the doctors who performed the autopsy at the National Naval Medical Center in Bethesda, Maryland, the night of the assassination. They were Commanders James J. Humes and J. Thornton Boswell of the Navy Medical Corps and Lieutenant Colonel Pierre Finck of the Army Medical Corps. All concede the expert qualifications of these military doctors. In addition to the medical personnel, FBI agents Francis X. O'Neill and James W. Sibert and Secret Service agents Roy Kellerman, William R. Greer, William O'Leary, and Clinton J. Hill were allegedly present during all or part of the autopsy, which was apparently conducted by Commander Humes.

The autopsy report, signed by the three doctors, states that the President died "as a result of two perforating gunshot wounds, fired from a point behind and somewhat above the level of the deceased." The fatal missile, the doctors found, entered the skull and fragmented; then a portion exited, carrying with it sections of the brain, skull, and scalp.

Much has been written in these books and elsewhere about the head wounds, their source and course. Obviously, the autopsy doctors were not at the scene of the assassination, nor at Parkland Hospital while the doctors there administered to the President in the fruitless effort to save him. The source of the autopsy doctors' conclusion that the fatal missile came from "behind and somewhat above" was necessarily a combination of hearsay and their own observation of the wounds.

These books contain the not unimpressive argument that the head wounds may have been caused by a bullet coming from in front and not from "behind and somewhat above," as the Report states, or even by more than one bullet, and that the bullet or bullets were not and could not have been fired from Oswald's rifle nor by him. Mark Lane's presentation is particularly effective. However, it is fair to say that the conflicts and contradictions and unsupported speculations in these books and the authors' theories on this aspect of the inquiry produce no satisfactory alternative. Here the Commission's Report is the most convincing. The limits of a magazine article do not permit a detailed analysis of the arguments. Nevertheless, on the basis of numerous scrutinies of the Warren Report and its exhibits, as well as each of the books under discussion and their respective exhibits, plus articles in the press and elsewhere, I am inclined to accept the Commission's conclusion that the shot which killed the President was fired from the sixth floor of the Texas School Book Depository by Lee Harvey Oswald, utilizing his Mannlicher-Carcano rifle. The physical evidence points there and nowhere else.

The other wounds in the President's body present far more difficulties, difficulties with the Commission's Report, but also difficulties with the theories advanced in each of these books. The autopsy report signed by the autopsy doctors states:

> The other missile entered the right superior posterior thorax above the scapula . . . and made its exit through the anterior surface of the neck.

This seems to be saying that one bullet, not the fatal one, entered the President's body just below and to the right of the President's neck above the shoulder bone and exited through the front of his neck. This would be consistent with a wound from above and behind, and with an artist's schematic drawing made later under Commander Humes's direction. However, it is inconsistent with a chart made by the Commander during or right after the autopsy, indicating a lower wound in the back and a higher wound in the front of the throat. It is also inconsistent with the FBI reports of the autopsy and certain newspaper reports, obviously founded on FBI leaks.

The autopsy report is undated. Commander Humes testified it was completed and forwarded to higher authority by November 24, within forty-eight hours of the autopsy. Humes's supplemental report was forwarded to The White House Physician on December 6 and shortly thereafter was turned over to the Secret Service. Thus it appears that in December 1963 the Secret Service had the doctors' autopsy reports indicating the President had been shot near the base of the neck from behind and that the bullet had followed a downward course and exited through the lower portion of the front of the neck or throat.

However, the FBI report turned over to the Commission on December 9, 1963, states:

> Medical examination of the President's body revealed that one of the bullets had entered just below his shoulder to the right of the spinal column at an angle of 45 to 60 degrees downward, that there was no point of exit, and that the bullet was not in the body.

The FBI supplemental report, dated January 13, 1964, states:

> Medical examination of the President's body had revealed that the bullet which entered his back had penetrated to a distance of less than a finger length.

The supplemental report also refers to evidence of "an exit hole for a projectile" in front of President Kennedy's shirt about one inch below the collar button.

These FBI reports to the Commission appear to have been founded upon two reports made and signed by FBI agents Sibert and O'Neill, the first on November 26, 1963, the second on November 29, 1963. The agents' November 26th report states in part that, during the autopsy Commander Humes located a bullet hole "below the shoulders and two inches to the right of the middle line of the spinal column"; that probing by the doctor indicated entry "at a downward position of 45 to 60 degrees" and that "the distance traveled by this missile was short inasmuch as the end of the opening could be felt with the finger." The agents' report notes that the doctors "were at a loss to explain why they could find no bullets"; "no complete bullet could be located in the body either by probing or X-ray" and "no point of exit" found.

The agents state a telephone call was made to the FBI laboratory, which advised that a bullet found on a stretcher in the emergency room at Parkland Hospital in Dallas had been turned over to the FBI; that Dr. Humes was told of it during the autopsy; that he immediately said this "accounted for no bullet being located which had entered the back region and that since external cardiac massage had been performed at Parkland Hospital it was entirely possible that through such movement the bullet had worked its way back out of the point of entry and had fallen on the stretcher."

Further examination of the body, and X-rays of pieces of the skull brought into the autopsy room during the autopsy satisfied Dr. Humes, the agents' report continues, that one bullet "had entered the rear of the skull and had fragmentized prior to exit through the top of the skull," and another "had entered the President's back and worked its way out . . . during external cardiac massage." The agents' November 29 report explains that the piece of skull brought into the autopsy room had been found on the floor of the Presidential car and was taken to Washington in another plane, as was the whole bullet found at Parkland Hospital.

It is obvious that these reports are the foundations for the FBI reports. It is equally obvious that they measurably undermine the elaborate speculations expounded in the books under review about the fatal shots coming from in front.

However, there is also an obvious inconsistency between these reports and the autopsy doctors' report stating that the bullet which entered in the back, near the base of the neck, exited through the throat, despite the doctors' earlier theorizing that this bullet had fallen out. Dr. Humes provided an explanation. During the autopsy he observed that a tracheotomy had been performed on the President at Parkland Hospital, but at the time he had no way of knowing that a projectile wound in the front of the President's neck was used as the point of the incision. Early on the morning of November 23, 1963, following the autopsy, he talked on the phone with Dr. Malcolm O. Perry, who had performed the tracheotomy, and learned of the throat wound, which damaged the trachea and other portions of the neck. From this he concluded that the bullet which entered the President from behind at the right of the base of the neck, or just below it, had exited from the front of the neck or throat. This is the substantiation for that portion of the autopsy report which describes these wounds, stating the back wound was one of entrance and the throat or neck wound one of exit.

It is, as I have said, inconsistent with the FBI reports. It is also inconsistent with newspaper reports based on interviews with the Parkland doctors and with TV statements made by them describing the wound in the front of the neck as a puncture wound, indicating a wound of entrance. Does this mean that the doctors' autopsy report is incorrect or was falsified to sustain a Commission theory or to fasten guilt upon Oswald? It is important to remember that the autopsy report was completed and forwarded to higher authority by November 24, 1963, within forty-eight hours after the assassination, well before the Commission was appointed and before any clear theories of how the assassination had occurred had been formulated. It was also signed by all three of the military doctors who performed the autopsy at Bethesda.

But none of this prevents five of our authors — Messrs. Weisberg, Popkin, Fox,

Lane, and Epstein — from launching more or less harsh attacks on Commander Humes and the doctors' autopsy report. The attacks are premised on three grounds: First, that the report is undated — overlooking the fact that the report form provides space only for the date and time of death and date and time of the autopsy, both of which are indicated. Second, that Commander Humes certified in writing on November 24, 1963, that he had "destroyed by burning certain preliminary draft notes." Third, that the autopsy report is inconsistent with the FBI reports. The last is particularly curious because these authors have all been extremely critical of the FBI with respect to this and other aspects of the investigation; they have freely attacked the FBI's credibility and implied that it was the main sponsor, in addition to the Dallas police, of the theory that Oswald alone was guilty. Sauvage, in his addendum, "American Postscript," uses the inconsistency to damn both the FBI and the Commission. Weisberg also seizes on the alterations made by Humes in his draft of the report and his notes of his telephone conversations with Dr. Perry as evidence of deliberate falsification of the record.

They all prove too much. Perhaps the autopsy report is inaccurate or contains excessive speculation. If we accept the FBI report we must remember it was founded on Humes's prior speculation; it remains undemonstrated that the autopsy report was falsified or altered at a later date to fit a Commission theory. The real animus for the onslaught on Commander Humes is the fact that the autopsy report cuts the ground from under the theories that the shots came from in front.

The most circuitous attack is made by Epstein. Having established to his own satisfaction that the dominant purpose of the Commission was to dispel rumors and establish political truth, he posits the theory that the FBI reports are accurate, that the

doctors' autopsy report was altered more than two months after the autopsy, and that the autopsy report published in the Warren Report is not the original one. Hedged with enough "ifs," he ventures that this indicates the conclusions of the Report "must be viewed as expressions of political truth."

His technique is interesting. He uses the phrase "purported to be the original" when referring to the published report, and he calls it the "Commission's autopsy report" rather than the "autopsy doctors' report." Like Sauvage, Epstein suggests that the inconsistency presents a dilemma, one horn of which is that if the FBI distorted its report on this basic fact, doubt is cast on the entire investigation because the Commission's investigation and conclusions were premised on the accuracy of the FBI reports. Epstein overlooks the fact that he himself has already spent a chapter attacking the credibility of the FBI. He also ignores the fact that the Commission accepted the doctors' autopsy report, not the report of the FBI, which indicates that the Commission's conclusions were not entirely premised on the FBI report. Sauvage sees the point and damns both.

Epstein, like the other authors, chooses to accept what the FBI and Secret Service bystanders at the autopsy report that they heard (obviously hearsay) but rejects what the doctors who did the autopsy wrote and have not denied.

The second horn of the dilemma, says Epstein, is that if the FBI reports are accurate, the doctors' report must have been altered after January 13. He and Sauvage imply that the alteration was designed to bolster the Commission's theory that the President and Governor John Connally were both hit by the same bullet, and that it went through the President's neck and was the bullet found at Parkland Hospital. Epstein ignores the fact that, as he himself reports, it was not until March, four months later, that the single-bullet theory was first

advanced and that it was never fully accepted. One might observe that his line of argument, supported by innuendoes such as
"purported," "purportedly," and well-
sprinkled "ifs," needs far greater demonstration. Lane advances the same argument and
concludes there was a belated alteration in
the doctors' report.

All of these books except *The Second Oswald* seem to ignore the fact that the FBI
reports were based on the reports of Sibert
and O'Neill, who were present at the autopsy; furthermore, that the doctors' autopsy report, which was revised or written in
final form the next day, after the phone
conversations with Dr. Perry at Parkland
Hospital, was forwarded to the Secret Service, not the FBI. As Popkin notes, the FBI
reports are phrased in the language of Sibert and O'Neill, rather than the technical
language of the doctors.

Why is it necessary to assume falsification
and a plot? Why cannot the third possibility, the unmentioned possibility — that
Commander Humes's explanation is the
truth — be accepted? It is not even discussed, except by Popkin. The alternatives
proposed by the others involve either falsification by Humes or distortion or worse by
the FBI. And although the FBI is their favorite whipping boy on other aspects of the
case, here they point the finger at Humes.
They do so, I suggest, because this fits
more easily into their theories of conspiracy
and plot. And if there was a plot to falsify
the record, is it inappropriate to ask, "Why
didn't somebody tell the FBI?"

It is interesting to note Epstein's comment that the FBI supplemental report implies that the wound in the front of the
neck was an exit wound, caused by a fragment from the other bullet, presumably the
bullet which entered the head and fragmented. The FBI supplemental report does
no such thing. It refers to a wound of exit
caused by a "projectile." Since Epstein does
not advance the theory of shots from the

front and wounds of entrance in front, he
has no need to attack the FBI reports, as
do the others.

I have expanded on this entire area because I believe it is typical. It is demonstrable that these books use the same technique
in dealing with such matters as the identification of the rifle, the proof that it belonged to Oswald, the identification of Oswald, the questions concerning Oswald's
marksmanship, the descriptions of J. D.
Tippit's murder, the proof that Oswald was
Tippit's killer, the source of the bullet
found at the Parkland Hospital, the question of how many shots were fired, the sequence of the shots, the number of shots
that hit Governor Connally, the source of
the shots — front, rear, or both — how
Ruby got into police headquarters, the alleged relationship between Oswald and
Ruby, etc. If one were to catalogue the way
each of these books treats each of these
matters and to list the theories put forth by
each writer as to what happened and who
was guilty, it would quickly appear that the
pattern of treatment reflects the theory advanced. This is perfectly proper if it does
not involve distortion and contradiction and
the easy assumption that all who disagree
are either corrupt, dishonest, or incredible.
That is nonetheless the practice. Only
Weisberg is consistent. He finds malevo-
lence everywhere.

Nor is the Warren Commission without
fault. With respect to the inconsistencies in
the doctors' autopsy reports, the FBI reports, and the FBI agents' reports, the
Commission had a clear duty. Its obligation
was to inquire into the inconsistencies, to
question all who were involved. It had a
duty to report the facts and to include all
the reports in its own Report. Unlike that
of a jury, the function of the Commission
was not merely to render a verdict of "innocent" or "guilty." Its duty was to disclose the facts and explain its conclusions. It
failed to do so.

1967

77.

Crime in a Free Society

The first paragraph of the selection below aptly and eloquently sums up a situation that is, or should be, of grave concern to every American citizen: "There is much crime in America. . . . Every American is, in a sense, a victim of crime." The selection is drawn from a report by the President's Commission on Law Enforcement and Administration of Justice, titled The Challenge of Crime in a Free Society, *published in February 1967. Reprinted here are portions of the work's introduction, and they make sobering reading.*

Source: *The Challenge of Crime in a Free Society*, Washington, 1967, pp. 1-14.

THERE IS MUCH CRIME in America, more than ever is reported, far more than ever is solved, far too much for the health of the nation. Every American knows that. Every American is, in a sense, a victim of crime. Violence and theft have not only injured, often irreparably, hundreds of thousands of citizens but have directly affected everyone.

Some people have been impelled to up-root themselves and find new homes. Some have been made afraid to use public streets and parks. Some have come to doubt the worth of a society in which so many people behave so badly. Some have become distrustful of the government's ability, or even desire, to protect them. Some have lapsed into the attitude that criminal behavior is normal human behavior and consequently have become indifferent to it, or have

adopted it as a good way to get ahead in life. Some have become suspicious of those they conceive to be responsible for crime: adolescents or Negroes or drug addicts or college students or demonstrators; policemen who fail to solve crimes; judges who pass lenient sentences or write decisions restricting the activities of the police; parole boards that release prisoners who resume their criminal activities.

The most understandable mood into which many Americans have been plunged by crime is one of frustration and bewilderment. For "crime" is not a single simple phenomenon that can be examined, analyzed, and described in one piece. It occurs in every part of the country and in every stratum of society. Its practitioners and its victims are people of all ages, incomes, and backgrounds. Its trends are difficult to ascertain. Its causes are legion. Its cures are speculative and controversial. An examination of any single kind of crime, let alone of "crime in America," raises a myriad of issues of the utmost complexity.

Consider the crime of robbery, which, since it involves both stealing and violence, or the threat of it, is an especially hurtful and frightening one. In 1965 in America there were 118,916 robberies known to the police: 326 robberies a day; a robbery for every 1,630 Americans. Robbery takes dozens of forms, but suppose it took only four: forcible or violent purse snatching by boys, muggings by drug addicts, store stickups by people with a sudden desperate need for money, and bank robberies by skillful professional criminals. The technical, organizational, legal, behavioral, economic, and social problems that must be addressed if America is to deal with any degree of success with just those four kinds of events and those four kinds of persons are innumerable and refractory.

The underlying problems are ones that the criminal justice system can do little about. The unruliness of young people, widespread drug addiction, the existence of much poverty in a wealthy society, the pursuit of the dollar by any available means are phenomena the police, the courts, and the correctional apparatus, which must deal with crimes and criminals one by one, cannot confront directly. They are strands that can be disentangled from the fabric of American life only by the concerted action of all of society. They concern the Commission deeply, for unless society does take concerted action to change the general conditions and attitudes that are associated with crime, no improvement in law enforcement and administration of justice, the subjects this Commission was specifically asked to study, will be of much avail.

Of the everyday problems of the criminal justice system itself, certainly the most deli-

cate and probably the most difficult concern the proper ways of dealing individually with individuals. Arrest and prosecution are likely to have quite different effects on delinquent boys and on hardened professional criminals. Sentencing occasional robbers and habitual robbers by the same standards is clearly inappropriate. Rehabilitating a drug addict is a procedure that has little in common with rehabilitating a holdup man. In short, there are no general prescriptions for dealing with "robbers." There are no general prescriptions for dealing with "robbery" either. Keeping streets and parks safe is not the same problem as keeping banks secure. Investigating a mugging and tracking down a band of prudent and well-organized bank robbers are two entirely distinct police procedures. The kind of police patrol that will deter boys from street robberies is not likely to deter men with guns from holding up storekeepers.

Robbery is only one of twenty-eight crimes on which the Federal Bureau of Investigation reports in its annual Uniform Crime Reports. In terms of frequency of occurrence, it ranks fifth among the UCR's "Index Crimes," the seven serious crimes that the FBI considers to be indicative of the general crime trends in the nation. (The others are willful homicide, forcible rape, aggravated assault, burglary, theft of $50 or over, and motor vehicle theft.) The Index Crimes accounted for fewer than 1 million of the almost 5 million arrests that the UCR reports for 1965. Almost half of those arrests were for crimes that have no real victims (prostitution, gambling, narcotics use, vagrancy, juvenile curfew violations, and the like) or for breaches of the public peace (drunkenness, disorderly conduct). Other crimes for which more than 50,000 people were arrested were such widely different kinds of behavior as vandalism, fraud, sex offenses other than rape or prostitution, driving while intoxicated, carrying weapons, and offenses against family or children.

Each of the twenty-eight categories of crime confronts the community and the criminal justice system, to a greater or a lesser degree, with unique social, legal, correctional, and law enforcement problems. Taken together they raise a multitude of questions about how the police, the courts, and corrections should be organized; how their personnel should be selected, trained, and paid; what modern technology can do to help their work; what kinds of knowledge they need; what procedures they should use; what resources they should be given; what the relations between the community and the various parts of the criminal justice system should be. . . .

Only 13 percent of the total number of Index Crimes in the UCR for 1965 were crimes of violence. The remaining 87 percent were thefts: thefts of $50 or over in money or goods, automobile thefts, and burglaries (thefts that involve breaking into or otherwise unlawfully entering private premises). Of these three kinds of stealing, burglary was the most frequent; 1,173,201 burglaries were reported to the FBI in 1965, approximately one-half of them involving homes and one-half commercial establishments. Burglary is expensive; the FBI calculates that the worth of the property stolen by burglars in 1965 was some $284 million. Burglary is frightening; having one's home broken into and ransacked is an experience that unnerves almost anyone. Finally, burglars are seldom caught; only 25 percent of the burglaries known to the police in 1965 were solved, and many burglaries were not reported to the police.

Because burglary is so frequent, so costly, so upsetting, and so difficult to control, it makes great demands on the criminal justice system. Preventing burglary demands imaginative methods of police patrol, and solving burglaries calls for great investigative patience and resourcefulness. Dealing with individual burglars appropriately is a difficult problem for prosecutors and judges; for while burglary is a serious crime that carries heavy penalties and many of its practitioners are habitual or professional criminals, many more are youthful or marginal offenders to whom criminal sanctions in their most drastic form might do more harm than good.

Burglars are probably the most numerous class of serious offenders in the correctional system. It is a plausible assumption that the prevalence of the two crimes of burglary and robbery is a significant, if not a major, reason for America's alarm about crime, and that finding effective ways of protecting the community from those two crimes would do much to make "crime" as a whole less frightening and to bring it within manageable bounds.

Larceny — stealing that does not involve either force or illegal entry — is by far the most frequent kind of stealing in America. It is less frightening than burglary because to a large, perhaps even to a preponderant extent, it is a crime of opportunity, a matter of making off with whatever happens to be lying around loose: Christmas presents in an unlocked car, merchandise on a store counter, a bicycle in a front yard, and so forth. Insofar as this is so, it is a crime that might be sharply reduced by the adoption of precautionary measures by citizens themselves. The reverse side of this is that it is an extremely difficult crime for the police to deal with; there are seldom physical clues to go on, as there are more likely to be in cases of breaking and entering, and the likelihood of the victim identifying the criminal is far less than in the case of a face-to-face crime, like robbery. Only 20 percent of reported major larcenies are solved, and the solution rate for minor ones is considerably lower.

A unique feature of the crime of automobile theft is that, although only a quarter of all automobile thefts — and there were 486,568 reported to the FBI in 1965 — are solved, some 87 percent of all stolen automobiles are recovered and returned to their owners. The overwhelming majority of automobile thefts are for the purpose of securing temporary transportation, often for "joyriding."

More than 60 percent of those arrested for this crime in 1965 were under eighteen years of age, and 88 percent were under twenty-five. However, automobile theft for the purpose of stripping automobiles of their parts or for reselling automobiles in remote parts of the country is a lucrative and growing part of professional crime, a Commission study of professional criminals indicates. What is especially suggestive about these facts is that, while much automobile theft is committed by young joyriders, some of it is calculating, professional crime that poses a major law enforcement problem. The estimated value of the unrecovered stolen automobiles in 1965 is $60 million. In other words, coping with automobile theft, like coping with every kind of serious crime, is a matter of dealing with many kinds of people with many kinds of motives. No single response, by either the community or the criminal justice system, can be effective.

These three major crimes against property do not tell the whole story about stealing. In fact, the whole story cannot be told. There is no knowing how much embezzlement, fraud, loan sharking, and other forms of thievery from individuals or commercial institutions there is, or how much price-rigging, tax evasion, bribery, graft, and other forms of thievery from the public at large there is. The Commission's studies indicate that the economic losses those crimes cause are far greater than those caused by the three index crimes against property. Many crimes in this category are never discovered; they get lost in the complications and convolutions of business procedures. Many others are never reported to law enforcement agencies. Most people pay little heed to crimes of this sort when they worry about

"crime in America," because those crimes do not, as a rule, offer an immediate, recognizable threat to personal safety. . . .

Two striking facts that the UCR and every other examination of American crime disclose are that most crimes, wherever they are committed, are committed by boys and young men, and that most crimes, by whomever they are committed, are committed in cities. Three-quarters of the 1965 arrests for Index Crimes, plus petty larceny and negligent manslaughter, were of people less than twenty-five years old. More fifteen-year-olds were arrested for those crimes than people of any other age, and sixteen-year-olds were a close second. Of 2,780,015 "offenses known to the police" in 1965 — these were Index Crimes — some 2 million occurred in cities, more than half a million occurred in the suburbs, and about 170,000 occurred in rural areas. The number of city crimes per hundred thousand residents was over 1,800, the suburban rate was almost 1,200, and the rural rate was 616.9.

In short, crime is evidently associated with two powerful social trends: the increasing urbanization of America and the increasing numerousness, restlessness, and restiveness of American youth. The two trends are not separate and distinct, of course. They are entangled with each other in many ways, and both are entangled with another trend, increasing affluence, that also appears to be intimately associated with crime. An abundance of material goods provides an abundance of motives and opportunities for stealing, and stealing is the fastest growing kind of crime. . . .

What appears to be happening throughout the country, in the cities and in the suburbs, among the poor and among the well-to-do, is that parental, and especially paternal, authority over young people is becoming weaker. The community is accustomed to rely upon this force as one guarantee that children will learn to fit themselves into society in an orderly and peaceable manner, that the natural and valuable rebelliousness of young people will not express itself in the form of warring violently on society or any of its members. The programs and activities of almost every kind of social institution with which children come in contact — schools, churches, social-service agencies, youth organizations — are predicated on the assumption that children acquire their fundamental attitudes toward life, their moral standards, in their homes. The social institutions provide children with many opportunities: to learn, to worship, to play, to socialize, to secure expert help in solving a variety of problems. However, offering opportunities is not the same thing as providing moral standards.

The community's social institutions have so far not found ways to give young people the motivation to live moral lives; some of them have not even recognized their duty to seek for such ways. Young people who have not received strong and loving parental guidance, or whose experience leads them to believe that all of society is callous at best, or a racket at worst, tend to be unmotivated people, and therefore people with whom the community is most unprepared to cope. Much more to the point, they are people who are unprepared to cope with the many ambiguities and lacks that they find in the community. Boredom corrodes ambition and cynicism corrupts those with ethical sensitivity.

That there are all too many ambiguities and lacks in the community scarcely needs prolonged demonstration. Poverty and racial discrimination, bad housing and commercial exploitation, the enormous gap between American ideals and American achievements, and the many distressing consequences and implications of these conditions are national failings that are widely recognized. Their effects on young people have been greatly aggravated by the technological revolution of the last two decades, which has greatly reduced the market for unskilled labor. A job, earning one's own living, is probably the most important factor in making a person independent and making him responsible. Today, education is a prerequisite for all but the most menial jobs; a great deal of education is a prerequisite for really promising ones.

And so there are two continually growing groups of discontented young people: those whose capacity or desire for becoming educated has not been developed by their homes or schools (or both) and who therefore are unemployed or even unemployable; and those whose entry into the adult working world has been delayed by the necessity of continuing their studies long past the point at which they have become physically and psychologically adult. Young people today are sorely discontented in the suburbs and on the campuses as well as in the slums.

However, there is no doubt that they more often express this discontent criminally in the slums. So do older people. It is not hard to understand why. The conditions of life there, economic and social, conspire to make crime not only easy to engage in but easy to invent justifications for. A man who lives in the country or in a small town is likely to be conspicuous, under surveillance by his community, so to speak, and therefore under its control. A city man is often almost invisible, socially isolated from his neighborhood, and therefore incapable of being controlled by it. He has more opportunities for crime. At the same time, in a city, much more than in a small community, he rubs constantly, abrasively, and impersonally against other people; he is likely to live his life unnoticed and unrespected, his hopes unfulfilled. He can fall easily into resentment against his neighbors and against society, into a feeling that he is in a jungle where force and cunning are the only means of survival.

There have always been slums in the cities, and they have always been places where there was the most crime. What has made this condition even more menacing in recent years is that the slums, with all their squalor and turbulence, have more and more become ghettos, neighborhoods in which racial minorities are sequestered with little chance of escape. People who, though declared by the law to be equal, are prevented by society from improving their circumstances, even when they have the ability and the desire to do so, are people with extraordinary strains on their respect for the law and society.

It is with the young people and the slum dwellers who have been embittered by these painful social and economic pressures that the criminal justice system preponderantly deals. Society insists that individuals are responsible for their actions, and the criminal process operates on that assumption. However, society has not devised ways for ensuring that all its members have the ability to assume responsibility. It has let too many of them grow up untaught, unmotivated, unwanted. The criminal justice system has a great potential for dealing with individual instances of crime, but it was not designed to eliminate the conditions in which most crime breeds. It needs help. Warring on poverty, inadequate housing and unemployment, is warring on crime. A civil rights law is a law against crime. Money for schools is money against crime. Medical, psychiatric, and family-counseling services are services against crime. More broadly and most importantly every effort to improve life in America's "inner cities" is an effort against crime. A community's most enduring protection against crime is to right the wrongs and cure the illnesses that tempt men to harm their neighbors.

Finally, no system, however well staffed or organized, no level of material well-being for all, will rid a society of crime if there is not a widespread ethical motivation and a widespread belief that, by and large, the government and the social order deserve credence, respect and loyalty. . . .

Each time a citizen fails to report an offense, declines to take the commonsense precautions against crime his police department tells him to, is disrespectful to an officer of the law, shirks his duty as a juror or performs it with a biased mind or a hate-filled heart, or refuses to hire a qualified man because he is an ex-convict, he contributes his mite to crime. That much is obvious. A further duty of every citizen is to familiarize himself with the problems of crime and the criminal justice system so that when legislatures are considering criminal laws or appropriations for the system, he can express informed views; and when politicians make crime an election issue, he will not be panicked or deceived. The money that is needed to control crime will come, ultimately, from the public. That, too, is obvious.

Beyond this, controlling crime depends to a great degree on interaction between the community and the criminal justice system. The need for the system and the universities to work together on research into crime and the ways to prevent or control it has been mentioned. Similarly, effective policing of slums and ghettos requires programs designed to improve relations between the police and the residents of such neighborhoods and enable them to work together. Community-based correctional programs require that organizations of many kinds, and individuals as well, involve themselves actively in the job of reintegrating offenders into the life of the community. Programs designed to reduce juvenile delinquency require the same kind of public involvement.

Above all, the Commission inquiries have convinced it that it is undesirable that offenders travel any further along the full course from arrest to charge to sentence to detention than is absolutely necessary for society's protection and the offenders' own welfare. Much of the congestion throughout the system, from police stations to prisons, is the result of the presence in the system of offenders who are there only because there is no other way of dealing with them. One of the system's greatest needs is for the community to establish institutions and agencies to which policemen, prosecutors, and judges can refer various kinds of offenders without being compelled to bring the full force of criminal sanctions to bear on them.

Doubtless, devising and instituting alternative ways of treating offenders is a long and complicated process. It must begin with an understanding by the community of the limited capacity of the criminal justice system for handling the whole problem of "crime." Until the public becomes fully aware of what the system can do and what it cannot do, it cannot give the system the help it needs.

78.

Gerald Stern: Public Drunkenness — Crime or Health Problem?

Public discussion of the proper use and of the abuse of alcohol was significantly stimulated in 1967 by the publication of Alcohol Problems *(a report to the nation by the Cooperative Commission on the Study of Alcoholism on the problems of changing national attitudes and policy), and by the general report of the President's Commission on Law Enforcement and Administration of Justice: "The Challenge of Crime in a Free Society." The latter report, which devoted a special chapter to drunkenness, made several recommendations, ranging from expanded research to the elimination of criminal treatment of drunkenness and the establishment of civil detoxification centers. These recommendations are discussed in the following article by Gerald Stern, who served as staff attorney on the President's Commission and devoted his primary attention to its* Task Force Report: Drunkenness.

Source: *Annals* of the American Academy of Political and Social Science, November 1967.

One out of every three arrests in this country is for the crime of public drunkenness. The effect of this disproportionate volume of drunkenness arrests on the criminal justice system was a major concern of the President's Commission on Law Enforcement and Administration of Justice. The Commission concluded that a heavy burden is imposed on the police, the courts, and correctional institutions and that attention and resources are diverted from serious crimes. Moreover, it found that people charged with drunkenness offenses are not being afforded the rights and protections

which should accrue in every criminal case.

Many accused drunkenness offenders are "repeaters" who have been arrested many times for the same offense. The vast majority of these chronic offenders are homeless alcoholics with complex medical and social problems; yet no substantial attempts have been made to treat these problems, which seem to be the underlying cause of the arrests.

It was in this setting that the National Crime Commission undertook its study of the handling of drunkenness offenders and published its findings and recommendations.

THE LAWS AND THEIR
IMPLEMENTATION

STATUTES AND LOCAL ORDINANCES in many areas prohibit public drunkenness and provide maximum jail sentences ranging from five days to six months for offenders. These laws generally prohibit being "drunk." Others sanction the arrest of any inebriate who is "unable to care for his own safety" [Wisconsin]. In some jurisdictions a two-year maximum sentence may be imposed for "habitual drunkenness" [North Carolina].

Supplementing the "public drunk" statutes are laws — often municipal ordinances — which prohibit drinking alcohol in public or being drunk in a "private house or place to the annoyance of any person" [New York]. A variation of the typical public drunkenness statute makes punishable drunkenness that causes a breach of the peace [Alabama; Georgia]. Also, there are provisions within some vagrancy statutes which punish "common" drunks [Alabama]. In Michigan, there is an omnibus statute which penalizes an assortment of conduct including: drunkenness, nonsupport, neglect, window-peeping, vagrancy, begging, loitering in a place of prostitution, jostling, loitering for the purpose of soliciting employment of legal services, and having an "illegal occupation."

Regardless of existing laws, police generally arrest inebriates who are impoverished, and charge any of an assortment of petty offenses. In Chicago, for example, the police, having no drunkenness law to enforce, resort to a disorderly conduct statute to arrest nondisorderly inebriates. This practice has only recently been terminated in New York City.

The primary purpose of the drunkenness laws appears to be two-pronged. The first is to clear the streets of homeless inebriates who might present an obnoxious appearance or otherwise annoy passers-by. The second is to assist inebriates who do not have the inclination or the resources to find shelter. Punishment and regulation of criminal conduct — the usual reason for criminal laws — are not significant factors in the enforcement of drunkenness laws.

To a lesser degree, drunkenness arrests are used to punish slum-area youths and others who act disrespectfully toward police and to hold for investigation people suspected of committing more serious crimes.

The volume of drunkenness arrests varies from city to city and appears to be determined by the community's concern for "clean streets." One high-ranking police official, from a large city which reports a high drunkenness-arrest rate, provided a succinct, although somewhat simplistic, description of police policies.

> There are three types of jurisdictions; the first is "take home," the second is "walk over," and the third is "book." We're the third. Our officers follow a "keep the streets clean" campaign.

The overriding concern to keep homeless, Skid Row, and other slum-area inebriates off the streets prompts some police departments to assign special police details to make mass drunkenness arrests. These "bum squads," patrolling Skid Row and border areas, are especially sensitive to complaints by storekeepers.

Given the keep-the-streets-clean motivation underlying most drunkenness-arrest policies, the arrest process, of necessity, discriminates against the poor. The very basis on which the decision to arrest is made depends largely upon the affluence of the inebriate. Wealthier people appear less in need of the safekeeping aspects of police custody because they generally have suitable living quarters and can get there safely and quickly. Skid Row residents, however, usually have neither the means to afford taxi fares nor homes in which to drink and sleep.

The inebriate is generally not arrested if he has the means to get home and gracefully accepts the police officer's suggestion. The homeless inebriate will tend to get arrested more than his wealthier counterpart merely because of his lack of a home — a home in which to drink and "sleep it off." The more in need of assistance he seems to be, the more likely he is to be arrested. Moreover, from a policeman's point of view, the white-collar inebriate, whether or not ordered to retire, will soon find his way home; however, the homeless inebriate, by definition, is more likely to remain in public.

Compounding the problem of the inherent discrimination in arrest practices is that many Skid Row residents are arrested, in effect, for being "drunk types." Some police assigned to Skid Row beats or to the "bum squads" see little distinction between the alcoholic who is inebriated and the alcoholic who, they think, is about to be inebriated. One offender recounted this experience:

> That ain't for intox alone that we get pinched. The Wagon circles around those alleys and streets, and if you're standing there with a couple of fellows, you're picked up. One day just after I got out of here [the House of Corrections], I hopped off the streetcar at Ninth and St. Clair. A couple of fellows I know were standing on the corner. "Hi Ya Charley," they says, and I stopped to pass the time of day. I'm not standing there more than a minute when the Wagon comes around, and I'm picked up. "I just got back from the Workhouse," I says. "Aw, you're drunk," they tells me, and I'm back in again — without even a drink. In the first precinct they have four paddy wagons alone. I guess those fellows have to pick us up to keep their jobs.

The police are often able to predict with certainty which Skid Row alcoholics will be drunk later in the evening. "Why not arrest them now (especially if the patrol wagon is on the scene and half-empty) instead of later?" was a question asked by one Skid Row policeman. A stronger case is made to justify the arrest of the Skid Row alcoholic who has alcohol in his possession; there is little doubt that, in due course, he will be inebriated and perhaps disorderly or injured.

Another reason for the arrest of sober people on drunkenness charges is accounted for by the unusually broad discretion given to the police officer. The decision to arrest is based upon the judgment of a police officer that a certain individual is "drunk in a public place." The policeman has neither the medical expertise nor any objective standards to make a judgment that an individual is "drunk." The consumption of even a small amount of alcohol may produce physiological effects, and not all persons under the influence of alcohol are drunk. The range of intoxication obviously varies from near-sobriety to unconsciousness. And the point at which arrests are made varies among jurisdictions and among individual police officers within any given jurisdiction. This broad discretion given to the police, unchecked by scientific tests or court contests, permits errors in judgment and, hence, the arrest, prosecution, and incarceration of innocent people.

The signs of intoxication, used by police to establish the criminal charge, are: "bloodshot" or "glassy" eyes, unsteady or staggering gait, the odor of alcohol, and unclear speech. Situations occur regularly in which people are arrested in the throes of a heart attack, epileptic seizure, or other serious illness showing symptoms similar to intoxication. Also vulnerable are poorly dressed people who are sober but have physical characteristics resembling the symptoms of intoxication.

Aggravating this problem of sober people being arrested for drunkenness is the incentive given to policemen assigned to Skid Row precincts to make arrests. Since Skid Row residents are generally not inclined to commit serious crimes, the only way to "keep up the figures" is to enforce drunkenness laws with added zeal.

FROM ARREST TO CORRECTIONS

FOLLOWING ARREST, the accused drunkenness offender is placed in a large barren cell called a "tank," a "sobering-up" facility which houses him for a few hours. One local government report noted wryly that, in view of the unsanitary facilities and other hazards in the tank, "it is questionable whether greater safety is achieved for the individual who is arrested for his safekeeping."

Perhaps the most serious deficiency in the criminal system following arrest is the lack of rehabilitation attempts and other medical and social services. It is widely known that chronic alcoholics and the Skid Row population in general suffer from a variety of serious ailments. Intoxication in many instances causes serious medical complications, and since the symptoms of intoxication so closely resemble other, more serious illnesses, it is difficult to detect or to diagnose these illnesses. People arrested for drunkenness sometimes become seriously ill without receiving adequate medical attention. During the period 1964-1965, sixteen persons arrested for drunkenness in Washington, D.C., died while in police custody.

After the sobering-up period, the defendant often has the opportunity of posting collateral or bail and obtaining his release. In many areas, the forfeiture of the nominal amount of collateral or bail posted permits the individual to avoid the disturbing aspects of the courtroom and the possibility of a jail sentence. Thus, the person who is able to post the few dollars required purchases his freedom. The result, of course, is to ensure that only the very poor need suffer the indignities of a courtroom appearance and the fear of incarceration.

Defendants charged with drunkenness in court are not afforded the procedural and due-process safeguards which attach in other criminal cases. They sometimes appear before the judge in groups of fifteen or twenty and, without the aid of counsel, plead guilty *en masse*. Those who plead not guilty are given brief trials. Because they are unrepresented by counsel, they are unable to articulate their defense.

Observations made by the Commission staff indicate that these defendants are not permitted even the most basic rights. Staff members observed one-minute trials in which the arresting officer testified that the defendant was drunk. Cross-examination of the police officer was not allowed. Not only was there a failure to advise the defendant of his right to remain silent, but the defendant was often directed to testify. And, in some instances, to make matters worse, as the defendant muttered his explanation, the judge interrupted with news of the guilty verdict. Sometimes, the arresting officer was not present, but the administration of justice was not to be delayed; the court officer, in violation of the most basic rules of evidence, testified in place of the prosecution's star witness. And, as is often the case in petty offenses, the absence of a prosecutor forced the judge to assume that role.

Defendants with prior records are the likeliest to be sent to jail, often because of inability to pay fines. In jail, the defendant is fed, sheltered, and given access to whatever recreational facilities are available. No attempt is made to provide treatment for these men, many of whom are alcoholics. Nor is there more than the most limited medical treatment available for existing illness. Austin MacCormack, a noted correctional authority, stated recently that the jails which house alcoholics are of "appallingly poor quality," are "a disgrace to the country . . . [and] have a destructive rather than a beneficial effect" on alcoholics and other petty offenders.

After serving a short sentence, the chronic offender is released to his former haunts on Skid Row without any money, job, or plans. He is often rearrested within a matter of days or hours.

EVALUATION OF THE EXISTING SYSTEM

THE PRESENT SYSTEM is highly discriminatory. There is no desire to arrest all drunks, only those "unable to care for themselves." So a procedure is instituted and adhered to whereby respectable drunks, very often alcoholics, are assisted home, and poor drunks are arrested. The few respectable drunks who have been arrested are generally released, and the poor drunks are prosecuted. When respectable drunks do face trial and sentencing, they are permitted the luxury of retained counsel and, if convicted, pay a small fine. But poor drunks are compelled to endure the indignity of a perverted trial procedure and a jail sentence solely because of lack of funds.

The effectiveness of the criminal justice system depends upon the respect it commands as an impartial forum. By failing to dispense due process in all cases, the entire system is weakened. Moreover, by handling cases which are regarded as noncriminal in nature, the system breeds disrespect for its institutions, thereby becoming less potent to deal with serious crimes.

The futility of using a penal approach to deter alcoholics from drinking, although never accurately measured, is best viewed in light of the startling recidivism records which exist. Some offenders are arrested ten to thirty times each year and may compile as many as three hundred drunkenness arrests during their lifetimes.

The accomplishments of the criminal justice system in the handling of the drunkenness offender are transient. Some drunks are removed from public view, given food, shelter, transportation to a hospital in some instances, and a brief period of forced sobriety and detoxification.

Present methods of handling the problem of public drunkenness are so routine a part of our criminal procedure that there is a tendency to become indifferent to the distortion of the criminal justice system. Necessary but inadequate welfare services are provided by the police and correctional institutions. Accordingly, when faced with providing services to the person in need, the question is asked: "Should he not be arrested so that he can be helped?" But since these services are regarded only in terms of arrest and incarceration, the entire analysis is distorted.

The cruel paradox of the system is that a man must be charged with a crime in order to be provided assistance and safekeeping. A recent newspaper article portrayed this dilemma. When the police in New York City decided to stop arresting drunks, there were complaints from those who had been habitually arrested. These complaints, rather than establishing a need for arrests, indicated the need for housing, food, and medical services. And if suitable welfare services were available in Lincoln, Nebraska, the police would not have to report in their annual arrest statistics the item called "sleepers," representing the number of people — not convicted of any crime — who use the jail for sleeping purposes.

SHORT-RANGE AND LONG-RANGE REFORM

THE ISSUE of whether or not to handle drunkenness within the criminal system may be debatable. Based upon purely moralistic principles, it is arguable that drunkenness is wrong and so contrary to our ethical code that it should be punished by criminal laws. But it is not arguable whether the law need be applied equally and in conformity to due-process models. Accordingly, if we choose to make drunkenness punishable, then such laws must be applied to all who are found inebriated in public. Arresting many more drunks and granting guaranteed rights to all people charged with drunkenness would greatly impede the smooth functioning of the system. But unless the criminal system is able to provide the due-process and procedural safeguards which have been held to be guaranteed under law, then it must forfeit its jurisdiction over the drunkenness offender.

Although the National Crime Commission failed to make any explicit recommendation on this point, it seems important to make the free services of counsel available for accused drunkenness offenders. Counsel is needed to raise applicable defenses. It is noteworthy, for example, that the involvement of counsel resulted in the two recent federal appellate decisions barring prosecutions of alcoholics in four states and the District of Columbia. Moreover, the trial of a drunkenness case involves some very complex issues. The burden of establishing intoxication in "drunk driving" cases is difficult to discharge because of the frequent involvement of defense counsel in this area of law, where the observations of police officers are subjected to barrages of cross-examination.

The presence of defense counsel would have a major impact on the quality of justice administered in "drunk court." Because counsel's insistence upon following procedural and substantive law would tend to delay the processing of drunk cases, this additional burden might, in fact, provide sufficient impetus to remove this entire problem from the already congested criminal courts.

The Crime Commission recommended that drunkenness not be considered a criminal offense. Disorderly-conduct statutes were regarded by the Commission as being sufficient to protect against any disorderliness stemming from intoxication. The Commission also recommended, as a necessary step to implement noncriminal handling, the establishment of comprehensive treatment programs.

The first part of such a treatment program would be a detoxification unit which would provide needed medical and social services, diagnosis for long-term treatment, and referral to an appropriate after-care facility. The after-care programs would embrace a variety of coordinated facilities and supportive residential housing. The need for expanded research and federal legislation was also recognized, but the establishment of a treatment program must begin immediately, as part of, not the result of, research projects.

While it was recognized that the police must continue to play a role in taking inebriates into custody, the Commission reported that homeless and other slum-area residents charged with drunkenness were observed being subjected to physical abuse by the police. One police officer was seen taking a bottle of ammonia from a patrol wagon and pouring it over a sleeping inebriate. Attempts to awaken sleeping inebriates by twisting their fingers were also observed. One police officer boasted to a Commission observer of having broken the fingers of inebriates by attempting to awaken them. Other examples of abuse range from sadism to unintentional mishandling. In view of these observations, the Commission deemed it appropriate to suggest additional training for the police in basic problems of alcoholism and the proper way of escorting inebriates to detoxification facilities.

Although the police could continue to transport inebriates, in the absence of public health workers assigned to this task, there would be no criminal prosecution and incarceration. Under the authority of civil legislation the police could be empowered to bring inebriates to a civil detoxification facility where the length of incarceration would not exceed a few hours. Few objections would be raised by civil libertarians if immobile drunks were taken to such a clinic. When the individual became sober he could leave the facility or elect to remain for a few days of detoxification purposes and, possibly, enter a voluntary long-term treatment regimen.

The Commission did not recommend any program of civil commitment beyond the initial three- or four-hour period of inebriation. The after-care program that it outlined was of a voluntary nature.

Undoubtedly, with the emergence of court decisions prohibiting criminal prosecution of alcoholics for drunkenness, attempts will be made to utilize civil commitment legislation. The result will be to continue incarcerating this homeless population, perhaps for even longer periods of time.

A graphic, and perhaps overly cynical, example of this trend was the initial attempt in Washington, D.C., to satisfy the requirements of a federal-court ruling barring the conviction of alcoholics. Part of the jail was "transformed" into a civil commitment, "health" facility. Under the new program, patients were quartered in "dormitories" which had formerly housed them as prisoners. According to published news reports, the patients complained bitterly — a rarity for this seemingly apathetic population — about their incarceration. They preferred being prisoners. The only attempt at rehabilitation noted was the color of the uniforms, which were changed from blue to white. Moreover, as prisoners, they had access to the recreational facilities and the grounds of the institution; as patients, they were restricted to their dormitories. The Washington, D.C., Director of Corrections testified in court that the patients had to be kept separate from the prisoners who had "free access around the institution."

Civil commitment need not always be less pleasurable for alcoholics than jail, but it will, in all likelihood, remain strikingly similar. The incarceration of people for treatment raises many serious problems, one of which is that successful treatment programs do not presently exist. The "hospital" will be nothing more than a detention facility, and the length of detention is likely to be far greater than the usual thirty-day jail sentence. Too often, the fundamental issues inherent in civil commitment are summarily dismissed under the guise of altruism. And faulty analogies between forcing sobriety upon an alcoholic and preventing a suicide — a favorite among some professionals — will not overcome the problems raised.

The concept of freedom has a long and noble tradition in this country. A difficult burden must be met before freedom can be taken from an individual. The person who drinks should be encouraged to stop. Treatment facilities should be made available to him. The product consumed may properly be regulated. But the government should not have the right to force sobriety upon the alcoholic by imprisoning him, especially in the absence of any attempt to provide a voluntary, comprehensive, rehabilitation program.

Further, and perhaps of more practical importance, there are serious questions raised within the law as to the constitutionality of such commitment statutes. Some laws permit the commitment of alcoholics without any showing of dangerousness. Others, more properly, require that the alcoholic be shown to be a danger to himself or to others. And, presumably, the requisite danger must constitute more than being addicted to alcohol and the consequent possibility of injury or illness. Thus, the alcoholic who does not pose a threat to the safety of others and who does not suffer from other serious committable mental disorders appears not to be a proper subject for commitment under existing laws.

The case for civil commitment is less convincing when it considers middle-class alcoholics with the financial independence to function, obtain necessary services, and continue drinking. The fact that drinking may foreshorten his natural life by a few years, though not a pleasant prospect, generally will not compel institutionalization in the absence of serious family difficulties. Civil commitment is more acceptable when it involves the unproductive resident of Skid Row, who presents such an unappetizing sight on the street. As in the existing criminal system, the distinction is based upon affluence. Civil commitment laws will most certainly be applied against the poorest, most apathetic, and least powerful of the population.

A mutual effort by attorneys, physicians, and behavioral and political scientists must be made to impress upon society that this forgotten population of homeless alcoholics has the right to freedom. And society has the corresponding obligation to make available appropriate health and welfare facilities, even the most basic of which will solve some of the existing problems.

79.

RICHARD N. GOODWIN: The Growth of Federal Power

No one would deny that the history of the United States shows a general trend in the direction of increasing federal or centralized power, although many different reasons are given for the change and widely varying assessments are made of it. Many of the other changes in American life in the past 200 years seem to reinforce this one, most notably, perhaps, the increasing ease and speed of transportation and communication owing to advances in technology. But the causes, as Richard N. Goodwin tried to show in an article, which is reprinted here in part, go much deeper than mere technological changes. The very formlessness and restlessness of American life, he suggested, may be at the heart of the matter; in a situation essentially mobile and fluid, there must be one strong and central point or force. Goodwin was not one of those who objected to centralization while at the same time misunderstanding it and naïvely accepting its many advantages. But he was nonetheless profoundly aware of the dangers, some of which are described here.

Source: *Commentary*, June 1967: "The Shape of American Politics." Reprinted from *Commentary*, by permission; copyright © 1967 by the American Jewish Committee.

THE REALITY of increased federal power is undeniable. The events and circumstances which have created it are more tangled and ambiguous. Most obvious is the necessity for federal leadership in the conduct of foreign affairs, accepted by even the most conservative. Thus, as America became a global power with swiftly spreading burdens and ambitions, government waxed. Our relations with other countries, deeply and even mortally consequential in themselves, inevitably seep into a hundred areas of national life, shaping the structure of our industrial system, setting priorities for education and scholarship, pushing us toward technology and away from other pursuits.

Through this indirect effect on other institutions, and through the immediate impact of particular decisions and acts, the conduct of foreign affairs pervades the attitudes of the nation, contributing to a national mood of enthusiasm or resignation, anger or despair, which unavoidably carries over into a wide range of unrelated public problems and private sensibilities. The war in Vietnam has crippled and drained the drive behind civil rights. The presence and potential of nuclear power has entered into our art, and probably into the psychological structure of every citizen. Yet this towering power is for the most part in the hands of a single man and his employees. Even the normal checks on public dissent are partially sterilized by ignorance, central control over information, and the fact that immediate self-interest is usually not involved, thus depriving protest of the passion which comes from simple personal engagement. It is part of the naïveté of the conservative position to believe that foreign affairs can be compartmentalized — that enormous power can be granted in the world arena while being withdrawn from domestic affairs. The truth is that authority over foreign affairs carries with it a new, wholly modern, ability to alter the nature and direction of our society.

In some measure the increase in central power is attributable to the converging flow of historical and psychological factors. The New Deal, out of necessity, created large new authority for government. More importantly, it led citizens to expect a great deal more than they previously had from Washington. Once this process had begun, it could not easily be arrested. For the natural inertia of the American system resists all but the most critical and revolutionary conditions, such as the Depression itself. The single conservative administration since Roosevelt could only consolidate, and not reverse, the flow. In our nation popular expectations and political power ride side-by-side. As demands increased, the central government was compelled to seek fresh authority. Those who chose conservative principle over political response met the fate of Taft and Goldwater.

Strengthening this domestic "revolution of rising expectations" is the natural tendency of political leaders to add to their power, to relish the "anguish" of decision, and to resent any effort to oppose their will. I do not mean this as criticism. It is a psychological condition of great leadership to want power and receive satisfaction from its exercise, just as a great artist must desire command over his materials. (Justice Frankfurter once told me no one could be a great President who didn't enjoy the job — even if he was occasionally tormented by its burdens. Of course, the fact that a man enjoys power does not in itself make him great.) It is natural for a leader, once in possession of power, to resist frustration. Our system is deliberately and instinctively designed to restrain this ominous psychological inclination. The great number of institutional "checks and balances" are combined with less formal limitations grounded in national traditions and values, political realities, popular sentiment, and the power of the press to criticize and expose. These are often the most potent restraints, not only limiting what a leader can do, but what he would think of doing. They are accepted and even cherished by men whose indoctrination in the American system is stronger than inner drives to power. Like most important political guides, they are rarely articulated, having been absorbed into character and personality. (For example, no one doubted that President Truman would relinquish the steel industry when the Supreme Court ordered him to do so. Yet it is hard to think of another country where a President would yield to a judicial body on a matter of such magnitude. Nor could the Court have made him act if he refused to. It was simply "unthinkable" that he should refuse.)

The price of this system is often inaction, or very slow progress. For radical and swift changes require great and concentrated authority, which, in turn, is extraordinarily dangerous in the wrong hands. We can see today how the concentration of power over foreign affairs in a single man — long a goal of that liberal thought which was contemptuous of congressional conservatism — has dissolved the normal checks of our institutional structure. And these restraints have been neutralized precisely in the area where political checks — public opinion and the press — are weakest, poorly informed, most prone to emotional reaction (especially since personal economic interests are rarely affected in any obvious way), and most willing, in resigned bafflement at complexities, to accept Presidential direction on faith. It is possible that conservatives have something to teach about the value of institutional arrangements, and the unwisdom of sacrificing them to immediate desires. At least we should understand that the hope for pure self-restraint in the use of power can be a very feeble guarantee, and often weakest in the temperament which wishes to accomplish the most for the country.

This interlocking psychological and historical process has been given a greater momentum by our increasing ability to shape events from the center. Economics and, to a far lesser extent, other social sciences have enabled us to achieve an improved mastery over the operations of society. We now try to control economic conditions in every section of the country, using newly refined tools of fiscal and monetary policy — raising and lowering taxes and interest rates in response to computerized projection and the counsel of experts and businessmen. (These tools are more doubtful than a few recent successes have led us to believe, and as presently used they have serious social costs, depriving the government of revenue to support needed social programs and generally aggravating maldistribution of income.) Mass communications and swift transportation have enabled government to bring its authority and assistance to bear in a de-

tailed and specific manner, allowing it to construct the rapidly responsive bureaucracy hitherto thought impossible in a nation of continental dimensions, and encouraging the natural tendency of local officials to turn to the federal government. Hardly a day passes without a phone call from a mayor asking for concrete advice or help. Task forces and experts are constantly dispatched to states and towns, not only in flood or famine, but to examine housing programs, evaluate complaints about pollution control, and to decide whether new power lines are going to blight a suburban area. Computerization of government, the next stage, will increase the possibilities of central control and influence and, unless we make some fairly radical structural changes, will in fact bring about such an increase.

Many of these new mechanisms and techniques are more efficient and result in greater justice — at least in the abstract sense of that term. It is hard to argue that we should not make sure everyone pays his taxes. Yet the knowledge that a giant computer in West Virginia is making a detailed analysis of the economic status of every American will add an inevitable, subtle, and pervasive tension to the financial transactions of each citizen — just as the sight of a police car in the rear-view mirror makes even the law-abiding motorist wary and self-conscious. That is a rather high price to pay to catch a few cheaters, especially when our tax laws give advantages to the privileged which no system of automation can remedy.

Access and communication, however, also work in reverse, occasionally yielding a political influence to disadvantaged groups greater than their economic and social power. We are past the time of the 1920s when millions of farmers could languish in desperation and cause scarcely a ripple in Washington. For example, the civil-rights movement owes much of its impact to the television cameras which displayed the cruelties of Bull Connor and the violence of Selma to an audience for whom racial injustice in the South had seemed as remote as apartheid in South Africa. Through modern communication, Negro leaders have become national celebrities, enhancing the power and possibilities of leadership. Similarly, the poverty program owes a great deal to books and articles: a series in the New York *Times* on Kentucky, Michael Harrington's book, and a piece by Dwight Macdonald in the *New Yorker* — all of which helped to stimulate conscience and political action by introducing thoughtful citizens and national leaders to the agonies of the previously unnoticed millions trapped beneath the surface of affluence.

These varied forces contributing to central power have a unifying theme: the mutually reinforcing concurrence of national demand and expectation with the assertion of power and the capacity to exercise it. There is, however, a more subtle, pervasive, and probably more significant factor. It is the gradual dissolution of alternative outlets for grievances, demands, ambitions, and inner needs. It is as if many small magnets and a single large one were scattered on a floor. If the smaller magnets steadily lost their force, particles would break away and take their place in the stronger field of force. Something like that has happened to American political life.

There are, after all, many ways for a man to change the conditions of his life or modify his environment. He can act through local government, social institutions, and private organizations. Or he can gain access to opportunities which do not rest on official action — by, for example, "going West" to an unsettled frontier.

All these possibilities have been dissolving. Large-scale opportunity outside settled institutions began to disappear when the West was closed. After that, migrants and minorities sought a path into society through unskilled labor. Its virtual elimina-

tion in modern times may prove as momentous an event as the end of the frontier. Certainly the distress of Northern Negroes, and their struggle, would have taken a different shape if this same opportunity had been open to them. Today it is no longer possible to avoid conflict with society while gathering strength to force an entrance. The confrontation must be direct and immediate, and the unequal odds in such a clash require the intervention of the federal government, now the necessary agent of social change — and thus more powerful still.

More important to the growth of central power than the destruction of frontiers is the dwindling influence of local government and private associations. This erosion has been produced by two major social changes. The first, and most obvious, is the enormous resistance and complexity of many modern problems, requiring an antagonist of great force and resources. The second is a loss of connection: the fraying of human, civic, and territorial bonds between the individual and the disembodied structures which surround him. In consequence, the individual loses confidence in the capacity of local structures to modify the political conditions of existence, a self-fulfilling distrust which accelerates the weakening process. Diminishing faith turns people, not away from authority, but toward a more powerful center. This is certainly one of the reasons that totalitarianism finds its moment of opportunity at times of relative chaos.

Added to the many social and psychological conditions which have assaulted these historic structures are the growth in population (diluting participation in local government) and our fantastic mobility (making it hard to retain local allegiances). Therefore, individuals again turn toward the central government where, it seems, grievances and hopes can be effectively aired, and to which citizens in all parts of the country, even the rootless and displaced, feel some connection.

These weakened structures confront a social order whose growing rigidity closes off many traditional non-governmental outlets for change and for those personal ambitions which depend on social justice. The power of large corporations, the sanctity of the search for profits, the desirability of swift economic growth (we measure our success by our Gross National Product), and the exaltation of technology, are all virtually beyond serious challenge. Private citizens, communities, and even states feel helpless to deal with abuses resulting from an unchallengeable ideology and, being small, they are most vulnerable to the interests which benefit from this ideology. Thus our suburbs become horrors of ugliness, discomfort, and spiritual devastation because the right to buy land and build on it is sacred. The blurred advance of technology makes it impossible for any but the most sophisticated and endowed to weigh the advantage of change against the social ills it may bring. Since so much of our system is fixed, it is necessary to turn to the one authority still capable of channeling our institutions, through coercion or guidance, toward desired change: the central government.

Rising wealth also adds to central power. Although new affluence encourages conservatism, the "new conservatives" are usually far more concerned with the content of authority than the fact of its exercise. They find it possible to oppose welfare programs on the ground that they are against big government while supporting larger police powers and a range of new coercive authority for the state. In addition, many modern conservatives favor an interventionist and aggressive foreign policy which would inevitably lead to more formidable and sweeping powers for the federal government. This is far less principled than the conservatism of Jefferson or even Taft. It is rooted in economic self-interest, but whereas the dominant emotion of classical New England conservatives was confidence in themselves and in local institutions coupled with resentment at intrusion, the dominant feeling behind much of the new conservatism is fear (reinforced by a temperamental preference for abstraction over compassion). Behind the paradoxical conservative contribution to growing central power is the desire for protection of the newly affluent against unpleasant, troubling, and threatening social forces. Much of the root of today's liberal-conservative tension is the clash between fear and confidence, which is why conservatism tends to rise in times of felt danger and crisis. Certainly some of the most successful reactionary and conservative movements have rested on uncertainty and apprehension, while liberalism has generally tried to fuse popular desires with elitist confidence. (This gives us some hope that the second and later generations of the newly affluent — even in California — will be less conservative.). . .

Our American culture, more intensely than any other, reflects the process of fragmentation. A man as perceptive as André Malraux can claim that the United States lacks a national culture, since he looks for that culture in its classical sense — a structure of values and meaning embodying itself in certain forms. Our culture is of a different kind, rooted in our history as a nation. It is a culture of restlessness. Its principal values are change and movement, all continuously feeding the hunger for experience. This culture is sweeping the world, in painting, in theater, in the changing beat of music, in the adoration of technology. It is the culture of an age of fragmentation, at once reflecting and feeding that process. For it does not demand or provide the resting-place that unity and wholeness require. It transforms values into psychology, drives, hungers, and actions; it replaces belief with "authenticity."

Whatever this process of fragmentation may yield us in scientific knowledge or artistic accomplishment, it is charged with danger for political and social man. In these arenas of human activity there is no possible unit smaller than the individual. And the most vital and passionate need of the individual is for mastery: both over himself, and through some shaping share in the world around him. It becomes enormously difficult to achieve such mastery in the midst of dissolution and constant movement. Yet those who are deprived of mastery for themselves are often driven to cede it to others, perhaps ultimately forfeiting their freedom.

Whether or not the foregoing description has psychological and philosophical validity, it provides an analytic lens through which we can view our political and social institutions. More conservative than science or thought, they still reflect — as already suggested in the above account of the forces behind rising central power — the more profound contemporary currents of fragmentation and dissolution. Family ties stretch and break as the gap between the experience of the generations widens, and as more spacious possibilities of geographical and occupational mobility remove the pressure to reconcile natural hostilities and make it easier to indulge them. The community disappears, as the comprehensible unit of living blends into the huge, accidental monstrosities our cities have become. Science describes our world in terms beyond all but the most specialized understanding, dissolving control in mystery. Most of us know little more about the working of our world than did the ancients who ascribed natural phenomena to spirits. They, however, had the advantage of believing in their explanation, while we are only aware of our ignorance. Cities and technology, production and population grow and change, powered by forces which seem beyond the control, and even the desire, of the individual person. A handful of men in remote capitals hold our existence hostage to their wisdom or impulse or sani-

ty. The small groups where we could once achieve a sense of belonging and of being needed, because we could encompass them with our knowledge and presence, are disappearing, while the activities they once guided — the life of a town and of its citizens — now seem hopelessly beyond their competence.

As these myriad enemies assault the private stronghold of influence and importance, alienation, rage, desperation, and a growing sense of futility increasingly scar our political life. Two principal forms of reaction emerge. Violent protests and extreme convictions reflect the frustration of many at their inability to assert their significance and to share in the enterprise of society. Men of vitality and passion matched against indifference and encumbered by futility have virtually no recourse but rage. The history of the civil-rights movement reveals how helplessness can drive the pursuit of unexceptionable goals toward violent rhetoric. "Black power" is more a cry of despair and a plea for attention than a signal for battle. Among larger numbers, less endowed with vitality and conviction, there is a rising determination to protect and conserve. They seek security for their present position in the face of receding confidence in their own ability to shape the future.

We see these basic impulses in manifold, sometimes terrifying, forms: more reasonably in the New Right and the New Left, irrationally violent among Minutemen and John Birchers, Black Muslims and Southern Secessionists. They are reflected in the compulsive search for a hero or an enemy, and in a deepening disgust with political life itself. (Nothing more ironically illuminates this point than the contrasting attitudes toward power in MacBird and in the Shakespearean plays of which it is a pastiche.) All these conflicting movements help serve the single purpose of giving the individuals who belong to them the inner sense of significance that comes from being a part of some larger purpose. They reveal how a feeling of impotence is charged with danger, polarizing groups and individuals and creating a nation of strangers, until even those with whom we sympathize glare at us across an impassable barrier of hostility. The gradual decline of the Vietnam debate into competing slogans and invective is our most recent example of this process in action. The result is not merely extremism, but resignation and lassitude embodied in an unwillingness to face problems, make personal commitments, or to act until difficulties have all but overwhelmed us.

Thus, whatever our particular political positions, the one overriding goal of political life must be to help restore and strengthen that faith of the individual in himself which is the source of national direction and generosity of deed.

This may be an illusory goal. Perhaps the machine is already out of control, hurling us toward a future where we will all blend into some grotesque organism, our sensations absorbed by discordant sound and flashing light — where life itself is an endless "trip." Yet no one who pursues the profession of politics can permit himself to regard the goal as illusory, any more than a novelist can permit himself to believe that the form in which he works is obsolete. Politics alone cannot remedy a condition whose causes are so manifold. But it is at least partly a political task.

80.

The Clorox Case

Procter and Gamble Co., the nation's leading soap manufacturer and, more important, its leading advertiser (its total advertising budget is about 20 percent more than that of General Motors), bought the Clorox Chemical Co., the country's biggest producer of liquid bleach, in August 1957. Two months later the Federal Trade Commission filed antitrust proceedings, and ten years later, on April 11, 1967, the Supreme Court ruled in a 7 to 0 decision that the merger had indeed violated the law. The circumstances are spelled out in the following article, which appeared in the July 1967 issue of Consumer Reports. *The consequences of the decision were merely hinted at by the anonymous author of the piece, but it seemed to him that they might be important in the future.*

Source: *Consumer Reports,* July 1967.

ON APRIL 11, 1967, the U.S. Supreme Court struck perhaps its biggest blow in years in the cause of the consumer. It did so by concurring, 7 to 0, with a Federal Trade Commission finding that the nation's largest advertiser, Procter & Gamble Co., violated the antitrust laws ten years ago when it acquired the Clorox Chemical Co. The FTC, in ordering the annulment of that corporate marriage, was largely persuaded in its course by the formidable television advertising power gained for *Clorox* household liquid bleach as a result of the merger. Television, the FTC said, can be a monopoly tool in the hands of a very large advertiser, who can get special discounts and other privileges unavailable to a small advertiser.

Most newspapers that covered the story put it on their business pages and reported it in terms of "conglomerate mergers," "product-extension mergers," and other such arcane language. The real story of what the Clorox case can mean takes a bit of telling.

The Procter & Gamble-Clorox wedding took place in August 1957. The FTC filed antitrust charges two months later. It was tackling a true behemoth. That year P&G spent more than $80 million to plug its various brands, mainly on television. It spent an additional $47 million on cents-off coupons, cooperative advertising deals with supermarket chains, bonuses for prominent shelf positions in supermarkets, and other marketing gimmicks. By 1965, P&G's direct-advertising budget had reached $177 million, of which 90 percent went into TV. Its total ad outlay that year was nearly $30 million more than that of General Motors, the world's largest manufacturer.

Somehow, in all its years of soap making, P&G had never put out a liquid bleach. Noting that it was thus neglecting a market of $80 million annual sales, P&G decided to neglect it no longer. There were two ways to get into the bleach business: by marketing a new brand or by acquiring an established brand.

P&G found merger more to its liking. Although some 200 firms were producing household liquid bleach, *Clorox* dominated the field. It was the only truly national brand and commanded 48.8 percent of total sales. Clorox Chemical Co.'s nearest rival, Purex Corp., had 15.7 percent of the market. Clorox owed its success to classic "creation" of product differentiation. Its house-

hold liquid bleach is essentially the same as any other brand. Household liquid bleach generally consists of 5¼ percent sodium hypochlorite solution — a humdrum fact that, as you can well imagine, gained something in the telling when Clorox "informed" the housewife of its bleach's virtues. The reward for convincing buyers that your product is superior to an essentially identical product made by a competitor was and is a handsome premium in the retail price. Typically, an A&P store in suburban New York recently offered *Clorox* at 53 cents a gallon alongside A&P's *White Sail* house brand at 47 cents — or 13 percent more.

It remained for the Supreme Court to describe how techniques of advertising can turn the theory of price competition upside down:

> Since all liquid bleach is chemically identical, advertising and sales promotion is vital. In 1957 Clorox spent almost $3.7 million on advertising, imprinting the value of its bleach in the mind of the consumer. In addition, it spent $1.7 million for other promotional activities. The [Federal Trade] Commission found that these heavy expenditures went far to explain why Clorox maintained so high a market share despite the fact that its brand . . . retailed for a price equal to or . . . higher than its competitors.

As a result of such merchandising efforts, largely through TV commercials, the FTC noted, Clorox grew well beyond the corporate size necessary for optimal production efficiency. The hearing record shows that the high cost of shipping liquid bleach puts a strict limit on plant size; a bleach plant can profitably serve an area no bigger than 300 miles in radius. At the time of merger, Clorox operated thirteen plants. The plants may have been no more or less efficient had each been operated by a different corporation. Efficiency, then, was not in this case a benefit of bigness.

The record shows further that most of

Clorox's rivals operated plants on capital investments of less than $75,000 and that a considerable number were turning out the product in cellars and garages. "The equipment, raw materials, and labor . . . are relatively inexpensive," the FTC noted, "and neither the product nor its processes is the subject of a patent or a trade secret." Clorox's many minuscule rivals could price their products well below the industry giant's and still make a nice profit. So bigness wasn't needed to produce the product profitably.

THE BIG BARRICADE

THE CLOROX DOMAIN drew the admiration and envy of Procter & Gamble. A memo from the promotion department to the top anagement said, "We would not recommend . . . trying to enter this market by introducing a new brand," and went on to explain how much more profitable it would be to buy out *Clorox* and market it as a P&G brand. That memo later very much impressed Associate Justice John Marshall Harlan, who observed in his concurring opinion that "the difficulties of introducing a new nationally advertised bleach were already so great that even a great company like Procter . . . believed that entry would not 'pay out.' " If Procter blanched at trying to compete with Clorox, a small company by P&G's standards, the Court reasoned, what company would dare compete nationally once Clorox merged with Procter & Gamble?

But if Clorox was already big enough to dominate the bleach market, what difference would it make, one might ask, if an even bigger company marketed the brand? The fact is, if effective national competition with Clorox was difficult before the merger, it became well-nigh impossible afterward. The power to preempt commercial time on network television presents a virtually impregnable barrier to other companies that might want to compete on a national scale. To grasp the advantages of bigness in advertising, one need only consider what it does for the big companies' bargaining power with the television networks and other national media. Advertising time and space are sold at quantity discounts. The FTC was able to show that Clorox, as an independent company, bought its TV time at no substantial discount. But with the discounts available to it as a P&G subsidiary, it could increase its commercial time by one-third without increasing its TV advertising costs at all. Advantageous discounts would also become available on magazine advertising.

Bigness also pays off in the supermarket. "Given Procter's position as a well-established producer of a broad range of common grocery items," the FTC observed, ". . . it would seem likely that Procter can obtain from retailers . . . certain advantages in the display or marketing of its products not available to a single-product producer. . . ."

Court precedent has established that federal antitrust laws give the government power to block incipient monopolies. But the Clorox evidence actually went beyond incipiency. In October 1957, two months after the Procter-Clorox marriage, Purex Corp. tried to break into one of Clorox's strongholds, Erie, Pa. Until then, *Purex* bleach was not sold there at all; Clorox held 52 percent of the market, and a local brand, "101," held 29 percent.

Purex mapped its attack along classic lines, flooding the area with cents-off coupons and cents-off labels. Although it shied away from out-and-out price war, brand loyalty melted fast, and soon *Purex* had a 30 percent share of the Erie market, most of it at the expense of *Clorox* and "101." But Purex should have known better than to make its bid at all. One big advantage of being a monopolist is that you can slash prices selectively wherever someone dares to challenge you. Procter & Gamble did just that. It also boosted its commercial time on Erie TV stations and offered to sell an ironing board cover at half price to buyers of *Clorox.*

Purex was licked. Its market share in Erie dropped to 7 percent. The next time it decided to break into a new market, it followed P&G's example, buying out an existing regional brand *(Fleecy White)* to increase its national market share painlessly. To the FTC, the Purex joust illustrated "the two-edged quality of Clorox's dominant position as a Procter company. Not only is it a significant impediment to new entry [of a competitor into the market]; it is also an effective barrier to the growth or expansion of Clorox's existing rivals in the bleach industry, and thus an inhibitor of vigorous competitive activity."

BIGGER THAN BLEACH

THAT SAME QUOTE would probably apply with equal truth to scores of other mergers of consumer-goods manufacturers over the past twenty years. Indeed, it is what the Clorox decision says about other mergers, past and future, that makes it such a landmark.

Television, remember, did not put its foot in the door as America's super-salesman until 1947. Is it only by coincidence that companies big enough to contract for network advertising time in the early days have tended to consolidate their positions as the giants of their industries?

In 1963, for example, General Motors sponsored as one of its TV enterprises the mass-audience program "Bonanza" at a cost in air time of more than $6 million. That was four times what American Motors budgeted for *all* its TV advertising that year. Like many other companies that can't

match a rival's huge advertising expenditures and the special advantages they bring, American Motors is now faced with difficulties that may lead to merger. The enormous and rising cost of national television promotions has in fact been paralleled by an unprecedented incidence of corporate matrimony — nay, corporate polygamy. In the era of expensive mass advertising, there is no doubt that two or three firms can live as cheaply as one.

One effect of TV-aided corporate bigness, of course, has been an excess quantity of commercials on the air; another has been a deficiency of program quality resulting from the quest for a mass audience to view the sponsor's commercials; a third has been a huge advertising bill, which consumers pay one way or another. But a more profound effect in the long run may very well prove to have been an overconcentration of production in too few industrial hands, with all the consequent possibilities for monopoly pricing.

The merger trend has taken place at a bad time, technologically. Production efficiencies in many industries, as in the bleach industry, no longer require anything like the giantism that has been achieved. According to some economists, the maximum cost savings of mass production are now being achieved in smaller factories than before. A study done as long ago as 1956 by Dr. Joe S. Bain, professor of economics at the University of California, found that the largest companies in eight out of ten industries producing highly advertised consumer goods could operate just as efficiently if they were substantially smaller. His findings were corroborated more recently by data presented to the Senate Antitrust and Monopoly Subcommittee by Dr. John M. Blair, its chief economist.

Dr. Blair, as a co-worker of the late Senator Estes Kefauver and now of Senator Philip A. Hart, has compiled a number of studies on monopoly trends, most notably in the drug industry. Some of his latest findings, relating television advertising to the increased share of the market won by the four largest companies in a number of consumer-goods industries, are to be found in Part 5 of the Subcommittee's 1966 hearings entitled "Economic Concentration." . . .

The big-four breakfast cereal makers (Kellogg, General Mills, General Foods, and Quaker Oats) had a 79 percent share of the market in 1947. By 1963 they had increased their share to 86 percent. Those companies, plus Ralston Purina Co., spent more than $27 million on network TV in 1963, the last year for which Dr. Blair could find figures. In the beer business, the big-four brewers ran up their market share from 21 percent to 35 percent, and in the process helped chug-a-lug out of business 200 local and regional rivals who simply couldn't afford to compete on TV with companies spending $30 million on network and spot commercial time. The story repeats itself in toiletries, pet foods, and so on.

The increasing share of the consumer-goods market won by big advertisers is at least partly the result of the unfair competitive advantages that bigness brings. Procter & Gamble and other big advertisers can buy more ad exposure with the same dollars; they can use their influence in TV to place their products' commercials in the middle of programs rather than at the beginning or end; and a giant multiproduct advertiser like Procter can concentrate commercials for one product only in those areas where competition starts to pose a threat. A company with a small advertising budget has none of those advantages.

Mass advertising in the industries charted by Dr. Blair also performs the job of conjuring up and sustaining an illusion of product differentiation in areas where no real difference exists. "The one characteristic which they [the more concentrated indus-

tries] share in common," he testified, "is not the nature of the industry but the ability of their leading producers to exploit the differentiated products in a manner and on a scale which is simply not available to their smaller competitors."

To put it less politely, too often it's the clever copywriter, rather than the research chemist or engineer, who invents the special qualities in a product, whether or not there are real quality differences. The consumer preference for *Clorox,* for example, was, as Professor Bain has noted about many other products, "built primarily on a nonrational or emotional basis, through the efforts of the 'ad-man.' " And he pinpointed the consequences: "With unrestricted promotional effort . . . the pattern of promotional advantages of large firms supports and perpetuates high concentration even in the face of substantial growth of markets."

As Bain and other disinterested economists point out, oligopolies in consumer-product industries rob the market of price competition. We can cite as another source one of advertising's foremost defenders. Dr. Jules Backman, an economist, recently published a study of advertising sponsored by a $45,000 grant from the Association of National Advertisers, a brand-name trade group. He said this:

> When competitive moves are initiated, an effort often is made to make them distinctive in some way so that other business firms cannot meet them easily. This is why companies prefer competition through quality, warranties, delivery, credit terms, service, advertising, and other nonprice means to price reductions, which can be easily and quickly met by their competitors.

For virtually identical products such as liquid household bleaches, the concept of quality competition becomes meaningless, and the burden of justifying the lack of price competition must fall on such purely emotional differentiation as advertising can weave into the product's mystique, perhaps accompanied by small convenience differences in packaging.

Most of the industrial snowballing disclosed in Dr. Blair's statistics was the result of "horizontal" mergers — industrial marriages of firms producing the same types of goods. Hidden from sight, however, were the "conglomerate" mergers, pairing makers of unrelated products. According to the FTC, many and perhaps most mergers of large companies these days are conglomerate. For example, the Radio Corp. of America recently acquired Hertz Corp., the nation's largest auto rental concern. "Of all types of merger activities," Dr. Blair once wrote, "conglomerate acquisitions have the least claim to promoting efficiency in the economic sense."

Procter & Gamble's purchase of Clorox fell, strictly speaking, into still another category. It was viewed by the FTC and the courts as a "product-extension" merger, because Procter & Gamble's purpose was to add another item to its line of wash-day products. But for practical purposes, including the purposes of legal precedent, it was essentially a conglomerate, or mixed, marriage.

It is interesting to note that Mr. Justice Harlan, considered one of the more conservative members of the Supreme Court, made these points in his concurring opinion:

Procter has merely shown that it is able to command equivalent resources at a lower dollar cost than other bleach producers. No peculiarly efficient marketing techniques have been demonstrated, nor does the record show that a smaller net advertising expenditure could be expected. . . . Economies in defense of a merger must be shown in what economists label "real" terms, that is, in terms of resources applied to the accomplishment of the objective.

One crucial test of a merger's legality, then, in the opinion of Mr. Justice Harlan, may be whether economies of bigness in advertising will be passed along to the consumer in the form of lower prices. It will be interesting, indeed, to see how many betrothed companies are willing to risk making that argument. Already, one big wedding has been called off. Shortly after the Clorox decision, Colgate-Palmolive Co. (the nation's sixth largest advertiser) broke its engagement with the National Biscuit Co.

The government would seem now to have the weapon it needs to reverse the trend toward unwarranted economic concentration in consumer-goods industries achieved through the use of unfair advantages available only to the giant advertiser. Vigorous use of the weapon could bring about de-emphasis of advertising as a substitute for price competition — and the consumer might ultimately benefit.

You wouldn't tell lies to your own wife. Don't tell them to mine. Do as you would be done by. If you tell lies about a product, you will be found out — either by the government, which will prosecute you, or by the consumer, who will punish you by not buying your product a second time.
        DAVID OGILVY, *Confessions of an Advertising Man*, 1963

81.

HERBERT A. DEANE: On the New Student Nihilism

The following article appeared in the June 1967 issue of the Graduate Faculties Newsletter *of Columbia University. Written by Herbert A. Deane, vice dean of Columbia's graduate faculties, the article (which was based on a speech given by Professor Deane at Muhlenberg College in November 1966) was an attempt to come to terms with what seems to many persons, both in education and out, to be a new attitude on the part of students in our time. The nihilist is one who holds that nothing about existing institutions is healthy or acceptable, and who urges instead that society start over from the beginning. This is a difficult position to uphold, and it may be that few or no students actually uphold it with reasoned arguments. But there is undoubtedly something of a nihilistic attitude among a considerable number of the youth of the country, and Professor Deane's efforts to understand it therefore merit consideration.*

Source: *Graduate Faculties Newsletter,* Columbia University, June 1967.

I HAVE BEEN INCREASINGLY CONCERNED in the last year or so about an attitude (or, perhaps, collection of attitudes), among some students in the present generation, of rejection and hostility towards many, if not all, established institutions, organizations, and standards. Let me say first that after eighteen years of college and university teaching I am keenly aware that generalizations about student attitudes and behavior are exceedingly perilous; today, as in the past, college students demonstrate at least as wide a variety of opinions and actions as their elders do.

Therefore, I recognize that the hostility to institutions and standards which alarms me is demonstrated by only a small minority of students, and it may be that it has not yet appeared at all campuses. Nevertheless, I fear that this attitude of rejection of organizations and traditional patterns of behavior will probably spread beyond the confines of the small group of students who now hold it. It has, for youth, all the attraction of an extreme position; it presents itself under the guise of a highly moral and principled refusal to compromise in any way with the world, the flesh, and the devil; and some aspects of our contemporary society may easily tempt more young people to an outright rejection of the institutions and practices in the world around them. There is hypocrisy, vulgar materialism, expensive ugliness, addiction to high-sounding ideals which are rarely permitted to interfere with shrewd, cold pursuit of narrow self-interest, widespread indifference to those who are not successful in the competitive race — the poor, the elderly, the handicapped, the disinherited minorities at home, and the "stupid" and impoverished masses of Asia, Africa, and Latin America abroad. All these obvious aspects of contemporary American life provide, I believe, a fertile soil for further growth of this attitude of total rejection among a larger number of students, many of whom will be the more intelligent, concerned, and sensitive members of their generation.

Yet, to this negative aspect there may be a hopeful complement. To an extent perhaps unequalled in history, conscientious self-examination is denying us the comfort of pretenses; there is great idealism, which is by no means confined to the young, and new striving to break through the accumulated parochialisms of ages; and in many minds there is concern approaching militant dedication to overcome inequities that have attended civilization from its beginnings. Nevertheless, the young lack sophistication born of experience, and tend, a priori, to resent wrongs and to discount the resistant causes of evil. Therefore the imperfections in the world about us provide ready pretexts for youthful hostility. The cause of that hostility is not so apparent as the syndrome. It is not clear whether the phenomenon is part of a rather fundamental change in basic values among students in general, or a consequence of the rapid pace of social change and the instability of values attendant on a high rate of geographical and social mobility.

Let me try to specify what I mean by an attitude of rejection of standards and institutions, and then to distinguish very sharply between that attitude and a radical critique of existing standards and organizations, no matter how extreme that critique may be. The new student attitude — and for want of a better term let me call it the "anarchistic" or "nihilistic" attitude — seems to reject all existing institutions and patterns of behavior. It seems to reject the state, the legal system, political parties, churches, colleges, and universities, and seems to deny objective standards of excellence in literature, the arts, and morals. I want, however, to distinguish between the attitude and the students. Although I cautiously use the term "nihilism," I do not wish to describe any of

the students as outright nihilists. A few of them seem to speak and behave as if they thought destruction were the only suitable solution for existing ills; but others are less dogmatic, and still others have more limited targets for their hostility. The attitude is expressed differently by different students, and is not confined to those who are adherents of any one ideological position such as, for example, that of the so-called "new left."

There is much talk about how individuals in the present-day world of large and complex organizations, find themselves in a state of "alienation" (a word which has become so amorphous and vague as its use has become popular that we would all do well to avoid it). Organizations, institutions, norms are condemned, root and branch, because they stifle the expression of the free, creative impulses of the individuals caught up in their toils and turn them into gray, faceless, conforming automata. In particular, our nonrational impulses — our capacities for pleasure, anger, sexual enjoyment, domination — are said to be in danger of being stamped out by the rationalism and conformity that are supposed to be characteristic of organizational and institutional life today.

Civilization — for that is the shorthand term for the whole complex of institutions, norms, and standards — is the enemy. In the new "anarchist" gospel, preached, for example, by Norman O. Brown in his book *Life Against Death,* which has been popular reading among undergraduates during the past decade, civilization and all its appurtenances must be smashed, or at least radically simplified, in order to liberate the primal human urges and capacities that are now being stifled or blunted by it. A corollary is that no activity should be organized, planned, or directed — that action (indeed even art) should follow the dictates of momentary impulse and "feeling," and that spontaneity, "genuineness," and the satisfaction of impulse should be the only guides to conduct. To follow any other path is, at best, to be "square" and stodgy, and at worst, to surrender one's individuality and integrity to soulless, dehumanized institutions or to cold, impersonal standards of behavior.

So, for example, we are now asked to go to the theatre, the concert hall, or the art gallery to see and hear spontaneous "happenings," whose authors and performers proudly proclaim that they do not know in advance what is going to happen and, after the event, are unable to tell us what has happened and what it all meant. One suspects that some of these "happenings" are not as spontaneous as they are pretended to be. But the terms in which they are rationalized are highly significant. This mood in the world of the arts is not confined to a small fringe group; it has made its way even into the commercial theatre of Broadway; and we in New York have had "happenings" of this sort for the edification of the public in Central Park under the patronage of an energetic high priest of "culture," ex-Parks Commissioner Thomas Hoving (Ph.D., Princeton).

Students who have become converted to this new libertarian or anarchist doctrine now tell us that colleges and universities in the present form are not fulfilling their true function of liberating and developing the potentialities of human beings. Indeed, organized courses and seminars, even regular, organized extracurricular activities, to say nothing of elaborately organized administrative apparatuses — committees, department chairmen, cold-faced deans, provosts, and presidents — constitute an elaborate contrivance to repress all real curiosity, imagination, and individuality that may still lurk within the student, and to turn him into another homogeneous, stereotyped product who will fit neatly into the adult world of "organization men" neatly arranged in corporate hierarchies, and who will never (or hardly ever) suspect that he has sold his soul for a mess of pottage.

In this anarchistic vision the only meaningful education would be found in a deeply personal, sustained, unorganized, and spontaneous relation between a single student and his teacher, who would presumably be available at any hour, day or night, when the student felt the urge to "communicate." There would be no courses, no structured curriculum, certainly no requirements and no grades to mar this ideal relationship.

While this dream is obviously a fantasy, it — or something close to it — is sometimes seriously advanced as an ideal by students who like to consider themselves nonconformist, radical, anti-organization men. Not too long ago one of my College students complained bitterly about the lack of "personal contact" of students with faculty and administration at Columbia — a perennial complaint on most campuses and one that is sometimes justified. I reminded him of the conversations that he and I had had after class, of the office hours during which members of the faculty made themselves available to students, and of the series of informal "fireside chats" which the Dean of the College and members of the faculty had been holding with reasonably small groups of undergraduates in the dormitories. He dismissed all these "contacts" as meaningless or "phony" because they were not spontaneous and "free" but were in some degree organized and planned. When I pushed him a bit on this issue, he finally admitted that the only "communication" with the Dean or a teacher that he would regard as satisfactory would be a meeting that occurred without plan and that led to an hour or so of conversation about life, love, death, war and peace, and basic values. When I pointed out that if this were to be the practice, we would have to reduce the size of the College to the forty or fifty students whom the Dean might be able to see and talk to during a week, he remained completely unshaken in his devotion to his ideal and in his opposition to the present "system."

A weaker but more popular version of

this same ideal is the Paul Goodman-supported vision of "participatory democracy" in the university. In this version, there is still a University and there are still courses and seminars, but students share with the faculty the decisions about what shall be taught, how it shall be taught, how the university shall be administered, and how faculty should be chosen and promoted to tenure posts. A few such "universities" have been started in makeshift ways, and provide us with examples of what the "students" and "faculties" have in mind. It might be added that many who attend these have not seen fit to cut themselves off completely from traditional education.

Lest I seem to be an unreconstructed Bourbon reactionary, let me say that I have no objection at all to student concern with college and university administrative decisions. Administrators who consult with student representatives on a variety of issues are likely to make wiser decisions and rules than those who never make any effort to discover what students want or what is troubling them. But I am concerned when some students spend far more of their time in discussions of the problems of university administration than they do on their academic pursuits. I am just as worried when a college student devotes too much time and energy to athletic or nonathletic extracurricular activities and virtually ignores his primary task as a student — his education.

The main responsibility of students, after all, is still studying, just as the primary task of teachers is teaching and of administrators is administering. If students do not want their teachers to decide what courses shall be taught and what should be included in them, if a course is only a discussion on some subject among students and teacher, who are all regarded as equals, if a course is just a sustained conversation or "bull-session," why should the student and his parents waste their time and money on a college education? Why should I (or any-

one else) be paid for teaching if all I do is to go into a classroom and ask, "Well, fellows, what do you think about all this?" and if what follows is an unstructured conversation to which I contribute no more than any of the students?

Another facet of this problem is the refusal of some students to admit that there are any valid, objective criteria for determining the worth of an idea or an interpretation of an event or a piece of writing. Personal reaction, sincerity, what one feels deeply — these are said to be the only real criteria. As one of my students said to me last year, "This is what I felt when I was reading Freud. Since I am reporting honestly and sincerely my emotional reactions to the work, you should accept my report as a valid account of what Freud really meant. This," he said, "is 'my Freud.' You are entitled," he acknowledged with great magnanimity, "to 'your Freud,' but don't force me to accept 'your Freud.'" When I asked whether despite all the problems of interpreting and understanding any text, we could not agree that there was a "real" Freud "out there," to whose writings we could both go to see whether his interpretation could be justified, he insisted that there was no such independent entity and that only his (or my) personal, emotional reactions to the words were real. Down this road, of course, lie absolute chaos and nihilism; the "communication" that these students value so highly becomes a total impossibility when nothing except the individual's subjective, emotional reactions are recognized as real and legitimate. Each of us ends up as a totally isolated self, locked in a soundproof room, and unable to communicate with any other human being.

One of the greatest ironies involved in this whole nihilistic critique of civilization and all its works is that the opponents of institutions and standards often rely, as Norman Brown does, on Freud as the basis for their condemnation of artifice, organization, and civilization and for their glorification of individual impulse and instinctual urges. Now it is clear that in *Civilization and Its Discontents* and in other works Freud argued that the whole fabric of increasingly complex institutions has been built up in large part on the basis of instinctual renunciation, especially on the repression or redirection of erotic and aggressive impulses, and that he urged that, precisely in order to preserve the fragile fabric of civilization and rationality, excessive and unnecessary restraints on impulses be lightened or removed so as to minimize the danger of an explosion of repressed instincts which might destroy civilization. But this is a far cry from arguing that the restraints imposed on instincts by civilization, by institutions, and by accepted standards of behavior should be smashed in order to liberate the full force of instinctual energy.

Freud, like Augustine, was far too much the sad-eyed realist to agree with the nineteenth-century anarchist view that human beings were by nature predominantly altruistic, cooperative, and reasonable, and that this essentially good human nature would exhibit itself in conduct once the distorting and warping influences of the political, economic, and legal orders were removed. He would, I am certain, be equally appalled by the views of the contemporary "anarchists" who see in institutions and standards of behavior nothing but forces repressing basically good and cooperative human impulses. For it was Freud who regarded the limited, hard-won gains of human reason in individual and social life as the most valuable achievement of men.

Nothing I have said in criticism of this anarchist or nihilist view should be taken as opposition to radical criticism of existing political, educational, religious, and other institutions, especially on the part of the young. There is always need for vigorous and fundamental criticism of existing norms and institutions, and, given the fact that most of us normally tend to become more conservative and more fearful of change as we grow older, such criticism must come primarily from the young. Without such critical assaults, institutions and standards tend to become ossified and decadent; the spirit that originally motivated them — the concern, ultimately, for the well-being of the individuals who make up the organization or the group — is gradually forgotten or relegated to a position of inferiority to the demands of the organizational machinery itself, and we are left with the dry husks of external forms from which the life has departed. So society needs its radical critics, along with its less radical reformers, and its intelligent conservatives, in order to prosper, even if the young radicals sometimes appear to their elders to be naive, utopian, and simplistic. The attitude of the radical, however, differs sharply from the nihilist attitude that I have been discussing; no matter how vigorous and fundamental his criticisms may be, his posture is essentially a constructive one, since he always believes that he can propose a new set of institutions or standards that will serve human needs and aspirations far better than do existing arrangements.

He may be wrong in this judgment, and he is often mistaken in his too-easy assumption that it is possible to move directly and smoothly from where we now are to where he would have us be (as Marx forcefully pointed out in his criticisms of the Utopian Socialists of his day). But he does recognize the need for some structure or order to give meaning and direction to human life, and his own positive proposals are presented for examination and criticism by those who are more satisfied with existing institutions or who would change them only gradually and slowly. Even if his proposals turn out to be utopian or visionary, statement and discussion of them sometimes help to clarify the present situation and to suggest reforms that were not part of the radical author's intention. The young radical does not propose to smash the existing order of institutions and standards without giving any thought to what shall be put in its place or what the disastrous consequences may be if the fabric of civilization is ripped apart and nothing is or can be substituted for it.

To the members of my generation who have seen the incredible barbarity and destructiveness of which men are capable if the restraining forces of the artifice we call civilization are destroyed, the nihilistic program — smash the constraints of civilization so that blind, spontaneous impulse and instinct may be unhindered and men may be "free" — is an open invitation to anarchy and destruction, and, finally, to tyranny, for men will not long endure the misery of anarchy, and they will prefer even the tyrant's order to no order at all.

82.

Tom Hayden: The Occupation of Newark

The eruption of Newark began on the evening of July 12, 1967. It was not the most terrible riot during the long hot summer of that year — Detroit was far worse — nor was it the most surprising — New Haven, which was supposed to be a model city, confounded all of the experts. But it was terrible enough, and also surprising because of the things that men who were there found out about themselves and about their fellows. Tom Hayden, who was there, described some of the events of the week following July 12, and tried to give some understanding of them, too, in an article in the New York Review of Books, *part of which is reprinted here. All of the instances cited in this article were documented by newspaper reports or eyewitness accounts.*

Source: *New York Review of Books*, August 24, 1967.

I. Wednesday: John Smith Starts a Riot

As if to prove its inevitability, the Newark riot began with an ordinary police-brutality incident against a man with an ordinary name: John Smith, driver of Cab 45, in the employ of the Safety Cab Company. Early Wednesday night, Smith's cab drove around a police car double-parked on 15th Avenue. Two uniformed patrolmen stopped the cab. According to the police story given to the *Star-Ledger* of July 14, Smith was charged with "tailgating" and driving the wrong way on a one-way street. Later they discovered his license had expired. The officers charged that Smith used abusive language and punched them. "They only used necessary force to subdue Smith, the policemen asserted."

This "necessary force" was described more fully by Smith at his bail hearing on July 13. "There was no resistance on my part. That was a cover story by the police. They caved in my ribs, busted a hernia, and put a hole in my head." Witnesses on the stoops saw Smith dragged, paralyzed, to the police station. Smith was conscious, however: "After I got into the precinct, six or seven other officers along with the two who arrested me kicked and stomped me in the ribs and back. They then took me to a cell and put my head over the toilet bowl. While my head was over the toilet bowl I was struck on the back of the head with a revolver. I was also being cursed while they were beating me. An arresting officer in the cell-block said, 'This baby is mine.'"

It was about 8 o'clock. Negro cab drivers circulated the report on Smith over their radios. Women and men shook their heads as they stood or sat in front of their homes. The word spread down 17th Avenue, west of the precinct, and across the avenue into Hayes Homes. Called the "projects" by everyone, Hayes Homes was erected in the wake of "slum clearance" in the mid-Fifties. Each of the six 12-story buildings holds about 1,000 people. People know them as foul prisons and police know them as "breeding grounds" for crime. As the word spread through Hayes Homes, people gathered at the windows and along the shadowy sidewalks facing the precinct.

What was unusual about John Smith's case was the fact that the police were forced to let respected civil rights leaders see his condition less than two hours after the beating. The police were trapped and nervous because they had been caught by civil rights leaders whose account could not be discredited. A neighborhood resident had called several of these leaders — including activists from CORE, the United Freedom Party, and the Newark Community Union Project — minutes after Smith was brought in.

After they had a heated argument about Smith with officers in the precinct, an inspector arrived from central police headquarters and agreed to let the group see the prisoner in his cell. "Don't listen to what he says. He's obviously upset and nervous as you might expect," the inspector told the group. The group was incensed after seeing

Smith's condition. They demanded that he be sent immediately to the hospital. The police complied, while others searched for witnesses, lawyers, and members of Smith's family.

It was at this point that witnesses who were in the precinct house say the police began putting on riot helmets. None of the activists felt there was going to be an explosion, and none remembers a crowd of more than a hundred in the street at this point. . . .

Just after midnight, two Molotov cocktails exploded high on the western wall of the precinct. A stream of fire curled fifty feet down the wall, flared for ten seconds, and died. The people, now numbering at least 500 on the street, let out a gasp of excitement. Fear, or at least caution, was apparent also: many people retreated into the darkness or behind cars in the Hayes parking lot.

After three years of wondering when "the riot" would come to Newark, people knew that this could be it. While city officials pointed with pride to Newark's record of peace, most of the community knew it was only a matter of time until the explosion: "And when Newark goes," according to street wisdom, "it's going to really go." Despite millions in antipoverty and job-training funds during the last three summers, the ailments which afflict every black community had become no better. According to the city officials themselves, Newark has the highest percentage of bad housing of any city in the nation, the highest maternal mortality rate, and the second highest infant mortality rate; the unemployment rate in the ghetto is higher than 15 percent. Every effort to create an organized movement for change has been discredited, absorbed, or met with implacable hostility by politicians. The city's 250,000 Negroes — a majority of the population — felt with good reason excluded from the institutions of business and government. . . .

On the front lines against the police that night were men between fifteen and twenty-five years old from the projects and the nearby avenues. They were the primary assailants and the most elusive enemy for the police. They were the force which broke open the situation in which masses of people began to participate. . . .

Fathers and mothers in the ghetto often complain that even they cannot understand the wildness of their kids. Knowing that America denies opportunity to black young men, black parents still share with the whites the sense that youth is heading in a radically new, incomprehensible, and frightening direction. Refusal to obey authority — that of parents, teachers, and other adult "supervisors" — is a common charge against youngsters. Yet when the riot broke out, the generations came together. The parents understood and approved the defiance of their sons that night.

So while the young men grouped their forces, shouted, and armed themselves against the helmeted police with whatever they could find on the ground, the older generation gathered in larger and larger numbers in the rear. The Hayes projects are a useful terrain for people making war. The police station is well lit, but the projects are dark, especially the rooftops 100 yards above the street. Each room in the projects can be darkened to allow people to observe or attack from their windows. There is little light in the pathways, recreation areas, and parking lots around the bases of the tall buildings. The police thus were faced with the problems of ambush and of searching through a shadow world where everybody appears to be alike to an outsider. It was in this sanctuary that parents came together. It was here also that their sons could return to avoid the police.

Less than an hour after the bomb hit the precinct, the looting phase began. A group of twenty-five young people on 17th Avenue decided that the time was ripe to break into the stores. They ran up 17th Avenue toward Belmont as the word of their mission spread along the way. "They're going up to Harry's," a mother excitedly said. She and her friends looked quizzically at each other, then started running up to the corner. A boom and a crash signaled the opening of the new stage. Within fifteen minutes burglar alarms were ringing up and down Belmont and 17th. People poured out from the project areas into liquor and furniture stores as the young people tore them open.

The police now began patrolling on foot in small teams. It was clear that they were both outnumbered and uncertain of themselves in the streets. Police violence grew. The next day Newark Human Rights Commission Chairman Al Black reported to the mayor what the police did when "order" collapsed: a Negro policeman in civilian clothes was beaten by white policemen when he entered the precinct to report for duty; Mrs. Vera Brinson was told to "get the hell upstairs" and hit on the neck with a club in Hayes Homes; Gregory Smith said police shouted, "All you black niggers get upstairs" at project residents; two men were seized by police as they returned from work, one beaten by eight police at the precinct and the other punched and kicked by fifteen police at the entrance to his building. These people were not "criminals," Black told the mayor, but were working people.

But in the first hours the police could not control the streets in spite of nearly 100 arrests and numerous attacks on people. After a while they developed an uneasy coexistence with the crowd, the police in twos and threes taking up positions to "protect" stores which were already looted, while the people moved on to other stores. More police tried in vain to regain control of 17th Avenue and Belmont but were trapped in a pattern of frustrating advance-and-retreat.

One hope of the police may have been to keep the riot from spreading. Again, however, this was beyond their control. If they had used greater force on Belmont and 17th, the result probably would have been to spread the riot by making people move beyond the zone of fire. Furthermore, though all of Newark's 1,400 police were being mobilized, it is doubtful there were enough men to cordon off effectively a spreading mass of rioters. Therefore the question of when and how the riot would spread was in the hands of the people rather than the police. That it did not spread may indicate the lack of real organization. All around the original riot zone people were sitting on their stoops or sleeping in their homes within earshot of the window. Yet word did not spread until the following day.

Moreover, an incident involving Smith's fellow cab drivers Wednesday night tends to indicate that the spreading word by itself is not sufficient to spread the action. The cab drivers were the one group equipped to let thousands of people in the city know what had happened. Within a few hours of Smith's arrest, the black cabbies were deciding by radio to meet at the precinct and form a protest caravan to City Hall. Between 1 and 2 A.M. at least twenty cars were lined up along Belmont at the corner of 17th, creating new noise, excitement, and fury. After nearly an hour of waiting and planning, the cabs roared down to police headquarters, located behind City Hall, to demand the release of Smith. They carried close to 100 passengers from the riot area with them. At headquarters they were able to secure a promise that Smith would be adequately treated and released after arraignment in the morning. At the same time the police closed off traffic on Broad Street in front of City Hall, thus helping further to alert citizens who had not been affected by the rioting or the cab-drivers' caravan. Police by this time were swinging their clubs freely, even at confused motorists, perhaps out of fear that bombs would

be thrown against the City Hall building itself.

Yet the riot did not spread. By 4 A.M. most of the participants had gone home. . . . By 5 A.M. everyone had vanished from the streets, except the police.

II. THURSDAY:
THE COMMUNITY TAKES POWER

Thursday morning's papers denied what everyone knew was true. Mayor Addonizio called the events of the previous evening an "isolated incident," not of genuine riot proportions. In their behavior, however, city officials showed that they were worried.

The mayor called in civil rights leaders, including both moderate ministers and some of his more militant opponents. Concessions were made. Addonizio decided to ask for City Council funds to allow additional police captaincies so that a qualified Negro officer, Eddie Williams, could become the first Negro captain. He requested that Human Rights Director James Threatt and Police Director Dominick Spina separately investigate Wednesday's conflict. He reassigned the two patrolmen who beat Smith to "administrative positions." He referred the Smith case to the County Prosecutor and FBI. He announced formation of a Blue Ribbon Commission, like the McCone Commission which investigated Watts, to examine this "isolated incident." The mayor was doing what militant politicians were demanding. But when someone told him point blank that the people had lost confidence in his administration, Addonizio replied, "That's politics. Sit down. You've said enough."

There was no civil rights leader, no organization capable of determining what was to come. Sensing this, some community activists refused to engage in what they felt were fruitless meetings downtown. Others tried to warn the mayor of what might happen, in full knowledge that the mayor was now powerless. Others worked desperately for a solution that could be brought into the community in a bargain for peace. Many jockeyed for position, worrying about who had the mayor's ear, who might be blamed, who would be the channel for resources from the establishment to the community.

Some community activists settled on the idea of a demonstration at the precinct in the evening. At a neighborhood antipoverty center near the precinct, they ran off a leaflet which simply said: "Stop! Police Brutality!" It would be given out to motorists, calling for a demonstration at the precinct at 7:30 P.M. Some organizers of this demonstration probably thought it might channel energy away from violence. Others knew the violence was there and was not to be channeled into conventional protest, yet protest was the only avenue of expression familiar to them. So they proceeded. Police Director Spina would later claim that this activity helped to "fuel" the explosion later that night.

Regardless of what the mayor did, regardless of what civil rights leaders did, regardless of what planners of the demonstration did, the riot was going to happen. The authorities had been indifferent to the community's demand for justice; now the community was going to be indifferent to the authorities' demand for order. This was apparent to community organizers who walked around the projects Thursday afternoon talking to young people. All the organizers urged was that burning of buildings be minimized so as to spare lives. . . .

Heavy looting soon began on Springfield Avenue, three blocks from the precinct and the largest commercial street in the ghetto. By midnight there was action everywhere in the ghetto, although the mayor announced that the disturbance was being brought to an end. Partly the expansion was caused by people moving in new directions, outward from the looted areas where police were concentrated. Partly it was people in new neighborhoods following the example of people in the original area. A human network of communication was forming, with people in the streets as its main conductors.

The youth were again in the lead, breaking windows wherever the chance appeared, chanting "Black Power," moving in groups through dark streets to new commercial areas. This was more than a case of youth stepping in where parents feared to tread. This was the largest demonstration of black people ever held in Newark. At any major intersection, and there are at least ten such points in the ghetto, there were more than a thousand people on the streets at the same time. A small number entered stores and moved out with what they could carry; they would be replaced by others from the large mass of people walking, running, or standing in the streets. Further back were thousands more who watched from windows and stoops and periodically participated. Those with mixed feelings were not about to intervene against their neighbors. A small number, largely the older people, shook their heads.

People voted with their feet to expropriate property to which they felt entitled. They were tearing up the stores with the trick contracts and installment plans, the second-hand televisions going for top-quality prices, the phony scales, the inferior meat and vegetables. A common claim was: This is owed me. But few needed to argue. People who under ordinary conditions respected law because they were forced to do so now felt free to act upon the law as they thought it should be. When an unpopular store was opened up, with that mighty crash of glass or ripping sound of metal, great shouts of joy would sound. "Hey, they got Alice's." "They gave that place what it deserved." "They did? G-o-o-d!"

The riot was more effective against gouging merchants than organized protest had ever been. The year before a survey was started to check on merchants who weighted their scales. The survey collapsed because of disinterest: people needed power, not proof. This spring the welfare mothers spent a month planning and carrying out a protest against a single widely hated store. The owner finally was forced to close his business, but only after nineteen people were arrested in a demonstration. There was no effective follow-up against the other stores, though frightened merchants cleaned up their stores, offered bribes to organizers, and chipped in money to outfit a kid's baseball team. It was too late for concessions.

The Negro middle class and "respectable" working people participated heavily on Thursday night. Well-dressed couples with kids in their cars were a common sight. One woman, who said she already could afford the "junk" sold in the ghetto, decided to wait until the rioting spread to fancier sections where she could get expensive furs. Doubtless the mayor's failure to act on issues such as education caused disaffection among the black middle class. Doubtless, too, the middle class's willingness to consider rioting legitimate made it more likely that a riot would happen.

But it is doubtful that any tactics by the mayor could have divided the black middle class from the ghetto in such a way as to prevent a riot. The poor were going to riot. The middle class could join. Many did because their racial consciousness cut through middle-class values to make property destruction seem reasonable, especially when the white authorities cannot see who is looting. During the Watts riot the story was told of a black executive who regularly stopped to throw bricks before attending suburban cocktail parties and barbecues; the same attitude was present in Newark. When police systematically attacked Negro-owned stores later in the week, they were

only confirming what the black middle class, reluctantly, was starting to understand: that racism ultimately makes no distinction between "proper" and "lowly" colored people.

Black unity, solidarity, spirit, the feeling of being home: by whatever name, the fact was plain. There is no question that a majority of Negroes gave support. People on the street felt free to take shelter from the police in the homes of people they did not know. What concerned Governor Hughes greatly the next morning was the "carnival atmosphere" of people looting even in daylight. What for Hughes seemed like "laughing at a funeral" was to many in the community more like the celebration of a new beginning. People felt as though for a moment they were creating a community of their own.

Economic gain was the basis of mass involvement. The stores presented the most immediate way for people to take what they felt was theirs. . . .

For the most part the rioting was controlled and focused. The "rampaging" was aimed almost exclusively at white-owned stores and not at such buildings as schools, churches, or banks. The latter institutions are oppressive but their buildings contain little that can be carried off. To this extent the riot was concrete rather than symbolic. There were no attacks by Negroes on "soul brother" stores. There were people injured by glass on the streets where they fell, but they typically fell because police chased them, not because of stampeding in the rush for goods.

Basic feelings of racial hate were released at white people far less often than was suggested by the media. Many missiles were thrown at cars driven by whites but not often with murderous intent. Several times such cars were stopped, the occupants jeered at and terrified, and a few actual beatings occurred. However, no white passersby or storeowners were killed and very few, if any, were shot at. No white neighborhoods were attacked, though rioting reached the borders of at least four separate white areas. Several white community workers felt able to move around on foot freely by day and even at night, especially in the company of Negroes. Driving was more difficult because all white people appeared to be outsiders motoring home. These conditions remained the same throughout the week, though the tensions between whites and blacks intensified as the stage of spirited looting was replaced by that of bitter confrontation with the troops.

Police behavior became more and more violent as the looting expanded. The size of the rebellion was far too large for 1,400 patrolmen. Their tactic seemed to be to drive at high speeds, with sirens whining, down major streets in the ghetto. Thus they were driving too fast for rock-throwers while still attempting a show of force. As a result of this maneuver a woman was run down and apparently killed on 17th Avenue. The sight and sound of the police also stirred the community into greater excitement.

As darkness fell, the number of arrests increased sharply. Police started firing blanks. According to the *Times* of July 14, police were asking by radio for "the word" to shoot, and when news came in that policemen in one car were shooting real bullets, another voice shouted over the radio: "It's about time; give them hell!" At midnight orders were given for police to use "all necessary means — including firearms — to defend themselves."

Murdering looters was now possible. A short time afterward, twenty-eight-year-old Tedock Bell walked out of his Bergen Street home to see what had happened to the nearby bar where he was employed. When the police came, his wife left in fright. But Tedock told his sister-in-law and her boyfriend not to run because they weren't doing anything. They did run, however, while he walked. He became the

first victim a minute later. About 4 A.M. patrolmen Harry Romeo and David Martinez reported they saw four men emerge with bottles from a liquor store on Jones Street. They called halt, the officers told the Newark *News* — calling halt is a preliminary to shooting someone — but the looters ran. Martinez shot and killed one of them going through a fence.

More than 250 people were treated at City Hospital that night, at least 15 reportedly for gunshot wounds. Less than one-quarter of them were held for further diagnosis and treatment. The police took over the ambulances from the Negro drivers and rescue workers. Snipers were shooting at the ambulance, police said. By 2:20 A.M. Mayor Addonizio was revising his midnight estimate that the situation was under control. Announcing that things had deteriorated, he asked Governor Hughes for aid in restoring order.

By early Friday morning 425 people were in jail. In addition to 5 dead, hundreds were wounded or injured. The Newark *News* that morning expressed hope that Newark might again become a city "in which people can live and work harmoniously in a climate that will encourage, not repel, the expansion of the business and industry that provide jobs for all."

III. The Occupation

"An obvious open rebellion," asserted Governor Hughes after his tour of Newark at 5 A.M. Friday. From that announcement until Monday afternoon, the black community was under military occupation. More than 3,000 National Guardsmen were called up Friday morning from the surrounding white suburbs and southern Jersey towns. Five hundred white state troopers arrived at the same time. By mid-afternoon Friday they were moving in small convoys throughout the city, both clockwise and counterclockwise, circling around seven parts of the ghetto. Guardsmen were moving in jeeps or small open trucks, usually led or followed by carloads of troopers or Newark police. Bayonets were attached to the Guard's 30-caliber M-1 rifles or 30-caliber carbines, which they carried in addition to 45-caliber pistols. Personnel carriers weighing as much as eleven tons and trucks mounted with machine guns appeared here and there among the jeeps and police cars. The presence of these vehicles was designed, according to Governor Hughes, to build the confidence of the Negro community. . . .

IV. THE TERROR

We will never know the full story of how these troops and the police hurt the black people of Newark. But there is now sufficient evidence to establish the main features of their behavior.

Less than 2 percent of the Guardsmen and troopers were Negro. Virtually none of the 250 Negro Newark policemen took part in the violent suppression. The New Jersey National Guard, like that in other states, is a lily-white organization which seems to have the character of an exclusive "club" for middle-income businessmen from the suburbs. The New Jersey state troopers also are predominantly white, and many are from conservative South Jersey towns where the troopers act as local police. It was understandable that these men would bring into the ghetto racist attitudes that would soon support outright sadism. A captain who commanded helicopter-borne infantry told a *New York Times* reporter on July 14:

> They put us here because we're the toughest and the best. . . . If anybody throws things down our necks, then it's shoot to kill; it's either them or us, and it ain't going to be us.

On Saturday, the 15th, troopers charged up the stairs of the Hayes houses, shouting, "Get back, you black niggers!" There was shooting up each flight of stairs as they charged. Later, a trooper pumped more than thirty bullets into the body of a fallen teen-ager while shouting, "Die, bastard, die." A Guardsman asked a witness, "What do you want us to do, kill all your Negroes?" A Newark policeman chipped in, "We are going to do it anyway, so we might as well take care of these three now."

These are not isolated examples but a selection from innumerable incidents of the kind that were reported throughout the riots. From them we can draw three conclusions about the soldiers and the police.

Trigger-happiness because of fear, confusion, and exhaustion: Many of the troops were assigned to round-the-clock duty. During that duty they were under conditions of extreme tension. They were kept moving about by incidents or reports of looting, burning, and shooting. They drove at speeds of more than fifty miles per hour; they ran continually along the streets after people. They were surrounded by unfamiliar and hostile faces. There were no foxholes or other shelters from attack. The troopers and Guardsmen knew little or nothing about the terrain and often were unable to tell the direction of shooting. . . .

General and deliberate violence employed against the whole community: On Friday night 10 Negroes were killed, 100 suffered gunshot wounds, 500 were "treated" at City Hospital, and at least as many were arrested or held. By Sunday night another 10 were dead, at least 50 more had gunshot wounds, and another 500 were in jail. People were stopped indiscriminately in the streets, shoved, cursed, and beaten and shot. On Thursday, Joe Price, a veteran of the Korean War and an employee of ITT for fifteen years, was beaten on the head, arms, stomach, and legs by five Newark policemen inside the Fourth Precinct. He had protested police harassment of neighborhood teen-agers earlier in the day. Later, Jerry Berfet, walking peacefully on the sidewalk with two women, was stopped by police who told him to strip, ripped off his clothes, and forced him to run naked down the street. No charges were entered against either man. A Negro professional worker was arrested while driving on a quiet street after 10 P.M. curfew, beaten unconscious, and then forced to perform what his lawyer describes as "degrading acts" when he revived in the police station.

Troops fired wildly up streets and into buildings at real or imagined enemies. On Saturday, before darkness fell, three women were killed in their homes by police fire. Rebecca Brown, a twenty-nine-year-old nurse's aide, was cut nearly in half as she tried to rescue her two-year-old child from the window. Hattie Gainer, an elderly twenty-year resident of her neighborhood, was shot at her window in view of her three grandchildren. Eloise Spellman was shot through the neck in her Hayes apartment with three of her eleven children present.

A child in Scudder Homes lost his ear and eye to a bullet. A man was shot while fixing his car as police charged after a crowd. When another man told police he was shot in the side, the officer knocked him down and kicked him in the ribs.

The most obvious act of deliberate aggression was the police destruction of perhaps 100 Negro-owned stores Saturday and Sunday. One witness followed police down Bergen Street for fifteen blocks, watching them shoot into windows marked "Soul Brother." Another storeowner observed a systematic pattern. On his block three white-owned stores were looted Thursday night; no Negro stores were damaged. There were no other disturbances on his block until well after midnight Saturday when he received calls that troopers were shooting into the Negro-owned stores or were breaking windows with the butts of their guns. . . .

Cold-blooded murder: An evaluation of the deaths so far reported suggests that the military forces killed people for the purposes of terror and intimidation. Nearly all the dead were killed by police, troopers, and Guardsmen. The "crimes" of the victims were petty, vague, or unproven. None were accused by police of being snipers; only one so far is alleged to have been carrying a gun. Several of the dead were engaged in small-scale looting at most. The majority were observers; ten, in fact, were killed inside or just outside their homes. Many were killed in daylight. Nearly all the dead had families and jobs; only a few had previous criminal records. Seven of the dead were women, two were young boys. Of those known to be dead, five were killed Thursday night; one by a hit-and-run car, one allegedly shot by mistake by a sniper, three others by Newark police. Ten were slain on Friday night; six between Saturday afternoon and the early part of Sunday; one on Monday night. All but one or two of these were police victims. . . .

Clearly the evidence points to a military massacre in Newark rather than to a two-sided war. This was not only the conclusion of the Negroes in the ghetto but of private Newark lawyers, professors of constitutional law, and representatives of the state American Civil Liberties Union. They charge that the police were the instrument of a criminal conspiracy "to engage in a pattern of systematic violence, terror, abuse, intimidation, and humiliation" to keep Negroes as second-class citizens. The police, according to the complaint, "seized on the initial disorders as an opportunity and pretext to perpetrate the most horrendous and widespread killing, violence, torture, and intimidation, not in response to any crime or civilian disorder but as a violent demonstration of the powerlessness of the plaintiffs and their class. . . ."

Thus it seems to many that the military, especially the Newark police, not only triggered the riot by beating a cab driver but then created a climate of opinion that supported the use of all necessary force to suppress the riot. The force used by police was not in response to snipers, looting, and burning but in retaliation against the successful uprising of Wednesday and Thursday nights. . . .

The riot made clear that if something is not done about the police immediately, the fears of white society will be transformed into reality: whites will be facing a black society which will not only harbor but welcome and employ snipers. The troops did not instill fear so much as a fighting hatred in the community. People of every age and background cursed the soldiers. Women spat at armored cars. Five-year-old kids clenched bottles in their hands. If the troops made a violent move, the primitive missiles were loosed at them. People openly talked of the riot turning into a showdown and, while many were afraid, few were willing to be pushed around by the troops. All told there were more than 3,000 people arrested, injured, or killed; thousands more witnessed these incidents. From this kind of violence which touches people personally springs a commitment to fight back. By the end of the weekend many people spoke of a willingness to die.

By Sunday the crisis was nearing a new stage. If the occupation of Friday and Saturday was going to continue, the community would have started to counterattack in a real way. "Why should we quit," one kid wanted to know, "when they got twenty-five of us and only two of them are dead?"

Perhaps some fear of this trend led Governor Hughes to pull the troops out Monday morning. Perhaps he could see what another three days of occupation and siege would bring. Perhaps, on the other hand, he had no choice. The troops were tired, riots were spreading to other cities of the state, a railroad strike was beginning, and there were all those political engagements awaiting a man with large ambitions. It may also be true that the governor knew the situation all along but knew as well that 90 percent of New Jersey is white and frightened. In this view, the governor took a tough line in support of the troops at the beginning so that withdrawal would be politically acceptable to white voters later on. As late as Sunday night, a top State Police official was concerned that his men would consider him "chicken" if a pull-out were discussed openly.

Does it matter what Richard Hughes believed? Whatever it was, the consequences are what matter finally. The average view of Negroes as "criminals" to be suppressed was reinforced throughout the suburbs of New Jersey. The Negro community learned more deeply why they should hate white people. The police remain a protected and privileged conservative political force, the only such force licensed to kill. With all this coming to pass, few people were joyous as the troops went home on Monday.

V. FROM RIOT TO REVOLUTION

This country is experiencing its fourth year of urban revolt. Yet the message from Newark is that America has learned almost nothing since Watts.

There is no national program for economic and social change which answers the questions black people are raising. On the national scene, youth unemployment is well over 30 percent in the ghettos, in spite of the draft and manpower and make-work programs. Congress can pass laws against guns and riots, the FBI and local officials can bring criminal conspiracy or red-baiting charges, but until this country does something revolutionary to support the needs and aspirations of its youth — black and white, as the youth themselves define them — there will be no end to social crisis. . . .

The use of force can do nothing but create a demand for greater force. The Newark riot shows that troops cannot make people surrender. The police had several advantages over the community, particularly in firepower and mechanical mobility. Their pent-up racism gave them a certain amount of energy and morale as well. But, as events in the riot showed, the troops could not apply their methods to urban conditions. The problem of precision shooting — for example, at a sniper in a building with forty windows and escape routes through rooftop, alley, and doorway — is just as difficult in the urban jungle as precision bombing is in Vietnam. There is a lack of safe cover. There is no front line and no rear, no way to cordon an area completely. A block which is quiet when the troops are present can be the scene of an outbreak the moment the troops leave.

At the same time, the morale supported by racism soon turns into anxiety. Because of racism, the troops are unfamiliar with both the people and layout of the ghetto. Patrol duty after dark becomes a frightening and exhausting experience, especially for men who want to return alive to their families and homes. A psychology of desperation leads to careless and indiscriminate violence toward the community, including reprisal killing, which inflames the people whom the troops were sent to pacify.

The situation thus contains certain built-in advantages for black people. The community is theirs. They know faces, corners, rooms, alleys. They know whom to trust and whom not to trust. They can switch in seconds from a fighting to a passive posture. It is impressive that state and local officials could not get takers for their offer of money and clemency to anyone turning in a sniper.

This is not a time for radical illusions about "revolution." Stagnancy and conservatism are essential facts of ghetto life. It is undoubtedly true that most Negroes desire the comforts and security that white people possess. There is little revolutionary consciousness or commitment to violence per se in the ghetto. Most of the people in the Newark ghetto were afraid, disorganized, and helpless when directly facing automatic weapons. But the actions of white America toward the ghetto are showing black people that they must prepare to fight back. The conditions are slowly being created for an American form of guerrilla warfare based in the slums. The riot represents a signal of this fundamental change.

To the conservative mind the riot is essentially anarchy. To the liberal mind it is an expression of helpless frustration. While the conservative is hostile and the liberal generous toward those who riot, both assume that the riot is a form of less-than-civilized behavior. The liberal will turn conservative if polite methods fail to stem disorder. Against these two fundamentally similar concepts, a third one must be asserted, the concept that a riot represents people making history.

The riot is certainly an awkward, even primitive, form of history-making. But if people are barred from using the sophisticated instruments of the established order for their ends, they will find another way. Rocks and bottles are only a beginning, but they get more attention than all the reports in Washington. To the people involved, the riot is far less lawless and far more representative than the system of arbitrary rules and prescribed channels which they confront every day. The riot is not a beautiful and romantic experience, but neither is the day-to-day slum life from which the riot springs. Riots will not go away if ignored and will not be cordoned off. They will only disappear when their energy is absorbed into a more decisive and effective form of history-making.

Men are now appearing in the ghettos who might turn the energy of the riot into a more organized and continuous revolutionary direction. Middle-class Negro intellectuals and Negroes of the ghetto are joining forces. They have found channels closed, the rules of the game stacked, and American democracy a system which excludes them. They understand that the institutions of the white community are unreliable in the absence of black community power. They recognize that national civil rights leaders will not secure the kind of change that is needed. They assume that disobedience, disorder, and even violence must be risked as the only alternative to continuing slavery.

The role of organized violence is now being carefully considered. During a riot, for instance, a conscious guerrilla can participate in pulling police away from the path of people engaged in attacking stores. He can create disorder in new areas the police think are secure. He can carry the torch, if not all the people, to white neighborhoods and downtown business districts. If necessary, he can successfully shoot to kill.

It is equally important to understand that the guerrilla can employ violence during times of apparent "peace." He can attack, in the suburbs or slums, with paint or bullets, symbols of racial oppression. He can get away with it. If he can force the oppressive power to be passive and defensive at the point where it is administered — by the caseworker, landlord, storeowner, or policeman — he can build people's confidence in their ability to demand change. Such attacks, which need not be on human life to be effective, might disrupt the administration of the ghetto to a crisis point where a new system would have to be considered.

These tactics of disorder will be defined by the authorities as criminal anarchy. But it may be that disruption will create possibilities of meaningful change. This depends on whether the leaders of ghetto struggles can be more successful in building strong organization than they have been so far. Violence can contribute to shattering the status quo, but only politics and organization can transform it.

The ghetto still needs the power to decide its destiny on such matters as urban renewal and housing, social services, policing, and taxation. Tenants still need concrete rights against landlords in public and private housing, or a new system of tenant-controlled living conditions. Welfare clients still need the power to receive a livable income without administrative abuse, or be able to replace the welfare system with one that meets their needs. Consumers still need to control the quality of merchandise and service in the stores where they shop. Citizens still need effective control over the behavior of those who police their community. Political structures belonging to the community are needed to bargain for, and maintain control over, funds from government or private sources.

In order to build a more decent community while resisting racist power, more than violence is required. People need self-government. We are at a point where democracy — the idea and practice of people controlling their lives — is a revolutionary issue in the United States.

Even cities have their graves.
HENRY WADSWORTH LONGFELLOW, *Amalfi*

83.

Daniel P. Moynihan: The Politics of Stability

The year 1967 seemed to many observers to be a crucial one in the career of modern American liberalism. Born in the populism of William Jennings Bryan and his farmer-followers, enjoying its first successes during the Progressive Era of Theodore Roosevelt, coming to maturity under Franklin D. Roosevelt and his New Deal the movement — perhaps it was more a general attitude than a specific political program — seems to some to have fallen on hard times in recent years. The old panaceas seem to be less and less relevant to the problems of today, and fewer and fewer people seem to listen, but the question is: What will replace liberalism, which has ruled the nation for most of the past sixty or seventy years? There are of course a good many different answers to the question, including the proposition that liberalism is still very much alive and does not have to be replaced at all. Daniel P. Moynihan, at the time an influential presidential adviser, suggested late in 1967 that what he called the "politics of stability," a kind of dynamic conservatism, might fill the bill.

Source: *New Leader*, October 9, 1967.

PRESIDENT JOHNSON is said to be fond of relating the experience of an out-of-work schoolteacher who applied for a position in a small town on the Texas plains at the very depths of the Depression. After a series of questions, one puckered old rancher on the school board looked at the applicant and asked, "Do you teach that the world is round or flat?" Finding no clues in the faces of the other board members, the teacher swallowed hard and allowed he could teach it either way.

That is the position of just about anyone who would assay the state of the American republic at this moment from that middling vantage point known generally as liberalism. Two views are possible: On the one hand, it may be argued that the nation is entering a period of political instability from which it will not emerge intact; on the other, that we have entered a troubled time and will not only survive but will emerge from it wiser and having demonstrated anew the deep sources of stability in American life.

I cannot imagine what would constitute irrefutable evidence for either stand, and I assume that persons adopt one or the other according to their personal taste and condition. The apocalyptic view has many supporters, of course, most notably those of the newly emergent Left who foresee a period of Right-wing oppression and excess, followed by the triumph of a new ideology — a conviction that will seem absurd to anyone who has ever visited East Berlin. The more sanguine view commends itself to those who would like to believe it true. This includes, almost without exception, any liberal who has shared considerably in the "rewards" of American life and who can look forward to continued sharing on, if anything, more favorable terms.

The alternatives, then, are to agree with Andrew Kopkind that this past summer the war abroad and the revolution at home contrived to "murder liberalism in its official robes" (with few mourners), or to conclude that although we are in a lot of trouble, we can think and work (and pray) our way out of it. It is worth stressing that no one whose views we have learned to trust over the years would offer us a happier option than the latter, which means that if we do not think well enough, or work hard enough, or if our prayers are not answered, we can bring this republic to ruin.

Certainly things have not turned out as we had every reason to think they would. Walter Lippmann, with merciless clarity, has argued that the unexampled mandate of the 1964 election was "to be quiet and uninvolved abroad and to repair, reform, and reconstruct at home." Fate took another direction and has exacted a double price: not only troubles abroad but disasters at home because of — or seemingly because of — the troubles abroad. Tom Wicker has stated the matter plainly, as is his failing. "The war," he wrote at the end of last August, "has blunted and all but destroyed the hopeful beginnings of the Great Society. It has produced the gravest American political disunity in a century, and it has aggravated the profound discontent with America of the postwar generations."

The violence abroad and the violence at home — regardless of political persuasion, all agree that these are the problems, that they are somehow interconnected, and that in combination they have the potential for polarizing, then fracturing, American society. But the situation is especially embarrassing for American liberals, because it is largely they who have been in office and presided over the onset both of the war in Vietnam and the violence in American cities. Neither may be our fault, yet in a

world not overmuch given to nice distinctions in such matters, they most surely must be judged our doing.

The Vietnam war was thought up and is being managed by the men John F. Kennedy brought to Washington to conduct American foreign and defense policy. They are persons of immutable conviction on almost all matters we would consider central to liberal belief, as well as men of personal honor and the highest intellectual attainment. Other liberals also helped to persuade the American public that it was entirely right to be setting out on the course which has led us to the present point of being waist deep in the big muddy. It is this knowledge, this complicity if you will, that requires many of us to practise restraint where others may exercise all their powers of invective and contempt. The plain fact is that if these men got us into the current predicament, who are *we* to say we would have done better?

This is more the case with respect to the violence at home. The summer of 1967 came in the aftermath of one of the most extraordinary periods of liberal legislation, liberal electoral victories, and the liberal dominance of the media of public opinion that we have ever experienced. The period was, moreover, accompanied by the greatest economic expansion in human history. And, to top it all, some of the worst violence occurred in Detroit, a city with one of the most liberal and successful administrations in the nation; a city in which the social and economic position of the Negro was generally agreed to be far and away the best in the nation. Who are we, then, to be pointing fingers?

The question is addressed as much to the future as to the past, for the probabilities are that the present situation will persist for some time. By this I mean that President Johnson will almost certainly be reelected in 1968 and that, with some modifications, the national government will remain in the hands of the same kinds of liberals who have been much in evidence for the last seven years. The war in Asia is likely to go on many years, too, although possibly in different forms. Most importantly, the violence in our cities, tensions between racial and ethnic groups, is just as likely to continue and, if anything, get worse (as indeed the war could get worse). But our responses will have to be sufficiently different from those of the immediate past to suggest that we are aware of some of our apparent shortcomings.

What, as someone once said, is to be done? I offer three propositions.

1. Liberals must see more clearly that their essential interest is in the stability of the social order; and given the present threats to that stability, they must seek out and make much more effective alliances with political conservatives who share their interest and recognize that unyielding rigidity is just as great a threat to continuity of the social order as an anarchic desire for change.

For too long we have been prisoners of the rhetoric that Republicans do not know or care about the social problems of the nation. This is not only a falsehood but, as any New York Democrat can testify, it is seen by the electorate to be a falsehood. In New York City, two years ago, Mayor Lindsay was elected because he was the most liberal of the three candidates. Last year, Governor Rockefeller was reelected for precisely the same reason. The hooting at the callous indifference of Republicans toward human needs recently reached considerable levels in the rumpus over the rat bill. I don't doubt they deserved what they got in that uproar. The argument can nonetheless be made that we would have more to show for it all if somewhere along the line the Democrats had taken at face value the statement of Congressman Melvin R. Laird (R.-Wis.) that he was in favor of "massive" federal aid to city governments,

but not through the techniques of proliferating grant-in-aid programs which he and many like him thought to be an ineffective form of administration.

Interestingly, in the area of foreign affairs, the idea that Republican congressmen and senators are supporters of a moderate course is more readily accepted. It is time the idea became familiar in domestic matters. It is pleasant to hear the New Left declare that the white liberal is the true enemy because he keeps the present system going by limiting its excesses, yet the truth is that the informed conservatives deserve the greatest credit for performing this function — the Robert Tafts of the nation — and at the present juncture they are needed.

2. Liberals must divest themselves of the notion that the nation — and especially the cities of the nation — can be run from agencies in Washington.

Potomac fever became a liberal disease under the New Deal and it has turned out not only to be catching but congenital, having somehow worked into the gene structure itself. The syndrome derives from one correct fact that is irrelevant and two theories that are wrong.

It is certainly a fact that strolling across Lafayette Park to endorse or to veto a public-works program is much more agreeable than having to go through the misery of persuading fifty state legislatures. But this has to do with the personal comfort of middle-aged liberals, not with the quality of government action, and, in a time of some trouble, comfort cannot be the sole consideration.

The first theory is that the national government and national politics are the primary sources of liberal social innovation, particularly with respect to problems of urbanization and industrialization. I do not believe history will support this notion, for the cities and to a lesser extent the state governments have been the source of the preponderance of social programs in the twentieth century — mostly the cities and states in the North, of course. Probably the most important reason for this is that until recently these were the areas where such problems first appeared, and where the wealth and intellect — and political will — existed to experiment with solutions.

There is another reason which we tend to be reluctant to talk about, but whose discussion is perhaps admissible in a time of trouble. In the spectrum of regional politics, the South has for a century been the most social and politically conservative part of the nation. In the spectrum of American religious groups, American Protestants have fairly consistently been more conservative than American Catholics, and Catholics, in turn, more so than American Jews. It happens that Washington is, for practical purposes, a Southern Protestant city which combines both these pervasive conservative tendencies — or at least has done so in the past. In an odd combination of historical events, the cities of the North have been dominated by Catholic votes and Jewish intellect, and the result very simply has been a much greater level of liberal political innovation. If this potential has not been much in evidence of late, it is mostly, I believe, because we have allowed state and local governments to get into such fiscal straits that they have no resources left for innovation. But the impulse and potential remain there rather than in Washington.

The second theory I have labeled false is that you can run the nation from Washington. I don't believe you can, at least not with respect to the kind of social change liberals generally seek to bring about. In the field of legislating social attitudes and practices, it is pretty clear that the old-time Tories had a point when they said you can't change human nature — for good or for ill — with a bill-signing ceremony in the Rose Garden. I would note that twenty years ago the Taft-Hartley Act outlawed the closed shop, and that today the closed shop is probably more completely in effect in our building trade unions than ever in history.

The record of social innovation through various public programs is equally unreassuring, largely because the American system of public administration has turned out not to be very good at that sort of thing. Richard Rovere recently noted that "the new federal agencies set up to deal with the distress of the cities — the Office of Economic Opportunity, the Department of Housing and Urban Development, and the Department of Transportation — have turned in generally disappointing performances." Not because of their leadership, which has often been brilliant, but because of the resources available, and particularly the bureaucracy available. Rovere continues: "In the new agencies, for example, almost everyone feels that there is no greater hindrance to the war on poverty and no greater force for the perpetuation of slums than the public-welfare system administered by, and providing a *raison d'être* for, a huge, entrenched, and complacent sub-bureaucracy in HEW." Think of the dreams that had to die before that sentence could be written! But it happens to be true.

"How one wishes," Nathan Glazer writes in a forthcoming article, "for the open field of the New Deal, which was not littered with the carcasses of half-successful and hardly successful programs, each in the hands of a hardening bureaucracy." But the pattern persists: the bright idea, the new agency, the White House swearing in of the first agency head, the shaky beginning, the departure eighteen months later of the first head, replacement by his deputy, the gradual slipping out of sight, a Budget Bureau reorganization, a name change, a new head, this time from the civil service, and slowly obscurity covers all. Who among us today could state with certainty exactly what did become of the Area Redevelopment Administration, that early, shining creation of the New Frontier?

But the biggest problem of running the nation from Washington is that the real business of Washington in our age is pretty much to run the world. That thought may not give any of us great pleasure, but my impression is that it is a fact and we had better learn to live with it. Martin Luther King, Jr., and many other liberals are no doubt correct in holding that the war in Vietnam has stalemated government efforts in behalf of Negroes at home, but they are wrong, I would think, in their proposed solution: the government should get out of Vietnam. As far as I can see, an American national government in this age will always give priority to foreign affairs. A system has to be developed, therefore, under which domestic programs go forward regardless of what international crisis is preoccupying Washington at a given moment. This, in effect, means decentralizing the initiative and the resources for such programs.

3. Liberals must somehow overcome the curious condescension that takes the form of defending and explaining away anything, however outrageous, which Negroes, individually or collectively, might do.

Over the course of the summer it became clear that there are two distinct, though related, groups in the Negro community. One is the vast Negro underclass that has somehow grown up in our Northern cities; a disorganized, angry, hurt group of persons easily given to self-destructive violence. Alongside it is a group of radical, nihilistic youth, not themselves members of this underclass but identifying with it, able to communicate with it, and determined to use it as an instrument of violent, apocalyptic confrontation with a white society they have decided is irredeemably militaristic and racist. I do not believe we have yet realized the depth and intensity of this second group's feelings, nor the extent to which it has succeeded in politicizing the always existing torment of the urban masses — persuading them both of the inevitability

and the desirability of a nihilistic solution. All the signs declare that the violence is not ended. Worse still, a new set of signs tells us something that is painful, even hateful to have to hear: We must prepare for the onset of terrorism. Indeed, it may already have begun. How widespread and how successful remains to be seen, but the probability is so great that ignoring it would be an act of irresponsibility or of cowardice.

For liberals, this poses a special problem that derives in a sense from our own decencies. Trying to be kind, trying to be helpful, we somehow have got into the habit of denying the realities of the life-circumstances of the lower class, and this has curiously paralyzed our ability to do anything to change these realities. Typically, we have blamed ourselves for the shortcomings of the poor — and left it at that. A terrifying example was the response in ultra-liberal quarters to the findings of James S. Coleman in his massive report on *Equality of Educational Opportunity*. Coleman, a distinguished social scientist, concluded that the disastrously low level of educational achievement on the part of most Negro youth was the result not nearly so much of the quality of their schools as of their own family background and that of their classmates at school. With the hand of the federal bureaucracy barely concealed, Coleman was labeled a racist by people who went on their way deploring conditions in slum schools and blaming Lyndon Johnson or John Lindsay; they were not disturbed by the thought that they might be wrong, or that the politics of stability might involve something more hardheaded than the untroubled indulgence of sado-masochistic fantasy.

The point is a simple one: There is nothing whatever to be done to change the minds of the Negro nihilists and their white associates, who have been so much in evidence of late. Their course is set. The only option for the nation is to deprive them of the Negro underclass, which is the source of their present strength. This means facing up to some of the realities of life in that class that liberals have been notoriously unwilling to acknowledge, so much so that I would not be surprised if it developed that this fact itself was an element in the rage that roared through the streets of America this past summer.

The situation of the Negro masses today is startlingly like that of Yank, the quintessential, apolitical proletarian stoker in one of Eugene O'Neill's plays. Determined to make the world of the first-class passengers recognize his existence, he makes his way to Fifth Avenue and the 50s and begins jostling top-hatted gentlemen and insulting bejeweled, befurred ladies. He elicits only politeness, which, actually is a refusal to acknowledge that he is what he knows himself to be. He is driven mad by "I beg your pardons," finally turns violent, and in the end is destroyed.

The time for confronting the realities of black and white has come in America. It will not be pretty. More is the reason that liberals, rather than avoiding or explaining away that reality, should be the ones to work hardest at moving the nation in sane directions. Such words come easy; the effort itself will go against most of our tendencies. But we would do well to remember similar times of crisis in the past when our failure to lead gave the direction of events to others whose purpose was more to destroy than to build. If the politics of stability are to come to anything, they must be translated into programs.

In foreign affairs, surely, this involves the recognition that getting out of Vietnam is not just a matter of summoning the will but also of finding a way. It is time to acknowledge that the prestige and the credibility of the Armed Forces is involved and is entitled to consideration, as is the self-regard of the tens of thousands of American youths who perform honorably and well in those jungles because they were asked or told to do so by their government. The task of liberals is to make it politically worthwhile and possible for the administration to disengage. This requires that we continue to work within the party system and to make clear that we do in fact love peace more than we love the Vietcong. It also requires us to be unrelenting in our exposure of what the war really is doing to the Vietnamese people and of the future obligations which we incur with every day of its prolongation. In this respect, it seems to me that Senator Edward Kennedy's inquiry into civilian casualties is a model of informed and effective liberal action.

In domestic affairs, we have got to become a great deal more rigorous in the assessment not only of the reality of problems but of the nature of proposed solutions. We have to pay attention to what it is we are good at and to work from strength. In particular, we must attend to what the federal government is good at. On examination, this becomes fairly clear. The federal government is good at collecting revenues and rather bad at disbursing services. Therefore, we should use the federal fisc as an instrument for redistributing income between different levels of government, different regions, and different classes. If state and local governments are to assume effective roles as innovative and creative agents, they simply must begin to receive a share of federal revenues on a permanent, ongoing basis. Let us be frank: The original, determining opposition to this proposition in Washington has come from liberals, not conservatives, and we should be ashamed of ourselves.

At stake is not just the viability of municipal governments but also the sense of urban populations controlling their own destinies. Fifty years of social reform has pretty well destroyed the bases of working-class politics in this country. It is not at all funny to note that having broken the power of the bosses, destroyed their control over city jobs, and cleaned up the police force to boot, we find the federal government pouring millions into what Bayard Rustin has termed a "bedlam" of community-action programs to overcome the sense of powerlessness among the urban poor, while private donations are sought to enable mayors to hire proletarians who could never pass civil service examinations, and the Justice Department laments the fact that organized crime rather than the police seems to control the streets. The next irony in the history of the Negro in America will be that having acquired a majority of the votes in a number of major American cities, he will find direction of city affairs has been transferred to Washington — unless we start now to reverse that trend.

Finally, it is also reasonably clear that we must begin getting private business involved in domestic programs in a much more systematic, purposeful manner. Making money is one thing Americans are good at, and the corporation is their favorite device for doing so. What aerospace corporations have done for getting us to the moon, urban housing corporations can do for the slums. All that is necessary, one fears, is to let enough men make enough money out of doing so. It is encouraging to note how much ferment there seems to be in this direction at this time; hopefully, the liberal community will support the effort to involve private business rather than oppose it.

The politics of stability are not at first exciting. It is only when we come to see how very probably our national life is tied to them that they acquire a sudden interest.

84.

An Interview with Gunnar Myrdal

Swedish sociologist Gunnar Myrdal's pioneering study, An American Dilemma, *was published in 1942. It was highly applauded by those who read its many closely written pages, but few except the most astute realized that it would turn out to be as accurate in its predictions as it was in its analysis of the situation obtaining at the time. In fact Myrdal was right — and Donald McDonald interviewed him twenty-five years later at the Center for the Study of Democratic Institutions to find out what might be expected in the next quarter century.*

Source: *Center Magazine,* October-November 1967.

McDonald: Dr. Myrdal, twenty-five years have elapsed since the publication of your classic study of the Negro in America, *An American Dilemma.* In the intervening quarter of a century, have the developments in race relations come as a surprise to you?

Myrdal: As an economist who has often made wrong prognoses, I hope I can be excused for being happy that twenty-five years ago I made a correct one. After all, I was practically the only one working in the field who saw that change was brewing. Interracial relations had been stagnant in the United States from the 1870s onward. In some respects, as a matter of fact, the status of the Negro had deteriorated. It was a common belief that "state ways cannot change folk ways." But in 1942, I saw the

Negro at a turning point. I predicted his status would rise.

Q.: But not evenly and not on all fronts.

Myrdal: In the midst of all the current difficult problems, we should remember that there has been progress on practically all fronts during this quarter of a century. More Negroes have gotten an education. More Negroes have placed themselves in labor organizations and achieved seniority rank. More Negroes have been voting. The courts in the South have been working with less discrimination against the Negro. It could be foreseen that at a certain point, the Negroes would rise in rebellion, as they did a few years ago, partly as a result of the improvement in their status. For when Negroes became more educated, they began to ask themselves, more sharply and insistently: "Why are we being kept down?" This is an expected result from the improved situation in race relations.

Q.: In your book you said that "the Negro problem is primarily a moral issue of conflicting evaluations." You described the American dilemma as a "raging conflict between valuations preserved by Americans on the general plane" — that is, ideas of "liberty, equality, humanitarianism, and progress" — and the American outlook on the practical level. . . . I take it that you now feel that the dilemma is less intense, that there is substantially less conflict between the white American's ideals and his actual practices.

Myrdal: No, I do not. I think, though, that there has been a greater focusing on the dilemma.

When I wrote the book, most people of a leftist view (and conservatives, too) thought I was an idealist. The leftists held that the Negro problem was part of the general class struggle. It could never be resolved, they held, except by a political and economic revolution. The conservatives said the same thing, only they didn't believe in, or want, such a revolution. But both the leftists and the conservatives thought the Negro problem amounted to a simple clash of interests.

I felt, on the other hand, that ideals are meaningful when they are really held by human beings and embodied in institutions like the American Constitution. That was my approach, an approach now obvious to everybody. You saw it when Congress was confronted by a rebellion. Congress then reacted to the racial issue as a moral issue. In all the civil rights legislation, in the voting legislation, there has been a recognition that the racial crisis is basically a moral issue. Some years ago, an American Negro sociology professor who visited me in Sweden said: "I don't believe you when you say that we have the better part of the white man's heart on our side and that we can fight on with his help and on the basis of the Constitution. I don't believe that at all. White men are cynical. They serve their own interests by wanting to press us down."

I said: "My friend, Negroes are just a tenth of the population and you have very much less than a tenth of the actual power in America. If this overwhelming white majority were as cynical as you say they are, they could dump you in the ocean, send you back to Africa, or enclose you in some district in Mississippi."

He said: "No, they could not. There is the Supreme Court."

I said: "What is the Supreme Court? The white American majority can remake the whole Constitution if they want to. Don't you see that?"

It is not easy to see the importance of institutions and ideals as social facts when they are embodied in people's lives. Even the worst Southerner talks the language of the American creed.

Q.: You said in your book that the development of race prejudice is analagous to what is known as an "irreversible process" in chemistry. But you also talked about the "theory of social self-healing." According to this theory, the high ideals which people embody in their institutions — in their churches, schools, labor and professional organizations, particularly on the national level — begin to exert a liberalizing and softening effect on the prejudices. Has this theory been verified?

Myrdal: It is the trend I am now talking about. Certainly you Americans have your reactionary periods. But on the whole, American history, as I read it, is a history of moving toward an ever greater realization of the nation's ideals. If you take the long view, American history is moving in the right direction. Of course, it is a slow process; there are reverses. There are many cities where half-literate Negroes are massing, coming in from the South, and where the schools are actually deteriorating. And you have examples of white backlashes.

Periods of reaction can last several years. However, if you get out of this horrible Vietnam war, I suppose America will resume its gradual progress in race relations. To me such progress is characteristic of American history. Remember the Americans who have had immortality bestowed on them, the men acclaimed as national heroes? Almost all of them were liberals, fighting for a greater realization of American ideals.

Q.: You are optimistic.

Myrdal: I've always been optimistic about America. But if America should stop making reforms, it could get into serious difficulty. I understand that in this country you can buy guns from mail-order houses. If you were to get the Negro minority really mad, you could bring about a dissolution of American society. You simply have no choice but to keep on with the reforms.

Q.: How do you relate your cautious optimism about the abatement of race prejudice to what has been happening over the past five or six years: the Negro's frustration and resentment as expressed in the burnings in Watts and in the continuing disturbances in cities like Chicago, Atlanta, Omaha, Newark, Detroit, Syracuse, Philadelphia, St. Louis? . . .

Myrdal: When I consider the present Negro rebellions, certain facts appear important to me. First, the revolt started in the South, not in the North. I believe the prospects for racial peace are very much more favorable in the South. The Southern Negro is really getting something he did not have. The rights Congress has legislated in recent years are things Negroes in the North have had for a long time. In some localities, they have always had them. In the South, precisely because that society has been more thoroughly segregated, Negroes have preserved their own natural leaders, their funeral directors, lawyers, preachers, teachers. But in the North, the Negro leaders have often been drawn into the city political machines. They have been given petty political advantages. As a result these leaders have come to be suspected by the rest of the Negro people. So, it is natural that the Negroes in the North have been seeking more radical leaders. Because of that, the situation in the North is much more explosive.

Now, how do you deal with that situation? In America, the only way to meet it, if you do not want to have a police state, is to go on with the reforms. I think, for example, the fact that Congress has failed to enact adequate housing legislation is most unfortunate.

Q.: One of the results of the Watts disturbance is that it forced white Americans to take a close look at the kind of life the Negro is compelled to live in the urban ghettoes. . . . Do you believe, as a result of Watts, that at least some white Americans have been correcting their beliefs about what social reality actually is for the American Negro?

Myrdal: I definitely think so, but there is still a long way to go. The average, comfortable, middle-class white American has been able to keep a distance from poor people, all poor people, not just the Negro poor. And now the reality of poverty is being brought to his knowledge. But, of course, there is a twofold reaction to this new knowledge. From some Americans, particularly the uneducated whites who see themselves in competition with the Negroes for jobs, there is backlash. But for the educated white Americans, the result is all to the good.

Q.: You said in your study that it is of the "highest strategic importance to the Negro people" to get publicity because you felt that the great majority of white people would, if they really knew the condition of the Negro, give them a better deal. How well do you think the mass communication media have reported the condition of the American Negro?

Myrdal: They have been improving. The pictures in the newspapers and on television, at the time of the Birmingham outbreaks, the pictures of police dogs biting Negro kids, for example, had a tremendous effect on the average American. When he saw those pictures, the teacher, the preacher, the lawyer, the farmer, the worker, the ordinary white American said: "Wait a minute. This is not right." I am certainly not advocating more racial violence so that we can have more pictures like those. But as a social observer, I should point out that even when terrible things happen, they sometimes have good effects.

Q.: Is there time enough left to accomplish what twenty-five years ago you foresaw as taking place, namely the "scientific truth-seeking and education" which will "slowly rectify the beliefs and thereby the valuations" of white Americans concerning the Negro's condition? Do we have time enough for this "slow" rectification to take place?

Myrdal: There is always the danger that you will lag behind and then get horrible

reactions. As a social reformer, I have to say that progress will be slow, but I think people like you and me should work to utilize the time we have.

Q.: In your original study, you said that what is needed is an "educational offensive against racial intolerance" which would go deeper than "reiteration of glittering generalities in the nation's political creed." And you added that such an offensive has never been seriously attempted. Have you noted any such attempts since you wrote those words?

Myrdal: I would say that the activity of my friend Martin Luther King represents such an educational offensive. He is a great leader. Some of the speeches and statements made by President Johnson and other prominent white political leaders are part of that educational offensive. The conferences on poverty held at the universities are also a part.

Note, please, that I said the "poverty" problem, not the "Negro" problem. The Negro is very poor, relatively speaking. But the Negroes are only a tenth of the nation; they make up only a third or a fourth of the poor in America. You have a poverty problem. You have a slum problem. You have an urban problem. You can't have a rational solution of the Negro housing problem if you approach it as only a Negro problem. It's a housing problem for people. This is very important.

Martin Luther King shares that view. We discussed it when he was in Stockholm. He and I agreed that there is no chance of getting out of this situation if we don't look upon it as a much bigger problem. Of course, poor people have to stick together. The Puerto Ricans and poor whites must not look down upon the Negroes as their enemy. They have to see that they have common interests. Getting them to do so is a great educational task which is not being carried out in America.

Q.: In that connection, I might recall for

you something you wrote about a mistake made by W. E. B. DuBois, who thought that after the Civil War a natural alliance between landless Negroes and poor whites should have developed. You noted that there has not been a feeling of identification between the two races and expressed doubts about the DuBois thesis of there being a natural solidarity between poor whites and poor Negroes.

Myrdal: It's not a natural solidarity, but there should be solidarity, nonetheless. The Negro has had to struggle all through history against poor people of the white race. White people with better education and a more secure position in society have taken a more liberal line toward the Negro. Every opinion study confirms that. Here, again, you have the great educational work of men like Martin Luther King. Dr. King is trying to get the poor whites and the poor Negroes to see that they have a common interest. The solidarity is not there naturally, as Marx believed. But through a process of education it can be developed. . . .

Q.: In the light of the recent emergence of a "black power" current in the Negro civil rights movement, do you still feel Negroes must have the help of the whites, or does Stokely Carmichael have hold of a fundamental truth and strategic weapon in his "black power" rallying cry?

Myrdal: Negro nationalism is an old thing. You had the Garvey movement, the Black Muslims, and now you have this "black power" movement. It is a very natural thing. The Negro intellectual or semi-intellectual who grows up in the present radical environment finds it natural to become violently Negro-nationalistic.

The effects are not all bad. Some white people who observe it may become convinced that they must improve the racial situation so that the Negro will not become a violent separatist. But, as I said earlier, the fundamental fact is that the power in this country is on the side of the whites. The Negro must not forget that.

Martin Luther King knows that white liberals are very often pussyfooting, retreating; but he has never forgotten that he must have the white liberal behind him. You can criticize the white liberal. In the end, however, the Negro has to rely upon the whites in order to change society. I think a great many of the Negro people understand this very well, even though you do not always hear from them. They may be silent, but they understand such matters perfectly. There is a fund of common sense in the Negro population.

I might add here that of all the various groups in America, no group on the whole has had more devoted and morally solid leaders than has the Negro. A boxer like Joe Louis, a singer like Marian Anderson, a ball player like Jackie Robinson, a trade unionist like A. Philip Randolph, a statesman like Ralph Bunche — all of them, as they were rising, have felt a great responsibility toward their own race. They have felt that they should conduct themselves in such a manner as to reflect honor on their people. Of course, you have had your Negro crooks and Negro gangsters; every race has its share of those. But fundamentally the Negro leadership is probably the soundest leadership you can find in American history.

Q.: I suppose that to the extent that "black power," whether as a slogan or a reality, makes the American Negro feel proud, instead of resentful, of his blackness, his negritude, that is all to the good.

Myrdal: Well, a Swedish-American might have lingering kind feelings of the "Old Country" or an Italian-American for his country. That gives a flavor to his self-respect. But people should not have too much pride in their origin. That is really illiberal, particularly if it reaches the level where it is actually a threat to the cohesion in the country. Some people are haughty because their ancestors came over on the *Mayflower.* If I were an American, I would say to them: "To hell with you. I'm just as good as you are." That is the ideal, isn't it?

Q.: Perhaps in order for the Negro to reach that ideal, it may be necessary for him to move toward a feeling of special pride in his race before he can overcome, or eliminate, the white-induced feeling of self-resentment because he is a Negro.

Myrdal: I agree completely.

Q.: What is your evaluation of non-violence as developed by Martin Luther King? The young militants among the Negroes are saying that they can no longer follow Dr. King, and that they refuse to get their heads battered in.

Myrdal: Dr. King's philosophy is not new, of course. The trade unions used it when they were very weak. And Gandhi was not the first to use it. I think Dr. King is right. The Negro has very little chance resorting to violence. The whole police power is against him. But when he comes with nonviolence he appeals to your conscience.

This was always discussed among American Negroes. Twenty-five years ago many of the so-called radical Negroes were very critical of the National Association for the Advancement of Colored People, not to speak of the Urban League. They thought the legal battles waged by the NAACP were too tedious, yielded too little in results, etc. My conclusion then, as it is today, was that the Negro needs all sorts of organizations. He needs organizations to fight civil rights battles all the way to the United States Supreme Court. He needs the Urban League, which is a social welfare organization. I remember an old Mississippi Negro preacher telling me on one occasion that he was chairman of something called the Citizens Cooperation Society. He was also a member of the NAACP. I asked him about the difference between the two. "Well," he said, "we're NAACP when we're fighting, and we're Citizens Cooperation Society when we're pussyfooting. We've got to use both feet."

Q.: You stated in 1942 that you had discerned that progress in the Negro's conditions had been related to white men's wars. As you know, many of the Negro leaders today, not only militants like Stokely Carmichael but also Dr. King, are pointing to what they see as a connection between the impoverished and discriminated-against condition of the American Negro, on the one hand, and the resources that are being diverted by the American government to wage war against men of another race in Vietnam.

Myrdal: Yes, but remember there is this difference: in the First World War and in the Second World War, the American people were almost unanimous in their support of the government's policies. Today, in the case of the war in Vietnam, not only many Negroes but also a large portion of American whites, and not least of all the intellectuals, are outraged by the government's actions. Against this background, Martin Luther King, seeing that the things the poor need are voted down by a Congress which is more interested in the Vietnam war, is concerned. It is natural for Dr. King to point out the connection between what is being done in Vietnam and what is not being done for the poor at home.

Q.: And one cannot, I believe, overlook the fact that white men are killing yellow men in Vietnam. The racial thing is not entirely absent. I sometimes wonder whether we would be so careless about our "accidental" killings of the Vietnamese peasants if they were of our own race.

Myrdal: All Asia, and not just Japan, is asking itself whether the Americans would have used the atomic bomb in Europe during the Second World War. Of course, the most horrible thing that could happen would be for conflicts in the world to become loaded by the racial issue. If that should happen I would say we would really be lost. All of us are playing down this racial element, including the leaders in poor countries. But it is smouldering under the surface.

Q.: I remember your commenting in your book that in general the poor are not radical, not even liberal. I believe you said that before people can become liberals, politically, they have to achieve some measure of security and education. Would you say that in some respects the experience of the government's current "war on poverty" which sought, apparently unsuccessfully, to engage the poor in active, participational, policy-making in the development of their own antipoverty programs bears out your contention? In asking this, I realize that many big-city political party bosses were not at all interested in getting the poor to play a policy-making role in antipoverty programming. But where there was such an effort made sincerely, it does not seem that the poor responded, at least not the way it was thought they would respond.

Myrdal: Every opinion study shows that the more educated people are, the more liberal their opinions will be. The American poor have been the least revolutionary proletariat in the world. They have not been educated to be anything else.

There are many other reasons. In the old days, the more aggressive of the poor could always go West, to the frontier and rise. And when you had the early open American society, a man could rise upwards, even if he was relatively uneducated, and go quite high before his progress was stopped by lack of education. And, of course, the trade unions in this country have not organized more than a quarter of the workers. Even that percentage is shrinking. The unions are generally not interested in the poor. Then, the political parties long ago realized that they didn't have to deliver on their campaign promises to the poor. For one thing, when they are not herded by the party machines, the poor are nonvoters. The politicians had nothing to fear from *them.* This explains why social legislation, farm legislation, and housing legislation has not taken care of those who are poorest in this country.

Q.: You declared twenty-five years ago that a "rational policy [on race] will never work by changing only one factor, least of all if attempted suddenly and with great force. . . . Do you think that in the intervening years there have been mistaken efforts of this kind? The Negroes are suspicious of the counsel of moderation today. They have been frustrated for so long and have been told for so many years to be patient, that perhaps now they are pressing on one or another front, say, against *de facto* segregation of schools in Northern cities, believing that if they could break *that* down, that would be the solution to many things. And, of course, they meet tremendous resistance from the white community when they try to mount a massive attack on any one of these fronts.

Myrdal: Of course, in the social process the fight must go on on all fronts simultaneously. On the whole, this is what has been happening. The Negro's status has been rising slowly all over the place. At one time, the push may be on the legislative side, but as soon as that happens, people begin to understand that that is not enough, they discover that the Negro has been suffering from a legacy of poverty for generations. I think there is widespread recognition in America among enlightened whites and Negroes that we have to move on the whole broad front if substantial progress is to be made.

Q.: You have not, then, seen an excessive effort made on one front?

Myrdal: No. And another thing that should be noted is that you cannot have a carefully planned social process in something like this.

Q.: Are you basically optimistic about the future of America and its ability to resolve its racial problems?

Myrdal: I've always been an optimist where America is concerned. I've never been among those who said "it can happen here." Despite many mistakes and many reactionary periods, America is going forward.

85.

J. ANTHONY LUKAS: The Case of a Runaway Flower Girl

On October 8, 1967, Linda Fitzpatrick, an eighteen-year-old girl from Greenwich,
Connecticut, was found beaten to death on the floor of a boiler room in the East Village
area of New York City. Dead beside her was James L. (Groovy) Hutchinson, her
twenty-one-year-old "hippie" friend. According to newspaper reports, Miss Fitzpatrick
had recently been taking methedrine, or "speed," a psychedelic drug allied to, but more
potent than, LSD. The murder created a furor among the general public and hippies
alike, and both the East Village and the Haight-Ashbury district of San Francisco, the
two capitals of hippieland, became objects of intense interest to the news media and
also to great numbers of parents whose children had run away from home during the
previous summer. The story of one of these, Pamela Rae Koeppel, was told by a
New York Times reporter on October 19. She was found unharmed after four days,
but at year's end several hundred thousand runaways were still eluding pursuit, a
fact, with all of its implications, that was causing growing concern in the country.

Source: *New York Times,* October 19, 1967.

LAST FRIDAY Pamela Rae Koeppel painted a blue flower on her right cheek. The following day the 14-year-old schoolgirl left home. Last night she was found in a 14th Street hotel. After two policemen had staked out her room there, Pamela called her parents and said, "You found my hideout. You'll get my friend in trouble. I'm coming right home."

Pamela's four-day sojourn in and around Greenwich Village illustrates the growing problem created by thousands of young runaways, particularly girls, who are flooding the Village area to live as hippies.

Yesterday, several hours before she was found, Pamela's father, Adolph, a lawyer, called the *New York Times* in hopes that publicity would not only help find her but also warn other parents of the difficulties in finding runaway girls. Interviewed as he paced the white marble corridors of Federal Court in Brooklyn, where he had just fin-

ished summing up in a complicated condemnation case, he said: "I've got a twitch in my eye, a belt in my stomach, a jury out with my case, and a daughter somewhere over there in that jungle."

Mr. Koeppel and his wife, Rhoda, who live in a $60,000 ranch house in the Long Island suburban community, Lake Success, had reason to believe that Pamela was in Greenwich Village living as a "flower child."

"I asked her about that flower on her cheek when she got into the car for me to drive her to school Friday," said Mr. Koeppel, who practices law in Mineola. "She said, 'Oh, daddy, I'm a flower child.' Where else do these flower children go around here but Greenwich Village?"

Mr. Koeppel also had discovered that his daughter was secretly seeing a youth known as "Chichi," who lived on West 14th Street, and frequented the Village. "I thought she might be with him," he said yesterday.

Four days after Pamela left home, the combined efforts of Mr. Koeppel, his family and friends, the Nassau County Juvenile Aid Bureau, and the New York Police Department had failed to trace her. "We heard from Pamela twice by telephone on Sunday, but nothing after that," Mr. Koeppel said between nervous puffs on his fourth cigarette since lunch. "I had visions of her lying dead somewhere like that Linda what's-her-name."

Linda Fitzpatrick, an 18-year-old girl from Greenwich, Conn., was found murdered on a boiler-room floor in the East Village on October 8. Dead beside her was her 21-year-old hippie friend James L. (Groovy) Hutchinson.

Since Linda's death, the Police Department's Missing Persons Bureau and police stations in Greenwich Village have been deluged with calls from worried parents trying to trace their children. The police said yesterday that for the first time in the city's history runaway girls were outnumbering runaway boys, and officials say this trend is apparently accelerating.

Pamela Koeppel's case may be representative from another point of view. Her parents say she was a "disturbed child" who had been seeing a psychiatrist once a week for almost a year. Some social workers and psychologists who have studied the hippie movement believe that many hippies have emotional or psychological problems and use the hippie scene as camouflage.

Until a few months ago Mr. and Mrs. Koeppel thought they had Pamela's problems well under control. Her psychiatrist apparently thought so, too — she let Pamela take the summer off from her therapy sessions. "As far as we could tell she went through the summer very well," Mr. Koeppel said. "She found some new girl friends — I guess there must have been seven or eight in and out of the house during the summer on Long Island — swimming, drive-in movies, dates at the malt shop."

But Mr. Koeppel said the family, which includes a "very happy and normal" 18-year-old daughter who is a college freshman in New York, began to notice a return of Pamela's troubles as school approached this fall. "There were too many highs, too many lows, and at times she was getting to be really low," he recalls. In mid-September she started seeing the psychiatrist again, and after a couple of visits, the psychiatrist recommended that she see Pamela twice a week instead of once.

"Naturally we were deeply concerned," said Mrs. Koeppel, who was interviewed later. "We asked the psychiatrist whether there was any identifiable illness. She said no, but that Pamela was disturbed and needed increased attention. At one point the psychiatrist even suggested a brief hospitalization for a series of tests."

Meanwhile Pamela was becoming more argumentative at home. "She began telling us that we were watching her too closely, that we weren't giving her enough freedom." At the same time Pamela began showing interest in the hippies, the flower children. She started wearing what her father calls "hippie beads," and she occasionally expressed admiration for the "new scene."

Only after her flight from home did the family discover just how deep that admiration was. This week they picked up a pile of her compositions for an English class at Great Neck South Junior High School. One of them read in part:

> What is a flower child? A flower child is a young person belonging to a new generation which is very idealistic and thoughtful. They believe in love, beauty, peace, understanding, freedom, sharing and helping each other. Flower children are trying to change the world with these ideas.
> They love to express themselves by wearing rings, beads, and flowers. Flow-

ers are beautiful because they are part of nature. Flowers are lovely, beautiful, peaceful, and don't do anybody any harm but be beautiful. The flower child is the same way.

She got a C-plus on the composition, with no comment from the teacher.

The family had several long discussions with Pamela about her attitude. "We tried to point out to her that the flower children and the hippies are not creative persons, not really doing anything useful," Mrs. Koeppel said. "We told her that you didn't do these things by talking, that if she really wanted to do creative, artistic things, we would support her fully when she was through school and prepared. Sometimes I felt we were getting through to her," the mother said, "but I guess we never really did. As hard as we tried, I guess we never really knew Pamela."

Several times in the last few weeks Pamela told her father she was going to run away from home. "What would you do?" she would ask. He replied. "I'd send the police after you."

"Think they could find me?" she would say.

"Certainly," he answered.

"Want to bet?" she would say with a little smile.

On Thursday night father and daughter held the last of their discussions. "It ended," Mr. Koeppel recalled today, "with Pamela marching up to her room saying, 'You just don't understand me.'" The following morning Pamela painted the flower on her cheek and went to school. On Sat-

urday morning, Mr. Koeppel wanted her to go shopping with her mother, but the girl said she planned to meet some friends in Great Neck.

"It was the same old doubletalk she'd been giving us when she went to meet Chichi," he said. "I don't know why we fell for it. We probably should have put her under lock and key."

Instead, he drove her into town in the family Cadillac (they also own a Rambler). At 11 A.M., Pamela got out of the car. She was wearing a white parka, an orange-and-blue striped dress, green suede boots, a string of the long hippie beads, and a small bag over her shoulder. Her long, lustrous, brown hair rose a little in the breeze as she said good-by to her father and promised to call him at about 7 P.M., so he could pick her up for dinner.

From then on her movements were unclear. The father later learned that she called a friend on the South Shore that night and asked whether she could stay at his place overnight. He was not enthusiastic, but about 2 A.M. she apparently arrived by train at the South Shore town, got somebody to drive her to the friend's house, and demanded a bed. She got one.

At precisely the same time — with her phone call now seven hours overdue — her father called the Great Neck police and formally reported her missing.

The Juvenile Aid Bureau of the Nassau County police said yesterday it got the notification four hours later, at 6 A.M., but apparently the full search did not begin until the following day.

———◆———

Flower Power.
Ironic (?) slogan of hippies, late 1960s

86.

DAVID SANFORD: The Seedier Media

A striking phenomenon of the 1960s was the emergence of the so-called underground press in the larger cities of the country (mainly Los Angeles and New York). Edited and largely written by the young, the underground magazines and other periodicals expressed the rebellion of a generation that had created the beat and hippie cultures, and that had not said its last word when, at the end of 1967, hippiedom seemed to have ceased to be a force in the life of American youth. The following review of the style and content of the underground press appeared in December 1967.

Source: *New Republic*, December 2, 1967.

THERE IS NOTHING very underground about the underground press. The newspapers are hawked on street corners, sent to subscribers without incident through the U.S. mails, carefully culled and adored by the mass media. About three dozen of them belong to the Underground Press Syndicate, which is something like the AP on a small scale; through this network they spread the word about what is new in disruptive protest, drugs, sex. Their obsessive interest in things that the "straights" are embarrassed or offended by is perhaps what makes them underground. They are a place to find what is unfit to print in the *New York Times.*

The *Berkeley Barb*, the *East Village Other*, the *Fifth Estate*, the *LA Free Press* are among the more familiar and successful of the papers. They make the aging *Village Voice* — of which they are all derivative — seem very Establishment indeed. The hippie thing brought them to flower; but the death of hippie (the funeral was in early fall and the obit was in *Newsweek*) has apparently not diminished them. They are all the things their admirers think they are — exciting, informative, In, irreverent, refreshing,

audacious, lively; they haven't sold out like everybody else. But they are also recklessly undisciplined, often badly written, yellow, and, taken in large doses, very, very boring.

Nevertheless these papers have been said to provide the most exciting reading in America. At least they try — by saying what can't be said or isn't being said by the staid daily press, by staying on the cutting edge of "In" for an audience with the shortest of attention spans. There is nothing worse for an underground paper or its readers than to be the last to know. It took months for the revelations about the psychedelic pleasures of smoking banana peels, for instance, to travel to the daily papers and news magazines. And by the time, a few weeks ago, that the daily press reported that scientists had concluded it was all a hoax on the hippies, nobody who reads the *East Village Other* particularly cared. They had gone on to other things. They could sneer and remember they had been at the source, at the beginning of that long trip through the media to obsolescence.

The underground press is a photographic negative of the bourgeois newspapers and magazines; it registers many of the same images but all the colors are reversed. Anyone who sat down a few years ago and asked himself what isn't being reported, what causes are without champions, what words can't be printed, then decided to put out a newspaper that did everything differently, would have invented the underground. What the *LA Times* is for, the *LA Free Press* is likely to be against. Daily papers report arrests, for example, but from the standpoint of the police. That is their mental set; they are in the law-and-order bag. The underground papers are prone to see arrested persons as *victims* of the cops: "On Friday between 8 A.M. and 8:30 A.M. Judy (an antiwar protester) was arrested at the intersection of 13th and Broadway. She was standing with a group of people in the intersection. A cop knocked her down and grabbed her. A group of protesters circled the cop and began arguing that she hadn't done anything. More cops arrived. The cop who had knocked Judy down then let go of her. She began to move down Broadway and was chased by the cop who knocked her down again and dragged her to a patrol car. She was charged with assault on an officer." Here the *Berkeley Barb* in simple, letter-to-a-friend didactic style leaves no doubt about its position on the police. Cops attack innocent girls and charge *them* with assault. No phony balanced coverage. No on-the-one-hand-on-the-other-hand TV documentary stuff. Judy is *Barb's* friend. The negative is black and white — a corrective to all the news about unruly demonstrators and police officers trying to maintain order. Police brutality has become a shibboleth for the underground papers, serviceable and pat. The treatment people get at the hands of police is "rough," "completely unnecessary," "totally unprovoked." "Cops are dumber and less imaginative than we usually suppose."

Since alienation is their thing it is understandable that underground papers sometimes seem to reject bourgeois journalistic values of accuracy and balance. The recent Pentagon demonstration as reported by the *Washington Free Press,* for example, included bayonetings, demonstrators who were knocked unconscious, the Pentagon as an "isolated house of death," rather like a gas oven in Nazi Germany. Such flights into fancy are characteristic of this spontaneous freak-out journalism, the purest lode of which is to be found in the *Oracles,* colorful Los Angeles and San Francisco publications, which are all mind excursion.

The underground press often reads like some kind of Harvard *Lampoon* parody of the tabloid press complete with news stories, editorials, reviews, classified ads, and advice columns. But instead of Heloise there is Hip-pocrates (Dr. Eugene Schoenfeld) — the motorcycling, demonstrating MD, whose syndicated advice appears in several UPS papers. Sometimes he is really helpful since he answers questions you wouldn't dare ask the family doctor. Sample question: "I've never had any sexual experience but my friends tell me it's groovy. . . . Please give me some advice on how to have intercourse." Answer: "My favorite occupational therapist thinks your friends are right. I suggest you read. . . ." In the same column that that dialogue appeared, Dr. Schoenfeld passed along tips on how to remove pubic hair, where to go for help if you suspect you're queer and don't like what you suspect, and a helpful anecdote on autoerotism: "There is a story about a little boy who was found masturbating and told that he would go blind unless he stopped. 'Well,' he pleaded, 'can I do it until I need eyeglasses?' " In another column Hip-pocrates was asked "Is there anything specially abnormal with having one breast slightly larger than the other? I find it inhibiting at times, though my lover says he doesn't even notice it. Is there any way to balance the situation?" Answer:

"Breasts are rarely exactly alike in size and shape. Your lover probably enjoys the variation; perhaps he even has a favorite."

The underground press is predictable. Some papers are more political, others more psychedelic, others more aberrant, but for the most part they care about Dow, drugs, the draft, abortion, cops, rock, flicks, and sex, perhaps not in that order. They are as current as this week's pot bust and draft-card burning. They oppose the war and their most interesting features are their want ads, especially if you are a sadist looking for a masochist.

87.

The View from Iron Mountain

A strange and disturbing book appeared during the summer of 1967. Entitled Report from Iron Mountain on the Possibility and Desirability of Peace, *it purported to be an account of some top secret discussions by a group of high-powered intellectuals recruited by the U.S. government to assess the feasibility of peace. According to the book, the group decided after many meetings that peace in the full sense of the word, and not just the temporary absence of war, was not only nearly impossible but also to all intents and purposes undesirable. The report was edited by "Leonard C. Lewin," but no one seemed to know who he was, and there was a rumor that it had actually been written by a leading economist and diplomat, whose real name was extremely well known. Whatever its authorship, the book posed important questions that would indeed have to be answered in entirely new ways if peace was ever to become a reality instead of a dream.*

Source: *Report from Iron Mountain,* with introductory material by Leonard C. Lewin, New York, 1967, pp. 4, 7-10, 17-47.

LETTER OF TRANSMITTAL

. . . Because of the unusual circumstances surrounding the establishment of this Group, and in view of the nature of its findings, we do not recommend that this Report be released for publication. It is our affirmative judgment that such action would not be in the public interest. The uncertain advantages of public discussion of our conclusions and recommendations are, in our opinion, greatly outweighed by the clear and predictable danger of a crisis in public confidence which untimely publication of this Report might be expected to provoke. The likelihood that a lay reader, unexposed to the exigencies of higher political or military responsibility, will misconstrue the purpose of this project, and the intent of its participants, seems obvious. We urge that circulation of this Report be closely restricted to those whose responsibilities require that they be apprised of its contents. . . .

INTRODUCTION

THE REPORT WHICH FOLLOWS summarizes the results of a two-and-a-half-year study of the broad problems to be anticipated in the event of a general transformation of American society to a condition lacking its most critical current characteristics: its capability and readiness to make war when doing so is judged necessary or desirable by its political leadership.

Our work has been predicated on the belief that some kind of general peace may soon be negotiable. The *de facto* admission of Communist China into the United Nations now appears to be only a few years away at most. It has become increasingly manifest that conflicts of American national interest with those of China and the Soviet Union are susceptible of political solution, despite the superficial contraindications of the current Vietnam war, of the threats of an attack on China, and of the necessarily hostile tenor of day-to-day foreign policy statements. It is also obvious that differences involving other nations can be readily resolved by the three great powers whenever they arrive at a stable peace among themselves. It is not necessary, for the purposes of our study, to assume that a general détente of this sort *will* come about — and we make no such argument — but only that it *may*.

It is surely no exaggeration to say that a condition of general world peace would lead to changes in the social structures of the nations of the world of unparalleled and revolutionary magnitude. The economic impact of general disarmament, to name only the most obvious consequence of peace, would revise the production and distribution patterns of the globe to a degree that would make the changes of the past fifty years seem insignificant. Political, sociological, cultural, and ecological changes would be equally far-reaching. What has motivated our study of these contingencies has been the growing sense of thoughtful men in and out of government that the world is totally unprepared to meet the demands of such a situation.

We had originally planned, when our study was initiated, to address ourselves to these two broad questions and their components: *What can be expected if peace comes? What should we be prepared to do about it?* But as our investigation proceeded it became apparent that certain other questions had to be faced. What, for instance, are the real functions of war in modern societies, beyond the ostensible ones of defending and advancing the "national interests" of nations? In the absence of war, what other institutions exist or might be devised to fulfill these functions? Granting that a "peaceful" settlement of disputes is within the range of current international relationships, is the abolition of war, in the broad sense, really possible? If so, is it necessarily desirable, in terms of social stability? If not, what can be done to improve the operation of our social system in respect to its war-readiness?

The word *peace*, as we have used it in the following pages, describes a permanent, or quasi-permanent, condition entirely free from the national exercise, or contemplation, of any form of the organized social violence, or threat of violence, generally known as war. It implies total and general disarmament. It is not used to describe the more familiar condition of "cold war," "armed peace," or other mere respite, long or short, from armed conflict. Nor is it used simply as a synonym for the political settlement of international differences. The magnitude of modern means of mass destruction and the speed of modern communications require the unqualified working definition given above; only a generation ago such an absolute description would have seemed utopian rather than pragmatic. Today, any modification of this definition would render it almost worthless for our purpose. By the same standard, we have used the word *war* to apply interchangeably to conventional ("hot") war, to the general condition of war preparation or war readiness, and to the general "war system." The sense intended is made clear in context. . . .

DISARMAMENT AND
THE ECONOMY

. . . General agreement prevails in respect
to the more important economic problems
that general disarmament would raise. . . .

The first factor is that of size. The
"world war industry," as one writer has
aptly called it, accounts for approximately a
tenth of the output of the world's total
economy. Although this figure is subject to
fluctuation, the causes of which are themselves subject to regional variation, it tends
to hold fairly steady. The United States, as
the world's richest nation, not only accounts
for the largest single share of this expense,
currently upward of $60 billion a year, but
also ". . . has devoted a higher *proportion*
[emphasis added] of its gross national product to its military establishment than any
other major free world nation. This was
true even before our increased expenditures
in Southeast Asia." Plans for economic conversion that minimize the economic magnitude of the problem do so only by rational-
izing, however persuasively, the maintenance of a substantial residual military budget under some euphemized classification.

Conversion of military expenditures to
other purposes entails a number of difficulties. The most serious stems from the degree of rigid specialization that characterizes
modern war production, best exemplified in
nuclear and missile technology. This constituted no fundamental problem after World
War II, nor did the question of free-market
consumer demand for "conventional" items
of consumption — those goods and services
consumers had already been conditioned to
require. Today's situation is qualitatively
different in both respects.

This inflexibility is geographical and occupational, as well as industrial, a fact
which has led most analysts of the economic impact of disarmament to focus their attention on phased plans for the relocation
of war industry personnel and capital instal-

lations as much as on proposals for developing new patterns of consumption. One serious flaw common to such plans is the kind
called in the natural sciences the "macro-
scopic error." An implicit presumption is
made that a total national plan for conversion differs from a community program to
cope with the shutting down of a "defense
facility" only in degree. We find no reason
to believe that this is the case, nor that a
general enlargement of such local programs,
however well thought out in terms of housing, occupational retraining, and the like,
can be applied on a national scale. A national economy can absorb almost any
number of subsidiary reorganizations within
its total limits, providing there is no basic
change in its own structure. General disarmament, which would require such basic
changes, lends itself to no valid smaller-scale
analogy. . . .

In general, discussions of the problems of
conversion have been characterized by an
unwillingness to recognize its special quality. . . .

One school of economists has it that
these patterns will develop on their own. It
envisages the equivalent of the arms budget
being returned, under careful control, to the
consumer, in the form of tax cuts. Another,
recognizing the undeniable need for increased "consumption" in what is generally
considered the public sector of the economy, stresses vastly increased government
spending in such areas of national concern
as health, education, mass transportation,
low-cost housing, water supply, control of
the physical environment, and, stated generally, "poverty."

The mechanisms proposed for controlling
the transition to an arms-free economy are
also traditional — changes in both sides of
the federal budget, manipulation of interest
rates, etc. We acknowledge the undeniable
value of fiscal tools in a normal cyclical
economy, where they provide leverage to
accelerate or brake an existing trend. Their

more committed proponents, however, tend to lose sight of the fact that there is a limit to the power of these devices to influence fundamental economic forces. They can provide new incentives in the economy, but they cannot in themselves transform the production of a billion dollars' worth of missiles a year to the equivalent in food, clothing, prefabricated houses, or television sets. At bottom, they reflect the economy; they do not motivate it.

More sophisticated, and less sanguine, analysts contemplate the diversion of the arms budget to a nonmilitary system equally remote from the market economy. What the "pyramid-builders" frequently suggest is the expansion of space-research programs to the dollar level of current armaments expenditures. . . .

Without singling out any one of the several major studies of the expected impact of disarmament on the economy for special criticism, we can summarize our objections to them in general terms as follows:

1. No proposed program for economic conversion to disarmament sufficiently takes into account the unique magnitude of the required adjustments it would entail.

2. Proposals to transform arms production into a beneficent scheme of public works are more the products of wishful thinking than of realistic understanding of the limits of our existing economic system.

3. Fiscal and monetary measures are inadequate as controls for the process of transition to an arms-free economy.

4. Insufficient attention has been paid to the political acceptability of the objectives of the proposed conversion models, as well as of the political means to be employed in effectuating a transition.

5. No serious consideration has been given, in any proposed conversion plan, to the fundamental nonmilitary function of war and armaments in modern society, nor has any explicit attempt been made to devise a viable substitute for it. . . .

DISARMAMENT SCENARIOS

. . . The economic implications assigned by their authors to various disarmament scenarios diverge widely. The more conservative models . . . emphasize economic as well as military prudence in postulating elaborate fail-safe disarmament agencies, which themselves require expenditures substantially substituting for those of the displaced war industries. Such programs stress the advantages of the smaller economic adjustment entailed. Others emphasize, on the contrary, the magnitude (and the opposite advantages) of the savings to be achieved from disarmament. One widely read analysis estimates the annual cost of the inspection function of general disarmament throughout the world as only between two and three percent of current military expenditures. Both types of plan tend to deal with the anticipated problem of economic reinvestment only in the aggregate. We have seen no proposed disarmament sequence that correlates the phasing out of specific kinds of military spending with specific new forms of substitute spending. . . .

WAR AND PEACE
AS SOCIAL SYSTEMS

WE HAVE DEALT only sketchily with proposed disarmament scenarios and economic analyses, but the reason for our seemingly casual dismissal of so much serious and sophisticated work lies in no disrespect for its competence. It is rather a question of relevance. To put it plainly, all these programs, however detailed and well developed, are abstractions. The most carefully reasoned disarmament sequence inevitably reads more like the rules of a game or a classroom exercise in logic than like a prognosis of real events in the real world. This is as true of today's complex proposals as it was of the Abbé de St. Pierre's "Plan for Perpetual Peace in Europe" 250 years ago.

Some essential element has clearly been lacking in all these schemes. One of our first tasks was to try to bring this missing quality into definable focus, and we believe we have succeeded in doing so. We find that at the heart of every peace study we have examined — from the modest technological proposal (e.g., to convert a poison gas plant to the production of "socially useful" equivalents) to the most elaborate scenario for universal peace in our time — lies one common fundamental misconception. It is the source of the miasma of unreality surrounding such plans. *It is the incorrect assumption that war, as an institution, is subordinate to the social systems it is believed to serve.*

This misconception, although profound and far-reaching, is entirely comprehensible. Few social clichés are so unquestioningly accepted as the notion that war is an extension of diplomacy (or of politics, or of the pursuit of economic objectives). If this were true, it would be wholly appropriate for economists and political theorists to look on the problems of transition to peace as essentially mechanical or procedural — as indeed they do, treating them as logistic corollaries of the settlement of national conflicts of interest. If this were true, there would be no real substance to the difficulties of transition. For it is evident that even in today's world there exists no conceivable conflict of interest, real or imaginary, between nations or between social forces within nations, that cannot be resolved without recourse to war — *if* such resolution were assigned a priority of social value. And if this were true, the economic analyses and disarmament proposals we have referred to, plausible and well conceived as they may be, would not inspire, as they do, an inescapable sense of indirection.

The point is that the cliché is not true, and the problems of transition are indeed substantive rather than merely procedural. Although war is "used" as an instrument of national and social policy, the fact that a society is organized for any degree of readiness for war supersedes its political and economic structure. War itself is the basic social system, within which other secondary modes of social organization conflict or conspire. It is the system which has governed most human societies of record, as it is today.

Once this is correctly understood, the true magnitude of the problems entailed in a transition to peace — itself a social system, but without precedent except in a few simple preindustrial societies — becomes apparent. At the same time, some of the puzzling superficial contradictions of modern societies can then be readily rationalized. The "unnecessary" size and power of the world war industry; the preeminence of the military establishment in every society, whether open or concealed; the exemption of military or paramilitary institutions from the accepted social and legal standards of behavior required elsewhere in the society; the successful operation of the armed forces and the armaments producers entirely outside the framework of each nation's economic ground rules: these and other ambiguities closely associated with the relationship of war to society are easily clarified, once the priority of war-making potential as the principal structuring force in society is accepted. Economic systems, political philosophies, and corpora jures serve and extend the war system, not vice versa.

It must be emphasized that the precedence of a society's war-making potential over its other characteristics is not the result of the "threat" presumed to exist at any one time from other societies. This is the reverse of the basic situation; "threats" against the "national interest" are usually created or accelerated to meet the changing needs of the war system. Only in comparatively recent times has it been considered politically expedient to euphemize war budgets as "defense" requirements. The necessity for governments to distinguish between "aggression" (bad) and "defense" (good) has been a by-product of rising literacy and rapid communication. The distinction is tactical only, a concession to the growing inadequacy of ancient war-organizing political rationales.

Wars are not "caused" by international conflicts of interest. Proper logical sequence would make it more often accurate to say that war-making societies require — and thus bring about — such conflicts. The capacity of a nation to make war expresses the greatest social power it can exercise; war-making, active or contemplated, is a matter of life and death on the greatest scale subject to social control. It should therefore hardly be surprising that the military institutions in each society claim its highest priorities.

We find further that most of the confusion surrounding the myth that war-making is a tool of state policy stems from a general misapprehension of the functions of war. In general, these are conceived as: to defend a nation from military attack by another, or to deter such an attack; to defend or advance a "national interest" — economic, political, ideological; to maintain or increase a nation's military power for its own sake. These are the visible, or ostensible, functions of war. If there were no others, the importance of the war establishment in each society might in fact decline to the subordinate level it is believed to occupy. And the elimination of war would indeed be the procedural matter that the disarmament scenarios suggest.

But there are other, broader, more profoundly felt functions of war in modern societies. It is these invisible, or implied, functions that maintain war-readiness as the dominant force in our societies. And it is the unwillingness or inability of the writers of disarmament scenarios and reconversion plans to take them into account that has so reduced the usefulness of their work, and that has made it seem unrelated to the world we know.

THE FUNCTIONS OF WAR

As we have indicated, the preeminence of the concept of war as the principal organizing force in most societies has been insufficiently appreciated. This is also true of its extensive effects throughout the many nonmilitary activities of society. These effects are less apparent in complex industrial societies like our own than in primitive cultures, the activities of which can be more easily and fully comprehended. . . .

The nonmilitary functions of the war system are more basic. They exist not merely to justify themselves but to serve broader social purposes. If and when war is eliminated, the military functions it has served will end with it. But its nonmilitary functions will not. It is essential, therefore, that we understand their significance before we can reasonably expect to evaluate whatever institutions may be proposed to replace them.

Economic

The production of weapons of mass destruction has always been associated with economic "waste." The term is pejorative, since it implies a failure of function. But no human activity can properly be considered wasteful if it achieves its contextual objective. The phrase "wasteful but necessary," applied not only to war expenditures but to most of the "unproductive" commercial activities of our society, is a contradiction in terms. ". . . The attacks that have since the time of Samuel's criticism of King Saul been leveled against military expenditures as waste may well have concealed or misunderstood the point that some kinds of waste may have a larger social utility."

In the case of military "waste," there is indeed a larger social utility. It derives from the fact that the "wastefulness" of war production is exercised entirely outside the framework of the economy of supply and demand. As such, it provides the only critically large segment of the total economy that is subject to complete and arbitrary central control. If modern industrial societies can be defined as those which have developed the capacity to produce more than is required for their economic survival (regardless of the equities of distribution of goods within them), military spending can be said to furnish the only balance wheel with sufficient inertia to stabilize the advance of their economies. The fact that war is "wasteful" is what enables it to serve this function. And the faster the economy advances, the heavier this balance wheel must be. . . .

It should also be noted that war production has a dependably stimulating effect outside itself. Far from constituting a "wasteful" drain on the economy, war spending, considered pragmatically, has been a consistently positive factor in the rise of gross national product and of individual productivity. A former Secretary of the Army has carefully phrased it for public consumption thus: "If there is, as I suspect there is, a direct relation between the stimulus of large defense spending and a substantially increased rate of growth of gross national product, it quite simply follows that defense spending *per se* might be countenanced *on economic grounds alone* [emphasis added] as a stimulator of the national metabolism." Actually, the fundamental nonmilitary utility of war in the economy is far more widely acknowledged than the scarcity of such affirmations as that quoted above would suggest.

But *negatively* phrased public recognitions of the importance of war to the general economy abound. The most familiar example is the effect of "peace threats" on the stock market, e.g., "Wall Street was shaken yesterday by news of an apparent peace feeler from North Vietnam, but swiftly recovered its composure after about an hour of sometimes indiscriminate selling." Savings banks solicit deposits with similar cautionary slogans, e.g., "If peace breaks out, will you be ready for it?" A more subtle

case in point was the recent refusal of the Department of Defense to permit the West German government to substitute nonmilitary goods for unwanted armaments in its purchase commitments from the United States; the decisive consideration was that the German purchases should not affect the general (nonmilitary) economy. . . .

Although we do not imply that a substitute for war in the economy cannot be devised, no combination of techniques for controlling employment, production, and consumption has yet been tested that can remotely compare to it in effectiveness. It is, and has been, the essential economic stabilizer of modern societies.

Political

The political functions of war have been up to now even more critical to social stability. It is not surprising, nevertheless, that discussions of economic conversion for peace tend to fall silent on the matter of political implementation, and that disarmament scenarios, often sophisticated in their weighing of international political factors, tend to disregard the political functions of the war system within individual societies.

These functions are essentially organizational. First of all, the existence of a society as a political "nation" requires as part of its definition an attitude of relationship toward other "nations." This is what we usually call a foreign policy. But a nation's foreign policy can have no substance if it lacks the means of enforcing its attitude toward other nations. It can do this in a credible manner only if it implies the threat of maximum political organization for this purpose — which is to say that it is organized to some degree for war. War, then, as we have defined it to include all national activities that recognize the possibility of armed conflict, is itself the defining element of any nation's existence vis-à-vis any other nation. Since it is historically axiomatic that the existence of any form of weaponry insures its use, we have used the word "peace" as virtually synonymous with disarmament. By the same token, "war" is virtually synonymous with nationhood. The elimination of war implies the inevitable elimination of national sovereignty and the traditional nation-state.

The war system not only has been essential to the existence of nations as independent political entities, but has been equally indispensable to their stable internal political structure. Without it, no government has ever been able to obtain acquiescence in its "legitimacy," or right to rule its society. The possibility of war provides the sense of external necessity without which no government can long remain in power. The historical record reveals one instance after another where the failure of a regime to maintain the credibility of a war threat led to its dissolution, by the forces of private interest, of reactions to social injustice, or of other disintegrative elements. The organization of a society for the possibility of war is its principal political stabilizer. It is ironic that this primary function of war has been generally recognized by historians only where it has been expressly acknowledged — in the pirate societies of the great conquerors. . . .

In advanced modern democratic societies, the war system has provided political leaders with another political-economic function of increasing importance: it has served as the last great safeguard against the elimination of necessary social classes. As economic productivity increases to a level further and further above that of minimum subsistence, it becomes more and more difficult for a society to maintain distribution patterns insuring the existence of "hewers of wood and drawers of water." The further progress of automation can be expected to differentiate still more sharply between "superior" workers and what Ricardo called "menials," while simultaneously aggravating the problem of maintaining an unskilled labor supply.

The arbitrary nature of war expenditures and of other military activities make them ideally suited to control these essential class relationships. Obviously, if the war system were to be discarded, new political machinery would be needed at once to serve this vital subfunction. Until it is developed, the continuance of the war system must be assured, if for no other reason, among others, than to preserve whatever quality and degree of poverty a society requires as an incentive, as well as to maintain the stability of its internal organization of power.

Sociological

The most obvious of these functions is the time-honored use of military institutions to provide antisocial elements with an acceptable role in the social structure. The disintegrative, unstable social movements loosely described as "fascist" have traditionally taken root in societies that have lacked adequate military or paramilitary outlets to meet the needs of these elements. This function has been critical in periods of rapid change. The danger signals are easy to recognize, even though the stigmata bear different names at different times. The current euphemistic clichés — "juvenile delinquency" and "alienation" — have had their counterparts in every age. In earlier days these conditions were dealt with directly by the military without the complications of due process, usually through press gangs or outright enslavement. But it is not hard to visualize, for example, the degree of social disruption that might have taken place in the United States during the last two decades if the problem of the socially disaffected of the post-World War II period had not been foreseen and effectively met. The younger, and more dangerous, of these hostile social groupings have been kept under control by the Selective Service System.

This system and its analogues elsewhere furnish remarkably clear examples of disguised military utility. Informed persons in this country have never accepted the official rationale for a peacetime draft — military necessity, preparedness, etc. — as worthy of serious consideration. But what has gained credence among thoughtful men is the rarely voiced, less easily refuted, proposition that the institution of military service has a "patriotic" priority in our society that must be maintained for its own sake. Ironically, the simplistic official justification for selective service comes closer to the mark, once the nonmilitary functions of military institutions are understood. As a control device over the hostile, nihilistic, and potentially unsettling elements of a society in transition, the draft can again be defended, and quite convincingly, as a "military" necessity.

Nor can it be considered a coincidence that overt military activity, and thus the level of draft calls, tend to follow the major fluctuations in the unemployment rate in the lower age groups. This rate, in turn, is a time-tested herald of social discontent. It must be noted also that the armed forces in every civilization have provided the principal state-supported haven for what we now call the "unemployable." . . .

In general, the war system provides the basic motivation for primary social organization. In so doing, it reflects on the societal level the incentives of individual human behavior. The most important of these, for social purposes, is the individual psychological rationale for allegiance to a society and its values. Allegiance requires a cause; a cause requires an enemy. This much is obvious; the critical point is that the enemy that defines the cause must seem genuinely formidable. Roughly speaking, the presumed power of the "enemy" sufficient to warrant an individual sense of allegiance to a society must be proportionate to the size and complexity of the society. Today, of course, that power must be one of unprecedented magnitude and frightfulness.

It follows, from the patterns of human behavior, that the credibility of a social "enemy" demands similarly a readiness of response in proportion to its menace. In a broad social context, "an eye for an eye" still characterizes the only acceptable attitude toward a presumed threat of aggression, despite contrary religious and moral precepts governing personal conduct. The remoteness of personal decision from social consequence in a modern society makes it easy for its members to maintain this attitude without being aware of it. A recent example is the war in Vietnam; a less recent one was the bombing of Hiroshima and Nagasaki. In each case, the extent and gratuitousness of the slaughter were abstracted into political formulae by most Americans, once the proposition that the victims were "enemies" was established. The war system makes such an abstracted response possible in nonmilitary contexts as well. A conventional example of this mechanism is the inability of most people to connect, let us say, the starvation of millions in India with their own past conscious political decision-making. Yet the sequential logic linking a decision to restrict grain production in America with an eventual famine in Asia is obvious, unambiguous, and unconcealed.

What gives the war system its preeminent role in social organization, as elsewhere, is its unmatched authority over life and death. It must be emphasized again that the war system is not a mere social extension of the presumed need for individual human violence, but itself in turn serves to rationalize most nonmilitary killing. It also provides the precedent for the collective willingness of members of a society to pay a blood price for institutions far less central to social organization than war. . . .

The existence of an accepted external menace, then, is essential to social cohesiveness as well as to the acceptance of political authority. The menace must be believable, it must be of a magnitude consistent with the complexity of the society threatened, and it must appear, at least, to affect the entire society.

AMERICAN ENVIRONMENT

The conservation of resources, the preservation of natural beauty, a rational approach to urban planning and development, a broad consideration of long-range human values in the environment: during the 1960s problems such as these began to move into the public debate. A long tradition of free exploitation and the dominance of the private over the public interest was at last being questioned. Free and unrestricted land use had been followed by free and unrestricted industrialization, and the threat to the environment had become subtle and insidious, from outright destruction to slow poisoning. The noxious effluvia of industry made the air and water more and more inhospitable to life. The physical structure of the cities became progressively less hospitable as well, again through the exercise of private initiative in the absence of public policy. The necessity for such a public policy was much clearer than the means for arriving at one, but there was no doubt that the anticipated huge cost of the required programs was exceeded only by the urgent need to begin immediately.

"The New York Times"

Factory chimneys, municipal incinerators, and the exhaust from countless automobiles combine to poison the air of every major American city. Hundreds, perhaps thousands, of deaths and uncounted cases of heart and respiratory disease are traceable directly to polluted urban air. The problem is not inevitable, but the solution depends upon the willingness to spend enough private and public money to develop alternate fuels, methods of waste disposal, and effective controls on waste discharge. The willingness is as yet lacking; the problems worsen almost daily.

Polluted air hanging over New York City, Thanksgiving Day, 1966, in the middle of a three-day period of smog. In 1953, some 240 New Yorkers died as a result of a two-week siege of smog

(Above) Fish killed by pollutants dumped into a river; (below) result of pollution of a river in Louisiana

(Above) West Virginia factory emptying waste products into the Monongahela River; (right) garbage dumped into a stream in the once-wild New Jersey meadows

Water pollution is, if anything, even more extensive than that of the air. Industrial wastes — minerals, poisonous chemicals, insecticides — are poured in huge quantities into America's rivers and lakes. The result is water unfit for drinking or swimming, the killing off of wild life, and often the permanent disruption of the ecology of an entire region. Lake Erie, for example, is already considered "dead" and the other Great Lakes are rapidly becoming so. As with air pollution, the answer will be enormously expensive; the consequences of inaction are, however, unthinkable.

(Above) View of the Kennedy Expressway, the main route into Chicago for the daily commuters from the northwestern suburbs; (below) an automobile graveyard outside Detroit, Mich.

Landing lights mark the way for a jet plane approaching the runway at John F. Kennedy Airport

The American dedication to mobility appeared sometimes to border on obsession as the ability to create traffic congestion continued to nullify seemingly good planning. Detroit poured a constant stream of big new cars onto the highways, and old discarded ones piled up at the other end of the economy. Urban expressways designed to speed the flow of traffic through and out of town simply drew more cars into town and made themselves obsolete in a very short time. Overhead, air traffic increased comparably; newer, bigger, and noisier jets made city living yet more unpleasant, and traffic delays over major airports often exceeded flight times.

City growth and construction is still largely unregulated and unconcerned with broad city planning. Much building is done seemingly for its own sake, replacing a large office building downtown with a larger, adding to automobile and pedestrian congestion but without actually improving the structure, the appearance, or the operation of the city. "Urban renewal" projects typically replace old delapidated slums with bleak high-rise apartments — poorly constructed, dismal, and more expensive — while uprooting an entire neighborhood. Again, the glaring need is for strong public policy and humane city planning.

(Left) Contrasts in architecture in San Francisco; (below) children playing in an empty sandbox near a New York housing project. OPPOSITE PAGE: (Top) Street scene during New York's garbage strike, 1967; (bottom) construction begins on a new building

Rene Burri from Magnum

Bruce Davidson from Magnum

Jim Jowers — Nancy Palmer Agency

Inge Morath from Magnum

Herbert Loebel

Burk Uzzle from Magnum

(Above) Clutter of signs along a road approaching New York City; (left) display of lawn decorations and a prefabricated church. OPPOSITE PAGE: Housing development near Philadelphia, adjacent to a superhighway

A prime example of the results of lack of planning has been the unregulated growth of the suburbs. Free even from the minimal restrictions of the city, suburbs grow randomly as those who build them seek only to accommodate the maximum number of people in the minimum time. All too often the results combine drab uniformity, chaos, and no beauty whatsoever. The increasingly intolerable city finds itself ringed by ugly, unplanned, and already decaying suburbs. In response, new suburbs spring up, farther out, and the process gradually repeats itself. The Eastern Seaboard's megalopolis stretching from Boston to Washington has grown up in this way and is itself an unanswerable argument in favor of rigorous and far-sighted planning.

Fred Ward from Black Star

THIS BUILDING TO BE DEMOLISHED
NEW MODERN STRUCTURE TO BE ERECTED ON THIS SITE

OWNER MARTIN SCHULMAN   ARCHITECTS: WECHSLER & SCHIMENTI, A.I.A.

Dennis Stock from Magnum

New York Historical Society

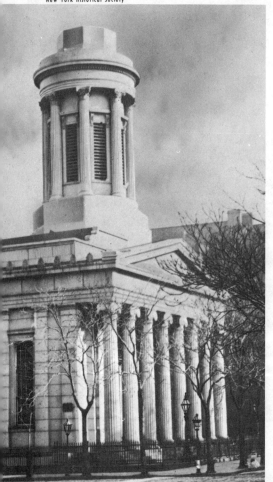

(Above) Protest signs in a Greenwich Village apartment building; (left) Collegiate Reformed Church and (below) Vanderbilt Mansion — two architecturally outstanding buildings demolished to erect modern structures

The Bettmann Archive

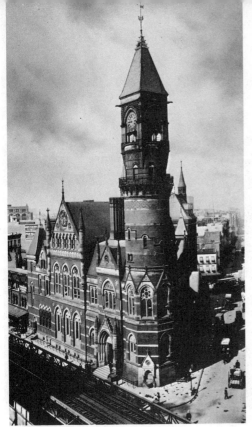

(Left) Jefferson Market Courthouse preserved as a library; (right) Disneyland recreates history

Humane values in urban planning would eliminate the now-prevalent belief that any new building is superior to any old building, or that new construction necessarily implies progress. Slum clearance programs are sometimes applied to run-down but viable and salvageable neighborhoods; much of an area's or a city's distinctiveness and real beauty can be and has been thus lost. On the other hand, new buildings have been known to be tax-penalized for architectural superiority.

Capen House in Topsfield, Mass., erected in 1683 and still standing in the 20th century

(Above) Erosion caused by careless mining practices in a Kentucky strip mine; (below) sightseers travel on mules to get a closer view of the Grand Canyon

America has a long tradition of exploiting nature, one that has outlived her ability to afford it. Many of the world's most magnificent natural regions have been destroyed by mining, logging, tourist development, or the suburban sprawl. Many areas of great beauty remain, of course, but even these are threatened on occasion; the virtual elimination of the California redwood and the flooding of the Grand Canyon have only with difficulty been forestalled. Until the terms of an intelligent, farsighted public policy are arrived at, the unimaginative, uncritical spread of technology which often masquerades as progress will continue to endanger what little unspoiled wilderness remains.

(Left) Fishing along a deserted Rhode Island beach; (below) family camping in the Colorado Rockies

Twentieth-century graffiti scrawled on a butte in a western state park

88.

Robert S. McNamara: Nuclear Strategy

One of the leading controversies in 1967, and one, moreover, that threatened to trouble the nation for some years to come, was over the question of whether the United States should construct a "heavy" or a "light" anti-ballistic missile defense system, or, indeed, whether it should construct any A.B.M. system at all. The arguments for both positions, in fact for all three, were spelled out by Secretary of Defense Robert S. McNamara in an address to the editors of United Press International in San Francisco, on September 18, 1967. (The speech is reprinted here in part.) McNamara, who believed that a light defense — adequate to protect against any attack mountable by China within the next decade or so — was the best choice, and who felt that the construction of a heavy or total defense system, involving the expenditure of fifty to a hundred billion dollars, would merely serve to speed up the arms race, resigned his post some ten weeks later.

Source: *New York Times*, September 19, 1967.

I WANT TO DISCUSS with you this afternoon the gravest problem that an American secretary of defense must face: the planning, preparation, and policy governing the possibility of thermonuclear war.

It is a prospect most of mankind would prefer not to contemplate. That is understandable; for technology has now circumscribed us all with a conceivable horizon of horror that could dwarf any catastrophe that has befallen man in his more than a million years on earth.

Man has lived now for more than twenty years in what we have come to call the Atomic Age. What we sometimes overlook is that every future age of man will be an atomic age. If, then, man is to have a future at all, it will have to be a future overshadowed with the permanent possibility of thermonuclear holocaust.

About that fact, we are no longer free. Our freedom in this question consists rather in facing the matter rationally and actions to minimize the danger. No sane citizen; no sane political leader; no sane nation wants thermonuclear war. But merely not wanting it is not enough. We must understand the difference between actions which increase its risk, those which reduce it, and those which, while costly, have little influence one way or another.

Now, this whole subject matter tends to be psychologically unpleasant. But there is an even greater difficulty standing in the way of constructive and profitable debate over the issues; and that is that nuclear strategy is exceptionally complex in its technical aspects. Unless these complexities are well understood, rational discussion and decision making are simply not possible.

What I want to do this afternoon is deal with these complexities and clarify them with as much precision and detail as time and security permit.

One must begin with precise definitions. The cornerstone of our strategic policy continues to be to deter deliberate nuclear attack upon the United States, or its allies, by maintaining a highly reliable ability to inflict an unacceptable degree of damage upon any single aggressor, or combination of aggressors, at any time during the course of a strategic nuclear exchange — even after our absorbing a surprise first strike. This can be defined as our "assured destruction capability."

Now it is imperative to understand that assured destruction is the very essence of the whole deterrence concept. We must possess an actual, assured destruction capability. And that actual assured destruction capability must also be credible. Conceivably, our assured destruction capability could be actual without being credible — in which case, it might fail to deter an aggressor. The point is that a potential aggressor must himself believe that our assured destruction capability is in fact actual and that our will to use it in retaliation to an attack is in fact unwavering.

The conclusion, then, is clear: If the United States is to deter a nuclear attack on itself or on our allies, it must possess an actual and a credible assured destruction capability.

When calculating the force we require, we must be "conservative" in all our estimates of both a potential aggressor's capabilities and his intentions. Security depends upon taking a "worst plausible case" — and having the ability to cope with that eventuality. In that eventuality, we must be able to absorb the total weight of nuclear attack on our country — on our strike-back forces; on our command and control apparatus; on our industrial capacity; on our cities and on our population — and still be fully capable of destroying the aggressor to the point that his society is simply no longer viable in any meaningful, twentieth-century sense. That is what deterrence to nuclear aggression means. It means the certainty of suicide to the aggressor — not merely to his military forces, but to his society as a whole.

Now let us consider another term: "first-strike capability." This, in itself, is an ambiguous term, since it could mean simply the ability of one nation to attack another nation with nuclear forces first. But as it is normally used, it connotes much more: the substantial elimination of the attacked nation's retaliatory second-strike forces. This is the sense in which "first-strike capability" should be understood.

Now, clearly, such a first-strike capability is an important strategic concept. The United States cannot — and will not — ever permit itself to get into the position in which another nation, or combination of nations, would possess such a first-strike capability which could be effectively used against it. To get into such a position vis-a-vis any other nation or nations would not only constitute an intolerable threat to our security but it would obviously remove our ability to deter nuclear aggression — both against ourselves and against our allies. Now, we are not in that position today — and there is no foreseeable danger of our ever getting into that position.

Our strategic offensive forces are immense: 1,000 Minutemen missile launchers, carefully protected below ground; 41 Polaris submarines, carrying 656 missile launchers — with the majority of these hidden beneath the seas at all times; and about 600 long-range bombers, approximately 40 percent of which are kept always in a high state of alert. . . .

Now what about the Soviet Union? Does it today possess a powerful nuclear arsenal? The answer is that it does.

Does it possess a first-strike capability against the United States? The answer is that it does not. Can the Soviet Union, in the foreseeable future, acquire such a first-strike capability against the United States? The answer is that it cannot. It cannot because we are determined to remain fully alert, and we will never permit our own assured destruction capability to be at a point where a Soviet first-strike capability is even remotely feasible.

Is the Soviet Union seriously attempting to acquire a first-strike capability against the

United States? Although this is a question we cannot answer with absolute certainty, we believe the answer is no. In any event, the question itself is — in a sense — irrelevant. . . .

But there is another question that is more relevant; and that is: Do we — the United States — possess a first-strike capability against the Soviet Union? The answer is that we do not. And we do not, not because we have neglected our nuclear strength. On the contrary, we have increased it to the point that we possess a clear superiority over the Soviet Union.

We do not possess first-strike capability against the Soviet Union for precisely the same reason that they do not possess it against us; and that is that we have both built up our "second-strike capability" to the point that a first-strike capability on either side has become unattainable. (A "second-strike capability" is the capability to absorb a surprise nuclear attack and survive with sufficient power to inflict unacceptable damage on the aggressor.)

There is, of course, no way in which the United States could have prevented the Soviet Union from acquiring its present second-strike capability — short of a massive, preemptive first strike on the Soviet Union in the 1950s. The blunt fact is, then, that neither the Soviet Union nor the United States can attack the other without being destroyed in retaliation; nor can either of us attain a first-strike capability in the foreseeable future.

The further fact is that both the Soviet Union and the United States presently possess an actual and credible second-strike capability against one another — and it is precisely this mutual capability that provides us both with the strongest possible motive to avoid a nuclear war.

The more frequent question that arises in this connection is whether or not the United States possesses nuclear superiority over the Soviet Union. The answer is that we do. . . . By using the realistic measure-

ment of the number of warheads available, capable of being reliably delivered with accuracy and effectiveness on the appropriate targets in the United States or Soviet Union, I can tell you that the United States currently possesses a superiority over the Soviet Union of at least three or four to one. Furthermore, we will maintain a superiority — by these same realistic criteria — over the Soviet Union for as far ahead in the future as we can realistically plan.

I want, however, to make one point patently clear: Our current numerical superiority over the Soviet Union in reliable, accurate, and effective warheads is both greater than we had originally planned and is, in fact, more than we require. Moreover, in the larger equation of security, our "superiority" is of limited significance, since even with our current superiority, or, indeed, with any numerical superiority realistically attainable, the blunt, inescapable fact remains that the Soviet Union could still — with its present forces — effectively destroy the United States, even after absorbing the full weight of an American first strike.

I have noted that our present superiority is greater than we had planned. Let me explain to you how this came about, for I think it is a significant illustration of the intrinsic dynamics of the nuclear arms race.

In 1961, when I became secretary of defense, the Soviet Union possessed a very small operational arsenal of intercontinental missiles. However, they did possess the technological and industrial capacity to enlarge that arsenal very substantially over the succeeding several years. Now, we had no evidence that the Soviets did in fact plan to fully use that capability. But, as I have pointed out, a strategic planner must be "conservative" in his calculations; that is, he must prepare for the worst plausible case and not be content to hope and prepare merely for the most probable.

Since we could not be certain of Soviet intentions — since we could not be sure that they would not undertake a massive buildup — we had to insure against such an eventuality by undertaking, ourselves, a major buildup of the Minuteman and Polaris forces. Thus, in the course of hedging against what was then only a theoretically possible Soviet buildup, we took decisions which have resulted in our current superiority in numbers of warheads and deliverable megatons. But the blunt fact remains that if we had had more accurate information about planned Soviet strategic forces, we simply would not have needed to build as large a nuclear arsenal as we have today.

Now, let me be absolutely clear. I am not saying that our decision in 1961 was unjustified. I am simply saying that it was necessitated by a lack of accurate information. Furthermore, that decision in itself — as justified as it was — in the end, could not possibly have left unaffected the Soviet Union's future nuclear plans.

What is essential to understand here is that the Soviet Union and the United States mutually influence one another's strategic plans. . . .

Now, in strategic nuclear weaponry, the arms race involves a particular irony. Unlike any other era in military history, today, a substantial numerical superiority of weapons does not effectively translate into political control or diplomatic leverage. While thermonuclear power is almost inconceivably awesome, and represents virtually unlimited potential destructiveness, it has proven to be a limited diplomatic instrument. Its uniqueness lies in the fact that it is at one and the same time an all-powerful weapon — and a very inadequate weapon. . . . Even with our nuclear monopoly in the early postwar period, we were unable to deter the Soviet pressures against Berlin, or their support of aggression in Korea. Today, our nuclear superiority does not deter all forms of Soviet support of Communist insurgency in Southeast Asia. . . .

This has been a difficult lesson both for us and for our allies to accept, since there is a strong psychological tendency to regard superior nuclear forces as a simple and unfailing solution to security, and an assurance of victory under any set of circumstances. What is important to understand is that our nuclear strategic forces play a vital and absolutely necessary role in our security and that of our allies, but it is an intrinsically limited role. Thus, we and our allies must maintain substantial conventional forces, fully capable of dealing with a wide spectrum of lesser forms of political and military aggression — a level of aggression against which the use of strategic nuclear forces would not be to our advantage, and thus a level of aggression which these strategic nuclear forces by themselves cannot effectively deter. . . .

I have pointed out that in strategic nuclear matters the Soviet Union and the United States mutually influence one another's plans. In recent years the Soviets have substantially increased their offensive forces. We have, of course, been watching and evaluating this very carefully. Clearly, the Soviet buildup is in part a reaction to our own buildup since the beginning of this decade. Soviet strategic planners undoubtedly reasoned that if our buildup were to continue at its accelerated pace, we might conceivably reach, in time, a credible first-strike capability against the Soviet Union.

That was not in fact our intention. Our intention was to assure that they — with their theoretical capacity to reach such a first-strike capability — would not in fact outdistance us. But they could not read our intentions with any greater accuracy than we could read theirs. And thus the result has been that we have both built up our forces to a point that far exceeds a credible second-strike capability against the forces we each started with. In doing so, neither of us has reached a first-strike capability. And the realities of the situation being what they are — whatever we believe their intentions to be and whatever they believe our intentions to be — each of us can deny the other a first-strike capability in the foreseeable future.

Now, how can we be so confident that this is the case? How can we be so certain that the Soviets cannot gradually outdistance us, either by some dramatic technology breakthrough or simply through our imperceptively lagging behind, for whatever reason — reluctance to spend the requisite funds; distraction with military problems elsewhere; faulty intelligence; or simple negligence and naïveté? All of these reasons — and others — have been suggested by some commentators in this country, who fear that we are in fact falling behind to a dangerous degree.

The answer to all of this is simple and straightforward. We are not going to permit the Soviets to outdistance us, because to do so would be to jeopardize our very viability as a nation. No President, no secretary of defense, no Congress of the United States — of whatever political party and of whatever political persuasion is going to permit this nation to take that risk.

We do not want a nuclear arms race with the Soviet Union primarily because the action-reaction phenomenon makes it foolish and futile. But if the only way to prevent the Soviet Union from obtaining first-strike capability over us is to engage in such a race, the United States possesses in ample abundance the resources, the technology, and the will to run faster in that race for whatever distance is required. But what we would much prefer to do is to come to a realistic and reasonably riskless agreement with the Soviet Union, which would effectively prevent such an arms race. . . .

Since we now each possess a deterrent in excess of our individual needs, both of our nations would benefit from a properly safeguarded agreement first to limit, and later to reduce, both our offensive and defensive strategic nuclear forces. We may, or we may not, be able to achieve such an agree-

ment. We hope we can. And we believe such an agreement is fully feasible, since it is clearly in both our nations' interests. But reach the formal agreement or not, we can be sure that neither the Soviets nor we are going to risk the other's obtaining a first-strike capability. On the contrary, we can be sure that we are both going to maintain a maximum effort to preserve an assured destruction capability.

It would not be sensible for either side to launch a maximum effort to achieve a first-strike capability. It would not be sensible because the intelligence-gathering capability of each side being what it is, and the realities of lead-time from technological breakthrough to operational readiness being what they are, neither of us would be able to acquire a first-strike capability in secret.

Now, let me take a specific case in point. The Soviets are now deploying an antiballistic missile system. If we react to this deployment intelligently, we have no reason for alarm. The system does not impose any threat to our ability to penetrate and inflict massive and unacceptable damage on the Soviet Union. In other words, it does not presently affect in any significant manner our assured destruction capability. It does not impose such a threat because we have already taken the steps necessary to assure that our land-based Minuteman missiles, our nuclear submarine-launched new Poseidon missiles, and our strategic-bomber forces have the requisite penetration aids — and, in the sum, constitute a force of such magnitude that they guarantee us a force strong enough to survive a Soviet attack and penetrate the Soviet ABM deployment.

Now, let me come to the issue that has received so much attention recently: the question of whether or not we should deploy an ABM system against the Soviet nuclear threat.

To begin with, this is not in any sense a new issue. We have had both the technical possibility and the strategic desirability of

Pictorial Parade

Robert McNamara, secretary of defense, 1961-68

an American ABM deployment under constant review since the late 1950s. While we have substantially improved our technology in the field, it is important to understand that none of the systems at the present or foreseeable state of the art would provide an impenetrable shield over the United States. Were such a shield possible, we would certainly want it — and we would certainly build it.

And at this point, let me dispose of an objection that is totally irrelevant to this issue. It has been alleged that we are opposed to deploying a large-scale ABM system because it would carry the heavy price tag of $40 billion. Let me make very clear that the $40 billion is not the issue. If we could build and deploy a genuinely impenetrable shield over the United States, we would be willing to spend, not $40 billion but any reasonable multiple of that amount that was necessary.

The money in itself is not the problem: The penetrability of the proposed shield is the problem. There is clearly no point, however, in spending $40 billion if it is not going to buy us a significant improvement

in our security. If it is not, then we should use the substantial resources it represents on something that will.

Every ABM system that is now feasible involves firing defensive missiles at incoming offensive warheads in an effort to destroy them. But what many commentators on this issue overlook is that any such system can rather obviously be defeated by an enemy simply sending more offensive warheads, or dummy warheads, than there are defensive missiles capable of disposing of them. And this is the whole crux of the nuclear action-reaction phenomenon. Were we to deploy a heavy ABM system throughout the United States, the Soviets would clearly be strongly motivated to so increase their offensive capability as to cancel out our defensive advantage.

It is futile for each of us to spend $4 billion, $40 billion, or $400 billion — and at the end of all the spending, and at the end of all the deployment, and at the end of all the effort, to be relatively at the same point of balance on the security scale that we are now. In point of fact, we have already initiated offensive weapons programs costing several billions in order to offset the small present Soviet ABM deployment, and the possibly more extensive future Soviet ABM deployments. That is money well spent; and it is necessary. But we should bear in mind that it is money spent because of the action-reaction phenomenon.

If we in turn hope for heavy ABM deployment — at whatever price — we can be certain that the Soviets will react to offset the advantage we would hope to gain. It is precisely because of this certainty of a corresponding Soviet reaction that the four prominent scientists — men who have served with distinction as the science advisers to Presidents Eisenhower, Kennedy, and Johnson, and the three outstanding men who have served as directors of research and engineering to three secretaries of defense — have unanimously recommended against the deployment of an ABM system designed to protect our population against a Soviet attack. These men are Doctors Killian, Kistiakowsky, Wiesner, Hornig, York, Brown, and Foster.

The plain fact of the matter is that we are now facing a situation analogous to the one we faced in 1961: We are uncertain of the Soviets' intentions. At that time we were concerned about their potential offensive capabilities; now we are concerned about their potential defensive capabilities. But the dynamics of the concern are the same. . . .

As you know, we have proposed U.S.-Soviet talks on this matter. Should these talks fail, we are fully prepared to take the appropriate measures that such a failure would make necessary. The point for us to keep in mind is that should the talks fail — and the Soviets decide to expand their present modest ABM deployment into a massive one — our response must be realistic. There is no point whatever in our responding by going to a massive ABM deployment to protect our population when such a system would be ineffective against a sophisticated Soviet offense. Instead, realism dictates that if the Soviets elect to deploy a heavy ABM system, we must further expand our sophisticated offensive forces and thus preserve our overwhelming assured destruction capability. But the intractable fact is that, should the talks fail, both the Soviets and ourselves would be forced to continue on a foolish and feckless course. . . .

It is important to distinguish between an ABM system designed to protect against a Soviet attack on our cities and ABM systems which have other objectives. One of the other uses of an ABM system which we should seriously consider is the greater protection of our strategic offensive forces. Another is in relation to the emerging nuclear capability of Communist China.

There is evidence that the Chinese are devoting very substantial resources to the development of both nuclear warheads and missile delivery systems. As I stated last January, indications are that they will have medium-range ballistic missiles within a year or so, an initial intercontinental-ballistic-missile capability in the early 1970s, and a modest force in the mid-'70s.

Up to now, the lead-time factor has allowed us to postpone a decision on whether or not a light ABM deployment might be advantageous as a countermeasure to Communist China's nuclear development. But the time will shortly be right for us to initiate production if we desire such a system.

China at the moment is caught up in internal strifes, but it seems likely that her basic motivation in developing a strategic nuclear capability is an attempt to provide a basis for threatening her neighbors and to clothe herself with the dubious prestige that the world pays to nuclear weaponry. We deplore her development of these weapons, just as we deplore it in other countries. We oppose nuclear proliferation because we believe that in the end it only increases the risk of a common and cataclysmic holocaust. President Johnson has made it clear that the United States will oppose any efforts of China to employ nuclear blackmail against her neighbors.

We possess now, and will continue to possess for as far ahead as we can foresee, an overwhelming first-strike capability with respect to China. And despite the shrill and raucous propaganda directed at her own people that "the atomic bomb is a paper tiger," there is ample evidence that China well appreciates the destructive power of nuclear weapons.

China has been cautious to avoid any action that might end in a nuclear clash with the United States — however wild her words — and understandably so. We have the power not only to destroy completely her entire nuclear offensive forces but to devastate her society as well. Is there any possibility, then, that by the mid-1970s China might become so incautious as to attempt a nuclear attack on the United States or our allies? It would be insane and suicidal for her to do so, but one can conceive conditions under which China might miscalculate. We wish to reduce such possibilities to a minimum. And since, as I have noted, our strategic planning must always be conservative and take into consideration even the possible irrational behavior of potential adversaries, there are marginal grounds for concluding that a light deployment of U.S. ABMs against this possibility is prudent.

The system would be relatively inexpensive — preliminary estimates place the cost at about $5 billion — and would have a much higher degree of reliability against a Chinese attack than the much more massive and complicated system that some have recommended against a possible Soviet attack. Moreover, such an ABM deployment designed against a possible Chinese attack would have a number of other advantages. It would provide an additional indication to Asians that we intend to deter China from nuclear blackmail and thus would contribute toward our goal of discouraging nuclear-weapon proliferation among the present nonnuclear countries.

Further, the Chinese-oriented ABM deployment would enable us to add — as a concurrent benefit — a further defense of our Minuteman sites against Soviet attack, which means that at modest cost we would in fact be adding even greater effectiveness to our offensive missile force and avoiding a much more costly expansion of that force.

Finally, such a reasonably reliable ABM system would add protection of our population against the improbable but possible accidental launch of an intercontinental missile by any of the nuclear powers.

After a detailed review of all these considerations, we have decided to go forward with this Chinese-oriented ABM deployment, and we will begin actual production of such a system at the end of this year.

I want to emphasize that it contains two possible dangers — and we should guard carefully against each. The first danger is that we may psychologically lapse into the old oversimplification about the adequacy of nuclear power. The simple truth is that nuclear weapons can serve to deter only a narrow range of threats. This ABM deployment will strengthen our defensive posture and will enhance the effectiveness of our land-based ICBM offensive forces. But the independent nations of Asia must realize that these benefits are no substitute for their maintaining and, where necessary, strengthening their own conventional forces in order to deal with more likely threats to the security of the region. The second danger is also psychological. There is a kind of mad momentum intrinsic to the development of all new nuclear weaponry. If a weapon system works — and works well — there is strong pressure from many directions to produce and deploy the weapon out of all proportion to the prudent level required.

The danger in deploying this relatively light and reliable Chinese-oriented ABM system is going to be that pressures will develop to expand it into a heavy Soviet-oriented ABM system. We must resist that temptation firmly, not because we can for a moment afford to relax our vigilance against a possible Soviet first strike but precisely because our greatest deterrent against such a strike is not a massive, costly, but highly penetrable ABM shield, but rather a fully credible offensive assured destruction capability. . . .

Let me emphasize — and I cannot do so too strongly — that our decision to go ahead with *limited* ABM deployment in no way indicates that we feel an agreement with the Soviet Union on the limitation of strategic nuclear offensive and defensive forces is any the less urgent or desirable. The road leading from the stone ax to the ICBM — though it may have been more than a million years in the building — seems to have run in a single direction. If one is inclined to be cynical, one might conclude that man's history seems to be characterized not so much by consistent periods of peace, occasionally punctuated by warfare; but rather by persistent outbreaks of warfare, wearily put aside from time to time by periods of exhaustion and recovery — that parade under the name of peace.

I do not view man's history with that degree of cynicism, but I do believe that man's wisdom in avoiding war is often surpassed by his folly in promoting it. However foolish unlimited war may have been in the past, it is now no longer merely foolish but suicidal as well. It is said that nothing can prevent a man from suicide if he is sufficiently determined to commit it.

The question is what is our determination in an era when unlimited war will mean the death of hundreds of millions — and the possible genetic impairment of a million generations to follow? Man is clearly a compound of folly and wisdom — and history is clearly a consequence of the admixture of those two contradictory traits. History has placed our particular lives in an area when the consequences of human folly are waxing more and more catastrophic in the matters of war and peace.

In the end, the root of man's security does not lie in his weaponry. In the end, the root of man's security lies in his mind. What the world requires in its twenty-second year of the Atomic Age is not a new race toward armament. What the world requires in its twenty-second year of the Atomic Age is a new race toward reasonableness. We had better all run that race; not merely we the administrators but we the people.

89.

Irving Kristol: American Intellectuals and Foreign Policy

Beginning in 1932, when Franklin D. Roosevelt gathered about him an influential group of academic advisers (dubbed the "Brain Trust") to help plan the policies of his administration in the face of the worst depression the country had ever known, the Democratic Party numbered among its adherents most of the intellectuals of the U.S. Never was this more true, perhaps, than in 1964, when the intellectuals, almost to a man, supported President Johnson in his bid for reelection against the challenge of Senatory Barry Goldwater of Arizona. By 1967, however, when the following article by Irving Kristol appeared in Foreign Affairs, *the situation had radically changed. Most American intellectuals no longer supported the President and his policies, many were actively and vigorously opposed, and there was even talk that the Democrats had lost the intellectuals for good. Kristol discussed the reasons for this change, which others suggested might be permanent and might spell the ultimate defeat of the Party. The article is reprinted here in part.*

Source: Reprinted by special permission from *Foreign Affairs*, July 1967.

A RECENT LETTER TO *The New York Times*, complaining about the role of the academic community in opposing President Johnson's Vietnam policy, argued that "it is not clear why people trained in mathematics, religion, geology, music, etc., believe their opinions on military and international problems should carry much validity." And the letter went on: "Certainly they [the professors] would oppose unqualified Pentagon generals telling them how to teach their course."

One can understand this complaint; one may even sympathize with the sentiments behind it. The fact remains, however, that it does miss the point. For the issue is not intellectual competence or intellectual validity — not really, and despite all protestations to the contrary. What is at stake is that species of power we call moral authority. The intellectual critics of American foreign policy obviously and sincerely believe that their arguments are right. But it is clear they believe, even more obviously and sincerely, that *they* are right — and that the totality of this rightness amounts to much more than the sum of the individual arguments.

An intellectual may be defined as a man who speaks with general authority about a subject on which he has no particular competence. This definition sounds ironic, but is not. The authority is real enough, just as the lack of specific competence is crucial. An economist writing about economics is not acting as an intellectual, nor is a literary critic when he explicates a text. In such cases, we are witnessing professionals at work. On the other hand, there is good reason why we ordinarily take the "man of letters" as the archetypical intellectual. It is he who most closely resembles his sociological forebear and ideal type: the sermonizing cleric.

Precisely which people, at which time, in any particular social situation, are certified as "intellectuals" is less important than the fact that such certification is achieved — informally but indisputably. And this process involves the recognition of the intellectual as legitimately possessing the prerogative of being moral guide and critic to the world. . . .

It is simply not possible to comprehend what is happening in the United States today unless one keeps the sociological condition and political ambitions of the intellectual class very much in the forefront of one's mind. What we are witnessing is no mere difference of opinion about foreign policy, or about Vietnam. Such differences of opinion do exist, of course. Some of the most articulate critics believe that the United States has, through bureaucratic inertia and mental sloth, persisted in a foreign policy that, whatever its relevance to the immediate postwar years, is by now dangerously anachronistic. They insist that the United States has unthinkingly accepted world responsibilities which are beyond its resources and that, in any case, these responsibilities have only an illusory connection with the enduring national interest. These men may be right; or they may be wrong. But right or wrong, *this* debate is largely irrelevant to the convulsion that the American intellectual community is now going through — even though occasional references may be made to it, for credibility's sake. One does not accuse the President of the United States and the Secretary of State of being "war criminals" and "mass murderers" because they have erred in estimating the proper dimensions of the United States' overseas commitments. And it is precisely accusations of this kind that are inflaming passions on the campus, and which are more and more coming to characterize the "peace movement" as a whole.

What we are observing is a phenomenon that is far more complex in its origins and far-reaching in its implications. It involves, among other things, the highly problematic relationship of the modern intellectual to foreign affairs, the basic self-definition of the American intellectual, the tortured connections between American liberal ideology and the American imperial republic and the role of the newly established academic classes in an affluent society. Above all, it raises the question of whether democratic societies can cope with the kinds of political pathologies that seem to be spontaneously generated by their very commitment to economic and social progress.

II

No MODERN NATION has ever constructed a foreign policy that was acceptable to its intellectuals. True, at moments of national peril or national exaltation, intellectuals will feel the same patriotic emotions as everyone else, and will subscribe as enthusiastically to the common cause. But these moments pass, the process of disengagement begins, and it usually does not take long for disengagement to eventuate in alienation. Public opinion polls generally reveal that the overwhelming majority of ordinary citizens, at any particular time, will be approving of their government's foreign policy; among intellectuals, this majority tends to be skimpy at best, and will frequently not exist at all. It is reasonable to suppose that there is an instinctive bias at work here favorable to government among the common people, unfavorable among the intellectuals.

The bias of the common man is easy to understand: he is never much interested in foreign affairs; his patriotic feelings incline him to favor his own government against the governments of foreigners; and in cases of international conflict, he is ready to sacrifice his self-interest for what the government assures him to be the common good. The persistent bias of intellectuals, on the other hand, requires some explaining.

We have noted that the intellectual lays claim — and the claim is, more often than not, recognized — to moral authority over the intentions and actions of political leaders. This claim finds concrete rhetorical expression in an ideology. What creates a community of intellectuals, as against a mere aggregate of individuals, is the fact that they subscribe — with varying degrees of warmth or with more or less explicit reservations — to a prevailing ideology. This ideology permits them to interpret the past, make sense of the present, outline a shape for the future. It constitutes the essence of their rationality, as this is directed toward the life of man in society.

Now, it is the peculiarity of foreign policy that it is the area of public life in which ideology flounders most dramatically. Thus, while it is possible — if not necessarily fruitful — to organize the political writings of the past three hundred years along a spectrum ranging from the ideological "left" to the ideological "right," no such arrangement is conceivable for writings on foreign policy. There is no great "radical" text on the conduct of foreign policy — and no great "conservative" text, either. What texts there are (e.g., Machiavelli, Grotius, in our own day the writings of George Kennan and Hans Morgenthau) are used indifferently by all parties, as circumstance allows. . . .

The reasons why this should be so are not mysterious. To begin with, the very idea of "foreign policy" is so amorphous as to be misleading. As James Q. Wilson has pointed out, it is not at all clear that a State Department can have a foreign policy in a meaningful sense of that term — i.e., one "policy" that encompasses our economic, military, political, and sentimental relations with nations neighborly or distant, friendly or inimical. Moreover, whereas a national community is governed by principles by which one takes one's intellectual and moral bearings, the nations of the world do not constitute such a community and propose few principles by which their conduct may be evaluated. What this adds up to is that ideology can obtain exasperatingly little purchase over the realities of foreign policy — and that intellectuals feel keenly their dispossession from this area.

It is not that intellectuals actually believe — though they often assert it — that the heavy reliance upon expediency in foreign affairs is intrinsically immoral. It is just that this reliance renders intellectuals as a class so much the less indispensable: to the extent that expediency is a necessary principle of action, to that extent the sovereignty of intellectuals is automatically circumscribed. It is only where politics is ideologized that intellectuals have a pivotal social and political role. To be good at coping with expediential situations you don't have to be an intellectual — and it may even be a handicap.

It is this state of affairs that explains the extraordinary inconsistencies of intellectuals on matters of foreign policy, and the ease with which they can enunciate a positive principle, only in the next breath to urge a contrary action. So it is that many intellectuals are appalled at our military intervention in Southeast Asia, on the grounds that, no matter what happens there, the national security of the United States will not be threatened. But these same intellectuals would raise no objection if the United States sent an expeditionary force all the way to South Africa to overthrow apartheid, even though South Africa offers no threat to American security. So it is, too, that intellectual critics are fond of accusing American foreign policy of neglecting "political solutions" in favor of crude military and economic action — thereby demonstrating their faith that, if foreign policy were suffused with sufficient ideological rationality, it would dissolve the recalcitrance that mere statesmen encounter. And when the statesman candidly responds that he is coping, not with problems, but with an endless series of crises, and that he really has no way of knowing beforehand what "solution," if any, is feasible, he is simply reinforcing the intellectual's conviction that the managers of foreign affairs are, if not more wicked than he is, then certainly more stupid. Usually, he will be willing to think they are both.

Charles Frankel has written that "international affairs are peculiarly susceptible to galloping abstractions" and has stressed that "intellectuals, more than most other groups, have the power to create, dignify, inflate, criticize, moderate or puncture these abstractions." In the event, intellectuals rarely moderate or puncture, but are diligent in inflation. Abstractions are their life's blood, and even when they resolutely decide to become "tough-minded" they end up with an oversimplified ideology of Realpolitik that is quite useless as a guide to the conduct of foreign affairs and leads its expounders to one self-contradiction after another. But the important point is not that intellectuals are always wrong on matters of foreign policy — they are not, and could not possibly be, if only by the laws of chance. What is striking is that, right or wrong, they are so often, from the statesman's point of view, irrelevant. And it is their self-definition as ideological creatures that makes them so.

III

IN THE UNITED STATES, this ideological self-definition has taken on a very special form, and the relation of the American intellectual to foreign policy has its own distinctive qualities. Just how distinctive may be gathered from asking oneself the following question: Is it conceivable that American intellectuals should *ever* disapprove of *any* popular revolution, anywhere in the world — whatever the express or implicit principles of this revolution? One can make this question even sharper: Is it conceivable for American intellectuals ever to approve of their government suppressing, or helping to frustrate, any popular revolution *by poor people* — whatever the nature or consequences of this revolution? The answer would obviously have to be in the negative; and the implications of this answer for American foreign policy are not insignificant. This policy must work within a climate of opinion that finds the idea of a *gradual* evolution of traditional societies thoroughly uninteresting — which, indeed, has an instinctive detestation of all traditional societies as being inherently unjust, and an equally instinctive approval, as being inherently righteous, of any revolutionary ideology which claims to incorporate the people's will.

As a matter of fact, even though official policy must obviously be based on other considerations, the makers of policy themselves find it nearly impossible to escape from this ideological framework. The State Department, for example, is always insisting that the United States is a truly revolutionary society, founded on revolutionary principles and offering a true revolutionary promise — as contrasted with the communists' spurious promises. The intellectual critics of American foreign policy deny that any such revolutionary intention or program exists — but think it ought to. There are precious few people in the United States who will say aloud that revolutionary intentions are inconsistent with a prudent and responsible foreign policy of a great power. Oddly enough, to hear this point made with some urgency these days, one has to go to the Soviet Union.

The American intellectual tradition has two profound commitments: to "ideals" and to "the people." It is the marriage of these two themes that has made the American mind and given it its characteristic cast — which might be called *transcendentalist populism.*

The "transcendentalist" theme in American thought is linked to a disrespect for tradition, a suspicion of all institutionalized authority, an unshakable faith in the "natural" (what once was called "divine") wisdom of the sincere individual, and incorruptible allegiance to one's own "inner light." The American intellectual sees himself as being in perpetual "prophetic confrontation" with principalities and powers. (That very phrase, "prophetic confrontation," has lately been used by Hans Morgenthau to define the proper stance of the intellectual vis-à-vis his government's policies.) Tell an American intellectual that he is a disturber of the intellectual peace, and he is gratified. Tell him he is a reassuring spokesman for calm and tranquillity, and he will think you have made a nasty accusation.

This transcendentalist "protestantism" of the American intellectual derives from the history of American Protestantism itself — as does his near-mystical celebration of "the people." . . . This evolution, which might be called the democratization of the spirit, has created an American intellectual who is at one and the same time (*a*) humble toward an idealized and mythical prototype of the common man (if the people have a quasiecclesiastical function, to oppose them in any consistent way partakes of heresy) and (*b*) arrogant toward existing authority, as presumptively representing nothing but a petrified form of yesteryear's vital forces. It has also had a peculiar effect upon the politics of American intellectuals, which is more often than not a kind of transcendentalist politics, focusing less on the reform of the polity than on the perfection and purification of self in opposition to the polity. Just as the intellectual opposition to slavery in the 1830s and 1840s paid little attention to the reform of particular institutions but focused primarily on the need for the individual to avoid being compromised and contaminated by this general evil, so in the 1960s what appears most to torment our academic intellectuals is the morality of their own actions — whether they should cooperate with Selective Service, accept government contracts, pay taxes, etc. At both times, the issue of individual, conscientious "civil disobedience" has become acute. . . .

Precisely what an American intellectual does *not* believe was most elegantly expressed by Sir Thomas More, in the discussion of an intellectual's obligation in his *Utopia:*

> If evil persons cannot be quite rooted out, and if you cannot correct habitual attitudes as you wish, you must not therefore abandon the commonwealth. . . . You must strive to guide

policy indirectly, so that you make the best of things, and what you cannot turn to good, you can at least make less bad. For it is impossible to do all things well unless all men are good, and this I do not expect to see for a long time.

There have been, of course, some American intellectuals who have followed Sir Thomas More's direction. For their efforts and pains, they have been subjected to the scorn and contempt of the intellectual community as a whole. (Arthur Schlesinger, Jr., Eric Goldman, and John Roche could provide us with eloquent testimony on this score.) . . .

IV

THE TRANSFORMATION of the American republic into an imperial power has sharply exacerbated the relations between the intellectual and the makers of foreign policy. The term "imperial power" is merely a synonym for "great power" and is not necessarily the same thing as "imperialistic" power. But there would seem to be a gain in clarity, and a diminution of humbug, in insisting on the use of the more provocative phrase. There are a great many people who appear to think that a great power is only the magnification of a small power, and that the principles governing the actions of the latter are simply transferrable — perhaps with some modification — to the former. In fact, there is a qualitative difference between the two conditions, and the difference can be summed up as follows: a great power is "imperial" because what it does *not* do is just as significant, and just as consequential, as what it does.

Which is to say, a great power does not have the range of freedom of action — derived from the freedom of inaction — that a small power possesses. It is entangled in a web of responsibilities from which there is no hope of escape; and its policy-makers are doomed to a strenuous and unquiet life,

with no prospect of ultimate resolution, no hope for an unproblematic existence, no promise of final contentment. It is understandable that these policy-makers should sometimes talk as if some particular redirection of policy, of any great power, is capable of terminating the tensions inherent in this imperial condition. But it is foolish for us to believe them; and it is even more foolish for them to believe themselves. It is no accident that all classical political philosophers, and all depicters of utopia, have agreed that, to be truly happy, a human community should be relatively small and as isolated as possible from foreign entanglements.

Indeed, this utopian ideal is a major historic theme of American foreign policy, being at the root of what we call "isolationism." And so long as the United States was not a great power, it was not entirely utopian. The American republic, until the beginning of the twentieth century, was genuinely isolationist, and isolationism made both practical and idealistic sense. Practical sense, because the United States was geographically isolated from the main currents of world politics. Idealistic sense, because the United States could feel — and it was no illusion — that it served as a splendid and inspiring example to all believers in popular government everywhere, and that this exemplary role was more important than any foreign actions it might undertake, with the limited resources at its command.

True, at the same time that the United States was isolationist, it also expansionist. But there is no necessary contradiction between these two orientations, even though some modern historians are shocked to contemplate their coexistence. Most of the territories that the United States coveted, and all that were acquired, prior to the Civil War, were thinly populated — there was no subjugation of large, alien masses. And the intent of this expansion was always to incorporate such territories into the United States on absolutely equal terms, not to dominate them for any reasons of state. The idea of "manifest destiny" was therefore easily reconcilable to the isolationist idea. This reconciliation became troublesome only when expansion threatened to disturb the regional balance of power within the republic. Thus, the opposition to the Mexican War among some Northerners was intense, because it meant a possible accretion to the power of the "slavocracy." But there would otherwise have been little opposition to westward and southwestern expansion; and, once the war was over, no one thought for a moment of giving these territories back to Mexico or permitting them to evolve into independent national entities.

In the end, of course, "manifest destiny" did write an end to American isolationism, by establishing the material conditions for the emergence of the United States as a great power. But the isolationist idea, or at least crucial aspects of it, survived — not simply as some kind of "cultural lag," but by reason of being so intimately conjoined to "the American way of life," and to the American intellectual creed. This way of life insisted upon the subordination of public policy to private, individual needs and concerns. It had little use for the idea of military glory, which Abraham Lincoln called "that attractive rainbow that rises in showers of blood — that serpent's eye that charms to destroy." It was intensely patriotic, but allergic to all conceptions of national grandeur.

The United States was tempted to a brief fling at European-style imperialism under Presidents McKinley and Theodore Roosevelt, but found the experience disagreeable, and that enterprise was gradually liquidated. When the American democracy entered World War I, it was in no imperial frame of mind. On the contrary, the whole point of the Wilsonian "crusade" was to rid the world of imperial politics. One can almost say that this crusade was a penultimate outburst of the isolationist spirit, in that its goal was a happy, self-determined existence for all the individuals on this earth — *une vie à l'Américaine* — without any further cruel violations of it by international power politics.

The disillusionment consequent upon this crusade prepared the way for the United States to enter history as an imperial power. To be sure, its most immediate effect was to stimulate a purely geographic isolationism that was shot through with streaks of xenophobia. But this attitude simply could not withstand the pressure of events and the insistent demands of world realities. In retrospect, the spectacle of the United States entering World War II has an almost dreamlike, fatalistic quality. There was never, prior to Pearl Harbor, any literal threat to the national security of the United States. And there was no popular enthusiasm, except among a small if influential group of "internationalists," for the United States' accepting responsibility for the maintenance of "world order." It all just seemed inescapable, and the alternative — retiring into a Fortress America — just too unmanly. The dominant mood was resignation, tinged with outrage at the Japanese bombardment of American soil. And resignation — sometimes sullen, sometimes equable — has remained the dominant popular mood ever since.

Strangely enough, this resigned acceptance of great-power responsibilities by the American people has been accompanied by a great unease on the part of the intellectuals. . . . Though this dissatisfaction affects only a minority, it is nevertheless a most serious matter. It is much to be doubted that the United States can continue to play an imperial role without the endorsement of its intellectual class. Or, to put it more precisely: since there is no way the United States, as the world's mightiest power, can avoid such an imperial role, the opposition of its intellectuals means that this role will be played out in a domestic climate of ideological dissent that will enfeeble the resolution of our statesmen and diminish the credibility of their policies abroad.

What is to be done? It is always possible to hope that this intellectual class will come to realize that its traditional ideology needs reformation and revision. It is even possible to argue plausibly that, in the nature of things, this is "historically inevitable." One can go so far as to say that, on intellectual grounds alone, this intellectual class will feel moved to desist from the shrill enunciation of pieties and principles that have little relevance to the particular cases our statesmen now confront, and to help formulate a new set of more specific principles that will relate the ideals which sustain the American democracy to the harsh and nasty imperatives of imperial power. All of this is possible. But one must add that none of these possibilities is likely to be realized in the immediate or even near future.

It is unlikely for two reasons. The first is that the burden of guilt such a process would generate would be so great as to be insupportable. It took three centuries to create the American intellectual as we know him today; he is not going to be recreated in one generation. . . .

Secondly, this crisis of the intellectual class in the face of an imperial destiny coincides with an internal power struggle within the United States itself. Our intellectuals are moving toward a significant "confrontation" with the American "establishment" and will do nothing to strengthen the position of their antagonist. Which is to say that the American intellectual class actually has an interest in thwarting the evolution of any kind of responsible and coherent imperial policy. Just what this interest is, and what this confrontation involves, we are only now beginning to discern. Behind the general fog that the ideology of dissent gen-

erates, the outlines of a very material sociological and political problem are emerging.

V

IT HAS ALWAYS BEEN ASSUMED that as the United States became a more highly organized national society, as its economy became more managerial, its power more imperial and its populace more sophisticated, the intellectuals would move inexorably closer to the seats of authority — would, perhaps, even be incorporated en masse into a kind of "power élite." Many writers and thinkers — and not only on the political left — have viewed this prospect with the greatest unease, for it seemed to them to threaten the continued existence of intellectuals as a critical and moral force in American life.

Well, it has happened here — only, as is so often the case, it is all very different from what one expected. It is true that a small section of the American intellectual class has become a kind of permanent brain trust to the political, the military, the economic authorities. These are the men who commute regularly to Washington, who help draw up programs for reorganizing the bureaucracy, who evaluate proposed weapons systems, who figure out ways to improve our cities and assist our poor, who analyze the course of economic growth, who reckon the cost and effectiveness of foreign aid programs, who dream up new approaches to such old social problems as the mental health of the aged, etc., etc. But what has also happened, at the same time, is that a whole new intellectual class has emerged as a result of the explosive growth, in these past decades, of higher education in the United States. And these "new men," so far from being any kind of élite, are a mass — and have engendered their own mass movement. . . .

Now, this new intellectual class, though to outsiders appearing to be not at all badly off, is full of grievance and resentment. It feels discriminated against — opinion polls reveal that professors, especially in the social sciences and humanities, invariably tend drastically to underestimate the esteem in which public opinion (and, more particularly, the opinion of the business community) holds them. It feels underpaid; you'll not find any credence on the campus for the proposition (demonstrably true) that the salaries of professors do not compare unfavorably with the salaries of bank executives. It feels put upon in all sorts of other familiar ways. The symptoms are only too typical: here is a new class that is "alienated" from the established order because it feels that this order has not conceded to it sufficient power and recognition.

The politics of this new class is novel in that its locus of struggle is the college campus. One is shocked at this — we are used to thinking that politics ought not to intrude on the campus. But we shall no doubt get accustomed to the idea. . . .

Just what direction this movement into politics will follow it is too early to say with certainty. Presumably, it will be toward "the left," since this is the historical orientation of the intellectual class as a whole. . . .

VI

THOUGH THERE IS MUCH fancy rhetoric, pro and con, about "the purpose of American foreign policy," there is really nothing esoteric about this purpose. The United States wishes to establish and sustain a world order that (a) ensures its national security as against the other great powers; (b) encourages other nations, especially the smaller ones, to mold their own social, political and economic institutions along lines that are at least not repugnant to (if not actually congruent with) American values; and (c) minimizes the possibility of naked, armed conflict. This is, of course, also the purpose of the foreign policies of such other great powers as Soviet Russia and Maoist China. Nor could it be otherwise, short of a fit of collective insanity on the part of the governing classes of these powers. Without the conflict, tension, and reconciliation of such imperial purposes there would be no such thing as "foreign affairs" or "world politics," as we ordinarily understand these terms.

But for any imperial policy to work effectively — even if one means by that nothing more than doing the least possible mischief — it needs intellectual and moral guidance. It needs such guidance precisely because, in foreign affairs, one is always forced to compromise one's values. In the United States today, a relative handful of intellectuals proffers such guidance to the policy-maker. But the intellectual community en masse, disaffected from established power even as it tries to establish a power base of its own, feels no such sense of responsibility. It denounces, it mocks, it vilifies — and even if one were to concede that its fierce indignation was justified by extraordinary ineptitude in high places, the fact remains that its activity is singularly unhelpful.

The United States is not going to cease being an imperial power, no matter what happens in Vietnam or elsewhere. It is the world situation — and the history which created this situation — that appoints imperial powers, not anyone's decision or even anyone's overweening ambition. And power begets responsibility — above all, the responsibility to use this power responsibly. The policy-maker in the United States today — and, no doubt, in the other great powers, too — finds this responsibility a terrible burden. The intellectuals, in contrast, are bemused by dreams of power without responsibility, even as they complain of moral responsibility without power. It is not a healthy situation; and, as of this moment, it must be said that one cannot see how, or where, or when it will all end.

90.

RICHARD H. ROVERE: Reflections on Vietnam

The United States at the end of 1967 was a deeply troubled nation. The coming of fall had put an end to the riots of the "long hot summer," but no one was so optimistic as to expect peace in the cities in the summer ahead. The basic problems of the Negro and of the poor in general were still unsolved, and in fact they seemed to become more desperate as time wore on. The young were disaffected, crime was on the upswing, the space program was not going well, and inflation threatened to undermine the dollar, which was also subjected to severe pressures from abroad. But all of these problems paled beside that of Vietnam. There was hardly an individual of high school age or over who was without an opinion on the subject, and there were many who feared that the war, bad as it was, would get worse before it would get better. In these circumstances Washington correspondent Richard H. Rovere wrote a long article for the New Yorker *in which he tried to come to terms both with the realities of Vietnam and his own deeply held beliefs about his country and its political and moral role in the world. The article is reprinted here in part.*

Source: *New Yorker*, October 28, 1967. Reprinted by permission; © 1967 The New Yorker Magazine, Inc.

This is not 1948; LBJ is not Harry Truman; and Vietnam is not Korea. — *From an editorial in the* New Republic, *September 30, 1967.*

SO SAY THE LIBERAL DOVES — or at least some among them who were adult and articulate in 1948 and 1950 and who must. somehow square past and present. . . .

It is always easier to deny than to establish the validity of any given historical analogy. If history really repeated itself, its study would be at once boring and terrifying. But analogy can have a limited validity and can, like metaphor, yield and enrich insights. Moreover, where a denial is so flat and emphatic, it is advisable to take a close, hard look. Why should anyone insist that "this is not 1948"? People are capable of keeping track of the years without assistance. . . .

There is, as it happens, one quite striking way in which presidential politics today very much resembles the presidential politics of 1948. Then, as now, many liberal Democrats wished very much to be rid of a liberal Democratic President. . . . True, the motives of the 1948 liberals were quite different from those that spur today's liberals into disowning Johnson and contemplating support for a conservative Republican, provided he is less of a hawk than the President. The dump-Truman people did not hate the then President, they merely scorned him and feared that the Democratic Party could not win with him; what the dump-Johnson people fear is precisely the opposite — a Democratic victory that would keep the despised incumbent in office. . . .

"LBJ is not Harry Truman." In many ways, the two men are as different as John F. Kennedy and William Howard Taft. Johnson is a consummate politician; Truman was only a persevering one. Truman was as artless as Johnson is artful. Truman was generally candid, and Johnson seems a compulsive dissembler. . . . Still, Johnson in late 1967 has more in common with Truman in 1948 than the hostility of some of the same liberals. Both were once Democratic senators and vice-presidents. Each took office upon the death of a beloved predecessor. Johnson, like Truman, has never been a child of the Establishment. From the Eastern liberals' point of view, both came from the wrong, or South, side of the tracks. Both had meager, or at least unfashionable, schooling. Both have rather coarse manners and offend by indelicacy of speech. (Liberals, I have no doubt, consider themselves large-minded people, concerned with principles, not personalities. Some are large-minded, others not. If Kennedy had lived, he might at some point have called a halt to the escalation he began. He might even have found a way to get us out of Vietnam altogether. If he had lived and, as seems to me entirely possible, found no better solution than Johnson's, then, of course, he would have faced today much the kind of opposition that Johnson faces. But I cannot help believing that it would have been somewhat less widespread and more restrained against a commander in chief who was a Harvard man with uncommon wit, intellectual poise, a passion for excellence, and gallantry of manner. Kennedy just might have managed to run a slightly more tasteful and elegant war.) But the relevant thing is that Johnson is, as Truman was, a liberal Democratic President of the United States in serious trouble on almost every front. . . .

"Vietnam is not Korea." They are 2,000 miles apart and considerably different in climate, terrain, and demography. Both, however, are relatively small and underdeveloped Asian countries partitioned into a Communist North and a non-Communist South by international agreements in the making of which they had no voice. Both abut China, both are peninsular, and both have long histories of colonial occupation and oppression. Each has been the site of large-scale warfare, with the United States in each case intervening to assist the anti-Communist government of the Southern region, and with China assisting — on a very large scale in Korea and on what is still a small scale in Vietnam — the Communist regime in the North. There are other parallels and, of course, many divergencies. Of the latter, all but one — the very different relationships of Korea in 1950 and Vietnam today to Soviet and Chinese power — seem to me to bear only tangentially on the soundness of our present policy and the consistency of liberal thinking. In any consideration of these matters, we must, I think, begin with the incontrovertible fact that the two countries are on the same continent. In both cases, United States policy toward Asia has been at issue. . . .

Do we, as a people, have any morally or politically legitimate concern with the political order in Asia? If we say no — or say perhaps, but not to the point of using force — then we simply have to ask ourselves what on earth we were doing in Korea seventeen years ago, and even what we were fighting the Japanese about twenty-five years ago. (It will not do to say that they attacked us at Pearl Harbor. That would not have happened if our foreign policy had not seemed a threat to theirs.) For, beyond all the talk about Fascism and imperialism and Communism and democracy and self-determination, the basic reality is that, for bad reasons or good, the United States has increasingly, through most of this century, been throwing its weight around in Asia to create or maintain a political order that several American governments have decided is best for the United States and possibly best for Asia.

I happen to think we would all be far better off if this decision had never been taken by anyone, but it was taken — and not by Lyndon Johnson in late 1963 or early 1964. The balance of power — that is what our three Asian wars have been about, and we might as well state the rest of this proposition, which is that this is what all foreign policy is and almost always has been about. If we ask ourselves why we shouldn't leave the balance of power in Asia to the Asians, we might as well reopen the question of whether we have, or ever had, any business messing about with the balance of power in Europe or anywhere else in the world or the cosmos. I can think of several quite compelling arguments for having different European and Asian policies, but I cannot see how the war in Vietnam can be regarded as some new and lamentable departure from established policy. Rather, it appears to me an application of established policy that has miscarried so dreadfully that we must begin examining not just the case at hand but the whole works. If this is where our foreign policy lands us, then we had better settle among ourselves whether the policy is, or ever was, any good, and even whether we ought to have any foreign policy at all.

For most liberals, the real clincher is that, as they see it now, in Korea we opposed an act of clear and premeditated aggression carried out by an army crossing an international boundary and seeking to annex by force the territory on the other side, whereas in Vietnam we are interfering in what is essentially a civil war, with the forces we oppose consisting of indigenous rebels. There is something in this, but, in my view, very little, and nothing, certainly, to destroy the strength of the analogy. In Korea, it was plainly a matter of troops from the North marching into the South. The people in the Southern war zones seemed to feel very little sympathy for the invaders, whereas in Vietnam the Vietcong guerrillas and, possibly to a lesser extent, the regulars from the North have a good deal of support. But this hardly demonstrates that one is a civil war and the other was not. Koreans fought Koreans in Korea, as Vietnamese are fighting Vietnamese in Vietnam. In each case, the issue was control of the Southern terri-

tory and unification of the country. In each case, the contested area has been part of the homeland of people with a more or less common history. . . .

If the war in Vietnam is in some sense "imperialist," as so many Americans have come to believe, so was the war in Korea. In any event, the ultimate soundness of a policy is not to be determined by who supports it and who does not. This is particularly the case when, as in the UN, the count is of nation states. The fact that a majority of General Assembly members has regularly opposed the admission of mainland China does not lend any moral or political force to the wisdom of mainland China's exclusion. The fact that the Organization of American States voted overwhelming support, *ex post facto*, of the American intervention in the Dominican Republic in 1965 has never been regarded as an acceptable sanction for the dispatch of troops.

In Korea, as in Vietnam, our intervention was undertaken on the President's initiative. War was never declared by Congress. Truman lacked even as questionable a mandate as the one that Congress gave Johnson in the 1964 Gulf of Tonkin Resolution. Dean Rusk can lecture congressmen today about our obligations under the SEATO treaty, but the treaty had not even been thought of in Dean Acheson's day. Yet I pick up an antiwar manifesto signed by many people who to my certain knowledge favored the Korean intervention and find them saying that because "Congress has not declared a war, as required by the Constitution," the war in Vietnam is "unconstitutional and illegal." For my part, I would be happy if the Supreme Court ruled the war unconstitutional next Monday morning. But I cannot imagine a theory of the war or of the Constitution that would hold our presence in Vietnam to be in violation of our fundamental law and would not require the same judgment on our earlier presence in Korea.

Nor can I see that it would make much difference if Congress did declare the existence of a state of war or if the Supreme Court certified the carnage as constitutional. Can any legislature turn an unjust cause into a just one by an observance of due process? Slavery was "constitutional" until it was smashed in a war of dubious constitutionality.

The signers of this antiwar manifesto were brought together by, they say, a common desire to assist young men in avoiding conscription. A worthy purpose it may well be, but the draft is legal; the Selective Service Act has been in force for twenty-seven years, and the Supreme Court has yet to strike it down. Such sticklers for law might consider turning themselves in for sedition and conspiracy. I find the names of some of them also attached to an appeal calling upon other citizens to join them and Henry David Thoreau — part of whose *Civil Disobedience* is used as the manifesto for this particular group — in withholding from the Internal Revenue Service that part of their taxes which, by their calculations, "is being used to finance the war." The income-tax laws are at least as legal and constitutional as Selective Service. Thoreau didn't want to help pay for the Mexican War, which may have been, as he passionately believed it was, immoral, but it was certainly not illegal or unconstitutional. Anyway, a "legal" war is a legal fiction.

The rhetoric of politics is always opportunistic. But war, which debases all discourse, makes it worse. The opportunism of the doves is no more to be censured than that of anyone else. If I could stop the war by talking, I would not mind talking nonsense or telling a few lies. I have brought up the whole question of the Korea-Vietnam analogy because I think it is important for all of us to see that there have been some profound changes in *us* as well as in the world in the last two decades.

To begin with, I think, the mere passage of time has had its effect. In 1950, with a great war only five years behind us, we had, as a people, the zeal and energy of crusad-

ers. There was then little dissent — and, compared with today, little cause for dissent — from the proposition that militarized Communism threatened the peace and stability of the world and that it was up to us, newly emerged as a superpower, to turn back its sorties with whatever force was called for. We did so, and I have no doubt that if the circumstances that had obtained in the late forties or early fifties were to obtain at present in Vietnam, most of today's doves would support our role in Vietnam with at least as much vigor as they supported our role in Korea.

But the *New Republic* is in a way profoundly right in insisting that things aren't the same. Much has happened in the Communist world that requires us to rethink our positions, but even if this were not so we could not look upon Vietnam today as we once looked upon Korea. Our crusading zeal has ebbed; affluence, much of it spent on education, has been accompanied by a heightened sophistication about the world and its affairs, a spreading skepticism and disenchantment, and, in the middle class, a new and rather strange hedonism that particularly and peculiarly affects the young. We are not, I think, a more attractive people than we were — rather, the contrary — but we are in many ways less self-righteous. Both the best and the worst spirits among us are turning inward more than they were before, given more to seeking individual grace and salvation — the consequences being, on the one hand, an admirable willingness to work and sacrifice on behalf of the disadvantaged and, on the other hand, a less admirable self-indulgence that increases the demand for everything from drugs to yachts and sports cars, from unrestricted sexual license to the right to behave as obnoxiously and irresponsibly as one's underdeveloped conscience may dictate. . . .

As a nation among nations, as a force in the world, we may be behaving more chauvinistically today than we have ever behaved in the past. This almost has to be true, because our power is so immense that any ugly display of it makes an impression commensurate with its magnitude. But among us, as a people, chauvinism and jingoism have been declining steadily since the First World War. Although Hitler's Germany was more detestable than Kaiser Wilhelm's, there was less Hun-hating in the Second World War than in the First. What was "liberty cabbage" in 1918 was sauerkraut in 1945. There was not much flag-waving in the Second World War, and still less in the Korean War. But now we seem to have made a really radical break with the past. This is the first war of the century of which it is true that opposition to it is not only widespread but fashionable. It is the first in connection with which it seems in downright bad taste to invoke patriotism. . . . Those who support the war, like those who oppose it, appeal not to the patriotic heart but to the bleeding one. This is without precedent. . . .

All wars are brutalizing, and perhaps in the random violence of the past few years (not merely the riots — not even so much the riots as the murders and assassinations) we are paying part of the price for sanctioned murder in the name of anti-Communism, self-determination, and democracy. But what seems already clear — from the size of the antiwar movements, from the muting of the eagles, from the outrage over atrocities and civilian losses — is that there is building up in this country a powerful sentiment not simply against the war in Vietnam but against war itself, not simply against bombing in Vietnam but against bombing anywhere at any time for any reason, not simply against the slaughter of innocents in an unjust conflict but also against the slaughter of those who may be far from innocent in a just conflict. The youthful protesters would probably acknowledge this without hesitation, only asking themselves why anyone should labor the point so heavily. (Some would no doubt go further, and

say that they oppose not only the wars this government runs but everything else it does.) Their elders, thinking of a past they find it necessary to be true to, cannot turn pacifist overnight. They must distinguish between this war and the wars they have supported in the past — up to and including the war in the Middle East a few months ago. But in fact our present war is different mainly in that it seems endless and hopeless.

Is it possible for us to come through this experience, if we come through at all, as a pacifist nation? I suppose not. "Pacifist nation" seems a contradiction in terms. If all of us, or most of us, were pacifists, we would have little reason to be a nation. Defense is the fundamental *raison d'être* for the modern state. And if a pacifist nation didn't come apart at the seams, some nonpacifist nation would tear it apart. It seems to me, though, that if the war goes on and if opposition to it continues to increase at the present rate, there will in time be a testing of this whole proposition. No government that is not totalitarian can go on indefinitely fighting a hard war that its people hate. Something has to give. Either the government yields to the popular will or it becomes oppressive and stifles the protest by terror. . . .

I want American democracy to survive. It is in many ways a fraud. It is not keeping its promises to the American Negroes. It has abused them and many other people. It has very little aesthetic or intellectual appeal. But under it there is at least a hope of redemption. Things do get done here that don't get done under other systems. But it now seems clear to me that if American democracy does survive it will be something quite different from what we have known. I find it hard at this stage to see how a victory for democracy will not also be a victory for pacifism. Those who will lead the struggle are, whether they acknowledge it or not, renouncing war as an instrument of policy. They may insist that of course they would fight the enemy at the gates, or perhaps take arms against a new Hitler if one should arise.

But the wars of the future — at least, those that would have any ideological content — are not going to be like the wars of the past. India and Pakistan or India and China may fight over bits and pieces of territory, but the Soviet Union and the United States are agreed on the need for common efforts to cool it when such disputes get hot. Most future wars are apt to be like the war in Vietnam — wars that will be called by their instigators "wars of national liberation." The Soviet Union, as Nikita Khrushchev long ago informed us, will support them. From its point of view, they are irresistible. They cost next to nothing and drive us Americans out of our minds. But if we survive as anything like a free society, we will not be entering them.

I simply cannot imagine this country, under any President chosen in a free election, taking on another Vietnam. If this is so, it may be good news. But it means that we won't have much in the way of a foreign policy. We will draw back from all difficult situations. We will leave the field to those who have not renounced war. . . .

We have sinned greatly and frequently since 1954, but not always in the ways that we think we have. We did not go into Vietnam hoping for a war; after all, we had just passed up a splendid opportunity to join the fighting with our then friends the French at our side. But we were not taken altogether by surprise at discovering that nothing really had been settled by Geneva. Two-fifths of our aid in the early days was military, but something beyond this figure persuades me that we were after something a bit more decent than the opening of a new firing range.

The non-Communist state that came into being as a consequence of the Geneva Conference looked to our foreign-aid people as if it might actually work, as if it might turn out to be a nice, prosperous, well-behaved little democracy. In the bright light of hindsight, this seems a ridiculous dream. And what may have been ridiculous about it was not that people like the Emperor Bao Dai and Ngo Dinh Diem would never let it happen but, rather, that Ho Chi Minh would never let it happen. We are always being told what awful people we have supported in Saigon while all along there has existed the alternative of supporting the Vietnamese Thomas Jefferson, Ho Chi Minh, and having him on our side. Ho sounds a lot more attractive than most of the types we have lately been dealing with, and it might have been very smart of us back before 1950, say, to try to strike up some sort of deal with him. And Ho could not have been much interested in us in the early fifties (and anyway think of what McCarthy would have said), and Diem then did not have, or was concealing, his cloven hoof.

Diem never seemed a Thomas Jefferson, or even a Lyndon Johnson, but he looked no worse than our man in Korea, Syngman Rhee. And one can at least advance the hypothesis that our troubles have grown not out of Diem's "failure" and ours to create a good society in South Vietnam but out of a certain amount of early success, or, if not that, out of Ho's fear that we might somehow succeed someday. It could also be that he was not unmindful of the possibilities for looting. The Americans had put a good many desirable things — including a lot of expensive and well-made weaponry — in South Vietnam, and if he could knock over the government without too much difficulty they would all be his.

Senator Fulbright has been saying for years that foreign aid is dangerous, because it can lead to war. I think he is right. We invest money and, more important, hope in a country, and when some thugs threaten to wreck the country and dash its hopes and ours we are tempted to police the place. Some of the most promising governments in Africa are likely to go to pieces because

Suspended here in Asia...
We think back
with chagrin...

How difficult
the getting out...
How easy getting in...

Courtesy, Hugh Haynie, "Los Angeles Times" Syndicate

Cartoon by Hugh Haynie in "The Courier-Journal," Louisville, Ky., 1968

the leaders of less hopeful neighboring states either can't stand the thought that the people across the way are going to make it or feel that neighbors ought to share and share alike.

In the late fifties and early sixties, many Americans who had no appetite for war and no thought that there would be one urged that we give Saigon enough military assistance to put down the Vietcong and enable the government at least to stand on its feet and have enough time and energy to make something of itself. They should have known better. But there was no reason then to think of the difficulties with the Vietcong as having much to do with the balance of power in Asia. Indeed — and here, perhaps, is another important difference between this war and Korea — it seems to have been *our* intervention on a large scale that gave the war a real balance-of-power meaning.

In the early sixties, when Laos was a more troublesome place than Vietnam, the Russians were looking the other way. In that period, too, the "domino theory" was generally discredited. There may then have been a chance for a President to reappraise — agonizingly, of course — the whole affair and order a phase-out. Vietnam was still an obscure place, and with us no longer involved it would have been still more obscure. I speak of a time when Kennedy was alive. He could probably have de-escalated, but instead he escalated. If he had lived, and if he had beaten Goldwater or some other Republican in 1964, he might have altered his strategy at some later point. But he died, and Johnson pursued his policy with a vengeance, thereby, in my view, giving the domino theory a strange validity it had earlier lacked: *The dominoes might fall in a certain way because we set them up that way.*

If we had got out of Vietnam five years ago, the balance of power in Asia might have been affected only insignificantly and imperceptibly. If we got out tomorrow, the consequences might be very serious indeed. We have painted ourselves in.

Until early in 1965, I felt that our role in Vietnam was defensible. The rulers of the country seemed an untrustworthy lot, but that did not appear a good reason for turning the place over to the Vietcong. Knowing that a developing nation cannot possibly manage war and reform at the same time without assistance, I felt that our assistance in putting down an insurgency was helpful. The fact that the insurgents were natives did not bother me; so were their antagonists, and I have never believed that civil wars are somehow more virtuous and rational than wars of any other kind.

From my point of view, the operations of the Vietcong were, and still are, every bit as irrational as I now believe ours are. They don't seem to mind destroying their country any more than we do. I can understand why some Americans should be indifferent to the fate of Vietnam — to a certain degree, and to my own dismay, I am coming to feel that way myself — but I cannot understand why any Vietnamese should be indifferent to it. I wish Johnson would swallow his pride, whatever the consequences, but it seems to me it is positively idiotic for Ho Chi Minh not to take Johnson and Rusk at their word and, if what they are saying is all a bluff, call it. Why not set a place and a date, and see whether Rusk shows up?

Everybody knows that unless American forces stay in Vietnam for the rest of history the Vietcong are going to have their triumphs anyway; if they negotiated us out of there tomorrow on any terms at all, the country would be theirs before long. (Tran Van Dinh, a former South Vietnamese diplomat, at odds with the Saigon regime, has speculated that this very knowledge may be a reason for Ho's not negotiating. Our departure would create a vacuum that would for a time be filled by the Vietcong but would ultimately be vulnerable to Chinese pressure. Tran Van Dinh believes that one of the last things Ho really wants is a complete American pullout.) If the Vietcong can remain as strong as they seem to be with all the Americans chasing them around the country, they should have no trouble at all seizing power after they sat down and told us enough lies about the future to make it impossible for us not to agree to get out.

The American people love to be lied to at peace conferences, and if that happened in this instance the guerrilla could put away his shooting irons, turn respectable, run for office, and run the country. General Ky could get a job with Pan American World Airways or just loll about on the Riviera, where he would be an authentic part of the scene and would find a lot of his old friends as well as many new ones.

Nothing so agreeable is going to happen. It is up to us to make the first move. Until recently, I felt that the best first move would be a relatively small one — small but visible: not necessarily putting an end to the bombing but announcing a plan for scaling it down. I know Air Force officers

who wouldn't object to this. Why, it may be asked, should they, since the targets are mostly gone anyway? But many other Air Force people would not object to something of the sort being done for political reasons even if they had strategic reservations. I did not think such a move would be of the least help in "bringing Hanoi to the conference table," but I thought that almost any de-escalation would put an end to our scaring everyone else about our intentions, particularly toward the Chinese, and would help prepare us for the inevitable. In time, Johnson or some other President may begin a phased withdrawal in that way.

But I now fear that it will soon be too late — by which I mean too late to undo the damage to us. And it is we ourselves in this moment of history that we must think of before we think of anyone or anything else. This is a terrible thing to feel compelled to say. Edwin Reischauer, in his *Beyond Vietnam: The United States and Asia*, argues that of the three options he thinks we have — escalation and a likely war with China, complete withdrawal as soon as possible, and plodding along on our present bloody and repugnant course — the last is the least disastrous and hence the most acceptable.

Reischauer, who was until recently our Ambassador in Japan, is a fine scholar and humanist who has great respect and affection for the people of Asia, among whom he lived and studied for many years before John F. Kennedy persuaded him to leave scholarship for diplomacy. He is no hawk, no imperialist, no warrior of any kind. He thinks we were crazy ever to get into this and crazy to have let it reach this point. But what he fears most of all is that if we abandon this undertaking now, we will tell ourselves that Asia is impossible, that we should never again have anything to do with it, and will abandon not only Vietnam but all of Asia, with the likely exception of Japan.

I share his fear. We might treat Asia as

we treated Europe after 1918. We must ask ourselves right now whether that wouldn't be a pretty good idea. From some points of view, it might be an excellent idea. If our foreign policy in Asia produces such a monstrosity as the Vietnam war, why not get out? But, as Reischauer sees it, and as I would like to see it, our foreign policy in Asia is more than just the war in Vietnam. Most of Asia needs our help desperately, and we can perhaps use a good deal of Asian help in growing up. I want to go on having an American presence in Asia, because I don't want people to starve to death if we can prevent it, and I don't want Asians to despise my children and grandchildren and plot to destroy them.

Anyway, the thing wouldn't work. In recent years, a good many people have urged the dismantling of NATO, on the ground that it is no longer needed and that what is sometimes called "the European system" can work on its own. Whenever such proposals were brought to the attention of George Ball, the former undersecretary of state and a dedicated Europeanist, he would ask their sponsors if they remembered what had happened to "the European system" in 1914 and in 1939. Things may have changed in Europe lately, but there has never been anything anyone could call "the Asian system," capable of settling what diplomats call "regional" problems — usually meaning wars. Even if China managed to contain itself, which doesn't seem very likely, there would still be a good deal of unpleasantness between India and Pakistan. Making their own nuclear weapons might seem more important to them than it does now. And there would be unpleasantness elsewhere in Southeast Asia. And who knows whether some of Japan's long-range planners might not start casting a speculative eye on the "power vacuums" we would be creating?

Until very recently, these considerations put me in substantial agreement with Reischauer that perhaps Johnson's way offers fewer dangers than any of the others. But now I think we have reached — or are just about to reach — a point at which the argument no longer holds water. For one thing, if we continue much longer we may pull out of Asia whether we win, lose, or draw in Vietnam. It happens to be the view of our people that they don't want their kids to be killed so that Asians can go on eating. Most of them would see no logic in saying there is a necessary connection between starvation in India and Americans getting shot in Vietnam, but even if the logic were self-evident they would reject it. Beyond all that, however, we seem as incapable as the South Vietnamese of running a war — or, at any rate, *this* war — and doing anything worthwhile at the same time. Congress insists on cutting our decent programs elsewhere in the world — to say nothing of those in this country — almost to the point of absurdity. In a literal sense, it is finding a way to make the wretched of the earth foot the bill for Vietnam. This isn't its intention, and as a nation we are still more generous than most, yet not only are innocent people dying in Vietnam but, because of the dollars-and-cents cost of the war, they are dying in Africa.

The war in Vietnam is heading too many of us for the loony bin. People who could once talk sensibly about politics are becoming unhinged and disoriented by it. Some are really thinking seriously of running Ronald Reagan for President. A young man who used to be a provocative analyst now screwily and oracularly proclaims that "morality, like politics, starts at the barrel of a gun." This is printed in a local high-brow journal, and it takes a professor from California to remind this well-educated ex-humanist, now evidently en route to some kind of New Left Fascism, that politics *ends* at the barrel of a gun.

Not long ago, a highly intelligent and attractive young Negro spokesman for a radical organization said that he couldn't see any reason anyone should write a book about poverty — he was talking of Michael Harrington's *The Other America* — because anyone who was really poor and had lived in a ghetto knew all there was to know about it anyway. He said he himself could tell it like it is, but thought a book about it was a waste of anyone's time.

The land is filling up with cranks and zanies — some well intentioned, some vicious. It can be contended that Vietnam is not the only cause of goofing off, of alienation. Of course it isn't. But it provides the occasion, and it heightens the degree. And so it seems to me that if we stay on in Vietnam we will render ourselves incapable of being of much help to Asians or anyone else. We will need all the help we can get ourselves. If Ronald Reagan became President, I'd say by all means let's not have a foreign policy.

I want us to get out and then try to recover our sanity, so that we may face the consequences. Some of them cause me almost no concern. The spread of Communism bothers me very little. It may be bad in some places and not so bad in others, but we can live with it just about anywhere — even ninety miles from Key West. Once, it was, or seemed to be, a world movement, and it was surely a brutally expansionist one. But its adventures in expansionism blunted its threat as a world movement.

By 1948, when Tito broke with Stalin, it should have been clear that ideology was no match for nationalism — at least in Europe. When China broke with Russia, it was obvious that the same thing went for Asia. Perhaps if we had borne in mind the history of earlier religious movements we could have seen all this fifty years ago. But we didn't see it, and neither, of course, did they. At any rate, we now know that the mere circumstance that a piece of real estate falls under Communist control doesn't constitute a threat to our existence, and doesn't even mean there is no more hope for the people involved.

Nor, with things as they are, can my first concern be with the indisputable fact that by pulling out we would be breaking our pledge not only to the Vietnamese but to the Thais and others to whom what would follow might be quite painful. We are going to get out sooner or later anyway, and when we do we will not go back in, so, no matter what happens in the near future, they are going to have to work out their relations with China without much support from us.

But some of the consequences of withdrawal disturb me greatly. By and large, I think that most of American foreign policy for the last thirty years has been admirable. I want us to continue to be part of the world and to use our considerable talents for the benefit of all mankind. I suspect that if we get out of Vietnam we won't have much left in the way of a foreign policy. And, most of all, I fear what will happen right here if we withdraw. Theodore C. Sorensen writes that since Khrushchev could admit a mistake in the missile crisis five years ago, and Kennedy could acknowledge one at the Bay of Pigs a year before that, Lyndon Johnson ought to be able to do the same thing now. Here are two analogies that do not work at all. The missile crisis was over in a few days, the Bay of Pigs in a few hours. No Russian soldiers died in the missile crisis, no American ones at the Bay of Pigs. It would take greater magnanimity and a greater dedication to the truth than we have any right to expect of any politician on earth for Lyndon Johnson to say that this whole bloody business is a mistake, and was from the start. He just cannot and will not do it. If he did, he would throw this country into worse turmoil than it has known at any time since the Civil War.

Could he pull out and either say nothing or tell some lies? Could he possibly use Senator Aiken's ploy and announce that we had achieved our ends in Vietnam and were withdrawing? Perhaps, but there would still be turmoil. There will be turmoil whether we stay or go, and I dread it. But, between the two, I have less fear of the consequences of withdrawal than of those of perseverance.

This war is intolerable. What does it mean to say that? Not much — talk is cheap. I haven't a clue as to how we can get out, and I have never much liked the idea of proposing without knowing of a means of disposing. I don't think we can write our way out, and I doubt very much if we can demonstrate our way out. But out is where I want us to be, and I don't know what a man can do except say what he thinks and feels.

91.

Robert McAfee Brown: The Draft and Civil Disobedience

In the fall of 1967 groups of clergymen, of academics, of parents, and of concerned citizens took the decisive step of stating that they were willing to collaborate with young men who refused to be drafted on grounds of conscience, even if it meant going to jail. Robert McAfee Brown, a professor of religion at Stanford University, gave reasons for his own civil disobedience in an article published in Look, *part of which is reprinted here. The editor's note reprinted below appeared with the article as originally published.*

Source: *Look,* October 31, 1967: "Because of Vietnam . . . 'In Conscience I Must Break the Law.' " By permission of the editors of *Look* Magazine, Copyright © 1967, Cowles Communications, Inc.

Editor's Note: Each escalation of the war in Vietnam has set off an escalation in the protest against it. Because arguments for and against the U.S. role are increasingly concerned with the moral issue, religious leaders in all denominations have been in the forefront of movements demanding an end to the bombings and an unconditional offer to negotiate. Prominent among these is Robert McAfee Brown, professor of religion at Stanford University, who was ordained to the Presbyterian ministry in 1944, earned his divinity degree at Union Theological Seminary and his doctorate at Columbia University. Later, he served as a chaplain at Amherst College. In 1962, the late Pope John XXIII invited Dr. Brown to be a Protestant observer at the Vatican Council in Rome. A few months ago, he called on the Catholic bishops of the U.S. to show their support for Pope Paul VI's cease-fire pleas by in-volving themselves more directly in protests against the war. Dr. Brown's disillusionment with those protests has led him to the stand for civil disobedience he takes in this article. The editors, recognizing the depth of passion aroused by Vietnam, present this statement by a responsible American who feels driven to what he knows are extreme measures.

"VIETNAM? I've got other things to worry about." There was a time when it was easy for me to say that. I was worried about the California battle over Proposition 14, in which the real estate interests were trying to palm off on the California voters legislation designed to discriminate against minority groups, a measure later declared unconstitutional by the United States Supreme Court. I was worried about the plight of the migrant workers in the San

Joaquin Valley, who were striking for the right to bargain collectively. I was also, if truth be told, worried about other things as well: getting tomorrow's lecture finished, scrounging up the extra dollars I was going to need when state-income-tax time rolled around, finding time to get acquainted with my kids, recouping some of the losses on the writing project on which I was currently so far behind.

In this, I was like many millions of Americans. In addition, also like many millions of Americans, I was probably afraid to face the issue of Vietnam, afraid that if I learned enough about it, I would have to join those radical, far-out types who two or three years ago were saying in such lonely fashion what many middle-class people are saying now: that our policy in Vietnam is wrong, that it is callous and brutalizing to those who must implement it, that it cannot be supported by thinking or humane people and that if one comes to feel this way, he has to engage in the uncomfortable and annoying and possibly threatening posture of putting his body where his words are.

In the interval since I discovered that I couldn't duck Vietnam any longer, I have tried to do my homework, read some history, examine the Administration's position, listen to its critics and come to a stand of my own. I've come to a stand, all right. And I only regret, not just for the sake of my own conscience, but for the sake of the thousands of Americans and the hundreds of thousands of Asians who have died in Vietnam, that I did not come to it with much greater speed. For I have now gone the full route — from unconcern

to curiosity
to study
to mild concern
to deep concern
to signing statements
to genteel protest
to marching
to moral outrage

to increasingly vigorous protest
to . . . civil disobedience.

The last step, of course, is the crucial one, the one where I part company with most of my friends in the liberal groups where I politic, with most of my friends in the academic community where I work and with most of my friends in the church where I worship. And since I am a reasonable man, not given to emotive decisions, one who by no stretch of the imagination could be called far-out, one who is not active in the New Left, one who still shaves and wears a necktie — a typical Establishment-type middle-class American WASP — I feel it important to record why it is that such a person as myself finds it impossible to stop merely at the level of vigorous protest of our policy in Vietnam and feels compelled to step over the line into civil disobedience.

My basic reason is also my most judgmental: I have utterly lost confidence in the Johnson Administration. Those who do not share that premise may shrink from the consequences I draw from it. All I can say by way of reply is that I tried for many months to work from the presupposition that the Administration was genuinely seeking peace and that it was trying to conduct foreign policy in honorable terms. But the record now makes patently clear to me that our Government is not willing to negotiate seriously save on terms overwhelmingly favorable to it and that it has refused to respond to many feelers that have come from the other side. I can no longer trust the spokesmen for the Administration when they engage in their customary platitudes about a desire to negotiate. What they do belies what they say, and at the moment they express willingness to talk with Hanoi, they engage in further frantic acts of escalation that bring us closer to the brink of World War III and a nuclear holocaust. I do not believe that they are any longer reachable in terms of modifying their senseless policy of systematically destroying a small nation of dark-skinned people so that American prestige can emerge unscathed. All of us who have written, spoken, marched, petitioned, reasoned and organized must surely see that in the moments when Mr. Johnson is not calling us unpatriotic, he is simply ignoring a mounting chorus of moral horror with benign disdain and proceeding day by day, week by week, month by month, to escalate the war far past the point of no return.

This means that if one believes that what we are doing in Southeast Asia is immoral, he has no effective way of seeking to change such a policy, for the policy, in the face of two or three years of increasing criticism, is only becoming more hard-nosed, more irrational, more insane. The procedures through which change can normally be brought about in a democracy are increasingly futile. Mr. Johnson emasculated Congress in August 1964 with the Gulf of Tonkin agreement, which he now uses to justify air war over China. Public protests are written off as examples of lack of patriotism or lack of fidelity to the Americans now in Vietnam or even, by members of the House Armed Services Committee, as treasonable. With each act of military escalation, the moral horror of the war is escalated. We have been killing women and children all along; now, we kill more of them. We have been destroying the villages of civilians all along; now, we destroy more of them. We have been breaking almost every one of the rules that civilized men have agreed constitute the minimal standards of decency men must maintain even in the indecency of war; now, we break them more often.

This escalation of military power demands the escalation of moral protest. Those of us who condemn this war, who are repulsed by it and who realize that history is going to judge our nation very harshly for its part in it, must see more and more clearly that it is not enough any longer to sign another advertisement or send an-

other telegram or give another speech — or write another article. The ways of genteel, legal protest have shown themselves to be ineffective. During the time of their impact, escalation has not lessened, it has increased. . . .

In the face of such conclusions, one is counseled, "Work for '68. Wait for '68." I will, of course, work for '68, just as, inevitably, being a child of time, I must wait for it. But I am no longer content to throw all my energies in that direction. . . .

In the face of such facts, an informed conscience does not have the luxury of waiting 12 months to see what the political machinery may or may not produce. Therefore, I find myself forced, by the exclusion of alternatives as well as by an increasing sense of moral imperative, to escalate my own protest to the level of civil disobedience. The war is so wrong, and ways of registering concern about it have become so limited, that civil disobedience seems to me the only honorable route left.

I make this judgment, foreseeing two possible consequences.

First, there is always the remote possibility (on which it is not wise to count too heavily) that civil disobedience might make a significant enough impact on the nation as a whole that the policy makers could not any longer ignore the voice and act of protest. If engaged in by significant enough numbers of people (and significant enough people), it could conceivably shock the nation and the world into a recognition that our actions in Vietnam are so intolerable that a drastic shift in our policy could no longer be avoided. There is the further remote possibility that others, not yet ready to escalate their protest to civil disobedience, might at least escalate somewhere in the spectrum and thus produce a total yield noticeably higher than in the past.

I would like to believe that such things might happen. I see little likelihood that they will. Why, then, protest by breaking the law, if such protest is not going to do any discernible good? Because there comes a time when the issues are so clear and so crucial that a man does not have the choice of waiting until all the possible consequences can be charted. There comes a time when a man must simply say, "Here I stand, I can do no other, God help me." There comes a time when it is important for the future of a nation that it be recorded that in an era of great folly, there were at least some within that nation who recognized the folly for what it was and were willing, at personal cost, to stand against it. There comes a time when, in the words of Father Pius-Raymond Régamey, one has to oppose evil even if one cannot prevent it, when one has to choose to be a victim rather than an accomplice. There comes a time when thinking people must give some indication for their children and their children's children that the national conscience was not totally numbed by Washington rhetoric into supporting a policy that is evil, vicious, and morally intolerable.

If such language sounds harsh and judgmental, it is meant precisely to be such. The time is past for gentility, pretty speeches and coy evasions of blunt truths. Evil deeds must be called evil. Deliberate killing of civilians — by the tens of thousands — must be called murder. Forcible removal of people from their homes must be called inhumane and brutal. A country that permits such things to be done in its name deserves to be condemned, not only by the decent people of other countries but particularly by the decent people who are its citizens, who will call things what they are and who recognize finally and irrevocably that the most evil deed of all is not to do bestial things but to do bestial things and call them humane.

In light of this, I no longer have any choice but to defy those laws of our land that produce such rotten fruits. I believe with Martin Luther King that such civil disobedience as I engage in must be done nonviolently, and that it must be done with a willingness to pay the penalties that society may impose upon me. I recognize the majesty of Law and its impregnable quality as a bulwark of a free society, and it is in the name of Law that I must defy given laws that are an offense against morality, making this witness wherever need be — in the churches, on the streets, in the assembly halls, in the courts, in jails.

Each person who takes this route must find the level at which his own conscience comes into conflict with laws relating to American presence in Vietnam, and the cardinal rule for those engaging in civil disobedience must be a respect for the consciences of those who choose a different point along the spectrum at which to make their witness; words like "chicken" or "rash" must have no place in their lexicon. Some will refuse to pay that portion of their Federal income tax directly supporting the war. Others will engage in "unlawful assembly" in front of induction centers. For myself, it is clear what civil disobedience will involve. I teach. I spend my professional life with American youth of draft age. And while I will not use the classroom for such purposes, I will make clear that from now on my concerns about Vietnam will be explicitly focused on counseling, aiding and abetting all students who declare that out of moral conviction they will not fight in Vietnam. I will "counsel, aid and abet" such students to find whatever level of moral protest is consonant with their consciences, and when for them this means refusing service in the armed forces, I will support them in that stand. In doing so, I am committing a Federal offense, for the Military Selective Service Act of 1967 specifically states that anyone who "knowingly counsels, aids or abets another to refuse or evade registration or service in the armed forces" opens himself to the same penalties as are visited upon the one he so counsels, aids and abets, namely up to five years in jail or up to $10,000 in fines, or both.

I will continue to do this until I am arrested. As long as I am not arrested, I will do it with increasing intensity, for I am no longer willing that 18- or 19-year old boys should pay with their lives for the initially bumbling but now deliberate folly of our national leaders. Nor am I willing to support them in action that may lead them to jail, from a safe preserve of legal inviolability for myself. I must run the same risks as they, and therefore I break the law on their behalf, so that if they are arrested, I too must be arrested. If this means jail, I am willing to go with them, and perhaps we can continue there to think and learn and teach and reflect and emerge with a new set of priorities for American life. If, as is far more likely, this means merely public abuse or ridicule, then perhaps a minority of us can be disciplined, chastened, and strengthened by that kind of adversity.

But whatever it means, the time has come when some of us can no longer afford the luxury of gentility or the luxury of holding "moderate" positions. The issue must be joined. Our country is committing crimes so monstrous that the only thing more monstrous would be continuing silence or inaction in the face of them.

92.

An End to the Draft?

U.S. military manpower policies have been apparently atypical since World War II. Previous to that conflict, the country depended on a small professional army between wars, and only initiated conscription when large numbers of men were needed quickly, as in the Civil War and in World Wars I and II. Since 1945, however, a civilian draft has been in existence more or less continuously (there was a short hiatus before the Korean War). Headed ever since 1941 by General Lewis B. Hershey, the Selective Service program has been highly controversial, especially in recent years, mainly because of alleged inequities in its operation. Protests against the draft grew particularly vehement during the summer and fall of 1967, which led to the action on the part of General Hershey that is described in the Nation *editorial reprinted here. The editorial predicted that the draft would be ended by the Congress elected in the fall of 1968. Such prophecies had been made before, however, and had not come true.*

Source: *Nation*, December 18, 1967: "Many Thanks, General."

GEN. LEWIS B. HERSHEY, becoming uneasy about resistance to the draft on college campuses, went to the White House and obtained consent for the drafting of a letter to Selective Service boards around the country advising the swift induction of student protesters who interfere with the operation of the Selective Service machinery by sitting-in at draft boards or induction centers, or by willfully getting in the way of Army recruiters. Although the letter did not mention students, it was clearly directed at them, since there is at present no other more or less homogeneous body of activist protesters. There was only one reference to demonstrations; clearly, Hershey did not wish to outlaw antiwar demonstrations as such — or did not have the temerity to try it.

The dimensions of the anti-Hershey reaction are impressive. The American Civil Liberties Union challenged him with three actions at law. Both Students for a Democratic Society and the National Student Association brought suit. Student newspapers were in full cry; professors wired individual protests. Recruiting facilities were denied at Columbia University, and at Stanford Pres. Wallace Sterling announced that "so long as the Hershey directive remains in effect" recruiting would be banned on that campus. The normally moderate president of Yale, Kingman Brewster, Jr., who had rebuked the university chaplain for his activities against the draft, termed Hershey's position an "absolutely outrageous usurpation of power." The academic dander was up.

Among politicians, reaction was equally forcible, with only an occasional voice, like that of the national commander of the American Legion, raised in Hershey's defense. Senator Javits denounced the move as "absolutely wrong." Rep. John Moss, one of the few Congressmen who work insistently for freedom of information in the government, demanded Hershey's resignation. In a shrewd move calculated to bring maximum embarrassment on the Administration, Sen. Philip Hart, a Democrat, called for "prompt" opinion from the Attorney General as to the legality of the Hershey proposal.

In view of the lawsuits directed against Hershey, Supreme Court Justice Abe Fortas' comment at Colgate University was perhaps ill advised, but it left no doubt as to where the Justice stood. He was quoted as saying that Hershey was "a law unto himself" and one who "responds only to his own conversation."

Hershey's proposal would have drawn protests under any circumstances, but the heat of the reaction can be accounted for, in part, by a widespread uneasiness about interference with civil liberties arising from the most frustrating war ever undertaken by the United States. There is a feeling, also,

that anything an official in Hershey's position says in condemnation of draft protesters is bound to have a multiplier effect on local draft boards. Many are itching to crack down on demonstrators, legal or illegal. To the same effect, there has been considerable harassment of students by the FBI. *El Gaucho*, the student newspaper of the University of California at Santa Barbara, reported in its November 20 issue that at least eight local students, six of them from UCSB, had been questioned by FBI agents concerning their nonpossession of draft cards. The story mentioned scattered reports of arrests in other parts of the country.

The most significant part of the furor, however, and the one in which General Hershey has undercut his own organization, is the damage done to the basic concept of conscription. It has few remaining friends except in the veterans' organizations. Businessmen are handicapped when they wish to hire draft-vulnerable applicants. The applicants are at even greater disadvantage. College and university administrators are annoyed. Middle-class families, including those who support the war in Vietnam, dislike having their own sons drafted.

GOP politicians sense a popular issue. A group of Republican Congressmen has written a book on *How To End the Draft* that makes excellent sense. Future wars are likely to be of the guerrilla type, which can be fought more effectively by professional soldiers, or so the argument runs. As for a nuclear exchange, soldiers will have little to do except die with the civilians.

A striking harbinger of the demise of the draft, probably at the hands of the Congress to be elected next November, is Nixon's endorsement of the concept of a volunteer professional army. In his usual slippery way, he would postpone any change until after the Vietnamese War, but when Nixon prepares to abandon a ship it must truly be sinking.

93.

Paul H. Douglas: Tax Loopholes

Paul Douglas, whose account of what he felt to be tax inequities is reprinted here in part, was U.S. Senator from Illinois for eighteen years and in 1967 was appointed chairman of the National Committee on Urban Problems. In 1955 Douglas became vice-chairman of Congress' Joint Economic Committee and in the same year was placed on the Senate Finance Committee, where he served for eleven years until defeated for a fourth term in 1966 by Charles Percy. His struggle to change the tax laws was directed against those who argued that it was a citizen's duty to pay as little in taxes as was legally possible.

Source: *American Scholar*, Winter 1967-68.

There were two general sets of facts that convinced me that there were great abuses within our federal tax system.

The first was that only about half of the total personal income in the country was subject to taxation, while the other half completely escaped being levied on. The basic exemption of $600 a person accounted for only a fraction of this latter amount. The remainder was income that most people believed was taxable, but that was exempted in reality by a series of devices.

Then we discovered and got the Treasury to confirm that in every year there were a considerable number of persons with annual incomes of over $500,000 who paid no taxes at all. As we gathered evidence we found this number would never fall below twenty-five and sometimes went above thirty. We also found an even greater number with huge incomes who paid less than 10 or 15 percent.

We found that the averages paid by the groups with incomes above $50,000 was only a fraction of the amount they were presumed to pay, and that the uppermost group with incomes over $250,000, who according to the schedules were presumed to pay nearly 90 percent, actually paid on the average only 25 percent or slightly less. The "effective" rate was therefore far less than the nominal rate.

All this, plus the evidence on specific "loopholes" or "truckholes" that enabled large quantities of income to slip through the tax net, still further convinced Senator Gore and me that we should expose these abuses and seek to cure them. We continued to be helped by public-spirited experts, who gave us surreptitious information, sometimes at real risk to themselves, and in particular by the ability of my former assistant, Mr. Philip Stern, who, building on some of our work and adding much of his own, produced his brilliant and witty book *The Great Treasury Raid* (New York, 1964), which is still the classic in this field. . . .

When the so-called Ruml plan for withholding a basic percentage of the federal income tax from wages and salaries was adopted by Congress, it did not apply the withholding principle to interest and dividends. Such income was, on the contrary, to be reported by the recipient and the taxes were to be paid by him.

The Economic Committee hearings that I held in 1955 showed that while virtually all of the wages and salaries were reported, there were a big volume of interest and an appreciable portion of dividends that were not. It became possible to estimate the size of this gap from the reports published by the Securities and Exchange Commission and by the Treasury. Our little liberal group in the Senate, therefore, began to advocate applying the withholding principle, or what the British term "payment at the source," to dividends and interest so that ownership would not receive any more favored treatment than employment.

In 1962, under President Kennedy and Secretary Dillon, the Administration adopted this provision, and the Office of Tax Analysis under Donald Lubig was most helpful in the preparation of evidence and in working out simple plans for collection. It was clear that in 1959 about $1 billion in dividends and $3 billion in interest were not reported, with a consequent annual loss in taxes of between $900 million and $1 billion. These unreported sums amounted to 8 percent of all dividends and 34 percent of all interest. The proportion of wages and salaries not reported in 1959 came, on the other hand, to only 3 percent. This showed the greater efficiency of the withholding method.

The administration tax bill for 1962, therefore, contained a provision for the automatic deduction and transmission to the Treasury of 20 percent from the total sums credited to dividends and interest without specifying the individuals or their amounts, and then for the filing of claims for any excess to be made periodically by the recipients. The plan was simple and just, and was adopted by the House Ways and Means Committee and by the House itself. Senator Gore and I prepared to support it in the Senate Finance Committee and, if necessary, on the floor of the Senate itself.

We had heard rumblings of opposition, but I must admit we were not prepared for the storm that followed. Suddenly, from all over the country, but especially from Illinois, thousands of protests poured into my office. By the end of a month, I had received over 65,000 such letters and other senators had received about as many. Inquiry proved that these had been stimulated by the building and loan associations, whose main national body had launched the campaign from Chicago. The banks also helped in the letter-writing blitz.

These letters showed an extraordinary misconception of the tax. A large proportion hotly attacked the requirement for withholding as the imposition of a completely new and additional tax. They apparently thought that interest either was not income or was so sacred that it should not be taxed. This very fact was in itself eloquent proof of the widespread evasion or avoidance of the tax. It was in vain that in my initial answer I pointed out to these protesters that this was not a new tax but merely a better means of collecting an existing tax that had been widely evaded and avoided, and that their confusion was indeed ample proof of an existing failure to report.

Another widely prevalent misconception was that the tax was a levy amounting to a 20-percent annual assessment on the total capital that a person owned. It was consequently attacked as part of a communist scheme to confiscate all capital. It was, of course, instead, a tax on income, not on capital. Thus on $1,000 of holdings that paid 4 percent, the 20 percent tax would be levied on the $40 of interest and not on the principal of $1,000.

I then prepared a brief article summarizing the way in which the income tax had been avoided and evaded, and how simple the proposal was — namely, to withhold one-fifth of all payments of dividends and interest and send the totals to the Treasury. In the event of overwithholding, the individuals would then be able to file quarterly requests for refunds. I pointed out to all my correspondents that the basic income tax on wages and salaries had been similarly withheld for twenty years with only annual refunds and asked why interest and dividends should be given such especially favored treatment.

It was all in vain. No one was convinced. The tide of angry letters continued to pour in. Virtually every senator received thousands, and many counted their letters in the tens of thousands.

The result was inevitable. By a vote of eleven to five, the withholding provision was stricken from the bill in the Finance Committee. Then, on the floor of the Senate, when I moved to restore the clause, I was overwhelmingly defeated and mustered only twenty votes.

Here we were deserted by the administration, which evidently decided that the struggle was useless. During the entire battle, the academic profession of economists was all but silent, so that Senator Gore and I felt that we had been allowed to die on an economic Berlin Wall without a hand ever being raised to help. . . .

The biggest and longest battle was, however, over the worst abuse of all, namely the 27½-percent depletion allowance on gas and oil. Billions of dollars are at stake here, and a little explanation of the present tax procedures in the oil industry is appropriate. The oil industry already had certain tax favors that I did not question. Of course, the deduction of operating costs from gross revenue is perfectly proper. Nor did I question the propriety of charging off the costs of the unsuccessful drillings or "dry holes" from the revenues obtained from the successful drillings when these are conducted

by the same enterprise. I did not raise any objection to granting the industry the right to charge off in the first year all the "intangible" drilling and development costs. These so-called developmental costs comprise from 75 to 90 percent of the total exploratory and drilling costs and were granted the fastest of all rates of accelerated depreciation — namely, a complete write-off in the initial year. Men in the industry who were secretly in favor of my stand (and there are a few) have repeatedly assured me that this is an even more important special favor than the depletion allowance itself. But this issue was complicated since these costs could always be alleged to be operating costs and hence deductible dollar for dollar from the immediate income realized from the oil and gas.

So I determined to concentrate on the 27½-percent depletion allowance, which Hubert Humphrey and I had originally attacked in 1951 and 1952. This exempted from taxation 27½ percent of all gross income in the oil and gas industry up to 50 percent of net income, and it did this without any limitation as to the length of time for which this exemption was to continue or the ratio of the tax rebate to the original investment.

This provision had been inserted in our tax laws during the 1920s when the corporation income tax was only 14 percent of net profits and when the total amount of the tax privilege thus conferred was not overwhelming, say, about 7 percent of the profits. But it continued to be retained after the corporate tax had risen to 52 percent and when the depletion allowance could and commonly did cut in half the taxes paid by this rich industry. Moreover, it had spawned a series of similar exemptions: sulfur had been granted a 23-percent exemption, and a number of minerals, including coal, had been allowed a 15-percent depletion grant. We had seen Tom Connally broaden this exemption by a 5-percent rate on clam and oyster shells, as well as on sand and gravel — although there was no danger of "dry holes" or unsuccessful explorations in these cases! Every mineral had come to be included.

We ultimately got the Treasury to tell us how much these exemptions amounted to, and their report was that in the late Fifties and early Sixties the total came to about $3.5 billion annually, with the Treasury losing about $1.5 billion. Today it is undoubtedly much more.

Long before this, however, I had prepared a counterproposal which I tried out in committee and on the floor nearly every year. This was to introduce a sliding scale allowance that would amount to granting the existing 27½ percent on the first million dollars of annual gross income but decreasing this to 21¼ percent on gross incomes of between $1 million and $5 million and then having it fall to 15 percent on all incomes over $5 million. This would have yielded in the earlier years from $350 to $400 million a year in revenue, while in later years the gain would have been around $500 million annually. Today it would probably be still more.

I justified this differential between small and large operators on the ground that the smaller operators were not able to distribute their risks to the same degree as the big operators and companies. Their fewer drillings exposed them, therefore, to higher risks.

I must confess, however, that I also hoped that this compromise would help to split off the small operators from the huge companies and make it more possible to pass the measure. In this, I was disappointed. Although there were only two or three concerns in Illinois that had gross receipts in excess of a million dollars, nearly all of the small operators lined up behind the big companies and in bitter opposition to me.

They were the dominant economic interest in one congressional district covering the southeastern section of the state. Most of them insisted that I was proposing to cut their allowance to 15 percent, although this was, of course, not the case. No explanation was effective, although finally the more knowledgeable would privately admit that while they understood that they would not be hurt, for the sake of industry solidarity they must oppose the Douglas amendment and me personally. Despite all their efforts and the oil money that came into the state in the 1954 and 1960 election campaigns, I had been able to beat off their attacks, and had even carried the oil district. Their opposition continued, however, and in the Senate I had no such luck.

Despite help from Senator Albert Gore and an honorable conservative, Senator John Williams of Delaware, we were periodically snowed under on the Finance Committee. Indeed, I sometimes suspected that the major qualification for most aspirants for membership on the Finance Committee was a secret pledge or agreement to defend the depletion allowance against all attacks. I suspected, also, that campaign funds reinforced these pledges.

Once again, we received little or no support from the administration, which evidently thought the depletion allowance to be "too hot to handle." And, once again, the economics profession was largely silent, except for a few scattered voices that correctly pointed out that the tax favors led to overinvestment in the industry, thus causing the average return, exclusive of tax favors, on the American investment to fall somewhat below the general average for all industry. . . .

The third great abuse lies in the field of the capital gains tax. Here the profits realized from the sale of a capital asset that has been held for longer than six months are taxed, when sold, at only one-half the income tax rate, but in no case at more than 25 percent. Moreover, the amounts not taxed are not counted as "taxable income," and hence do not appear in the statistics issued by the Treasury Department. Like the murdered victims of the criminal syndicate, they, with the oil and mineral depletion allowances, are given an anonymous burial so that even the buried bodies disappear.

Philip Stern estimated in 1962 that this favored treatment shrunk the tax base by $6 billion a year and cost the Treasury $2.4 billion annually. But this is only the beginning. An even greater leakage occurs when property is bequeathed. Let us take the case of a father who buys property for $100,000 during his lifetime, which by the time of his death is worth $1 million, or $900,000 more. His son inherits the estate and a year later sells this same property for $1.1 million. He will pay a capital gains tax only on the $100,000 that has accrued during his ownership, while the $900,000 gain inherited from his father not only will go tax free but will be unrecorded. Stern estimates that from $12 to $13 billion thus escape taxation every year and that the Treasury annually loses an approximate added $2.9 billion. . . .

The treatment of stock options was, and is, an especially antisocial use of the capital gains principle.

It had been the custom of many corporations to give to a chosen group of executives the right to buy added quantities of stock and for gains realized upon this to be taxed at capital gains and not at income tax rates. Very commonly this stock could be purchased at less than the market rate, thus extending the practice of the "preferred lists" that had been the common custom during the 1920s of such financial giants as the Morgan firm and Samuel Insull. If the stock fell while the option was being held, then the beneficiary was commonly freed from his option. . . .

Due to the valiant efforts of Senator Gore, we succeeded in ending some of the worst abuses of the stock option plans. How much we have saved by these modifications is still unknown, but I estimate that while the gains are real they are still minor.

Another persistent loophole is the exemption from federal taxation of the interest on the bonds of state and local governments. This exemption was first enacted because of the fear that such a tax would be held unconstitutional by the courts, and also by a desire to make the financing of capital improvements easier for the state and local governments. That it has helped in the latter direction is shown by the fact that while high-grade municipals are still much less safe than federal issues, their yield in March of 1967 was a full percentage point below the latter, namely, 3½ instead of 4½ percent. Without this tax advantage, the municipalities would probably have had to pay at least 4¾ percent interest and possibly 5 percent in order to float their loans. Since the total outstanding bonds issued by the state and local governments amount to approximately $100 billion, the total in interest that is saved for these bodies probably comes to somewhere around $1.25 to $1.5 billion a year.

Such tax-free issues, however, become tax havens or sanctuaries for men and women in the upper income and tax brackets. Thus when Mrs. Horace Dodge, Sr., inherited $56 million from the estate of her husband, she immediately invested all of it in state and municipal bonds and thereby removed the entire income from her fortune from federal taxation. This is a particularly attractive tax route for those in the upper income tax brackets who do not wish to play an active role in the business world. If only the existing income from these bond issues were taxed, federal receipts would be at least 50 percent on the $3.5 billion that is now immune from federal taxation. This would amount to $1.75 billion. If the federal government were to pay in outright subsidy to the local governments to compensate for these lost tax benefits, this would still net at least a half billion dollars a year for the federal government. It might indeed net more since the interest rate, and hence the total interest payments on state and municipals, would rise. Assuming that the total interest could increase to $4.5 billion, at an average tax rate of 50 percent, this could net $2.25 billion, or $1 billion more than the compensating subsidy. Unless some such action is taken, the amount of lost income will probably increase as retired men and women of wealth seek these privileged sanctuaries. . . .

The depreciation allowances on buildings are computed on the money cost of the property to the last purchaser and not on the book value of the physical structure of the building itself. Thus if a man constructs an office building at a cost of $5 million, he can take accelerated depreciation for several years and use this as a credit against the net income from that property, or any other property that he may own. At 5 percent a year, he would thus get a credit of $250,000. If his net income from the building was $200,000, this would mean that he would pay no taxes and would have an additional credit, to be carried over, of $50,000. This could go on for at least five years, when the accelerated depreciation amounting to approximately $1.7 million would have to be greatly reduced. But office buildings enhance somewhat in value during the first years of occupancy, and it would be quite possible to sell the property for $5 million or more instead of the depreciated book value of approximately $3.3 million. The original owner would pay a capital gains tax only on the $1.7-million profit made from selling at above book value, although he had used his depreciation allowance to reduce his higher regular income tax rate.

The newcomer could, however, start taking his double depreciation on his $5-million purchase price instead of on the $3.3 million of book value. This, as a matter of fact, would be an important reason why he would pay the full $5 million.

After a few years a third comer might even be willing to pay $5 million, although the $3.4 million taken for depreciation might have left but $1.6 million of the original cost of $5 million.

This process could be kept up almost interminably, with the ultimate total amounts deducted for depreciation far exceeding the original cost. This practice also puts a premium upon a frequent change of ownership, which is especially injurious in the case of tenements. . . .

There are many other quirks and loopholes in the taxation of commercial real estate that result in great losses of tax revenue, among them the "sell and lease back" arrangement. Here any gains will be taxed later only at capital gains rather than at income tax rates, while the rent payments can be deducted from gross profits as an operating cost. Time forbids going into all these complexities. But as the publications of various tax services demonstrate, they are complex and, for those who practise them, lucrative.

In 1962, the Treasury presented a mass of evidence showing excessive tax-deduction claims for travel and for entertainment. The instances presented were at once ludicrous and also, in a sense, nauseating. We were able to tighten the rules somewhat, most notably in limiting travel expenses (exclusive of actual transportation) to twice the amount allowed government employees and at a present figure of $32 a day. We also restricted the deductibility of business presents to $25 from one person to another. But the major expenses for entertainment have been largely legalized, and the evils of an expense-account civilization are still largely unchecked. . . .

I began my senatorial career in a quandary, and when I left, the quandary was even bigger than when I started. It was this: Can and will the people under the best system of government in the world, and with an able and high-minded Congress, ever be able to protect the public interest in tax matters and enforce equal justice for all?

I must admit that the eighteen years have, on the surface, been disillusioning. We have made a few improvements during that time and may have saved a billion dollars or more a year, but the big loopholes and truckholes remain. Indeed, new ones have been opened, sometimes over our opposition and sometimes, as I have pointed out, without our knowledge. I daresay that there may be still other financial time bombs, presumably concealed in innocent-sounding verbiage, which will turn out to free still more income from taxation. The summing up that Philip Stern gave in his *The Great Treasury Raid* is substantially true today.

For a raid of its magnitude, the time (high noon) and setting (the United States Treasury, a stone's throw from the White House) showed a breathtaking boldness of design and planning. From out of nowhere, it seemed, they appeared — old people and young, rich and poor, an oil millionaire here, a factory worker there, a real estate tycoon, a working mother, several well-known movie stars, some corporation presidents, even the chairman of a powerful Congressional committee. It was a mixed lot, all right, that converged on the Treasury Building that high noon. Into the building they strolled, gloriously nonchalant. No one stopped them; not a guard looked up to question them. Quickly and quietly they found their way to the vaults; opened them noiselessly with the special passkeys each had brought with him. Like clockwork, with split-second timing, each went to his appointed spot, picked up a bag and walked out as calmly as he had entered. At the exits the guards sat motionless. At precisely 12:04 it was all over. Each of the "visitors" had vanished into thin air.

So had forty billion dollars from the United States Treasury. . . .

James Madison saw this danger to our democracy at the very founding of our Republic and tried to develop an answer in the tenth essay of *The Federalist*. He thought he had found a partial answer to the peril in the mutual checks and balances that the divergent producing interests, called into being by a national market, would exercise upon each other.

This form of countervailing power is helpful in many fields. But I did not find it to be an adequate protection for the consumers or the small taxpayers. For producers seldom think of consumers, while those with big potential tax bills are commonly not solicitous about the other taxpayers. There is, moreover, a kind of fellow feeling among the powerful that makes it bad form for one group to balk another in a matter in which they are not themselves directly concerned.

We owe it to our country to pay our taxes without murmuring; the time to get in our fine work is on the valuation.

EDGAR WILSON ("BILL") NYE

94.

Daniel S. Greenberg: The Politics of Pure Science

Pure science, says Daniel S. Greenberg, is the institutionalization of Huck Finn's curiosity. There is no doubt, at least, about the institutionalization. Scientific research, only a third of a century ago the concern of a few academics, has become a major affair not only for most industrial firms but also for the federal government, which spent billions of dollars yearly in the 1960s on scientific pursuits of one kind and another (mainly the Apollo program). Institutionalization and so much money bring with them political power, the extent and character of which Greenberg discussed in the 1967 article part of which is reprinted here. News editor of Science, *Greenberg expanded the article in a book published early in 1968.*

Source: *Saturday Review*, November 4, 1967.

IN STUDYING the American scientific community, it would be useful to discover a scientific Establishment, a group small in number, associated with venerable institutions, that commands affairs regardless of what the *pro forma* processes may be. A cursory examination of the community suggests existence of such an Establishment, but to the extent that it does exist, emphasis upon it can mislead more than enlighten in understanding the politics of science. Therefore, let us begin with a paradox: There is no American Scientific Establishment. Yet Harvard, Massachusetts Institute of Technology, California Institute of Technology, and the University of California are its Oxbridge. Two World War II research centers, the MIT Radiation Laboratory (famous for radar) and the Los Alamos Scientific Laboratory (of A-bomb fame), are its Eton. The Cosmos Club in Washington is its Athenaeum, the physicists are its aristocracy. The National Academy of Sciences is its established church, and the President's Science Advisory Committee is its Privy Council.

The Establishment has two branches. The eastern wing is headed by a triumvirate: Jerome B. Wiesner, provost of MIT and science adviser to the late President John F. Kennedy; George B. Kistiakowsky, science adviser to former President Dwight D. Eisenhower, professor of chemistry at Harvard, and vice president of the Academy; and Detlev Bronk, president of Rockefeller University and former president of the Academy. The western wing is headed by Lee DuBridge, another former Eisenhower science adviser who is president of the California Institute of Technology.

I. I. Rabi, still another Eisenhower confidant and recently retired professor of physics at Columbia, is the *eminence grise*, and *Science*, the weekly magazine of the American Association for the Advancement of Science, is the quasi-official journal. The National Science Foundation is the bank; Frederick Seitz, president of the Academy, is the peacekeeper; and Emanuel R. Piore, vice-president of International Business Machines Corporation, is the chief troubleshooter. Harvey Brooks, dean of engineering and applied physics at Harvard, is the political theoretician. The late J. Robert Oppenheimer is the tragic hero.

Illusion or reality, I do not think the Establishment concept provides much help for examining the politics of science. So, at the outset, I would like to dispel any hopes for elitist theories, compact tables of organization, or directions to a central command post. We are examining a very untidy subject.

The part of our society that is conveniently referred to as "the scientific community" is an agglomeration of people and institutions generally centered about workshops called laboratories and engaged in activities called research. This definition takes us only to the gates of the community. Once inside, it is common for the visitor to direct his attention to the substance of science, to what scientists are doing, to what their work is about. But we are concerned with something else — the political behavior of science, both in its relations with the nonscientific world and in its internal aspects. What we want to know is how it works, in terms of the people and the forces, traditions, policies, and practices that determine who gets what. For this purpose, it is necessary, first, to look upon the scientific community not simply as the location for a particular type of activity; rather, it is necessary to look upon it as a way of life, as a collection of particular and persistent sensitivities, values, and vulnerabilities, and as a style of behavior distinct unto itself. And then, after having looked at its internal characteristics, we will be in a better position to examine and understand the community's dealings with other segments of our society.

If we are looking at the substance and practice of science, we find the common denominator is a dedication to the understanding of the physical universe through systematic investigation and measurement,

through the harnessing of curiosity, training, discipline, and instruments. (Some would add intuition and good luck.) But if we direct our attention to the politics of science, internal and external, we find that the common denominator involves different matters.

From the political perspective, the scientific community can be seen as bound together by a twofold ideology: first, a desire for society to support, but not govern, science; second, for the community of science to exist as a loosely organized entity — meritocratic anarchy may be the best description of it — in which hierarchy and tables of organization bear little relation to the realities of power. This dual ideology is important not because it governs events but rather because it affects the vision of scientists and influences the stances that they adopt, both in relation to each other and in their dealings with nonscientists. In its starkest theoretical formulation, the ideology is contained in the assertion of Michael Polyani: "The pursuit of science can be organized . . . in no other manner than by granting complete independence to all mature scientists. They will then distribute themselves over the whole field of possible discoveries, each applying his own special ability to the task that appears most profitable to him. The function of public authorities is not to plan research, but only to provide opportunities for its pursuit. All they have to do is to provide facilities for every good scientist to follow his own interest in science."

Derivations of this puristic concept are to be found in the statements of men very much concerned with the practical problems of administering the affairs of the scientific community. In the words of Alan T. Waterman, former director of the National Science Foundation: "Basic research is a highly specialized activity; it is not one where the judgment of laymen has validity. Consequently, planning for basic research and such evaluation of its performance as is needed for the continuation of existing programs must be left in the hands of competent and experienced scientists." Or consider the words of a group of chemists: "To understand how research is organized at the universities, one must realize that a university does not operate through a chain of command. Each member of the faculty is expected to develop a research program of his own. His research is not subject to review or criticism by anyone in his own department, except on his own initiative."

Polyani, Waterman, and the chemists were addressing themselves more to what is desirable than to what is actually in the world of science, but in science, as in politics and religion, theoretical formulations can tinge perceptions, stir up passions, and move men to action.

If education and place of employment are the criteria, it is relatively simple to locate the American scientific community and identify the institutions through which it works. Statistics on the size and cost of science are harder to use, however, because it is difficult to pluck science from the mass of scientific and technical endeavors that are often lumped together as "science." First, a quick survey of the dimensions of the scientific community.

In 1960, the latest year for which comprehensive figures are available, 335,300 persons gave "scientist" as their occupation, 822,000 said they were engineers and 775,100 said they were technicians. Of the total who considered themselves scientists, 176,500 were employed by industry, 98,100 by colleges and universities, and 60,700 by federal, state and local governments.

These figures are grossly swollen, probably by self-flattering definition. If we are to locate the segment of the mass that conducts the politics of science, it is necessary first to seek out a particular identifying characteristic: possession of the doctoral degree, for the leaders almost invariably possess the advanced scientific training that precedes the degree. Again, definite figures are lacking. But a good assessment is to be found in the federal government's *National Register of Scientific and Technical Personnel*, which is based on a biennial survey that is believed to cover some 90 percent of all science doctorates, and 75 percent of all persons, with or without degrees, whose work calls for a scientific background. In 1964 according to the *Register*, the statistical profile of American science showed only 56,457 Ph.D.s in the natural and physical sciences. The number of Ph.D.s in engineering totaled only 10,000.

Now two important points. First, in terms of place of employment, educational institutions accounted for the largest group of doctorates in science, 47 percent; industry employed 29 percent, and government 14 percent. Second, the gross number of Ph.D.s is rather small, and when we deduct those at the end of their careers, plus those who hold degrees but do not practice science, we have to conclude that, while we hear a great deal about the incredibly rapid expansion of scientific research, real scientific research — as distinguished from technological activity — actually absorbs a rather minuscule portion of the nation's working force.

The rank and file of science, as is the case with the rank and file of any group or profession, goes about its business and generally leaves the politics to a handful of leaders. How big is this handful in the case of science? Christopher Wright, of Columbia University, a longtime observer of the science and government relationship, estimates the number at 200 to 1,000. James Killian of MIT, who has been at the inner core of the relationship, uses the lower figure to describe the "consistently influential." The numbers shift with time and issues, but there is no doubt that the politics of science is generally conducted by a remarkably small number of people.

Now, to move to the financial resources available to the practitioners of science and the institutional array in which these resources are employed: The amounts that this country spends under the heading of "research and development" and the rate of growth of these expenditures during the past twenty-five years are spectacular.

In 1940, the nation's total spending in these categories is estimated to have been $345 million. The commonly used figure for the federal portion of that total is $74 million. The 1940 total for research and development was approximately .03 percent of the gross national product, and the federal contribution constituted about .08 percent of the federal budget.

By 1962-63, the nation's total research and development (R&D) expenditures had risen to $16.4 billion, of which the federal government provided $12.2 billion. The 1962-63 total was close to 3 percent of the gross national product, and the federal contribution constituted approximately 14 percent of the federal budget. But again, as was the case with gross figures on employment in science, it is necessary to move on to more refined numbers to arrive at an understanding of the financial component of the politics of science.

In assessing the finances of what comes under the heading of research and development, it is difficult but necessary to attempt to locate boundaries between various segments of scientific and technical endeavor. And here we have to be content with shadings rather than with precise demarcations. Let us start with an idealized compartmentalization, consisting of "development," "applied research," and "basic research."

If development is the translation of existing knowledge into hardware, gadgets, techniques, or new material, then development accounts for the vast majority of R&D expenditures — somewhere around 68 percent. An example of development would be the employment of existing knowledge about electromagnetic propagation to devise a new radio communications device. In general, this is the function of engineers.

If applied research is the quest for a new understanding that is specifically needed to make possible a new development, then applied research accounts for about 22 percent of R&D expenditures. Again taking radio communications as a case in point, an example of applied research would be the creation of a smaller, or perhaps less resistant, transistor to meet the weight or power requirements of the radio device. This generally involves more science than engineering, but the two often tend to merge in this area.

If basic research is the quest for fundamental knowledge, regardless of the purpose to which it might be applied, then basic research is the smallest portion of R&D, amounting to only about 10 percent of the total. In the field of electromagnetic studies, its findings might ultimately be incorporated into communications devices.

But — and this is what a lot of the politics of pure science is all about — the basic researcher is not primarily, and perhaps not at all, concerned with utility. His objective is an understanding of fundamental phenomena, regardless of their utility. Therein lies the fundamental political dilemma of basic research in the United States. Patronage, public and private, comes to basic research for many reasons, but the strongest reason is a belief that utilizable results may ensue. . . .

At the honorary apex of American science sits the National Academy of Sciences. This is a ponderous, self-perpetuating body with a current membership of approximately 780. Established during the Civil War through the machinations of a number of scientific luminaries who were disturbed by government's indifference to science, the Academy is designated by Congressional charter as scientific adviser to the federal government. The charter, however, specifies that the Academy is to advise only when advice is asked, and, until quite recently, the government did not often ask.

To the numerical limits of its membership, the Academy is supposed to encompass the most professionally distinguished members of the American scientific community; but with the average age of admission being 49.1 years and the average age of the total members 61.6 years, there are many distinguished young scientists outside the Academy. And, regardless of age, there are some rather undistinguished ones inside.

On the whole, however, the Academy represents the best of post-middle-age science in America. Election is by a process that rivals the papacy for mystery. Through an infinitely complex screening process, those who are inside select forty-five new members for admission each year, and, in general, the selections are made with great care, for in the hierarchy of scientific honors, admission to the Academy is second only to winning the Nobel Prize. Nevertheless, despite the time, care, and occasional politicking that go into selecting Academy members, it is illuminating to note that since 1950, the Nobel Prize has been awarded to nine scientists who, at the time of the award, were not Academicians. In all but two cases, Academy membership was swiftly bestowed upon them after bestowal of the prize. (One of the two exceptions died after receiving the prize, and one still has not made it, though he got the prize in 1954.)

Around the half-century mark in its history, which came during World War I, the Academy recognized that its honorary and advisory functions did not mix well. Accordingly, the National Research Council was established to draw upon the scientific community at large for advisory services. Today NRC annually obtains the services — without cost, except for travel expenses — of some 4,000 scientists and engineers throughout the country, to provide advice

on an incredibly broad array of matters, ranging from the nutritional requirements of laboratory animals to selection of a site for the most costly research center ever constructed.

The proper name of the overall organization is the National Academy of Sciences-National Research Council (NAS-NRC). Appended to this, in a loose fashion, is the recently established National Academy of Engineering, the creation of which, several years ago, underlined the fact that NAS-NRC had become almost wholly a creature of pure science. The engineers, writhing from inadequate representation, were initially going to set up their own independent Academy, but eventually agreed to begin their existence in confederation with the scientist-dominated Academy. So far, the arrangement has worked out fairly well.

The Academy's power and influence are open to question. The institution has been called the Supreme Court of Science and science's League of Women Voters. But, whatever the role of the Academy may be, there is no doubt that the internal politics of science is heavily weighted with Academy members. Academy membership is not a prerequisite for entry to the political arena, but membership certifies scientific accomplishment and scientists generally prefer to entrust their political affairs to those who have demonstrated scientific or technical creativity. Occasionally, a career administrator, such as Killian of MIT, will go to the top in the politics of science; but, on the whole, the ranking politicians, such as Wiesner, Seitz, Rabi, DuBridge, Kistiakowsky, and Bronk, first made their marks in the substantive work of their professions, and then moved into the politics.

It is important to note that this route often leads to interlocking positions. Thus, Seitz not only is president of the Academy but also chairs the Defense Science Board, which is the highest ranking science advisory body in the Pentagon; he is also a member of the President's Science Advisory Committee. When Bronk was president of the Academy, he sat on PSAC and also chaired the National Science Board, which is the top advisory board of the National Science Foundation.

The most influential of the government's science advisory bodies is the President's Science Advisory Committee (PSAC), an eighteen-member group that by custom is chaired by the President's Special Assistant for Science and Technology. But whatever its standing in the hierarchy of influence, its members as often as not go about muttering that the federal Establishment is impervious to scientific sense.

PSAC is a post-Sputnik outgrowth of a Science Advisory Committee established by President Truman in 1951. With one brief exception, the chairmanship of both bodies has always been filled by alumni of the World War II atomic bomb laboratory at Los Alamos or the radar laboratory — the Radiation Laboratory — at MIT. Academy members have always predominated on PSAC and its predecessor. Until recently approximately one-third of the members came from Harvard or MIT. Now, however, Cambridge, Massachusetts, is down to one or two members on PSAC, a decline which reflects the powerful presence of Lyndon Johnson in scientific politics.

In 1964, a study found that the so-called "hard sciences" (physics, chemistry, mathematics, and engineering) accounted for 77 percent of the membership; the rest were from the so-called "life sciences," or other fields, but none was from the behavioral or social sciences which was still the case in 1967. It was also found that the "hard scientists" were more likely to endure as PSAC members while their "life scientist" colleagues came and went. The same study showed that two-thirds of all PSAC members were employed by thirteen universities: California, Caltech, Chicago, Columbia, Cornell, Duke, Harvard, Illinois, Johns Hopkins, MIT, Pennsylvania, Princeton, and Stanford.

The prevalence of university-based scientists in the government's science advisory councils is a source of no little concern to scientists who are employed in the government's own laboratories or in industrial laboratories. Thus, Alvin Weinberg, director of the Atomic Energy Commission's Oak Ridge National Laboratory, notes that "even the professor of purest intent must be in some measure loyal to the Estate which he represents. As a result, government scientific advisory circles tend to be preoccupied with science at the universities, rather than with science in industry or in government laboratories; the whole structure and cast of thinking is geared to the problem of university science, and the limitations of the university as an instrument of government are overlooked. It would not be a great exaggeration to describe the advisory apparatus . . . as a lobby for the . . . university."

Laymen, upon first acquaintance with the scientific community's ways, often are appalled and outraged. That scientists should be both recipient and principal adviser to their public patron runs counter to popular notions of man's capacity for integrity in the face of temptation. But, as was noted earlier, science is unlike any other activity, and the scientific community is unlike any other organization. When confronted with the layman's lack of understanding, skepticism, and, at times, ill will, the inhabitants of the scientific community are first of all reverently patriotic toward the methodology and mores of their craft; secondly, they are anxiously poised to expel intruders who would usurp the name of science or meddle in its internal affairs; and, finally, they simply wish the rest of us would convert to science.

In one way or another, all professions share these characteristics. Whether the scientific community exceeds the norm for devotion to them defies precise measure; nor do all scientists partake equally of the trinity. Science's ever growing dependence upon government support, as well as the arrival of younger, less-traditional-minded scientists in positions of influence, has highlighted the difference between those who insist upon the preeminent importance, sovereignty and self-government of science and those who believe that science must recognize that it is only one of many legitimate claimants for public support. In 1960, for example, former NSF Director Waterman declared that "in the broadest sense national policy for science is a matter primarily to be determined by the scientists themselves. The scientists of the country are unquestionably the ones most capable of deciding what is best for progress in science, in the true meaning of the word." Six years later, a member of the new generation of federal science officials, Ivan B. Bennett, deputy director of the White House Office of Science and Technology, while not contesting Waterman's thesis, did add a note of political realism: "Science . . . can no longer hope to exist, among all human enterprises, through some mystique, without constraints or scrutiny in terms of national goals, and isolated from the competition for allocation of resources which are finite."

95.

Virlis L. Fischer: Water and the Southwest

During the 1960s the United States slowly began to face up to a crisis in the use of its natural resources: pollution of air and water, destruction of wildlife, unrestricted use of pesticides, and the problem of how to dispose of all the "garbage" (from used cars to sewage) that 200,000,000 people produce. In the southwestern part of the United States the central problem is one of water supply. Other regions of the country have been threatened with water shortages at various times, but in the Southwest, where the annual rainfall is small and often irregular, the problem has been perpetual and is worsening, especially with the increase in population. The widespread use of irrigation has greatly increased the agricultural productivity of the region, but it has also made great demands on the already overextended water supply. The following article by Virlis L. Fischer of the Western Forestry and Conservation Association details the problem of water supply in the Southwest and what steps are being taken to solve it.

Source: *American Forests*, November 1967.

THE CRITICAL WATER SUPPLY problems of the Pacific Southwest cannot go unsolved without disastrous consequences to both the region and the nation. Inaction on such a scale would have far-reaching effects. And yet this region is but symptomatic of a growing national problem in which serious water shortages have already been experienced in New York, New England, and other areas. While aggravated by temporary drought conditions, the shortages of usable water are basically due to population, pollution, and progressively increasing demands caused by our standard of living. Thus, it's a people problem. According to a U.S. Geological Survey water supply paper of 1965, nine regions will experience a drastic deficit in water by the year 2000. These nine regions comprise 55 percent of the contiguous forty-eight states.

Perhaps the ultimate in plans for solving water supply problems on a continental scale is an engineering concept developed by The Ralph M. Parsons Co. This plan is known as NAWAPA (North American Water & Power Alliance). It would collect some of the surplus water in Alaska and northwest Canada now flowing unused into northern oceans and transfer it to water-deficient areas of Canada, the United States, and Mexico. This project would cost an estimated $100 billion, require thirty years to build, and utilize as the heart of the system a 500-mile-long storage reservoir in the Rocky Mountain trench of Canada at 3,000 feet elevation. It would generate its own power for the necessary pumping and create an enormous saleable surplus. In the process, the Canada-Great Lakes canal network would provide ship and barge transportation, besides stabilizing levels of the Great Lakes and St. Lawrence Seaway.

Howsoever NAWAPA may sound like a panacea, the complexities of international agreements, financing, authorization, right-of-way acquisition, studies of impact on fish and wildlife and other resources, and plans for mitigation of losses would add years to the starting date of this ambitious project. Meanwhile, the problems of the Pacific Southwest are immediate and pressing, and it would appear that a regional approach is logical at this point in time.

For purposes of identity, the Pacific Southwest region consists of southern California, most of Arizona, southern Nevada, southwestern Utah, and a portion of western New Mexico. Within this region are the metropolitan centers of Los Angeles, San Diego, Phoenix, Tucson, and Las Vegas. These are among the nation's fastest growing cities. Growth accelerated in the 1930s when drought-ridden thousands from the dust bowl of the Midwest flocked to southern California. With the wartime economy of the 1940s and development of air-conditioning, the migratory pattern had been set. Winter-weary persons by the thousands have continued to swarm southwestward, seeking opportunity, recreation, and retirement in the land of sunshine. Percentagewise, Arizona and southern Nevada are growing even faster.

Present supplies of water in the arid Southwest are not adequate to sustain the level of development that already exists. Its principal source, the Colorado River, is one of the great drainages in the nation but its flow is tiny compared to the discharge into the ocean from the mighty Columbia. Rainfall is scant in the desert lowlands — averaging only 2.5 inches annually at Yuma, 4.85 at Las Vegas, 7 at Phoenix. Precipitation falls mainly in the higher mountains, so that well over half of the total water yield of the Colorado Basin is a product of the national forests. The importance of watershed management and research in the forestry program is readily apparent.

But the Colorado River is already over-committed. Los Angeles long ago tapped the Owens Valley on the eastern slope of the Sierra Nevada Mountains, and in 1928 the Metropolitan Water District of Southern California was formed to import water 240 miles from the Colorado River. It serves most cities in southern California. In recent years the diversion from the Colorado has exceeded 5.5 million acre-feet. This is considerably greater than the 4.4 million acre-feet allocated by the Supreme Court, and southern California stands to lose this excess diversion when the Central Arizona project permits that state to utilize

Joe Munroe from Photo Researchers

One of the problems facing the Southwest is the formation of deep cracks in the earth
as a result of pumping off the underground water supply for irrigation purposes. This
scene is outside Phoenix, Ariz.

more of its allocated share of 2.8 million
acre-feet.

In 1959 the California State Water Plan
was enacted, which will permit southern
California to import 1.9 million acre-feet
per year from the surplus waters of northern California coastal streams upon completion of an aqueduct down the great central
valley of that state. The Pacific Southwest
Water Plan contemplates enlargement of
these facilities to permit an additional 1.2
million acre-feet for southern California and
a second like amount for the Pacific Southwest on a long-range basis. California thus
leads the way in displaying the kind of
statesmanship needed to solve water problems of a magnitude involving large-scale
transfer of water from areas of surplus to
areas of need.

Arizona long ago fully developed the water potential from its Salt River and Gila
River basins and is temporarily getting by
with an alarming overdraft of its groundwater supplies. Her situation is rapidly ap-

proaching one of desperate urgency, and its
alleviation depends on early authorization of
the Central Arizona Project, which is designed to provide 1.2 million acre-feet from
the lower Colorado River. This involves an
aqueduct to bring water from Lake Havasu
to Phoenix and Tucson, plus pumping facilities for the uphill pull. Seriousness of the
situation can be seen when it is realized that
the groundwater overdraft in the Gila Basin
is 2.2 million acre-feet per year. Obviously
the well will run dry soon without additional supplies becoming available.

Southern Nevada has an allocation of
300,000 acre-feet, whose utilization in large
part depends upon a project, now authorized, to bring water uphill 1,000 feet from
Lake Mead to Las Vegas. In the meantime,
besides a small existing supply from Lake
Mead, the Las Vegas area is rapidly deplet-
ing its groundwater reserves which accumulated from the melting snows of the nearby
Spring and Sheep mountains.

The underground storage throughout the

Pacific Southwest is a legacy from past ages, and its depletion has resulted in salt-water intrusion in coastal areas, land subsidence, and nearly 300,000 acres of developed land lying idle in Arizona for lack of water.

The water supply outlook is further depressed by the need for fulfilling our treaty obligations with Mexico, and the fact that the lower basin states are benefiting temporarily from water allocated to the upper Colorado Basin states but which they are not yet consumptively using. It is little wonder, therefore, that Congressman Wayne Aspinall, an eminent authority on Western resources, recently stated that the Colorado River would have to be augmented by 2.5 million acre-feet annually just to provide quantities *already* committed. Future growth of the area will require even more water.

While most of the future use will be for municipal and industrial purposes, an effort is being made to maintain agriculture at its present level and also provide for fish and wildlife and outdoor recreation. The area is agriculturally important to the nation with its production of much of our supply of winter vegetables and for many specialty crops.

To the question, "Is greater utilization of the existing supplies possible?", the answer is yes. There is loss from seepage, evaporation, operational spills, and consumption by undesired vegetation. The Pacific Southwest Water Plan contemplates the lining of canals and irrigation efficiencies to conserve water research in evaporation control, facilities for groundwater recovery, channelization and phreatophyte eradication.

Channelization and phreatophyte control have caused some problems in aesthetics and wildlife habitat. The Bureau of Reclamation has coordinated this work with the Bureau of Sports Fisheries and Wildlife, state game and fish agencies, and park planners in a program aimed at maximizing recreation values to the extent possible in the overall water conservation effort. This includes fish hatcheries, federal wildlife refuges, state wildlife management areas, state parks, and preservation of backwater sloughs where feasible. The Bureau has a professional biologist on the job.

The reuse of treated sewage effluent for agricultural and certain industrial purposes is an important potential source of supplemental water. Likewise, a program for improving the quality of return-flow waters to reduce the salt load even moderately would permit unrestricted reuse of additional amounts. There is also a theoretical potential for increasing precipitation through weather modification, but this is only in the research state.

Even after stretching present supplies, however, it is clear that the future water supply problems of the Pacific Southwest can only be met through importation from areas of surplus outside the region and by desalination of ocean water. Recent technological advances have lifted desalination beyond the pilot plant level, and we are now on the threshold of large-volume production. But whether by importation, desalination, or a combination of both, the day of cheap water is over.

Desalination will go a long way toward solving future water problems for populous southern California coastal areas. It may even be feasible for a giant desalination plant in Mexico's Gulf of California, then bringing the water to the Yuma area, 140 feet above sea level. Costs are not yet competitive, however, for overcoming much distance and elevation, and this brings us back to the urgent need for action on the Central Arizona Project. It would be tragic to allow this region to wither by our failure to face up to this critical problem.

Unfortunately, the proposed means for financing the Central Arizona Project touched off one of the most vigorous preservation battles in the nation's history and delayed congressional authorization. This was the Bureau of Reclamation's plan to build two single-purpose power dams in the Grand Canyon. The proposed Marble Canyon Dam is now officially dropped, but Hualapai Dam (formerly Bridge Canyon) is still under congressional consideration. Hualapai is the best remaining damsite on the lower Colorado and could finance the Central Arizona Project, as there is a ready market for the power. Its location led to storms of protest against "inundation" of the Grand Canyon and invasion of the national park system with commercial developments. "Inundation" was an exaggeration, of course, but it traveled like "the shot heard 'round the world."

Actually, the dam would back the water up through Grand Canyon National Monument entirely and along one boundary of Grand Canyon National Park for thirteen miles. The lake could not be seen from any existing rim viewpoint in the national park. Aesthetic damage to the national park would be extremely minute, but alteration to the national monument would be considerable. The National Park Service has never developed Grand Canyon National Monument for public use and enjoyment except for a rough, dusty access road to the spectacular Toroweap viewpoint above Lava Falls. If the final decision is not to build the dam, the area should be added to the national park. If the dam is built, it should be added to the Lake Mead National Recreation Area. In either case the scenery is so awesome that it shouldn't be hidden away in mothballs from the public. A little more development here might have spared the nation from the whole argument.

The controversy has forced the Department of the Interior to look beyond the traditional dam building at possible alternatives for financing the project, such as thermonuclear power on the lower river. Whichever plan wins final preference, this writer suspects that economics will outweigh aesthetics in deciding the issue.

When the water situation in the Southwest becomes desperate enough, the aesthetics of a highwater mark on a lakeshore are likely to be no more objectionable than the fluctuating shoreline of the Lake Mead National Recreation Area. This area has developed into a highly popular, year-round outdoor playground which had more than 3.6 million recreational visits last year — and consistently outdraws every National Park Service area in the nation with the exception of five associated with Shenandoah-Blue Ridge Parkway-Great Smoky Mountains in the populous East. Hualapai Lake would have limited access, however, compared to other Colorado reservoirs. But when it comes to drinking water for the wife and kiddies, aesthetics can bend a little if that's the only way. But there may be another way — a potentially competitive alternative — that would spare the Grand Canyon, even though not much has been said in this controversy about the aesthetics of thermonuclear power generation. If so, this may be the place to bend.

Central Arizona is but one phase of the complicated Western water problem. The question of interbasin transfers of surplus water from one region to areas of need is the crux of a much larger issue which will require statesmanship and cooperation of the highest order. So far, the "haves" bristle at the very approach on the theory that the surplus of today may not be surplus tomorrow. Obviously, guarantees will have to be made giving first priority to areas of origin if this hurdle is to be overcome.

One big question which may have to be reopened follows: Are interstate surplus waters flowing unused into the ocean the property of a region or the nation? This is a little remindful of the recent argument that the Grand Canyon is not the exclusive property of Arizona — it belongs to all.

1968

96.

Eugene Rabinowitch: Turning the Clock Toward Midnight

The Bulletin of the Atomic Scientists, a journal of science and public affairs founded in 1945 by Hyman G. Goldsmith and Eugene Rabinowitch to give voice to the concern of the scientists who had worked on and knew the potential effects of the atomic bomb, prints on the cover of every issue a small clock. From 1960 to the end of 1967 the clock showed about twelve minutes to midnight. It was front page news around the country when the January 1968 issue appeared, for the minute hand had been moved up. Rabinowitch explained why in an editorial, part of which is reprinted here.

Source: *Bulletin of the Atomic Scientists,* January 1968: "New Year's Thoughts, 1968."

THE DISMAL RECORD

EIGHT YEARS AGO, on January 1, 1960, the clock on the *Bulletin* cover was moved a few minutes back in recognition, we said then, "of the growth, in the preceding decade, of understanding that the advent of nuclear weapons had made war between major technological nations irrational." A year later the outcome of the Cuban crisis seemed to confirm this judgment: faced with the threat of nuclear war, the Soviet Union withdrew its missiles, and the United States promised not to renew assaults on Cuba.

An interval of half-hearted East-West rapprochement followed. But it did not go fast, and it did not go far. It was enough, however, to loosen the rigidity of the two ideological power camps. A trend back to international anarchy ensued, with each nation pursuing again its own "national interest."

De Gaulle's France and Mao's China led the way. Both devoted enormous efforts to the development of nuclear weapons as a visible sign of their sovereignty and a guarantee of their freedom of action.

Stirrings of military nationalism appeared all over the globe. India and Pakistan went to war in 1965; Israel and the Arab countries did the same in 1967. And the United States was already embarked on a growing military intervention in Southeast Asia, without the UN label that had so irritated American nationalists in the Korean conflict.

A return to international anarchy had followed very quickly the end of World War I. After World War II it took a little longer. The blasts that leveled Hiroshima and Nagasaki, incinerating a hundred thousand human beings, were not as easily forgotten as the booms of the Big Berthas, or the year-long slaughter in the trenches around Verdun. But when the Cuban crisis was over, and no nuclear bombs went off, the belief spread that these would never again be used in war. And if so, did they not provide an "umbrella" under which nations could resume the pursuit of "national interests" by any other means, including if need be, aerial bombs, tear gas, and napalm?

By January 1965 the hopes that had caused the *Bulletin* clock to be moved back in 1960 were fading. But the editor was urged to give the new American administration time to show its hand. Was the new President not elected with the enthusiastic support of American scientists, receiving an overwhelming majority over an Air Force reserve general who embodied traditional nationalist thinking?

But the new President, although he had once sat at the feet of Franklin Delano Roosevelt, was not an inspired world leader, able to stem the rising tide of nationalism. He had inherited American commitment to defend an anti-communist perimeter threatened in Vietnam — a logical succession to American involvement in Korea. True, the geographical and political situation in Vietnam was much less favorable than in Korea. Instead of an easily fortifiable, hundred-mile-long line from sea to sea, a thousand-mile-long, indefensible jungle frontier; instead of a crusty old veteran fighter for Korean independence, a choice of ambitious officers, most of whom had fought with the French against the national revolution; instead of communist politicians imported by the Soviet troops to North Korea, a victorious leader in the war against the French.

Still, in terms of power politics, the second intervention was the logical conse-

quence of the first. The decision President Johnson made was one any tradition-bound President would have made — to fight it out rather than to risk a disintegration of the American sphere of influence in East Asia.

This is not said to justify the American policy in Vietnam, but merely to suggest that a valid alternative to this policy cannot be found in the framework of traditional power politics — a framework in which retreat and appeasement inevitably lead to fighting later, and probably under more difficult conditions. For a true alternative, a new framework is needed — a policy in which building the world community is given a higher priority than winning the contest for spheres of economic, political, and ideological influence.

The need for restructuring the international society seems clear at the end of a great war, whether in 1918 or 1945. But years go by, and nations return to self-centered pursuit of divergent national interests, until this pursuit leads them again into a deadly confrontation.

But such confrontations mankind cannot again afford. The breakaway from history now has to be sought in the doldrums of "politics as usual." Can it succeed? As of January 1968, the record is dismal.

THE FAILURE OF THE LEADERSHIP

AMERICAN POLITICAL LEADERS will say indignantly that they have not remained narrow traditionalists. Did they not defy domestic criticism and offer aid to practically all needy nations? Did they not battle congressional opposition year in and year out for greater foreign aid appropriations? Did they not pour American money into Latin America, Africa, and Southeast Asia? Did they not send Peace Corpsmen to teach English and child-rearing, hygiene and well-digging, to the remotest corners of the world? Did not American wheat rescue the hungry in India in 1965 and 1966, as it did the hungry in the Ukraine in the 1920s?

All this is true. But it is also true that these constructive efforts have been made with a weak left hand, while the mighty right hand was extending and strengthening the American empire in the world — defeating the Soviet blockade in Berlin, reestablishing the violated truce line across Korea, training and paying allied armies, outdoing the Soviet Union in a multibillion-dollar missile and bomb race. Even the two or three billions of dollars allocated to the space program are expressions of a will for victory in the race to the moon rather than signs of enlightened concern with mankind's desire to know more about its cosmic habitat.

Now, as the Vietnam war is beginning to pinch, Congress, offering no resistance to a $30-billion military expenditure, thinks it's time to cut down the "nonessentials" such as foreign aid, urban rehabilitation, and the research budget, and the administration offers no strong opposition.

It is not true that American resources are insufficient to support vast constructive efforts, even while financing the war in Vietnam. When a war comes, undreamed-of financial and technological resources suddenly become available to multiply many times the military appropriations and increase manyfold the production of planes or ships. It is all a question of urgency or priorities, and it is in the weighing of priorities that this administration, as well as its predecessors, has failed.

Whatever the pressure of war, it is still within American power to hold the constructive aims above those of destruction. Yet we easily find $2 billion monthly for military ends, but fail to find the few millions (and to organize the effort) needed for decent resettlement, feeding, protecting the health, and securing the education of the millions of people our military operations have displaced. What could have been made in the last decades, what can be made even now, if America's wealth, America's technological manpower and know-how, were invested as liberally in constructive tasks as they are invested in fighting the war!

As other nations are settling back into the grooves of self-serving national policies, America is failing to show the vision, the will, and the leadership to make our tentative international programs grow and ultimately to become the main content of world politics — as if they were not our main hope for the future, but fringe embellishments of power politics.

It is always too late and too little. A Lower Mekong development, pushed forward with all the immense American technological power, could have perhaps forestalled the civil war in Vietnam and prevented the division of Laos. But American commitment of $1 billion to this program came only when the war in Vietnam was beyond the point of no return. Plans for provision of fresh water to convert deserts into pastures, pushed ahead with a will several years ago, could have perhaps forestalled the Israel-Arab war and put nations of this area onto the path of constructive cooperation. Building the Aswan Dam in cooperation with the Russians could have perhaps prevented the sharpening of the contest between the countries for influence in the Near East.

The administration may have erred in committing American manpower to a war in a politically and geographically unprofitable area; perhaps a less committed leadership could extricate the United States. But this tactical error, if any, is not where the failure of American postwar policy lies, and extrication is not how it can be truly repaired.

The great failure, the crime before the future generations of mankind, has been not a sin of commission, but a sin of omission: a failure to stem the worldwide trend toward pre-atomic "normalcy" by an imaginative, large-scale use of American power and wealth, to lead in a worldwide mobilization of technical, economic, and intellectual resources for the building of a viable world community.

The day of reckoning may be approaching, not in the form of American withdrawal and communist takeover in the Far East but in a wave of world hunger and the accompanying surge of world anarchy predicted by many thoughtful analysts for the next decade.

THE SINS OF THE OPPOSITION

THE VIETNAM WAR has created grave dissension in America. A large part of the academic community have turned away from the administration they helped to install three years earlier.

The ethical and emotional basis of this opposition is admirable — as was that of the students at Oxford who adopted, in the Thirties, a resolution never again to fight "for king and country." It expresses a healthy revulsion against extending into the scientific civilization the barbaric traditions of the past; against misusing man's love for his people and his country to force him to participate in mass murder.

This revulsion is much more widespread and stronger now than it was thirty years ago. It is clearly nonsensical, if not criminal, to appeal to patriotic devotion and the fighting spirit of youth; as if they were being called to prove their mettle in hand-to-hand fighting, rather than to destroy innocent people by the hundreds by burning them in the sticky flow of napalm, or by the millions by exploding thermonuclear missiles over "enemy" cities — or to die themselves and to sacrifice their families in a mass elimination of humans as if they were cockroaches.

The outburst of Oxford students encouraged the German militarists into believing in England's decadence and helped to unleash World War II. Those same students then joined the RAF and turned the tide in the Battle of England.

Now, we are told, the marches and the riots of the pacifist youth also encourage the enemy to think that American society is in decay. And yet, even more than in the days of the Oxford resolution, the young men who burn their draft cards represent the sound instinct of mankind clamoring for survival. But it is also true that much of the power in the world is now, as it was in the Thirties, in the hands of men convinced that they have the right — in the service of a political ideal, or for the sake of their personal power — to send millions to die and to kill other millions; and peace hangs by the slender thread of mutual deterrence. This places heavy responsibility on the political and intellectual leadership of those who oppose war. The liberal and intellectual leaders of France and England did fail before World War II; they had refused to see the reality of the German drive for power; our present leaders deceive themselves and others about the realities of today's world.

The air resounds with speeches, the magazine pages are filled with articles proposing easy, honorable ways out of the Vietnam deadlock. Informed, closely reasoned criticisms of America's action in Vietnam by men as respected as Senator Fulbright or Professor Galbraith end with proposals which make one ask: On what planet have these men lived in the last decades? . . .

In proposing cheap but "honorable" solutions in Vietnam, those leaders of political opposition smooth the path to new American isolationism — to end in another rude, if not catastrophic, awakening. . . . The real short-range alternatives in Vietnam are: continuation of the war — whose success, under the geographical and political conditions, is remote — or withdrawing, leaving the power to the NLF without delusions about the consequences of such withdrawal, about the probable new crises to ensue in Korea, Laos, and Thailand, if not in Malaya and Burma.

More important long-range alternatives face America, whether she stays in Vietnam or not; and whether, after withdrawal she returns to fight, if need be, in Korea, Laos, or Thailand; or, sobered by Vietnam, she leaves the whole area alone. The triple alternatives are: continued participation in the contest for world power; retiring into "fortress America"; or putting America's world involvement onto a new track — investing, with a will and with whatever sacrifice may be needed, our unique wealth and technological power, in closing the gap between the prosperous city civilization of the North and Lin Piao's "world village" of the South.

It has been said that each government has the opposition it deserves. The American government of today offers a mirage of approaching military victory in Vietnam and subsequent withdrawal to build the "great society" at home. This has engendered an opposition that is equally reluctant to face realistically the situation, to proclaim the need for a radical change rather than a mere readjustment of American world policy — not retrenchment and isolationism but a different and perhaps more costly but more creative American involvement in the future of mankind.

James Reston, in the *New York Times*, recently wrote:

> Are they [the American people] really for the vast economic aid appropriations that have to be voted to avoid anarchy in other parts of the world, or are they bored or even disgusted with foreign aid? Do they really believe that we are on the verge of a new class war between the rich white nations and the poor nonwhite nations?

His answer is that the American people don't even want to think about these questions. "They want to preach at home and abroad, but will not pay the price." Neither the American government nor its opposition has risen above this popular attitude. To say that, in a democratic country, they cannot do so would mean to despair of the viability of democracy in the age of science!

There is little reason to feel sanguine about the future of our (and the whole Western) society on the world scale. There is a mass revulsion against war, yes; but no sign of conscious intellectual leadership in a rebellion against the deadly heritage of international anarchy. There is no broad recognition of the breathtaking perspectives of the scientific revolution — from all-destroying nuclear and biological war, likely if the international anarchy continues; from unprecedented world hunger, inevitable if man's procreation and food production are not brought into harmony by rational effort, to practically unlimited supply of energy, fresh water, food, shelter, and clothing for all — if stable peace is maintained and worldwide constructive cooperation is established.

In sad recognition that the past six years have brought mankind no closer to choosing the creative path, but have brought it farther down the road to disaster, the *Bulletin* clock is moved, on this sad New Year's Day, closer to midnight.

97.

Daniel X. Freedman: The Use and Abuse of Psychedelic Drugs

The psychedelic ("mind-manifesting") effects of LSD, a synthetic preparation of lysergic acid diethylamide, were first discovered by the Swiss chemist Albert Hofmann in 1943. Interest in this and similar drugs was routinely scientific for a few years following the discovery, but in the 1950s professional groups began to explore the use of the psychedelics as adjuncts to psychotherapy and also for other, more arcane, purposes. LSD was proposed as an aid in the treatment of neurosis and, with more success, in the cure of alcoholism. At the same time, its use outside of medical circles, especially on college campuses, became widespread; claims were advanced that it had great educational and religious value; and various cults sprang up, dedicated to a mystique characterized by the slogan "Turn on, tune in, and drop out." It was at this juncture that the psychedelics became a center of controversy. In 1966 a federal law was passed restricting (with a few exceptions) their manufacture, sale, and general use, and a flourishing black market resulted. The following assessment by Daniel X. Freedman, chairman of the department of psychiatry at the University of Chicago, is taken from a condensed version of a paper given at the University of California San Francisco Medical Center.

Source: *Bulletin of the Atomic Scientists*, April 1968.

Magic, drugs, drama, festival rites, utopian ideologies, and (with biological regularity) dreams have abetted man throughout history in his unceasing urge to transcend limits and escape dreary reality or anxiety. Given the prevalence of such wishes for omnipotence, it is not surprising that drugs play a role, not only in the behavior of individuals but in social and ideological processes. A pertinent question is whether the data of ethnology, pop culture, and clinical use indicate that there are drugs which specifically enhance these varied purposes. If so, how do they? Why and how exclusively or to what extent do they work? At what cost?

There are problems complicating such assessment. With the appropriate motives and occasions, almost any psychoactive drug can provide a brief "ego disruption," producing a moment of being "out of it." This disruption *in itself* may promote the release of powerful effects, and this ego state will be welcomed for its value as a remarkable trip from reality. Etched upon it may be the specific pattern of the drug. While I believe that drugs such as LSD extend and accent this primary ego state in a salient and sustained way, it is true that sufficiently strong motives can capture any opportune occasion to generate uninhibited or cultist behavior. . . .

The reported consequences of drugs such as LSD range from isolated awe or benign or even bored surprise to shifts of values.

They range from transient to long-term psychoses, to a gamut of confusional states and depression, to varieties of religious or aesthetic experience and insight, to clique formation and ritual. There are now conflicting reports of therapeutic efficacy in alcoholism, depression, character disorders, and severe neurosis. There is also a mushrooming psychedelic culture. This underlies the tribal motions (or Brownian movements) of young and aging dropouts, rebels disavowing society's "games" if not all (nonmusical) instrumental behavior. The paraphernalia of fringe fashions, music, and art comprise the trappings and trippings commercialized as psychedelic "go-go." Some serious theologians and some hippies, as well as our peripatetic prophets, now seek the drugs as a promoter of love, of religious or self-enhancement; apparently Western society will be a Zen Elysium. Enthusiasts are sincere and private, or provocative and evangelistic, and there are variant subgroups whose rapidly evolving ideologies and behavior are as yet unrecorded.

The recurrent historical theme is that certain drugs are compellingly related to "learning," to self-revelation, and that they are involved in some mystical, often ritual, use. The American Indian states that "peyote teaches." This theme does not dominate ordinary accounts of marijuana usage. The potent preparations of cannabis — charas and ganja — are an exception and have been used in India to enhance contemplative states as well as for a "high," and are not without paranoid and other psychotomimetic effects. Apparently there is a continuum of effects along the dimension of self-revealing and ritual usages.

To the extent that there are classes of agents which reveal normally suppressed components of the mind — exposing these dimensions to our attention — we can say that both use and abuse stem from an amazed response to a drug-induced subjective experience. If this is what Humphrey Osmond meant by the term "psychedelic" (or "mind-manifesting") it is an apt though not novel description. Whatever the outcome, the mode of functioning and experiencing called psychedelic — or psychotomimetic — reflects an innate capacity (like the dream) of which the *waking* human mind is capable. The fact that a certain class of drugs so sharply compels this level of function (with all the variability inherent in less organized states) and does so for a chemically determined package of time is what intrigues the bio-behavioral scientist. . . . There are few drugs which can so readily . . . unhinge us from the constancies which regulate daily life or so clearly present us with unevaluated data from the "inside world" and from the many inutile perceptions potentially available to us. . . .

During the first four-and-a-half hours of the drug state there is generally a clear-cut self-recognition of effects — an internal "TV show" — which is followed by another four- or five-hour period in which a subjective sense of change is not marked but during which heightened self-centeredness, ideas of reference, and a certain "apartness" are observed. At twelve to forty-eight hours after drug ingestion, there may or may not be some letdown and slight fatigue. There is no craving for a drug to relieve this and no true physiological withdrawal, as is the case with opiates, alcohol, and certain sedatives and tranquilizers. Tolerance (diminished effect with daily dosage) does occur, requiring three or four days of abstinence for recovery of full sensitivity to the drug.

It is the intense experience without clouded consciousness — the heightened "spectator ego" witnessing the excitement — which is characteristic for these drugs in usual dosages. Thus there is a split of the self, a portion of which is a relatively passive monitor and a portion of which experiences. Some people seem to repeat this long after the drug state; they turn away from the prosaic world, or else are turned away by society as well as turned on by the drug. They may find a clique or a group which tolerates this disposition.

During the drug state, awareness becomes intensely vivid while self-control over input is remarkably diminished; thus there is the lurking threat of loss of inner control, of the "dying of the ego" so often reported in bad trips or in phases of mystical experiences with the drug. Customary boundaries become fluid and the familiar becomes novel and portentous. The loosening of boundaries and carelessness or an indifference to the habitual and customary may characterize certain chronic drug abusers. This may border on a supercilious posture of superiority which the elect of many cults can assume (or which the outsider feels to be the attitude of those who know something he does not).

Events — internal or external, memories or perceptions — take on a trajectory of their own; qualities become intense and gain a life of their own. Redness is more interesting than the object which is red; meaningfulness more important than what is specifically meant; connotations balloon into cosmic allusiveness; the limits of sobriety are lost. Sexual experience may or may not remain "sexual." The very definition of the importance and stability of the external world shifts. And, after the drug state, we may find more tolerance for ambiguity and a diminished readiness for the quick answer; we also can find an associated inability to decide, to discriminate, to make commitments.

Most neurotic symptoms have been viewed as misguided attempts at cure, and it may be that for many the drug experience — like certain symptomatic acts — represents a beginning which, without luck or expertise, cannot easily come to a useful conclusion. Thus many of the immediate aftereffects of LSD could depend largely on the motive for taking the drug and in fact could be transient rather than transforming.

How to reinforce any shifts in attitude which do occur with the drug without running the risk of repeated drug sessions is a largely unstudied issue. One good "trip" does not predict a second.

Since judgment is not enhanced *during* the drug state and since isolation or apartness, even when sanctioned by a minority group, bring their own problems, it is clear that persons who continually overvalue the experience of the drug state could develop or reinforce patterns of poor practical judgment. The consequences of long-term and frequent use of the drug — at present the rarest form of experimentation with LSD — would probably have to be evaluated in this context.

In the drug state, the experience of compelling immediacy diminishes the normal importance of past and future. It also is related to the overvaluation of "nowness," the pursuit of the novel in certain youth subcultures. The ability to see the familiar in a new light, the temporary loss of normal anticipations, may be relevant to the still poorly understood creative process. Yet there is nothing about the drug effect which specifically enhances the synthetic and organizing facility. It is, in fact, the need for synthesis — not the ability to synthesize — that is enhanced in the drug state.

An important feature of the state is an increased dependence upon the environment for structure and support as well as greater vulnerability to the milieu. With the loss of boundaries, persons or a group are used for such elemental functions as control — for helping one to know what is inside and what is outside, for comfort, and for binding and balancing the fragmenting world. Persons or objects in the environment have positive or negative value in quite elemental terms: for example, as threats or as anchors in maintaining control. Persons are seen as objects — either to be clung to or to be contemplated in an essentially self-centered, aesthetic, or ideologic frame of reference.

Eugene Anthony from Black Star

Timothy Leary, leader of a cult which champions the unrestricted use of LSD

The claims for a different perspective on personal relationships have to be evaluated in terms of how this is integrated into the user's life, as well as in the internal rearrangements of his values.

With the fusion of self and surroundings some of the strain between harsh authority, social limits, and personal strivings can for the moment be transcended or dissolved. At the same time there is a leaning on others for structure and control. Hence, when the drugs are taken in a group setting, the breach with reality can be filled by the directive mystique and support of the group. This is, in part, why I have termed these drugs "cultogenic." . . .

Some persons endure all this without evident harm. The spectator ego can simply be interested in the reversal of figure and ground, the visual tricks, or — with higher doses — the spectator is entranced or totally absorbed. The experiencing ego can, especially with increasing dosage, be overwhelmed. At any level, defensiveness can

appear: the struggle for control may dominate; the spectator shuts his eyes and fights.

There are different modes of coping with the drug state which could be called protective. One protection is *not* to fight the multiplicity of experiences during the drug state. When the traditional defensive operations come too strongly into play temporary panic may ensue even in relatively stable people. Thus a certain yielding and surrender of ambition and personal autonomy help some individuals to have a good experience, but this requires, if not group support, a special kind of personal strength. It also requires stable groups.

Some people achieve an overall stability by a disposition to react with an astounded pleasure to the whole flux of events. Others, like the Peyote Indians, are encouraged or equipped to transcend the fragmented disparate elements and visions, letting them flow into a mystique, or be steered by latent guiding interests or memories. With higher dosages and the increasing loss of the capacity to focus, the importance of guiding "sets" (music, mystique, or affective expectations such as the doctrine of boundless love) is enhanced.

The drug experience is compelling; it is hard to convey but incredibly vivid. No doubt the rearrangements of reality which can occur produce a memorable experience, but one is reminded of Sidney Cohen's remark that most people get what they deserve or what they are equipped at the time to experience. . . .

In a state of altered consciousness where control over awareness is diminished, there is no way to bind the intensities experienced and symptoms may ensue. Thus people may "act" to produce vivid consequences or experiences in order to see them in a new light and grasp thereby for control. What often is lacking in this repetitive remembering or acting is the element of guidance, correction, reflection, and structure which leads to authentic self-mastery.

This may be the chief source of danger of LSD — the lack of structure and autonomy and the traumatic and potent intensity of individual experiences.

Thus "acting out" behavior with or without a drug often compels external control, correction, and guidance and appears as a provocative accusation against authority. The young do not merely "turn on" themselves, but seem to display great anger at the guides who, they feel, failed them. They thereby keep a link — and a very strong one — to the very strictures which had previously absorbed them, just as a misbehaving child is tied to his parents by evoking their involved irritation or punishment. Some kind of continuity with reality is sought. The bridge may be a book as it was with Huxley, silent synthesis or change of values and tastes, or the understanding of a group or person. In the Native American Church, the Indian utilizes all these elements — religious explanation and adherence, specific ceremonies, and the group with its ideology — to integrate the experience which serves a purpose in the total fabric of his life. The Indian does not accordingly seek a simple "high" or thrill with the drug. . . .

Some psychotherapists have attempted to use the loosening of associations and the intense experiencing produced by the drug in order to influence behavior change. Yet the history of LSD therapy by physicians represents a picture of both use and abuse. In the late 1950s many physicians were not only struck by the drug-induced phenomena but apparently were addled by taking the drug concurrently with their patients. Yet what is rational about therapy as distinct from healing cults is our obligation to study and control that with which we work.

There are a number of continuing controlled projects in this country and a long history of experience with the use of LSD in therapy. Two major modes of treatment prevail. That employed by many European workers (often called "psycholytic") represents a method by which certain defenses are breached. With a strong drug-enhanced tie to the therapist, feelings and memories are allowed to emerge vividly and unforgettably before the eye of consciousness, and their strength discharged. The events are later worked over with care. The integration which follows is a collaborative venture requiring the active participation and output of the patient.

In the so-called psychedelic therapies as they are now being tested there is an awareness of an immense amount of preparation, of salesmanship with an evangelical tone in which the patient is confronted with positive displays of hope before he has his one great experience with very high doses of drug. The experience is structured by music and by confident good feelings. With the support of the positive therapist throughout this experience, the patient is encouraged to see his life in a new light, to think of his future accordingly.

Obviously careful follow-up is essential since the immediate glow which occurs with drug-induced personality change can be deceptive. Even if these results are occasionally positive, such therapies are taxing upon the time, emotions, and good sense of all involved and are not likely to be extensively used. Yet the fact that under LSD the therapist can often readily suggest basically positive or negative attitudes toward a wide range of life experiences and promote a state in which struggle may be diminished should arouse our fundamental curiosity — not only about LSD therapy and its possible efficacy but about the mechanisms, utility, resistances, and pitfalls in behavior change achieved through persuasion.

We should recall that the increasing problem of drug abuse in most countries is with alcohol, followed by the barbiturates, amphetamines, opiates, and mild tranquilizers. In this context the consequences to national health of hallucinogens are not as yet truly startling — either in terms of the utility of LSD or its harm. In the long run, debates about whether or not to use LSD are hardly as socially consequential as the use of "the pill." The agent most frequently used by youth for illicit purposes and with lethal effect is the automobile. This is an interesting generation, but they have not as yet gone completely to pot.

Not all users are the young, nor are all youthful users initially unconventional and unproductive. A few current illicit self-help groups employ the drug and religion to achieve a conventional outcome, for example, a group of ex-convicts and a group of homosexuals. Many practices (half-way houses, group therapies, cathartic therapy, confrontation therapy) built into the total fabric of psychiatric work are imitated by ever proliferating self-help groups which frequently tap our society's long tradition of distrust of medical science.

Estimates of the incidence of psychedelic drug "use," however defined, are always vulnerable to criticism. They range from 1 to 15 percent on certain campuses. Figures higher than 5 percent probably do not distinguish single trials from habitual use, nor LSD from other drugs of abuse; for example, proselytizers frequently tell us about the "inevitable" increase in the use of marijuana and LSD. Only a small fraction of persons who have taken the truly potent hallucinogenic drugs can be said to constitute a reliable base for study of long-term users. The problem is that some are always first discovering the drug (available now for twenty years) and acclaiming it, while the silent others are experiencing disillusion after a year or two of absorption. Still others actively seek or passively accept one or two experiments. . . .

Complications for research also arise from sensational publicity. The select as well as the popular press provide a structure for the curious, restless, and lost as they compete to announce or denounce drug usage. The psychedelic hucksters — for a bandwagon effect — confidently announce that growing hordes of youngsters are independently dedicated chronic users. To the mature, their message is that this is a revolution in which adults are helpless; to the young it is a subtle invitation to revolt under the sanction of inevitability. The establishment reacts with irritation and fright. As the advertising escalates and the empirical problem grows, the young and their frequently confused and permissive parents must enter the debate and assess the claims of value. Government agencies were not immune; they delayed for well over a year before setting up appropriate means for the approval, distribution, and control of LSD for research — a significant problem for scientists. Physicians hysterically crying alarm have joined the melee, lumping all bad reactions into one dire outcome: permanent madness. They now also cite somatic dangers. . . .

The fact is that dangerous and tragic psychological consequences are now unequivocally established, and it is just this fact which users deny, as if it were concocted to attack their autonomy and self-esteem. From our own campus experiences it appears that users who end up in hospitals with prolonged and serious psychoses are initially a quite unstable group. They are, in any event, a small group. Suicides and violence are also uncommon. . . .

A fair number of people have had LSD without apparent serious untoward effects. The majority of acute untoward reactions with LSD — while severely troublesome — are not as yet proven to be inevitably permanently crippling. The suggestibility, despair, confusion, and latent disorganization of those who unwisely take LSD is, I believe, as crucial a variable as the chemical which renders them — unexpectedly — vulnerable to more trauma than they can handle.

The habitual *long-term* use of LSD for pleasure or escape produces the *possibility* of chronic impairment of good sense and maturation. In this sense, abuse of the drug can surely reinforce a dissociative trend, leading to acute reactions or insidious disorganization and failure successfully to integrate life crises. . . .

With skilled therapists, 1 percent or less of drug experiences may be unexpectedly traumatic. Certainly under these circumstances less than 1 percent is traumatic in outcome. With proper immediate follow-up most of these reactions should be therapeutically resolved. This appears to have been the case even though attempts to screen subjects in order to predict reactions have not yielded clear-cut guidelines; nor has it been established that the drug is necessarily traumatic when given to severely mentally ill persons with the structure and follow-up available in therapeutic settings. We can be confident — from the experience in responsible research centers in the 1950s and in European clinics — that the setting and the ability to manage the experience and its aftermath are crucially important. There is no question that good sense and trained skills can help to control bad LSD experiences and outcomes. In all probability older subjects (past twenty-five years) are less likely to have prolonged reactions linked to a single bad experience. Impressions are that 10 percent of any batch of trips (whether or not the first) have the potential for trouble. The inescapable problem is that, except within narrow limits, a bad experience and an unwelcome outcome need not be associated and neither can they always be predicted.

My current opinion is that the chief abuse of LSD is irresponsible, alluring, and provocative advertising by the bored mass media. Couched in the language of drugs, an ideology has been insinuated into youth culture by a band of articulate writers and vagrant professionals. These have replaced the old medicine show with an updated campus version complete with readings and

tempting arguments, if not pills, to sell: "Tune in, turn on, drop out." A drug mystique has been welded to the serious shifts and strains inherent in the experience of the potentially most unstable group of any society — the adolescent and young adult.

We need not determine whether this is indeed a "now" generation valuing honesty, love, direct confrontation, uncomplicated action, and avoiding ideologies in favor of simple justice. These values, however germane to the LSD experience, were not born from the drugged mind. The Pied Pipers of LSD — peddling a drug which *can* enhance poor judgment — would lure youth from the acquisition of competence, or even from the serious study of man's attempts to deal with the two orders of reality in his personal development and in his religious, artistic, philosophical, and scientific endeavors. If we attempt to account for the fact that the greatest abuse has been among the well-educated — or those who might be — we would in all honesty have to question the strange tolerance for these psychedelic follies in campus cultures. Forgetting both Freud and James, many of our teachers and intellectuals are either entranced or perplexed by stories of LSD-induced revelations. They appear neither to have learned, nor to teach, from experience. . . .

If we ask whether there have been cultures which have eradicated mental disorders and disease with these drugs, or groups which have seen the dissolution of deviant behavior or even drug-linked behaviors (for example, alcoholism), we find some slight association, but no clear-cut, overall differences. In fact, the use of these drugs is often associated with some form of psychosocial deprivation or, equally, with marked privilege, as in Brahmins and college students. That private satisfactions might have been achieved, that some groups using these drugs could have attained some spiritual equilibrium seems apparent, but whether the drugs and their effect are both necessary and sufficient to get such results — whether no alternative means exist within a culture — is another question.

We should not forget to assess the cost of sustained euphoria or pleasure states; we have to wonder whether the mind of man is built to accommodate an excess of either pleasure or rationality. We do not know whether or not there are individuals with sufficient strength to take these drugs for growth or pleasure within the social order without increased and credulous alienation from it. . . .

In general, it seems to me that we have been more awed than aided by our experience with these drugs. They still remain agents which reveal but do not chart the mental regions; to do that we must employ mental faculties available in the undrugged state. Accordingly we should do better than repeat the ontogeny of past encounters with mind-revealing drugs. We should strive to make distinctions so that, if we learn, in the future, how the elements of mind are related, we can specify for the chemist the designs he should seek. But first we have to learn to analyze what these drugs can teach us about the ways in which the chemical organization of the brain is related to the dimensions of mind.

98.

RICHARD S. LEWIS: The Kennedy Effect

President Kennedy's call, in May 1961, for a national commitment to land a man on the moon and return him safely to earth before the end of the decade had an electrifying effect on the U.S. space program. Vast sums were appropriated, and the energies and skills of thousands of scientists and researchers were marshalled in behalf of the effort. For a time all went well. But a combination of events — notably the escalation of the Vietnam war and the terrible Apollo fire of January 1967 — caused many Americans to have second thoughts. The effects of Kennedy's decision on the space program as a whole, and especially on its future after the moon landing, were assessed by Richard S. Lewis, science editor of the Chicago Sun-Times, *in an article that appeared early in 1968.*

Source: *Bulletin of the Atomic Scientists*, March 1968, pp. 2-5.

THE THUNDERING SUCCESS of the 364-foot Saturn 5 launch vehicle on its maiden test flight last November marked a dramatic upturn in the fortunes of the U.S. space program, which had been sliding downhill since the Apollo fire in January 1967. It has revived the possibility that a manned lunar landing can be made in this decade. While the deadline has lost much of the urgency which impelled President Kennedy to set it, in 1961, it is still considered important by the Johnson administration. The principal reason is that it would demonstrate a technological capability of meeting the most ambitious commitment in the history of technology within a predictable time frame.

On Capitol Hill, this is regarded as an exhibition of strategic importance in the context of present rivalries, wherein spectacular developments in technology appear to be evidence of a society's vitality and power.

In retrospect, Mr. Kennedy's request to Congress in May 1961 that "this nation should commit itself to achieving the goal before this decade is out of landing a man on the moon and returning him safely to Earth" appears to be one of the most important acts of his administration. He, himself, came to regard it so, and his technical advisers believed it would become as monumental in history as the Louisiana Purchase or the Panama Canal.

The request was rapidly translated into a mandate, to which Congress acquiesced. It galvanized the lagging, directionless space effort around a dramatic, not-too-distant goal which, the President's technical adviser assured him, was within the state of the art and which, if all went well, might be achieved during a second term of office. The mandate provided the impetus for enlarging the American space work establishment, thus enabling the United States to overtake Russian space technology within an acceptable time frame of reference.

However, the impact of the mandate was not confined to providing the fledgling manned space flight program with a destination. It became much more far-reaching than that, possibly because the potential in science and technology amplifies military and political decisions affecting their development. The military decision creating the Manhattan Project led to scientific and engineering developments not clearly foreseen in 1942. The political decision to send men to the moon also led to unexpected results in the development of space technology, but in a different way.

In the long range, it has determined the priorities, the engineering designs, and the scientific objectives of the space program in this decade, and it is quite likely to control future space work for the remainder of this century. This unforeseen result might be called the Kennedy Effect. While its intent in the beginning was to enlarge American competence in space, its implementation has built a Procrustean bed and the American space program has been severely mutilated to fit it.

A critical element of the Kennedy Effect is the commitment implicit in the original call to the moon. By imposing what has turned out to be an inflexible goal of the greatest priority, President Kennedy and his advisers limited the space agency's options in the present tight budget era. As a result of budget cuts, the cost of fulfilling the lunar landing commitment prevents NASA from undertaking, or preparing to undertake, any other program of magnitude before the end of the decade. Project Voyager, designed to soft-land a life-seeking capsule on Mars by 1973, has been postponed indefinitely and other planetary exploration programs after 1969 have been shelved on this account. This situation has alarmed James A. Van Allen of the University of Iowa, a member of the Space Science Board of the National Academy of Sciences, who warned that the United States is abandoning *in situ* study of the planets to the Soviet Union (*Science*, December 15, 1959).

In addition to this withdrawal, the once imposing edifice of graduate-student training and university research in space-related science which NASA began to build earlier in the decade has crumbled for lack of continuing appropriations. In this way, the national competence in science is being diminished. ·

The time frame is a second critical element of the Kennedy Effect. It dictated the decision to develop the Saturn 5 as the lunar launch vehicle for Project Apollo and shaped the final configuration of the Apollo spacecraft.

The time limitation forced NASA to adopt lunar orbit rendezvous as the mode for the lunar landing rather than direct ascent to the moon as originally planned. Instead of broadening American performance in space, the Kennedy Effect has narrowed it to a single line of launch vehicles and spacecraft and a single *modus operandi.*

This was not intended, but the history of Project Apollo, which has not been an entirely happy one, shows it was inevitable.

On July 11, 1961, the late Hugh Dryden, deputy administrator of NASA, explained to the House Committee on Science and Astronautics that there were at least five ways of going to the moon. Each called for a different technical approach.

One was by direct ascent, using a powerful, liquid-fuel rocket. The second was by direct ascent using a solid-fuel rocket. The third was refueling by means of rendezvous in earth orbit. The fourth was refueling by lunar orbit rendezvous. And the fifth technical approach was rendezvous on the moon with a previously landed fuel supply.

The overall feasibility of landing on the moon had been established so far as NASA was concerned early in 1961 by a manned lunar landing task force set up in the Eisenhower administration. It now remained to determine the landing mode. Three weeks before Kennedy called for the landing, an ad hoc task group was appointed to make a study of how to accomplish the landing in a time frame of six and one-half to eight and one-half years.

The ad hoc task group, chaired by William Fleming of NASA, reported in June 1961 that the mission could be performed by a huge launch vehicle NASA had in mind, called Nova. It was to be 360 feet tall, "60 feet taller than a football field is long," as Administrator James E. Webb described it at the first National Conference on the Peaceful Uses of Space, at Tulsa, Oklahoma. In their most powerful configuration, the Nova's three stages would develop a total of 17 million pounds of thrust to propel a 150,000-pound Apollo spacecraft directly to the moon.

However, a later study by Nicholas Go-

lovin of NASA and Laurence Kavanau of the Department of Defense asserted that Nova posed technical and reliability problems which were not likely to be resolved in time to meet the Kennedy deadline. At the end of 1961, NASA began to consider developing a smaller launch vehicle, the Saturn 5, capable of developing a total of 8.7 million pounds of thrust in three stages. Nevertheless, NASA announced in January 1962 that it had selected the Aerojet General Corporation to develop the M-1 engine for the Nova second stage and in March called for industry proposals for detailed systems definition and preliminary design of the Nova. Northwest of Cape Canaveral [Kennedy], the space agency began to acquire thousands of acres for the Nova development and launch facility.

But even as development work was started on the M-1 engine, it was eliminated from Project Apollo, along with the Nova concept. The Manned Space Flight directorate decided on Saturn 5 as the only lunar launch vehicle that could be developed in time to put a man on the moon in this decade.

The formal explanation for the switch was given to the House Committee on Science and Astronautics in July of 1962 by D. Brainerd Holmes, then director of the Office of Manned Space Flight. Of all the methods studied for going to the moon, he said, direct ascent by Nova would take the longest to develop. Time could be saved by developing Saturn 5, which did not require the M-1 engine. The M-1 engine was new, existing only in blueprint. On the other hand, the F-1 kerosene-oxygen engine for the first stage of Saturn 5 and the J-2 upper-stage hydrogen-oxygen engine were already in development.

However, Saturn 5 was not powerful enough to lift an Apollo weighing 75 tons to the moon. It would boost only 45 tons to escape velocity. There were two approaches to solving this problem.

One was to lighten the Saturn 5 third

stage by leaving out the 95 tons of liquid oxygen it would normally carry at launch. This would enable the first two Saturn stages to put the third stage and the Apollo in low earth orbit as inert payload. A rendezvous would then be made with a liquid oxygen tanker, previously orbited, and the third stage's oxygen tank would be filled. Its J-2 liquid hydrogen-liquid oxygen engine would then be capable of accelerating the 75-ton Apollo to the moon.

This approach called for a double launch of two Saturn 5's — one to establish the liquid oxygen tanker in orbit and the other to put up the third stage and the Apollo. The problem of rendezvous in earth orbit, it was felt, could be readily solved.

A second approach was to lighten the Apollo configuration to 45 tons. This could be done if Apollo did not land on the moon but remained instead in lunar orbit. Then the spacecraft's braking and descent engines and the fuel they required could be eliminated from the payload. In their place, a relatively lightweight skiff (Lunar Module) could be substituted to take two of the three Apollo crewmen to the lunar surface, while the third remained on watch in the orbiting mother craft.

The return mode required the two crewmen to lift their skiff off the moon and make a rendezvous with the Apollo in lunar orbit. After reentering the spaceship, the crewmen would cast off the skiff and leave it afloat in lunar orbit. Then they would ignite the Apollo engine and return home.

Holmes advised the House committee that lunar orbit rendezvous was the way NASA had decided to go. "As far as time is concerned," he said, "direct ascent is the latest — twenty months later than lunar orbit rendezvous. It requires the most additional development. We must develop the modules not under contract — the braking stage, the lunar touchdown stage, and the Nova. We would not like to develop the Nova today on a rush basis."

In lunar orbit rendezvous, the only new requirement was the lunar module skiff. All the other equipment, Holmes pointed out, was already under contract.

"The mode selection is not a question of basic feasibility," Wernher von Braun, director of the Marshall Space Flight Center, told the Committee's Manned Spaceflight Subcommittee later. "There are many ways to go to the moon. It is a question of time, cost, and so forth."

The Nova program was abandoned, since, as Holmes explained to the House committee, it was not financially possible to develop it and the Saturn 5 at the same time. While M-1 engine development continued for several years, funding steadily declined until fabrication plans were shelved.

Once the launch vehicle and spacecraft design was decided on these terms, the Kennedy Effect froze them into a rigid development and testing schedule. Also, it did not allow for any alternative ventures to the moon in the manned program. For example, after rendezvous and docking were mastered in Project Gemini during 1965-66, it would have been possible to launch a two-man crew around the moon in a Gemini spacecraft, using the Air Force Titan 3D and Centaur launch vehicles. Alternatively, a circumlunar flight was possible by another route, by docking a Titan 2-launched Gemini in orbit with a Centaur rocket, instead of the less powerful Agena. Estimates by engineers of the Convair Division of General Dynamics show that the hydrogen-oxygen powered Centaur rocket has more than enough propulsion to boost a Gemini spacecraft in earth orbit to an orbit encompassing the earth-moon system.

These options were ruled out by Apollo's cost, which rose from the initial estimate of $20 billion to more than $23 billion. A circumlunar flight was planned as a goal after Project Mercury in 1959, and it has remained as a possible exercise in Apollo, although cost considerations dictate that the objective of any moon mission in Apollo should be a landing.

The Kennedy Effect produced fabrication and testing schedules which became so rigid that unforeseen delays or accelerations of the pace of development had cost repercussions. After 1963, NASA contended, it was no longer possible to accelerate or stretch out the development schedule without significant cost increases.

Pressure on the contractors for meeting schedules was high. The Grumman Aircraft Engineering Company went ahead with the development of the Lunar Module (LM) before it was known what kind of surface the LM would land on. There was not enough time to wait for the results of lunar reconnaissance in Projects Ranger and Surveyor.

Incomplete spacecraft were shipped from the North American Aviation factory at Downey, California, to the John F. Kennedy Space Center in Florida, with the expectation they would be tidied up there while undergoing checkout. On Apollo 012, the craft in which Astronauts Virgil I. Grissom, Edward H. White II, and Roger B. Chaffee were asphyxiated in the January 27, 1967, fire, there were 113 uncompleted engineering change orders when the vehicle was delivered to NASA, and 623 more were released later. A second spacecraft, Apollo 017, was the subject of a report showing 109 malfunctions and discrepancies six months after it was delivered to NASA. Among the problems in this spacecraft was a dead battery installed upside down so that it interfered with the deployment of one of the parachutes.

However, Apollo 017 eventually was put in flight condition and performed perfectly on the maiden flight test of Saturn 501 on November 9, 1967.

During congressional hearings into the Apollo fire, North American executives complained that they could not keep up with the changes ordered by NASA and meet delivery schedules. Was tight scheduling to blame for the slipshod workmanship

in Apollo 012? The Apollo Review Board never said so. The fire was clearly the result of poor work practices and inspections, it said. Contributory negligence was exhibited by NASA's inability to perceive the risk of testing an electrically defective spacecraft with a pure-oxygen atmosphere and flammable materials in the crew compartment.

A year after the Apollo fire, the Senate Space Committee issued a report accusing NASA of overconfidence and complacency. These attitudes together with the space agency's evasiveness in revealing the production problems it was having with the contractor, North American Aviation, Inc., contributed to the accident, the report stated. It was released January 31, 1968, and received a minimum of attention in the press.

A member of the committee's Democratic majority, Senator Walter F. Mondale of Minnesota, said in a separate report that NASA's "lack of candor" and "patronizing attitude" toward Congress after the tragedy "can only produce a loss of congressional and public confidence in NASA programs."

The Republican committee members, Edward W. Brooke of Massachusetts and Charles H. Percy of Illinois, called for further discussion of the space agency's capability of achieving the lunar landing on the Kennedy timetable. It wasn't worth sacrificing safety, they said in a separate report, adding:

> In our opinion, a delay of the landing into the next decade brought about in the interest of safety or as a result of efforts to avoid excessive costs that might develop in holding to the present schedule would in no way be a political or technical disaster.

Following the fire, however, the Kennedy Effect produced a speed-up in the lunar landing flight sequence. Originally, fifteen Saturn 5-Apollo flights were to be made before 1970 and the landing was to be attempted near the end of the sequence. Budget cuts made it impossible for NASA to purchase or fly all fifteen vehicles before the end of the decade, and during the Apollo fire hearings, Webb told the House committee it was planned to attempt the lunar landing on the eleventh Saturn 5 flight.

Further cuts in the budget reduced to nine the number of moon rockets NASA could purchase and fly in this decade. Webb amended his earlier estimate and said it might be possible to accomplish the landing on the ninth flight — but only if all went well on the other flights.

An enormous burden was placed on each step in the flight test program. Unless every one was successful, the deadline could not be met. Any significant delay would enhance a suggestion in Congress that the entire Apollo Project be put in mothballs until after a settlement of the Vietnam war.

Under the pressure of scheduling and keeping down costs, NASA resorted to "all up" testing of the first Saturn 5, without any preliminary flight tests of the first and second stages. The Apollo and the third stage had been test flown before on the uprated Saturn 1, but the booster stage, with its 7.5 million pounds of thrust, and the second stage, producing 1 million pounds of thrust, had never been off the ground under their own power. In addition, the equipment at Launch Complex 39 was getting its first workout.

The odds against the "all up" test succeeding were regarded as inordinately high. Saturn 501 was the first American rocket to be tested in full flight configuration, with payload, and even though computerized checkout systems constantly monitored thousands of components in the rocket and spacecraft, the gamble looked like a desperate one. If the "all up" test had failed, it was "all up" with the effort to meet the Kennedy deadline.

The flight of Saturn 501-Apollo 017 turned out to be the most successful test in American space technology. There was no important discrepancy. And that success must be attributed to the Kennedy Effect, as a failure would have been.

In the context of budget stresses imposed by the war overseas, and by poverty at home, the Kennedy Effect has sustained Apollo by reducing the space program essentially to a single priority. Projects of lesser priority have been shelved into the next decade or into limbo.

No new programs can be started under these conditions. That implies little progress in space technology or science in the next decade, for new programs require years of lead-time.

In fact, one of the grand results of the Kennedy Effect is the probability that the Saturn 5 is the last major launch vehicle which the United States is likely to develop in this century. The Nova is dead and no other launch vehicles are in view. There are no missions for them in any case.

By its stringent singularity of purpose, the Kennedy Effect has tended to confine rather than extend the national potential in space. It will realize its objective of putting astronauts on the moon, but for a long time after that they will not be able to do anything else.

It will free man from his remaining chains, the chains of gravity which still tie him to this planet. It will open to him the gates of heaven.
    WERNHER VON BRAUN, *referring to travel in outer space*

99.

Constitutional Reform in Maryland

The writing of constitutions, if one includes the making of the Mayflower Compact, is perhaps the oldest American political tradition. The traditional vehicle for producing such documents has been the constitutional convention, a device widely used in the Revolutionary period, in the period of constitutional reform of the 1820s, and also today. A new Maryland constitution, replacing an antiquated one dating from the Civil War, was drawn up by 142 popularly elected delegates in a convention that opened at Annapolis on September 12, 1967, and that produced a finished document on January 10, 1968. It was disapproved by the voters on May 14. The account of the new constitution reprinted here was written by Dr. Clinton I. Winslow, professor emeritus of political science at Goucher College and a delegate to the convention from Baltimore County. Richard Homan's account of the rejection appeared in the Chicago Sun-Times *two days after the voting. Other states that are considering constitutional revisions are Pennsylvania, Hawaii, Illinois, New Mexico, Arkansas, Georgia, Nebraska, and Washington.*

Source: *Baltimore Sun,* January 10, 1968: "Local Government and the Courts."
Chicago Sun-Times, May 16, 1968.

I.

CLINTON I. WINSLOW:
Description of the
Proposed Constitution

THE NEW MARYLAND constitution is intended to replace the constitution of 1867 with its 200 amendments. But it is not a revolutionary document — the general structure, powers, and interrelationships of governmental institutions, as well as the place of the people in the body politic, remain fundamentally the same.

Maryland will continue to have a tripartite governmental structure with the governor, the legislature, the courts operating under the familiar "separation of powers"

doctrine. The General Assembly will continue as a bicameral body, concerned chiefly with lawmaking and altered somewhat in size and basis of representation.

The courts will still have the assignment of interpreting and applying the law to individual cases, operating under a revised structure at the trial level and an unchanged one at the appeal level. The governor's office remains intact with some modifications in powers and relationships.

The charter counties and Baltimore city remain much as they are in structure, with some changes in power. Municipalities retain their present organization and powers in large part. Noncharter counties, on the other hand, face reorganization.

The position of the people vis-à-vis the

constitution remains largely the same. The new Declaration of Rights, it is believed, safeguards the liberties of the people even more completely than does the existing one. The controls over government in the hands of the people are, on balance, increased rather than diminished.

One of the major changes written into the new constitution concerns local government. For much too long a time, Maryland has followed a practice by which the General Assembly has been the legislative body for the counties. Determination of petty matters in each county has been the business of the state legislature to the point that more than half of the bills considered by almost every session are "local" bills. A few of the counties have escaped by adopting "Home Rule."

The new constitution proposes to solve this "local legislation" problem by a new approach. All counties will now have "home rule" with an instrument of government or charter of their own choosing, or alternatively one written by the General Assembly as a general substitute. When so reorganized, the twenty-four counties of the state (Baltimore city will be treated as a county) will operate under a new arrangement of powers. Rather than having a list of "expressed powers" at the hands of the General Assembly, they will possess "shared powers."

Counties will be endowed with broad unenumerated powers except for certain stated restrictions and a basic power of the General Assembly to withdraw any area of power and exercise it through a general public law applicable statewide. Responsibility for local government is thus placed rather squarely upon local officials.

Some changes have been made in the General Assembly. There will be fewer members in each house for the sake of greater efficiency. The members will be selected from single member districts — so as to gain visibility and responsibility. Longer sessions will be in order so that there will be ample time for attending to the legislative business of the state without undue haste and last minute pressure.

In line with the general policy of having no constitutional determination of salaries, the present provision of a fixed amount, with the resulting temptation to provide additional emoluments, disappears. The General Assembly will have new powers of investigation and must keep more complete records open to the public.

The governor's control over his own administration is strengthened. He is being provided with a lieutenant governor, to whom the governor can delegate many time-consuming functions.

At no point probably does the new constitution depart more widely from the old than in the judicial branch. The new document provides for a system of unified courts, in a four-tiered arrangement. The Court of Appeals and the Intermediate Appellate Court will remain much as they now are in organization.

At the trial level, now occupied chiefly by the circuit courts and the Supreme Bench of Baltimore City, there is to be a Superior Court, statewide in jurisdiction and subject to the supervision of a chief judge. The aim is to make full use of available judges and to approach more nearly to a single standard of justice than is likely with separate courts. At the fourth tier, the existing police magistrates, municipal courts, people's courts, justices of the peace will give way to a unified District Court manned by judges trained in the law and, like the judges of the Superior Court, directed by a chief judge and assignable where needed.

The process of selection of judges is being changed considerably. There will be nominating commissions composed of equal numbers of lawyers and lay members whose task it will be to create lists of candidates for vacancies on the bench. The number on any list varies with the court in case as do the sizes of the commissions. In every situation, however, the governor must select a judge from the list presented.

Such an appointee then serves for a stated period before a general election at which time his name will appear on the ballot so that the voters may determine whether to continue him in office. If retained, he will then serve a term of eight years. Constitutional retirement remains at the age of seventy and provisions are made for judicial removal either for disability or misconduct.

In the area of suffrage and elections, the means of popular control over governmental matters have been somewhat altered. Residence requirements have been eased; the length of the ballot has been shortened. Single-member districts for the General Assembly tend to make it easier for the voter to know his representatives and provide him with a more direct approach to the General Assembly.

While the number of signers to referendum petitions has been increased, the process by which the people can get a constitutional convention has been simplified. The proposed statewide supervision of elections should discourage irregularities and bring more uniformity into the electoral processes. Probably the most talked about change is the lowering of the voting age to nineteen years.

Has the Convention done what it was set up to do? As the people of Maryland examine what is now before them, they will discover much that was promised before the Convention assembled. Most people, doubtless, will also find provisions not exactly to their liking.

But constitution-making in a democratic society can hardly be expected to produce a perfect document. If that were the question before the people, the answer would be easy. But that is not the question. It is rather: To what degree do the good features of the new constitution outweigh the less desirable ones? To what extent is the new constitution an improvement upon the one we now have?

As one who has been in this movement for more than thirty years, the present writer can answer without reservation: "The Constitutional Convention of the State of Maryland has done a very good job."

II.

RICHARD HOMAN:
Account of the Defeat

IT's HARD TO IMAGINE how the people of a state could rebuff their leadership more completely than Maryland's voters did Tuesday.

After a poorly financed campaign led by a smattering of low-level courthouse officials, the proposed new state constitution was rejected by a margin that shocked its supporters and even startled its opponents. Rejection was total and followed no geographic patterns, as do many issues of reform in Maryland.

The defeat clearly took the state's establishment by surprise. Government, political, civic, business, and religious leaders had campaigned for ratification. It was the rank-and-file trampling the officers — the little man deciding for himself what kind of government he would have.

The rejection drew on a current mood of fear and resentment that extends well beyond Maryland: fear of change, during a period of unsettled social conditions, especially when it is proposed by urban liberals and labeled as reform, and resentment at the apparent expansion of an already big government that seems to be helping the wrong people.

The fears and resentments mobilized the biggest turnout in any special election in Maryland's history. The 650,000 who voted were 43 percent of the total registered.

The manpower to lead the campaign against ratification was supplied by the constitutional reformers' decision to eliminate several elected local offices from the constitution. Almost to a man, these officials in each of the counties campaigned against the document. It would jeopardize their jobs, but the argument they made to voters was that it would end the citizens' right to elect these officials.

The outcome raises serious questions about how much the "establishment" really leads and how attuned the leaders are to the wishes of their constituency. Defeat of Maryland's proposed constitution could be a setback for constitutional reform efforts throughout the nation. Government scholars had considered Maryland's vote one that would reverse the trend against proposed new constitutions.

100.

Robert F. Kennedy: Vietnam — Illusion and Reality

The critics of U.S. policy in Vietnam advanced three main arguments in 1967 and, with growing intensity, in early 1968. First, they said, the war was a civil conflict, and the United States therefore had no business in it. Second, the use of napalm and other modern technological weapons on the people of a small, underdeveloped nation was tantamount to mass murder and close to genocide. Third, the specter of monolithic communism, against which American efforts were presumably directed, was no more than that — a specter — and did not justify drawing the conclusion: "Better dead than red." Much of the criticism came from the young, many of whom looked to Senator Robert F. Kennedy of New York as their spokesman. Kennedy delivered the following speech in Chicago on February 8, 1968, shortly after the peak of the Viet Cong's New Year offensive. The speech marked Kennedy as a leading anti-administration critic in the Senate and catapulted him into the race for the nomination (although he did not declare until a month later). On June 5, Kennedy became the victim of the second major assassination in a single year. He was shot in a Los Angeles hotel minutes after delivering a speech celebrating his victory in the California presidential primary. He died the following morning.

Source: *Chicago Sun-Times*, February 11, 1968.

THE EVENTS OF THE LAST few weeks have demonstrated anew the truth of Lord Halifax's dictum that although hope "is very good company by the way . . . (it) is generally a wrong guide."

Our enemy, savagely striking at will across all of South Vietnam, has finally shattered the mask of official illusion with which we have concealed our true circumstances, even from ourselves.

But a short time ago we were serene in our reports and predictions of progress. In

April, our commanding general told us that "the South Vietnamese are fighting now better than ever before . . . their record in combat . . . reveals an exceptional performance." In August, another general told us that "the really big battles of the Vietnam war are over . . . the enemy has been so badly pummeled he'll never give us trouble again." In December, we were told that we were winning "battle after battle," that "the secure proportion of the population has grown from about 45 percent to 65 percent and in the contested areas the tide continues to run with us."

That is what we were told, and what we were told at the highest possible level.

Those dreams are gone. The Viet Cong will probably withdraw from the cities, as they were forced to withdraw from the American Embassy. Thousands of them will be dead. But they will, nevertheless, have demonstrated that no part or person of South Vietnam is secure from their attacks: neither district capitals nor American bases, neither the peasant in his rice paddy nor our ambassadors nor the commanding general of our own great forces.

No one can predict the exact shape or outcome of the battles now in progress, in Saigon, in Hue, or at Khe Sanh. Let us pray that we will succeed at the lowest possible cost to our young men. But whatever their outcome, the events of the last two weeks must have taught us something. For the sake of those young Americans who are fighting today, if for no other reason, the time has come to take a new look at the war in Vietnam — in fact the time is long past — not by cursing the past but by using it to illuminate the future.

And the first and necessary step is to face the facts. It is to seek out the austere and painful reality of Vietnam, freed from wishful thinking, false hopes, and sentimental dreams. It is to rid ourselves of the "good company" of those illusions which have lured us into the deepening swamp of Vietnam.

"If you would guide by the light of reason," said Holmes, "you must let your mind be bold."

We will find no guide to the future in Vietnam unless we are bold enough to strip away the illusions and to confront the grim anguish, the reality of that battlefield which was once a nation called South Vietnam, stripped of deceptive illusions. It is time for the truth.

We must, first of all, rid ourselves of the illusion that the events of the past two weeks represent some sort of victory. That is not so.

It is said the Viet Cong will not be able to hold the cities. This is probably true. But they have demonstrated despite all our reports of progress, of government strength and enemy weakness, that half a million American soldiers with 700,000 Vietnamese allies, with total command of the air, total command of the sea, backed by huge resources and the most modern weapons, are unable to secure even a single city from the attacks of an enemy whose total strength is about 250,000. It is as if James Madison were able to claim a great victory in 1814 because the British only burned Washington instead of annexing it to the British Empire.

We are told that the enemy suffered terrible losses; and there is no doubt he did. They cannot, however, be as devastating as the figures appear. The secretary of defense has told us that "during all of 1967 the Communists lost about 165,000 effectives," yet enemy main force strength "has been maintained at a relatively constant level of about 110,000-115,000 during the past year." Thus it would seem that no matter how many Viet Cong and North Vietnamese we claim to kill, through some miraculous effort of will, enemy strength remains the same.

Now our intelligence chief tells us that of 60,000 men thrown into the attacks on the cities in the last two weeks, more than

"The Train Robbery"; cartoon from "Punch" giving English view of the effect of the Vietnam war on the United States' economy

20,000 have been killed. If only two men have been seriously wounded for every one dead — a very conservative estimate — the entire enemy force has been put out of action. Then, I ask, who is doing the fighting?

Again it is claimed that the Communists expected a large-scale popular uprising which did not occur. How ironic it is that here in the United States our public officials should claim a victory because a people whom we have given 16,000 lives, billions of dollars, and almost a decade to defend did not rise in arms against us. More disillusioning and painful is the fact the population did not rise to defend its freedom against the Viet Cong.

Thousands of men and arms were infiltrated into populated urban areas over a period of days, if not of weeks. Yet few, if any, citizens rushed to inform their protectors of this massive infiltration. At best they simply shut their doors to concern, waiting for others to resolve the issue. Did we know the attack was coming? If so, why did we not strike first, and where were the forces needed for effective defense?

For years we have been told that the measure of our success and progress in Vietnam was increasing security and control for the population. Now we have seen that none of the population is secure and no area is under sure control. Four years ago, when we only had about 30,000 troops in Vietnam, the Viet Cong were unable to mount the assaults on cities they have now conducted against our enormous forces. At one time a suggestion that we protect enclaves was derided. Now there are no protected enclaves.

This has not happened because our men are not brave or effective, because they are. It is because we have not conceived our mission in this war. It is because we have misconceived the nature of the war. It is because we have sought to resolve by military might a conflict whose issue depends upon the will and conviction of the South Vietnamese people. It is like sending a lion to halt an epidemic of jungle rot.

This misconception rests on a second illusion — the illusion that we can win a war which the South Vietnamese cannot win for themselves.

Two Presidents and countless officials have told us for seven years that although we can help the South Vietnamese, it is their war and they must win it; as Secretary of Defense McNamara told us last month, "We cannot provide the South Vietnamese with the will to survive as an independent nation . . . or with the ability and self-discipline a people must have to govern themselves. These qualities and attributes are essential contributions to the struggle only the South Vietnamese can supply." Yet this wise and certain counsel has gradually become an empty slogan, as mounting frustration has led us to transform the war into an American military effort.

The South Vietnamese Senate, with only one dissenting vote, refuses to draft eighteen- and nineteen-year-old South Vietnamese, with a member of the Assembly asking, "Why should Vietnamese boys be sent to die for Americans," while nineteen-year-old American boys fight to maintain the Senate and Assembly in Saigon.

Every detached observer has testified to the enormous corruption which pervades every level of South Vietnamese official life. Hundreds of millions of dollars are stolen by private individuals and government officials while the American people are being asked to pay higher taxes to finance our assistance effort. Despite continual promises, the Saigon regime refuses to act against corruption. Late last year, after all our talks and all our pressure for reform, two high Army officers were finally dismissed for "criminal" corruption. This was applauded here in the United States. Last month, these same two officers were given new and powerful commands.

In the meantime, incorruptible officers resign out of frustration and out of despair.

Perhaps we could live with corruption and inefficiency by themselves. However, the consequence is not simply the loss of American lives. For government corruption is the source of the enemy's strength. It is, more than anything else, the reason why the greatest power on earth cannot defeat a tiny and primitive foe.

You cannot expect people to risk their lives and endure hardship unless they have a stake in their own society. They must have a clear sense of identification with their own government, a belief they are participating in a cause worth fighting and dying for. Political and economic reform are not simply idealistic slogans or noble goals to be postponed until the end of the fighting. They are the principal weapons of battle. People will not fight — they will simply not fight — to line the pockets of generals or swell the bank accounts of the wealthy. They are far more likely to close their eyes and shut their doors in the face of their government — even as they did last week.

More than any election, more than any proud boasts, that simple fact reveals the truth. We have an ally in name only. We

support a government without supporters. Without the effort of American arms that government would not last a day.

The third illusion is that the unswerving pursuit of military victory, whatever its cost, is in the interest of either ourselves or the people of Vietnam. For the people of Vietnam, the last three years have meant little but terrible, terrible horror. Their tiny land has been devastated by a weight of bombs and shells greater than Nazi Germany knew in the whole of the Second World War. We have dropped twelve tons of bombs for every square mile in North and South Vietnam.

Whole provinces have been substantially destroyed. More than 2 million South Vietnamese are now homeless refugees. Imagine the impact in our country if an equivalent number — over 25 million Americans — were wandering homeless or interned in refugee camps, and millions more refugees were being created as New York and Chicago, Washington and Boston, were being destroyed by a war raging in their streets. Whatever the outcome of these battles, it is the people we seek to defend who are the greatest losers.

Nor does it serve the interests of America to fight this war as if moral standards could be subordinated to immediate necessities. Last week, a Viet Cong suspect was turned over to the chief of the Vietnamese Security Services, one of our leading allies, who executed him on the spot, a flat violation of the Geneva Convention on the Rules of War. And what has been done about it?

Of course, the enemy is brutal and cruel and has done the same thing many times. But we are not fighting the Communists in order to become more like them — we fight to preserve our differences. Moreover, such actions — like the widespread use of artillery and air power in the centers of cities — may hurt us far more in the long run than it helps today.

The photograph of the execution was on front pages all around the world — leading our best and oldest friends to ask, more in sorrow than in anger, what has happened to America? I believe we asked the same question of ourselves that morning, and the fact is that we do not have a satisfactory answer.

The fourth illusion is that the American national interest is identical with — or should be subordinated to — the selfish interest of an incompetent military regime.

We are told, of course, that the battle for South Vietnam is in reality a struggle for 250 million Asians — the beginning of a Great Society for all of Asia. But this is pretension. We can and should offer reasonable assistance to Asia; but we cannot build a Great Society there if we cannot build one in our own country. We cannot speak extravagantly of a struggle for 250 million Asians, when a struggle for 15 million in one Asian country so strains our forces, that another Asian country, a fourth-rate power which we have already once defeated in battle, dares to seize an American ship and hold and humiliate her crew.

And we are told that the war in Vietnam will settle the whole course of the future of Asia. But that is a prayerful wish based on unsound hope, meant only to justify the enormous sacrifices we have already made. The truth is that communism triumphed in China twenty years ago and was extended to Tibet. It lost in Malaya and the Philippines, met disaster in Indonesia, and was fought to a standstill in Korea. It has struggled against governments in Burma for twenty years without success, and it may struggle in Thailand for many more.

The outcome in each country depends and will depend on the intrinsic strength of the government, the particular circumstances of the country, and the particular character of the insurgent movement. The truth is that the war in Vietnam does not promise the end of all threats to Asia and ultimately to the United States; rather, if we proceed on our present course and follow our present policy, it promises only years and decades of further draining conflict on the mainland of Asia — conflict which, as our finest military leaders have always warned, could lead us only to national tragedy.

There is an American interest in South Vietnam. We have an interest in maintaining the strength of our commitments — and surely we have demonstrated that. With all the lives and resources we have poured into Vietnam, is there anyone to argue that a government with any support from its people, with any competence to rule, with any determination to defend itself, would not long ago have been victorious over any insurgent movement, however assisted from outside its borders?

And we have another, more immediate interest: to protect the lives of our gallant young men and to conserve American resources. But we do not have an interest in the survival of a privileged class, growing ever more wealthy from the corruption of war, which after all our sacrifices on their behalf can ask why Vietnamese boys have to fight for Americans.

The fifth illusion is that this war can be settled in our own way and in our own time on our own terms. Such a settlement is the privilege of the triumphant, of those who crush their enemies in battle or wear away their will to fight. We simply have not done this, nor is there any prospect we will achieve such a victory.

For twenty years, first the French and then the United States have been predicting victory in Vietnam. In 1961 and in 1962, as well as 1966 and 1967, we have been told that "the tide is turning"; "there is 'light at the end of the tunnel' "; "we can soon bring home the troops — victory is near — the enemy is tiring." Once, in 1962, I participated in such predictions myself. But for twenty years we have been wrong.

The history of conflict among nations does not record another such lengthy and consistent chronicle of error as we have shown in Vietnam. It is time to discard so proven a fallacy and face the reality that a military victory is not in sight and that it probably will never come.

Unable to defeat our enemy or break his will — at least without a huge, long, and ever more costly effort — we must actively seek a peaceful settlement. We can no longer harden our terms every time Hanoi indicates it may be prepared to negotiate; and we must be willing to foresee a settlement which will give the Viet Cong and the National Liberation Front a chance to participate in the political life of the country. Not because we want them to but because that is the only way in which this struggle can be settled.

No one knows if negotiations will bring a peaceful settlement, but we do know there will be no peaceful settlement without negotiations. Nor can we have these negotiations just on our own terms. Again, we might like that. We may have to make concessions and take risks, and surely we will have to negotiate directly with the NLF as well as Hanoi. Surely it is only another illusion that still denies this basic necessity. What we must not do is confuse the prestige staked on a particular policy with the interest of the United States; nor should we be unwilling to take risks for peace when we are willing to risk so many lives in war.

A year ago, when our adversary offered negotiations if only we would halt the bombing of the North, we replied with a demand for his unconditional surrender. Officials at the highest level of our government felt that we were on the edge of a military victory and negotiations, except on our terms, were not necessary. So, therefore, we made that demand in February 1966. We made that demand that they surrender before we would go to the negotiating table.

Now, a year too late, we have set fewer conditions for a bombing halt, conditions which clearly would have been more acceptable then. And the intervening year, for all its terrible costs, the deaths of thousands of Americans and South Vietnamese, has not improved our condition one single bit. When the chance for negotiations comes again, let us not postpone for another year the recognition of what is really possible and necessary to a peaceful settlement.

These are some of the illusions which must be discarded if the events of last week are to prove not simply a tragedy but a lesson: a lesson which carries with it some basic truths.

First, that a total military victory is not within sight or around the corner; that, in fact, it is probably beyond our grasp; and that the effort to win such a victory will only result in the further slaughter of thousands of innocent and helpless people — a slaughter which will forever rest on the national conscience of our country.

Second, that the pursuit of such a victory is not necessary to all of our consciences and the national interest and is even damaging that interest.

Third, that the progress we have claimed toward increasing our control over the country and the security of the population is largely illusory.

Fourth, that the central battle in this war cannot be measured by body counts or bomb damage but by the extent to which the people of South Vietnam act on a sense of common purpose and hope with those that govern them.

Fifth, that the current regime in Saigon is incapable or unwilling to be an effective ally in the war against the Communists.

Sixth, that a political compromise is not just the best path to peace, but the only path, and we must show as much willingness to risk some of our prestige for peace as to risk the lives of young men in war.

Seventh, that the escalation policy in Vietnam, far from strengthening and consolidating international resistance to aggression, is injuring our country through the world, reducing the faith of other peoples in our wisdom and purpose and weakening the world's resolve to stand together for freedom and peace.

Eighth, that the best way to save our most precious stake in Vietnam — the lives of our soldiers — is to stop the enlargement of the war, and that the best way to end casualties is to end the war.

Ninth, that our nation must be told the truth about this war, in all its terrible reality, both because it is right and because only in this way can any administration rally the public confidence and unity for the shadowed days which are before us.

This kind of approach is painful to give and I am sure it is painful to listen to.

No war has ever demanded more bravery from our people and our government —

not just bravery under fire or the bravery to make sacrifices but the bravery to discard the comfort of illusion — to do away with false hopes and alluring promises. Reality is grim and painful. But it is only a remote echo of the anguish toward which a policy founded on illusion is surely taking us.

This is a great nation and a strong people. Any who seek to comfort rather than speak plainly, reassure rather than instruct, promise satisfaction rather than reveal frustration — they deny that greatness and drain that strength. For today as it was in the beginning, it is the truth that makes us free.

101.

Eugene V. Rostow: The Choice in Foreign Policy

The speech from which the following selection is taken was given by Rostow, then in the State Department, before the Women's Forum on National Security in Washington, on February 20, 1968. It was delivered about five weeks before President Johnson announced the partial halt in the bombing of North Vietnam that eventually led to peace talks with the North Vietnamese at Paris in May. Rostow was of course defending administration policy in Southeast Asia. During the month or so before the speech was delivered, the North Vietnamese had launched their Tet offensive, which had thrown the Americans and their South Vietnamese allies on the defensive and suggested to many in the United States that the war could not be won.

Source: VSD, April 1, 1968.

For the first time since the early 1950s, the foreign policy we have pursued since the end of the war is facing a fundamental challenge. The issues in the debate are familiar to all of us. We have been arguing with each other about them since the age of Theodore Roosevelt and Woodrow Wilson. . . .

At this grim and fateful moment, the issue before the American people is exceedingly simple: What do we do now — now, in 1968 — taking into account the

consequences of the strength or weakness of what we do in every area of tension in the world, from the Middle East and South America to Berlin and Tokyo? That is the question, and it concentrates the mind to restate it.

Many of the answers that come thundering forth, eloquent and concerned, are worthy of classic faculty meetings in this or any other country. Perhaps one reason for their high quality is that several of the chief speakers have had years of experience as professors, deans, or college presidents. Responding to the issue before us, they say that President Eisenhower should never have signed the SEATO Treaty in 1955, and the Senate should never have ratified it, or the Tonkin Gulf Resolution ten years later. President Kennedy should never have increased the presence of American military advisers in Vietnam, starting in 1961. There should have been a referendum in Vietnam in 1956, we are told, as if free, secret elections could have been held in North Vietnam in 1956, and as if a failure to hold elections justified war in Vietnam any more than it would in other countries divided by circumstance against their will — that is, in Germany or Korea. There is too much corruption in Vietnam, others say — this of a small, fragmented Asian society, without the administrative machinery of a modern state, which has endured more than twenty years of guerrilla warfare! We are solemnly advised to negotiate — to negotiate *now* — or call the Geneva Convention, or neutralize the country, or use the machinery of the United Nations, as if the government had not explored every hint of a negotiating possibility, and pressed the Soviet Union for years to reconvene the Geneva Conference, or allow the issue of Vietnam to be considered by the Security Council, or to cooperate in other ways to bring about a fair political settlement of the conflict. . . .

But the passion of the debate is more significant than its defects in logic. Beyond the words is a protest of the utmost importance — a protest against the 20th century and against the responsibilities the 20th century requires the United States to assume in defense of our national security. The debate is not really concerned with the past, present, and future of the hostilities in Vietnam. It is addressed to the fact that we are involved in world politics and no longer live as we did in the 19th century, isolated and safe in a system of power maintained by others. Senator Aiken remarked the other day that

we have inherited the responsibilities of the British Empire but not its privileges. There is a good deal to his wise comment. The real issue we are debating is whether we continue to carry responsibilities of this order, with the help of Europe, Japan, Australia, New Zealand, and other countries who may wish to join us in regional efforts for peace, or whether we try once again to retreat into the world of the past, a world which isn't there and cannot be recreated.

It is an old debate, difficult to resolve precisely because it pits reality against memories that are part of our bone. And it is a debate of the utmost importance, to us and to every other people in the world.

Let no one be confused about what is at stake. If the American people falter, or seem to falter now, before we have completed the work of organizing a stable system of peace, our friends and our rivals will alike conclude that safety and peace are in peril: our rivals will see opportunities opening, and our friends will wonder how good America's word really is, when the going gets rough. The risks of miscalculation will be increased.

Such an atmosphere of anxiety and uncertainty is the breeding ground of war. Three times in this century men have misread the will of America, confusing our natural grumblings for our ultimate purpose.

I hope the same mistake is not being made once more. However much we dislike the burden of responsibility, the United States will not again abandon the defense of our national interests to chance. The United States and many other countries would take the gravest view of any renewal of hostilities in the Middle East or in Korea. And they regard the pattern of military support for North Vietnam with growing concern.

The facts of life in the 20th century, and the nature of our civilization, require us to pursue the foreign policy which has been developed by our four Presidents since 1945. Our history keeps us from a Roman solution. We cannot and will not impose Pax Americana on the world. But the changing map of world power in this century makes it necessary for us — for the first time in our history — to play a leading part in seeking to build a secure and stable system of world order. The old system is gone, destroyed in the aftermath of two world wars. A new one has not yet been established. The European states which organized the balance of world power in the 19th century are no longer capable of accomplishing that goal. The Soviet Union, the United States, and Japan are states on a new scale of power. The nuclear weapon has transformed the problem of power. The dissolution of Empire and the rise of Communist movements have created new focal points of danger throughout the world.

For twenty years we have held the line, organizing regional coalitions of peace to join us in the search for stability. Obviously, we cannot hold the world together single-handed. But we have a vital national interest in peace. And we cannot delegate the protection of that interest to anyone else. There is no one to pick up the torch if we let it fall.

This is the implacable subject matter of our debate over foreign policy. It is a debate between facts and nostalgia, between realities and dreams. We have to accustom ourselves to the unpleasant situation with which we must live: that there are no quick, cheap solutions, and that we shall have to continue to exert ourselves, with regional alliances of increasing strength, until the Communist nations accept a rule of live-and-let-live and join us in a regime of peaceful coexistence.

The debate over our course in Vietnam is one stage in a great debate which has lasted for more than forty years.

After the First World War, we repudiated President Wilson and sought to return to a "normalcy" that we refused to believe had gone forever. In the 1930s, we followed an inward-looking isolationism that

placed our own vital interests in mortal peril. Our internal debate raged until the moment when the enemy's attack mocked our irresolution.

The postwar administration of President Truman provides a happier parallel for the present debate. President Truman was, in fact, the main architect of the policies we are following today. Like President Johnson, he had the courage not to run away from an unpopular war, whatever the political cost to himself. And like President Johnson, he had to fight not only the Communists abroad but the extremists at home — those on the right, who were for total, uncompromising, unrestrained war against Communism, and those on the left, like Henry Wallace, who wanted us to stay home and leave the world to whoever could take it.

President Truman, as you remember, gave in to neither extreme. Instead, he laid down what has been our basic foreign policy ever since, the policy of coexistence. In the world of nuclear bombs, President Truman believed it was mad to talk about a holy war against Communism throughout the world. America wanted to live in peace within a reasonably stable world of broad horizons, a world in which we and our friends could seek the blessings of freedom and progress. We had no desire to launch military attacks against Communist systems, but we could not tolerate Communist aggression. What we sought was Communist acceptance of the idea that force could not be used to change the boundaries of the two systems: a principle we upheld in supporting the territorial integrity and political independence of Iran, Greece, Turkey, and Korea, and in preventing the absorption of Berlin. When they sought to change the balance of power by force or the threat of force, we reacted firmly. That, in broad terms, was the meaning of the famous Truman Doctrine, announced in response to Communist designs on Greece and Turkey.

Following that Doctrine, successive

American Presidents faced down Communist aggression time and time again. This principle is the essence of our position in Vietnam. On each occasion, we have made it perfectly clear that we were not trying to destroy the Communists in their own countries but only helping others to resist their aggression into the non-Communist world.

For four administrations we have followed the same doctrine of convincing the Communists that while aggression would get them nowhere, peaceful coexistence was theirs for the asking.

Resisting aggression, of course, is only half our foreign policy. To be sure, in order to have a decent society, either at home or abroad, there must be law and order. Force must be kept under control. But we all know that law and order, by itself, is not enough; there must be progress and hope. One-half of President Truman's policy is symbolized by the Truman Doctrine, the other by the Marshall Plan and the Point Four Program. These were not "giveaway" programs, as their shortsighted critics so often called them, but were designed to help other people back on their feet so that they could look after their own affairs.

In Europe, with the Marshall Plan, our policy fostered a brilliant success. With our help at a critical moment, the Western Europeans have made themselves more stable and prosperous than at any time in their history. No one talks any more about Western Europe "going Communist." Today the Western Europeans contribute a major share to Atlantic defense through NATO and give large quantities of aid to developing countries around the world. The recent Resolutions of the NATO Council open a new chapter in the evolution of the Alliance. In those Resolutions, the Allies undertook to join us in the search for a stable peace, not only in continental Europe but in the Mediterranean, where new threats have emerged, and in areas of tension beyond Europe itself.

We look forward to the Europeans taking a greater role in world affairs. We are pleased by the increasing influence exerted in Asia by the Japanese, whose prosperity has made them the world's third largest economy. We believe that the key to the future lies in interdependence. And we accept that that interdependence means a partnership of equals.

In short, in the developed parts of the free world, in Europe and in Japan, our policy of peacekeeping and aid has been a success. We have helped others achieve stability. We have been gradually building regional coalitions based on genuine cooperation, not for war but to safeguard world order and give a rational structure to the world's economic relations.

But as we have achieved success in one area, we have been faced by a growing challenge in another — in the whole "Third World" of developing countries — many only recently freed from centuries of colonial rule.

Our strategy throughout the Third World is the same as our strategy in Europe. We are helping countries in the various regions of the world to develop their own strong and stable political and economic institutions and encouraging them to work together in international groupings for defense and economic development. The nations of Latin America are cooperating with us in the Alliance for Progress. Many of the free nations of Asia are likewise banding together in a number of organizations promoting trade, economic development, and defense.

We have helped these peoples of the Third World, both with our military power to shield them against aggression and with our aid to prime the whole process of their economic development. We hope that the various regional groupings that are forming will, in time, give an orderly and progressive structure to the Third World and enable it to resist the many forces of confusion, violence, and despair that are inevitable in a world undergoing such rapid and radical transformations.

In many places in this Third World, we have had notable successes. In Latin America, with the help of the Alliance for Progress, many countries have made impressive steps toward modern economies. In the Middle East, Turkey, Israel, Tunisia, and Iran have shown dramatic improvements. So, farther east, have such countries as Pakistan, Thailand, the Republic of China, and South Korea. Others, like Indonesia, have recently taken encouraging steps to put themselves on the road to steady economic growth and progress. In short, there has been advance in many areas.

But there is no point in fooling ourselves by looking only at the bright spots. There is a tremendous job to be done in many parts of the world before peoples can achieve stable political systems and throw off the poverty and despotism they have known for centuries. All over the world, ancient societies have suddenly had to face up to life on their own in a world that is strange to them, and often hostile. There is going to be local turmoil in many places for a long time to come.

This would be true even if there were no Communists, but, of course, there are. They wait, like scavengers, to feast off the wounds of struggling societies. It is ridiculous to see them behind all the troubles in the world, but it is equally ridiculous to pretend that they do not exist. In most of the troubled areas of the world, they are active, adding to the confusion, waiting for the opportunity to extend their own brutal and dreary system.

Nowhere have the Communists taken the offensive more openly than in Southeast Asia. There is, quite literally, not one nation in this part of the world that has not had to contend with a Communist threat to its plans for peaceful development. Mindful of the rebuff the free world dealt the North Korean attempt at direct aggression in 1950, Communists in Southeast Asia are trying a newer and more sophisticated form of aggression. They call it the "War of Na-

tional Liberation." It is a formidable weapon, as we have reason to know.

The nations of Southeast Asia are still weak, militarily and economically. Left to their own resources, it is unlikely that even the most determined of them would be able to resist the combination of external pressure and subversion from within. Should this Communist strategy succeed, a Communist-dominated Southeast Asia would result.

I am not raising the specter of "monolithic Communism." Even the State Department has heard about divisions among Communist leaders and ideologies. But Communist oligopoly is not necessarily an improvement over Communist monopoly, from our point of view. We know that Hanoi is not a satellite of Peking. But, would Hanoi's rule in Laos or Cambodia be any less oppressive, or any more welcome, to the local populations than Peking's rule in Burma or Malaysia? The danger posed by the resulting alliance of Peking and Hanoi, and other states made into their images, would be at least as dangerous to us, to India, to Indonesia, and to other countries as any single "monolithic" power dominating the same area. It might be even more aggressive, as each sought to demonstrate his superior zeal. If this happened we would be confronted, in our "small world" of supersonic jet aircraft and missiles, with the threat of a hostile Asia quite similar to the threat which we perceived thirty years ago as a serious menace to our own security.

Another straw man some people like to set up for themselves to attack is the image of America as a "world policeman," determined to intervene willy-nilly everywhere and anywhere in the world where there is even the hint of a Communist threat. Nothing could be farther from the truth. We realize that, in the last analysis, only the Asians themselves can prevent a Communist Asia. Today, despite the evident imbalance of power between them and mainland China and its allies, peoples and governments are resisting Communism successfully now in Thailand, in Indonesia, in Malaysia, and elsewhere. They will continue to do so provided we and our Allies prevail in Vietnam, and they remain confident that they are not alone in facing up to Hanoi and Peking.

To enhance their efforts at economic development and in defense, the nations of Southeast Asia have formed a number of useful regional organizations. But, both militarily and economically, even their combined power does not right the balance. What does right it, what does give them the confidence to pursue their own efforts, is America's demonstrated willingness to support Asian governments who are making their own self-development and self-defense efforts in the face of Communist insurgency. Formally, I recall to you, this willingness was expressed in the SEATO Treaty, signed in 1954, a treaty which specifically recognizes the possibility of the new form of aggression which now confronts our Asian friends and Allies.

Far from making us a world policeman, it is this *willingness* to assist, provided it remains *credible*, which is in fact the best guarantee that we and the Asians have that no new world war, no new critical situations requiring a military intervention will ever be reached. As long as they remain convinced of American willingness to stand behind them and help them, the small nations of Asia can continue to face up to Hanoi and Peking, deal with Communist insurgency at home, and develop in the ways of their own choosing.

This is what is at stake in Vietnam — the credibility of America's support in Southeast Asia, and, indeed, in the many other areas in whose security we have a national interest. Remove this credibility and we will indeed be placed in the position of becoming world policemen, or captives in a fortress America. In theory, there may be better places to fight than Vietnam; in fact, we have no alternative.

Although the import of my address today is directed at our policy throughout the world, I believe the events in Vietnam in the last few weeks suggest that I give special emphasis to that corner of the world this evening.

First of all, what is our enemy in Vietnam? Our enemy in Vietnam is aggression, conducted by the Communist government of North Vietnam and supported by other Communist governments. We do not maintain that this Communist government in Hanoi is a satellite of Peking — but neither do we accept the notion that it is a great bulwark against it. The two are allies — desiring the same goals, using the same means. When we resist one ally in South Vietnam, the lesson is not lost on the other, in Peking.

Aggression in South Vietnam is directed and supplied by, and increasingly manned by personnel of the government of Hanoi headed by Ho Chi Minh. That Ho Chi Minh is a Vietnamese nationalist, no one will deny. But what some people would like us to forget is that he is also a Communist. As a Communist, he has made himself the enemy of every kind of Vietnamese nationalism not his own. By 1951, he had driven the last of the nationalist non-Communists out of the Viet Minh. In 1955 and 1956, he drove some 840,000 non-Communist Vietnamese out of North Vietnam, imprisoned about 100,000 others, and liquidated outright at least another 50,000. Not content to have eliminated any contending schools of thought from his own domain, he set about deliberately to impose his own system on them from the other half of Vietnam, South Vietnam, as well. He planned to do this not through political agitation, or through anything resembling the democratic process — but by force. His plans were made early. After the cease-fire of 1954, he instructed some of his followers to go underground, in the South. Others, he called to the North for training, and re-infiltration. By 1957, he had turned these forces loose, beginning a campaign of political and military action and outright terror, which has gradually grown in size to the proportions it has reached today.

To be sure, this campaign operated on fertile ground. In any country with such a history of chaos as Vietnam in the 20th century, there are bound to be many disaffected people and much difficulty in establishing a central government based on consent. The Communists have recognized this from the beginning and are skillful in linking their political efforts to the exploitation of popular grievances. Because of these grievances and through the use of terror — against individuals, groups, and recently, against entire cities, the Communists have succeeded in building an infrastructure with roots buried in the soil of South Vietnam. As long as this infrastructure remains, the war in Vietnam will not be won. When it is destroyed, victory in Vietnam will be as assured as the victory over the guerrillas in Malaysia some ten years in the past. This is the key to understanding the war in Vietnam, a war which is, despite the battles and their casualties, primarily a political one.

The events of the first part of this month, the so-called Tet, or New Year's, offensive, reveal to us how important this basic fact is. During the Tet offensive, the Communists attacked some thirty-eight of forty-four of Vietnam's provincial capitals, plus the capital city of Saigon itself. They did this at the cost of tremendous losses to their own forces — estimated to be as high as 38,000 men killed alone — not to mention over 6,000 prisoners and uncounted wounded. Their purpose in these attacks was not a purely military one. Nor would they sacrifice so many men merely to create a "diversion," as some commentators have suggested, from the more purely military confrontation at Khe Sanh. Their primary purpose, rather, was to weaken, or even to destroy, the government of South Vietnam. For the Communists know, and we must never forget, that if they ever did succeed in destroying the constitutionally elected polit-

ical authority in South Vietnam, they would indeed have won the war. They would have won it even if a Khe Sanh, a Dak To, a Loc Ninh, or any other point in geography, and dozens others to boot, were successfully defended.

They did not succeed in their maximum goals. The popular uprisings which they told their troops would greet them in the cities never materialized. Indeed, the urban population of Vietnam has clearly demonstrated it is not willing to throw in its lot with the Viet Cong. This was a failure, and hopefully, a revealing failure to the Vietnamese Communists. But we cannot yet say whether or not it was a decisive failure.

Were the Vietnamese government now to stand by, inactively, in the face of the recent destruction, in the face of people made homeless, in the face of the fear that the Viet Cong have brought, for the first time, to the peoples of the cities, then the Communists would not consider their losses to have been in vain. This would be no less true if the Vietnamese government were to abdicate its responsibilities, either for civic action or for the maintenance of security, to us Americans. For, in that case, it would only be a matter of time before the cycle would repeat itself again and again. And sooner or later, losses and overwhelming "kill ratios" notwithstanding, the people's patience with a government that can neither [help] nor protect them would crumble, and the Communists would have won their political war.

I say this not to be dramatic but to point out to you that the U.S. government has never lost sight of the fact that as much as this is a political war, it is a South Vietnamese war. And the South Vietnamese alone can win it. Although the final analysis, the definitive report, has yet to be made, the reactions of the South Vietnamese so far give a strong indication that they are determined to do just that.

The South Vietnamese government has remained in place, in Saigon, and in every province capital of Vietnam. It has organized a relief committee which has succeeded in coordinating the efforts of a great number of Vietnamese ministries and authorities and in channeling these efforts directly [wherever] they are needed among the victims of the Communist offensive. Local authorities throughout the country are taking similar actions. Equally significant, a vast array of Vietnamese individuals and groups outside the government, Buddhists and Catholics, Cao Dai and Hoa Hao [Wa How], labor leaders and students, eminent political leaders outside of the government as well as in it, have expressed their willingness to unite to combat an enemy whose destructive capacity and will have never been more graphically illustrated. The government of South Vietnam has expressed its willingness to collaborate with all of these forces. As the Nazis came to learn after the worst of their efforts against Britain had been exhausted, adversity can serve to unite a people and fire its determination. There are signs that this is what the Communist attacks may be producing in Vietnam. . . .

By assisting the Vietnamese in this effort, we will have successfully defended our own interests as well. We will have convinced the Communists that they cannot succeed in a war of national liberation in Southeast Asia any more than in a more conventional aggressive action in Korea or in Europe.

Only by convincing them of the firmness of our resolve and our willingness to carry out our promises will there be any hope of achieving in Asia the same kind of stability that we and our Allies have been able to reach in Europe.

But if our resolve gives way, it will be the old story. Successful aggression in one place will encourage aggression everywhere and sap the courage of those who are now prepared to resist. South Vietnam is not unique. The same potential for subversion exists in any number of countries in the Third World. If Communist aggression succeeds in preventing Vietnam from building

a progressive non-Communist society, the emboldened Communists will not unreasonably expect to succeed — and to succeed mainly by threat — in many other places.

Why do we care? That is the real question, the question that only a few critics of our policy occasionally raise. Why are we making this great effort to help sustain the Vietnamese in their revolution and to sustain other nations in their economic development? Why do we not, as they propose, withdraw back to the developed countries and abandon the Third World to Communism, racism, and chaos? We can protect ourselves in our fortress. And we have problems enough at home.

This is the new version of the old isolationism. It has led us to disaster in the past and if we follow it now, it can only lead us to disaster in the future. It is based on a fundamental illusion that we have inherited from the 19th century: that America can somehow ignore the rest of the world and still be safe. But to return to the beginning of my remarks. We Americans must face the facts of life in this, the 20th century. In the last century, we were protected by a wide ocean and a reasonably stable balance of power maintained by Europeans among themselves and through their empires around the world. We could count on their rivalries to make sure that no one was powerful enough to threaten us. Today that old balance, and the world order that went with it, is swept away. If we retreated from the world, no purely local forces could stop Russia from dominating Europe or no purely local forces could stop Communist China and its Allies from dominating all the Far East.

Those who advocate withdrawing into our own continental fortress should ask themselves what sort of country we might be if large parts of the world were united in hostility toward us. A fortress under siege is not a pleasant place to live. A garrison state is an uncongenial environment for freedom. We can, in fact, only continue to exist as a free society in a world that is stable and friendly and open.

It is sometimes said that we must turn our backs on the world because we have too many problems at home, because we cannot afford to rebuild our cities and eliminate poverty and still maintain our foreign commitments. Of course, as the President recently said, all this is bunk. We have enormous resources in this country; what we need is the will. Many of the people who now use Vietnam as the excuse for not getting on with new programs at home have always been against domestic reform.

In today's world, selfishness and irresponsibility cannot start or stop at the water's edge. Irresponsibility at home and irresponsibility abroad go together. We cannot retreat from our cities and hide out in the suburbs. We cannot abandon the Third World and withdraw to America. We must find the will and the means to meet our responsibilities both at home and abroad if we are to be true to ourselves, our friends, and the interests of the generations that follow us. That is the basic policy of this administration; that is where the President has been leading us.

102.

Lyndon B. Johnson: Withdrawal Speech

As 1967 drew to a close it was evident that the Vietnam war was causing serious divisions in the United States. Public disenchantment with the conduct of the war and with the war itself was becoming more widespread. Even the President's own party was sharply divided on the issue — so much so, in fact, that Senator Eugene McCarthy of Minnesota began campaigning for the Democratic presidential nomination on an antiwar platform. By his impressive showing in the New Hampshire primary election in March 1968, Senator McCarthy demonstrated the reality of the divided opinions about the war. Hawkish candidates for office started to sound more dovelike, and other antiwar candidates entered the field. Then on March 31 President Johnson made an address to the nation on Vietnam policy, in which he announced a cutback in the bombing of North Vietnam and made another offer to start peace negotiations with the Hanoi regime. But the most startling — and totally unanticipated — portion of the speech was his closing announcement that he would not be a candidate for reelection. This statement, coupled with the fact that North Vietnam did accept the offer to begin talks toward a negotiated settlement, radically changed the political picture in the United States in an election year. Portions of President Johnson's address are reprinted below.

Source: *Chicago Sun-Times*, April 1, 1968.

Tonight I want to speak to you on peace in Vietnam and Southeast Asia.

No other question so preoccupies our people. No other dream so absorbs the 250 million human beings who live in that part of the world. No other goal motivates American policy in Southeast Asia.

For years, representatives of our government and others have traveled the world — seeking to find a basis for peace talks. Since last September, they have carried the offer I made public at San Antonio.

It was this: that the United States would stop its bombardment of North Vietnam when that would lead promptly to productive discussions — and that we would assume that North Vietnam would not take military advantage of our restraint.

Hanoi denounced this offer, both privately and publicly. Even while the search for peace was going on, North Vietnam rushed their preparations for a savage assault on the people, the government, and the allies of South Vietnam.

Their attack — during the Tet holidays — failed to achieve its principal objectives. It did not collapse the elected government of South Vietnam or shatter its Army — as the Communists had hoped. It did not produce a "general uprising" among the people of the cities. The Communists were unable to maintain control of any city. And they took very heavy casualties.

But they did compel the South Vietnamese and their allies to move certain forces from the countryside, into the cities. They caused widespread disruption and suffering. Their attacks, and the battles that followed, made refugees of half a million human beings.

The Communists may renew their attack. They are, it appears, trying to make 1968 the year of decision in South Vietnam — the year that brings, if not final victory or defeat, at least a turning point in the struggle.

This much is clear: If they do mount another round of heavy attacks, they will not succeed in destroying the fighting power of South Vietnam and its allies. But, tragically, this is also clear: Many men — on both sides of the struggle — will be lost. A nation that has already suffered twenty years of warfare will suffer once again. Armies on both sides will take new casualties. And the war will go on.

There is no need for this to be so. There is no need to delay the talks that could bring an end to this long and bloody war.

Tonight, I renew the offer I made last August — to stop the bombardment of North Vietnam. We ask that talks begin promptly and that they be serious talks on the substance of peace. We assume that during those talks Hanoi would not take advantage of our restraint. We are prepared to move immediately toward peace through negotiations.

Tonight, in the hope that this action will lead to early talks, I am taking the first step to deescalate the conflict. We are reducing — substantially reducing — the present level of hostilities. And we are doing so unilaterally, and at once.

Tonight, I have ordered our aircraft and naval vessels to make no attacks on North Vietnam, except in the area north of the Demilitarized Zone (DMZ) where the continuing enemy build-up directly threatens allied forward positions and where movements of troops and supplies are clearly related to that threat. . . .

Now, as in the past, the United States is ready to send its representatives to any forum, at any time, to discuss a means of bringing this war to an end. I am designating one of our most distinguished Americans, Ambassador Averell Harriman, as my personal representative for such talks. In addition, I have asked Ambassador Llewellyn Thompson, who returned from Moscow for consultations, to be available to join Ambassador Harriman at Geneva or any other suitable place just as soon as Hanoi agrees to a conference.

I call upon President Ho Chi Minh to respond positively and favorably to this new step toward peace.

But if peace does not come now through negotiations, it will come when Hanoi understands that our common resolve is unshakable and our common strength is invincible. . . .

Every American can take pride in the role

we have played in Southeast Asia; we can rightly judge — as responsible Southeast Asians themselves do — that the progress of the past three years would have been far less likely — if not impossible — if America and others had not made the stand in Vietnam.

At Johns Hopkins University, three years ago, I announced that we would take part in the great work of developing Southeast Asia, including the Mekong Valley — for all the people of the region. Our determination to help build a better land — for men on both sides of the present conflict — has not diminished. Indeed, the ravages of war have made it more urgent than ever. I repeat tonight what I said at Johns Hopkins — that North Vietnam could take its place in this common effort just as soon as peace comes.

Over time, a wider framework of peace and security in Southeast Asia may become possible. The new cooperation of the nations of the area could be a foundation stone. Certainly friendship with the nations of such a Southeast Asia is what we seek — and all that we seek.

One day, my fellow citizens, there will be peace in Southeast Asia. It will come because the people of Southeast Asia want it — those whose armies are at war today and those who, though threatened, have thus far been spared. Peace will come because Asians were willing to work for it — to sacrifice for it — to die for it. But let it never be forgotten: Peace will come also because America sent her sons to help secure it. . . .

I believe that a peaceful Asia is far nearer to reality, because of what America has done in Vietnam. I believe that the men who endure the dangers of battle there are helping the entire world avoid far greater conflicts than this one.

The peace that will bring them home will come. Tonight I have offered the first in what I hope will be a series of mutual

Wide World

President Lyndon Johnson photographed while preparing his withdrawal speech in late March 1968

moves toward peace. I pray that it will not be rejected by the leaders of North Vietnam. I pray that they will accept it as a means by which the sacrifices of their own people may be ended. And I ask your support, my fellow citizens, for this effort to reach across the battlefield toward an early peace. . . .

Finally my fellow Americans, let me say this. Those to whom much is given, much is asked. I cannot say — no man could say — that no more will be asked of us. Yet I believe that now — no less than when the decade began — this generation of Americans is willing to "pay any price, bear any burden, meet any hardship, support any friend, oppose any foe, to assure the survival and the success of liberty."

Since those words were spoken by John F. Kennedy, the people of America have kept that compact with mankind's noblest cause. We shall continue to keep it. Yet I believe we must always be mindful of this one thing: Whatever the trials and tests ahead, the ultimate strength of our country and our cause will lie, not in powerful weapons or infinite resources or boundless wealth but in the unity of our people.

This, I believe very deeply.

Throughout my public career, I have followed the personal philosophy that I am a free man, an American, a public servant, and a member of my party — in that order, always and only. For thirty-seven years in the service of our nation — first as congressman, as senator, as Vice-President, and now as your President, I have put the unity of the people first, ahead of any divisive partisanship.

In these times, as in times before, it is true that a house divided against itself — by the spirit of faction, of party, of region, of religion, of race — is a house that cannot stand. There is divisiveness in the American house now. There is divisiveness among us all tonight. Holding the trust that is mine — as President of all the people — I cannot disregard the peril to the progress of the American people and the hope and the prospects of peace for all peoples. I would ask all Americans, whatever their personal interest or concern, to guard against divisiveness and all of its ugly consequences.

Fifty-two months and ten days ago in a moment of tragedy and trauma, the duties of this office fell upon me. I asked then for "your help and God's" that we might continue America on its course, binding up our wounds, healing our history, moving forward in new unity to clear the American agenda and to keep the American commitment for all our people. United, we have kept that commitment, and united, we have enlarged that commitment.

Through all time to come, America will be a stronger nation, a more just society, a land of greater. opportunity and fulfillment because of what we have done together in these years of unparalleled achievement. Our reward will come in the life of freedom and peace and hope that our children will enjoy through ages ahead. What we won when all our people united must not now be lost in suspicion, distrust, and selfishness or politics among any of our people.

Believing this as I do, I have concluded that I should not permit the presidency to become involved in the partisan divisions that are developing in this political year. With America's sons in the field far away, with America's future under challenge here at home, with our hopes and the world's hopes for peace in the balance every day, I do not believe that I should devote an hour or a day of my time to any duties other than the awesome duties of this office, the presidency of your country.

Accordingly, I shall not seek and I will not accept the nomination of my party for another term as your President. But, let men everywhere know, however, that a strong and a confident, a vigilant America stands ready to seek an honorable peace and stands ready tonight to defend an honored cause, whatever the price, whatever the burden, whatever the sacrifice that duty may require.

Thank you for listening. Goodnight, and God bless all of you.

A mandate for unity.
> LYNDON B. JOHNSON, Speech in Austin, Texas, Nov. 4, 1964, commenting on the landslide victory he had just scored in the presidential balloting.

103.

Thomas A. Johnson: The Negro in Vietnam

Negroes constituted about 20 percent of the U.S. combat troops in Vietnam during 1967-1968, a fact that led some critics to charge the government with prejudicial treatment. There were good reasons for the disproportionately high numbers of Negroes who saw action: both the Negro primary enlistment rate and the Negro reenlistment rate were higher than those for whites, and a higher proportion of Negroes were drafted. There were thus more Negroes in the Army and available for duty. But there were reasons for the criticism, too, for all of these factors reflected the unequal economic and social status of the Negro at home, which tended to keep him from acquiring a deferred status in the draft, and which also made a combat career relatively attractive. The problems thus created for an orderly transition back to civilian life were treated in three articles written by Thomas A. Johnson for the New York Times. Portions of the first and third articles are reprinted here.

Source: *New York Times*, April 29, May 1, 1968.

Saigon, South Vietnam — The Army sergeant with the coal-black face muttered: "What in the hell am I doing here? Tell me that — what in the hell am I doing here?" But there was a smile on his face.

At the moment, he and the men of his understrength platoon — about half of them Negroes — were crouching on a jungle trail as artillery shells pounded the brush 100 yards away.

At the same time, some 50,000 other Negroes in Vietnam were unloading ships and commanding battalions, walking mountain ranges and flying warplanes, cowering in bunkers and relaxing in Saigon villas. They were planning battles, moving supplies, baking bread, advising the South Vietnamese Army, practising international law, patrolling Mekong Delta canals, repairing jets on carriers in the Tonkin Gulf, guarding the United States Embassy, drinking in sleazy bars and dining in the best French restaurants in Saigon, running press centers, burning latrines, driving trucks and serving on

the staff of Gen. William C. Westmoreland, the American commander.

They were doing everything and they were everywhere. In this highly controversial and exhaustively documented war, the Negro, and particularly the Negro fighting man, has attained a sudden visibility — a visibility his forefathers never realized while fighting in past American wars.

Fourteen weeks of interviews with black and white Americans serving here reveal that Vietnam is like a speeded-up film of recent racial progress at home. But Vietnam also demonstrates that the United States has not yet come close to solving its volatile racial problem.

Why was the sergeant — a thirty-four-year-old career soldier — in Vietnam?

He talked with good humor of the "good Regular Army" to a Negro correspondent, he shuddered with anger recalling that his hometown paper in the Deep South called his parents "Mr. and Mrs." only when referring to their hero son, and he pointed out that he had stayed in the Army because his hometown offered only "colored" jobs in a clothing factory where whites did the same work for higher pay.

Most often, Negro and white civilians and career soldiers see Vietnam as a boon to their careers and as a source of greater income than at home. It was not unusual to hear civilians and career soldiers — Negro and white — express such views as, "Hell, Vietnam's the only war we've got."

For the Negro there is the additional inducement that Southeast Asia offers an environment almost free of discrimination.

One civilian remarked, "Bread and freedom, man, bread and freedom."

"THE BIG QUESTION is whether the black cat can walk like a dragon here in South Vietnam and like a fairy back in the Land of the Big PX. Also, can America expect him to?"

The speaker, who said he had observed "America's wars both at home and abroad," was at a Negro civilian's villa on Cong Ly Street, near Independence Palace.

The year 1968 was just a few hours old, and a "soul session" was in full swing at the villa.

The answers to the questions about Negroes in the war zone and Negroes back home in a bountiful America were, for the most part, that "the black cat" could not accept a double standard and should not, but that "while America could not honestly expect him to, she would — in that undying hypocrisy for which she is so justly famous."

The session was a gathering of "soul brothers" — Negro military men and civilians, including a correspondent. Earlier, several had made their appearances at the American community's most "in" New Year's party, on Phan Thanh Gian Street (the invitation had read: "The flower people of Saigon invite you to see the light at the end of the tunnel"), and now they had got down to "the problem."

Saigon's 11 P.M. curfew was not strictly enforced that night, and the first dawn of 1968 found the soul-session participants in general agreement that the presence of the Negro in Vietnam raised more questions than it answered.

With his sudden visibility on the battlefield, the Negro has achieved the most genuine integration and the fullest participation in policies that America has yet granted. "And," it was pointed out during the soul session, "the brother is dying in order to participate — again."

The Negro is 9.8 percent of all United States military forces here, close to 20 percent of the combat forces, about 25 percent of the front-line combat leaders, and currently 14.1 percent of those killed in action.

Front-line commanders are partial to whoever will volunteer to fight, white or black. And the prime requirement, when a GI, black or white, looks for a bunker companion, is a man who will stick with him when the shooting starts.

But the Negro here has achieved his blood-spattered "equality" in America's most unpopular war. While some Americans praise him as a hero, others condemn him as a mercenary.

While he battles the Viet Cong and the North Vietnamese, he reads of racial outbreaks at home, and of authorities putting down these outbreaks with varying degrees of force and counterviolence. He hears predictions of more to come.

Discharged from the service, he is approached by black ultramilitants eager to capitalize on his battle skills and on his resentment — a resentment that the militants are certain will follow when a former serviceman realizes that at-home America has not reached the state of racial integration that Vietnam-America has.

Those who stay in the service — especially in the elite units — can expect to be used to help put down any racial outbreaks.

The Negro in Vietnam has achieved this war-zone integration 10,000 miles from home and at a time when the loudest black voices — if not the most representative — clamor for racial separation. And there is an undeniable truth in the most effective argument of these voices: The degree of equality that has been struggled into here is not available in some places in the United States and is not yet a hope in many places at home.

This is the first time in the history of American wars that national Negro figures are not urging black youths to take up arms in support of American policy to improve the lot of the black man in the United States. . . .

THE REV. DR. MARTIN LUTHER KING, JR., who was perhaps the most charismatic of contemporary Negro spokesmen, directly opposed the war.

Also opposed to the war are H. Rap Brown and Stokely Carmichael, the present and former chairmen of the Student Nonviolent Coordinating Committee, who are believed to have significant influence among young Negro militants in the ghettos. Floyd B. McKissick, head of the Congress of Racial Equality, which seeks to carry its economic, social, and political concept of black power into Negro population centers, is also opposed to the war.

The national board of the largest civil rights organization, the 450,000-member NAACP, has refused to take a public stand on the war, stating that peace efforts and civil rights should not be mixed. But the New York State Conference of the association, the largest state unit, voted last autumn, after a stormy session in Albany, to oppose the war.

Whitney M. Young, Jr., executive director of the Urban League, a civil rights group that enjoys good cooperation with government and industry, takes an after-the-fact position: "since" the Negro performs well in Vietnam, he should not suffer discrimination in America.

The most hawkish statements from blacks on the war in Vietnam have come from Negro military men. A Negro field-grade officer commented:

"You won't find many public doves — if any at all — among Negro or white career military men, no more than you'd find ambitious executives in a Ford plant urging company workers to buy Chevrolets. An executive is product-conscious."

The war's lack of popularity at home seems to have had little effect on the Negro soldier's willingness to fight it. The job, the mission, takes precedence. . . .

Most Negro servicemen interviewed in Vietnam over three and a half months felt that their uniforms kept them from participating in traditional civil rights activities, but many career men contended that their staying in the service was in itself a civil rights battle.

"We were working our show the same as Negroes back home," said Sgt. George Terry of the Army. "We brought democracy to the service by sticking it out."

"Many people called us Uncle Toms, but we were actually holding the line," said Lieut. Col. Felix L. Goodwin, a twenty-seven-year veteran who is information officer for the First Logistical Command.

Another Negro lieutenant colonel recalled that when he was graduated from Infantry Officer Candidate School at Fort Benning, Ga., in the late 1940s, a party was given in the back room of a Negro beauty parlor in "colored town" for the few Negro graduates. "A Negro chaplain told us 'not to make trouble by insisting on attending the main graduation party on the base,'" he said. "We should have 'made trouble,' but we did not. I simply can't conceive of anything happening like that nowadays. Anyway, I went back to Benning a few years ago and I lived on Colonels' Row." . . .

Should recent trends continue, about two-thirds of the first-term Negro servicemen will reenlist. Some 41,000 Negroes will be discharged this year, and about 5,000 of these will have served in Vietnam.

While some Negro militants predict that the returning Vietnam veteran will supply the cadre for a black-vs.-white civil war, some government spokesmen say he will be a leader for integration.

There is evidence to support both predictions.

Some groups that are considered extremist have added returning veterans to their number. One such recruit in New York remarked to a Negro correspondent: "I saved two white boys' lives in Vietnam. I must have been out of my Goddamn mind."

"You were," said the militant who had recruited him, "but you're on Straight Street now."

On the other hand, some returning veterans have ignored the pleas of ultramilitants.

Melvin Murrel Smith, a Negro from Syracuse who served as a Marine sergeant, maintains that "the friendships formed between whites and Negroes in Vietnam will never die because of what we went through together." Mr. Smith, whose organization of self-defense units in the Vietnamese village of Tuyloan caused the Viet Cong to place a $1,700 price on his head, said that he and several white buddies from Vietnam now often telephoned and visited one another. "Civilians can't see this because they've never been through what we went through together," Mr. Smith said.

The big question is still what will happen to the Negro grunt whose skills with the M-16 rifle and the M-79 grenade launcher are hardly marketable and who, if historical patterns prevail, will find employers much less interested in him than front-line commanders were.

There are programs trying to reverse the historic patterns. The Urban League and the American Legion are seeking jobs for the returning veteran. And an armed forces training program — Project Transition, set up on 86 military posts — gives courses in civilian skills for the serviceman who is to be discharged. . . .

And the speculation continues over whether the Negro veteran will integrate or disintegrate: Will he riot?

A young Negro naval officer at Camranh Bay called this "a white question, since whites like to convince themselves that people start riots intentionally." "I say yes," the officer added. "He will riot — if white people make him."

S. Sgt. Hector Robertin, a Puerto Rican born in Spanish Harlem who supervises an Army photography team, said it was hard for most people to "realize just why people do riot."

"Take a middle-class white of nineteen from Oregon," he said. "You could never make him understand the resentment of a cop pushing you off a street corner just because you're there, the credit gyps and landlord leeches and the feeling you come to have that if you ever get anything, you're going to have to take it."

"People talk about burning down their own neighborhood. Hell, the people there don't own a damn thing, and the government should've burned down those rat traps years ago to give people a chance for a better life. But how do you make people understand that who've never seen it, lived it?"

A Negro field-grade officer took a related view, if more gently. "There is no doubt about it," he said. "You'll have a new Negro coming out of Vietnam who has seen that America will allow him to die without discrimination, and he'll want to live without discrimination.

"You've also got a new Negro on the streets back home demanding only what white people take for granted every day.

"But what will happen? That's a question for America — for white people, not me.

"I think we stumbled into this war in Vietnam. God, I hope we don't stumble into another one back home."

Then the question was asked: "And what about you? What about you when and if we 'stumble' into a civil war back home?"

"I honestly don't know," the officer said. "I'm a soldier, yes, and I believe in America, yes, and I'm certain that it is the only country capable of bringing about a true democracy and a good standard of living for all people — but I really don't know.

"Those kids on the street — they are angry, they are inarticulate and nobody can talk to them, but do you realize they are saying no less than what Patrick Henry said?"

104.

The Dollar Crisis

Responding to intense pressures exerted on it in the international market, Great Britain devalued the pound in November 1967. The action, necessary from a British point of view and approved by the United States, nevertheless had the effect of transferring some of the pressure to the dollar, which was already in trouble owing to three factors: the high cost of the Vietnam war, a relatively low rate of domestic taxation, and the huge U.S. capital investment in foreign countries during the preceding decade. At the beginning of January President Johnson proposed several measures to reduce the deficit in the U.S. balance of payments, but there was widespread feeling that some of these, at least, were too little, too late, or both. In March 1968 there was a run on gold, which the United States was pledged to support, and thereafter the situation continued to grow worse instead of better. The head of the Federal Reserve Bank warned in March that the country was in worse financial trouble than at any time since 1931, a date that many Americans could still remember; and dire predictions were made by many other authorities, including the President himself, who said in May that the average home mortgage rate might reach 10 percent — an unprecedented level — by the end of the year. To control both internal inflation and the balance of payments deficit, he strongly urged a tax increase that, after long hesitation by Congress, was finally passed. Reprinted here are a set of questions from readers and the answers to them by Richard A. Nenneman, which appeared in The Christian Science Monitor *in January, and an editorial that appeared in the* New York Times *in March.*

Source: Reprinted by permission from *The Christian Science Monitor*, January 18, 1968: "What About This Dollar Mess?" © 1968 The Christian Science Publishing Society. All Rights Reserved. *New York Times*, March 15, 1968.

I.

RICHARD A. NENNEMAN:
On the President's Measures

How can the richest country in the world have a balance-of-payments problem? Is this just some bookkeeping entry?

It's a bookkeeping entry, all right — and a lot more! Very simply, this is what happens: Nations trade with each other, but each nation has its own currency. In order to pay for what it buys abroad, it has to earn foreign currency through such ways as selling goods or services abroad and earning money on its foreign investments. When all

"Funny — They all come from friends that I'd saved so many times."; cartoon by Hugh Haynie in "The Courier-Journal," Louisville, 1967

its foreign transactions — trade in goods and services, investment abroad and income from that investment, and government spending abroad — don't cancel each other out, we say that its payments are not in balance.

What happens, then, if a nation has a deficit in its balance of payments?

The nation in deficit has to settle its foreign accounts through a transfer of gold or a reserve currency — the American dollar or the pound sterling. All three are classed as international reserves (along with certain borrowing rights at the International Monetary Fund) under the Bretton Woods agreement of 1944. But, since every nation's reserves are limited, it can't go on settling its accounts this way indefinitely. It has to get its trade and foreign investments and governmental commitments abroad into balance before its reserves run out.

Is this what happens when the United States has a deficit, too?

Not necessarily. Since the United States and Great Britain run reserve currencies, individuals or foreign central banks that get dollars or sterling in the course of their business may continue to hold them; or they can swap them for other currencies or turn them in for gold. If they hold onto the reserve currencies, this increases total world reserves. The United States dollar in foreign hands is a claim against future American production. It can be invested (this is the major source of the flourishing Eurodollar market today), and becomes a kind of quasi-international currency, *as long as* the holder has no qualms about its eventual purchasing power. In the case of the pound last November, enough holders of sterling became uneasy about its future value and turned in sterling to force Britain to devalue.

If these circumstances forced the British to devalue, is this also apt to happen in the United States eventually?

It isn't likely. Britain has for a long time had major economic problems at home. Sterling was marginally overvalued; that is, the prices of British goods were slightly on the high side in relation to other nations' manufactures. Anxiety by holders of sterling that Britain would use devaluation as a means of solving its trade imbalance helped precipitate the devaluation.

In view of the ripples the British devaluation has caused in worldwide finance, such as the questions it has raised about the dollar, it might have been better if devaluation had not been forced on the British. But there was too much feeling that the basic British situation was not righting itself. Confidence is a matter of emotion as well as logic. There was much emotion and some logic behind what happened.

The United States, on the other hand, is not in any basic economic trouble at home (although its rate of inflation needs to be cut). In foreign trade, it had a surplus of over $4 billion last year (remember, the trade surplus is only one part of the balance-of-payments accounts). There is no general feeling that American prices are not competitive.

If the dollar were to be devalued, this would be in terms of gold — that is, the price of gold would rise. Most other nations would follow such action with a devaluation of their own, keeping their currencies in line with their old relation to the dollar. The only net change would be a higher gold price.

What's so bad about raising the price of gold? Wouldn't that be better than taking these sudden measures to defend the dollar?

It would be better if it accomplished something. But most opinion says that it wouldn't. Since the United States has long told all who hold dollars that they are redeemable at $35 for an ounce of gold, raising the gold price would undermine confidence in our integrity. There would be a deep distrust in holding dollars in the future, and the present reserve system might collapse.

Tinkering with the gold price also would raise gold to a preeminence it is fast losing. Present French policies, which would combine a rise in the gold price and a return to a pure gold standard (no reserve currencies), seem to be founded on some simplistic notions about how automatically the gold standard functioned in the late 19th century.

Dr. Arthur Bloomfield, economics professor at the University of Pennsylvania, has noted in a monograph on that period, "Clearly, the pre-1914 gold standard system was a managed and not a quasi-automatic one from the viewpoint of the leading individual countries. Nor did that system work as 'smoothly' as is often believed."

Most central bankers are beginning to think seriously of an international system less dependent on the world's limited supply of gold. What needs attention now is not the gold price but the United States payments deficit.

How successful is the President's five-point program going to be?

Two points are apt to work very well. Cutting back overseas lending by $500 million can be easily controlled by the Federal Reserve System: the banks will comply. And the cutting back of corporate investment abroad by $1 billion should be equally successful — it is mandatory.

The other three points, involving $1.5 billion, are more problematic. Congress will seriously question restrictions on tourism; the President hopes to save $500 million here. This area may well be left to individual conscience. Also, exports cannot easily be raised, and $500 million more is expected from them. Increased financing and insurance for exports should be an aid, however. Finally, the $500 million to be saved in offset costs for United States troops abroad is largely dependent on the decisions of other nations.

If the program is reasonably successful, will everything be fine then?

Not at all. These are emergency measures, apparently devised in some haste to soften the blow of the huge fourth-quarter payments deficit and gold loss. They do not befit the world's economic giant. Over a long period, they would even work against our own balance of payments. For example, limiting investment today cuts off future income from abroad. Also, large corporations can't plan intelligently if their investments abroad are going to be puppets on a string jerked by the government.

The United States deficit has two main causes: the Vietnam war and capital investment abroad. The end of the war would restore some $1.5 billion to the balance, but also bring demands to end the emergency measures. So the problem would still remain. Capital investment is a "cause" of the deficit only in the sense that it is a very large item that could be curtailed without being cut off. There had even been some signs that American investment in Europe would fall off somewhat anyway in 1968.

I've heard that some European countries don't like the war and are using their growing monetary weight to make us end it. Is this true?

Only the British (in Europe) support the war with any enthusiasm. The Continentals feel their willingness to increase their holdings of dollars would have the effect of supporting that part of the American deficit caused by the war — and thus of supporting the war itself.

I object to the President's saying we shouldn't go to Europe next summer. I haven't been for five years and was already planning a trip. Why should I stay home when the government spends so much money abroad?

The President was trying to identify those areas where big savings could be made easily. He would also like those European countries in surplus to cut down their surpluses. If you don't go to Europe, you help him achieve both ends. The tourist doesn't cause the deficit any more than any other single item in the total balance sheet. The government is looking for ways to get a dramatic turnaround. (Over the longer run, of course, tourism abroad increases foreign spending here for travel offices and new jets.)

Looking at the statistics, incidentally, I might suggest that we cut down on the almost $500 million we spend on imported alcoholic beverages. And did you know that we import over $1 billion in coffee annually? But changes such as these would hit more Americans than travel restrictions and also hit hard at a couple of countries' chief exports to the United States. The President was trying to avoid this.

I've heard that the American deficit actually helps other countries. Are there conditions under which a limited deficit might be acceptable?

Yes, I think there are. And there is an analogy in history — the expansion of the American West after the Civil War. The West was built with Eastern and European money. But it got built! Eastern money owned the railroads and the mines, but it also developed a part of the nation. And who owns Western industry today? Easterners *and* Westerners.

The analogy has a flaw, because the United States had a common currency. But the same thing was happening that happens when an American company invests abroad. As the largest supplier of capital in the world today, United States investment abroad is needed. With it come advanced production and marketing techniques. What the world hasn't adjusted to is the role of the United States as a major supplier of capital.

Perhaps American business went too heavily into a few burgeoning industries in the European Common Market area. But that part of the world is most like the United States, and American techniques could easily be adapted to Europe.

Are you suggesting that the balance-of-payments figures don't really measure what is going on?

To some extent, yes. They are correct, but somewhat arbitrary. For instance, when foreigners buy a short-term United States government bond, that counts in the American deficit; bonds of more than one-year maturity don't. Beyond that, though, the idea of a perfect balance for every country doesn't take into account the world we live in, many economists say. The United States leads in the supply of capital and technology. For it to balance its payments at the expense of these will hurt other nations.

What is difficult is that, unlike the opening of the West, if the United States overspends abroad, foreigners are in effect asked to hold on to extra dollars. While the dollar is a reserve currency, at the same time it remains our domestic currency. But until there is some kind of universal money unit, holding on to extra American dollars may be preferable to a lag in the growth of international reserves.

So are you saying the deficit doesn't really need to be overcome?

Oh, no. The rules of the game are that each nation balance its external accounts. And the French and other Europeans have a valid point in saying that Americans have abused the "privilege" of having a deficit that their reserve-currency status gives them. Other nations do realize that the size of the United States and the reserve-currency status of the dollar cause special problems for any adjustment in its payments position. But now the time is here to do something decisive.

Doing it, Americans can hope that other countries will see the need for a broader approach to world monetary problems. Even the limited establishment of Special Drawing Rights (SDRs) as agreed on tentatively at Rio de Janeiro last fall is not a big enough step forward. But if the United States follows the rules of the game now, it may nudge other countries forward to genuine monetary reform. I have a hunch this may be part of the Johnson administration's aim.

Business is the most aggressive force toward internationalism today. One might say that businessmen have vaulted ahead of their central banks and their governments. Now it is time for governments to catch up. Until there is further evolution toward truly international reserves, one way out might be to accept a United States deficit of limited amount each year. But this initiative must come from outside the United States.

II.

The Dollar Under Siege

THE RUSH INTO GOLD has taken on stampede proportions. Private individuals and corporations have joined the speculators and hoarders in a massive demand for gold that reflects their fear and distrust of the present international monetary system.

It was futile to believe that the fever for gold could be calmed by the fraternity of central bankers, led by William McChesney Martin, Jr., expressing solidarity all over again last weekend. The markets see no hope in such statements. They recognized that Mr. Martin, as head of the independent Federal Reserve Board, could not commit Congress or the administration, even though he could — and last night did — arrange to make credit more expensive by raising the discount rate to 5 percent, the highest this country has seen since 1929.

Admittedly, it is easy to find fault with the system. It is even easier to criticize its operators. But the current gold rush is a manifestation of much deeper feelings — rational and irrational. In a real sense, it represents a massive vote of no confidence in the way that the world's most powerful and richest nation is managing its political and economic affairs.

There is no other explanation for this unprecedented flight from the dollar. Probably most of those now buying gold are not after a quick killing. Nor do they want to sink the dollar. They are seeking protection against a nation that has squandered much of its vast resources, that has become mired in an escalating war that they think it cannot win, that appears paralyzed and divided, undisciplined and leaderless.

The handwriting, unmistakable and indelible, has been on the wall for a long time now. And even before sterling's devaluation sent the alarm bells ringing last November, it was obvious that the United States was flirting with disaster.

Yet the administration and Congress refused to heed the signs. Instead, they have engaged in a futile tug-of-war over whether spending should be cut or taxes raised while spending ran out of control and dollars flowed out of the country. The President finally bestirred himself to introduce a balance-of-payments program, but it was a hastily drawn-up package of inadequate half-measures that helped to sow fresh seeds of doubt about the nation's determination to defend the dollar. Even this week, special-interest senators from gold-mining states such as Colorado were tying up the Senate in a sterile debate over eliminating the gold cover, a move that should have been made long ago.

Now, with time and the gold stock both running out, there are no cosmetics left and no promises that have credibility. If the existing system is to be preserved until something stronger can replace it, then the administration, Congress, and the nation must face up to the need for swift and decisive action. At this late stage the frenetic rush into gold can only be thwarted by a positive demonstration of discipline and sacrifice. The huge cost of the war in Vietnam must be paid for; the extravagances of nonessential domestic programs must be stopped.

This newspaper has long advocated a flexible fiscal policy. We strongly favored an increase in taxes when the war in Vietnam first began to place the budget and the economy under strain. Later, we favored a stringent reduction in spending for the supersonic transport budget, agriculture, the space race, highways, and other domestic programs that were sheer extravagances in time of war. The failure to proceed on either front is largely responsible for the gold crisis — and for today's closing of the London gold market by the Treasury.

Now, the pressure of events combined with previous inaction in Washington to meet those events compels us to urge an immediate increase in taxes to make clear that the nation will bear the burden of financing the cost of Vietnam. We have steadily resisted the administration's proposed 10-percent surcharge because we did not believe that it could do the job and also because we thought it preferable to regain control over nonessential spending.

But a nation in an escalating war, with its currency under siege, has few options. If the existing monetary system is to be preserved, it is essential to take the harsh deflationary medicine of a tax increase of major proportions. The rebuilding of international confidence must start with a show of national purpose.

The nation is in the midst of the worst financial crisis since 1931. In 1931 the problem was deflation. Today it is inflation, and equally intolerable.

WILLIAM McCHESNEY MARTIN, JR., Chairman of the Federal Reserve Board, after a 5½% discount rate (the highest since 1929) was announced in April 1968.

Chester Sheard

POWER AND PROTEST

The social and political ferment of the 1960s was led by a new group, the student activists. Typically they were idealistic, committed college students, middle-class, secure, above average in intelligence. Free of economic struggle, and able therefore to see the inadequacy of mere material well-being, they struck out, albeit sometimes blindly, at the injustices and shortcomings of the American political and social system. The system, the "Establishment," as they began to conceive it, was a complex interrelationship of government, industry, and university that was at once ubiquitous and unapproachable. It was faceless, unresponsive, and often irresponsible. It was essentially antidemocratic for it followed its own internal logic, that of existing power relations and of technology, and not the will of the people. Democracy had become attenuated as the institutions of society moved away from social values; when challenged, normal paths of protest and change quickly became blind alleys, and the "open" society turned repressive. The amorphous New Left, unideological and more a condition than an organization, turned to physical protest and sought a major redistribution of power.

(Above) Oil millionaire Sam Ross of Texas standing next to his Cadillac with his oil wells in the background; (below) pipelines of an oil refinery in Houston, Texas

Ted Rozumalski — Pix from Publix

The oil industry is, traditionally, the symbol of successful entrepreneurship, built by giant men and growing from nothing to an empire by dint of force and cunning. It is at the same time, however, the outstanding example of an imperial industry, arrogating to itself quasi-governmental powers on both the domestic and international levels. Vast economic power is easily — and necessarily — convertible to political power; on the highest levels, indeed, the two are not easily distinguishable. The tacitly acknowledged penetration of state legislatures and of Congress by the oil industry maintains the powers and privileges of each in a symbiotic status quo.

(Above) Fish-eye view of the Humble Building. When completed in 1963, the Humble Oil Company's 44-story office was Houston's tallest and most expensive structure. (Below) "How far into our fiscal year do we carry our spontaneous outburst of anti-West feeling?"

Ben Roth Agency

(Above) A Consolidated Edison plant pours smoke into the otherwise clean air over New York City, early 1967; (below) sign promoting homes built with federal funds, 1940; (right) Lyndon Johnson and Frederick Kappel celebrate the launching of Telstar communications satellite, 1962

The other side of the coin is the penetration of private industry by government. Since the "internal improvements" dispute of the 1820s the issue of government's proper sphere has remained unsettled. Instead of policy, the government has followed an ad hoc pattern of gradually increasing involvement in nominally private business; this is particularly true of the defense business of recent decades. The problem created by the interlocking of business and government — or the "military-industrial complex" that President Eisenhower warned of — is one of accountability. How is the oil industry to be held to account for its foreign policy activities? How is the government to be held to account for its business ventures into communications satellites or supersonic aircraft?

(Right) Multiple-exposure photo showing variable-sweep wing on supersonic transport, designed by Boeing, which won government approval, 1967; (below) a 365-foot Apollo Saturn V rocket outside vehicle assembly building at Cape Kennedy, Florida

The defense industry, bolstered by the arms race and then the space race, became a government-subsidized business. Again, accountability is the issue; when in 1968 Congress simultaneously raised taxes and slashed welfare and social spending to finance the increasingly unpopular Vietnam war, and then eagerly committed $50 billion to a dubious new anti-missile program, no public debate on priorities influenced the decisions.

OPPOSITE PAGE: Mercury capsule atop a Redstone rocket displayed in New York. (Top) Changing shifts at McDonnell Aircraft's plant producing government-ordered Phantom jets; (center) "Brain Drain"; cartoon from "Punch"; (bottom) Grumman Aircraft assembly line

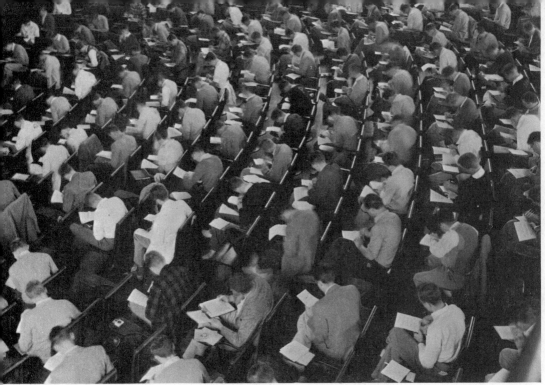

(Top) Large lecture hall, Princeton University; (bottom left) student demonstration at the University of California; (bottom right) Mario Savio, leader of the Berkeley protest, 1964

Anti-Vietnam demonstration in Washington, D.C., 1965

Activist groups, composed overwhelmingly of college students, protested against the facet of the "Establishment" nearest them: the huge, impersonal university. In the radical critique, the university was seen as a processing machine intended to turn out engineers and technicians for an expanding technological society while neglecting humane education and the traditional critical role of the university. Underlying all the local issues and concerned splinter groups was the maddening and seemingly insoluble Vietnam war, the focus around which broader protest was centered.

Military police confront protesters during a peace march in Washington, D.C.

Civil rights group trying to halt construction of a school in Cleveland, Ohio, which they feel will resegregate the neighborhood. Police arrested the demonstrators

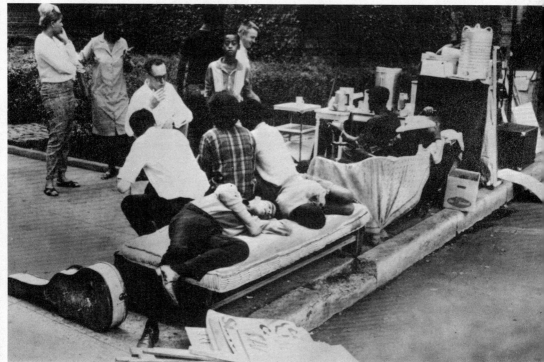

(Above) Tenants evicted from their integrated apartment building in Chicago following a rent strike to protest the landlord's failure to maintain the property; (right) demonstration outside an empty classroom during a Teachers' Union strike in New York City, September 1967

The activist approach spread rapidly as a response to other faceless institutions. When no line of responsibility was discoverable, when complaint and petition were met with blank complacency, the only resolution seemed to be a totally-committed physical act. The roots of this method lay in the early civil rights movement, of course, but there was a difference: the early sit-in had been pure demonstration, but the object of the new sit-in and its many variations was more and more the obstruction of the system. While this was usually a hopeless goal, the act dramatized the helplessness of people excluded from decision-making power over their own lives.

(Above) Mark Rudd, leader of the student takeover at Columbia, explains its purpose to reporters; (below) Chicago, August 1968

A striking example of the new temper came in April 1968. Student groups at Columbia University had become concerned over some apparently discriminatory real estate practices of the university. Normal channels of investigation and dissent were tried — the established modes for "redress of grievances" — and were found inadequate. The university, in the students' view, simply ignored meetings and petitions. In desperation, then, the students took over Columbia for four days. The university tried at first to avoid adverse publicity, both about its real estate policies and its treatment of dissent; finally, however, the police were sent in.

105.

John W. Gardner: Poverty

"A government of unprecedented power appears to be impotent," wrote John W. Gardner, "in the face of the threat of social disintegration and the promise of social justice." Thus did Gardner express his disillusionment with the attitude of the Johnson administration and of the 90th Congress toward the problems of poverty and urban blight; and, expressing it even more eloquently, he resigned his post as secretary of health, education, and welfare in January 1968 to become chairman of the Urban Coalition, a private organization supported by the Carnegie Foundation and pledged to try to deal with poverty on a national scale. The following article by Gardner appeared as the conclusion of a Life *special report titled "The Cycle of Despair: the Negro and the City."*

Source: *Life*, March 8, 1968.

THE COMFORTABLE AMERICAN does not enjoy thinking about the human misery festering at the other end of town. He does not enjoy knowing that many of his fellow citizens live in conditions that breed every variety of social evil. It is not easy for him to acknowledge that his own infant, dropped into that ruinous environment, would just as surely fall victim to it. He averts his eyes from the human damage that occurs there.

In the absence of medical attention, physical deficiencies that could be corrected early become lifelong handicaps. In the absence of early mental stimulation, minds that could be awakened settle into lifelong dullness. Crime, drugs, prostitution claim their victims. So do apathy, degradation, and despair. Ultimately, all Americans bear the cost.

A disintegrating neighborhood and its social casualties are in every way a burden on the community and the nation.

The American dream is based on the conviction that every individual is of value. Or so we have always told ourselves. A free society should produce free and responsible individuals as a tree bears fruit. That is its purpose.

It should enable the talented to develop their talent. It should enable each person to achieve the best that is in him. It should help the lame to walk, and the despairing to hope, and the ignorant to know. It should fight every condition that stunts human growth or warps the mind or dulls the spirit. By doing so, it should make men more free, more responsible, more self-sufficient.

Poverty is not easy to eliminate, whether the poor are black or white. In the case of the Negro it is made harder by the evil of racism.

But we cannot afford to be discouraged by the difficulty of the problems. If they were easy, we would have solved them long ago. When we formed this free society we did not commit ourselves to solve only the easy ones.

The tough problems are the ones that test our resolve.

I have heard the authentic voices of hatred, and the threats of violence — from white men and black. But those who hate cannot save us; they can only destroy.

What can save us is, first of all, a great effort on the part of white Americans to understand and extend a hand across the gulf of fear and anger. They must make a full commitment to right injustices and build a better future. What is also needed is a recognition on the part of the Negro community that that better future cannot be built instantly. The wrongs of centuries cannot be righted in a day or a year. But a common commitment to act now can create the climate in which solutions are possible.

We must begin with a massive resolve on the part of the great, politically moderate majority of whites and blacks — to transform destructive emotion into constructive action. The time has come when the full weight of community opinion, white and Negro, should be felt against those within their own ranks who hate and destroy.

We *can* solve our problems. But it will take moral courage, intelligence, and stamina. We have summoned these qualities before at critical times in our history. At no time has the need been greater than it is now.

We cannot have two nations, one white and one black. Every time we salute the flag we pledge allegiance to "one nation indivisible."

One nation indivisible it must remain.

106.

Hunger in the United States

In July 1967 the Citizens' Crusade Against Poverty in Washington, D.C., established a Citizens' Board of Inquiry into Hunger and Malnutrition in the United States, with Benjamin Mays and Leslie Dunbar as cochairmen. Hearings were conducted in nearly all parts of the country, and data was collected bearing on the pervasiveness of hunger among the population. The report of the board, published in April 1968, showed that very few states did not have counties with serious hunger problems. National, state, and local welfare programs were found to be almost wholly inadequate to cope with the situation. The following selection includes portions of the Foreword and of the Introduction to the report.

Source: *Hunger, U.S.A.*, Washington, 1968, pp. 4-5, 8-9.

IF YOU WILL GO LOOK, you will find America a shocking place.

No other Western country permits such a large proportion of its people to endure the lives we press on our poor. To make fourfifths of a nation more affluent than any people in history, we have degraded onefifth mercilessly. . . . Wherever we have gone we have seen the multitudinous cast-offs of an economic system which, bewilderingly, can build up ever greater national achievements without affecting the immense and economically useless pockets of the impoverished. Curiously, the desolate poor are heavily weighted on the side of old inhabitants: Indians, Negroes, Appalachian whites, Spanish-speaking residents of the Southwest. . . .

We feel fairly confident that most Americans must believe — if they think of it at all — that the federal food programs (including the school lunch program) are designed to serve the interests and needs of beneficiaries. This is not true. They are designed and administered within the context of the national agricultural policy. That policy, as led by the Department of Agriculture and congressional committees and subcommittees of agriculture and agricultural appropriation, is dominated by a concern for maximizing agricultural income, especially within the big production categories.

Other objectives always yield to this one. Those other objectives include farm production, soil conservation, the welfare of individual farmers, and farm employment. Our agricultural policy can be and often is attentive to those other objectives, but *only when they do not conflict with the dominant objectives of maximizing income.* But almost never does our agricultural policy take a direct concern with the interests of consumers and, certainly, not of poor consumers.

Rather than criticize this we think it preferable (*a*) to recognize that the Department of Agriculture and the committees of Congress that it is responsive to have this dominant concern; and (*b*) to remove from their care the administration of the food programs which are and have always been extraneous to this primary concern.

The second main direction that our recommendations follow is toward freeing the poor, as far as we can see possible, from the special and often oppressively undignified guardianship of any bureaucracies. We think those who are poor can be safely assumed to have a concern for their own and their children's best interests and can, therefore, be trusted to look after themselves. The principal recommendation of this Board is, therefore, a free food stamp program keyed to need and to the objective of a completely adequate diet, and one which would be administered with minimum controls. . . .

IN ISSUING THIS REPORT, we find ourselves somewhat startled by our own findings, for we too had been lulled into the comforting belief that at least the extremes of privation had been eliminated in the process of becoming the world's wealthiest nation. Even the most concerned, aware, and informed of us were not prepared to take issue with the presumption stated by Michael Harrington on the opening page of his classic *The Other America*:

> To be sure, the other America is not impoverished in the same sense as those poor nations where millions cling to hunger as a defense against starvation. This country has escaped such extremes.

But starting from this premise, we found ourselves compelled to conclude that America has not escaped such extremes. For it became increasingly difficult, and eventually impossible, to reconcile our preconceptions with statements we heard everywhere we went:

— that substantial numbers of newborn, who survive the hazards of birth and live through the first month, die between the second month and their second birthday from causes which can be traced directly and primarily to malnutrition.

— that protein deprivation between the ages of six months and a year and one-half causes permanent and irreversible brain damage to some young infants.

— that nutritional anemia, stemming primarily from protein deficiency and iron deficiency, was commonly found in percentages ranging from 30 to 70 percent among children from poverty backgrounds.

— that teachers report children who come to school without breakfast, who are too hungry to learn, and in such pain that they must be taken home or sent to the school nurse.

— that mother after mother in region after region reported that the cupboard was bare, sometimes at the beginning and throughout the month, sometimes only the last week of the month.

— that doctors personally testified to seeing case after case of premature death, infant deaths, and vulnerability to secondary infection, all of which were attributable to or indicative of malnutrition.

— that in some communities people band together to share the little food they have, living from hand to mouth.

— that the aged living alone subsist on liquid foods that provide inadequate sustenance.

We also found ourselves surrounded by myths which were all too easy to believe because they are so comforting. We number among these:

Myth: The really poor and needy have access to adequate surplus commodities and food stamps if they are in danger of starving.

Fact: Only 5.4 million of the more than 29 million poor participate in these two government food programs, and the majority of those participating are not the poorest of the poor.

Myth: Progress is being made as a result of massive federal efforts in which multimillion-dollar food programs take care of more people now than ever before.

Fact: Participation in government food programs has dropped 1.4 million in the last six years. Malnutrition among the poor has risen sharply over the past decade.

Myth: Hunger and starvation must be restricted to terrible places of need, such as Mississippi, which will not institute programs to take adequate care of its people.

Fact: Mississippi makes more extensive use of the two federal food programs than any state in the United States.

In addition to the hearings, the site visits, the personal interviews, the anecdotal stories, we learned from government officials, statistics, studies, and reports that where, by accident or otherwise, someone looked for malnutrition, he found it — to an extent and degree of severity previously unsuspected. If this report is marred by any single element, it is the anomaly of asserting that a phenomenon exists, and that it is widespread, without being able to ascertain its exact magnitude or severity because no one ever believed it existed.

To the best of our knowledge, we have collected the studies and information compiled by all who have gone before us and have supplemented it with the best evidence that our own direct efforts could uncover. At best, we can make an educated guess as to the order of magnitude of the problem. But the chief contribution we can make does not rest with engaging in a numbers game.

It lies elsewhere — with the reversal of presumption. Prior to our efforts, the presumption was against hunger, against malnutrition; now the presumption has shifted. The burden of proof has shifted. It rests with those who would deny the following words of one of our members, "There is sufficient evidence to indict" on the following charges:

1. Hunger and malnutrition exist in this country, affecting millions of our fellow Americans and increasing in severity and extent from year to year.

2. Hunger and malnutrition take their toll in this country in the form of infant deaths, organic brain damage, retarded growth and learning rates, increased vulnerability to disease, withdrawal, apathy, alienation, frustration, and violence.

3. There is a shocking absence of knowledge in this country about the extent and severity of malnutrition — a lack of information and action which stands in marked contrast to our recorded knowledge in other countries.

4. Federal efforts aimed at securing adequate nutrition for the needy have failed to reach a significant portion of the poor and to help those it did reach in any substantial and satisfactory degree.

5. The failure of federal efforts to feed the poor cannot be divorced from our nation's agricultural policy, the congressional committees that dictate that policy, and the Department of Agriculture that implements it; for hunger and malnutrition in a country of abundance must be seen as consequences of a political and economic system that spends billions to remove food from the market, to limit production, to retire land from production, to guarantee and sustain profits for the producer.

Perhaps more surprising and shocking is the extent to which it now rests within our power substantially to alleviate hunger and malnutrition. While new programs are needed, and new legislation is desired and urged, there are now reserves of power, of money, of discretionary authority, and of technical know-how which could make substantial inroads on the worst of the conditions we have uncovered — and this could be commenced not next year or next month — but today.

107.

ROBERT B. RIGG: Military Occupation of the Cities

The issue of the use of force to control and combat civil disorder received much attention following the disturbances in American cities during 1967. Because such widespread disorder was unprecedented in this century, police and National Guard officials were frequently unsure of precisely what measure of force to use. The Kerner Commission Report cited the danger of overreacting by the police, and this conclusion of the report seemed borne out by the April 1968 disturbances, when police and military action was more restrained than in 1967 and the loss of life also much less. The threat of future disorders led many police departments and National Guard units to undertake programs of riot control. In the following article, reprinted here in part, a professional soldier who specializes in long-range military strategy told what steps would be taken by both National Guard and Army units to deal with urban violence in the United States.

Source: *Army,* January 1968: "Made in USA."

DURING THE NEXT FEW YEARS organized urban insurrection could explode to the extent that portions of large American cities could become scenes of destruction approaching those of Stalingrad in World War II. This could result from two main causes:

Man has constructed out of steel and concrete a much better "jungle" than nature has created in Vietnam.

There is the danger and the promise that urban guerrillas of the future can be orga-

nized to such a degree that their defeat would require the direct application of military power by the National Guard and the active Army.

This degree of destruction can easily come about because of these two circumstances. After all, we have seen many square blocks totally ruined in Watts, Detroit, and elsewhere, where there was no organized resistance. Were organized insurrection to break out and military power needed to suppress it, destruction in city square miles could mount tremendously over what we have seen.

However, while application of pure military firepower would be a poor solution, political efforts might prove not much better. There are measures that offer a better solution if we are to keep our cities from becoming battlegrounds: penetration by police intelligence, application of military intelligence, and reliance on traditional FBI methods. Such efforts must begin now so as to prevent organized urban guerrilla violence from gaining momentum.

To prevent and to curb urban violence of any order we must establish an effective system of intelligence in the ghettos of urban America. If penetration were professionally effective, such a system could warn of any plans for organized violence by subversive elements. Further, should organized violence break out, such an espionage system would be able to keep riot control and counterviolence forces informed during a disturbance.

The real prevention of urban violence and insurrection begins with social, economic, and political efforts. But alongside these measures and efforts there must be the "peripheral insurance policy" of an inside intelligence system that can warn of serious outbreaks and help curb them.

Furthermore, there will also be needed among the well-established political-tactical-military informants those who can help guide troops and police through the maze of buildings, stairwells, streets, alleyways, tunnels, and sewers that may be the key to tactical success. In the countryside we would call this elementary or "grass roots" intelligence; in the city there will be a similar need.

Just as China was plagued with rural guerrilla warfare from the 1920s to the late 1940s, so, too, if present trends persist, could the United States experience similar strife and violence. The singular difference is that the fighting would be urban in nature. Furthermore, it is likely to be of such a special brand that can bear only the unique label, "Made in the U.S.A." Thus, the United States may inadvertently provide the world with a new brand of internal warfare that could haunt and harass large metropolitan areas for decades to come.

This possibility is alarming in light of the population explosion and the urban growth which by the 1980s may result in strip cities extending from Miami to Boston, from Chicago to Detroit, from San Francisco to San Diego — not to mention similar areas abroad. Of further import for the near future is the fact that the older "core cities" — such as Chicago, New York, Detroit, Newark, Oakland, Los Angeles, and others — could become concrete jungles where poverty could spread with their growth. Additionally, such cement-and-brick "jungles" can offer better security to snipers and city guerrillas than the Viet Cong enjoy in their jungles, elephant grass, and marshes. This suggests protracted warfare of a very new kind if city guerrilla forces become well organized by dissident and determined leaders.

City warfare is not new. What would make this type of conflict new, different, and more terrifying would be two elements. One would be the very geographical extent of the concrete jungles that are now simply called ghettos; such slum areas can expand rapidly as suburbia grows and absorbs the more affluent. The other would be lawless forces intoxicated by the ease and security with which they might successfully defy police, National Guardsmen, and Army regulars. The concrete blocks of our great ghettos have vertical acreage and horizontal mileage that offer such tactical protection and vantage points as to make future snipers much "braver" and city guerrillas much bolder than unorganized rioting mobs have been so far.

These are only a few of the trends in the United States which flash warning that our nation could be in for such violent street disorders that to suppress them would ultimately require the civil use of military power on a scale never heretofore visualized.

Racial issues, poverty, political unrest among minorities, the population explosion, and the rapid growth of strip cities that absorb the decaying old core cities — all these represent a combination of future factors and trends that could plague metropolitan areas and breed more violent and better-organized disorder. That urban violence has spread significantly makes the outlook grim, because street violence has found acceptance among minorities.

Today's riots bring more than temporary disorder. They instill a new frame of mind among minorities — an outlook that visualizes rebellion against society and authority as a successful venture for the future. So far the unruly elements, with no real organization, have demonstrated that they can do unusual damage wantonly and indiscriminately. But the sick seed can grow into a menacing weed if in the future the potentials of organization are exploited.

So far the causes of urban violence have been emotional and social. Organization, however, can translate these grievances into political ones of serious potential and result in violence, or even prolonged warfare. Thus, we may find that the danger to a free America is greater from within than from without.

If present trends persist, it is possible that in the next decade at least one major metropolitan area in the United States could be faced with guerrilla warfare of such intensity as to require sizable U.S. Army elements in action and National Guard units on active duty for years. No doubt such an urban conflict could be contained, subdued and defeated, but the effort could possibly require years of concerted military action before even effective social improvements could have impact. This is what the war in South Vietnam has demonstrated. Further, if organized guerrilla resistance spreads to several cities and requires the use of many military units, a national paralysis of very serious proportions might ensue. . . .

Urban riot has been established as an instrument of racial rebellion. But the riots have not been strictly one of Negroes clashing with whites; often the rioters were relieving their frustrations at their ghetto surroundings and relative poverty, and upon authorities. It is important to remember this, especially where it pertains to slums. Violence in the future may even be by whites protesting against poverty and their environment. White or black, here is where the political aspect looms large because Communist elements can penetrate urban America and foment serious trouble.

The future brand of trouble may not necessarily be Communist-inspired. Activists of the left who now expend their energies in protesting against the Vietnam war could become a growing source of urban unrest and trouble. The future problem of city violence bears no particular political label at the moment but it does indicate that trouble can arise from the left or right, or from black or white. Poverty and social problems exist in rural areas, but they can reach explosive and serious proportions only in our cities.

The personal right to own firearms is being seriously debated in Washington today. The argument will linger, and probably with no conclusive results, for a long time. The stark fact remains that from Chicago to the Congo, anyone who wants to shoot can buy small arms and even mortars. World War II, the many limited wars since, and all the military-aid programs have flooded the world with arms and ammunition. If a subversive force or organization wants arms, they are available. If their leaders want them on a wholesale scale, arms for the urban guerrillas of the United States will not be hard to obtain.

Today, one trend is self-evident: metropolitan police cannot cope with even disorganized violence where it reaches high proportions. Tomorrow, police and National

Guard units may not be able to cope with urban violence that is well organized. . . .

While the patterns of future urban insurrection may vary, there will be certain problems to confront, if the violence is organized.

Problem No. 1 would be organization itself. To combat this would require political and intelligence penetration of high order and expertise. Here, penetration must be deep enough so as to warn of secret subversive plans, to pinpoint leaders, and to disrupt organization itself.

Problem No. 2 would concern the identification of hideouts, areas where weapons are stored, sources of arms, guerrilla means of transportation, access and escape routes, and probably resistance spots. In other words, we must have intimate and accurate information on the facilities used by urban guerrillas before and during trouble.

Problem No. 3 relates to tactical military action against organized resistance once conflict begins. Hopefully, this assumes that at least fair intelligence and espionage would continue to meet the problems mentioned. But no intelligence report has ever been prepared that included complete information on the enemy *after* the fighting started. Tactical action has always had to rely on what little was known and what could be learned through intelligence gathered by scouting and combat. Imagine a building, or a block of buildings, that houses innocent people but is used at night by snipers and insurrectionists with fire bombs. Tactical action here would take on the proportions of search-and-plant operations by day and retaliation, maneuver, and fighting by night. Night fighting will call for a very delicate decision as to which darkened window to shoot at and which rooftop to blast by mortar fire or to assault by helicopter. A whole new manual of military operations, tactics, and techniques needs to be written in respect to urban warfare of this nature. There are none on the subject today.

Problem No. 4 includes police-Guard-Army and local authority (particularly political) coordination, communications, and control. Here also is a very big problem that can be greatly aggravated by chaos and street fighting. For every city, for every emergency, this one requires much planning in depth. Planning is vital, particularly in terms of political and military control and coordination of all efforts. Once chaos and conflict ensue, command and coordination become even more crucial and necessary. Communications in terms of standing operating procedure, integrated radio networks, liaison, procedures, and the like are big problems that must be solved before conflict and modified to meet the demands of the situation.

Problem No. 5 can be termed "Mixture X." It includes everything from control and safety of a few dozen (or hundreds) of refugees fleeing from buildings to hostages being held by seasoned guerrillas or being used by them as escape shields. It includes the sick and wounded among the innocent. It includes the supply of food and medicine — and medical treatment — to trapped people. It includes evacuation by helicopters and by fire fighters of people trapped in burning buildings. It includes the protection of firemen from sniper fire, the need of which last summer's Detroit riot demonstrated in very grim and dramatic fashion. Plainly, firemen need the Red Cross badge of safety to protect them in their valor and work. They didn't have even this in Detroit. They may suffer heavy casualties during organized urban insurrection of the future unless they are somehow more respected by some agreement or other measure.

Success in coping with organized urban warfare will not rest on agreements but rather depend on tactics and techniques yet to be formulated. The overall problem, and success in meeting it, depend heavily on a new measure of organization, coordination, and study among officials of the city, state,

National Guard, police, active Army, and FBI. While these organizations understand the problem and are alert to it, much work lies ahead.

The implications are clear. American military and political plans must now, more than ever before, be based upon meeting a new kind of internal violence. . . .

Such planning must include training troops for urban insurrection. For the National Guard this means a complete change of direction in training as something of first priority. For the active Army, such training has serious overtones to the extent that it must train for the concrete jungle as well as for the other kind. Further, it means that Army units must be oriented and trained to know the cement-and-asphalt jungle of *every* American city. It means that maneuvers

and exercises, heretofore carried out about the countryside, in the future can be conducted in large cities. Possibly the sight of such maneuvers in several cities could prove a deterrent to urban insurrection. Today's trend implies that very soon American troops will be maneuvering in metropolitan areas to an extent more than ever before imagined. Here they will be required to learn about and memorize details of many metropolitan communities, their buildings, streets, alleyways, rooftops, and sewers, just as once they learned the use of terrain features of open country. This is the only way to solve the intelligence, social, economic, and political problems associated with serious Third Front warfare which could bear the unfortunate label of "Made in the U.S.A."

108.

Business and the Urban Crisis

To aid the nation in dealing with the severe and complex social issues represented by the urban ghetto, President Lyndon B. Johnson, in January 1968, called upon business executives to provide jobs for the hard-core unemployed. In response, a National Alliance of Businessmen, headed by Henry Ford II, initiated a program called JOBS (Job Opportunities in the Business Sector). To augment government programs, the administration also urged businessmen to tackle other problems in the cities, especially housing and education. In February 1968 McGraw-Hill Publications issued a special report on "Business and the Urban Crisis," outlining the responsibilities of American enterprise toward the problems of urban disintegration and poverty. Portions of the report are reprinted below.

Source: *Business Week,* February 3, 1968.

THE PROBLEM

"IF YOU CATS can't do it, it's never going to get done."

The speaker: Frank Ditto, a Black militant leader in Detroit.

The cats: a group of Detroit businessmen

who visited Ditto's Voice of Independence headquarters after last summer's riots.

"The government can't lick this problem," Ditto added. "So business has to."

Of course, business *has* to do nothing of the sort. What's more, no one — business included — can expect to come up with a swift cure for the ills that plague the cities.

But, if only for intelligently selfish reasons, businessmen can't afford to ignore the urban crisis. Here's why:

If you ignore the crisis, no one else may be able to cool the anger that boils up in riots. So far at least, no one else has gotten more than token results — not the government, not the labor unions, not the churches, and not the civic organizations.

Make no mistake — the riots are not yet revolutionary, nor do they involve more than a tiny fraction of the Negro population. They are significant only as a headline-grabbing symbol that focuses attention on the resentment felt by Negroes, now 11 percent of the nation's population. The real problem is not the riots but the frustration that generates them.

That frustration often explodes in rioting just when conditions are improving. Reason: Deprived people feel most frustrated when their hopes and expectations have been raised but not completely satisfied. . . .

If you ignore the crisis, you may be overlooking a big potential market. The city has always been a social and economic necessity for businessmen. Markets thrive in healthy cities, waste away in sick ones.

If today's sick cities can be cured — if ghetto dwellers can be better housed, better educated, and, above all, better employed — new and profitable markets will open up for business.

Even the very process of saving the cities creates opportunities for some industries — construction, for example. Between now and the year 2000, the city ghettos will need some 10 million new dwelling units. No matter who builds these units — private operators or public authorities — they will add up to $200 billion in today's dollars in new business for developers, contractors, and building-product manufacturers. . . .

The income gap between this country's whites and non-whites is wide and getting wider. Today, in the midst of general prosperity, over 30 million Americans live in poverty (family incomes under $3,130), and almost 30 million more live in deprivation (incomes from $3,130 to $5,000). Roughly half of each group is clustered in the city slums.

To be sure, slum dwellers' incomes are rising — but not at the same pace as the incomes of everyone else. And in the worst slums, incomes are actually falling. In New York's central Harlem, for instance, the average dropped from $3,997 in 1960 to $3,907 in 1966. Meanwhile, consumer prices in the New York metropolitan area rose 12 percent. . . .

But the income gap is just one of the barriers that trap non-whites in the city ghettos. Here are four others:

1. Zoning bars low-income families from the suburbs — first, by stipulating lot sizes (and thus house prices) that are beyond their reach; second, by keeping out blue-collar industry that could provide jobs for people now living in the city.

2. Welfare often hinders more than it helps. First of all, the welfare burden (annual cost: $7 billion) falls heavily on the Northern cities and lightly on the areas where the bulk of the poor came from. Second, even states and cities with liberal benefits fail to meet federally defined minimum-income levels. Finally — and this is the crux of the matter — welfare practices kill the slum dweller's incentive to find a job and hold his family together. If the father of a family on welfare gets a job, whatever he earns is deducted from his family's welfare payments. In effect, he is taxed 100 percent on his earnings. So he may face a hard choice: Quit the job or abandon his family.

3. A new legislative coalition has little sympathy for the sick cities. In state legislatures and Congress, there has always been an understandable rivalry between represen-

tatives of the cities and the rural areas. Now — and for equally understandable reasons — the rural spokesmen have a potent new ally: representatives of the burgeoning suburbs. This new coalition reinforces suburban zoning and limits the ability of urban-based legislators to put across programs aimed at solving the cities' problems.

4. Cities lack the financial base to do the job that must be done — to tackle adequate housing programs, for instance. The basic problem: Property taxation — source of most municipal revenue — is inequitable; it puts the biggest burden on business, the smallest on slum-housing owners. So, not surprisingly, many companies flee the city — which only loads a bigger burden on those who stay, puts the city in a worse financial bind than ever, and makes it less and less likely that slum problems will be solved with local money.

In theory at least, removing all those barriers is every American's problem. But this report is about what businessmen can do — if they get involved. And since this report stresses the purely practical reasons for business action, it goes without saying that getting involved invites economic risks.

When the president of Detroit's largest department store led a state open-housing fight last November, more than 10,000 customers closed out their accounts in 10 days. Every time Henry Ford II has made a pronouncement in behalf of Negro rights, Ford Motor Co. sales have tumbled in the South.

But Henry Ford still maintains: "People who don't face up to this issue are stupid. It's a great opportunity for business. It's shortsighted not to step in and do something to solve the problem."

What, then, can business do to ease the frustration of the ghetto dwellers?

Business can turn the staggering need for low-rent city housing into a big and profitable market — if some of the government-imposed rules that now regulate housing construction are changed.

Business can also put its influence and special skills behind sorely needed changes in the city school systems.

And business alone holds one key to breaking the vicious slum cycle of unemployment, poverty, poor housing, poor education, and low productivity. That key is jobs.

JOBS

How many jobs are needed? Secretary Wirtz estimates a half-million for 100 city slums, another half-million for the rest of the country.

In a growing economy that produces a million and a half new jobs a year, the need to place half a million slum dwellers — or even a million — does not sound all that tough.

But it is. Business has found that hiring and training the people at the bottom of the ghetto barrel — "making the transition from the street corner to a job," as a Los Angeles training executive puts it — is tougher than it sounds.

Yet business must face up to it. President Johnson, for one, has issued a direct challenge: ". . . Help me find jobs for these people or we are going to have to offer every one of them a job in government."

Members of the Urban Coalition, which includes the nation's top industrialists, recently pledged a million jobs. And many businessmen cite practical reasons for action.

Says Chester Brown, Allied Chemical's chairman: "Business can broaden its markets by increasing people's purchasing power. One way to do this is to lift the economic status of poverty-stricken slum dwellers." . . .

HOUSING

THE PROBLEM OF SUPPLYING HOUSING in the cores of cities is not a problem of logistics or construction technology. It is purely a problem of economics.

Under present taxation and finance practices, no one can supply the volume of housing needed. But if the rules that force these practices are changed — if some new form of government subsidy is accepted and if red tape is trimmed from federal housing programs — a staggering need can be turned into a profitable market.

Business' stake in changing the rules is pretty simple and direct. Just replacing the substandard housing in cities would involve more new construction than the total volume of housing starts over the past five years.

The 1960 housing census uncovered more than 4 million urban dwelling units that were completely dilapidated, some 3 million more that were badly deteriorated, and another 2 million with serious code violations or serious overcrowding. If that is not a bad enough problem — or a big enough market — recent Census studies indicate the 1960 figures may have underestimated the number of dilapidated units by as much as one-third.

What's more, revitalizing the cities would encourage the return of hundreds of thousands of families who have fled to the suburbs — and thus would generate new demand for middle- and upper-income housing.

So sitting right there in the city slums is a market for well over 7 million new and rehabilitated housing units and all the building products that go into them — everything from flooring and dry wall to lighting and plumbing fixtures. And, points out Raymond H. Lapin, president of HUD's Federal National Mortgage Assn.: "The profit earned on a sheet of gypsum board is the same whether the board is used in a low-rent apartment or a $50,000 house." . . .

EDUCATION

AT THE U.S. OFFICE OF EDUCATION, Commissioner Harold Howe II spells out the problem:

"There is a vast psychological gap between the clientele of today's city schools (students and parents) and the suppliers of education (teachers, administrators, and school board members)."

This gap is steadily widened by the spreading Negro ghettos, the flight of white families to the suburbs, and the mushrooming non-white population of city schools.

An example that scares everybody is Washington, D.C., where 93 percent of public-school pupils are Negroes and the percentage is still rising. Elsewhere, worried school administrators watch the trend and see their systems as "Washington minus five years" or "Washington minus three years." In Detroit, non-whites represent 57 percent of the school population; in Chicago, 54 percent; in Cleveland, 53 percent; in St. Louis, 62 percent.

When the Negro school population reaches such high levels, the quality of education suffers. Negro pupils begin to feel segregated and lose their motivation to learn. Teachers have to spend more time keeping order than teaching. So, not surprisingly, the most experienced teachers tend to shun the very schools that most need them.

Total solution of the educational problem may not be possible. But ghetto schools can be vastly improved — if there are major changes in attitude and action not only among educators but also among businessmen.

109.

On Civil Disorders

During the summer of 1967 nearly 150 cities in the United States experienced civil disorders, of which the most severe were the July riots in Newark and Detroit. In their wake President Johnson established a National Advisory Commission on Civil Disorders, with Governor Otto Kerner of Illinois as chairman, to investigate the origins of the disturbances, the means by which they could be controlled, and the role of the local, state, and federal governments in dealing with them. The Commission's report, portions of which appear below, was issued on March 1, 1968, and immediately gained a large audience. Reactions to the findings were mixed, ranging from strong disapproval to warm praise. The President himself did not endorse the report, and elected officials generally showed themselves unwilling to embrace the vast programs for social renewal recommended by the Commission.

Source: *Report of the National Advisory Commission on Civil Disorders,* Washington, 1968, pp. 5-16, 63-74, 91-93, 147, 218-231.

Preface

LAST SUMMER over 150 cities reported disorders in Negro — and in some instances, Puerto Rican — neighborhoods. These ranged from minor disturbances to major outbursts involving sustained and widespread looting and destruction of property. The worst came during a 2-week period in July when large-scale disorders erupted first in Newark and then in Detroit, each setting off a chain reaction in neighboring communities.

It was in this troubled and turbulent setting that the President of the United States established this Commission. He called upon it "to guide the country through a thicket of tension, conflicting evidence and extreme opinions." . . .

Much of our report is directed to the condition of those Americans who are also Negroes and to the social and economic environment in which they live — many in the black ghettos of our cities. But this Na-

tion is confronted with the issue of justice for all its people — white as well as black, rural as well as urban. In particular, we are concerned for those who have continued to keep faith with society in the preservation of public order — the people of Spanish surname, the American Indian and other minority groups to whom this country owes so much.

We wish it to be clear that in focusing on the Negro, we do not mean to imply any priority of need. It will not do to fight misery in the black ghetto and leave untouched the reality of injustice and deprivation elsewhere in our society. The first priority is order and justice for all Americans.

In speaking of the Negro, we do not speak of "them." We speak of us — for the freedoms and opportunities of all Americans are diminished and imperiled when they are denied to some Americans. The tragic waste of human spirit and resources, the unrecoverable loss to the Nation which this denial has already caused — and continues to produce — no longer can be ignored or afforded.

Two premises underlie the work of the Commission:

That this Nation cannot abide violence and disorder if it is to ensure the safety of its people and their progress in a free society.

That this Nation will deserve neither safety nor progress unless it can demonstrate the wisdom and the will to undertake decisive action against the root causes of racial disorder.

This report is addressed to the institutions of government and to the conscience of the Nation, but even more urgently, to the mind and heart of each citizen. The responsibility for decisive action, never more clearly demanded in the history of our country, rests on all of us.

We do not know whether the tide of racial disorder has begun to recede. We recognize as we must that the conditions underlying the disorders will not be obliterated before the end of this year or the end of the next and that so long as these conditions exist a potential for disorder remains. But we believe that the likelihood of disorder can be markedly lessened by an American commitment to confront those conditions and eliminate them — a commitment so clear that Negro citizens will know its truth and accept its goal. The most important step toward domestic peace is an act of will; this country can do for its people what it chooses to do. . . .

PATTERNS OF DISORDER

DISORDERS ARE OFTEN DISCUSSED as if there were a single type. The "typical" riot of recent years is sometimes seen as a massive uprising against white people, involving widespread burning, looting, and sniping, either by all ghetto Negroes or by an uneducated, Southern-born Negro underclass of habitual criminals or "riffraff." An agitator at a protest demonstration, the coverage of events by the news media, or an isolated "triggering" or "precipitating" incident, is often identified as the primary spark of violence. A uniform set of stages is sometimes posited, with a succession of confrontations and withdrawals by two cohesive groups, the police on one side and a riotous mob on the other. Often it is assumed that there was no effort within the Negro community to reduce the violence. Sometimes the only remedy prescribed is application of the largest possible police or control force, as early as possible.

What we have found does not validate these conceptions. We have been unable to identify constant patterns in all aspects of civil disorders. We have found that they are unusual, irregular, complex, and, in the present state of knowledge, unpredictable social processes. Like many human events, they do not unfold in orderly sequences. . . .

Based upon information derived from our surveys, we offer the following generalizations:

1. No civil disorder was "typical" in all respects. Viewed in a national framework, the disorders of 1967 varied greatly in terms of violence and damage: while a relatively small number were major under our criteria and a somewhat larger number were serious, most of the disorders would have received little or no national attention as "riots" had the Nation not been sensitized by the more serious outbreaks.

2. While the civil disorders of 1967 were racial in character, they were not *inter*racial. The 1967 disorders, as well as earlier disorders of the recent period, involved action within Negro neighborhoods against symbols of white American society — authority and property — rather than against white persons.

3. Despite extremist rhetoric, there was no attempt to subvert the social order of the United States. Instead, most of those who attacked white authority and property seemed to be demanding fuller participation

in the social order and the material benefits enjoyed by the vast majority of American citizens.

4. Disorder did not typically erupt without preexisting causes as a result of a single "triggering" or "precipitating" incident. Instead, it developed out of an increasingly disturbed social atmosphere, in which typically a series of tension-heightening incidents over a period of weeks or months became linked in the minds of many in the Negro community with a shared reservoir of underlying grievances.

5. There was, typically, a complex relationship between the series of incidents and the underlying grievances. For example, grievances about allegedly abusive police practices, unemployment and underemployment, housing, and other conditions in the ghetto, were often aggravated in the minds of many Negroes by incidents involving the police, or the inaction of municipal authorities on Negro complaints about police action, unemployment, inadequate housing, or other conditions. When grievance-related incidents recurred and rising tensions were not satisfactorily resolved, a cumulative process took place in which prior incidents were readily recalled and grievances reinforced. At some point in the mounting tension, a further incident — in itself often routine or even trivial — became the breaking point, and the tension spilled over into violence.

6. Many grievances in the Negro community result from the discrimination, prejudice, and powerlessness which Negroes often experience. They also result from the severely disadvantaged social and economic conditions of many Negroes as compared with those of whites in the same city and, more particularly, in the predominantly white suburbs.

7. Characteristically, the typical rioter was not a hoodlum, habitual criminal, or riffraff; nor was he a recent migrant, a member of an uneducated underclass, or a person lacking broad social and political concerns. Instead, he was a teenager or young adult, a lifelong resident of the city in which he rioted, a high school dropout — but somewhat better educated than his Negro neighbor — and almost invariably underemployed or employed in a menial job. He was proud of his race, extremely hostile to both whites and middle-class Negroes and, though informed about politics, highly distrustful of the political system and of political leaders.

8. Numerous Negro counterrioters walked the streets urging rioters to "cool it." The typical counterrioter resembled in many respects the majority of Negroes, who neither rioted nor took action against the rioters, that is, the noninvolved. But certain differences are crucial: the counterrioter was better educated and had higher income than either the rioter or the noninvolved.

9. Negotiations between Negroes and white officials occurred during virtually all the disorders surveyed. The negotiations often involved young, militant Negroes as well as older, established leaders. Despite a setting of chaos and disorder, negotiations in many cases involved discussion of underlying grievances as well as the handling of the disorder by control authorities.

10. The chain we have identified — discrimination, prejudice, disadvantaged conditions, intense and pervasive grievances, a series of tension-heightening incidents, all culminating in the eruption of disorder at the hands of youthful, politically-aware activists — must be understood as describing the central trend in the disorders, not as an explanation of all aspects of the riots or of all rioters. Some rioters, for example, may have shared neither the conditions nor the grievances of their Negro neighbors; some may have coolly and deliberately exploited the chaos created by others; some may have been drawn into the melee merely because they identified with, or wished to emulate, others. Nor do we intend to suggest that the majority of the rioters, who shared the adverse conditions and grievances, necessari-

ly articulated in their own minds the connection between that background and their actions.

11. The background of disorder in the riot cities was typically characterized by severely disadvantaged conditions for Negroes, especially as compared with those for whites; a local government often unresponsive to these conditions; Federal programs which had not yet reached a significantly large proportion of those in need; and the resulting reservoir of pervasive and deep grievance and frustration in the ghetto.

12. In the immediate aftermath of disorder, the status quo of daily life before the disorder generally was quickly restored. Yet, despite some notable public and private efforts, little basic change took place in the conditions underlying the disorder. In some cases, the result was increased distrust between blacks and whites, diminished interracial communication, and growth of Negro and white extremist groups.

I.

The Pattern of Violence and Damage

Levels of Violence and Damage

BECAUSE DEFINITIONS of civil disorder vary widely, between 51 and 217 disorders were recorded by various agencies as having occurred during the first 9 months of 1967. From these sources we have developed a list of 164 disorders which occurred during that period. We have ranked them in three categories of violence and damage, utilizing such criteria as the degree and duration of violence, the number of active participants, and the level of law enforcement response:

Major Disorders

Eight disorders, 5 percent of the total,

were major. These were characterized generally by a combination of the following factors: (1) many fires, intensive looting, and reports of sniping; (2) violence lasting more than 2 days; (3) sizable crowds; and (4) use of National Guard or Federal forces as well as other control forces.

Serious Disorders

Thirty-three disorders, 20 percent of the total, were serious but not major. These were characterized generally by: (1) isolated looting, some fires, and some rock throwing; (2) violence lasting between 1 and 2 days; (3) only one sizable crowd or many small groups; and (4) use of state police though generally not National Guard or Federal forces.

Minor Disorders

One hundred and twenty-three disorders, 75 percent of the total, were minor. These would not have been classified as "riots" or received wide press attention without national conditioning to a "riot" climate. They were characterized generally by: (1) a few fires or broken windows; (2) violence lasting generally less than 1 day; (3) participation by only small numbers of people; and (4) use, in most cases, only of local police or police from a neighboring community.

The 164 disorders which we have categorized occurred in 128 cities. Twenty-five (20 percent) of the cities had two or more disturbances. New York had five separate disorders, Chicago had four, six cities had three and 17 cities had two. Two cities which experienced a major disorder — Cincinnati and Tampa — had subsequent disorders; Cincinnati had two more. However, in these two cities the later disorders were less serious than the earlier ones. In only two cities were later disorders more severe.

Three conclusions emerge from the data:

The significance of the 1967 disorders

cannot be minimized. The level of disorder was major or serious, in terms of our criteria, on 41 occasions in 39 cities.

The level of disorder, however, has been exaggerated. Three-fourths of the disorders were relatively minor and would not have been regarded as nationally-newsworthy "riots" in prior years.

The fact that a city had experienced disorder earlier in 1967 did not immunize it from further violence. . . .

II.

The Riot Process

THE COMMISSION has found no "typical" disorder in 1967 in terms of intensity of violence and extensiveness of damage. To determine whether, as is sometimes suggested, there was a typical "riot process," we examined 24 disorders which occurred during 1967 in 20 cities and three university settings. We have concentrated on four aspects of that process:

The accumulating reservoir of grievances in the Negro community;

"Precipitating" incidents and their relationship to the reservoir of grievances;

The development of violence after its initial outbreak;

The control effort, including official force, negotiation, and persuasion.

We found a common social process operating in all 24 disorders in certain critical respects. These events developed similarly, over a period of time and out of an accumulation of grievances and increasing tension in the Negro community. Almost invariably, they exploded in ways related to the local community and its particular problems and conflicts. But once violence erupted, there began a complex interaction

of many elements — rioters, official control forces, counterrioters — in which the differences between various disorders were more pronounced than the similarities.

The Reservoir of Grievances in the Negro Community

OUR EXAMINATION of the background of the surveyed disorders revealed a typical pattern of deeply held grievances which were widely shared by many members of the Negro community. The specific content of the expressed grievances varied somewhat from city to city. But in general, grievances among Negroes in all the cities related to prejudice, discrimination, severely disadvantaged living conditions, and a general sense of frustration about their inability to change those conditions.

Specific events or incidents exemplified and reinforced the shared sense of grievance. News of such incidents spread quickly throughout the community and added to the reservoir. Grievances about police practices, unemployment and underemployment, housing, and other objective conditions in the ghetto were aggravated in the minds of many Negroes by the inaction of municipal authorities.

Out of this reservoir of grievance and frustration, the riot process began in the cities which we surveyed.

Precipitating Incidents

IN VIRTUALLY every case a single "triggering" or "precipitating" incident can be identified as having immediately preceded — within a few hours and in generally the same location — the outbreak of disorder. But this incident was usually a relatively minor, even trivial one, by itself substantially disproportionate to the scale of violence that followed. Often it was an incident of a type which had occurred frequently in the same community in the past without provoking violence.

We found that violence was generated by an increasingly disturbed social atmosphere, in which typically not one, but a series of incidents occurred over a period of weeks or months prior to the outbreak of disorder. Most cities had three or more such incidents; Houston had 10 over a 5-month period. These earlier or prior incidents were linked in the minds of many Negroes to the preexisting reservoir of underlying grievances. With each such incident, frustration and tension grew until at some point a final incident, often similar to the incidents preceding it, occurred and was followed almost immediately by violence.

As we see it, the prior incidents and the reservoir of underlying grievances contributed to a cumulative process of mounting tension that spilled over into violence when the final incident occurred. In this sense the entire chain — the grievances, the series of prior tension-heightening incidents, and the final incident — was the "precipitant" of disorder.

This chain describes the central trend in the disorders we surveyed and not necessarily all aspects of the riots or of all rioters. For example, incidents have not always increased tension; and tension has not always resulted in violence. We conclude only that both processes did occur in the disorders we examined.

Similarly, we do not suggest that all rioters shared the conditions or the grievances of their Negro neighbors: some may deliberately have exploited the chaos created out of the frustration of others; some may have been drawn into the melee merely because they identified with, or wished to emulate, others. Some who shared the adverse conditions and grievances did not riot.

We found that the majority of the rioters did share the adverse conditions and grievances, although they did not necessarily articulate in their own minds the connection between that background and their actions. . . .

The Development of Violence

ONCE THE SERIES of precipitating incidents culminated in violence, the riot process did not follow a uniform pattern in the 24 disorders surveyed. However, some similarities emerge.

The final incident before the outbreak of disorder, and the initial violence itself, generally occurred at a time and place in which it was normal for many people to be on the streets. In most of the 24 disorders, groups generally estimated at 50 or more persons were on the street at the time and place of the first outbreak.

In all 24 disturbances, including the three university-related disorders, the initial disturbance area consisted of streets with relatively high concentrations of pedestrian and automobile traffic at the time. In all but two cases — Detroit and Milwaukee — violence started between 7 p.m. and 12:30 a.m., when the largest numbers of pedestrians could be expected. Ten of the 24 disorders erupted on Friday night, Saturday, or Sunday.

In most instances, the temperature during the day on which violence first erupted was quite high. This contributed to the size of the crowds on the street, particularly in areas of congested housing.

Major violence occurred in all 24 disorders during the evening and night hours, between 6 p.m. and 6 a.m., and in most cases between 9 p.m. and 3 a.m. In only a few disorders, including Detroit and Newark, did substantial violence occur or continue during the daytime. Generally, the night-day cycles continued in daily succession through the early period of the disorder.

At the beginning of disorder, violence generally flared almost immediately after the final precipitating incident. It then escalated quickly to its peak level, in the case of 1-night disorders, and to the first night peak in the case of continuing disorders. In Detroit and Newark, the first outbreaks began within two hours and reached severe, although not the highest, levels within 3 hours.

In almost all of the subsequent night-day cycles, the change from relative order to a state of disorder by a number of people typically occurred extremely rapidly — within 1 or 2 hours at the most.

Nineteen of the surveyed disorders lasted more than 1 night. In 10 of these, violence peaked on the first night, and the level of activity on subsequent nights was the same or less. In the other nine disorders, however, the peak was reached on a subsequent night.

Disorder generally began with less serious violence against property, such as rock- and bottle-throwing and window-breaking. These were usually the materials and the targets closest to hand at the place of the initial outbreak.

Once store windows were broken, looting usually followed. Whether fires were set only after looting occurred is unclear. Reported instances of fire-bombing and Molotov cocktails in the 24 disorders appeared to occur as frequently during one cycle of violence as during another in disorders which continued through more than one cycle. However, fires seemed to break out more frequently during the middle cycles of riots lasting several days. Gunfire and sniping were also reported more frequently during the middle cycles. . . .

III.

The Riot Participant

The Profile of a Rioter

THE TYPICAL RIOTER in the summer of 1967 was a Negro, unmarried male between the ages of 15 and 24. He was in many ways very different from the stereotype. He was not a migrant. He was born in the state and was a lifelong resident of the city in which the riot took place. Economically his position was about the same as his Negro neighbors who did not actively participate in the riot.

Although he had not, usually, graduated from high school, he was somewhat better educated than the average inner-city Negro, having at least attended high school for a time.

Nevertheless, he was more likely to be working in a menial or low status job as an unskilled laborer. If he was employed, he was not working full time and his employment was frequently interrupted by periods of unemployment.

He feels strongly that he deserves a better job and that he is barred from achieving it, not because of lack of training, ability, or ambition, but because of discrimination by employers.

He rejects the white bigot's stereotype of the Negro as ignorant and shiftless. He takes great pride in his race and believes that in some respects Negroes are superior to whites. He is extremely hostile to whites, but his hostility is more apt to be a product of social and economic class than of race; he is almost equally hostile toward middle class Negroes.

He is substantially better informed about politics than Negroes who were not involved in the riots. He is more likely to be actively engaged in civil rights efforts, but is extremely distrustful of the political system and of political leaders.

The Profile of the Counterrioter

THE TYPICAL COUNTERRIOTER, who risked injury and arrest to walk the streets urging rioters to "cool it," was an active supporter of existing social institutions. He was, for example, far more likely than either the rioter or the noninvolved to feel that this country is worth defending in a major war.

His actions and his attitudes reflected his substantially greater stake in the social system; he was considerably better educated and more affluent than either the rioter or the noninvolved. He was somewhat more likely than the rioter, but less likely than the noninvolved, to have been a migrant. In all other respects he was identical to the noninvolved. . . .

THE BASIC CAUSES

THE RECORD before this Commission reveals that the causes of recent racial disorders are imbedded in a massive tangle of issues and circumstances — social, economic, political, and psychological — which arise out of the historical pattern of Negro-white relations in America.

These factors are both complex and interacting; they vary significantly in their effect from city to city and from year to year; and the consequences of one disorder, generating new grievances and new demands, become the causes of the next. It is this which creates the "thicket of tension, conflicting evidence, and extreme opinions" cited by the President.

Despite these complexities, certain fundamental matters are clear. Of these, the most fundamental is the racial attitude and behavior of white Americans toward black Americans. Race prejudice has shaped our history decisively in the past; it now threatens to do so again. White racism is essentially responsible for the explosive mixture which has been accumulating in our cities since the end of World War II. At the base of this mixture are three of the most bitter fruits of white racial attitudes:

Pervasive discrimination and segregation. The first is surely the continuing exclusion of great numbers of Negroes from the benefits of economic progress through discrimination in employment and education and their enforced confinement in segregated housing and schools. The corrosive and degrading effects of this condition and the at-

titudes that underlie it are the source of the deepest bitterness and lie at the center of the problem of racial disorder.

Black migration and white exodus. The second is the massive and growing concentration of impoverished Negroes in our major cities resulting from Negro migration from the rural South, rapid population growth, and the continuing movement of the white middle class to the suburbs. The consequence is a greatly increased burden on the already depleted resources of cities, creating a growing crisis of deteriorating facilities and services and unmet human needs.

Black ghettos. Third, in the teeming racial ghettos, segregation and poverty have intersected to destroy opportunity and hope and to enforce failure. The ghettos too often mean men and women without jobs, families without men, and schools where children are processed instead of educated, until they return to the street — to crime, to narcotics, to dependency on welfare, and to bitterness and resentment against society in general and white society in particular.

These three forces have converged on the inner city in recent years and on the people who inhabit it. At the same time, most whites and many Negroes outside the ghetto have prospered to a degree unparalleled in the history of civilization. Through television — the universal appliance in the ghetto — and the other media of mass communications, this affluence has been endlessly flaunted before the eyes of the Negro poor and the jobless ghetto youth.

As Americans, most Negro citizens carry within themselves two basic aspirations of our society. They seek to share in both the material resources of our system and its intangible benefits — dignity, respect, and acceptance. Outside the ghetto, many have succeeded in achieving a decent standard of life and in developing the inner resources which give life meaning and direction. Within the ghetto, however, it is rare that either aspiration is achieved.

Yet these facts alone — fundamental as

they are — cannot be said to have caused the disorders. Other and more immediate factors help explain why these events happened now.

Recently, three powerful ingredients have begun to catalyze the mixture.

Frustrated hopes. The expectations aroused by the great judicial and legislative victories of the civil rights movement have led to frustration, hostility, and cynicism in the face of the persistent gap between promise and fulfillment. The dramatic struggle for equal rights in the South has sensitized northern Negroes to the economic inequalities reflected in the deprivations of ghetto life.

Legitimation of violence. A climate that tends toward the approval and encouragement of violence as a form of protest has been created by white terrorism directed against nonviolent protest, including instances of abuse and even murder of some civil rights workers in the South, by the open defiance of law and Federal authority by state and local officials resisting desegregation, and by some protest groups engaging in civil disobedience who turn their backs on nonviolence, go beyond the constitutionally-protected rights of petition and free assembly and resort to violence to attempt to compel alteration of laws and policies with which they disagree. This condition has been reinforced by a general erosion of respect for authority in American society and the reduced effectiveness of social standards and community restraints on violence and crime. This in turn has largely resulted from rapid urbanization and the dramatic reduction in the average age of the total population.

Powerlessness. Finally, many Negroes have come to believe that they are being exploited politically and economically by the white "power structure." Negroes, like people in poverty everywhere, in fact lack the channels of communication, influence, and appeal that traditionally have been available to ethnic minorities within the city and which

enabled them — unburdened by color — to scale the walls of the white ghettos in an earlier era. The frustrations of powerlessness have led some to the conviction that there is no effective alternative to violence as a means of expression and redress, as a way of "moving the system." More generally, the result is alienation and hostility toward the institutions of law and government and the white society which controls them. This is reflected in the reach toward racial consciousness and solidarity reflected in the slogan "Black Power."

These facts have combined to inspire a new mood among Negroes, particularly among the young. Self-esteem and enhanced racial pride are replacing apathy and submission to "the system." Moreover, Negro youth, who make up over half of the ghetto population, share the growing sense of alienation felt by many white youth in our country. Thus, their role in recent civil disorders reflects not only a shared sense of deprivation and victimization by white society but also the rising incidence of disruptive conduct by a segment of American youth throughout the society.

Incitement and encouragement of violence. These conditions have created a volatile mixture of attitudes and beliefs which needs only a spark to ignite mass violence. Strident appeals to violence, first heard from white racists, were echoed and reinforced last summer in the inflammatory rhetoric of black racists and militants. Throughout the year, extremists crisscrossed the country preaching a doctrine of violence. Their rhetoric was widely reported in the mass media; it was echoed by local "militants" and organizations; it became the ugly background noise of the violent summer.

We cannot measure with any precision the influence of these organizations and individuals in the ghetto, but we think it clear that the intolerable and unconscionable encouragement of violence heightened tensions, created a mood of acceptance and an expectation of violence and thus contributed to the eruption of the disorders last summer.

The police. It is the convergence of all these factors that makes the role of the police so difficult and so significant. Almost invariably the incident that ignites disorder arises from police action. Harlem, Watts, Newark, and Detroit — all the major outbursts of recent years — were precipitated by arrests of Negroes by white police for minor offenses.

But the police are not merely the spark. In discharge of their obligation to maintain order and insure public safety in the disruptive conditions of ghetto life, they are inevitably involved in sharper and more frequent conflicts with ghetto residents than with the residents of other areas. Thus, to many Negroes, police have come to symbolize white power, white racism, and white repression. And the fact is that many police do reflect and express these white attitudes. The atmosphere of hostility and cynicism is reinforced by a widespread perception among Negroes of the existence of police brutality and corruption and of a "double standard" of justice and protection — one for Negroes and one for whites. . . .

THE COMMUNITY RESPONSE

The racial disorders of last summer in part reflect the failure of all levels of government — Federal and state as well as local — to come to grips with the problems of our cities. The ghetto symbolizes the dilemma: a widening gap between human needs and public resources and a growing cynicism regarding the commitment of community institutions and leadership to meet these needs.

The problem has many dimensions — financial, political, and institutional. Almost all cities — and particularly the central cities of the largest metropolitan regions — are simply unable to meet the growing need for public services and facilities with traditional sources of municipal revenue. Many cities are structured politically so that great numbers of citizens — particularly minority groups — have little or no representation in the processes of government. Finally, some cities lack either the will or the capacity to use effectively the resources that are available to them.

Instrumentalities of Federal and state government often compound the problems. National policy expressed through a very large number of grant programs and institutions rarely exhibits a coherent and consistent perspective when viewed at the local level. State efforts, traditionally focused on rural areas, often fail to tie in effectively with either local or Federal programs in urban areas.

Meanwhile, the decay of the central city continues — its revenue base eroded by the retreat of industry and white middle-class families to the suburbs, its budget and tax rate inflated by rising costs and increasing numbers of dependent citizens and its public plant — schools, hospitals, and correctional institutions deteriorated by age and long-deferred maintenance.

Yet to most citizens, the decay remains largely invisible. Only their tax bills and the headlines about crime or "riots" suggest that something may be seriously wrong in the city. . . .

THE FUTURE OF THE CITIES
Choices for the Future

The complexity of American society offers many choices for the future of relations between central cities and suburbs and patterns of white and Negro settlement in metropolitan areas. For practical purposes, however, we see two fundamental questions:

Should future Negro population growth be concentrated in central cities, as in the past 20 years, thereby forcing Negro and white populations to become even more residentially segregated?

Should society provide greatly increased special assistance to Negroes and other relatively disadvantaged population groups?

For purposes of analysis, the Commission has defined three basic choices for the future embodying specific answers to these questions:

The Present Policies Choice

Under this course, the Nation would maintain approximately the share of resources now being allocated to programs of assistance for the poor, unemployed, and disadvantaged. These programs are likely to grow, given continuing economic growth and rising Federal revenues, but they will not grow fast enough to stop, let alone reverse, the already deteriorating quality of life in central-city ghettos.

This choice carries the highest ultimate price, as we will point out.

The Enrichment Choice

Under this course, the Nation would seek to offset the effects of continued Negro segregation and deprivation in large city ghettos. The enrichment choice would aim at creating dramatic improvements in the quality of life in disadvantaged central-city neighborhoods — both white and Negro. It would require marked increases in Federal spending for education, housing, employment, job training, and social services.

The enrichment choice would seek to lift poor Negroes and whites above poverty status and thereby give them the capacity to enter the mainstream of American life. But it would not, at least for many years, appreciably affect either the increasing concentration of Negroes in the ghetto or racial segregation in residential areas outside the ghetto.

The Integration Choice

This choice would be aimed at reversing the movement of the country toward two societies, separate and unequal.

The integration choice — like the enrich-

ment choice — would call for large-scale improvement in the quality of ghetto life. But it would also involve both creating strong incentives for Negro movement out of central-city ghettos and enlarging freedom of choice concerning housing, employment, and schools.

The result would fall considerably short of full integration. The experience of other ethnic groups indicates that some Negro households would be scattered in largely white residential areas. Others — probably a larger number — would voluntarily cluster together in largely Negro neighborhoods. The integration choice would thus produce both integration and segregation. But the segregation would be voluntary.

Articulating these three choices plainly oversimplifies the possibilities open to the country. We believe, however, that they encompass the basic issues — issues which the American public must face if it is serious in its concern not only about civil disorder, but the future of our democratic society. . . .

Conclusions

The future of our cities is neither something which will just happen nor something which will be imposed upon us by an inevitable destiny. That future will be shaped to an important degree by choices we make now.

We have attempted to set forth the major choices because we believe it is vital for Americans to understand the consequences of our present drift.

Three critical conclusions emerge from this analysis:

1. The nation is rapidly moving toward two increasingly separate Americas.

Within two decades, this division could be so deep that it would be almost impossible to unite:

a white society principally located in suburbs, in smaller central cities, and in the peripheral parts of large central cities; and a Negro society largely concentrated within large central cities.

The Negro society will be permanently relegated to its current status, possibly even if we expend great amounts of money and effort in trying to "gild" the ghetto.

2. In the long run, continuation and expansion of such a permanent division threatens us with two perils.

The first is the danger of sustained violence in our cities. The timing, scale, nature, and repercussions of such violence cannot be foreseen. But if it occurred, it would further destroy our ability to achieve the basic American promises of liberty, justice, and equality.

The second is the danger of a conclusive repudiation of the traditional American ideals of individual dignity, freedom, and equality of opportunity. We will not be able to espouse these ideals meaningfully to the rest of the world, to ourselves, to our children. They may still recite the Pledge of Allegiance and say "one nation . . . indivisible." But they will be learning cynicism, not patriotism.

3. We cannot escape responsibility for choosing the future of our metropolitan areas and the human relations which develop within them. It is a responsibility so critical that even an unconscious choice to continue present policies has the gravest implications.

That we have delayed in choosing or, by delaying, may be making the wrong choice, does not sentence us either to separatism or despair. But we must choose. We will choose. Indeed, we are now choosing. . . .

RECOMMENDATIONS FOR NATIONAL ACTION

THE DISORDERS are not simply a problem of the racial ghetto or the city. As we have seen, they are symptoms of social ills that have become endemic in our society and now affect every American — black or white, businessman or factory worker, suburban commuter or slum-dweller.

None of us can escape the consequences of the continuing economic and social decay of the central city and the closely related problem of rural poverty. The convergence of these conditions in the racial ghetto and the resulting discontent and disruption threaten democratic values fundamental to our progress as a free society.

The essential fact is that neither existing conditions nor the garrison state offers acceptable alternatives for the future of this country. Only a greatly enlarged commitment to national action — compassionate, massive, and sustained, backed by the will and resources of the most powerful and the richest nation on this earth — can shape a future that is compatible with the historic ideals of American society. . . .

Objectives for National Action

Just as Lincoln, a century ago, put preservation of the Union above all else, so should we put creation of a true union — a single society and a single American identity — as our major goal. Toward that goal, we propose the following objectives for national action:

Opening up all opportunities to those who are restricted by racial segregation and discrimination, and eliminating all barriers to their choice of jobs, education, and housing.

Removing the frustration of powerlessness among the disadvantaged by providing the means to deal with the problems that affect their own lives and by increasing the capacity of our public and private institutions to respond to those problems.

Increasing communication across racial lines to destroy stereotypes, halt polarization, end distrust and hostility and create common ground for efforts toward common goals of public order and social justice.

There are those who oppose these aims as "rewarding the rioters." They are wrong. A great nation is not so easily intimidated. We propose these aims to fulfill our pledge of equality and to meet the fundamental needs of a democratic and civilized society — domestic peace, social justice, and urban centers that are citadels of the human spirit.

There are others who say that violence is necessary — that fear alone can prod the Nation to act decisively on behalf of racial minorities. They too are wrong. Violence and disorder compound injustice; they must be ended and they will be ended.

Our strategy is neither blind repression nor capitulation to lawlessness. Rather it is the affirmation of common possibilities, for all, within a single society.

110.

MARTIN LUTHER KING, JR.: Showdown for Nonviolence

Early in 1968 Memphis garbage collectors struck against the city government, charging prejudicial treatment of Negroes in municipal hiring practices. Memphis' newly elected mayor was adamant, and the strike dragged on. The Reverend Martin Luther King, Jr., the foremost American apostle of nonviolence, the leading Negro moderate, and a Nobel Peace Prize winner, went to Memphis to lead a protest in behalf of the strikers. There, on Thursday, April 4, he was shot and killed while standing on a motel balcony. The irony of his death, as well as genuine grief at the passing of a greatly distinguished man, convulsed the country for a week. Riots in a number of Northern cities occurred, his funeral monopolized the air waves, and Congress passed a watered down version of an open housing bill that it had been long considering. The eulogists at the funeral said he had not died in vain. But Mike Royko, Chicago columnist, wrote that King had been "executed by a firing squad that numbered in the millions" — the white racists who, he charged, had hated King from the beginning and were unmoved by his death. "We have pointed a gun at our own head," he concluded, "and we are squeezing the trigger. And nobody we elect is going to help us. It is our head and our finger." Reprinted here is an article by King that appeared shortly before he died.

Source: *Look*, April 16, 1968.

THE POLICY of the federal government is to play Russian roulette with riots; it is prepared to gamble with another summer of disaster. Despite two consecutive summers of violence, not a single basic cause of riots has been corrected. All of the misery that stoked the flames of rage and rebellion remains undiminished. With unemployment, intolerable housing, and discriminatory education a scourge in Negro ghettos, Congress and the administration still tinker with trivial, halfhearted measures.

Yet only a few years ago, there was discernible, if limited, progress through nonviolence. Each year, a wholesome, vibrant Negro self-confidence was taking shape.

The fact is inescapable that the tactic of nonviolence, which had then dominated the thinking of the civil rights movement, has in the last two years not been playing its transforming role. Nonviolence was a creative doctrine in the South because it checkmated the rabid segregationists who were thirsting for an opportunity to physically crush Negroes. Nonviolent direct action enabled the Negro to take to the streets in active protest, but it muzzled the guns of the oppressor because even he could not shoot down in daylight unarmed men, women, and children. This is the reason there was less loss of life in ten years of Southern protest than in ten days of Northern riots.

Today, the Northern cities have taken on the conditions we faced in the South. Police, National Guard, and other armed bodies are feverishly preparing for repression. They can be curbed, not by unorganized resort to force by desperate Negroes but only by a massive wave of militant nonviolence. Nonviolence was never more relevant as an effective tactic than today for the North. It also may be the instrument of our national salvation.

I agree with the President's National Advisory Commission on Civil Disorders that our nation is splitting into two hostile societies and that the chief destructive cutting edge is white racism. We need, above all, effective means to force Congress to act resolutely — but means that do not involve the use of violence. For us in the Southern Christian Leadership Conference, violence is not only morally repugnant, it is pragmatically barren. We feel there is an alternative both to violence and to useless timid supplications for justice. We cannot condone either riots or the equivalent evil of passivity. And we know that nonviolent militant action in Selma and Birmingham awakened the conscience of white America and brought a moribund, insensitive Congress to life.

The time has come for a return to mass nonviolent protest. Accordingly, we are planning a series of such demonstrations this spring and summer, to begin in Washington, D.C. They will have Negro and white participation, and they will seek to benefit the poor of both races.

We will call on the government to adopt the measures recommended by its own commission. To avoid, in the Commission's words, the tragedy of "continued polarization of the American community and ultimately the destruction of basic democratic values," we must have "national action — compassionate, massive, and sustained, backed by the resources of the most powerful and the richest nation on earth."

The demonstrations we have planned are of deep concern to me, and I want to spell out at length what we will do, try to do, and believe in. My staff and I have worked three months on the planning. We believe that if this campaign succeeds, nonviolence will once again be the dominant instrument for social change — and jobs and income will be put in the hands of the tormented poor. If it fails, nonviolence will be discredited and the country may be plunged into holocaust — a tragedy deepened by the awareness that it was avoidable.

We are taking action after sober reflection. We have learned from bitter experience that our government does not correct a race problem until it is confronted directly and dramatically. We also know, as official Washington may not, that the flash point of Negro rage is close at hand.

Our Washington demonstration will resemble Birmingham and Selma in duration. It will be more than a one-day protest — it can persist for two or three months. In the earlier Alabama actions, we set no time limits. We simply said we were going to struggle there until we got a response from the nation on the issues involved. We are saying the same thing about Washington. This will be an attempt to bring a kind of Sel-

ma-like movement, Birmingham-like movement, into being, substantially around the
economic issues. Just as we dealt with the
social problem of segregation through massive demonstrations and we dealt with the
political problem — the denial of the right
to vote — through massive demonstrations,
we are now trying to deal with the economic problems — the right to live, to
have a job and income — through massive
protest. It will be a Selma-like movement
on economic issues.

We remember that when we began direct
action in Birmingham and Selma, there was
a thunderous chorus that sought to discourage us. Yet, today, our achievements in
these cities and the reforms that radiated
from them are hailed with pride by all.

We've selected fifteen areas — ten cities
and five rural districts — from which we
have recruited our initial cadre. We will
have 200 poor people from each area. That
would be about 3,000 to get the protests
going and set the pattern. They are important, particularly in terms of maintaining
nonviolence. They are being trained in this
discipline now.

In areas where we are recruiting, we are
also stimulating activities in conjunction
with the Washington protest. We are planning to have some of these people march to
Washington. We may have half the group
from Mississippi, for example, go to Washington and begin the protest there, while
the other half begins walking. They would
flow across the South, joining the Alabama
group, the Georgia group, right on up
through South and North Carolina and
Virginia. We hope that the sound and sight
of a growing mass of poor people walking
slowly toward Washington will have a positive, dramatic effect on Congress.

Once demonstrations start, we feel, there
will be spontaneous supporting activity taking place across the country. This has usually happened in campaigns like this, and I
think it will again. I think people will start

moving. The reasons we didn't choose California and other areas out West are distance
and the problem of transporting marchers
that far. But part of our strategy is to have
spontaneous demonstrations take place on
the West Coast.

A nationwide nonviolent movement is
very important. We know from past experience that Congress and the President won't
do anything until you develop a movement
around which people of goodwill can find a
way to put pressure on them, because it really means breaking that coalition in Congress. It's still a coalition-dominated, rural-
dominated, basically Southern Congress.
There are Southerners there with committee chairmanships, and they are going to
stand in the way of progress as long as they
can. They get enough right-wing Midwest-
ern or Northern Republicans to go along
with them.

This really means making the movement
powerful enough, dramatic enough, morally
appealing enough, so that people of goodwill, the churches, labor, liberals, intellectuals, students, poor people themselves begin
to put pressure on congressmen to the point
that they can no longer elude our demands.

Our idea is to dramatize the whole economic problem of the poor. We feel there's
a great deal that we need to do to appeal to
Congress itself. The early demonstrations
will be more geared toward educational
purposes — to educate the nation on the
nature of the problem and the crucial aspects of it, the tragic conditions that we
confront in the ghettos.

After that, if we haven't gotten a response from Congress, we will branch out.
And we are honest enough to feel that we
aren't going to get any instantaneous results
from Congress, knowing its recalcitrant nature on this issue, and knowing that so
many resources and energies are being used
in Vietnam rather than on the domestic situation. So we don't have any illusions
about moving Congress in two or three

weeks. But we do feel that, by starting in Washington, centering on Congress and departments of the government, we will be able to do a real educational job.

We call our demonstration a campaign for jobs and income because we feel that the economic question is the most crucial that black people, and poor people generally, are confronting. There is a literal depression in the Negro community. When you have mass unemployment in the Negro community, it's called a social problem; when you have mass unemployment in the white community, it's called a depression. The fact is, there is a major depression in the Negro community. The unemployment rate is extremely high, and among Negro youth, it goes up as high as 40 percent in some cities.

We need an Economic Bill of Rights. This would guarantee a job to all people who want to work and are able to work. It would also guarantee an income for all who are not able to work. Some people are too young, some are too old, some are physically disabled, and yet, in order to live, they need income. It would mean creating certain public-service jobs, but that could be done in a few weeks. A program that would really deal with jobs could minimize — I don't say stop — the number of riots that could take place this summer.

Our whole campaign, therefore, will center on the job question, with other demands, like housing, that are closely tied to it. We feel that much more building of housing for low-income people should be done. On the educational front, the ghetto schools are in bad shape in terms of quality, and we feel that a program should be developed to spend at least a thousand dollars per pupil. Often, they are so far behind that they need more and special attention, the best quality education that can be given.

These problems, of course, are overshadowed by the Vietnam war. We'll focus on the domestic problems, but it's inevitable that we've got to bring out the question of the tragic mix-up in priorities. We are spending all of this money for death and destruction and not nearly enough money for life and constructive development. It's inevitable that the question of the war will come up in this campaign. We hear all this talk about our ability to afford guns and butter, but we have come to see that this is a myth, that when a nation becomes involved in this kind of war, when the guns of war become a national obsession, social needs inevitably suffer. And we hope that as a result of our trying to dramatize this and getting thousands and thousands of people moving around this issue, that our government will be forced to reevaluate its policy abroad in order to deal with the domestic situation.

The American people are more sensitive than Congress. A Louis Harris poll has revealed that 56 percent of the people feel that some kind of program should come into being to provide jobs to all who want to work. We had the WPA when the nation was on the verge of bankruptcy; we should be able to do something when we're sick with wealth. That poll also showed that 57 percent of the people felt the slums should be eradicated and the communities rebuilt by those who live in them, which would be a massive job program.

We need to put pressure on Congress to get things done. We will do this with First Amendment activity. If Congress is unresponsive, we'll have to escalate in order to keep the issue alive and before it. This action may take on disruptive dimensions, but not violent in the sense of destroying life or property: it will be militant nonviolence.

We really feel that riots tend to intensify the fears of the white majority while relieving its guilt, and so open the door to greater repression. We've seen no changes in Watts, no structural changes have taken place as the result of riots. We are trying to find an alternative that will force people to confront issues without destroying life or property. We plan to build a shantytown in Washington, patterned after the bonus marches of the Thirties, to dramatize how many people have to live in slums in our nation. But essentially, this will be just like our other nonviolent demonstrations. We are not going to tolerate violence. And we are making it very clear that the demonstrators who are not prepared to be nonviolent should not participate in this. For the past six weeks, we've had workshops on nonviolence with the people who will be going to Washington. They will continue through the spring. These people will form a core of the demonstration and will later be the marshals in the protests. They will be participating themselves in the early stages, but after two or three weeks, when we will begin to call larger numbers in, they will be the marshals, the ones who will control and discipline all of the demonstrations.

We plan to have a march for those who can spend only a day or two in Washington, and that will be toward the culminating point of the campaign. I hope this will be a time when white people will rejoin the ranks of the movement.

Demonstrations have served as unifying forces in the movement; they have brought blacks and whites together in very practical situations, where philosophically they may have been arguing about Black Power. It's a strange thing how demonstrations tend to solve problems. The other thing is that it's little known that crime rates go down in almost every community where you have demonstrations. In Montgomery, Ala., when we had a bus boycott, the crime rate in the Negro community went down 65 percent for a whole year. Anytime we've had demonstrations in a community, people have found a way to slough off their self-hatred, and they have had a channel to express their longings and a way to fight nonviolently — to get at the power structure, to know you're doing something, so you don't have to be violent to do it.

We need this movement. We need it to bring about a new kind of togetherness between blacks and whites. We need it to bring allies together and to bring the coalition of conscience together.

A good number of white people have given up on integration too. There are a lot of "White Power" advocates, and I find that people do tend to despair and engage in debates when nothing is going on. But when action is taking place, when there are demonstrations, they have a quality about them that leads to a unity you don't achieve at other times.

I think we have come to the point where there is no longer a choice now between nonviolence and riots. It must be militant, massive nonviolence, or riots. The discontent is so deep, the anger so ingrained, the despair, the restlessness so wide, that something has to be brought into being to serve as a channel through which these deep emotional feelings, these deep angry feelings, can be funneled. There has to be an outlet, and I see this campaign as a way to transmute the inchoate rage of the ghetto into a constructive and creative channel. It becomes an outlet for anger.

Even if I didn't deal with the moral dimensions and questions of violence versus nonviolence, from a practical point of view, I don't see riots working. But I am convinced that if rioting continues, it will strengthen the right wing of the country, and we'll end up with a kind of right-wing take-over in the cities and a Fascist development, which will be terribly injurious to the whole nation. I don't think America can stand another summer of Detroit-like riots without a development that could destroy the soul of the nation, and even the democratic possibilities of the nation.

I'm committed to nonviolence absolutely. I'm just not going to kill anybody, whether it's in Vietnam or here. I'm not going to burn down any building. If nonviolent protest fails this summer, I will continue to preach it and teach it, and we at the Southern Christian Leadership Conference will still do this. I plan to stand by nonviolence because I have found it to be a philosophy of life that regulates not only my dealings in the struggle for racial justice but also my dealings with people, with my own self. I will still be faithful to nonviolence.

But I'm frank enough to admit that if our nonviolent campaign doesn't generate some progress, people are just going to engage in more violent activity, and the discussion of guerrilla warfare will be more extensive.

In any event, we will not have been the ones who will have failed. We will place the problems of the poor at the seat of government of the wealthiest nation in the history of mankind. If that power refuses to acknowledge its debt to the poor, it will have failed to live up to its promise to insure "life, liberty, and the pursuit of happiness" to its citizens.

If this society fails, I fear that we will learn very shortly that racism is a sickness unto death.

We welcome help from all civil rights organizations. There must be a diversified approach to the problem, and I think both the NAACP and the Urban League play a significant role. I also feel that CORE and SNCC have played very significant roles. I think SNCC's recent conclusions are unfortunate. We have not given up on integration. We still believe in black and white together. Some of the Black Power groups have temporarily given up on integration. We have not. So maybe we are the bridge, in the middle, reaching across and connecting both sides.

The fact is, we have not had any insurrection in the United States because an insurrection is planned, organized, violent rebellion. What we have had is a kind of spontaneous explosion of anger. The fact is, people who riot don't want to riot. A study was made recently by some professors at Wayne State University. They interviewed several hundred people who participated in the riot last summer in Detroit, and a majority of these people said they felt that my approach to the problem — nonviolence — was the best and most effective.

I don't believe there has been a massive turn to violence. Even the riots have had an element of nonviolence to persons. But for a rare exception, they haven't killed any white people, and Negroes could, if they wished, kill by the hundreds. That would be insurrection. But the amazing thing is that the Negro has vented his anger on property, not persons, even in the emotional turbulence of riots.

But I'm convinced that if something isn't done to deal with the very harsh and real economic problems of the ghetto, the talk of guerrilla warfare is going to become much more real. The nation has not yet recognized the seriousness of it. Congress hasn't been willing to do anything about it, and this is what we're trying to face this spring. As committed as I am to nonviolence, I have to face this fact: if we do not get a positive response in Washington, many more Negroes will begin to think and act in violent terms.

I hope, instead, that what comes out of these nonviolent demonstrations will be an Economic Bill of Rights for the Disadvantaged, requiring about ten or twelve billion dollars. I hope that a specific number of jobs is set forth, that a program will emerge to abolish unemployment, and that there will be another program to supplement the income of those whose earnings are below the poverty level. These would be measures of success in our campaign.

It may well be that all we'll get out of Washington is to keep Congress from getting worse. The problem is to stop it from moving backward. We started out with a poverty bill at $2.4 billion, and now it's back to $1.8 billion. We have a welfare program that's dehumanizing, and then Congress adds a Social Security amendment that will bar literally thousands of children from any welfare. Model cities started out; it's been cut back. Rent subsidy, an excellent program for the poor, cut down to nothing. It may be that because of these demonstrations, we will at least be able to hold on to some of the things we have.

There is an Old Testament prophecy of the "sins of the fathers being visited upon the third and fourth generations." Nothing could be more applicable to our situation. America is reaping the harvest of hate and shame planted through generations of educational denial, political disfranchisement, and economic exploitation of its black population. Now, almost a century removed from slavery, we find the heritage of oppression and racism erupting in our cities, with volcanic lava of bitterness and frustration pouring down our avenues.

Black Americans have been patient people, and perhaps they could continue patient with but a modicum of hope; but everywhere, "time is winding up," in the words of one of our spirituals, "corruption in the land, people take your stand; time is winding up." In spite of years of national progress, the plight of the poor is worsening. Jobs are on the decline as a result of technological change, schools North and South are proving themselves more and more inadequate to the task of providing adequate education and thereby entrance into the mainstream of the society. Medical care is virtually out of reach of millions of black and white poor. They are aware of the great advances of medical science — heart transplants, miracle drugs — but their children still die of preventable diseases and even suffer brain damage due to protein deficiency.

In Mississippi, children are actually starving, while large landowners have placed their land in the soil bank and receive millions of dollars annually not to plant food and cotton. No provision is made for the life and survival of the hundreds of thousands of sharecroppers who now have no work and no food. Driven off the land, they are forced into tent cities and ghettos of the North, for our Congress is determined not to stifle the initiative of the poor (though they clamor for jobs) through welfare handouts. Handouts to the rich are given more sophisticated nomenclature such as parity, subsidies, and incentives to industry.

White America has allowed itself to be indifferent to race prejudice and economic denial. It has treated them as superficial blemishes, but now awakes to the horrifying reality of a potentially fatal disease. The urban outbreaks are "a fire bell in the night," clamorously warning that the seams of our entire social order are weakening under strains of neglect.

The American people are infected with racism — that is the peril. Paradoxically, they are also infected with democratic ideals — that is the hope. While doing wrong, they have the potential to do right. But they do not have a millennium to make changes. Nor have they a choice of continuing in the old way. The future they are asked to inaugurate is not so unpalatable that it justifies the evils that beset the nation. To end poverty, to extirpate prejudice, to free a tormented conscience, to make a tomorrow of justice, fair play, and creativity — all these are worthy of the American ideal.

We have, through massive nonviolent action, an opportunity to avoid a national disaster and create a new spirit of class and racial harmony. We can write another luminous moral chapter in American history. All of us are on trial in this troubled hour, but time still permits us to meet the future with a clear conscience.

111.

Erwin N. Griswold: Dissent, Protest, and Disobedience

Erwin N. Griswold, U.S. solicitor general, delivered the address from which the following selection is taken at the Tulane University School of Law on April 16, 1968. During the previous ten days the nation had been convulsed by the civil disorders following the murder of Martin Luther King, Jr., and shortly afterward a wave of violent student revolts, notably at Columbia University, convulsed it once again.

Source: The George Abel Dreyfous Lecture on Civil Liberties, 1968.

WE MUST DRAW two fundamental distinctions when we speak of dissent; the first involves primarily legal and moral variables and divides permissible from unpermissible dissent; the second presupposes that the dissent is tolerable but involves the social and political considerations of whether, or when or how, the protest *should* be made. The latter is not a question of right but of judgment and morals, even of taste, and a proper sense of restraint and responsibility, qualities which are or should be inherent in the very concept of civil liberties.

We must begin any analysis of these questions with the undoubted fact that we live in a society, an imperfect and struggling one no doubt, but one where government and order are not only a necessity but are the preference of an overwhelming majority of the citizenry. The rules that society has developed to organize and order itself are found in a body of law which has not been imposed from outside, but has been slowly built up from experience expressed through the consent of the governed and now pervades all aspects of human activity. Inevitably there are occasions when individuals or groups will chafe under a particular legal bond, or will bridle in opposition to a particular governmental policy, and the question presents itself, what can be done?

Vocal objection, of course — even slanderous or inane — is permissible. But the fact that one is a dissenter with a right to express his opposition entitles him to no special license. Thus, in expressing views that are themselves wholly immune to official strictures, he gains no roving commission to ignore the rules and underlying assumption of society that relate in a neutral way to activity rather than to the maintenance or expression of ideas. Thus, I submit that one cannot rightly engage in conduct which is otherwise unlawful merely because he intends that either that conduct or the idea he wishes to express in the course of the conduct is intended to manifest his dissent from some governmental policy. I cannot distinguish in principle the legal quality of the determination to halt a troop train to protest the Vietnam war or to block workmen from entering a segregated job site to protest employment discrimination, from the determination to fire shots into a civil rights leader's home to protest integration. The right to disagree — and to manifest disagreement — which the Constitution allows to the individuals in those situations

— does not authorize them to carry on their campaign of education and persuasion at the expense of someone else's liberty, or in violation of some laws whose independent validity is unquestionable.

This distinction runs deep in our history, but has too frequently been ignored in this decade. But the line is a clear one, and we should reestablish it in the thinking and understanding of our people. While I share Professor Harry Kalven's assessment that the "generosity and empathy with which [public streets and parks] are made available [as a "public forum"] is an index of freedom, I regard as unassailable the limitation that the mere fact that a person wishes to make a public point does not sanction any method he chooses to use to make it. Yet there seems to be currently a considerable tendency to ignore, if not to reject, this limitation. Certainly many of the modern forms of dissent, including those I have just mentioned, proceed on the basis of the contrary proposition. Only last term the Supreme Court was asked to sustain the right of demonstrators active in a cause that most of us here and the Court itself no doubt regarded as laudable, to lodge their demand for an end to segregation on the grounds of a city jail where, it seemed, biased treatment was being accorded prisoners. The argument was made that a demonstration at that site was "particularly appropriate," irrespective of the consequences. Speaking for the Court, Justice Black rejected this rationale, explaining that

> such an argument has as its major unarticulated premise the assumption that people who want to propagandize protests or views have a constitutional right to do so whenever and however and wherever they please.

That notion the Court expressly "vigorously and forthrightly rejected."

Another form of protest that can never, in my view, be excused or tolerated is that which assumes the posture of a violent and forcible assault on public order, whatever the motivation. The interests at stake in such a situation must transcend the validity of the particular cause and the permissibility of adhering to it. Violent opposition to law — any law — or forcible disregard of another's freedom to disagree falls beyond the pale of legitimate dissent or even of civil disobedience, properly understood; it is nothing short of rebellion. The utter indefensibility of violent opposition to law is that it proceeds on the foolhardy and immoral principle that might makes right. . . .

These reflections have dealt with the question when law and government may tolerate dissent, or dissent manifested in certain ways, and I have suggested that it is illicit to violate otherwise valid laws either as a symbol of protest or in the course of protest, and secondly that I regard it as indefensible to attempt to promote a viewpoint either by flagrant violence or by organized coercion. Now I will turn . . . to the second distinction. . . . That is, assuming a legal or moral right to protest, what considerations of prudence and responsibility should infuse the determination to exercise these rights.

First, you will note that I imply that a line may be drawn between legal and moral rights to dissent. I am not now referring to what I accept as the genuine possibility that one may exercise his constitutional right to dissent in a way that, because of recklessness or unfairness, makes his conduct ethically improper. I mention this distinction, however, because I believe awareness and evaluation of it should always be taken into account in considering an exercise of the right to dissent. But for the present, I mean to concentrate on the converse of this distinction, that there may be a moral right to dissent without a corresponding legal privilege to do so. It is in this context that "civil disobedience" must be viewed.

Earlier, I observed that our system contemplates that there may be a moral right to "civil disobedience" (properly understood) that exists notwithstanding a "legal" duty to obey. I also referred to the source of this moral right: the ultimate sanctity of a man's own conscience, as the intellectual and volitional composite that governs his conception of his relation to Eternal Truth. I wish now to emphasize the considerations which, in my view, condition the existence and exercise of this moral right, because I believe the current rhetoric — which sometimes seems to consecrate "civil disobedience" as the noblest response in the pantheon of virtues — has obscured the nature and consequence of this activity. To define my term — I mean by "civil disobedience" the deliberate violation of a rule ordained by constituted government because of a conscientious conviction that the law is so unjust that it cannot morally be observed by the individual.

The most important point to be stressed is that this decision is one that should be made only after the most painful and introspective reflection, and only when the firm conclusion is reached that obedience offends the most fundamental personal values. It is self-evident that routine or random noncompliance with the law for transient or superficial reasons would negate the first principles of civilized behavior. Unless society can safely assume that *almost* without exception individuals will accept the will of the majority even when to do so is grudging and distasteful, the foundation of secure liberty will rather rapidly erode. . . .

Henry David Thoreau is generally regarded as the most notable American exponent of civil disobedience, and all of us share admiration for his determination. But we must not ignore the vital aspect of Thoreau's nonconformity — his passionate attempt to dissociate himself from society. He was, as Harry Kalven has put it, "a man who does not see himself as belonging very intensely to the community in which he was raised," and who sought constantly but futilely to reject the society to which he had not voluntarily adhered.

Thoreau's poignant attitude was charming enough in mid-19th-century America. But it was, essentially, an effort to withdraw from the realities of life and it was, I suggest, myopic even then, for it was painfully inconsistent with the fact that man is a part of society by nature, by geography, and by citizenship. Unlike a member of a purely artificial group, like a bar association or country club, a citizen cannot resign from the "social compact" because he protests policies of the regime. Now in the last third of the 20th century, we must be even more cognizant that there is nothing noble or salutary about foredoomed attempts to abdicate membership in society. Complex problems demand rational attention that can come only from personal focus on solutions and never from stubbornly turning one's back on harsh and unpleasant realities.

This is precisely what nonconformity as a way of life is. It is the essential irrationality of the "hippie movement" — a mass endeavor to drop out of life. It is a protest of sorts, of course, but one that can bear no fruit because it takes issue with what is not only inevitable but, more importantly, indispensable — social regulation of individual behavior.

Stretched to its logical extreme, this also is civil disobedience, and for this reason I urge that before any man embarks upon a unilateral nullification of any law, he must appreciate that his judgment has not merely a personal significance but also portends grave consequences for his fellows.

In determining whether and when to exercise the moral right to disobey the dictates of the law, it must also be recognized that society not only does not but cannot recognize this determination as entitled to legal privilege. It is part of the Gandhian tradition of civil disobedience that the sincerity of the individual's conscience presupposes that the law will punish this assertion of personal principle. In the very formation of our country, in the *Federalist* papers, Hamilton explained the reason why government cannot compromise its authority by offering a dispensation for individual conscience:

> Government implies the power of making laws. It is essential to the idea of a law that it be attended with a sanction; or, in other words, a penalty or punishment for disobedience. If there be no penalty annexed to disobedience, the resolutions or commands which pretend to be laws will, in fact, amount to nothing more than advice or recommendation.

Thus, it is of the essence of law that it is equally applied to all, that it binds all alike, irrespective of personal motive. For this reason, one who contemplates civil disobedience out of moral conviction should not be surprised and must not be bitter if a criminal conviction ensues. And he must accept the fact that organized society cannot endure on any other basis. His hope is that he may aid in getting the law changed. But if he does not succeed in that, he cannot complain if the law is applied to him. . . .

We are all aware of the fact that for many long years the legal structure was often used to perpetuate deprivations which were at odds with the most basic constitutional and moral values. During this time, conditions of political, social, and economic inequality made ineffective meaningful attempts to change these regulations and policies by petition within the customary channels of reform. In this situation, the only realistic recourse was deliberate refusal to abide by the restrictions any longer. Lunch-counter sit-ins and freedom rides are among the most dramatic examples of the techniques that were used to expose the injustices that were perpetrated under the banner of law. In many of these cases, these actions were not, indeed, illegal, since the restrictive laws were plainly invalid if one had the time, energy, and money to take them up to higher courts. In other cases, though, the line was not clear, and sometimes the actions taken were undoubtedly illegal. We cannot fail to recognize the fact that it was these tactics which succeeded in putting the basic issues squarely before the courts and the public. And it was in this way that the law was clarified in the courts and that legislative changes were brought about.

There are great lessons to be learned from this experience. Perhaps the greatest of these is that what mattered was not merely the moral fervor of the demonstrators, or the justice of their cause, but also the way in which they conducted themselves. They and their leaders were aware of the moral dimensions of their cause, and they knew that this required an equal adherence to morality in the means by which they sought to vindicate their cause. Because of this, rigid adherence to the philosophy of nonviolence was sought and widely achieved. In retrospect, I am sure that our nation will point with pride, not only to the courage of those who risked punishment in order to challenge injustice, but also to the morality of their actions in scrupulously avoiding violence, even in reaction to the force which was exerted on them. The affirmation of the close relation between morality and nonviolence will be one of the many monuments of the Rev. Martin Luther King, Jr.

As this experience shows, the ultimate legal success as well as the intrinsic moral quality of civil disobedience turns on the restraint with which it is exercised. This is an extremely hard line to draw, but it is one which must be earnestly sought out. Unfortunately, some of those who claim this mantle today do not appreciate the moral quality of thought and action which made their predecessors worthy to wear it.

112.

Student Revolt

*The job of a college president during the early part of 1968 was about as thankless
as a job can be. Pressures on him from students and younger faculty members, on
the one hand, and from trustees and alumni, on the other hand, grew more intense
as the academic year drew to a close. "Basically," Time magazine put it, "today's
undergraduate rebels hope to be taken seriously as a responsible voice in shaping
their university — which means influencing basic policy decisions, securing better
teachers, helping create a more meaningful curriculum, and insisting on autonomy
in their personal lives." And, it added, "none of these requests are at all absurd."
However, the methods used at many institutions to attain these goals were almost
wholly disruptive. At Columbia University, students occupied several buildings for
a week beginning on April 23 and were finally dislodged in a police raid that saw 150
people hurt and that shocked the city and the country. At the University of Denver,
later in the month, a small group of students apparently hoped to produce a similar
situation, but Chancellor Maurice B. Mitchell moved quickly to nip the affair in the
bud. Reprinted here are two documents bearing on student revolt in general, and
on the question of punishment for student rebels in particular. The first is a portion
of a pamphlet issued by a group of Columbia students shortly after the police raid,
which occurred early in the morning of April 30. The second is a portion of a letter
from Chancellor Mitchell explaining his action. It was dated April 30.*

Source: *Why We Strike,* n.p., n.d., pp. 12-14.
Letter to Friends of the University of Denver, April 30, 1968.

I.

Statement of Columbia Student Strikers

WHAT IS THE POLITICAL JUSTIFICATION for not
disciplining the demonstrators?

There are two basic reasons why the
demonstrators should not be punished.
First, they took the only actions they could
have to successfully win just demands. Second, the authority that promulgated the
laws that the demonstrators are accused of

violating — the Columbia administration
— is totally illegitimate and doesn't have
the right to discipline — or pass laws providing for the disciplining of — anyone.

The justice of the demonstrators' goals
has been admitted by nearly everyone.
Some people object to the tactics we use;
they think we should have employed the
"legitimate channels" to achieve our demands. We ask these people: Where were
you earlier this year when 400 students
marched peacefully into Low Library to
present Grayson Kirk a letter asking for dis-

affiliation with IDA? The official response to this letter was, "We cannot answer because there was no return address." Where was the legitimate means for discussion when SDS challenged Kirk to debate on IDA and there was no answer at all? Where were you when peaceful demonstrations were held at the gym site and the university pressed charges against a minister for trespassing? And where were you when SDS presented a petition on IDA with 1,700 signatures to the administration and their response was to put the six on disciplinary probation for marching into their building? We ask that you ask yourself if the reason you now care about our demands is because we are using the very tactics we are at this time.

In short, we have used the "legitimate channels." The administration apparently considered them less legitimate than we did, for they never spent a minute paying any attention to them. Lack of administration response to these methods over a long period of time, plus their lack of response to traditional tactics of civil disobedience, convinced us that the tactics we have used over the past two weeks were the *only* way we could achieve our just demands.

Strict civil libertarians argue that those who commit civil disobedience must suffer the legal consequences even if their cause is just. But we say people should not be disciplined for doing what is necessary to achieve what is right.

We also point to the basic illegitimacy of the Columbia administration. As the strikers said in their policy statement of April 28,

> We . . . believe in the right of all people to participate in the decisions that affect their lives. An institution is legitimate only if it is a structure for the exercise of this collective right. The people who are affected by an illegitimate institution have the right to change it.
> Columbia University has been governed undemocratically. An administra-

tion responsible only to the Trustees has made decisions that deeply affect students, faculty, and the community. It has expropriated a neighborhood park to build a gym. It has participated, through IDA, in the suppression of self-determination throughout the world. It has formulated rules and disciplined students arbitrarily and for the purpose of suppressing justified protest. The actions of the administration in the present crisis have exposed it to students and faculty as the antidemocratic and irresponsible body it has always been.

Our goal is to create a functioning participatory democracy to replace the repressive rule of the administration and Trustees of this university. The acceptance of amnesty by the administration is a fundamental part of this transition because it establishes the illegitimacy of the existing structure. The granting of amnesty is the formal establishment of a new order — the right and power of all people affected by the university not to be judged by illegitimate authority.

For students who took the only actions possible to successfully achieve necessary and just demands to be disciplined for the violation of rules set up by a totally discredited and illegitimate authority would be a travesty.

II.

MAURICE B. MITCHELL: Statement of the Chancellor of the University of Denver

THIS UNIVERSITY has dismissed more than forty students on this day. Their dismissal is the result of willful disobedience of the rules and regulations for orderly and proper conduct.

For several days now, a small group of students has made demands and issued threats to the administration of the university. Specifically, they have threatened to occupy the chancellor's office and administra-

John Loengard, "Life," © Time Inc.

Student protest at Amherst College in 1965

tion building and to sit-in in other essential university buildings and to disrupt university activities.

The issues on which these protests are based are improper, illegal, and go against the orderly processes by which institutions can and should operate. This university will not be run by threats and intimidation. It will not respond to ultimatums from students, and it will not be intimidated by the pressures of groups who are dedicated to the disruption of institutions of higher learning or seek disorganization to the point where such institutions can be controlled by violence and run under constant threat of disruption. . . .

I make myself fully responsible for these decisions. In the simplest language in which I can put it, the time has come for society to take back control of its functions and its destiny. If we condone the abandonment of the rule of law in the university, we have no right to expect those who attend it and later move on into outside society to conduct themselves in any other manner.

There is the assumption on the part of some disaffected students at the university that it is immoral for them to tolerate conditions not of their liking and that they have some sort of moral obligation to engage in acts of defiance and violence. There is no way to prevent this, but there is every reason to hold those who engage in such practices fully responsible for the consequences of their acts. To those who insist that improper activities are the only answer to their problems, I have replied that the decision to engage in such activities carries with it the full responsibility to accept punishment; and punishment on this campus under these circumstances and for such acts is going to be instant and sufficient to the cause. . . .

The overwhelming majority of the members of the student body of this university appear to be in full support of the comments I have made above. They are humiliated and deeply distressed by what they see happening on this campus today. A certain sympathy for severe punishment meted out to classmates is understandable, but they have carefully avoided taking any overt action, and it is my hope that they will continue to do so. . . .

As I have undoubtedly said above, the time has come to make the stand, and we are doing it in the very beginning. We want no Columbia University or Berkeley or Howard or Wilberforce situation on this campus, and we simply are not going to have it.

113.

Irving Kristol: The Strange Death of Liberal Education

Many attempts were made in the spring of 1968 to determine the cause of the student revolts that broke out on a number of U.S. campuses and also in universities abroad. Some viewed the disturbances, which involved the near-destruction of Columbia University and pitched battles in other places, as the work of iconoclastic conspirators who were set on undermining the total fabric of American life. Others saw them as inevitable effects of the frustrating conflict in Vietnam; and still others said that they reflected the ennui of a generation with too much money to spend and too much time on its hands. Sociologist Irving Kristol suggested another cause for the widespread troubles, which may, in retrospect, turn out to be the most significant phenomenon of the year. The article reprinted here first appeared in Fortune.

Source: *Fortune*, May 1968.

MOST STUDENTS who go to college are under the impression that, in addition to preparing themselves for their future vocations, they will partake of something called "a liberal education." Certainly most of their parents think this to be the case. Neither seem to be aware that liberal education, to all intents and purposes, no longer survives on the American campus. To be sure, there are some rare exceptions among the small colleges. But in the overwhelming majority of universities, liberal education is extinct.

Popular ignorance of this fact is not surprising. Liberal education is still a marketable (if nonexistent) commodity, and the educational conglomerates that we persist in calling universities are highly sales-oriented institutions. Practically all of them offer "general education" courses that, to an untrained eye, look like the real thing. But there is an unbridgeable gulf between the actuality of "general education," that is, a smattering or casual acquaintance with the various academic disciplines, and "liberal education," which explores the great ideas of the past as the source of living possibilities for students and teachers alike.

What is involved here is not so much deception as self-deception. The very meaning of "liberal education" has become so foreign to the academic community that almost no one can be bothered to notice its demise. However, a recently published collection of essays edited by Robert A. Goldwin, *Higher Education and Modern Democracy* (Rand McNally), reveals that not all professors are willing to reconcile themselves to a system of education that is "illiberal" in the traditional sense of the term. The contributors are distinguished scholars and educators — Leo Strauss (University of Chicago), Allan Bloom (Cornell), Daniel Bell (Columbia), Thomas K. Simpson (St. John's of Annapolis), Martin Meyerson (president of the University of Buffalo), and others. Their papers are marked by an awareness that the death of liberal education is no mere academic incident. It is, rather, very near the roots of that turbulent and bewildering crisis which our universities are now experiencing.

When students demand that they not be bent, folded, or mutilated, they are all too easily misunderstood — especially since they themselves have only a dim awareness of what they mean. It is generally assumed that they want greater individual and personal attention, and everyone promptly agrees that it should be provided them through counseling, smaller classes, greater participation in academic government, etc. We are then dismayed when these reforms seem not to make the slightest difference — as, indeed, they have not, at Berkeley or elsewhere.

But the students only *seem* to be rebelling against the university as a bureaucratic institution. In truth, they are rebelling against it as a soulless institution — which is not quite the same thing. It is not the external arrangements of their education that upset them so much; it is the internal void. Specifically, it is the disappointing discovery, in the words of Allan Bloom, of "a great disproportion between what they study and the lives they wish to lead."

The problem of the "multiversity" is a problem of purpose. The multiversity is very good at *training* scholars and specialists. It is very bad at *educating* young men and women. And while many young people doubtless benefit from the training they get, the frustration of those who *need* education — a liberal education, above all — has explosive consequences. As Professor Bloom writes: "The multiversity does not appeal to the students' longings for an understanding of the most serious problems, in particular their doubts about the route to follow in order to live a good life and their questions about the nature of justice. . . . This is not a particularly disturbing situation for the great majority of young people who are content to make careers and do not feel called upon to reflect generally about themselves or the whole of society. But for that most interesting few who can become leaders, pathfinders, and revolutionaries, this is a great source of dissatisfaction. . . . [These] students must turn elsewhere to educate themselves and satisfy their cravings."

The "elsewhere" to which dissatisfied students have turned in an effort to make "a connection" between their lives and the world of ideas is familiar enough. Drugs, sex, apocalyptic politics, Oriental mysticism, amateur existentialism — the list is only too familiar, and sometimes seems endless. All these together constitute the "popular culture" of the campus — a culture constantly being reshaped by fad and fashion, demanding no real intellectual or moral effort on the part of its consumers, pandering to unformed taste and uninstructed feelings, capable of being agitated by every passing wind of doctrine. The excitement this culture proposes is factitious, superficial, and quickly exhausted. Anyone who can compare it with the truly gripping experience of being personally involved with great ideas, great books and great minds knows that it is but a pale imitation of the real thing. But, for today's students, the real thing is a matter of hearsay, and most of them can only have hazy views of it, as across a vast credibility gap.

The unwitting villain in the piece is the graduate school. The fantastic expansion of graduate education was obviously inevitable, given our society's need for skilled professionals with advanced specialized training. What was not inevitable, however, was the extent to which the graduate school has come to tyrannize the entire process of higher education. More and more, the undergraduate curriculum is oriented toward the real or imagined needs of the graduate degree. More and more, the undergraduates' tuition fees and alumni contributions go to maintain the graduate establishment. More and more, the brightest students are recruited, at the earliest possible moment, into the various academic and professional disciplines. And more and more, a professor's status is defined by his relation to the graduate program. If he is active in it, his prestige is high. If he is not, he is viewed as not having "made it."

This last point probably represents the greatest single obstacle to any revival of a program of liberal education. The teachers for such a program just do not exist. Not only is there an absolute shortage of college teachers throughout the nation; there is a further relative shortage of teachers who are competent to provide a liberal education, even under the most propitious circumstances. As Thomas Simpson points out, an education in "liberal scholarship" is very different from the training in "research" that our professors now get in their graduate years.

Liberal scholarship's purpose, says Simpson, "is understanding rather than information; its methods are wide reading of a literature which is classical as well as contemporary, together with open and critical speculation; its product is ideas, sometimes new ones and sometimes old, but always living thoughts in the mind of someone who has learned, as all human beings have to learn, through humble and arduous study. This liberal scholarship does not come packaged with the familiar academic labels. . . . As a result, it has no home in our universities, or among our academic societies."

How to break out of this vicious circle is indeed a baffling problem. Professor Simpson's own proposal, for a *graduate* school of the liberal arts that would keep the tradition of liberal education alive and maintain a supply of qualified teachers, is an excellent and ingenious one. But it is only too likely to encounter massive indifference, if not active hostility, from the academic world, as now constituted.

Meanwhile, down on the campus, the restlessness and rootlessness gather momentum. Even the professors are infected, in ways they are not always conscious of. The hippie professor is now a familiar campus figure. He, too, feels that the mere conveyance of specialized information and skills is not what he had in mind when he dreamed of becoming a teacher to the young. More often than not, he will join the rebellious students in their assaults against school and society.

Over the past year, there has been a student-faculty movement toward the founding of off-campus "anti-universities," where the prevailing academic conventions are ignored and where students can study (or play at studying) whatever and however they wish. This is a kind of *reductio ad absurdum* of the campus revolt. But it is also, in a perverse way, witness to the tendency of our higher educational institutions to impoverish the educational experience and to leave discussion of "the most important things" — touching on the meaning of the good life and the good society — to amateur enthusiasts or cynical popularity seekers.

———◆———

A child miseducated is a child lost.
JOHN F. KENNEDY, State of the Union Address, January 11, 1962.

114.

Scott Buchanan: A Message to the Young

The following selection is the concluding portion of an article by Scott Buchanan, philosopher, educator, and writer on politics, which was published in the Center Magazine *early in 1968. Buchanan died within a few days of the appearance of the article. It was therefore in effect his last word to the young people he had long both studied and served.*

Source: *Center Magazine*, March 1968.

SOME OF YOU of the younger generation, probably the larger portion, will want to forget the infinity of possible worlds that you can create or that you have inherited, even the best possible of possible worlds, and you will decide to cultivate your suburban gardens. If you do, you will, as you know, have eminent philosophical authority for your decision. Realizing this, you may want to reread some of the great books to help you choose your style of garden — the Epicurean, or possibly a Stoic porch. I hope you will acquire the comic spirit, should you so decide, because I am afraid you will not be left alone and undisturbed; your protecting hedge will have to be a stout sense of humor.

A few others will smell adventure in a wide open world, and your curiosity will lead you to explore all the possible worlds that you can get passports to. You may be frightened by the monsters that you meet, as well as by the monsters you will help to create, but you will probably escape all of them, one after another. In the end you will find that each world through which you have passed was a university, offering credits toward a Bachelor of Experience degree.

Some of you may already have fallen in love with an actual world of the past. Not realizing that a past actual world, although it was once possible, is now an impossible world, you may even seek to defend it with your life. In the end, you may leave an island for some Sancho Panza to govern and after many battles against evil will find your own Dulcinea and final victory in heaven.

Still others, I presume a very few, will be bored with the dreams found in the books of the past and seek your escape in the future. You will think it your duty to smash this sorry scheme of things into bits in order to build the only really possible world, the city of the future. You may remember that Aristophanes wrote his *Birds* about you and realize, when you do, that you are probably already a citizen of a city not built with hands.

The rest will, I take it, become citizens of the actual world we have here and now. You must already know that it is a feverish, impatient place, not very tolerant of any full exercise of the liberal arts, especially those which contemplate alternative possibilities, neither generous nor sympathetic with those who find it necessary to measure and redefine their loyalties to it. You may find any simple loyalty that you have suddenly canceling other loyalties that you wish to keep, and you may be charged with several treasons within a single hour. You will also find that the words you use and the deeds you do are marvelously ambiguous. All these things will be so because you have made the *idea* of the world the rule of your life and yet you have found a way of accepting the actual world, and of accepting the fate it offers as the necessary condition of life. This may mean that you see the need for a world government or a universal church, as Toynbee suggested; but it more probably will mean that you will want to see that the laws you live under are made truly universal and the God you serve is more than an idol. It should lead you to see that the persons with whom you live and work are not merely useful but serve common ends with you, that the parts of nature you exploit are made useful not only to yourselves but to your fellows as well, that the science you know and the skill you acquire is made available through education to everybody.

These simple-sounding truths were accepted by the Founding Fathers of this country; they have regularly been accepted in the Western world; and they are now being accepted by the rest of mankind. They are all rules of world law. With the possible worlds that they comprehend and permeate, they are making the world revolution that will probably continue through the rest of your lives.

Perhaps the most important thing the present citizen of the world has to remember is that the world lives and moves, it revolves; revolution, indeed, is its natural property. The sudden and explosive phenomena that we often call revolutions are mere symptoms of the deeper and larger work of the world, the rattling and wobbling of the wheels of the great chariot of time.

The answer is to rely on youth — not a time of life but a state of mind, a temper of the will, a quality of imagination, a predominance of courage over timidity, of the appetite for adventure over the love of ease. The cruelties and obstacles of this swiftly changing planet will not yield to obsolete dogmas and outworn slogans. They cannot be moved by those who cling to a present that is already dying, who prefer the illusion of security to the excitement and danger that comes with even the most peaceful progress.

It is a revolutionary world we live in; and this generation, at home and around the world, has had thrust upon it a greater burden of responsibility than any generation that has ever lived.

ROBERT F. KENNEDY, Speech to the young people of South Africa on their Day of Affirmation in 1966.

Index of Authors

The numbers in brackets
indicate selection numbers
in this volume

BALDWIN, JAMES (Aug. 2, 1924-   ), author and lecturer on civil rights. Member of the national advisory board of the Congress of Racial Equality; wrote *Go Tell It on the Mountain* (1953), *Notes of a Native Son* (1955), *Nobody Knows My Name* (1961), *Another Country* (1962), *The Fire Next Time* (1963). [28]

BLACK, HUGO L. (Feb. 27, 1886-   ), political leader and jurist. U.S. senator from Alabama (1927-37); associate justice (1937-   ) of the U.S. Supreme Court. [65] See also Author Index, Vol. 16.

BRENNAN, WILLIAM J., JR. (April 25, 1906-   ), jurist. Judge (1949-50) of the Superior Court of New Jersey and (1950-52) of the Appellate Court; justice (1952-56) of the New Jersey Supreme Court; associate justice (1956-   ) of U.S. Supreme Court. [23, 65]

BROWN, ROBERT MCAFEE (May 28, 1920-   ), theologian and educator. On faculty of Union Theological Seminary (1953-62); professor of religion at Stanford University (1962-   ). Author of *The Significance of the Church* (1956); *The Spirit of Protestantism* (1961). [91]

BUCHANAN, SCOTT (March 17, 1895-March 25, 1968), philosopher and educator. Dean of St. John's College, Annapolis, Md. (1937-47); trustee of the Foundation for World Government (1948-58); consultant, Fund for the Republic (1957-68). Author of *Possibility* (1926); *Poetry and Mathematics* (1929); *Essay in Politics* (1953). [114]

CARMICHAEL, STOKELY (Sept. 12, 1942-   ), civil rights activist. Former field secretary for the Student Nonviolent Coordinating Committee; enunciator of the "black power" slogan in the civil rights movement; co-author of *Black Power* (1968). [69]

CARSON, RACHEL (May 27, 1907-April 14, 1964), scientist and author. Taught zoology (1931-36) at the University of Maryland; aquatic biologist (1936-49) with U.S. Bureau of Fisheries; editor in chief (1949-52) of U.S. Fish and Wildlife Service publications; wrote *The Sea Around Us* (1951), *Silent Spring* (1962). [18]

CAUDILL, HARRY M. (May 3, 1922-   ), lawyer and author. Wrote *Night Comes to the Cumberlands* (1963) and articles on the problems of Appalachia. [61]

CLARK, THOMAS CAMPBELL (Sept. 23, 1899-   ), lawyer and jurist. Attorney General of the United States (1945-49); associate justice of the U.S. Supreme Court (1949-67). [74]

COLEMAN, JAMES S. (May 12, 1926-   ), sociologist and educator. Assistant professor of sociology at the University of Chicago (1956-59); professor of social relations at Johns Hopkins University (1959-   ). Author of *Community Conflict* (1957); *The Adolescent Society* (1961); *Adolescents and the Schools* (1965). [72]

DEANE, HERBERT A. (May 26, 1921-   ), educator. Vice-dean of the graduate faculties at Columbia University. Author of

(1953-64); Republican Party candidate (1964) for President of the United States; wrote *The Conscience of a Conservative* (1960). [9]

GOODWIN, RICHARD N. (Dec. 7, 1931-), lawyer and government official. Deputy assistant secretary of state on inter-American affairs (1961-63); author of *Triumph or Tragedy: Reflections on Vietnam* (1966). [79]

GREENBERG, CLEMENT (Jan. 16, 1909-), art critic. Former editor of *Partisan Review*; author of *Joan Miro* (1948) and *Art and Culture* (1961). [20]

GREENBERG, DANIEL S. (Dec. 31, 1927-), scientist and educator. News editor of *Science* magazine; research fellow in history of science at Johns Hopkins University. [94]

GRISWOLD, ERWIN N. (July 14, 1904-), lawyer and educator. Special assistant to the U.S.; attorney general (1929-34); professor of law at Harvard Law School (1935-46); solicitor general of the U.S. (1967-). Author of *The Fifth Amendment Today* (1955). [111]

GUSTAFSON, W. ERIC (Nov. 18, 1933-), economist and educator. Instructor in economics at Harvard University. [17]

HACKER, ANDREW (Aug. 30, 1929-), professor of government at Cornell University; author of *Congressional Redistricting* (1963). [73]

HALL, EDWARD T. (May 16, 1914-), anthropologist. Professor (1946-48) at the University of Denver, (1948-51) at Bennington College, and (from 1963) at Illinois Institute of Technology; director (1950-55) of the teaching program of the Foreign Service Institute, U.S. State Department; president (1955-60) of Overseas Teaching and Research, Inc. [14]

HARRIMAN, W. AVERELL (Nov. 15, 1891-), businessman, public official, and diplomat. Chairman of the board (1932-46) of Union Pacific Railroad; partner in Brown Brothers Harriman & Co.; ambassador (1943-46) to Russia and (1946) to Great Britain; secretary of commerce (1946-48) under H. S. Truman; governor of New York (1955-59); ambassador at large (1961, 1965-); assistant secretary of state (1961-63) and undersecretary of state (1963-65) under J. F. Kennedy and L. B. Johnson. [59]

HARRINGTON, MICHAEL (Feb. 24, 1928-), author. Member (from 1960) of the national executive committee of the Socialist Party; editor (1961-62) of *New America*; chairman (from 1964) of the League for Industrial Democracy; edited *Labor in a Free Society* (with Paul Jacobs, 1959) and wrote *The Other America* (1963). [16]

HARRIS, HERBERT, journalist, editor, and government official. [42]

HAYDEN, THOMAS (Dec. 11, 1939-), a founder of Students for a Democratic Society. Community worker at Newark, N.J.; active in antiwar and protest movements; made an "unauthorized" trip to North Vietnam in December 1965, in company with Staughton Lynd and Herbert Aptheker. Co-author of *The Other Side* (1967); author of *Rebellion in Newark* (1967). [82]

HOMAN, RICHARD, correspondent for the *Washington Post*. [99]

JOHNSON, LYNDON B. (Aug. 27, 1908-), political leader and statesman. Thirty-sixth President of the United States (1963-69); U.S. representative from Texas (1937-49); U.S. senator (1949-61) and Democratic majority leader (1955-60); Vice-President of the United States (1961-63) under J. F. Kennedy; succeeded to the presidency upon Kennedy's death (Nov. 22, 1963). [38, 40, 41, 68, 102] See also Author Index, Vol. 17.

JOHNSON, THOMAS A. (Oct. 11, 1928-), correspondent for the *New York Times*. [103]

KENNEDY, JOHN F. (May 29, 1917-Nov. 22, 1963), political leader and statesman. Thirty-fifth President of the United States (1961-63); U.S. representative from Massachusetts (1947-53); U.S. senator (1953-60); wrote *Why England Slept* (1940), *Profiles in Courage* (1956), *The Strategy of Peace* (1960); assassinated Nov. 22, 1963. [2, 3, 12, 26, 29, 35, 36] See also Author Index, Vol. 17.

general counsel (1963-65) of Encyclopaedia Britannica, Inc.; director of National Education Television WTTW, Chicago; partner (from 1965) in Liebman, Williams, Bennett, Baird & Minow. [4]

MITCHELL, MAURICE B. (Feb. 9, 1915-   ), educator and publisher. Associated with Encyclopaedia Britannica (1953-67), president (1962-67); chancellor of the University of Denver (1967-   ). [112]

MORGAN, HOWARD (1914-   ), government official. Member (1961-63) of the Federal Power Commission. [32]

MOYNIHAN, DANIEL P. (March 16, 1927-   ), government official and educator. Official of the Department of Labor (1961-65); director of the Joint Center for Urban Studies of Harvard University and Massachusetts Institute of Technology (1966-   ). Co-author of Beyond the Melting Pot (1963). [83]

NADER, RALPH (Feb. 27, 1934-   ), author and social critic. Gained national fame over the issue of safety in automobiles with the publication of his book Unsafe at Any Speed (1965). Member of the board of directors of Consumers Union (1967-   ). [55]

NENNEMAN, RICHARD A. (Oct. 13, 1929-   ), business and financial editor of the Christian Science Monitor (1965-   ). [104]

POWERS, CHARLES F. (Nov. 5, 1925-   ), scientist. Associate research oceanographer at Great Lakes Research Division, University of Michigan. [63]

RABINOWITCH, EUGENE (April 27, 1901-   ), chemist, writer, and educator. Worked on the Manhattan Project (1944-46); research professor at the University of Illinois (1947-   ); editor in chief of the Bulletin of the Atomic Scientists. Author of Minutes to Midnight (1950); Dawn of a New Age (1964). [96]

RIDGEWAY, JAMES (Nov. 1, 1936-   ), journalist. Associate editor of the New Republic (1962-   ). [51]

RIGG, ROBERT B. (Oct. 27, 1913-   ), army officer. Former intelligence officer and expert in military strategy. Author of War: 1974 (1958). [107]

ROBERTSON, ANDREW (Sept. 15, 1936-   ), scientist. Assistant research limnologist at the Great Lakes Research Division, University of Michigan. [63]

ROSTOW, EUGENE V. (Aug. 25, 1913-   ), lawyer and economist. Professor (1944-   ) and dean (1955-65) at Yale Law School; adviser to U.S. State Department (1942-44, 1961-   ) member (1961-   ) of the Advisory Council to the Peace Corps. [101] See also Author Index, Vol. 16.

ROVERE, RICHARD H. (May 5, 1915-   ), editor and writer. Staff writer (1944-   ) for the New Yorker; author of Senator Joe McCarthy (1959); The American Establishment (1962); Waist-deep in the Big Muddy (1968). [90]

RUSK, DEAN (Feb. 9, 1909-   ), diplomat and public official. Professor of government and dean of the faculty (1934-40) at Mills College; special assistant to the secretary of war (1946-47); director (1947-49) of the Office of UN affairs, U.S. State Department; assistant secretary (1949, 1950-52) and deputy undersecretary of state (1949-50) under Truman; president (1952-60) of the Rockefeller Foundation; secretary of state (1961-   ) under Kennedy and L. B. Johnson. [5]

SANFORD, DAVID, associate editor of the New Republic. [86]

SCAMMON, RICHARD M. (July 17, 1915-   ), political scientist. Associate producer (1939-41) of the University of Chicago-NBC Round Table; U.S. political officer in Germany (1945-48); chief (1948-55) of research for Western Europe, U.S. State Department; director (1955-61, from 1965) of elections research, Governmental Affairs Institute; director (1961-   ) of the Bureau of the Census, U.S. Commerce Department. [53]

SHRIVER, R. SARGENT, JR. (Nov. 9, 1915-   ), lawyer and government official. Director (1961-66) of the Peace Corps; director (1964-68) of the Office of Economic Opportunity; special assistant to the President (1964-68); U.S. Ambassador to France (1968-   ). Author of Point of the Lance (1964). [33]

STERN, GERALD (May 16, 1933-   ), corporation counsel. Assistant district attor-

Times and Harry M. Caudill for Selection 61, from *The New York Times Magazine,* ® 1966 by The New York Times Company. The New York Times and J. William Fulbright for Selection 67, from *The New York Times Magazine,* ® 1966 by The New York Times Company. The New York Times and Andrew Hacker for Selection 73, from *The New York Times Magazine,* ® 1966 by The New York Times Company.

Oak Publications for Selection 31 ("Oh Freedom," "We Shall Not Be Moved," "Keep Your Eyes on the Prize," "Woke Up This Morning With My Mind Stayed on Freedom," "Ain't Gonna Let Nobody Turn Me Round," "This Little Light of Mine," "We Shall Overcome"), from *We Shall Overcome!* Songs of the Southern Freedom Movement, compiled by Guy and Candie Carawan for The Student Nonviolent Coordinating Committee.

The Progressive for Selection 32, from *The Progressive,* Copyright ® 1963 by The Progressive, Inc.

Saturday Review and Arnold L. Fein for Selection 76, from *Saturday Review,* ® 1966 by Saturday Review, Inc.

Science for Selection 44, from *Science,* Copyright 1964 by the American Association for the Advancement of Science.

Student Nonviolent Coordinating Committee for Selection 69, from *The New York Review of Books,* Copyright ® 1966 by Student Nonviolent Coordinating Committee.

Time Inc. for Selection 52. This article, which originally appeared in the March 1965 issue of *Fortune,* is Chapter 1 of Mr. Faltermayer's book *Redoing America,* published by Harper & Row; ® 1965 Time Inc. Time Inc. and Irving Kristol for Selection 113, from the May 1968 issue of *Fortune Magazine,* ® 1968 by Time Inc.

Washington Post for Selection 99 (Richard Homan, "Account of the Defeat"), a *Washington Post Special* appearing in the May 16, 1968, issue of the *Chicago Sun Times.*